Helen Fairbairn, Gareth McCormack

Hiking
IN IRELAND

DUBLIN & WICKLOW

1 HOWTH PENINSULA

This pleasant ramble along the cliffs of the Howth Peninsula (p43) offers wild coastal scenery within easy reach of the capital. An extremely scenic excursion, on a clear day you can see both the Mourne Mountains to the north and the Wicklow Mountains to the south. Howth is also home to the largest seabird colony on Ireland's eastern seaboard.

2 WICKLOW WAY HIGHLIGHT

The best section of Ireland's most famous long-distance walk, this three- or four-day route begins in Dublin's suburbs and travels through increasingly dramatic scenery to the heart of the Wicklow Mountains (p48). Along the way it crosses wild moorlands, high mountain rises and several marvellous glens.

3 LUGNAQUILLA

At 925m, Lugnaquilla (p62) stands over 100m higher than the next tallest peak in the Wicklow Mountains. The climb to the vast summit plateau brings you through the wild hanging valley of upper Fraughan Rock Glen. Then, having enjoyed tremendous views from the top, there's the secluded beauty of Art's Lough to look forward to on the descent.

SOUTHEAST

1 KNOCKANAFFRIN RIDGE

The 755m-high summit of Knockanaffrin (p76) crowns a long ridge in Waterford's Comeragh Mountains. Dotted by fascinating clusters of rock that thrust skyward from the apex of the arête, the ridgeline just begs for further exploration.

2 MAHON FALLS

The Comeragh Mountains are endowed with many topographical wonders, yet two features are celebrated above all others. The first of these is the 80m-high Mahon Falls (p80), one of the most striking mountain cascades in Ireland. Second is the astounding glacial amphitheatre of Coumshingaun. This energetic tour allows you to visit both in a single outing.

3 GALTYMORE

At 919m, Galtymore (p86) stands proud of the rest of the Galtee range by almost 100m. The classic horseshoe route over the summit provides magnificent panoramic views, as well as thrilling glimpses into the awesome corries far below. It also includes an ascent past Lough Curra, the highest and most dramatic lake in the area.

SOUTHWEST

1 BRANDON MOUNTAIN
This classic route takes you up one of Ireland's best-loved mountains (p97). Begin by climbing past a line of paternoster lakes, through a series of glacial corries. Once you see the summit views you'll appreciate why this charismatic peak is such a favourite.

2 DINGLE WAY
Long sandy beaches, ancient ruins and a mountain crossing are highlights of one of the most scenic Way-marked Ways in Ireland. The three-day route (p100) follows country roads, coastal paths and open mountainside as it makes its way around the very tip of the Dingle Peninsula.

3 COOMLOUGHRA HORSESHOE
This challenging mountain circuit crosses the three highest peaks in Ireland, featuring tremendous views and an exciting, narrow rock ridge. A highly recommended and rewarding day out, it is arguably the finest circular walk in the country (p108).

4 TORC MOUNTAIN
The compact summit of Torc Mountain (535m, p116) provides some the best views available over Killarney National Park. Yet the route to the top involves a relatively easy climb up a mountain path, making it the perfect introduction to Irish hill-walking.

5 SHEEP'S HEAD WAY HIGHLIGHT
A high-quality coastal circuit (p130), this walk explores wild scenery at the tip of the Southwest's most remote peninsula. Highlights include wonderful views of the western seaboard and the chance to immerse yourself in the interior's rural beauty.

CENTRAL WEST

1 BENBULBIN

The classic route to Sligo's most famous summit (p167) takes you up a gully and out to the mountain's precipitous western tip. A superbly scenic ascent of one of Ireland's most distinctive mountains, rewarded by thrilling aerial views of Donegal Bay.

2 MINAUN HEIGHTS

This impressive route (p173) takes you along a series of spectacular sea cliffs, offering a bird's-eye view of Achill Island. From the moment you reach the clifftop you're met by a breathtaking panorama over 4km-long Trawmore Strand, and the scenery just keeps improving all the way to Dooega Head.

3 MWEELREA

The highest peak (p185) in the province of Connaught soars dramatically above Killary Harbour and the sandy beaches of the Atlantic coast. This approach, via the cliff-lined, glacial corrie of Coum Dubh, offers the most spectacular ascent option.

4 DIAMOND HILL

A charismatic little peak, Diamond Hill (445m, p190) is the most accessible mountain in Connemara National Park. Enjoy fantastic views from the narrow, quartzite summit, with a recently constructed path easing progress and navigation.

5 BLACK HEAD

The unique, shattered limestone landscape of the Burren is among Ireland's most treasured natural assets. This route (p198) crosses rocky terraces and natural pavements, showcasing many of the plant species that make the region a botanist's delight.

ATLANTIC ISLANDS

1 TORY ISLAND

There's a palpable feeling of remoteness as you stand on the cliffs at Tory's northwestern tip, watching the Atlantic spray blowing across the island. A 10th-century round tower, puffin colonies and a wonderfully rugged coastline are among the highlights of the walk around the island (p146).

2 INISHTURK

This charming island (p151) strikes the perfect balance between rugged scenery and welcoming hospitality. The walk explores soaring sea cliffs and a modest mountain summit, with friendly inhabitants, sandy coves and a picturesque harbour thrown in for good measure.

3 GREAT BLASKET ISLAND

Exploring perhaps the most evocative of the Atlantic Islands, this rugged outpost exudes a wonderfully natural atmosphere. There's some exhilarating walking too, taking you past the poignant ruins of an abandoned village to the island's 292m high point (p158).

NORTHWEST

1 HORN HEAD

Horn Head (p218) boasts the most impressive coastal scenery of north Donegal and for hikers, the trip around the headland is right up there among the country's classic coastal routes. The attraction is the tremendous coastal architecture, which includes a natural sea-arch, sheer cliffs and swathes of golden sand.

2 ERRIGAL

A classic of the northwest, the highest and most distinctive mountain in Donegal is an obligatory outing for visiting hikers. With its volcanic profile and unbeatable location within Glenveagh National Park, this route (p222) has few rivals in terms of scenic splendour.

3 GLENCOLMCILLE CIRCUIT

Situated amid some of the country's wildest coastal scenery, the remote village of Glencolmcille (p230) exudes an other-worldly atmosphere. Follow part of an ancient pilgrimage route to explore the dramatic coastline, numerous ancient monuments and the evocative deserted village of Port.

NORTHERN IRELAND

1 CAVE HILL

Cape Town has Table Mountain; Belfast has Cave Hill (p243). The 368m-high escarpment rises directly from the city's suburbs, offering unbeatable views over the capital of the north. The trip to the top is short, accessible and highly rewarding.

2 SLIEVE BINNIAN & THE ANNALONG VALLEY

The fabulous Mourne Mountains are a magnet for outdoor enthusiasts, and there are countless fine routes to choose from. This circuit begins with an ascent of Slieve Binnian (747m, p259), whose 1.5km-long summit ridge is littered with fascinating granite tors.

3 CAUSEWAY COAST WAY HIGHLIGHT

This superb route (p268) follows a signed trail along the celebrated Antrim coast, taking you past sandy beaches, sea arches and towering cliffs. The journey links two of the country's premier natural tourist attractions: Carrick-a-Rede, with its thrilling rope bridge, and the World Heritage Site of the Giant's Causeway.

4 ANTRIM HILLS WAY HIGHLIGHT

Some of the most enjoyable upland walking in County Antrim can be found along this scenic Waymarked Way (p273). Explore the sheer escarpments and coastal summits of the Glens of Antrim, with dramatic scenery, fantastic views and firm terrain just some of the treats on offer.

HIKING IN IRELAND

Gentle mountains, rugged ridges, wild moorlands, spectacular sea cliffs, remote islands, warm hospitality and the infamous Irish weather – all are part of the wonderful experience that is hiking in Ireland.

This guide details 85 walks and outlines many more, helping you explore Ireland's remarkable range of hiking areas. Routes extend across the most spectacular landscapes of Northern Ireland and the Republic, and vary in length from one hour to three days.

From the rolling Wicklow Mountains to the spiky summits of Connemara, from the sandy beaches of the Dingle Peninsula to the dramatic coastal cliffs of the northwest, hiking in Ireland can be at once peaceful and exhilarating. The sheer variety of terrain means there are top-class options for everybody, novice and enthusiast alike. Anybody can share the pleasure of a boat trip to walk on the Atlantic Islands for example, while some of the country's challenging mountain ridges are best left to more experienced souls.

Besides the physical grandeur of the scenery, Ireland also enchants its visitors with more ephemeral characteristics. The evocative ruins of an abandoned village, the humbling presence of remote antiquities, even the way the mist drifts over the valley on more sombre days – there's a timeless atmosphere to the place that catches many in its thrall. Observe it, absorb it and then head to the pub with a better understanding of what makes the country so unique.

There's a different experience waiting here to captivate each visitor, but one thing you can be sure of is that hiking in Ireland is guaranteed to exceed your expectations.

Contents

THE MAPS

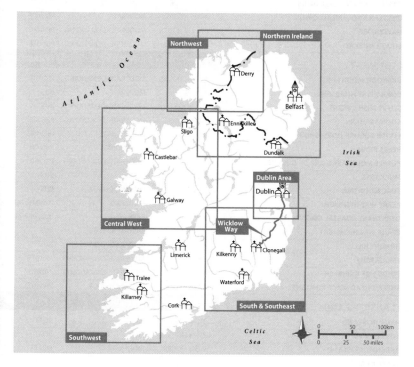

Table of Hikes

DUBLIN & WICKLOW	DURATION	DIFFICULTY	TRANSPORT
PHOENIX PARK & RIVER LIFFEY	3½–4 HOURS	EASY	BUS
VIKING & MEDIEVAL DUBLIN	2 HOURS	EASY	BUS
HOWTH PENINSULA	3½–4 HOURS	EASY–MODERATE	TRAIN, BUS
BRAY HEAD	4–4¼ HOURS	EASY–MODERATE	TRAIN, BUS
GREAT SUGAR LOAF	1–1¼ HOURS	MODERATE	PRIVATE
WICKLOW WAY HIGHLIGHT	3 DAYS	MODERATE	BUS, TAXI
MAULIN CIRCUIT	2½–3 HOURS	MODERATE	PRIVATE
CAMADERRY	4¾–5¼ HOURS	MODERATE	PRIVATE, BUS
MULLACOR	4–4½ HOURS	MODERATE	BUS
LUGNAQUILLA	5½–6 HOURS	MODERATE–DEMANDING	PRIVATE

SOUTHEAST	DURATION	DIFFICULTY	TRANSPORT
BLACKSTAIRS MOUNTAIN	5¼–5¾ HOURS	MODERATE–DEMANDING	PRIVATE
BARROW WAY HIGHLIGHT	5–5½ HOURS	EASY	BUS, PRIVATE
KNOCKANAFFRIN RIDGE	4½–5 HOURS	MODERATE–DEMANDING	PRIVATE
NIRE VALLEY COUMS	5–5½ HOURS	MODERATE–DEMANDING	PRIVATE
COUMSHINGAUN CIRCUIT	4–4½ HOURS	DEMANDING	PRIVATE
MAHON VALLEY	4–4½ HOURS	MODERATE	PRIVATE
EASTERN KNOCKMEALDOWNS	6½–7 HOURS	MODERATE–DEMANDING	PRIVATE
WESTERN KNOCKMEALDOWNS	4–4½ HOURS	MODERATE	PRIVATE
GALTYMORE	5¾–6¼ HOURS	MODERATE–DEMANDING	PRIVATE
LOUGH MUSKRY	4–4½ HOURS	MODERATE–DEMANDING	PRIVATE

SOUTHWEST	DURATION	DIFFICULTY	TRANSPORT
BRANDON MOUNTAIN	5½–6½ HOURS	MODERATE–DEMANDING	PRIVATE
DINGLE WAY HIGHLIGHT	3 DAYS	MODERATE	BUS
SLIEVE MISH CIRCUIT	5–6 HOURS	MODERATE–DEMANDING	BUS
COOMASAHARN	5–5½ HOURS	MODERATE–DEMANDING	PRIVATE
COOMLOUGHRA HORSESHORE	6–7 HOURS	DEMANDING	PRIVATE
REEKS RIDGE	6–7 HOURS	DEMANDING	PRIVATE
PURPLE MOUNTAIN & GAP OF DUNLOE	6–7 HOURS	MODERATE–DEMANDING	PRIVATE
MUCKROSS	4–5 HOURS	EASY	BUS
TORC MOUNTAIN	3½ HOURS	EASY–MODERATE	BUS
KERRY WAY HIGHLIGHT	2 DAYS	MODERATE	PRIVATE, BUS, BO
DERRYNANE COASTAL CIRCUIT	3 HOURS	EASY	BUS, PRIVATE
BEARA WAY HIGHLIGHT	2–3 DAYS	EASY–MODERATE	BUS
HUNGRY HILL	4–5 HOURS	MODERATE–DEMANDING	BUS
ESKATARRIFF	5½–6 HOURS	MODERATE–DEMANDING	PRIVATE
POCKET OF AKINKEEN	4–4½ HOURS	MODERATE–DEMANDING	PRIVATE
SHEEP'S HEAD WAY HIGHLIGHT	5½–6 HOURS	EASY–MODERATE	PRIVATE

ATLANTIC ISLANDS	DURATION	DIFFICULTY	TRANSPORT
RATHLIN ISLAND	3½–4½ HOURS	EASY	BOAT
TORY ISLAND	3½–4 HOURS	EASY	BOAT
ARRANMORE ISLAND	5–5½ HOURS	MODERATE	BOAT
CLARE ISLAND	5–5½ HOURS	MODERATE	BOAT
INISHTURK	3½–4½ HOURS	MODERATE	BOAT
INISHMORE	6–6½ HOURS	MODERATE	BOAT, PLANE

ATLANTIC ISLANDS continued

	DURATION	DIFFICULTY	TRANSPORT
INISHEER	4½–5 HOURS	MODERATE	BOAT, PLANE
GREAT BLASKET ISLAND	3½ HOURS	EASY–MODERATE	BOAT

CENTRAL WEST

	DURATION	DIFFICULTY	TRANSPORT
BENBULBIN	4–5 HOURS	MODERATE	PRIVATE
ACHILL HEAD & CROAGHAUN	5–5½ HOURS	MODERATE–DEMANDING	PRIVATE
SLIEVEMORE	4 HOURS	MODERATE	BUS
MINAUN HEIGHTS	5–5½ HOURS	MODERATE	PRIVATE
DÚN CAOCHÁIN CLIFFS	5½–6½ HOURS	MODERATE	PRIVATE
CORRAUN HILL	5–5½ HOURS	MODERATE–DEMANDING	PRIVATE
CORRANBINNA	5½–6 HOURS	DEMANDING	BUS, PRIVATE
CROAGH PATRICK	4–4½ HOURS	MODERATE–DEMANDING	BUS, PRIVATE
MWEELREA	6½–7 HOURS	DEMANDING	PRIVATE
KILLARY HARBOUR	3½–4 HOURS	EASY	PRIVATE
DIAMOND HILL	2½–3 HOURS	EASY–MODERATE	BUS
GLENCOAGHAN HORSESHOE	7–7½ HOURS	DEMANDING	BUS
CENTRAL MAUMTURKS	5–5½ HOURS	MODERATE–DEMANDING	PRIVATE
ERRISBEG	2–3 HOURS	EASY–MODERATE	BUS
BLACK HEAD	5 HOURS	MODERATE	BUS, PRIVATE

NORTHWEST

	DURATION	DIFFICULTY	TRANSPORT
RAGHTIN MORE	3½–4 HOURS	MODERATE	PRIVATE
MELMORE HEAD	4–4½ HOURS	EASY–MODERATE	PRIVATE
ARDS	2–2½ HOURS	EASY	PRIVATE, BUS
HORN HEAD	5–6 HOURS	MODERATE	PRIVATE
MUCKISH	2½–3 HOURS	MODERATE	PRIVATE
ERRIGAL	3½ HOURS	MODERATE	PRIVATE
GLENVEAGH NATIONAL PARK	5–6 HOURS	MODERATE–DEMANDING	PRIVATE
SLIEVE SNAGHT & THE POISONED GLEN	6½–7 HOURS	DEMANDING	PRIVATE
SLIEVE LEAGUE	4½–5½ HOURS	MODERATE–DEMANDING	PRIVATE, BUS
GLENCOLMCILLE CIRCUIT	4–5 HOURS	MODERATE	BUS, PRIVATE
BLUE STACK CIRCUIT	6–7 HOURS	MODERATE–DEMANDING	PRIVATE

NORTHERN IRELAND

	DURATION	DIFFICULTY	TRANSPORT
CAVE HILL	2–2½ HOURS	EASY–MODERATE	BUS
NORTH DOWN COASTAL PATH	4½–5 HOURS	EASY	TRAIN, BUS
LAGAN TOWPATH	4¼–4¾ HOURS	EASY	TRAIN
CASTLE WARD	2–3 HOURS	EASY	BUS, PRIVATE
SLIEVE BEARNAGH & SLIEVE MEELMORE	5–5½ HOURS	MODERATE–DEMANDING	BUS, PRIVATE
SLIEVE DONARD	4½–5 HOURS	MODERATE–DEMANDING	BUS
BRANDY PAD	6½–7½ HOURS	MODERATE	BUS
SLIEVE BINNIAN & THE ANNALONG VALLEY	5–5½ HOURS	MODERATE–DEMANDING	BUS, PRIVATE
CUILCAGH MOUNTAIN	5–5½ HOURS	MODERATE	PRIVATE
CUILCAGH WAY HIGHLIGHT	3–3½ HOURS	EASY–MODERATE	PRIVATE
SAWEL & DART	5–5½ HOURS	MODERATE–DEMANDING	BUS
BINEVENAGH CLIFFS	2–3 HOURS	EASY–MODERATE	PRIVATE
CAUSEWAY COAST WAY HIGHLIGHT	5–5½ HOURS	MODERATE	BUS, TRAIN
GLENARIFF FOREST PARK	2½–3 HOURS	EASY	BUS
ANTRIM HILLS WAY HIGHLIGHT	5–6 HOURS	MODERATE	BUS

The Authors

HELEN FAIRBAIRN

An appreciation of the natural environment and the love of a challenge have led Helen to explore many of the world's dramatic landscapes over the years, and she has worked on six Lonely Planet walking titles to destinations as diverse as the American Rockies and the European Alps. Now leading a more settled life in Ireland, Helen continues to enjoy the outdoors whilst introducing her children to the adventures of life. Other writing achievements include a hiking guidebook to Northern Ireland and regular contributions to *Walking World Ireland* magazine.

MY FAVOURITE HIKES

The countless rewards of walking in Ireland keep me coming back. Even after decades exploring the country, there's always something else to discover. A recent approach to **Clare Island** (p150) by sea kayak enabled me to explore a series of spectacular shoreline caves I never knew existed. Then on **Tory** (p146), I spent five minutes enthralled by an unobscurred view of the corncrake, a rare bird I had often heard but never seen. Alongside the countless highs of Irish walking, ranges like the **Twelve Bens** (p191) and the **MacGillycuddy's Reeks** (p110) guarantee a prize every time – it's little wonder I can't drag myself away.

GARETH McCORMACK

A professional landscape photographer, Gareth spends much of his time scouring the Irish countryside for that perfect photo. Born in Northern Ireland, he now lives in county Sligo and occasionally swaps the lens for the keyboard and works as a hiking author; his list of publications include eight Lonely Planet walking guides and 12 years' worth of articles for hiking magazines. Gareth's photographic interpretation of Ireland's wild places can be viewed online at www.garethmccormack.com.

Route Descriptions

This book contains 85 route descriptions ranging from day trips to three-day walks, plus suggestions for other walks, side trips and alternative routes. Each walk description has a brief introduction outlining the natural and cultural features you may encounter, plus information to help you plan your walk – transport options, level of difficulty, time frame and any permits required.

Day walks are often circular and are located in areas of uncommon beauty. Multiday walks include information on campsites, hostels or other accommodation, and places where you can obtain water and supplies.

TIMES & DISTANCES
These are provided only as a guide. Times are based on actual walking time and do not include stops for snacks, taking photographs, rests or side trips. Be sure to factor these in when planning your walk. Distances are provided but should be read in conjunction with altitudes. Significant elevation changes can make a greater difference to your walking time than lateral distance.

LEVEL OF DIFFICULTY
Grading systems are always arbitrary. However, having an indication of the grade may help you choose between walks. Our authors use the following grading guidelines:

Easy – a walk on flat terrain or with minor elevation changes usually over short distances on well-travelled routes with no navigational difficulties.
Moderate – a walk with challenging terrain, often involving longer distances and steep climbs.
Demanding – a walk with long distances and difficult terrain with significant elevation changes; may involve challenging route-finding.

TRUE LEFT & TRUE RIGHT
The terms 'true left' and 'true right', used to describe the bank of a stream or river, sometimes throw readers. The 'true left bank' simply means the left bank as you look downstream.

Planning

Variety is what walking in Ireland is all about, from precipitous mountain ridges to level canal paths, from windswept cliffs tops to woodland waterfalls. There are well-marked paths, firm forest tracks and wild, cross-country excursions. Such variety within a relatively small space means you can be standing atop a panoramic summit one day, and strolling across a golden beach the next. It's possible to cover a significant amount of the country in a couple of weeks, though locals will confirm that there are so many intriguing nooks and crannies it takes a lifetime to explore it all properly.

Most Irish walking comes in the form of one-day outings, whether it's a short three-hour stroll or an energetic, eight-hour mountain traverse. However there are also multiday walks in the form of the country's Waymarked Ways, the best sections of which are highlighted in this book. The length and accessibility of Ireland's walks means the logistics of planning a trip are relatively simple, though you'll appreciate your own transport if you're travelling to rural areas outside the summer months.

Though it could never be described as a budget destination, independent travellers can move around relatively inexpensively by staying in a combination of hostels and camping grounds. Of course there's also a wide range of B&Bs, guesthouses and hotels for those who prefer more comfort. In addition to the information given here, Lonely Planet's *Ireland* guide is indispensable as a general travel guide to the country.

WHEN TO WALK

Ireland's relatively mild climate means walking is not restricted to particular times of the year like it is in places with more extreme seasonal variations. Though walking in winter requires different preparation from summer outings, most Irish hikers keep enjoying the outdoors all year round. Some routes are actually at their best on crisp, sunny winter days, when the bog is frozen underfoot and crystal-clear air makes views stretch forever.

See Climate (p291) for more information.

That said, it's important to appreciate that walks present different challenges at different times of the year, and you may need to adapt your route decisions and equipment accordingly. Many mountain routes that are relatively accessible during the summer become serious undertakings on the rare days they're covered with snow and ice, when they should be tackled only by hikers with appropriate winter mountaineering experience and equipment.

The driest months in Ireland are April, May and June, with July not far behind; this is a particularly important consideration in western areas where rainfall is relatively high. The coldest months are January and February, and the mountains are generally covered by snow several times during this period. However, the snow rarely lasts more than a few days before thawing, and lowland areas receive just one or two modest falls each year.

Whatever time of year it is, it's often unwise, if not downright dangerous, to go out in poor visibility or strong winds. The potential hazards of making a navigational error in such conditions are especially acute on mountain or coastal routes that involve high cliffs and significant drop-offs. Rain also makes grass and rock slippery underfoot, and can cause rivers to rise rapidly – a gentle stream can become a raging torrent almost

---

DON'T LEAVE HOME WITHOUT...

- Your sea legs for boat trips to the Atlantic Islands (p142)
- A compass for mountain navigation (p318)
- Insect repellent to combat summer midges (p323)
- A flask for hot drinks during and after the walk (p296)
- Waterproofs and sunglasses – for a fickle climate (p291)
- A three-flat-pin plug adapter for international electrical appliances (p288)

---

as you watch. The general rule is to check the weather forecast carefully before heading out on any walk.

Besides the weather, the other seasonal consideration for hikers is the amount of daylight. In mid-December the sun rises around 8.45am and sets at 4pm, giving just seven hours of daylight. If you want to complete a long mountain circuit at this time of the year, there's no choice but to start and finish in the dark. By mid-June, the sun doesn't set until 10pm and there are 18 hours of daylight. It's quite possible to start an eight-hour walk at lunchtime and still finish with daylight to spare.

During the peak tourist season of July and August accommodation can be tight in popular areas, and it's essential to book ahead. Some accommodation options – especially those in rural areas – also close during the off-peak season from October to Easter. Many useful bus services are strictly seasonal, so a trip outside June to September really means private transport if you want to travel extensively.

COSTS & MONEY

The collapse of the economy in six short months between 2008 and 2009 has left the country in a state of flux: prices are coming down in many areas, but they're coming down from such a height that to many visitors Ireland remains a fairly expensive destination. For a decade Irish wallets were at the mercy of a rip-off culture that stung everybody, including visitors, who felt it most when it came to bed and board.

In Dublin, the bare minimum to survive is about €50 a day: €20 to €25 for a hostel and €20 for sustenance, which leaves enough for a pint. If your purse strings are a little more relaxed, you can get a decent bed for around €50 in the capital, €40 outside it. For €100 you can sleep pretty luxuriously almost anywhere. Outside the capital things can be significantly cheaper, depending on the area and season: in rural areas outside July and August, prices are around two-thirds what you might pay in Dublin.

In the Republic the economic downturn has resulted in supermarket prices coming down, in response to competition from the North. Although restaurants are closing down all over the country, there hasn't been a marked decrease in the price of eating out – yet. For less than €10, don't expect much more than soup and what comes between two slices of bread. Very ordinary bar meals will cost €15 or more; the better restaurants won't blink twice when charging €30 for fish in a fancy sauce.

In Northern Ireland, the bite isn't as deep. The 'rip-off Republic' tag that for so long dogged the South wasn't as much of an issue over of the border. But price differences certainly hurt when northerners head south: current exchange rates make the eurozone very expensive for anyone using sterling (as they do in Northern Ireland, which is part of the United Kingdom).

HOW MUCH?

Dorm bed in a hostel
€18/£15

B&B (per person sharing)
€35–45/£30–35

OS Map €8.60/£6.90

Pint of beer in a bar
€4/£3

Car hire per week
€200/£150

Once in the North though, you can get by on £35 a day without too much bother – if you limit yourself to a budget lifestyle. Accommodation costs generally mirror the Republic, but you'll find real savings on food – you can get excellent two-course lunches in lots of good restaurants for £10 or less, while main courses in Belfast's best eateries range from £14–18.

Car rental is costly throughout the island. Be sure to check your car-insurance policy back home before accepting the exorbitant insurance policies offered at car-rental agencies. If your credit card usually covers car-rental insurance, it's a good idea to confirm that the policy applies in Ireland before you leave.

BACKGROUND READING

To get you in the mood for your trip, here's a selection of our favourite Irish walking literature. Details of specific area guidebooks are given in the relevant regional chapters.

The Way that I Went by Robert Lloyd Praeger. First published in 1937, this is the classic reference for Irish walkers and conservationists. Written by Ireland's greatest field botanist, it's the result of 5000 miles of walking from Donegal to Kerry. Along the way Praeger crossed hills and bogs, swam through flooded caverns, sifted through fossil bones and explored ancient tombs. He was the first to describe much of the landscape he crossed, and is also credited with discovering several important archaeological sites.

A Walk in Ireland by Michael Fewer: subtitled 'An Anthology of Walking Literature in Ireland 1783–1993'. This offering from one of Ireland's best known walkers is a selection of accounts of pedestrian travel through the country during the last 200 years. Experience the beauty of the Irish landscape as described in articles, excerpts, letters and journal entries from authors as diverse as John Keats and Paul Theroux.

Footloose in the West of Ireland by Mike Harding. An account of the author's love affair with the West, lasting more than 30 years and distilled into descriptions of 27 walks. Each route details wanderings around ancient sites and scrambles up mountains, as well as recounting the area's history, folklore and poetry.

INTERNET RESOURCES

The internet has become an indispensable planning tool for hikers. Ireland is well wired, so there's a lot of useful information available online. Here are a few sites to get you started:

BBC Weather Service (http://news.bbc.co.uk/weather) Provides detailed weather forecasts; the meteorological charts for the British Isles include Ireland.

Fáilte Ireland (www.discoverireland.ie) The Republic's official tourist information site has heaps of practical information, including a huge accommodation database. Follow their walking link for maps and descriptions of the country's numerous National Loop Walks.

Irish Mountain Views (www.mountainviews.ie) A fantastic resource for Irish hillwalkers, listing all the country's summits, with members' accounts of routes and experiences on each peak. Great for checking out approaches to mountains that don't normally appear in guidebooks.

Lonely Planet (www.lonelyplanet.com) Comprehensive travel information and advice, with a hiking, trekking and mountaineering branch on the Thorn Tree.

TOP FIVES

COASTAL WALKS

Ireland's wonderfully fragmented coastline rises to its full glory along the western seaboard, where you can expect kilometre upon kilometre of exhilarating walking past soaring rock formations and crashing ocean waves.

- Gaze at Marble Arch and the amazing rock architecture around Horn Head (p218).
- Explore Europe's highest sea cliffs beneath Slieve League (p228).
- Appreciate a fine panorama of mountain and sea from Knockmore on Clare Island (p150).
- Revel in the exposure of the Dún Caocháin cliff-line in remote north Mayo (p176).
- Discover beautiful sandy beaches and hidden coves around the Dingle Peninsula (p96).

SPOTTING WILDLIFE

There's something special about observing wild creatures in their natural habitat. Whether it's laughing at the antics of clown-like puffins or feeling awed by the power of a fully-grown stag, there's nothing like walking to get you close to Ireland's wildlife.

- Watch herds of wild red deer roam along the first wild stretch of the Kerry Way (p117).
- Catch a glimpse of a playful otter along the tranquil River Barrow (p72).
- See basking seals and breaching whales from Great Blasket Island (p158).
- Lift binoculars for close-up views of puffins, guillemots and razorbills on Rathlin Island (p144).
- Keep an eye open for golden eagles in Glenveagh National Park (p224).

GEOLOGICAL WONDERS

A complex geological history has left a legacy of intriguing landforms, from weird volcanic shapes and extensive limestone plateaus to chiselled reminders of the ice age.

- Visit the unique volcanic rock formations of the Giant's Causeway (p268).
- Gaze in awe at the massive glacial corrie of Coumshingaun (p79).
- Wander across the fascinating limestone moonscape around Black Head (p198).
- Descend deep into the Marble Arch Caves from the Cuilcagh Way Highlight (p263).
- Count the submerged drumlins in Clew Bay from the top of Croagh Patrick (p182).

ARCHAEOLOGICAL SITES

Countless ancient sites offer reminders of ten millennia of human habitation, with Neolithic, Bronze Age, pagan and Christian structures sprinkled along walking routes around the country.

- Find inspiration in Glendalough's Monastic City on the way to Mullacor (p61).
- Explore stone circles and ancient tombs on the Beara Way (p122).
- Visit the plethora of pagan and early-Christian sites around Glencolmcille (p231).
- Discover seven huge, pre-Christian forts perched on the cliff edge in the Aran Islands (p153).
- Pass the gaunt remains of a deserted village beneath Achill Island's Slievemore (p172).

MOUNTAIN SUMMITS

Hillwalkers and adrenaline junkies are spoilt for choice in Ireland, where sharp arêtes and lofty ridges lead to incredible summit views.

- Enjoy some of the finest views in Ireland from the coastal peak of Brandon (p97).
- Relax on Lugnaquilla's broad summit plateau after an absorbing ascent (p62).
- Climb a steep ramp to reach an airy ridge near the top of Mweelrea (p185).
- Scramble along tremendous, knife-edged ridges to Ireland's highest point on the Coomloughra Horseshoe (p108).
- Clamber across the knobbly tors of Slieve Bearnagh for lofty views of the Mournes (p252).

THE IRISH MUNROS

The term 'munro' is an import from Scotland, and has come to indicate a mountain that is more than 3000ft (900m) in height. The name was coined in memory of Sir Hugh Munro, who completed a survey of all the Scottish peaks and, in 1891, published the first comprehensive list of Scottish mountains over 3000ft high.

The list of Scottish munros has been revised several times, with current accounts detailing 284 summits. The task of listing Irish munros is somewhat easier, thanks to the lower elevation of the country's high ground. It is generally accepted that there are just 12 munro peaks in Ireland, though the list can vary depending on the definition of a mountain 'top'.

The Irish munros are located in four regions of the country. The MacGillycuddy's Reeks, on the Iveragh Peninsula (County Kerry), contain nine of the 12. Brandon Mountain, on the Dingle Peninsula (County Kerry), is the country's eighth-highest summit. Lugnaquilla in the Wicklow Mountains (County Wicklow) and Galtymore (County Tipperary), just slip in as Ireland's 11th and 12th munros respectively. Routes over all of these summits are detailed in this book, and the small number of peaks means that experienced mountain enthusiasts should be able to 'bag' all the Irish munros in a single visit.

Northern Ireland Tourist Board (www.discovernorthernireland.com) Northern Ireland's official tourism information site is particularly strong on accommodation and attractions.

Hikers Association of Ireland (www.hikersassociation.ie) An online forum for Irish walkers, with details of public walking events and links to walking clubs and organisations around the country.

Hike Northern Ireland (www.hikeni.com) A searchable directory of hundreds of walking routes across Northern Ireland, with maps and descriptions for each walk featured. Includes full details of all the province's Waymarked Ways.

Waymarked Ways of Ireland (www.hikeireland.ie) Provides stage-by-stage descriptions of all the Waymarked Ways in the Republic.

GROUP WALKS

Joining an organised walking tour can be a great option for people who are new to walking, who want an introduction to the country before embarking on an independent trip, or who simply like the idea of having company along the trail. See p296 for a list of companies that provide commercial walking tours around Ireland.

If you like the idea of walking with a group, but don't want to get involved with a commercial operator, why not consider joining one of Ireland's walking festivals. A typically Irish invention, walking festivals are a lively mix of organised walks and social events spread over two to four days. Festivals take place all round the country and are anything but local events, with participants often coming from Europe, Japan and the USA. They're a great way of meeting Irish hikers and often offer the opportunity to visit more out-of-the-way places. An entry fee is charged to help cover organising costs, refreshments en route and a certificate and/or T-shirt at the end of it all. For a list of the major festivals around the country, see the Walking Festival Calendar on p295.

GUIDED WALKS

There are numerous commercial operators that offer walking tours of Ireland. Two types of tour are usually offered: fully guided, where you have the services of a guide from beginning to end; and self guided, where the company organises your accommodation and luggage transfers, and provides maps and route notes, but you actually walk on your own.

Companies offering guided trips along the Waymarked Ways featured in this book are listed in the relevant walk descriptions. For a list of larger companies, both in Ireland and abroad, that offer organised walking holidays in Ireland see Guides in the Walkers Directory chapter, p296. Even if you don't book a tour, the itineraries outlined on their websites can be a great source of information.

INDEPENDENT WALKS

Ireland offers independent travellers several different types of walking experience: wild trips across open countryside, short trips along signed trails and long-distance Waymarked Ways. This book details the best routes in all three categories. However, it's also worth finding out a bit more about the country's collection of Waymarked Ways and National Loop Walks. If you particularly like long-distance routes or short, signed trails, these offer a host of additional options around the country.

Waymarked Ways

Ireland has more than 3000km of official Waymarked Ways, or designated long-distance walking trails. Crossing the length and breadth of the country and taking hikers to some of the most beautiful parts of the Republic and Northern Ireland, these vary in length from the 214km-long Kerry Way to the 26km Cavan Way in the upper Shannon Valley.

The Waymarked Way project was launched in the South in 1982 with the opening of the Wicklow Way (see p49), and in the North in 1983 with the opening of the Ulster Way (see Changing Fortunes of the Ulster Way, p242). Today there are a total of 36 official routes, all signed with posts bearing yellow arrows and a 'walking person' logo.

Before dashing out and buying guidebooks however, think about these points. With a few exceptions (notably the canal towpaths), most of the Ways spend the majority of their time on forest tracks and/or public roads. Finding accommodation each night can necessitate time-consuming detours or very long days between stops. Maintenance is also inadequate along many of the less-frequented trails – paths have become overgrown and waymarkers are hidden by vegetation.

Nevertheless the Ways provide a rich resource, and judicious route selection offers hikers the opportunity to discover Ireland off the beaten track. In this book we describe the highlight sections of the best routes around the country. At the end of each regional chapter you'll also find a list of additional Waymarked Ways in that area. For full descriptions of routes in the Republic see www.hikeireland.ie, and for routes in Northern Ireland see www.hikeni.com.

Loop Walks

The antithesis to Ireland's Waymarked Ways is its network of National Loop Walks. Developed in 2007 to provide signed routes for more casual hikers, the scheme has burgeoned into a veritable plethora of walks around the Republic of Ireland (it does not, as yet, extend to the North).

The routes vary from 1½ to 4½ hours in length and are clearly signed throughout, with a map board at the start and finish. They're designed to avoid roads as much as possible (many routes follow tracks, old boreens or river-side paths), though there may be some linking sections along minor roads. The large number of trails means that wherever you are in the country, you can look up the website and find a route in the vicinity.

HISTORY OF IRISH WALKING

For centuries people have walked through the Irish countryside for practical reasons: searching for itinerant work, herding stock, attending distant events before the advent of road-borne transport. Pilgrimages to sites of religious significance, notably Croagh Patrick in County Mayo and Glendalough in the Wicklow Mountains, had always been made on foot.

Recreational walking is a relatively recent phenomenon however, coinciding with increases in car ownership and leisure time. By the time the Mountaineering Council of Ireland (now Mountaineering Ireland) was founded in 1971, several walking clubs were well established, including the Holiday Fellowship Hiking Club (1930), Irish Mountaineering Club (1948), Tralee Mountaineering Club (1954) and North West Mountaineering Club (1955).

The 1960s and 1970s were eventful decades: the country's first outdoor adventure centres were opened, offering training in activities such as hiking and climbing, and the Irish Mountain Rescue Association was established. The appointment of the Long Distance Hiking Routes Committee in 1978 was soon followed by the opening of the Wicklow Way, Ireland's first official long-distance walk. The number of government-supported walking routes, both long and short, has since grown steadily, the official response to the ever-growing popularity of walking.

Ireland's oldest walking festival, the Castlebar International, dates from 1967. Since then numerous other walking festivals and public challenge events have been launched as tourism bodies and charities have grasped the revenue-generating potential of the activity.

Many new walking clubs were set up during the 1980s and 1990s, and the country's first dedicated magazine, *Hiking World Ireland*, was first published in 1994. By then, local and all-Ireland walking guides had already been on bookshop shelves for several years. Interest in walking continues to proliferate today, and by 2009, Mountaineering Ireland counted some 130 walking clubs among its membership. Not bad for a country of such diminutive size!

Note, however, that the walks have been developed with inexperienced, 'occasional' hikers in mind, rather than dedicated enthusiasts. The loops avoid terrain that might endanger hikers in any way, keeping away from steep slopes, deep water, crags or cliffs. They also bypass environmentally sensitive areas such as wildlife reserves and heritage sites. Unfortunately this means they often skirt around an area's most interesting features. For example, many of the routes on the Atlantic Islands keep to inland tracks and roads, and never actually approach the spectacular sea cliffs that make the location so attractive in the first place.

Nevertheless, the scheme does contain some walking gems, and if you're based in one place for a significant amount of time, it's definitely worth checking out routes nearby. The scheme is administered by Fáilte Ireland, the main tourism body in the Republic, and the best place to see what's available is on their website, www.discoverireland.ie/walking, where you'll find an interactive map of all the country's loop walks, with maps and descriptions for each route.

Environment

THE LAND

The Irish landscape exerts a powerful sway on the people who live in it, and you can't help but agree that the vibrant greenness of the fields, the fearsome violence of the jagged coastline and the ever-changing light of the mountain valleys are integral to experiencing Ireland.

Ireland stretches just 486km north to south and 275km east to west, so its impressive topographical variety may come as a surprise. The extensive central lowlands generally rise no more than 120m above sea level, and host the expected green fields and cultivated farmland. But travel a short distance away, and you're confronted by mountain ridges that rear sharply skyward.

Many of these ranges were formed about 450 million years ago, when great heat and immense pressure transformed sedimentary rocks into quartzite and schist, the main building blocks of Connemara, Donegal, Mayo and Tyrone. Near the end of this era, granite also emerged from beneath the earth's surface to form the foundations of the Wicklow Mountains and Donegal's Derryveagh Mountains.

There followed a relatively tranquil period when Ireland was part of the European landmass; vast areas of sandstone were laid down and later covered by limestone deposits. The immense, other-worldly landscape of the Burren originated during this period.

Ireland's second mountain-building era took place between 340 and 280 million years ago and mainly affected the south of the island. The high, sandstone ridges of the southwestern peninsulas and more isolated ranges such as the Comeraghs were formed at this time. Then, around 60 million years ago, a period of intense volcanic activity gave rise to Northern Ireland's Mourne Mountains and the extraordinary hexagonal stone columns of the Giant's Causeway in County Antrim.

Then came various ice ages, ending about 10,000 years ago, when much of Ireland was buried under ice for long periods. The erosive impact of the ice shaped much of the landscape we know today, with three classic features in mountain areas being corries, U-shaped valleys and arêtes (see the boxed text Signs of a Glacial Past, p30)

Centuries after the end of the ice age, extensive forests of oak, hazel and other species developed, only to be felled by Neolithic farmers around 3000 BC. Blanket bog – accumulations of decayed plant material – gradually spread across one-fifth of the island, and still covers huge swaths of Connemara, Mayo and Donegal. Further forest clearances took place from the 17th century, and by 1800, Ireland was the least wooded country in Europe. Even today, only 8% of its area is forested. Most of that consists of unsightly commercial plantations of lodgepole pine and sitka spruce, with native woodlands confined to tiny, sheltered pockets around the country.

Besides its fertile lowlands and varied mountains, Ireland's other outstanding feature is its coastline, which measures an incredible 5631km. In the west, the Atlantic coast is rugged and deeply indented, presided over by high cliffs and mountains that drop directly to the sea. The east coast has a relatively smooth, low profile in comparison, though still enjoys its share of sandy beaches. Hundreds of small islands, more than 20 of them inhabited, also dot the country's shoreline, many supporting unique ecosystems.

Look for *Reading the Irish Landscape* by Frank Mitchell and Michael Ryan for an understanding of Ireland's geology, archaeology, urban growth, agriculture and afforestation.

The illustrated pocket guide *The Animals of Ireland* by Gordon D'Arcy is a handy, inexpensive introduction to the country's fauna.

WILDLIFE

Ireland's flora and fauna is, by and large, shy and subtle, but as in any island environment, travellers who set out on foot will discover a country that is resplendent with interesting species.

SIGNS OF A GLACIAL PAST

Many of Ireland's finest walks are through landscapes that have been substantially shaped by glaciers. As a glacier flows downhill with its great weight of ice and snow it creates a distinctive collection of landforms, many of which are preserved once the ice has retreated or vanished.

The most obvious is the U-shaped valley (1), gouged out by the glacier as it moves downhill, often with a bowl-shaped corrie (2) at its head. Corries are found along high mountain ridges or at mountain passes or cols (3). Where an alpine glacier – which flows off the upper slopes and ridges of a mountain range – has joined a deeper, more substantial valley glacier, a dramatic hanging valley (4) is often the result. In a post-glacial landscape, hanging valleys and corries commonly shelter hidden alpine lakes or tarns (5). The thin ridge, which separates adjacent glacial valleys is known as an arête (6).

As a glacier grinds its way forward it usually leaves long, lateral moraine (7) ridges along its course – mounds of debris either deposited along the flanks of the glacier or left by sub-ice streams within its heart. At the end – or snout – of a glacier is the terminal moraine (8), the point where the giant conveyor belt of ice drops its load of rocks and grit. Both high up in the hanging valleys and in the surrounding valleys and plains, moraine lakes (9) may form behind a dam of glacial rubble.

The plains, which surround a once-glaciated range, may feature a confusing variety of moraine ridges, mounds and outwash fans – material left by rivers flowing from the glaciers. Perched here and there may be an erratic (10), a rock carried far from its origin by the moving ice and left stranded in a geologically alien environment; for example, a granite boulder sitting in a limestone landscape.

View of area before glacier's retreat

Animals

Ireland has 25 species of mammal, none of which is endemic, although some have been isolated from Continental forms of the same species long enough to evolve into a distinct Irish subspecies.

Fallow deer are a fairly common sight in Dublin's Phoenix Park (see p38) and other large wooded parklands. These deer are predominantly deep fawn in colour with dense white spotting on the back. The stags' antlers are flattened at the ends and resemble small hands.

Thanks mainly to a concerted conservation program, **red deer** persist in the wild after centuries of hunting and the destruction of their forest habitat. The only truly native herd is in Kerry (see p117); the herd in Donegal's Glenveagh National Park was introduced (see p225). During summer the mature stags are a magnificent sight, standing up to 1.4m high at the shoulder. Their multi-branched antlers are shed after the autumn rut (mating season).

The **fox** has survived persecution for eating game and domestic birds, and still ranges widely across the country. Unmistakable with its reddish-brown coat and long bushy tail, it is sometimes seen by hikers during the day despite the fact it's mainly nocturnal.

The Irish **hare** is another creature that hikers often spot scampering away. A living link with animals resident in Ireland during the last ice age, the hare can be seen throughout the country in a variety of habitats. It has brown fur, a white tail and relatively short ears (for a hare), and can run at speeds of up to 60km/h.

In mature woodlands, watch out for the **grey squirrel**, an avid eater of hazelnuts, that was introduced to Ireland in the early 20th century. The native **red squirrel** is now relatively rare, but hikers will still see them jumping through the boughs of Muckross Estate in Kerry (see p113).

Ireland also has a wide range of water mammals, both in its fresh-water rivers and coastal seas. Although mainly nocturnal, **otters** can sometimes be seen around rivers and lakes and on rocky western shores. About 1.5m long, dark brown with a white face, they are very agile in the water. Their tracks resemble a cat's paw print, and can often be traced along the banks of watercourses.

Half of Europe's population of **grey seals** is found along Ireland's north, west and south coasts. The bull is dark grey with black blotches, while the cow (female) is lighter in colour. The other main species of seal found in Ireland is the **common seal**, the largest colony of which lives around Strangford Lough and can be seen by hikers from Castle Ward (p250).

If you're tackling a coastal route, keep an eye open too for the oceanic mammals that skirt the Irish coast during their migratory travels. **Blue** and **killer whales** can sometimes be seen, though sightings are a rare privilege. Much more common are the **porpoise** and **dolphin**, which are most likely to be seen from August to October, travelling as part of a pod off the south and west coasts.

BIRDS

Many travellers visit Ireland specifically for the birdwatching. The number of bird species recorded in Ireland totals 424, although only about one-third of these are resident; the rest use Ireland as a stopover point during migrations from the Arctic to warmer climes.

From May to August coastal hikers are certain to see many breeding seabirds, particularly along rugged cliffs, where they sometimes congregate in huge colonies. Species that find a haven here include the **fulmar**,

The largest independent conservation group in Ireland, BirdWatch Ireland (www.bird watchireland.ie) works to protect the country's wild birds and their habitats. Ornithologists will love their website.

Ireland has 220 sq km of peatlands, vastly more than any other European nation. Even so, 81% of the country's original peatlands have now disappeared.

one of Ireland's most common coastal species, and the **kittiwake**, a small member of the gull family. **Guillemots**, meanwhile, are dark brown with a white breast, and lay their eggs on bare rock ledges.

Gannets are among the largest seabirds in Irish waters, and form dense breeding colonies on more isolated outcrops, notably off the coast of Kerry. Pure white with a yellow head and black tips to its 1.8m wingspan, hikers often spot them as they plunge arrow-like into the water in search of fish.

The species that most hikers want to see is the **puffin**. This endearing auk looks like a cross between a penguin and a parrot, and has an unmistakable, vividly coloured triangular bill and orange feet. Puffins come to Irish coasts in March and nest in mud burrows at the top of cliffs. The best places to see them are on Rathlin Island (p144) and along the Donegal, Mayo, Kerry and Cork coasts.

Summer visitors to Tory Island (p146) are also likely to come across the endangered **corncrake**. This elusive bird is adept at hiding in long grass, but its distinctive cry (similar to the raspy call of a cricket) will be heard by most visitors. A summer migrant from Africa, the corncrake is also found in County Galway and around the Shannon Callows.

Inland, **kestrels** are likely to be seen over most of the country, hovering above fields and open ground or perched on fence posts. This common bird of prey has pointed wings and a wedge-shaped tail; the brick-red male sports a blue-grey head and dark brown markings on its back and wings.

However Ireland's birds of prey are adapting to competition from two newly reintroduced species. In 2001, 46 **golden eagle** chicks were released into Donegal's Glenveagh National Park (see p224), and have now begun to breed successfully. A more recent project involves the release of some 35 **white-tailed sea eagles** into Killarney National Park in Kerry (p113), an attempt to re-establish the bird after a 100-year absence from the country.

> By the 1930s, Ireland's once-extensive forests had been reduced to just 1% of the country's total area.

> The rowan tree was once believed to have protective properties, and was planted to prevent places being bewitched.

Plants

Although Ireland is sparsely wooded, its range of surviving plant species is larger than many other European countries, thanks in part to the comparatively late arrival of agriculture.

There are remnants of the original **oak forest** in Killarney National Park (p113) and in southern Wicklow near Shillelagh. Far more common are pine plantations, which are growing steadily. Hedgerows, planted to divide fields and delineate land boundaries throughout Ireland, actually

TRADITIONAL MEDICINE CABINET

Long before antibiotics and wonder drugs, Irish people used wild plants to treat all manner of ailment.

- Bogbean for boils
- Chamomile as a remedy for whooping cough and Tuberculosis
- Cowslip to treat shattered nerves
- Dog rose hips as a source of Vitamin C
- Milkwort juice to cure warts
- Self-heal to treat strokes
- Tormentil for burns

host many of the native plant species that once thrived in the oak forests –
it's an intriguing example of nature adapting and reasserting herself.
The **Burren** in County Clare (p196) is one of Ireland's most intriguing
botanical showpieces, home to a remarkable mixture of Mediterranean,
alpine and arctic species.

The bogs of Ireland are home to a unique flora adapted to wet, acidic,
nutrient-poor conditions and whose survival is threatened by the deple-
tion of bogs for energy use. **Sphagnum moss** is the key bog plant and
is joined by plants such as **bog rosemary**, **bog cotton**, **black-beaked
sedge** (whose spindly stem grows up to 30cm high) and various types of
heather and **lichen**. Carnivorous plants also thrive, such as the **sundew**,
whose sticky tentacles trap insects, and **bladderwort**, whose tiny explo-
sive bladders trap aquatic animals in bog pools.

The Greenbox (www
.greenbox.ie) offers a
range of eco-friendly
activities and tours in
northwest Ireland.

NATIONAL PARKS & RESERVES
National Parks
There are six national parks in the Republic of Ireland: the Burren
(p196), Connemara (p188), Glenveagh (p224), Killarney (p113), Wicklow
Mountains (p48) and Ballycroy National Park in County Mayo. These
have been developed to protect, preserve and make accessible areas of
significant natural heritage. Northern Ireland does not have any national
parks as yet, though there is an ongoing consultation process to consider
the implications of designating the Mourne Mountains as the province's
first such area – see p259.

Forests & Forest Parks
Coillte Teoranta (Irish Forestry Board; ☎ 01-661 5666; www.coillte
.ie; Leeson La, Dublin) administers about 3500 sq km of forest, which
constitutes about 70% of the Republic's forested land. Most are
commercial projects, but there are also 12 forest parks and numerous
public picnic areas. These parks open year-round and have a range of
visitor facilities. Coillte forests are visited on several routes described,
including the Maulin Circuit (p57) and Ards (p216).

In the North there are 124 state forests, overseen by the **Northern
Ireland Forest Service** (☎ 028-9052 4480; www.forestserviceni.gov.uk;
Dundonald House, Upper Newtownards Rd, Belfast). Many sites have
also been developed for recreational use, complete with walking trails and
caravan parks; Glenariff (p271) is one such site detailed in this book.

For Ireland, one of
the most worrying
consequences of global
warming concerns the
future of the Atlantic
Gulf Stream. If it stops
circulating as many
scientists suggest, the
mild Irish climate would
suddenly resemble
Canada or Scandinavia.

National Nature Reserves
The Republic has 78 National Nature Reserves, the vast majority of which
are owned by the state and managed by the **National Parks & Wildlife
Service** (NPWS; ☎ 01-888 2000; www.npws.ie; 7 Ely Pl, Dublin 2).

In Northern Ireland there are over 40 nature reserves, which are either
leased or owned by the Department of the Environment. These reserves
are defined as areas of importance for their special flora, fauna or geology,
and include the Giant's Causeway (visited on the Causeway Coast walk,
p268) in County Antrim. More information is available from the **Environment & Heritage Service** (☎ 028-9054 6533; www.ehsni.gov.uk).

ENVIRONMENTAL ISSUES
Ireland does not rate among the world's biggest offenders when it comes
to polluting the environment, but the country's recent economic growth
has led to an increase in industry and consumerism, which in turn
generates more pollution and waste. The last 10 years has seen the

RESPONSIBLE WALKING

COUNTRYSIDE ACCESS

Traditionally, hikers in Ireland enjoyed almost unhindered access to the mountains, moors and coasts, based on a genuine respect for the property and livelihood of the people through whose land they passed. However, these traditions have never been enshrined in law, and there are few 'rights of way' where public access is guaranteed. Unfortunately the absence of a legal framework has now led to a rather fraught situation, and in recent years numerous disputes have blown up across the country, forcing the closure or re-routing of many traditional walking routes.

Given the lack of legal backup, it's easy to see how inconsiderate behaviour by hikers might provoke landowners and jeopardise the status of apparently established routes. To avoid worsening the situation, the best advice is to walk in a responsible manner at all times – see the guidelines below.

For further information contact **Leave No Trace Ireland** (☎ 028-9030 3938; www.leaveno traceireland.org; The Stableyard, Barnetts Demesne, Malone Rd, Belfast), an organisation that promotes responsible outdoor recreation. Their website offers full advice on appropriate walking behaviour in Ireland.

FARMLAND

- Be considerate of landowners and respect anybody you meet on your walk.
- Take care not to damage property, especially walls, fences and crops. Leave gates as you find them.
- Avoid disturbing farm animals, especially at sensitive times such as when they are breeding or have young. Observe them from a distance and don't offer them food.
- In general, dogs should not be brought onto hills or farmland.

CAMPING

- In remote areas, use pre-existing sites wherever possible. Keep at least 30m from watercourses and paths and move on after a night.
- Pitch your tent away from hollows where water is likely to accumulate – so that it won't be necessary to dig damaging trenches if it rains heavily.
- Leave your site as you found it – with no trace of your use.

untrammelled expansion of suburban development around all Ireland's major towns and cities, and the amount of waste produced has risen substantially since the early 1990s. While the population density is among Europe's lowest, the population is slowly rising.

Needless to say, concern for the environment is growing and the government has taken some measures to offset the damage that expanding societies can cause. On an immediate level, a number of recycling programs have been very successful, especially the 'plastax' – a 21c levy on all plastic bags used within the retail sector – which has seen their use reduced by a whopping 90%. The Republic has also established 35 wind farms in an effort to reduce the country's growing reliance on fossil fuels. Up north, another groundbreaking project pioneers the use of tidal energy – see the boxed text Harnessing Strangford's Power on p250.

While these are positive signs, they don't really put Ireland at the vanguard of the environmental movement. Polls seem to indicate the Irish are slightly less concerned about the environment than citizens of most other European countries, and the country is a long way from meeting its Kyoto Protocol requirement for reduced emissions. The government isn't pushing the environmental agenda far beyond ratifying

FIRES

○ Use existing fireplaces rather than creating a new one. Don't surround it with rocks – they're just another visual scar – but clear away all flammable material for at least 2m. Keep the fire small (under 1 sq m) and use a minimum of dead, fallen wood.

○ Be absolutely certain the fire is extinguished. Spread the embers and drown them with water, then examine the remains to ensure all heat is gone. Scatter the charcoal and cover the fire site with soil and leaves.

HUMAN WASTE DISPOSAL

○ If you need to go to the toilet in the wild, bury your waste. Dig a small hole 15cm deep and at least 30m from any stream, 50m from paths and 200m from any buildings. Take a lightweight trowel or a large tent peg for the purpose. Cover the waste with a good layer of soil. Toilet paper should be burnt or carried out.

○ Contamination of water sources by human faeces can lead to the transmission of giardia, a human bacterial parasite.

RUBBISH

○ If you've carried it in, you can carry it back out – everything, including citrus peel, cigarette butts and sanitary napkins, can be stowed in a dedicated rubbish bag. Make an effort to pick up rubbish left by others.

○ Buried rubbish takes years to decompose and will probably be dug up by wild animals who in turn may be injured or poisoned by it.

WASHING

○ Don't use detergents or toothpaste near streams or lakes; even if they are biodegradable they can harm fish and wildlife.

○ To wash yourself, use biodegradable soap and a water container at least 50m from the watercourse. Disperse the waste water widely so it filters through the soil before returning to the stream.

○ Wash cooking utensils 50m from watercourses using a scourer or gritty sand instead of detergent.

EU agreements, although it must be said these have established fairly ambitious goals for reduced air pollution and tighter management of water quality.

The annual number of tourists in Ireland far exceeds the number of residents (by a ratio of about 1.5 to one), so travellers can have a huge impact on the local environment. (See the boxed text, under Climate Change & Travel, p308 for more information on travelling sustainably).

Eco-tourism is not really burgeoning in a formalised way, although an organisation called The Greenbox (www.greenbox.ie) has established standards for eco-tourism on the island and promotes tour companies that comply to these standards. The rising popularity of outdoor activities – including walking – create economic incentives for conserving Ireland's environment, though increased activity in wilderness areas can also be harmful if not managed carefully.

Dublin & Wicklow

HIGHLIGHTS

- Rambling around the surprisingly unspoiled coastline of the **Howth Peninsula** (p43)
- Enjoying three days of consecutive scenic walking along the **Wicklow Way** (p49)
- Exploring Glendalough's awesome cliffs and lakes on the ascent to **Camaderry** (p59)
- Discovering the high-hanging valley on the climb to the top of mighty **Lugnaquilla** (p62)

Highest peak in the region: Lugnaquilla, Wicklow Mountains, 925m

Standing amid the urban bustle of O'Connell St on a busy afternoon, the idea of Dublin as a walking destination might seem ludicrous. Yet the truth is that Dubliners are blessed with a wide variety of walks within easy reach. For a flavour of the city itself, there's no better way to explore the capital's historic buildings, cultural sites and countless pubs than on foot. But if you prefer to escape the streets, you'll find green spaces and wild terrain are surprisingly close by. At the heart of the metropolis lies Phoenix Park, the largest urban park in Europe, where you can lose yourself for hours on end. To the north is Howth Peninsula with its scenic cliff walk, while to the south there's more rugged coastline between Bray and Greystones.

And then there are the Wicklow Mountains, which extend south from Dublin's fringes. Here you'll find 39 summits above 600m, culminating at the region's highest peak of Lugnaquilla (925m). Given the quality of the landscape and its proximity to the capital, it's not surprising that this is one of the most popular walking destinations in the country. With numerous mountain routes and the famous Wicklow Way, here's a perfect excuse for venturing beyond the city limits.

If time is short and you are restricted to a day trip, any of the walks described in this chapter are feasible from Dublin. Ideally, of course, your visit to Wicklow would last significantly longer, and you would base yourself closer to the mountains while exploring that area. Access is generally easy too – the remote valley of Glenmalure in the southern Wicklow Mountains is the only part of the region that's beyond the reach of public transport.

DUBLIN & WICKLOW

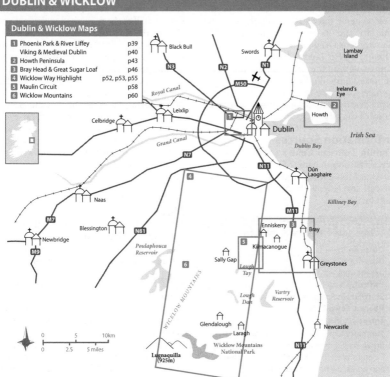

Dublin & Wicklow Maps

DUBLIN & WICKLOW

PLANNING
Maps & Books
The OSI 1:250,000 Holiday map *East* is best for general planning. Details of larger scale topographical maps are included in each walk description.

New Irish Walk Guides: East of Ireland, by Jean Boydell, David Herman and Miriam Joyce McCarthy, describes 67 walks and has interesting background information on the region.

GATEWAY
See Dublin (p65).

DUBLIN AREA

Though the city of Dublin is as busy and densely populated as any modern capital, it also benefits from close proximity to a number of natural assets. The reason a settlement was established here in the first place was, of course, that this is where a major river flows into the sea, making it a perfect location for a port of trade. The same features that have allowed the city to thrive down the centuries are also those that make it attractive to today's walkers; namely the existence of the River Liffey and the surrounding coastline. With fine coastal paths to the north and south, a huge river-side park right at the heart of things, and talismanic peaks such as Great Sugar Loaf on the southern boundaries, this is a capital with surprisingly wild enclaves within easy reach of the city centre.

PLANNING
Maps & Books
The OSI 1:50,000 *Dublin City & Environs Motoring Map* is invaluable for navigating the road maze.

DUBLIN & WICKLOW

Lonely Planet's *Dublin City Guide* and *Dublin Encounter Guide* provide the best general information about exploring the city and its culture. *Walking Dublin: Twenty-four Original Walks in and Around Dublin*, by Pat Liddy, describes a range of routes within the city and in the outer suburbs. *Easy Walks Near Dublin* by Joss Lynam takes you out into the countryside with descriptions of 40 outings within an hour of the city.

Information Sources
Dublin Tourism Centre (☎ 01-605 7700; www.visitdublin.com; 2 Suffolk St; daily Jul & Aug, Mon-Sat Sep-Jun) is the main port of call for help with city sights, services and facilities.

PHOENIX PARK & RIVER LIFFEY

Duration 3½–4 hours
Distance 12.7km
Ascent 30m
Difficulty easy
Start/Finish Parkgate St entrance
Nearest Town Dublin (p65)
Transport bus

Summary Explore Europe's largest enclosed urban park, home to herds of fallow deer, Ireland's president, a variety of monuments and an excellent visitor centre.

Phoenix Park is a miracle; a 350-year-old park that, at 709ha, is larger than all London's major parks put together. Occupying an oval-shaped tract of open fields and woodlands, it lies above the north bank of the River Liffey and is surrounded by busy roads and Dublin's midwestern suburbs. Its name is believed to be an anglicised version of the Irish *fionn uisce*, which refers to the stream that trickles through the park. Originally set aside in 1662 (see the boxed text Phoenix Park at a Glance, p42), it has been the site of all manner of events from murders to a Papal mass and just about everything in between. The unifying threads throughout its history are countless people doing nothing more adventurous than walking, jogging or cycling, and simply enjoying the open space and relative tranquility it provides.

The park's extensive network of paths means a great variety of walks are possible

within its boundaries. The roughly circular route described here concentrates on the eastern half of the park, then makes a diversion to the surprisingly quiet banks of the River Liffey, before returning to the park for a final triumphal stroll past the towering Wellington Monument.

The best time to visit depends on whether you want to enjoy the open spaces unhindered during the week, or join the crowds and visit some sporting or cultural event at the weekend. Either way there's no need to carry food or drink – you'll pass a kiosk and restaurant on the walk, and a couple of shops and a pub en route to the River Liffey.

PLANNING
Maps
The OSI 1:50,000 map No 50 shows the park but not all the paths. More useful is the OSI 120,000 *Dublin Street Map*, which covers the area within the M50 motorway.

GETTING TO/FROM THE WALK
Iarnród Éireann's (☎ 01-836 6222; www.irishrail.ie) Heuston station is only 10 minutes' walk from the park via St John's Rd West and Parkgate St. As well as direct train connections from most cities in the south and west of the country, there are numerous **Dublin Bus** (☎ 01-873 4222) and **Luas** (www.luas.ie) connections from all round the city.

Numerous Dublin Bus services also pass the park's Parkgate St entrance, including Nos 25, 25A, 26, 66 and 67 from Pearse St, and Nos 51, 68 and 69 from Aston Quay. The single fare is €1.60.

THE WALK
Pass through the impressive pillars of the Parkgate St entrance, then turn right into the **People's Garden**, the only formal part of the park. Soon bear left at a junction, then right along a path between colourful flower beds, past a pond on your right and then a statue of Sean Heuston (a leader of the 1916 Rising) on the left. Cross a road and continue down a path; a 19th-century bandstand sits in Band Hollow on your right and you soon reach a well-preserved 19th-century timber building housing **Phoenix Park Tea Rooms** (snacks €3-7.50; daily).

PHOENIX PARK & RIVER LIFFEY

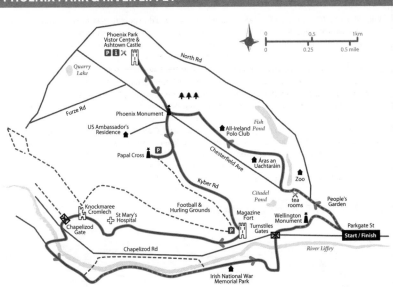

Cross the road on the far side of the building and follow a path bending right beside the fence of **Dublin Zoo** (☎ 01-677 1425; www.dublinzoo.ie; € 14 /9.50/40 adult/child/family; daily), which is one of Europe's oldest zoos. Continue north, parallel to a road, passing a polo field on the left. At a road junction turn left; behind the gates on the right is **Áras an Uachtaráin**, the Irish president's residence. Walk along the road past the **All-Ireland Polo Club** building. Where the road ends, follow a grassed path beside the wall on your right; a gap in the hedge soon allows a fine view of the imposing presidential quarters.

With the **Phoenix Monument** on your left, cross another road leading to the presidential home and follow signs along a narrow road towards the visitor centre. Beyond the car park you come to **Ashtown Castle**, which dates from the 17th century. The oak trees at the castle entrance are as old as the building itself. Next to the **restaurant** (lunch daily) are the only public toilets you'll easily find in the park.

Next door is **Phoenix Park Visitor Centre** (☎ 01-677 0095; € 2.75 /1.25/7 adult/child/family; daily Apr-Oct, Mon-Sat Nov

& Dec, Sat & Sun Jan-Mar), which provides excellent audio-visual displays about the park's history and natural heritage, and also organises tours of Ashtown Castle. Return down the road from the visitor centre car park to Chesterfield Ave, cross the road and pass the entrance to the **US Ambassador's Residence**. Now follow a path south beside the road to another car park near the **Papal Cross**, erected in 1979. From here, join the road and continue right for a short distance, then left along the road ahead (Kyber Rd), which is closed to vehicles.

Pass through a wide, shallow valley to a car park below **Magazine Fort** – worth a diversion for its view of Dublin. Continue to a road junction and turn right, passing below the fort. Now bear right up to a narrow path beside football fields and go on to Acres Rd. Bear left, cross a road close to the gate of St Mary's Hospital, then descend the steps to a road and turn right. Continue down to a wider road and turn right again. Opposite the entrance to Cheshire Home, a respite care facility, is a roadside plaque describing the nearby **Knockmaree Cromlech**, a prehistoric burial chamber. With luck you might find this site in the long

A WALK THROUGH DUBLIN'S HISTORY & CULTURE

With its colourful history and enterprising inhabitants, you'd expect Dublin to come with one or two sites worth a visit. Reality does not disappoint. The city boasts scores of buildings associated with famous and notorious people and events, and countless pubs, coffee shops and bistros where you can gather strength between excursions. Naturally the best way to explore all this is on foot, and there's a wide variety of urban walking trails to chose from.

Dublin Tourism Centre (☎ 01-605 7700; www.visitdublin.com; 2 Suffolk St; daily Jul & Aug, Mon-Sat Sep-Jun) provides details of guided walking tours around the city, with prices ranging from €10–12 per person. If you prefer to make your own way round, Lonely Planet's *Dublin City Guide* can help. It describes five urban itineraries, all between 2.5km and 5km long, and taking two to three hours to complete. The walks are organised around different themes, beginning with Dublin's literary landmarks and the city's faded Viking and medieval past. Then there's the staggered walk that many people come to Dublin for – the pub crawl. Finally there are two routes that leave the centre and explore the northern and southern quarters of the capital. To whet your appetite, here's a sample of what's on offer:

VIKING & MEDIEVAL DUBLIN

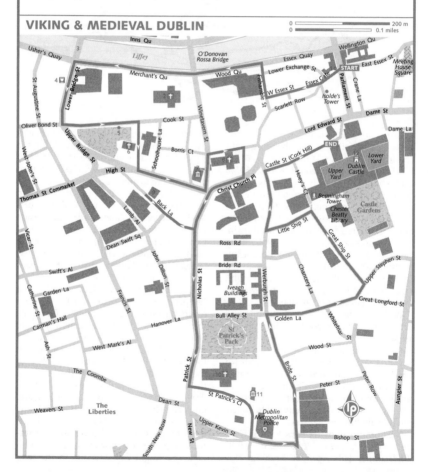

VIKING & MEDIEVAL DUBLIN

Duration   at least 2 hours
Distance   2.5km
Difficulty   easy
Start   Essex Gate, Parliament St
Finish   Dublin Castle

1 **Essex Gate** Begin your walk at the corner of Parliament St and Essex Gate, once a main entrance gate to the city. A bronze plaque on a pillar marks the spot where the gate once stood. Further along, you can see the original foundations of Isolde's Tower through a grill in the pavement, in front of the pub of the same name.

2 **Church of St Francis** Head west down Essex Gate and West Essex St until you reach Fishamble St; turn right towards the quays and left into Wood Quay. Cross Winetavern St and proceed along Merchant's Quay. To your left is the Church of St Francis, aka Adam & Eve's, after a tavern through which worshippers gained access to a secret chapel during Penal Law times in the 17th and 18th centuries.

3 **Father Mathew Bridge** Further down Merchant's Quay you'll see this bridge, built in 1818 on the spot of the fordable crossing that gave Dublin its Irish name, Baile Átha Cliath (Town of the Hurdle Ford).

4 **Brazen Head** Take a left onto Lower Bridge St and stop for a drink at Dublin's oldest pub, dating from 1198 (although the present building dates from 1668).

5 **St Audoen's Arch** Take the next left onto Cook St, where you'll find one of the only remaining gates of 32 that were built into the medieval city walls, dating from 1240.

6 **St Audoen's Church** Climb through the arch up to the ramparts to see one of the city's oldest existing churches. It was built around 1190, and is not to be confused with the newer Catholic church next door.

7 **Dvblinia** Leave the little park, join High St and head east until you reach the first corner. Here on your left is the former Synod Hall, now a museum, where medieval Dublin has been interactively re-created.

8 **Christ Church Cathedral** Turn left and walk under the Synod Hall Bridge, which links it to one of the city's most important landmarks and, in medieval times, the most important church inside the city walls.

9 **Tailors' Hall** Exit the cathedral onto Christ Church Place, cross over onto Nicholas St and turn right onto Back Lane. Proceed to Dublin's oldest surviving guild hall, built between 1703 and 1707 (though it says 1770 on the plaque) for the Tailors Guild. It's now the headquarters of An Taisce, the National Trust for Ireland.

10 **St Patrick's Cathedral** Do an about-turn, head back along the lane and turn right into Nicholas St, which becomes Patrick St. To your left you'll see Dublin's most important cathedral, which stood outside the city walls.

11 **Marsh's Library** Along St Patrick's Close, beyond the bend on the left, is this stunningly beautiful library, named after Archbishop Narcissus Marsh, dean of St Patrick's. Further along again on your left is the Dublin Metropolitan Police building, once the Episcopal Palace of St Sepulchre.

12 **Dublin Castle** Finally, follow our route up Bride St, Golden Lane and Great Ship St, and finish up with a long wander around Dublin Castle. Be sure not to miss the striking powder-blue Bermingham Tower and the nearby Chester Beatty Library, south of the castle, which houses one of Dublin's most fascinating collections of rare books and manuscripts.

PHOENIX PARK AT A GLANCE

Given its long existence and prime location, it's no surprise that Phoenix Park has been the site of several landmark events in Irish history. Some of the key dates in the park's past are:

1662 – Royal Deer Park is set aside by order of King Charles II, and later populated with English fallow deer.

1684 – The park reaches its present size.

1735 – Magazine Fort is built.

1747 – The park opens to the public; Phoenix Monument is unveiled by Lord Chesterfield, who also planted thousands of trees in the park.

1751 – Work starts on Vice-Regal Lodge, now Áras an Uachtaráin (the official residence of Ireland's president).

1764 – Royal Hibernian Military School opens, now St Mary's Hospital.

1776 – Deerfield Park is built to house the British chief secretary for Ireland.

1817–61 – Wellington Monument is built to commemorate the achievements of Arthur Wellesley, the famous Duke and a Dubliner.

1831 – Dublin Zoo is founded.

1864 – People's Garden opens.

1875 – Demonstrations in favour of Sunday closing of pubs.

1882 – British Chief Secretary, Frederick Cavendish, and Under Secretary, Thomas Burke, are murdered in the park.

1903 – 3000 trees are damaged by a fierce storm.

1927 – US Embassy opens in former Deerfield Park.

1932 – 31st Eucharistic Congress is held in the park.

1979 – 1.25 million people attend Mass celebrated by Pope John Paul II.

1980s – Dutch elm disease kills trees planted in 18th century; extensive replanting begins.

1986 – Phoenix Park is declared a National Historic Park.

---

grass at the top of the hill behind you (as you read the plaque), on the left beside the railings around the lodge.

Go on to the next plaque, featuring **Chapelizod Gate**, and walk down a paved path through the gate. Head along Park Lane to meet Martin's Row and turn left into Chapelizod village (this strange sounding name is thought to be a corruption of Chapel of Isolde). There's a small shop here and, a few steps to the left, Kelly's Grocery in a 400-year-old building. Continue to traffic lights, cross the River Liffey bridge ahead and turn left beside the Bridge Inn along St Laurence Rd. About 700m further on, go through a gateway between stone pillars to reach the riverbank. A paved path makes for easy walking downstream beside the remarkably peaceful river, through a couple of gates into the **Irish National War Memorial Park**, the main features of which are some distance from the river.

At the eastern end of the park, bear right along a minor road, then left again to cross the Liffey and Conyngham Rd. Pass through the **Turnstile Gates** back into Phoenix Park. Climb the steps and bear right to a roadside path for about 250m, then continue to the 67m-high **Wellington Monument**. In its day this was the world's tallest obelisk; the bronze bas-reliefs, made from captured cannons, depict Wellington's battlefield victories. Cross the grass to Chesterfield Ave and turn right to return to the Parkgate St exit.

Designed by renowned architect, Sir Edwin Lutyens, the Irish National War Memorial commemorates the estimated 49,000 Irishmen – all volunteers – who died during WWI. Lutyens' design features a Great War stone surrounded by circular fountains, which are, in turn, enclosed by pairs of 'book rooms' and pergolas. The 'book rooms' are small limestone pavilions which originally contained books listing the names of the war dead.

DUBLIN & WICKLOW

HOWTH PENINSULA

Duration 3½–4 hours
Distance 10km
Ascent 240m
Difficulty easy–moderate
Start/Finish Howth DART Station
Nearest Town Dublin (p65)
Transport train, bus

Summary This pleasant ramble along the cliffs of the Howth Peninsula offers wild coastal scenery within easy reach of the capital.

Situated 13km northeast of Dublin city centre, the Howth Peninsula forms the northern shore of Dublin Bay. Despite the relentless march of suburbia elsewhere around the capital, it has managed to retain a sizeable tract of wild, open space and stretches of quite rugged coastline. The peninsula has long attracted day-trippers from Dublin, but the recent development of a series of National Loop Walks means the various paths across the clifftops and heathland are now clearly marked. This route follows the longest marked trail in the area, the 'Bog of Frogs Loop', and is well signed throughout by purple arrows.

It's an extremely scenic excursion, and on a clear day you can see both the Mourne Mountains to the north and the Wicklow Mountains to the south. At different times of the year these vistas are framed by bright yellow gorse, vivid pink sea thrift, and the deep mauve of heath and ling heather.

Surprisingly perhaps, given Dublin's proximity, Howth is also home to the largest seabird colony on Ireland's east coast. Thousands of birds, including fulmars, kittiwakes and guillemots, nest on the steep quartzite cliffs between Balscadden Bay and Baily lighthouse. A short distance offshore, Ireland's Eye and Lambay Island are other important seabird sanctuaries. Tidal mudflats along the southern shore of the peninsula also provide an internationally important wintering ground for waders and wildfowl, such as redshank and brent geese.

The name Howth perpetuates the Viking visitation here centuries ago and is derived from the Norse word *höfuth*, meaning 'head'. The harbour dates from 1812, when the village became the main port for passengers and mail arriving from England, though the channel soon silted up and traffic moved south to Dún Laoghaire. Nowadays

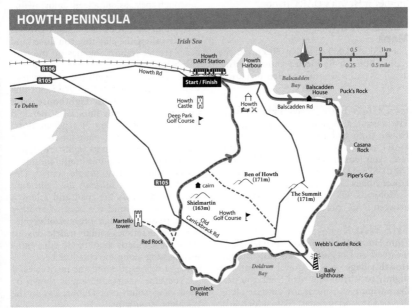

HOWTH PENINSULA

DUBLIN & WICKLOW

A TOWER OF STRENGTH

Still a fairly common feature along Ireland's coast, Martello towers form part of the scenery on both the Howth Peninsula and Bray Head walks near Dublin. In the Howth area no less than three towers survive – one on the southwest coast and two above the western shore of Balscadden Bay.

These elegant structures date from colonial times. Between 1804 and 1814, 27 of them were built along the east coast – around one-third of the total planned for the whole country. The intention was to defend the country against French invasion, an indignity already endured twice during the 1790s and perceived as a real threat as long as Napoleon remained in power. Ironically based on a prototype from Napoleon's birthplace, Corsica, the towers were three storeys high, had 2.5m-thick walls, sported huge, rail-mounted cannons on the roof and could house a small band of troops.

Many of the towers were guarded for just a few short years, before being gradually abandoned after 1815. As structures they've endured remarkably well, however, and now often serve more harmless purposes as restaurants and private residences.

Perhaps the most interesting tower in the Dublin area can be found at Sandycove Point, around 1.5km east of Dún Laoghaire in the south of the city. It was here that the writer James Joyce set the first chapter of his novel *Ulysses*. Today the building houses the **James Joyce Museum** (☎ 01280 9265; admission €7.25; daily Apr-Oct) where you can view letters, photographs and first editions of Joyce's works.

the harbour is full of sailing craft and on fine weekends the village is jammed with beach-starved Dubliners seeking a day by the sea. The moral is, of course, to travel via public transport, so the following walk starts and finishes at Howth's DART station.

PLANNING
Maps
The OSI 1:50,000 map No 50 covers the walk, although it doesn't show the fine detail of paths around the Ben of Howth area.

GETTING TO/FROM THE WALK
The easiest and quickest way to get to Howth from Dublin city centre is on the DART (€2.20, 20 minutes). For the same fare, you could also take **Dublin Bus** (☎ 01-873 4222) service 31 or 31A from Lower Abbey St.

Motorists will find a large parking area between DART station and the harbour.

THE WALK
From Howth DART station, turn left along the road and begin to head east through **Howth village**. A wide gravel footpath set slightly back from the road leads you past the **harbour** and marina. Continue along the road around the coast (Balscadden Rd),

climbing past **Balscadden House** on the left, which was home to the poet WB Yeats between 1881 and 1887. You soon reach the **car park** at the end of the road, where the cliff path begins. Follow the path up the rough coastal slope ahead, enjoying fine views north over Lambay Island and the precipitous pinnacles of Ireland's Eye. As you pass along the cliff-top, you'll see (and hear) several seabird colonies on the rock face below.

At the Nose of Howth the route swings south, tracing the beautiful, wild cliff-line for a further 2km. **Baily Lighthouse**, built in 1814, now comes into view, perched dramatically on the tip of a promontory. Here you come to a path junction. The area's three shorter loop walks are signed off to the right, but this route continues ahead, following lone purple arrows. Descend past a house to reach the lighthouse access road. Cross the road and follow a narrow path around the back of another house, passing through a tunnel of vegetation. The sometimes-muddy trail leads west along the southern shore of Howth Peninsula, passing along the cliff-line beneath a series of houses. Beyond the intricacies of the coastline, your attention is drawn by good views south over Dublin Bay to the Wicklow Mountains.

The path rounds **Drumleck Point** then descends closer to the shore, sometimes passing over the boulders at the back of a series of coves. Soon after descending a flight of steps cut into the rock, an angular **Martello tower** comes into sight ahead (see the boxed text A Tower of Strength, p44). Around 200m before the tower, a sign indicates the trail inland to the right (2½ hours from the start). Leave the coast here and climb to a grassy meadow, where a left then a right turn brings you to a road. Cross straight over this, climbing through gorse and bracken with great views northwest over the narrow, sand-fringed neck of land that connects Howth to the mainland.

The path now brings you to Howth Golf Course, where a series of white stones mark the route around the greens and fairways. Re-enter wilder terrain and continue along the western slopes of the **Ben of Howth** (171m). At a path junction, the red route comes down from the masts to the right, and the two routes continue ahead in tandem. Descend through deciduous woodland to the end of a suburban street. Now follow the arrows through a series of turnings, keeping generally left at the junctions. This brings you to a paved footpath that leads down a tree-lined alley and exits opposite Howth DART station, where the route began.

BRAY HEAD

Duration 4–4¼ hours
Distance 10km
Ascent 290m
Difficulty easy–moderate
Start Greystones DART station
Finish Bray DART station
Nearest Town Dublin (p65)
Transport train, bus

Summary A dramatic hike above coastal cliffs separating two popular seaside towns; far-reaching vistas from Bray Head's summit.

The southern seaside suburbs of Greystones and Bray, though fast spreading inland towards the foothills of the Wicklow Mountains, are still recognisable as the traditional seaside resorts to which Dubliners escaped on holidays. They remain extremely popular on weekends – places where kids play happily in the sand and water, shops sell dreadful souvenirs, and people enjoy ice-cream parlours and strolling along the promenade.

Besides the pleasures of the two towns, it's the land that separates them that appeals to walkers. Between the resorts lies a marvellously rugged stretch of coastline, traversed by a well-used path – so well-used, in fact, that on a Sunday afternoon it feels almost like O'Connell St in the centre of Dublin. Don't miss the ascent to the summit of Bray Head (206m) towards the end of the route – the climb is well worth the effort for the fine view over Dublin Bay below.

The walk is described starting from Greystones and finishing in Bray. Of course, it can also be done in the opposite direction, but remember that there are many more trains back towards Dublin from Bray than from Greystones. For refreshments, there's a wide selection of interesting cafés around Greystones station, while a choice of ice-cream parlours and fast-food joints can be found at the southern end of Bray Beach.

PLANNING
Maps
The OSI 1:50,000 map No 56 is the one to carry.

GETTING TO/FROM THE WALK
Greystones is at the southern end of Dublin's **DART** (☎ 01-836 6222; www.irishrail .ie) line (€2.70, 55 minutes to Dublin Connolly). Alternatively, **Dublin Bus** (☎ 01-872 0000) service No 84, from Dublin's Eden Quay stops near Greystones station (€3.50, one hour 20 minutes, at least 13 daily).

Bray is also on the **DART** (€2.50, 45 minutes to Dublin Connolly). **Dublin Bus** services No 45 and 84 run from Bray station to Eden Quay in Dublin (€2.50, one hour 10 minutes, every 20 minutes daily).

THE WALK
From the entrance to Greystones DART station, turn right for about 200m, then take the first left along a nameless lane. Cross a footbridge over the railway and go on to the promenade beside the rocky shore. Here you come to the **harbour**. At the time of writing the harbour area was subject to

BRAY HEAD & GREAT SUGAR LOAF

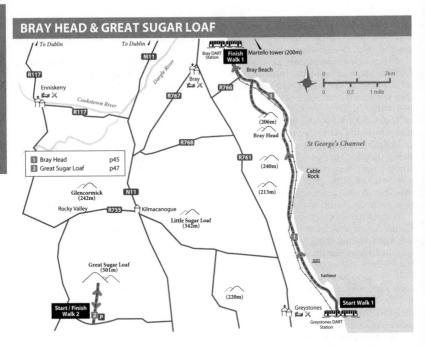

major construction work, with plans for shops, restaurants and cafés. When the work is complete you should simply be able to follow the path north past Greystones Sailing Club and onwards along the coast. While work is in progress, keep right and follow the boarding past the sailing club, then continue between metal fencing to re-join the coastal path 500m further north. This is where the walk really gets going along a wide gravel track. From here you have a good view of conical **Great Sugar Loaf** (501m) to the west (see p47), while Bray Head fills the prospect northwards.

The track now dwindles to a footpath underfoot. Continue past a playing field, and soon dip left to bypass a washed-away bridge. The path gradually rises along the low cliff-top, passing **Cable Rock** below. Continue through several hundred metres of woodland and tall scrub, then across the precipitous, open slopes of **Bray Head**. In places you look straight down to the railway line, perched precariously on a wide ledge. Eventually you round a bend and Dalkey Hill and its adjacent island come into view ahead. Now begin the gradual descent towards

Bray Beach. Well down the slope towards the strand you come to a gap in the stone wall and a flight of steps on the left (2-2¼ hours from Greystones). This is where you can leave the coastal path and climb to the top of Bray Head.

The concrete steps soon end, but continue ahead on a steep, rough path that leads up through woodland. Keep more or less straight ahead, ignoring all paths diverging right and left. From a crude rubbish tip in the trees, veer left, keeping to the widest trail. Soon you emerge from the trees and the path winds around, up through gorse, heather and rocks, to the summit and a large cross. The wide view takes in the Howth Peninsula and Dublin to the north, and Great Sugar Loaf to the southwest.

Retrace your steps back to the wide coastal path, having taken about 1¼ hours for the ascent and descent. Turn left and head into **Bray**, either strolling along the promenade or taking to the beach if the tide is out. Bray's **Martello tower**, now a private home, is partly hidden among houses a short distance inland from the marina (see the boxed text A Tower of Strength, p44). Roughly

250m before the harbour breakwater and marina at the northern end of Bray Beach, turn left along a side street; there are two pubs here – Hibernia and Katie Gallagher's. Cross the railway line and continue to the station, situated a short distance to the left (45 minutes from the summit path).

GREAT SUGAR LOAF

Duration 1–1¼ hours
Distance 3km
Ascent 210m
Difficulty moderate
Start/Finish Lay-by at GR O235119
Nearest Town Enniskerry (p67)
Transport private

Summary A steep ascent to the breezy summit of an unmistakable landmark between the coast and the Wicklow foothills.

A perfect cone from most angles, Great Sugar Loaf (501m) is an icon of the north Wicklow/Dublin area. It stands isolated but proud, a constant feature of the skyline from both Dublin's southern suburbs and from the Wicklow hills to the west. Quartzite boulders and scree spill over the summit and down the steep slopes, lending it a dramatic profile reminiscent of a volcano. Its location as the most easterly outlier of the Wicklow Mountains also means it commands fantastic views over the coast below.

The mountain's unique form makes it a popular destination, and a well-worn path leads up the southern slopes. The trail may be short, but don't underestimate the nature of the challenge; this is a peak of such character that even experienced walkers will enjoy the trip to the top. In particular, it's an ideal destination for active families – children from six years and up can be seen attacking the rock scramble near the top with gusto, and proclaiming themselves conqueror of the world once they reach the summit.

Note that the final ascent to the top crosses steep rock, which becomes slippery in wet conditions. It's best therefore to avoid this route after rain.

PLANNING
Maps
The OSI 1:50,000 map No 56 covers the walk.

GETTING TO/FROM THE WALK
The route starts and finishes at a parking area on the southern side of Great Sugar Loaf. Approach via the N11 Dublin–Wicklow road. Take the exit around 2.5km south of Kilmacanogue village and head east, past the Glenview Hotel. Follow this minor road uphill, keeping right at a T-junction almost a kilometre later. Park in a lay-by on the northern side of the road roughly 2km further on.

St Kevin's Bus (☎ 281 8119; www.glen daloughbus.com) runs along the R755 – less than 1km from the parking area – on its way from Dublin and Bray to Roundwood, Laragh and Glendalough. The driver should be able to drop you off at the closest point if you arrange it in advance. For full details of the service, see Glendalough (p67).

THE WALK
From the **parking area**, head north through the heather along a wide, grassy path. The climb begins immediately, but the angle of ascent is relatively benign until you reach the foot of the mountain proper. Here the path veers left and morphs into a steep, rocky trail that sweeps up the hill's southwestern flank. Keep straight ahead along the trail, and a short distance beneath the top, bear right (east) for the final ascent to the top.

The last 100m of the climb is by far the most challenging section of the route. A well-worn stone gully marks the passage of previous visitors, though a more stable route can be found off to the right. Whichever way you go up, hands will be needed as you scramble over the steep rock, and you should take care to avoid stepping on loose stones. Children of an adventurous nature love the experience, but will also appreciate an adult's presence close behind them.

The small summit is unadorned by trig pillar or cairn, the sharp tip providing the only landmark necessary (40 minutes from the start). The exhilaration of the climb makes the view doubly impressive; among the multifarious features on display are Howth Peninsula and Dublin city to the north, **Bray Head** and the Irish Sea to the east, and the northern peaks of the Wicklow Mountains to the west.

For the descent, simply retrace your outward route, taking particular care over the steep section beneath the summit.

WICKLOW MOUNTAINS

Right on Dublin's southern doorstep, the Wicklow Mountains are one of the most popular walking areas in Ireland. Highlights include numerous accessible summits and the famous Wicklow Way (p49), the first official Waymarked Way in the country. It's the scenic variety that makes this an obvious choice for walkers; the region overflows with natural drama in the form of waterfalls, lakes, woodlands, open moors and mountains of all shapes and sizes. The big, rounded hills and deep valleys have a unique character, and even the most well-travelled visitor will find much to enjoy.

The unfortunate cost of its proximity to Dublin is an over-spill of the sort of problems that are normally restricted to cities. Theft from parked cars is commonplace (see the boxed text Beware Thieves, p50), while high volumes of weekend traffic can cause chaos along the region's narrow roads.

Fortunately it's a simple matter to take a few basic security precautions, and you'll discover it's equally easy to escape the crowds. And with so many quality routes within a compact area, it's perfectly feasible to do several walks from one location. In fact, all of the routes in this section can be linked together without the need to ever set foot in a vehicle (see the boxed text A Wicklow Odyssey). Whether you choose the vagabond lifestyle or a relaxing break in one of the region's villages, this is the perfect place to kick back, relax, and still get some quality distance beneath your boots.

ENVIRONMENT

The geology of the Wicklow Mountains is at once simple and intricate. Essentially the mountains have a granite core surrounded by metamorphic rock, mainly schist. Complex chemical processes in the contact zone also produced outcrops of lead, silver and zinc. Over millennia the various rocks have eroded to leave broad, undulating mountain uplands.

During the last ice age glaciers covered Wicklow's upland terrain and carved out deep, steep-sided valleys. Evidence of their passing can be seen most notably at Glendalough. After the glaciers had vanished here, a single lake filled the glen, but Lugduff Brook subsequently dumped vast amounts of mud, sand and gravel on the valley floor. The resulting barrier (or alluvial fan) created two lakes, now known as Upper Lake and Lower Lake (see the boxed text Signs of a Glacial Past, p30).

Many of the higher reaches of the Wicklow Mountains are covered with blanket bog, but the steeper and drier ground supports mats of ling, bell heather and bilberry. In the valley woodlands, sessile oaks and their natural companions – birch, rowan, holly, hazel and ash – have staged a recovery from near extinction. Plentiful for 1000 years or more, these forests were decimated from the 17th century onwards to provide building materials, and charcoal to fuel iron-ore smelters. Although the woodlands were coppiced (periodically cut down to near ground level to promote regular regrowth) rather than felled, the frequency of coppicing was excessive. Since the establishment of state forests in the 1930s, more enlightened practices have encouraged

A WICKLOW ODYSSEY

If you have a week or more to spend in the Wicklow Mountains, why not take the challenge of completing all the routes in this section without ever resorting to mechanised transport. A fantastic adventure for any fit walker, and especially suited to those who are travelling without their own vehicle.

The journey would begin at Dublin's Marlay Park. From here, follow the first two and a half days of the Wicklow Way as far as the chiselled valley of Glendalough. Pause long enough to complete the Camaderry and Mullacor routes, two circuits exploring the peaks at the head of the valley. Then rejoin the Wicklow Way and continue southwest to Glenmalure. Here your odyssey would be finished in style with an ascent of the region's highest peak, Lugnaquilla. See what you're made of and complete it all in a week, or spare the legs and throw in a few rest days as you go. Either way, you could truly claim to know the Wicklow hills by the end of the trip.

WICKLOW MOUNTAINS NATIONAL PARK

Wicklow Mountains National Park is a patchwork of upland areas that together cover much of the high terrain of Wicklow. Stretching from the county's northern border, just a few kilometres from the suburbs of Dublin, the park extends south for some 35km to end south of Lugnaquilla.

Mapping the park's exact boundary is a difficult task, however, given the state's continual and piecemeal enlargement policy. Since it was established in 1991, several parcels of land have been transferred from Coillte Teoranta, the state forestry body, while other areas have been purchased from private landowners when land comes to public market. At the time of writing the park measured an impressive 170 sq km, making it the largest national park in the country, and it will continue to grow as new lands are acquired.

The primary purpose of the park is the conservation of local biodiversity and landscape. Of course, it also provides an invaluable recreational space for visitors, with walkers as particular beneficiaries. Annual visitor numbers are estimated at more than a million; not bad for a country with a total population just four times that figure.

Several roads cross park lands and traditional sheep grazing continues, but there are no settlements of any size within its boundaries. Numerous major mountain summits are encompassed, though spectacular Glendalough remains the undisputed showpiece. To find out more about the park, see www.wicklownationalpark.ie or visit the National Park Information Centre near Glendalough's Upper Lake.

the expansion of oak woods; Glendalough Woods Nature Reserve protects one of the few oak woods left in Ireland. There is also a fine stand of Scots pines on the northern side of Glendalough.

Hybrid red and sika deer are now plentiful in the area, and with luck you may see some. Red squirrels live in the conifers beside Upper Lake, and on a quiet day you may see foxes and hares on the higher ground, and smell, if not see, feral goats. The moors are also home to birds typical of such areas: red grouse, skylarks, meadow pipits and the more elusive kestrel and peregrine falcon (see Environment, p31, for more details).

PLANNING
Books
David Herman's *Hill Walkers' Wicklow* describes 30 one-day mountain walks and is the best walking guide to the area.

Information Sources
Wicklow County Tourism (☎ 0404-20070; www.visitwicklow.ie; Wicklow Enterprise Park, Wicklow Town) is the region's official point of contact for visitor information.

ACCESS TOWNS
See Glendalough (p67) and Roundwood (p68).

WICKLOW WAY HIGHLIGHT

Duration 3 days
Distance 69km
Difficulty moderate
Start Marlay Park
Finish Glenmalure
Nearest Towns Dublin (p65), Enniskerry (p67), Roundwood (p68), Glendalough (p67), Glenmalure (p68)
Transport bus, taxi

Summary The best section of Ireland's most famous long-distance walk. Begin in the suburbs of Dublin and travel through increasingly dramatic scenery to the heart of the Wicklow Mountains.

The 132km-long Wicklow Way passes through some of the finest mountain landscape in Ireland, crossing wild, breezy moorlands, high mountain rises, and several marvellous glens. This highlight describes the best section of the longer route, following the first half of the six-day trail.

The route was conceived by JB Malone, one of Ireland's best-known walkers, and it opened in 1982. Almost three decades later, it's still immensely popular and attracts walkers from many countries. This means that a trip along the Way is also a great social experience, and a natural camaraderie builds up through meeting the same people along the trail and in the villages at the end of each day.

It's a fantastic feeling to leave the busy suburbs of the capital on foot, arrive a couple of days later amidst some of the most dramatic mountain scenery in the country, and to know you've made the entire journey under your own steam. Plentiful vantage points along the way offer a seductive sense of progress as well as superb views. The route follows a mixture of moorland paths and forest tracks, with road walking kept to a minimum. This is achieved by keeping to the hills as much as possible and avoiding most of the area's villages and towns. This gives the trail an enjoyably remote feel, but it does mean that some of the accommodation options are a short detour away from the path.

The route is well marked throughout, with black posts bearing a yellow walking figure. You'll also find signposts at some road and track junctions, indicating direction, and sometimes distance, to the next significant landmark. Many signs bear the route's Irish name, *Slí Cualann Nua*. *Cuala* is an old name for the area embracing much of southern County Dublin and northern County Wicklow. One of the roads linking this area to Tara, Ireland's pre-Christian seat of political power and pagan worship, was known as *Slí Cualann*. Thus *Slí Cualann Nua* translates as the 'New Cualann Way'.

The southern section of the route, the part not described here, is less dramatic in terms of scenery and also spends significantly more time along roads. If you're determined to complete the entire trail, however, you'll find a summary of the remainder of the route (See the boxed text If You Just Can't Get Enough of a Good Thing…, p56).

BEWARE: THIEVES

Sadly, it's necessary to warn visitors to the Wicklow Mountains to lock vehicles and remove any valuables from sight. The best policy is to leave nothing at all inside your car, wherever it's parked. Thefts from vehicles are rife in the area and the perpetrators will smash windows in search of plunder.

PLANNING

The only commercial camping ground along the route is at Roundwood (see p68). Opportunities for wild camping are limited, largely because it is prohibited within Wicklow Mountains National Park, where you spend much of your time. That said, you will see signs of previous campers, especially in wild mountain valleys and forest clearings, though sites are often less than ideal.

Fortunately there is plenty of serviced accommodation, from hostels to B&Bs and hotels. This means there are numerous options for splitting the route into different stages. In particular the third day described – from Roundwood to Glenmalure – may be too long for some at 26km. The alternative here is to break the journey at Glendalough, splitting the stage into two legs of 12km and 14km respectively.

Note that the only ATM along the three-day section described is in Roundwood. Many B&Bs and hostels only accept cash, so make sure to carry enough to get you through the trip.

Maps & Books

Two OSI 1:50,000 maps, No 50 and No 56, are needed for the route. Alternatively, use two EastWest Mapping 1:30,000 sheets, *The Dublin & North Wicklow Mountains* and *Lugnaquilla & Glendalough*.

The Wicklow Way by Jacquetta Megarry and Sandra Bardwell was revised in 2008 and has the most up-to-date descriptions. It contains 1:100,000 strip maps, great photos and a comprehensive description of the route from north to south. Alternatively, *The Wicklow Way Map Guide* by EastWest Mapping was updated in 2005. It has maps at 1:50,000 and background information on local and natural history.

Information Sources

The website www.wicklowway.com is an invaluable resource when it comes to planning your trip, and provides accommodation listings as well as trail notes, maps and a host of background information.

Guided Walks

To simplify trip logistics, you may want to enlist the help of a company offering self-guided trips along the route. This means

VARYING FORTUNES OF MARLAY PARK

The rather elegant estate house and surrounding lands of Marlay Park were the work of David La Touche, a Huguenot by birth who made his fortune running a successful banking business in Dublin. He purchased the estate in 1768 and over the years poured vast sums of money into reconstructing the early-18th-century building and landscaping the extensive grounds. Waterfalls and ponds were created by impounding the waters of the Little Dargle River, and large numbers of trees and shrubs were planted. Once it was finished, the entire estate was named in honour of his wife Elizabeth Marlay.

La Touche's descendants sold the estate in 1872, and it was subsequently broken up by developers. A century later Dublin County Council acquired the house and surviving 86 hectares, and a regional park was established in 1975. The house was rescued from semi-dereliction by a major refurbishment scheme between 1992 and 2000, a project that also helped to revive traditional building skills by training numerous apprentices in old-fashioned craft techniques.

you walk on your own, at your own pace, but benefit from back-up support such as pre-paid accommodation, luggage transfers and comprehensive route notes and maps. Prices are per person sharing a double room; expect to pay a supplement for singles. Alternatively, if you're happy to organise your own accommodation but like the idea of someone else carrying your bags, you could opt just for a baggage transfer service.

Reputable Irish companies offering such services for the Wicklow Way are:

Footfalls (☎ 0404-45152; www.walking hikingireland.com; Trooperstown, Roundwood) This local company offers a variety of walking tours along the Wicklow Way, including a self-guided trip of eight days starting in Tinahely and finishing in Enniskerry for €549.
Tailor-Made Tours (☎ 066-976 6007; www.tailor-madetours.com; Ferry Rd, Keel, Castlemaine, Co Kerry) An eight-day, self-guided trip from Tinahely to Enniskerry costs €496 with this group.
Wicklow Way Baggage (☎ 086 269 8659; www.wicklowwaybaggage.com; Roundwood) This company will simply transport your baggage from one stage to another for €7.50 per bag per day.

GETTING TO/FROM THE WALK

To get to Marlay Park and the start of the Way, catch the **Dublin Bus** (☎ 01-872 0000) service No 16 from Upper O'Connell St (outside Burger King) in central Dublin (€2, 40 minutes, every 20 minutes). Alight at the Marley Grange stop opposite the park entrance.

At the southern end, Glenmalure is not served by a bus service, so you'll have to get back to Glendalough to access the nearest public transport. Taxis operating in the area include **Mick Dunbar** (☎ 087 817 6630) and **Andy Burke** (☎ 087 285 5406). Expect to pay around €20 for the ride. See Glendalough (p67) for onward transport details.

THE WALK
Day 1: Marlay Park to Knockree
5½–6½ hours, 20km, 630m ascent
The Way gets off to a good start through the woodlands of Marlay Park, and you'll soon leave all thoughts of the city behind as you tackle the Wicklow foothills. Reaching Knockree at the end of the day, the big hills loom ahead. Much of the day follows quiet roads, forest tracks and footpaths where boggy places are few.

From the gates at the main entrance to **Marlay Park**, bear left towards the signposted craft centre, keeping the main estate buildings on the right. Continue to a car park just inside the eastern entrance. Where this car park meets a grassy playing area, a plaque marks the official start of the Wicklow Way.

The route begins along wide paths through the beautifully wooded grounds, and is well marked as it follows the Little Dargle River upstream. At a T-junction turn right along a path parallel to the M50 motorway. Soon, cross a car park and head left out of the gates, then turn immediately right along a path and go down to a junction. Pass under the motorway and bear left up a minor road, soon beginning to climb quite steadily. Fork left into **Kilmashogue Wood** around 1¼ hours from Marlay Park.

DUBLIN & WICKLOW

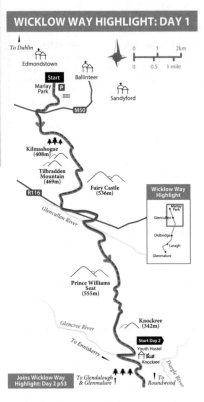

WICKLOW WAY HIGHLIGHT: DAY 1

Now keep left along a forest track, soon catching sight of Dublin Harbour and the Howth Peninsula to the north.

Roughly 2km from the wood entrance, bear left at the top of a series of zigzags and descend gently for 300m. Now turn right up a rocky path that leads to the forest edge. Pass out of the trees and turn left, and almost immediately you find yourself amid open moorland. The next change of direction is right turn at a T-junction (a left turn would take you to the top of 536m **Fairy Castle**; 1km return). Then a steep descent lands you at a bitumen road – the R116 – in the vale of Glencullen (1½ hours from Kilmashogue Wood entrance). Turn left, watching out for traffic along the fairly busy road.

It takes about 30 minutes to cover the distance to Boranaraltry Lane on the right. Follow this down across the **Glencullen River**, and continue up the side of the glen

through a series of turnstiles. Roughly 15 minutes beyond the river you come to a junction; here the Wicklow Way sweeps round to the right and begins to wind upwards to open moorland. It's well worth pausing here and looking behind you to savour the final views over Dublin. Pass through a line of pines, and the forest track beneath your feet morphs into a newly laid gravel path. Drainage channels guide the surface water away, making the once-boggy trip around the summit of **Prince William's Seat** (555m) a far more comfortable task.

The initial part of the descent is obvious as the path heads down through an impressive jumble of boulders. You now cross into an area where the trees have been cleared, and you'll need to keep an eye open for a couple of less obvious marker posts and rocks splashed with red paint. Fortunately you soon join another new section of path, where it's easier to enjoy the fantastic views of Great Sugar Loaf (p47) to the east. Join a forest track and descend steadily, past the first view of peaceful Glencree and across several track junctions, to a road (two hours from Glencullen). If you intend to stay in Enniskerry (p67) and can arrange a lift from your accommodation host, this would be a convenient place for a rendezvous. Otherwise, it's a 4km walk left along the road to the village.

To continue to Knockree, turn right and follow the road for about 200m to a junction. Turn left here and head along a narrow lane for roughly 800m. Then turn left onto a path that skirts Knockree hill and drops down to a minor road near the youth hostel (45 minutes from the Enniskerry road).

Just a few metres from the Way, **Knockree Youth Hostel** (☎ 01-276 7981; www .anoige.ie/hostels/knockree; Lackan House, Knockree; dm/tw €21/55) is located in a former farmhouse. It was completely refurbished in 2008 to 'five star hostel' standard, and now offers fantastic facilities including an optional continental breakfast for €3.

Just 1km east of the Way along a minor road, **Oaklawn B&B** (☎ 01-286 0493; www.oaklawnhouse.com; Glaskenny, Enniskerry; s/d €55/90) provides alternate accommodation in a large, two-storey home. The helpful owners can provide transport into Enniskerry for an evening meal.

Day 2: Knockree to Roundwood
5–6 hours, 22km, 680m ascent

Today you enter the heart of the Wicklow Mountains. The day begins impressively with the highest waterfall in Ireland, and the scenery just keeps getting better. There are long stretches across open moorland with excellent views, and highly recommended walks to the summit of Maulin (570m) and Djouce (725m). The hiking is almost exclusively off-road, along a series of high footpaths and forest tracks.

Rejoin the Way and cross the road, following first a forest track and then a path on the left. This brings you down to Glencree River, where a grassy riverbank path gives delightful walking downstream for about 1km. Here you come to a footbridge; cross this and continue up a path then forest track to a road. Turn left and follow the road for about 250m to the entrance to Crone Wood and a car park. **Coolakay House** (☎ 01286 2423; www.coolakayhouse.com; Enniskerry; s/d €60/90) offers B&B in a 19th-century farmhouse and is located 1.5km further southeast along the road. Evening meals are served in the on-site restaurant.

From Crone Wood car park, the route heads south and southeast along forest roads for some 2km, then begins to climb steeply above the Dargle Valley. Around 1¼ hours from the start you suddenly emerge into the open, to be greeted by a spectacular view of Powerscourt Waterfall. At 119m, this is the highest waterfall in Ireland, and it can be seen dropping down sheer cliffs into the wide valley below. Continue along a narrow path that snakes across the precipitous flanks of the valley, then veer into an adjacent conifer plantation. After five minutes in the trees, you pass onto more open ground where the trees have been cleared. Continue to a stone wall, and cross through a gap to a path junction on the other side. This is where you must decide if you want to make the ascent of Maulin. If so, turn right here, and refer to the Maulin Circuit description on p57 for further instructions to the top.

To continue along the Wicklow Way, turn left immediately after the stone wall. Now descend into the **Dargle River** in wild **Glensoulan**, an impressive valley dominated by the bulk of Djouce Mountain ahead. Cross the Dargle via a footbridge

and follow a wide path beside a plantation to a stile over a stone wall. From here a moorland trail rises across the northeastern flank of Djouce, reaching a much-trodden junction at the top of the mountain's eastern ridge (an hour from the waterfall view). The remarkably wide coastal view extends north to the Howth Peninsula and south to Wicklow Head. Continue across the steep slope and up to a shallow saddle roughly 800m south of Djouce's summit. This is the best take-off point for the ascent to the top of Djouce – see the side trip on p59 for full details of this much-recommended detour.

Just south of here, inside the boundary of Wicklow Mountains National Park, you join a raised boardwalk built of railway sleepers. This is intended not only to give walkers an easy ride but, more importantly, to give the much-trampled peat bog a chance to regenerate. The path carries you effortlessly

WICKLOW WAY HIGHLIGHT: DAY 2

THE MONASTIC CITY

Glendalough's Monastic City is focussed on the monastery founded by St Kevin in AD 570, which continued to operate for almost a millennium until the dissolution of Irish monasteries in 1537. In its heyday, the monastery was both a centre of learning and a magnet for pilgrims who arrived via St Kevin's Way (see p65). The tradition of pilgrimage continued until well into the 19th century, with particular focus on 3 June, St Kevin's feast day. Today the monastic settlement remains an atmospheric place to visit, with its splendid, 30m-high round tower, the substantial remains of a cathedral, a priests' house and three churches.

---

across **White Hill** (630m) and down to a lookout over beautiful Lough Tay with its white sandy beach. At this lookout there's a simple **memorial** to JB Malone, the founder of the Wicklow Way. Follow a forest path left and right through a small plantation to a car park beside the R759 (1¼ hours from the first Djouce path junction).

Turn left onto the road and continue for 14km, where a wide path on the right leads into the plantation. Follow forest tracks south for about 3.3km, then diverge to the right and follow a path through the trees for about 300m. Continue along another forest track, which bends around to the right and brings you down to a gate. Now cross open grassland, interspersed by a few stiles, to a vehicle track. Turn left here to reach a minor road at a T-junction.

The Wicklow Way heads to the right here. However if you intend to spend the night in **Roundwood** (p68) this is where you must take your leave. Cross over the junction and follow this road straight ahead, ignoring all minor side roads. You will arrive in the centre of the village just over 2km later, around 1½ hours from the R759.

Day 3: Roundwood to Glenmalure
6½–7½ hours, 27km, 750m ascent

With a fantastic variety of scenery, this section provides a fitting finale to the three-day walk. Highlights include the much-vaunted landscape around Glendalough, along with its Monastic City, and fantastic views over Lugnaquilla, Wicklow's highest mountain. The only significant stretch of road comes at the start of the day.

If you can arrange a lift from Roundwood, it's possible to avoid the 6km of road walking that marks the start of the day. If not, return by foot to the junction where you left the Way and turn left. Follow this road for a

further 4km, heading southwest through attractive countryside with fine views of Scarr, a large sprawling hill to the west. An initial descent through fine oak woodland leads to a bridge over the **Avonmore River** and the hamlet of Oldbridge (45 minutes from **Roundwood**). Here the road begins to rise steeply again, soon passing **Wicklow Way Lodge** (☎ 01-281 8489; www.wicklowway lodge.com; s/d €60/90), a very welcoming B&B with beautiful big rooms and lovely views from the deck. The owners can provide lifts to Roundwood for evening meals.

About 400m south of a small stream, turn right along a vehicle track. This brings you up to two stiles and a path heading south beside a forestry plantation. A short moorland path then leads to a track across **Paddock Hill** (360m), where the felling of trees has revealed fantastic sweeping views to the east. As you pass over the brow of the hill, the cliff-lined corrie above Glendalough is added to the scene to the southwest, while the triangular summit of Lugnaquilla (p62) peeps over the intervening hills to the south. A fairly rapid descent along paths lands you on the **R115**. Head left along the bitumen for about 200m, then turn right down a wide path to a footbridge across the beautiful Glenmacnass River. Soon you will come to a junction where the trail forks (1¾ hours from Oldbridge). The Wicklow Way turns right here.

If you want to detour to the village of **Laragh** (p68), the shortest route is to veer left at this junction and follow a path to a forest road. Cross over this and pursue a narrow trail through the vegetation to a minor road. At a car park beside the parish church, bear left to reach the centre of the village.

After turning right at the junction, the official route crosses through lovely mixed woodland above the **Glenmacnass River**.

This leads to a forest road, where you should turn right. Cross straight over a junction of tracks and climb out into the open, turning left near the top of the rise. As you round a bend and begin the descent, a magnificent view of **Glendalough's Lower and Upper Lakes** is revealed below. Continue through a gate and briefly along a forest road. Then turn left onto a path that winds down through the trees to a cluster of four stiles. Cross over a road beneath this section, and continue down to reach another minor road opposite Glendalough Hotel (45 minutes from the Laragh path junction). If you're feeling peckish, there are several options near here for a snack – see Glendalough (p67) for information on services in the area.

Head left along the road for 150m, then turn right into the Glendalough Visitor Centre. The trails following also form part of the valley's hiking network, and are likely to be busy with strolling tourists. Pass between the car park and main building, then cross a lawn and footbridge. Follow signs to the 'Green Rd', then turn right towards Upper Lake. After 100m on the Green Rd, a short side path on the right leads across a footbridge to the Monastic City, a fascinating site that's well worth a visit (see the boxed text The Monastic City, p54).

The path soon turns to gravel and passes along the shore of Lower Lake. Continue up the valley through beautiful oak woodland until you reach the small Wicklow Mountains National Park Visitor Centre, approximately 1.5km from the Monastic City. Just beyond this building, turn left across a bridge and climb a series of steps beside the verdant chutes of Lugduff Brook and **Pollanass Waterfall**. Veer left when you meet a forest track, then left again at a junction and cross two bridges. The Way

WICKLOW WAY HIGHLIGHT: DAY 3

DUBLIN & WICKLOW

IF YOU JUST CAN'T GET ENOUGH OF A GOOD THING...

The walk described here is a selected highlight of the Wicklow Way, covering roughly the first half of the 132km-long route. There's little doubt that if you walk only the section described, you will have seen the finest mountain scenery and covered the most interesting terrain. However, for purists who yearn for the satisfaction of completing the entire trail, the remainder of the route is outlined below. OSI 1:50,000 maps No 61 and No 62 are needed for this part of the route.

DAY 4: GLENMALURE TO MOYNE
5½–6½ hours, 21km, 550m ascent
This stage leads out of the high mountains and into the rolling hills of southwest Wicklow. Begin by climbing forest tracks almost to the top of Slieve Maan (550m), then descend across a tributary of the Aghavannagh River and follow a wide path over Carrickashane Mountain (508m). A descent along tracks and roads brings you down to Iron Bridge, roughly three hours from Glenmalure.

For those who prefer a shorter day's walk of around 14km, this is the jump-off point for **Aughrim**, a pretty village with a small supermarket located around 8km southeast of the Way. Accommodation hosts offer a collection service by arrangement. B&Bs include the helpful and friendly **Butler's Byrne** (☎ 0402-36644; Rednagh Hill; s/d €45/72). Alternatively, **Lawless's Hotel** (☎ 0402-36146; www.lawlesshotel.ie; s/d €60/90) is a large, popular establishment in the centre of the village, with meals available in both the bar and restaurant.

From Iron Bridge a series of forest tracks and roads takes you south through tranquil countryside, reaching the tiny Georgian hamlet of **Moyne** around 2½ hours later. The very hospitable **Jigsaw Cottage** (☎ 059-647 1071; www.jigsawcottage.com; s/d €65/84) and, slightly further on, **Kyle Farmhouse** (☎ 059-647 1341; s/d €45/70) are both around 500m from the trail, and both serve evening meals.

DAY 5: MOYNE TO SHILLELAGH
6¼–7¼ hours, 29km, 500m ascent
The Way passes through gentle hill-country from now until the end of the route. The day begins on narrow roads and tracks, and along a delightful grassy boreen that meanders past lovely rural views. Beautiful beech trees in Coolafunshoge Wood are a particular highlight before the route swings around a hillside and descends to the small village of **Tinahely** (2¼ hours from Moyne). Many walkers finish the Way here and take advantage of the limited bus service back to Dublin. The village has a supermarket, an ATM and several options for evening meals, and is a recommended stopping point for those who stayed overnight at Iron Bridge.

leads northeast for about 600m then, from a tight right bend, heads almost directly south and across Lugduff Brook again. The ascent is steady as you follow waymarkers up through the conifer plantation, turning left then right at clearly marked junctions. Around 1¾ hours from Glendalough, you emerge onto open ground at a **saddle** between Lugduff and Mullacor (p61). On a clear day the view is fantastic. Glenmalure lies ahead, with massive Lugnaquilla sprawling across skyline. Behind you, the long ridge of Camaderry (p59) is framed against the bulk of Tonelagee (p64).

Follow a wooden boardwalk across the col towards another forestry plantation. Veer left here onto a path that contours above the trees, before turning right and descending a flight of rock steps to a forest track. Turn left here. If you're planning to stay at **Glenmalure Youth Hostel**, rather than go all the way down to the crossroads in Glenmalure, continue along the official route for roughly 1km. At an oblique junction where the Way veers southeast, turn right and descend steeply to a road. Turn right and follow the bitumen for roughly 2km to the hostel.

To continue along the Way, keep following the waymarkers as you descend a series of tracks through the plantation. Eventually you swing northeast and drop down to a minor road beside a bridge. Turn right here and follow the road to a crossroads beside Glenmalure Lodge, around 1¼ hours from the saddle. For information on facilities in the area, see Glenmalure (p68).

The first place you come to is **Sunindale House** (☎ 0402-238 170; www.sunindale.com; s/d €50/80), a large, modern home by the road. **Madeline's Guest House** (☎ 0402-38590; s/d €50/80) is in the centre of the village and has an adjoining restaurant. If you're heading back to Dublin, take the **Bus Éireann** (☎ 01-836 6111) service No 132 (€13.50, one hour 50 minutes). The service runs from Tinahely to Dublin on Thursdays and Sundays, and from Dublin to Tinahely on Thursdays, Fridays and Sundays.

Walkers who continue will cross the 100km line at Mullinacuff, a short distance before the Strankelly crossroads. A long stretch of road hiking then brings you westward across a pair of hills and onto a forest track at Raheenakit (3½ hours from Tinahely). From here, a 3km detour leads to the village of **Shillelagh**. Accommodation options include **Kealys** (☎ 053-942 9113; s/d €45/70), on the main street. Alternatively, **The Olde Shillelagh** (☎ 053-942 9113; s/d €45/70), also the main street, is affiliated to a workshop where traditional Blackthorn shillelaghs – Irish fighting sticks – are still manufactured. The locally sourced timber is seasoned and hardened, and fashioned into walking sticks, clubs, and cudgels which are hopefully only used as souvenirs these days.

DAY 6: SHILLELAGH TO CLONEGAL
4½–5½ hours, 17km, 300m ascent
This stage begins with a stretch through Raheenakit Forest, and alternates between tracks and minor roads all the way from here to the end. The countryside remains attractive all the way, with pastoral hills giving way to the broad Derry River Valley as you near Clonegal. There's nothing obvious to welcome you once you arrive, but if you look around you'll find a noticeboard with a map by JB Malone (the Way's founder) in the park to the left of the village's wide intersection. There's only one thing to do here – head for Osbourne's, a fine old pub down the road on the right, to mark your achievement in your own personal way.

Clonegal itself is a pretty village with a handful of pubs and shops but little else. The town of Bunclody, around 5km to the south, is the nearest place with a choice of accommodation, restaurants, ATMs and a bus service back to Dublin. Most accommodation hosts will collect you from Clongal by arrangement. There are comfortable rooms at **Meadowside** (☎ 053-937 7459; Ryland St; s/d €50/80), a welcoming B&B on the main road in the centre of town. A five-minute walk from the centre, **Moss Cottage** (☎ 053-937 7828; www.mosscottageireland.com; s/d €48/80) is a grand Victorian home with comfortable rooms and beautiful gardens.

The **Bus Éireann** (☎ 01-836 6111) service No 5 to Dublin (€12, two hours, two Mon-Sat and three Sun) stops in Market Square.

MAULIN CIRCUIT

Duration 2½–3 hours
Distance 7km
Ascent 420m
Difficulty moderate
Start/Finish Crone Wood car park
Nearest Town Enniskerry (p67)
Transport private

Summary An accessible and relatively easy mountain that provides fine coast and waterfall views, with an optional extension to the summit of Djouce.

Maulin (570m) is a compact, modest-sized peak that offers some of the best mountain walking as you delve into the Wicklow Mountains from Dublin. This accessible and relatively easy circuit provides all the reward of reaching a wild mountain summit, without much of the slog often associated with getting there. The other main attraction of the route is spectacular views over Powerscourt Waterfall, the highest waterfall in Ireland.

Navigation is greatly facilitated by the existence of two marked hiking routes. The first section of the route follows the yellow 'walking man' symbols of the Wicklow Way, while the descent is marked by the red footprint icon of a National Loop Walk. These sections are separated by 2.5km across open mountain terrain, though paths provide constant guidance underfoot.

DUBLIN & WICKLOW

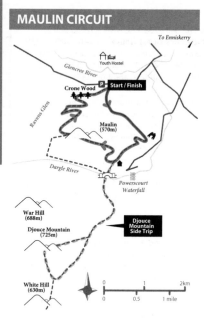

MAULIN CIRCUIT

To Enniskerry

Glencree River

Youth Hostel

Crone Wood   Start / Finish

Ravens Glen

Maulin
(570m)

Dargle River

Powerscourt
Waterfall

War Hill
(688m)

Djouce
Mountain
Side Trip

Djouce Mountain
(725m)

White Hill
(630m)

0   1   2km
0   0.5   1 mile

If you want to extend the walk, the side-trip to the summit of 725m-high Djouce Mountain is a good choice. Djouce (pronounced 'jowss') towers above the wild and lonely valley of Glensoulan. The extra elevation allows great views southwest over the bulk of the Wicklow Mountains. Including this detour doubles the day's distance and total ascent however, and merits a grade of moderate to demanding.

PLANNING
Maps
Carry the Harvey 1:30,000 map *Wicklow Mountains*, EastWest Mapping's 1:30,000 *The Dublin & North Wicklow Mountains*, or the OSI 1:50,000 map No 56.

GETTING TO/FROM THE WALK
From Enniskerry, drive south along the R760 for 3km to a junction on the right. Follow this minor road across the Dargle River and then northwest to the clearly signed 'Crone Wood' car park. A map board at the top of the car park indicates the route of both the Wicklow Way and the National Loop Walk, while a sign near the entrance lets you know what time the

car park gate will be locked (8pm in the summer, earlier in winter).

THE WALK
The route starts along the Wicklow Way. Pick up the waymarkers at the upper end of the car park and follow the marked trail south and southeast along forest roads for some 2km. Here you begin to climb steeply above the Dargle Valley. Almost an hour from the start you suddenly you emerge into the open, greeted by a spectacular view of **Powerscourt Waterfall**. At 119m, this is the highest waterfall in Ireland, and it can be seen dropping down sheer cliffs into the wide valley below.

Around 80m beyond the viewpoint you come to a map board, where the red footprint symbols of the loop walk head off to the right. Keep left along the main track, continuing along the Wicklow Way. A flatter section of trail leads past several more waterfall views, then the trail veers right over the tree-stumps of a clear-felled forest. This brings you to a gap in a wire fence and an old stone wall. Pass through these and join a rocky path. The Wicklow Way turns left here, descending steeply to Glensoulan. Head this way if you want to add the sidetrip to the summit of Djouce (see p59). However the main circuit turns right here, climbing along the rocky path towards Maulin.

After roughly 400m, the path swings northwest away from the wall and climbs across an open, heather-clad shoulder. The wide trail leads directly to the small cairn that marks the summit of **Maulin** (570m) – 45 minutes beyond the waterfall. Superb coastal views embrace Dublin Bay to the north, while Great Sugar Loaf forms a conspicuous cone in the centre of the scene.

Continue straight ahead from the summit, following a narrower path west towards the col beneath Tonduff South. An old stone wall on the right provides navigational guidance. Descend along the boggy trail, keeping close to the wall as it swings north near the col. Now turn right through a gap in the stones and follow the path to a wooden gate and stile at the corner of a forestry plantation. On the other side of this you meet a forestry track and re-join the red footprint symbols of the loop walk.

DUBLIN & WICKLOW

MIRACULOUS ESCAPE ON DJOUCE

On 12 August 1946, low cloud and mist enveloped Djouce Mountain and much of the eastern half of Ireland. This is nothing unusual, but at the same time, a severe storm triggered flash floods and unroofed houses.

Around midday a plane crossed the coast just south of Dublin, flying at an altitude of roughly 600m. On board more than 20 French Girl Guides were travelling to an international camp. The plane headed straight for the Wicklow Mountains, whose peaks reach over 700m. The inevitable happened and the plane collided with Djouce's southern ridge, bounced off and thumped down on the far side. Miraculously, the fuselage remained intact and a fire did not break out.

Two of the leaders extricated themselves from the wreckage and went in search of help, heading in opposite directions. One, accompanied by the pilot, eventually reached a farm in Glencree after just missing the Powerscourt Waterfall cliffs. The other made it to Luggala Lodge beside Lough Tay. After heroic efforts by rescuers, the entire party and crew were eventually brought down from the mountain. Despite some serious injuries, all survived.

The remaining section of the route is signed by markers for the loop walk, some of which are nailed to tree trunks. The signs direct you through numerous zigzags and junctions as you follow a series of tracks and paths down through the forest. Eventually you emerge onto a track just above the starting point, and turn left to return to the **car park** (one hour from the summit of Maulin).

SIDE TRIP: DJOUCE MOUNTAIN
2½ hours, 7.5km, 420m ascent

From the junction beside the stone wall, turn left and descend along the Wicklow Way into wild Glensoulan. Cross the **Dargle River** via a **footbridge**, then climb along a wide path beside a plantation to a stile over a stone wall. From here a moorland trail rises across the northeastern flank of Djouce, reaching a much-trodden junction at the top of the mountain's eastern ridge. You will return via this path on your homeward journey. For now, continue to follow the Wicklow Way southwest across the slope and up to a shallow saddle between Djouce and White Hill (688m). This is where you should leave the waymarked route, and turn right (north) onto a path that climbs the mountain's southern slopes. Follow this up to the summit of **Djouce** (725m), decorated with rock outcrops and a trig pillar perched atop one of the crags (1½ hours from the start of the sidetrip). The magnificent view includes a fine coastal panorama, plus the main Wicklow Mountains to the southwest.

From the summit, descend east along a wide path to the junction on the eastern ridge. Turn left here and retrace your steps back along the Wicklow Way to the junction beneath Maulin (around 45 minutes from Djouce). Follow the remainder of the Maulin Circuit back to the start.

CAMADERRY WALK

Duration 4¾–5¼ hours
Distance 14km
Ascent 600m
Difficulty moderate
Start/Finish Upper Lake car park
Nearest Towns Glendalough (p67), Laragh (p68)
Transport bus, private

Summary Experience the isolation of Glendalough's mining village, then the wide open spaces of a beautiful ridge high above the valley.

Overlooking Glendalough from the north, Camaderry (698m) is the highest point on a long, sloping ridge of peaks. Its location at the centre of the Wicklow Mountains means its summit offers fine 360° views that encompass most of the surrounding uplands. The route described takes in some cross-country walking between the Glenealo River and Turlough Hill, otherwise you're on tracks and paths all the way.

The wild and relatively natural environment on Camaderry stands in stark contrast to the ruined miners' village, which you pass above the western end of Upper Lake. At the peak of activity in the mid-19th century, this settlement contained at least four dwellings and a large building housing a water-powered ore crusher. Lead, zinc, copper and silver were the minerals mined in most abundance. For further information about the area's mining industry, see the boxed text Of Mines & Monks, p54.

PLANNING
Maps
Use the Harvey 1:30,000 map *Wicklow Mountains*, EastWest Mapping's 1:30,000 *Lugnaquilla & Glendalough,* or the OSI 1:50,000 map No 56.

GETTING TO/FROM THE WALK
The Upper Lake car park is located at the end of the Glendalough road, about 1.3km west of Glendalough Visitor Centre. The parking fee is €4 per car and facilities include public toilets and the Lakeside Take-away.

The walk can also start at the Glendalough Visitor Centre, from where you should cross the footbridge and head west along the Green Rd (The Mullacor Walk, p61). At the National Park Information Office, turn right to reach the Upper Lake car park.

THE WALK
Begin by following a gravel road west from the car park entrance, passing just above the lake shore and through Scots pines. Soon you catch a glimpse of Kevin's Bed – the remains of a tiny cottage that is the reputed resting place of St Kevin – on a small grassy shelf across the lake. Near the western end of the lake you emerge into the open and reach the site of the **old mines**. Drop down to the remains of the stone buildings of the miners' village and make your way through, crossing and re-crossing several small streams. Pick up a clear track from a long, low stone wall, and zigzag up beside the tumbling **Glenealo River**. The track becomes a walker's path by the upper cascades and generally keeps close to the stream. Pass an outlying mine near the top of the cascades. Ignore a solid footbridge across the river and follow a narrow path westward beside the stream into a wide glen.

Keep a watercourse on your left, and you'll soon turn northwestward alongside a major tributary of the Glenealo River. Soon you should catch sight of an unnaturally flat-topped, elongated mound that is

WICKLOW MOUNTAINS

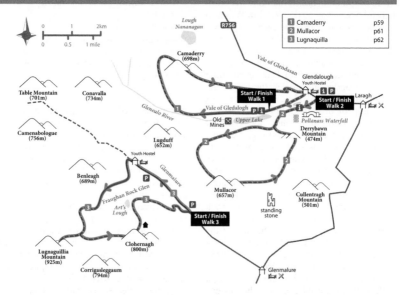

GLENDALOUGH HIKING TRAILS

For those who want to explore the scenery around Glendalough without committing to a full mountain excursion, it's worth considering one of the trails that have been developed by park authorities. There are nine walks to choose from, ranging from 1.7km to 11km in length. All the routes start at the National Park Information Office near the Upper Lake car park, and are fully signposted with colour-coded arrows. The Wicklow Way, Camaderry and Mullacor routes described in this book all follow part of the network of trails for some distance.

A leaflet containing a map and trail descriptions can be purchased for €0.50 from the National Park Information Centre. Details can also be found online at www.wicklownationalpark.ie.

Turlough Hill (located near the reservoir). Head for the hill, crossing some minor streams and fairly rough, heathery ground. There is a narrow path lurking among the heather, but its exact location is impossible to pinpoint so it's a matter of luck as to whether you hit upon it. Make your way up the glen and almost to the base of Turlough Hill, where you should come across a wide track leading southeast down to a saddle. It's easy to follow this dry, well-trodden track through a maze of peat hags then up through boulders to the spread-eagled summit plateau of **Camaderry** (698m) (about three hours from the start). The mountain's highest point is unmarked by a cairn, but distinguished by fine views of Lugnaquilla to the southwest, Mullacor to the south and massive Tonelagee to the north.

From the summit, continue southeastwards along the ridge on a good track, passing over point '677', which is marked by a small cairn. Now descend steadily on a clear path through the northern end of a line of old conifers. A secondary trail forks right here and descends very steeply, leading directly to the upper car park. However, the easiest option is to keep straight ahead and follow a grassed path through an ocean of bracken and into mixed woodland with Scots pine, larch and a few oaks. This track zigzags down to a minor junction. Turn left here and join a narrow path through the bracken to a boardwalk and steps made of railway sleepers. You now enter the forest and descend northwestwards to a forest road beside the Glendasan River. Turn right and follow this to the Glendalough road (nearly two hours from Camaderry). The visitor centre is located 250m to the left, the youth hostel and Upper Lake car park 250m and 1.25km respectively to the right.

MULLACOR WALK

Duration 4–4½ hours
Distance 14km
Ascent 600m
Difficulty moderate
Start/Finish Glendalough Visitor Centre
Nearest Towns Glendalough (p67), Laragh (p68)
Transport bus
Summary An exceptionally scenic ridge-walk high above Glendalough's lakes, starting and finishing amid picturesque oak woodlands.

At 657m, Mullacor is the highest point on the southern side of Glendalough and a deservedly popular destination. This walk makes a circuit of Lugduff Brook via the Spink – an airy, scenic cliff-top crossed by one of the most rewarding sections of trail in the national park. After visiting Mullacor, the route returns to Glendalough Valley via the summit of Derrybawn Mountain (474m).

Navigation is relatively straightforward, with route-finding simplified by a network of paths. The vast majority of the route follows wide forest tracks, steep walkers' paths, or a long section of boardwalk, built out of old railway sleepers to counteract the erosion caused by countless passing feet. The route starts and finishes at Glendalough Visitor Centre (see p67), and a wander around the exhibits is highly recommended before or after your excursion.

PLANNING
Maps

Use the Harvey 1:30,000 map *Wicklow Mountains*, EastWest Mapping's 1:30,000 *Lugnaquilla & Glendalough,* or the OSI 1:50,000 map No 56.

DUBLIN & WICKLOW

GETTING TO/FROM THE WALK

This route starts and finishes at Glendalough Visitor Centre, at the eastern edge of the settlement in Glendalough Valley. The centre is well signed and parking is free.

THE WALK

From the visitor centre car park, cross the **Glenealo River** footbridge and follow a broad path signposted 'Green Road' towards Upper Lake. About 1.5km along you come to the small **Wicklow Mountains National Park Visitor Centre** (daily May-Aug, weekends at other times), which houses informative displays about the parks natural and cultural heritage. Take time to stroll across to the shore of **Upper Lake** for the beautiful views, especially of the awesome cliffs above, which you'll soon be hiking.

Just 50m beyond the centre, turn left up a wide path towards **Pollanass Waterfall**, spelt 'Poulanass' on the sign. A long flight of steps beside Lugduff Brook and the falls takes you onto a forest track; turn left and walk uphill for a short distance and then turn right at a T-junction. Follow the track uphill and look out for a path on the right, which climbs steeply up through mixed woodland using sections of stone steps and some boardwalk. At the top of this steep section you reach open ground on a shoulder overlooking Glendalough. Here the boardwalk continues, making relatively easy, bog-free work of the long ascent of the Spink; the views of the Upper Lake and the old mine workings at the head of Glendalough are magnificent.

Eventually bear left at a fork; a few metres on from the end of the sleepers, continue along a path by the forest edge. After another short section of boardwalk you're back on the ground and a wide path leading directly towards the Lugduff–Mullacor ridge ahead (southwest). Contour south and southeast across the slope to the crest of the ridge and down to the col along more sleepers. Here you briefly meet the Wicklow Way (see p49) crossing the col, where there are excellent views south across Glenmalure to Lugnaquilla. Head up the wide path, across peaty terrain, to the amorphous summit of **Mullacor** (2¼ hours from the start).

Descend generally east from the summit, following a wide path to a broad saddle. Here you'll find a stile over a fence on the left, about 200m south of the forest corner. Cross the stile, turn left and descend beside the fence to the top corner of the forest. Now turn diagonally right on a narrow path. This crosses the wide glen below Cullentragh; cross a forest track and follow a clear path along the narrow rocky ridge to **Derrybawn Mountain** (474m) – 45 minutes from Mullacor.

Continue along the ridge for a short distance on a worn path, then drop down to the left to a small col. Keep left to descend an eroded path to a stile over the forest fence. Continue downhill through the conifers; cross a forest road and keep descending along a narrow path to another forest road. Turn left here, rejoining the Wicklow Way. Soon cross two bridges and turn right with the Way, heading towards the signposted 'car park'. Descend beside Lugduff Brook, turn right and continue back to Glendalough Visitor Centre (an hour from Derrybawn Mountain).

LUGNAQUILLA WALK

Duration 5½–6 hours
Distance 15km
Ascent 800m
Difficulty moderate–demanding
Start/Finish Parking area at GR T079929
Nearest Town Glenmalure (p68)
Transport private

Summary Lug your pack up Wicklow's highest mountain for huge views from its vast summit.

At 925m, Lugnaquilla (popularly known as 'The Lug') stands over 100m higher than the next tallest peak in the Wicklow Mountains, and is one of Ireland's 12 Munros (see the boxed text The Irish Munros, p26). It's a massive mountain that dominates Glenmalure, with generously proportioned spurs reaching north, south and east.

This immensely scenic route begins from upper Glenmalure, a valley whose lower slopes are unfortunately blighted by unsightly conifer plantations. However, the forestry is soon left behind, surpassed by the more natural wildness of a spectacular hanging valley, upper Fraughan Rock Glen. Having enjoyed tremendous views from the wide summit, there's the secluded beauty of Art's Lough to look forward to on the descent. There are fairly obvious signs of the passage of walkers for most of the way, but you need to remain alert across two tricky sections that require a little route-finding knowledge – the upper reaches of the glen and the descent from Art's Lough to a forest track.

It goes almost without saying that Lugnaquilla is very exposed, and conditions can change from full sunshine to zero visibility with alarming rapidity. Solid navigational skills are required in poor conditions to ensure you don't stumble over the ominously named corries, North Prison and South Prison, or into the firing range on the mountain's northwestern slopes (see the Warning).

PLANNING
Maps
Use the Harvey 1:30,000 map *Wicklow Mountains*, EastWest Mapping's 1:30,000 *Lugnaquilla & Glendalough,* or the OSI 1:50,000 map No 56.

GETTING TO/FROM THE WALK
The best place to start this circuit is the parking area at GR T079929. It's located about 2.7km northwest of the Glenmalure crossroads, but it's not signposted on-site. You can also start 1.2km further west along the road, at a larger car park beside the ford, or across the river at the youth hostel.

There is no public transport to the area.

THE WALK
Walk up the Glenmalure road and either cross the ford or a bridge about 60m upstream. Continue past **Glenmalure Youth Hostel** (see p68) to a T-junction. Turn left here and follow the forest road deep into magnificent **Fraughan Rock Glen**, beneath the fractured cliffs of its northwestern rim. About 45 minutes from the T-junction, the track peters out at the base of a waterfall. Cross the stream (an easy matter unless it's in spate) and tackle a short, steep ascent through bracken and boulders to the lip of a wide hanging valley above.

Stay generally near the stream, which is still on your right. Hop across some damp

> ## WARNING
> The northwestern side of Lugnaquilla lies within the Glen Imaal Artillery Range, an active training ground for the Irish military. Even when live firing is not taking place, this land may contain unexploded shells and other dangerous missiles. The boundary is marked by frequent signs and walkers are strongly advised to keep out of the area for their own safety. For further information, contact the **Army Range Warden Service** (☎ 045-404 653).

ground and start to climb again, crossing two streams coming down from the left. Make straight for the head of the valley, trending left to the base of some vertical rock slabs. Continue south up through scattered boulders for a few hundred metres to a steep gully on the right. This provides a relatively straightforward route to more open, broken ground. Keep heading generally south, climbing a slight ridge to reach the top of Lug's broad eastern spur. From here the route to the summit is easy, heading west then southwest across mostly firm, sheep-cropped turf. Pass the cliffs of the North Prison to find the summit of **Lugnaquilla** marked by a trig pillar nesting on a sprawling cairn (about three hours from the start). There's an almost overwhelming sense of space on this vast summit, with most of the Wicklow Mountains in view. A direction finder nearby identifies every feature of the panorama.

To start the descent, retrace your steps northeast and east; here you get the best views of the rugged cliffs of the South Prison. Continue east along the mainly grassy spur, taking care in poor visibility not to charge off southeast towards Carrawaystick Mountain. Head for the slight rise of **Clohernagh** (800m), where a **cairn** stands just east of the summit. Follow the well-worn path that descends eastwards from here for no more than 200m. You should now pick up a path leading northeast then north down an increasingly well-defined spur, bypassing steep fractured cliffs overlooking beautiful **Art's Lough**. With the lough clearly in view, swing northwest. The rough path doesn't go all the way to the rocky shore, but on a hot day it's tempting

REBELLION IN THE MOUNTAINS

It may seem like a long way from the wilds of Glenmalure, to the riotous streets of 1789 Paris, to Australia, but there was once a connection linking all three.

The ideals of the French Revolution –'Liberty, Equality and Fraternity' – inspired many Irish people to seek a truly national government and Catholic emancipation. The United Irishmen, an organisation with these aims, was founded in 1791 but was forced underground when war broke out between Britain and France two years later. French support for the Irish cause was readily forthcoming, but a French-led invasion in 1796 foundered. In the aftermath, the British launched an indiscriminately brutal search for United Irishmen and captured many of their leaders.

With nothing to lose, the survivors hit back, unleashing the 1798 Uprising. Fighting was largely confined to Antrim and Down in the North and Wexford in the southeast, but as local memorials reveal, also took place in Glenmalure and elsewhere (see Blackstairs Mountain, p71). The Battle of Glenmalure raged briefly and, according to a commemorative plaque near the end of the road there, more than a score of people died. The rebels were soon crushed, and the Act of Union with Britain came into force on New Year's Day 1801.

Many rebels eluded capture for several years, including a group from Glenmalure and neighbouring Glen of Imaal, led by Michael Dwyer and John Mernagh, who grew up at the foot of Lugnaquilla. The outlaws were eventually transported to Botany Bay (Australia) in 1805 and given land to start farming. Dwyer, an apparently rumbustious character, died in 1825, one week before his Irish children arrived in Sydney; Mernagh lived on until 1857.

to wade through the heather to cool off in its limpid waters.

Cross a stile near the corner of the fence parallel to the lough and turn left. A soggy, well-used path leads on beside the fence, swings left at a corner and descends, gradually trending away from the fence on the left to drop steeply and muddily to a conifer plantation. Continue to descend gently northeast for a few hundred metres, with trees on your left. The path isn't particularly clear here; you need to turn left and pass through a small gap in the conifers for 10m to arrive at an old fire break in the trees. Follow the fire break to a rough forest track that soon becomes better defined. After about 15 minutes' walking you arrive at a T-junction; turn left and descend through a series of zigzags. A final bridge crossing brings you to the Glenmalure road and the car park (about 2½ hours from the summit).

MORE WALKS

DUBLIN AREA
Fairy Castle

Fairy Castle (536m) and its satellite points Three Rock and Two Rock Mountains form an obvious landmark at Dublin's southern edge. Fantastic views over the capital and as far afield as Northern Ireland's Mourne Mountains more than reward the modest effort required to reach the top. Access the area by taking the R117 Enniskerry road, or **Dublin Bus** (☎ 01-872 0000) service 44, to Stepaside. Head south for 1km along the road signed to Glencullen, then turn sharp right and quickly left to reach the start of the route (GR O187233). Continue on foot up the road and onto a forest track. Keep to the main forest road, veering left then right to exit the trees near the collection of communication masts that mark Three Rock Mountain. Return to the track and follow it left to the trig point at the summit of Fairy Castle. Now descend southeast along a path to the twin granite outcrops of Two Rock Mountain. Continue down to the edge of the trees, then follow a rough track along the southern edge of the forest to a stile. Cross this to reach a forest road. After 20 minutes, keep right at two junctions, then swing left to return to your outward trail. The circuit involves 6km and 310m ascent, so allow around 2½ hours. Use OSI 1:50,000 map No 50.

WICKLOW MOUNTAINS
Tonelagee & Brockagh Mountain

Tonelagee (817m) is the third-highest summit in the Wicklow Mountains. It rises steeply from Wicklow Gap to the south and from Glenmacnass to the northeast, and can be climbed directly from the roads through both places. A longer and more scenic approach is via Brockagh Mountain along the long southeastern ridge, starting along the Wicklow Way near Laragh (see p68). The simplest return route from here is simply to retrace your steps. Allow at least six hours for this 19km walk, which involves 800m of ascent. Carry the Harvey 1:30,000 map *Wicklow Mountains* or OSI 1:50,000 map No 56.

WAYMARKED WAYS
Besides the Wicklow Way (see p49) and St Kevin's Way (see below), there are two main Waymarked Ways that radiate out from Dublin. First of these is the 1.25km-long Grand Canal Way, which meanders west along the canal's largely intact towpath to the River Shannon. Alternatively, you could follow the 77km stretch of the Royal Canal Way northwest to Mullingar. Check www.walkireland.ie for full descriptions of both routes.

St Kevin's Way
One of Ireland's five Pilgrim Paths, the 30km-long St Kevin's Way links the village of Hollywood on the northwestern edge of the Wicklow Mountains, through Wicklow Gap and Glendasan, to the Monastic City in Glendalough. It follows the probable route of the monk Kevin, who later became a saintly hermit (see the boxed text The Monastic City, p54). Small sections of a primitive road, possibly built for him, have been identified; examples can be seen at Wicklow Gap. About half the distance follows paved roads, including a perilous section near the western end. Much of the rest follows forest tracks and paths, some very wet. The route is generally well marked.

There is no public transport to Hollywood itself, though B&B accommodation is available in the village – contact **Wicklow County Tourism** (☎ 0404-20070; www .visitwicklow.ie). For details of transport and facilities in Glendalough, see p67. A free map guide to the route is available from the **Heritage Council** (☎ 056-777 0777). Part of the route is shown on the Harvey 1:30,000 map *Wicklow Mountains*; two OSI 1:50,000 maps, Nos 55 and 56, also cover the area but don't mark the route.

TOWNS & FACILITIES

DUBLIN
☎ 01 / pop 1.3 million

In 2007, Ireland's intimate capital was a city bursting with confidence, which was hardly surprising considering that the previous two decades had seen Dublin transformed from delightful backwater into a modern metropolis with no limits on its ambitions. The subsequent economic downturn may mean that some of the worst decadence has gone, but this is still a city where heritage and hedonism can live side by side.

Information
The city's main tourist office is **Dublin Tourism Centre** (☎ 605 7700; www.visitdublin .com; 2 Suffolk St; daily Jul & Aug, Mon-Sat Sep-Jun), a busy place where you can pick up maps, guides and information. The accommodation booking service is always in demand; alternatively call ☎ 1800 668 668.

Dublin's **National Map Centre** (☎ 476 0471; www.irishmaps.ie; 34 Aungier St; Mon-Fri) stocks the entire OSI and OSNI ranges and also sells maps online. **Hodges Figgis** (☎ 677 4754; 56-58 Dawson St) is a large bookshop and perhaps the best place to buy hiking guides and Irish titles generally.

Supplies & Equipment
If you need equipment for your excursions, try **Great Outdoors** (☎ 679 4293; www .greatoutdoors.ie; Chatham St) or the **Lowe Alpine Shop** (☎ 672 7088; 17-18 Temple Lane, Temple Bar). Self-caterers will also find supermarkets, groceries and street markets scattered throughout the city.

Sleeping
Dublin has hundreds of accommodation and eating options; here we offer a brief selection of places around Grafton St and Temple Bar, at the very heart of the city.

Avalon House (☎ 475 0001; www.avalon house.ie; 55 Aungier St; dm/s/d €18/30/60) occupies an attractive Victorian building and has great lounges for relaxing. Make sure to book ahead.

Close to the Temple Bar, **Ashfield House** (☎ 679 7734; www.ashfieldhouse.ie; 19-20

D'Olier St; dm/s/d from €22/36/72) is a modern hostel in a converted church. A continental-style breakfast is included in the price.

Grafton House (☎ 679 2041; www .graftonguesthouse.com; 26-27 South Great George's St; s/d from €70/100) is a heritage hotel with 17 en-suite rooms. Expect contemporary fittings and all mod cons.

Split between a chichi coach house and a more gracious Georgian house, **Number 31** (☎ 676 5011; www.number31.ie; 31 Leeson Close; s/d/t from €115/150/225) serves gourmet breakfasts in the conservatory. Young children are not permitted.

The Shelbourne (☎ 676 6471; www .theshelbourne.ie; 27 North St Stephen's Green; r from €200) is arguably the city's most iconic hotel, and recent refurbishment means the rooms have rediscovered their grandeur.

Eating

For many restaurants, particularly those in the centre, it's worth booking ahead to ensure a table.

Busy **Gruel** (☎ 670 7119; 68a Dame St; dinner mains €9-15; daily) serves super-filling breakfasts, tasty lunchtime roasts-in-a-roll, and an exceptional evening menu. It doesn't accept bookings, but the wait is worth the effort.

The epitome of Temple Bar chic, **Eden** (☎ 670 5372; Meeting House Sq; mains €15-25; lunch & dinner daily) offers trendy, minimalist surroundings and outstanding modern Irish cuisine prepared with organic seasonal produce.

Getting There & Away
BUS
Dublin's main bus station, Busáras, is located on Store St, just north of the river behind Custom House. **Bus Éireann** (☎ 836 6111; www.buseireann.ie) runs regular services from here to all major destinations in the Republic and Northern Ireland.

TRAIN
The city has two main train stations. **Connolly Station** (☎ 836 3333), just north of the Liffey and the city centre, is the station for Belfast, Derry, Sligo and other northern destinations. **Heuston Station** (☎ 836 5421), just south of the Liffey and well west of the centre, is the station for Cork, Galway, Killarney, Kilkenny and other destinations south and west of Dublin. For general train information, contact **Iarnród Éireann Travel Centre** (☎ 836 6222; www .irishrail.ie; 35 Lower Abbey St).

AIR
Dublin Airport (☎ 814 1111; www.dublin airport.com), 13km north of the centre, is Ireland's major international gateway airport. For international flight information, see p305. A number of bus services link the airport to the city centre. **Aircoach** (☎ 844 7118; www.aircoach.ie; €7) runs from 18 destinations throughout the city, including the main central streets. Coaches run every 10 to 15 minutes between 6am and midnight, then hourly through the night. Alternatively, **Airlink Express Coach** (☎ 872 0000, 01-873 4222; www.dublin bus.ie; adult €6) bus 747 runs every 10 to 20 minutes from 5.45am to 11.30pm between the airport, central bus station (Busáras) and Dublin Bus office on Upper O'Connell St; bus 748 runs every 15 to 30 minutes from 6.50am to 10.05pm between the airport, and Heuston and Connolly Stations.

Getting Around
Given the motorised madness that is driving around Dublin, public transport is a very convenient, inexpensive alternative. Indeed, public transport is the preferred option for all the walks within the city's boundaries.

BUS
Dublin Bus (☎ 872 0000; www.dublin bus.ie; 59 Upper O'Connell St) services run from around 6am to 11.30pm. Fares are calculated according to stages: one to three stages costs €1.15, four to seven stages €1.60, eight to 13 stages €1.80, and 14 to 23 stages €2.20. Make sure to have exact change for tickets when boarding buses.

TRAIN
The **Luas** (www.luas.ie) light-rail system operates from around 5.30am to 12.30am. There are two lines: the Green Line (trains every five to 15 minutes), which connects St Stephen's Green with Sandyford in south Dublin; and the Red Line (trains every 20 minutes), which runs from Lower Abbey St to Tallaght via Heuston Station. There are

ticket machines at every stop or you can buy tickets from newsagencies throughout the city centre; a typical short-hop fare will cost you €1.90.

DART (Dublin Area Rapid Transport; ☎ 836 6222; www.irishrail.ie) trains also run along the coast, going as far north as Howth and as far south as Greystones. There are services every 10 to 20 minutes from around 6.30am to midnight Monday to Saturday. Services are less frequent on Sunday. A one-way ticket from Dublin to Dun Laoghaire or Howth costs €2.20.

ENNISKERRY
☎ 01 / pop 2700

On a summer's day there are few lovelier spots than picturesque Enniskerry, replete with its art galleries and organic gourmet cafés.

Sleeping & Eating

Apart from offering good-sized rooms, **Cherbury B&B** (☎ 282 8679; www.cherbury.ie; s/d €50/90) is a helpful place serving hearty breakfasts. A pick-up and drop-off service is available for walkers by arrangement.

The **Powerscourt Arms Hotel** (☎ 282 8903; s/d €45/80; mains from €12.50) is a traditional pub that also offers comfortable, if slightly old-fashioned, en-suite rooms. Food is available in both the bar and restaurant.

Alternatively **Ferndale** (☎ 286 3518; www.ferndalehouse.com; s/d/tr €70/90/100) is a listed Victorian house, beautifully furnished in period style.

The village has a decent-sized supermarket for self-caterers.

A good spot for dinner is **Emilia's Ristorante** (☎ 276 1834; The Square; mains €12-16), which serves organic soups, perfect steaks, thin-crust pizzas and gorgeous meringue desserts.

Getting There & Away

Enniskerry is 18km south of Dublin, approximately 3km west of the M11 along the R117. **Dublin Bus** (☎ 872 0000) service 44 (€2.20, every 20 minutes) generally takes about 1¼ hours to get to Enniskerry from Hawkins St in Dublin.

Alternatively, you can take the **DART** (☎ 836 6222; www.irishrail.ie) train to Bray (€2.75) and catch bus 185 (€1.60,

hourly) from the station, which takes an extra 40 minutes.

GLENDALOUGH
☎ 0404

Rugged Glendalough (*Gleann dá Loch*, 'Valley of the Two Lakes') is one of Ireland's most beautiful corners and promises to be a highlight of any trip along the eastern seaboard. Although strictly speaking the name refers to the whole valley, we use it here to refer to the scattering of buildings around the monastic settlement, 2km west of Laragh.

Information

The small **tourist information office** (☎ 45688; Mon-Sat May-Sep), located next to the Glendalough Hotel, can answer general visitor inquiries and also has a selection of local maps and guides.

Just east of Glendalough Hotel, **Glendalough Visitor Centre** (☎ 45325; www .heritageireland.ie; €3/1 adult/child; daily) offers audiovisual presentations and exhibits on the monastic settlement.

The **National Park Information Centre** (☎ 45425; daily May-Sep, Sat & Sun Oct-Apr) is the best place for hiking-related queries. It's located near the Upper Lake car park and also sells local maps and hiking guides.

Sleeping & Eating

Modern **Glendalough International Hostel** (☎ 45342; www.anoige.ie; dm/tw €24/56) is a five-star hostel conveniently located near the round tower. Facilities include a drying room and internet access, while breakfast and packed lunches are available for €5/6.

The large **Glendalough Hotel** (☎ 45135; www.glendaloughhotel.com; s/d €118/164; three-course lunch €21, bar mains €10) dates back to the 19th century, but the interior decor is right up to date. There are 44 fairly luxurious bedrooms, while the bar and restaurant both do a roaring summer trade in food.

Getting There & Away

St Kevin's Bus (☎ 281 8119; www.glen daloughbus.com) runs from Glendalough to Laragh, Roundwood, Bray and Dublin (€13, 1½ hours, at least twice daily). The arrival/departure point in Dublin is outside the Mansion House on Dawson St.

GLENMALURE

☎ 0404

The remote valley of Glenmalure stretches beneath the western slopes of Lugnaquilla. The few facilities in the area are scattered around the crossroads near the Avonbeg River bridge, at the valley's southern mouth. The nearest shop is 8km northeast in Laragh and the nearest ATM is 11km east in Rathdrum.

Sleeping & Eating

The isolated **Glenmalure Youth Hostel** (☎ 01-830 4555; www.anoige.ie; Greenane; dm €15; daily Jun-Aug, Sat only Sep-May) is set at the northern head of the valley beneath Lugnaquilla. A rustic two-storey cottage, it has no phone or electricity (lighting is by gas). Bring all your food supplies with you.

Coolalingo (☎ 46583; s/d €40/60) is a very homely and friendly B&B, located close to Glenmalure Lodge Hotel.

By far the biggest place in the valley is **Glenmalure Lodge** (☎ 46188; s/d €40/80; mains €10.75-25), a friendly, old-world hotel located beside the crossroads. Food is served all day in the bar, and packed lunches can be provided on request.

Glenmalure is 8km southwest of Laragh via the 'Military Rd'. There is no public transport to the area.

LARAGH

☎ 0404 / pop 300

This busy little village lies at the eastern end of the Glendalough Valley and has plenty of accommodation options. The nearest tourist office is in the hamlet of Glendalough, 2km west. The nearest ATMs are in Roundwood, 7km north, or in Rathdrum, 10km south.

Sleeping & Eating

In the centre of Laragh, at the bottom of the road to Glendalough, you'll find **Dunroamin House** (☎ 45487; s/d €45/70), a traditional Irish home that offers large rooms and fine breakfasts.

Glendale B&B (☎ 45410; www.glendale -glendalough.com; Laragh East; s/d €70/80) is immaculate with comfortable rooms.

Glendalough River House (☎ 45577; www.glendaloughriverhouse.ie; s/d €58/82) is a delightful, 200-year-old restored farmhouse, beside the river at the start of the Green Rd pedestrian path to Glendalough.

The largest place in the village centre is **Lynham's Hotel** (☎ 45345; www.lynham soflaragh.ie; s/d €85/130; bar mains from €13). The bar dates back to 1777, but other facilities were renovated in 2002.

The **Wicklow Heather Restaurant** (☎ 45157; www.thewicklowheather.com; Main St, Laragh; mains €16-26; daily lunch & dinner) is also recommended.

Getting There & Away

St Kevin's Bus (☎ 01-281 8119; www.glen daloughbus.com) links Laragh to Glendalough, Roundwood, Bray and Dublin. For full details of the service, see Glendalough (p67).

ROUNDWOOD

☎ 01 / pop 600

Reputed to be Ireland's highest village, Roundwood is a popular stopping point for walkers along the Wicklow Way. It has a good supermarket with an ATM.

Sleeping & Eating

At the northern end of the village you'll find **Roundwood Caravan & Camping Park** (☎ 281 8163; www.dublinwicklowcamping .com; site & two adults from €24; Apr-Sep). Facilities include a well-equipped kitchen and TV lounge.

In the middle of Main St, handsome **Tochar House** (☎ 281 8247; s/d from €35/64) has sizeable, comfortable rooms. There's a pub downstairs, which can get a little noisy.

Riverbank B&B (☎ 281 8117; Dublin Rd; s/d €45/70) occupies a family home north of the village centre. The owners can collect walkers from the Wicklow Way, and also provide packed lunches.

Alternatively, **The Coach House** (☎ 281 8157; www.thecoachhouse.ie; s/d €45/90; mains from €12.50) is centrally located. It has large, comfortable rooms and a varied menu in the bar and restaurant.

Another good spot for food is the 17th-century **Roundwood Inn** (☎ 281 8107; Main St; mains €16-32, bar food €10-16).

Getting There & Away

St Kevin's Bus (☎ 01-281 8119; www .glendaloughbus.com) has regular services linking Roundwood to Laragh and Glendalough, Bray and Dublin. See Glendalough (p67) for full details.

Southeast

HIGHLIGHTS

- Watching for otters along the peaceful and verdant **River Barrow** (p72)
- Admiring spectacular waterfalls and glacial lakes in the **Comeragh Mountains** (p75)
- Scaling five peaks in a single day in the **Eastern Knockmealdowns** (p82)
- Standing tall atop the 900m-plus summit of **Galtymore** (p86)

Highest peak in the region: Galtymore, Galtee Mountains, 919m

If you're someone who appreciates the relaxed atmosphere of rural Ireland and enjoys a variety of walking terrain, odds are you'll love Ireland's southeastern corner. The region may lack the rugged grandeur and wildness of the west, but its patchwork of farmland, villages and woodland – not to mention several fine mountain ranges – exude a captivating charm. If you enjoy mountain climbing you'll have the opportunity to discover some of the country's better-kept secrets, or if lowland routes are more your style, there's a gem or two on offer.

The mountains in these parts – the Comeragh, Knockmealdown, Galtee and Blackstairs ranges – rear abruptly skyward from pastoral surrounds. They tend to be just a single ridge wide, geological anomalies that provide fantastically scenic viewpoints over the surrounding landscape. Here you can escape the crowds that gather round Ireland's more popular peaks, then soak up the atmosphere of a quiet village pub in the evening.

The only disadvantage of the rural setting is a lack of public transport, and though the routes are all easily accessible by road, you'll appreciate having your own vehicle to reach them at your convenience.

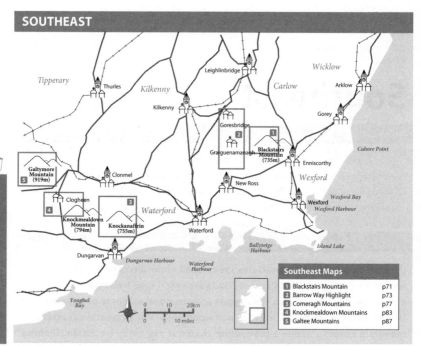

Southeast Maps	
1 Blackstairs Mountain	p71
2 Barrow Way Highlight	p73
3 Comeragh Mountains	p77
4 Knockmealdown Mountains	p83
5 Galtee Mountains	p87

PLANNING
Maps
The OSI 1:250,000 Holiday map *East* is best for general planning. Details of larger scale topographical maps are included in each walk description.

Information Sources
The official tourist office for the region is **Fáilte Ireland South East** (☎ 051-875 823; www.discoverireland.ie/southeast; 41 The Quay, Waterford). It's worth visiting their website to get a general overview of the area, as well as checking practical information such as accommodation listings. The site features a section on special offers where discounts on travel and accommodation, activity-based packages and a range of seasonal deals in the area are listed. It's also a good source of information on various local festivals and events, and on traditional and historic attractions.

GATEWAY
See Kilkenny (p92).

BLACKSTAIRS & BARROW

Blackstairs Mountain and the River Barrow are a marriage of opposites – a rugged peak that rises high above a tranquil river. The mountain forms the eastern boundary of the river's catchment area, and provides an impressive backdrop to the patchwork of woodlands, fields and villages on the broad valley floor. Cutting through the heart of it all, the River Barrow once thronged with boats carrying cargo and people between Dublin and the south coast, but is now the preserve of fishermen and walkers. The small, historic town of Graiguenamanagh is a perfect base from which to explore the area – and don't overlook Brandon Hill (p73), just south of the town, from where you can contemplate both mountain and river and their beautiful setting.

ACCESS TOWN
See Graiguenamanagh (p92).

BLACKSTAIRS MOUNTAIN

Duration 5¼–5¾ hours
Distance 18km
Ascent 750m
Difficulty moderate–demanding
Start/Finish Sculloge Gap
Nearest Town Graiguenamanagh (p92)
Transport private
Summary Exceptionally far-ranging vistas on a superb ridge hike east of the Barrow Valley, returning along an ancient track and country lanes.

From the west, Blackstairs Mountain (735m) looks like a huge humpback whale basking on the skyline, its long spine rising gracefully to the summit plateau. The long ridge affords magnificent views that encompass all three mountains ranges covered later in this chapter: the Comeraghs, Knockmealdowns and Galtees.

The only features punctuating the mountain's otherwise smooth profile are a few bristly tors on the southern ridge. During the last ice age, the tops of some peaks were left poking through the ice as nunataks. This exposed ground was then subject to severe erosion, with any earth stripped away to reveal the underlying rock beneath. In this case all that remained were elongated columns of hard granite – what is now visible as the tors.

The route described follows firstly forest tracks, then a rough stretch over heather leads to a good footpath across the mountain. The return is along a hill track, following what was long ago the main road to Wexford. The final leg of the walk is along very quiet country roads. It's hard to avoid this final road section even if you have two vehicles at your disposal because there are few safe parking places where you meet the road.

The route also passes two reminders of the region's turbulent past. In the small car park at the start, a memorial is dedicated 'To the men and women who gave their lives for liberty, equality and fraternity'. This was unveiled in 1998 to commemorate the bicentenary of the 1798 Uprising (see the boxed text Rebellion in the Mountains, p64). The other landmark is Caher Roe's Den, the hiding place of one Cathaoir

na gCapall, which was once set among the cluster of tors on the ridge. After his family lands in County Laois were forfeited to the Crown in the 18th century, Cathaoir took to horse trading and set up a network of horse thieves who sold their haul at country fairs. The law eventually caught up with him and he was hanged in Portlaoise in 1735.

PLANNING
Maps
This walk is covered by OSI 1:50,000 map No 68.

GETTING TO/FROM THE WALK
The walk starts and finishes at a small car park beside a minor road through Sculloge Gap, just 30m from its junction with the R702 (GR S827477). From Graiguenamanagh, follow the R703 (signposted to Borris) to a T-junction at the western end of the village of Ballymurphy. Turn right here and continue along the R702 to the car park.

THE WALK
Walk east along the R702 for 200m and turn right along a narrow road. Keep left round a bend, then take the second turn on the right, going through a metal gate and along a forest track. Pass through another

BLACKSTAIRS MOUNTAIN

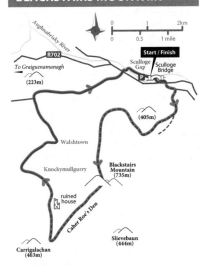

wooden gate and continue straight ahead on the gravel track. About 300m further on, turn right along a rough, vegetated track leading through a gap in the trees. At the top of the gap, pass over a wire fence (the top wire is clipped to allow access) and continue to climb along what is now a footpath weaving through gorse and heather. About 200m beyond the fence, turn sharp left (south) along a grassy track, gaining height close to the forest edge. The track swings west and widens the distance from the forest edge and levels out as it skirts the hill mapped simply as '405'. At a distinct corner of the plantation, the track starts to drop noticeably southwards you'll notice a small metal gate on the left. Turn right here along a rough track through more gorse and heather. Unfortunately the path soon peters out; simply head west, over heather wherever possible for the driest terrain, to reach the ridge crest on the skyline.

Once at the top of the ridge turn left (south), and you should be able to see the dark line of a path through heather ahead – this is the next objective. It proves to be a well-used footpath, which leads you all the way up the ridge to the small summit plateau, where the top of **Blackstairs Mountain** is marked by a cairn perched on a peat hag (two hours from the start). There's also a small cross marked 'RIP.' nearby. The magnificent view encompasses Mt Leinster, the Galtee Mountains, Slievenamon, the Knockmealdowns, the Comeraghs and the south coast.

Descend southwest over steep, rocky ground to **Caher Roe's Den**, the series of spiky tors on the southern ridge that once served as Cathaoir na gCapall's hiding place. After exploring the rocks, continue down to the prominent gap below (45 minutes from the summit). Turn right here along an old track known locally as the Wexford Rd, which it once was: its wide course, bound by stone walls, is still evident across the lower slopes of the mountain. Follow the track as it bends right after 200m and loses height; its course is generally easy to see, mostly with a stone wall on one or both sides. It has become overgrown across a few patches of marshy ground, which may demand acrobatics in wet conditions. If in doubt, just keep heading northwestward – in one place, the wall of a **ruined building**,

punctuated with a window, serves as a useful objective.

Eventually you come to a dense gorse thicket. Swing left and descend over wet ground to a stone-walled field. Turn right beside the wall, then veer left to a gate and a road at **Knockymullgurry**, which is little more than a handful of farm buildings (45 minutes from the gap). From here to the T-junction after **Walshtown** you follow the way-marked route of a local *Sli na Sláinte* (Highway to Health) walk. Turn right along the road, then take the first right after about seven minutes. This road leads northeast and uphill, then swings northwest at Walshtown and wanders up and down to a T-junction (GR S790473). Turn right here and follow this lane across the northern shoulder of Blackstairs Mountain and down to an intersection on the R702. Cross this road diagonally to the right, heading up a short lane to a T-junction. Bear right here a few hundred metres, across Sculloge Bridge, back to the start (1¾ hours from the gate).

BARROW WAY HIGHLIGHT

Duration 5–5½ hours
Distance 21km
Ascent 20m
Difficulty easy
Start Goresbridge
Finish St Mullins
Nearest Town Graiguenamanagh (p92)
Transport bus, private

Summary A tranquil, easy-going walk along the bank of a verdant waterway, passing through the medieval town of Graiguenamanagh and the historic hamlet of St Mullins.

The River Barrow, Ireland's second longest river, is one of the Three Sisters – the name given to the trio of rivers that drains southeastern Ireland. It rises in the Slieve Bloom Mountains in County Offaly, right in the middle of the country, and flows southeast to reach the sea at Waterford Harbour. In the late 18th and early 19th centuries, the Barrow was linked to the Grand Canal at Robertstown by a system of canals, opening up a navigable waterway from Dublin to Waterford.

Today the Barrow Way is a way-marked walking route that extends along the river

BARROW WAY HIGHLIGHT

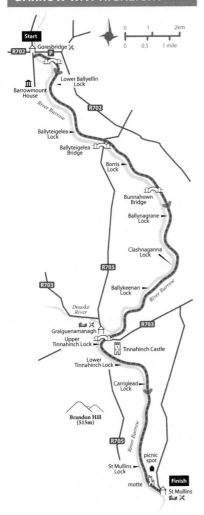

Start Goresbridge
R702
Lower Ballyellin Lock
Barrowmount House
River Barrow
R702
Ballyteigelea Lock
Ballyteigelea Bridge
Borris Lock
Bunnahown Bridge
Ballynagrane Lock
Clashnaganna Lock
R705
Ballykeenan Lock
R703
River Barrow
Douske River
Graiguenamanagh
Upper Tinnahinch Lock
R703
Tinnahinch Castle
Lower Tinnahinch Lock
Carriglead Lock
Brandon Hill (515m)
R705
River Barrow
picnic spot
St Mullins Lock
motte
Finish St Mullins

0   1   2km
0   0.5   1 mile

for 114km. The southern section, from Goresbridge to St Mullins, is easily the most beautiful part of the trail and is described here. The route meanders along a peaceful, green corridor a world away from distractions of the modern world. The towpath is grassed almost the whole way and the views change constantly as the river winds through farmland, woodland and a cliff-lined valley. On the water you should see swans, herons and ducks, and perhaps even a lively otter, whose wonderfully agile displays will imprint the route in your memory for a long time to come.

Despite its linear format, it's still possible to complete the route without private transport. Local bus services mean Goresbridge, at the start of the route, is accessible from both Kilkenny and Graiguenamanagh (p92). From Graiguenamanagh it's no hardship to do the remainder of the walk as an out-and-back excursion, with a break to explore the monastic ruins at St Mullins.

PLANNING
Maps & Books
OSI 1:50,000 map No 68 *Guide to the Barrow Navigation of Ireland* is aimed at boat travellers but has plenty of detailed descriptions that are also of interest to walkers.

GETTING TO/FROM THE WALK
Kilbride Coaches (☎ 051-423 633) run regular buses through Goresbridge from both Graiguenamanagh (35 minutes, first service leaving Graiguenamanagh at 7.45am) and Kilkenny (30 minutes, first service leaving Kilkenny at noon). There are two services daily from Monday to Saturday, and the first service each day is convenient for walkers.

Goresbridge is on the R702 about 6km east of its junction with the N9 at Gowran, and 19km from Kilkenny.

THE WALK
From the car park and picnic area beside the river at Goresbridge, cross the nine-arched bridge and skirt an old building on the right to reach the towpath. During the first hour you pass two locks that, like all on the waterway, are now manually operated. The first is **Lower Ballyellin**, and the adjacent lock keeper's cottage is painted an incongruous bright pink. **Barrowmount House**, standing mute and uninhabited across the river, was once the residence of the Gore family, whose name lives on in the nearby village. Brandon Hill (515m) to the south soon makes the first of many appearances during the walk; the prominent feature on the summit is a mission cross.

Next comes **Ballyteigelea Lock**. A kilometre or so further on, the peace is disturbed

SOUTHEAST

THE RIVER BARROW – AN HISTORIC WATERCOURSE

As you wander along the banks of the Barrow you'll see barges and other pleasure craft negotiating the old locks, and it's not difficult to imagine how busy it was in its heyday. The river has a long history as a water highway, which is scarcely surprising since St Mullins was settled from about the 7th century and Graiguenamanagh was well established by the mid-13th century.

By this time the area was already a major centre of farming and a rich source of timber, and Claraums – flat-bottomed boats of up to five tonnes – were pulled along by rope from the river bank or punted with a long pole.

In 1761 the Barrow Navigation Company started work above St Mullins, the limit of navigation on the tide upstream from New Ross. Huge sums were spent building short canals (or cuts) with locks to bypass shallow or rough stretches so that boats could reach Graiguenamanagh. At each lock a keeper, who lived nearby, worked the lock gates and collected tolls. Weirs were also built across the river nearby to control the flow through the canals, though the river usually had the last word when it fell to inconveniently low levels in summer and winter.

By 1801 work was complete: 23 locks were spread over a distance of 67km, making the river navigable as far upstream as Athy, where another link to Robertstown started. Barges up to 20m long could now be pulled along the towpath by two horses, carrying grain and flour to and from the mills beside the river. Corn, timber, manure and foodstuffs also kept the barges busy. The local pubs benefited too; consignments of malting barley were transported to Dublin to be used as raw material for Guinness stout, which was then transported back downstream in its finished state. In the early years a passenger boat even plied the river, but though hotels were built at Graigue and Carlow, the service never caught on and it ended in 1809. Engines replaced horses around 1911, and the advent of railways then motor vehicles eventually put the canal out of business in 1959. Today the barges and ponies have been replaced by cruise boats, canoeists, fishermen and walkers.

as **Ballyteigelea bridge** carries the R705 across the river. The South Leinster Way joins the towpath at the bridge and follows it down to Graiguenamanagh. Tranquillity is restored as you continue southeast, soon reaching a very long weir leading to **Borris Lock**. The mature woodlands that line the eastern side of the river are part of the Borris demesne, once held by the Kavanagh family. In the midst of this, the Barrow is joined by Mountain River, spanned by the stone-built **Bunnahown Bridge**.

From **Ballynagrane Lock**, about 30 minutes further on, the river glides through more open countryside of fields and scattered woodlands, and soon you reach **Clashaganna Lock**. Now the river is pushed away from its southward course by spurs reaching out from the nearby hills, and heads southwest then southeast. **Ballykeenan Lock**, unique on the waterway for being a double lock, soon marks the end of an unusually long cut. Continue for another half-hour then round a bend to find civilisation in the shape of the small town of **Graiguenamanagh** (three to 3¼

hours from Goresbridge). Even if you're continuing to St Mullins, it's well worth pausing here for lunch and taking a bit of extra time to explore the pretty and historic town.

Back on the river bank, the path is surfaced with bitumen for a while. Pass a broad weir and the tall remains of **Tinnahinch Castle**, built by the Butler family before the 16th century, to reach Upper Tinnahinch Lock. The bitumen gives way to grass beside a long cut bypassing river rapids; opposite, **Brandon Hill** (515m) rises steeply to its domed moorland summit. Deciduous woodland now lines the river, making this a delightful stretch, particularly in spring and autumn. A few hundred metres beyond **Lower Tinnahinch Lock** the river bends south into a steep-sided valley. The granite from these cliffs was used in the construction of the bridges, weirs and locks on the canal. The valley only widens well beyond the next lock at Carriglead, shortly before you arrive at **St Mullins Lock**, the end of the navigable river for most boats.

CALLING ALL ANGLERS

As well as being a fine location for a walk, the River Barrow is renowned for the quality of its fishing. The towpath provides easy access and the water holds species such as brown trout, salmon, roach, rudd, pike, perch and tench. Abundant stocks of pike are one of the main attractions, with many fish weighing in excess of 10kg.

It's another species that makes the Barrow unique however. Every year the river supports a run of Twaite Shad, one of the few places in Europe where these fish are recorded in such numbers. Anglers come from far and wide to take part in Ireland's only shad competition, an international catch-and-release event that takes place each May.

The Twaite Shad is a member of the herring family and is found in coastal areas from Norway and Iceland to the northeastern Mediterranean. It's a distinctive and colourful fish, with a brilliant blue back, silver belly, and yellow sides to its head. It spends most of the year in coastal waters, but swims to the tidal limit of rivers to spawn. Its habits make it particularly susceptible to estuarine pollution and practices such as dredging and raising barrages. Little is known about the fish's distribution and biology, but numbers are sufficiently low for it to be classified as 'vulnerable' in Ireland and a 'priority species' in Britain.

You're sure to learn more from anglers if you walk the towpath in May. If you're interested in trying your own luck for other species later in the summer, ask at local tackle shops for information. No permits are required for coarse angling from the towpath, though licences are required for salmon and fishing in side rivers.

The path turns back to bitumen at this point and a sign warns that the banks are liable to flooding at high tide. Follow the broad track into **St Mullins**; the tall buildings by the river were once a mill, one of many in the area that used water power to grind grain. If you continue past the mill for a hundred metres and cross a small stream, you'll come to a grassy riverside picnic area. To reach the pub and ruins at the centre of St Mullins, turn left up the road just before the mill. At the top of the hill you'll find a monastic site with the remains of at least three churches and the base of a round tower. Nearby the Norman motte – a large green mound, which once held a timber tower – is also well presented.

COMERAGH MOUNTAINS

Many walkers consider the Comeraghs the finest mountain range in Ireland's central south. They certainly offer plenty of variety, and you could easily spend a week exploring the region. The central part of the massif consists of a high, undulating plateau rather than distinct individual peaks. The exception to the rule comes at the northernwestern corner of the range, where the distinctive Knockanaffrin Ridge stretches away in a steep, linear arête.

With the River Suir and its tributaries to the north and various other streams flowing into the Atlantic elsewhere, the Comeraghs rise steeply from the surrounding farmland. The main rock is old red sandstone, laid down when Ireland was part of the European landmass and a desert-type climate prevailed. The tough sandstone survives in the long ridge and central plateau structure of the range, although the rock visible above ground is more likely to be a dark, pebbly conglomerate.

There are two obvious impacts of later glaciation. Most spectacular are the precipitous corries – or coums – that give the range its name. These amphitheatres were carved from the rock by lingering bodies of ice, and some of the old moraine walls now cradle lakes. (See the boxed text Signs of a Glacial Past, p30, for more on the sculpting forces of glaciation). The most spectacular example, Coumshingaun, has a headwall almost 400m high and is commonly described as 'the finest example of a glacial corrie in Ireland'. Not surprisingly, it forms the focal point of one of the walks described in this section.

The remaining three routes visit the other outstanding natural features of the area: the isolated ridge of Knockanaffrin; the superb corries on the western face of the mountains; and Mahon Falls, a beautiful, 80m-high cascade in a spectacular location.

ACCESS TOWNS

See Ballymacarbry (p90) and Clonmel (p91).

KNOCKANAFFRIN RIDGE

Duration 4½–5 hours
Distance 12km
Ascent 670m
Difficulty moderate–demanding
Start/Finish Nire Valley car park
Nearest Towns Ballymacarbry (p90), Clonmel (p91)
Transport private
Summary Magnificent panoramic views from a very scenic ridge-line dotted with extraordinary knobbly tors.

The 755m-high summit of Knockanaffrin crowns a long ridge that stretches northwest from the main Comeragh Plateau. Among the highest summits in the range, it commands wonderful panoramic views. The precipitous drop to the northeast means the outlook is particularly expansive in that direction, and on a very clear day it's possible to see as far as the Wicklow Mountains. The ridge is crowned by fascinating clusters of rock that thrust skyward from the apex of the arête, just begging for further exploration. Short grass underfoot also ensures easy yet airy walking – which may come as something of a relief after the rough ground of the main plateau.

This route follows minor roads for roughly 4km before accessing the open slopes, though the narrow lanes and the beauty of the surrounding scenery render this a painless task. A straightforward ascent then leads to the summit of Knocksheegowna (687m), where you join the ridge itself. Incidentally, Knockanaffrin's Irish name, *Cnoc an Aiffrin*, translates as 'hill of the mass', perhaps recalling the harsh laws of penal times when Roman Catholic mass was officially outlawed but still celebrated in isolated places in the open air.

PLANNING
Maps

The OSI 1:50,000 map No 75 covers the walk.

GETTING TO/FROM THE WALK

From Ballymacarbry on the Clonmel–Dungarvan road (R671), turn east at a junction opposite Melody's Nire View bar and head along the Nire Valley Scenic Drive. At a junction 5.2km further on, keep right and follow the road for 4.2km to its end at a large car park (GR S276128).

THE WALK

Begin by walking northwest and west down the road from the car park for about 2.5km. Take the second bitumen road on the right and follow this northeast, keeping straight ahead at all junctions and climbing steadily for about one kilometre. The road ends at an old farmhouse and numerous derelict farm buildings, but this route continues ahead along a farm track. Keep straight on at a track junction about 100m beyond the farm, then pass a stone building and gate on the left. The track now becomes a rocky path between stone walls and trees, and brings you to a gate. Beyond this, cross a fence and a stream, then follow a rough track north for a few hundred metres to a pretty little rivulet (an upper tributary of Glennanore Stream).

Bear right and walk along the bank of the stream for about 500m, with the line of ascent to Knocksheegowna clearly visible to the northeast. Before you launch up the slope however, you must cross to the left-hand side of a series of small, grassy gullies. Use an old stone wall as a guide for the easiest passage between the deepest gullies. Once across these obstacles nothing remains but the climb to the top. The angle of ascent is sustained throughout, but short grass makes progress relatively easy.

The summit of **Knocksheegowna** (678m) – 2½ hours from the start – is marked by a trig pillar perched atop a rock outcrop. The location is fantastically airy and the view is fabulous, taking in the Galtee and Knockmealdown Mountains, the south coast, and Lough Mohra sheltering beneath the precipice to the east.

Turn southeast and follow the ridge-line down to a flat saddle, then begin to climb

COMERAGH MOUNTAINS

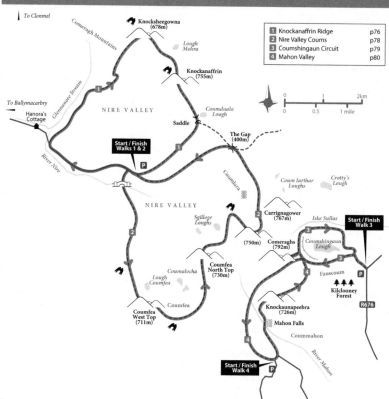

To Clonmel

Comeragh Mountains

Knocksheegowna
(678m)

Lough
Molira

Knockanaffrin
(755m)

Glennanore Stream

To Ballymacarbry

Hanora's
Cottage

NIRE VALLEY

Coumduala
Lough

Saddle

The Gap
(400m)

Start / Finish
Walks 1 & 2

River Nire

Coumlara

NIRE VALLEY

Coum Iarthar
Loughs

Crotty's
Lough

Sgilloge
Loughs

Carrignagower
(767m)

Iske Sullas

Start / Finish
Walk 3

(750m)

Comeraghs
(792m)

Coumshingaun
Lough

Counalocha

Coumfea North Top
(730m)

Fauscoum

Lough
Coumfea

Kilclooney
Forest

Coumfea

R676

Coumfea
West Top
(711m)

Knockaunapeebra
(726m)

Mahon Falls

Coummahon

Start / Finish
Walk 4

River Mahon

1	Knockanaffrin Ridge	p76
2	Nire Valley Coums	p78
3	Coumshingaun Circuit	p79
4	Mahon Valley	p80

0   1   2km
0   0.5   1 mile

SOUTHEAST

once more. During the ascent you pass several angular clusters of conglomerate rock teetering on the brink of the drop. Most of these are passed on the right but when you reach the summit tor, a faint path veers left and you must step over the rocks above the drop. The official summit of **Knockanaffrin** (45 minutes from Knocksheegowna) is distinguished by a tiny cairn set atop the tor itself. The view is unsurpassed, especially of the Comeragh Plateau and its corries, and the rural landscape of green fields that cover the lowlands to the east. Not surprisingly, (depending upon the time of year) you're likely to encounter the odd intrepid hiker who is also a landscape painter or photographer, perched atop the summit, balancing their gear and quietly capturing the sweeping landscape below to re-live another day.

Continue south along the ridge, soon crossing a simple stile over a fence. As you descend, keep on the eastern side of several more tors, following a well-trodden path down to a narrow gap high above **Coumduala Lough**. A short climb now brings you to an east-west fence. Don't cross the fence but follow it westwards, descending on a clear path through the heather. As soon as you can see the Nire Valley car park, the path swings right (west) and joins a grassy track, sunken at first, which leads to a widely spaced line of white posts. Continue along this line and at the last of these, bear left and follow a succession of sheep paths through the heather to the car park (1¼ hours from Knockanaffrin).

NIRE VALLEY COUMS

Duration 5–5½ hours
Distance 18km
Ascent 650m
Difficulty moderate–demanding
Start/Finish Nire Valley car park
Nearest Towns Ballymacarbry (p90), Clonmel (p91)
Transport private
Summary A spectacular outing around four dramatic coums hollowed out of the rugged western face of the Comeraghs.

Glacial corries and lakes are the glories of the Comeraghs – no less than 10 coums cluster around the periphery of the massif, giving the range its name. The eastern side of the mountains is graced by magnificent Coumshingaun and a few others, but the western flanks also have their fair share. These are generally less enclosed and more accessible than their eastern counterparts, making them easier targets for exploration.

This route climbs around the rims of no less than four coums. It's a fantastic route because the region's natural architecture is best appreciated from above: from this vantage point you not only appreciate the scale of the corries themselves, but can also clearly make out the jumbled hummocks formed by old glacial moraines. In many ways, this is also a trip around the lifeblood of the Nire Valley. Each of the coums is drained by a stream, which gather together at the base of the slope to form the Nire River, the centrepoint of the entire, beautiful valley.

The walk takes you along the western rim of the Comeragh Plateau. Surprisingly perhaps, given the vast expanses of bogland on the central plateau, the ground is mostly dry and peat-free. For this we may have to thank sheep, who have worn narrow paths along the edge. The only rough terrain is on the upper part of the descent from the plateau rim towards the Gap, from where an old track – with just one boggy patch – leads back to the start.

PLANNING
Maps
Use OSI 1:50,000 map No 75.

GETTING TO/FROM THE WALK
See Getting to/from the Walk for Knockanaffrin Ridge (p76).

THE WALK
From the car park, walk northwest down the road for about 500m and pass through a gate on the left. Follow a vehicle track down to a **bridge** over the River Nire. Cross this and continue along the track for several hundred metres to a gate, which provides access to open moorland. From here, head south. Cross the stream above a small gorge then make your way generally south, climbing up a broad spur towards the domed heights of Coumfea. Keep on the eastern side of the spur higher up for the best views of **Lough Coumfea** and **Coumalocha**, set amid green moraine hummocks and nearly enclosed by steeply tiered cliffs (1¾ hours from the start).

From the tiny cairn that marks **Coumfea West Top** (711m), progress is remarkably easy as you arc southeast then northeast around the plateau rim. The ground underfoot is mostly covered by firm, dry grass, and there are spectacular views of the pastoral Nire Valley and the Knockmealdown and Galtee Mountains beyond.

The terrain grows slightly rougher as you cross **Coumfea North Top** (730m) to reach the rim above **Sgilloge Loughs** (an hour from Coumalocha). Cross the stream tumbling into the lough, then contour northwards across the steep spur on clear sheep paths. This brings you to an **outlook** over **Coumlara** and its slender waterfall. Now head southeast, keeping above broken cliffs on the western side of the coum and crossing the stream well above the falls. Work your way generally north from here, picking a line part way up the steep slope and passing west of **Carrignagower** summit (767m). Eventually you reach a prominent outcrop of conglomerate boulders perched above the Gap.

To reach the Gap comfortably, start the descent in a northwesterly direction, bypassing precipitous crags and weaving through conglomerate boulders. Then head back towards a fence on your right (east), and generally follow this to **The Gap** (1½ hours from Sgilloge Loughs). The line of the old track from the Gap is marked with white-painted posts. After a dry start the trail becomes wet and disjointed across lower-lying ground, but soon improves again and provides fine views of the ground you've just covered. The posts come to an end once the Nire Valley car park is in sight. Bear left and follow sheep paths through the heather to the car park (45 minutes from The Gap).

COUMSHINGAUN CIRCUIT

Duration 4–4½ hours
Distance 8km
Ascent 650m
Difficulty demanding
Start/Finish Kilclooney Forest car park
Nearest Town Clonmel (p91)
Transport private

Summary A classic but challenging scramble around a truly spectacular corrie, with a short, low-level alternative to the lough shore.

The deep hollow of Coumshingaun is often called the finest example of a glacial corrie in Ireland. This may be a contentious claim to present to hillwalkers, but there's no doubting the coum's rugged impact. The rock walls were carved from the old red sandstone massif by ancient glaciers, leaving virtually sheer cliffs some 380m high. The walls sweep tightly round to form a deep amphitheatre, and in the heart of the pit, constrained by old moraine, lies Coumshingaun Lough, a 700m-long lake that legend claims to be bottomless.

The trip around the corrie is one of the classic hillwalks of the region, but it isn't for everyone. The circuit involves some easy scrambling and – more serious – a section of steep, eroded grass set above exposed drops. A slip here could have serious consequences, and only those with a cool head and experience over such ground should proceed. Needless to say, this section is best avoided in the wet.

If this circuit sounds too much for you, consider visiting the corrie as part of the Mahon Valley walk (see the following description, p80). Alternatively, you can appreciate the coum's natural splendour with much less effort on a low-level walk to the lough shore. Simply follow the route described as far as the lake, then retrace

THE HERMIT OF COUMSHINGAUN

Whether you gaze over the deep corrie of Coumshingaun from above or below, it's easy to imagine what an oppressive place this might be in poor weather. Spare a thought then for one Jim Fitzgerald, who became known as the Hermit of Coumshingaun. Born in the area in 1886, Fitzgerald fought overseas during WWI and returned home rather shaken by his experience. His solution was to retreat here and make a rough dwelling in one of the caves cut into the old red sandstone walls of the corrie. Once a fortnight he made a quick trip out to buy essential provisions with his army pension, but apart from that he existed for 40 years, alone in the shadowy depths of Coumshingaun.

your steps when you're ready. Allow 1½ hours for the return trip, which involves about 5.22km ascent.

PLANNING
Maps
The walk is covered by OSI 1:50,000 map No 75.

GETTING TO/FROM THE WALK
From Clonmel, use the R678 to reach the R676 Carrick-on-Suir to Dungarvan Rd. Head south along this road for roughly 6km to a signed right turn for Kilclooney Forest. The circuit starts and finishes here at the forest car park (GR S341103).

THE WALK
From the car park, follow a well-used path through the conifers to a forest road. Turn right here and climb past a communications mast disguised as a fake tree to reach the end of the road. Cross a fence and continue ahead over open mountain slopes, veering left and following a rough path towards the ridge ahead.

The top of the ridge marks the divergence of the low-level and high-level routes. To visit the lough shore, simply descend to the lake from here. For the longer circuit, continue to follow the path up along the crest of ridge. Large rocky outcrops soon begin to thrust through the grass, with plunging cliffs on both sides, so it pays to take care if you're walking in foggy or misty conditions. Some easy scrambling is required as you clamber enjoyably over and between the boulders, and a bit of exploration may be required to find the best route through the maze.

Where the rocks end a long, grassy ridge continues ahead. Follow the path along the southern side of the ridge to a point where the ground rears steeply skyward. This is the crux of the route – 50m of very steep grass that has been eroded into a series of tall, muddy steps. You'll need to be quite selective about where you step to ensure you have a firm foothold. The exposure is significant on both sides and extreme care is required, especially in the wet.

After the tribulations of this sometimes precarious section, it may come as something of a relief to emerge onto the flat ground of the Comeragh Plateau. Now begin to work your way around the rim of Coumshingaun, enjoying fine views both into the corrie below and further afield to the Blackstairs Mountains and the south coast. It's a chance to take a breath and enjoy the rewards of your exertions. If you want to visit the highest point in the range, detour 500m southwest from back of the corrie to the cairn that marks point 792m, then retrace your steps to the edge of the cliff.

Round the northwestern corner of the corrie and pass over point 704m. Now descend east along the ridge, keeping the Iske Sullas stream to your left. Avoid the temptation to veer south too early because steep ground surrounds the lake. Instead, keep to the crest all the way to the base of the slope, where you cross another path leading to the lake. Here's an opportunity to take a little side-trip to rest and recuperate if you need to. If you haven't already visited the lough shore, turn right along this path. Otherwise, continue straight across and follow sheep trails until you merge with your ascent route at the bottom of the south ridge. Now simply retrace your initial steps back through the forest to the car park, and you'll have completed a challenging but invigorating hike.

MAHON VALLEY

Duration 4–4½ hours
Distance 8km
Ascent 680m
Difficulty moderate
Start/Finish Mahon Falls car park
Nearest Town Clonmel (p91)
Transport private

Summary A magnificent waterfall, an awesome glacial corrie and the highest point in the Comeraghs – all on an energetic tour around the Mahon Valley.

The Comeragh Mountains are endowed with many topographical wonders, yet two features are celebrated above all others. First of these is the 80m-high Mahon Falls, one of the most striking mountain cascades in Ireland. Second is the astounding glacial amphitheatre of Coumshingaun. These sites deservedly form the area's two most popular tourist attractions, and their accessibility means they can be busy with summer picnickers.

Here we describe a fantastic route that takes in both landmarks in a single outing, and also throws in a visit to the highest point in the Comeraghs for good measure. While Coumshingaun can be easily reached at lake level, its awesome ruggedness is best appreciated from the top of the soaring headwall. The previous route (see Coumshingaun Circuit, p79) describes a challenging circuit around the entire coum, but steep, exposed terrain means it's restricted to experienced and confident hikers only. By approaching the area from the Mahon Valley, this walk offers an alternate way to approach the corrie yet avoid the steepest terrain. The route finishes with a rough trip over part of the main Comeragh Plateau and a scenic descent overlooking the falls.

PLANNING
Maps
Use OSI 1:50,000 map No 75.

GETTING TO/FROM THE WALK
From Clonmel, use the R678 to reach the R676 Carrick-on-Suir to Dungarvan Rd. Head south along this road to the River Mahon bridge, then turn right along a road

AN ANONYMOUS HIGHPOINT

This route takes you over the highest point of the Comeragh massif, a landmark known variously as either 'point 792m' or 'Fauscoum'. Purists argue that the name Fauscoum translates from the Irish as 'empty hollow', and properly refers to the corrie just south of Coumshingaun. Apparently an Ordnance Survey printing error once misplaced the name on the map, and it has since been used to refer to the peak rather than the hollow. The upshot of all the confusion is that the highest point in the entire Comeragh range may have no proper name attached at all.

signposted to Mahon Falls, and almost immediately right again. Nearly 2km along this narrow road, bear right towards the falls. The car park (GR S314081) is 2km further on. Note that visitors are warned not to leave valuables in their vehicles.

THE WALK

This walk starts easily, along the wide gravel path that leads from the car park to the foot of **Mahon Falls**. Cross the river beneath the falls and follow a faint path up the northern bank of the cascade, keeping close to the water initially then veering right and climbing beneath a bulging cliff. Though care is required across the steep terrain, the ascent is nowhere near as hair-raising as it looks from below.

When you're clear of the cliffs at the top of the falls, swing east and climb steadily over the heather-cloaked slope towards **Knockaunapeebra** (726m). With luck you'll locate the odd sheep track to ease your progress. The summit itself is marked by twin cairns and excellent views over the south coast. Press on northeastwards across a shallow gap then contour across the slope, negotiating patches of rough grass and peat hags as you go. Aim to reach the cliff-line somewhere at the back of **Fauscoum**, the corrie just south of Coumshingaun. Now turn north and begin to walk along the cliff-top, soon passing a spur and arriving at a bluff overlooking awesome **Coumshingaun** (two hours from the start).

Continue generally north around Coumshingaun to the highest point on the rim. Now turn sharply southwest and cross 500m of peaty ground to the highest point in the **Comeraghs** (792m), marked by a modest cairn and views of the Knockmealdown and Galtee Mountains to the west.

Descend southwest over heather and thick grass, and cross the **River Mahon** just north of the falls (45 minutes from Coumshingaun). From here there's a final, gradual climb onto Comeragh Mountain to the south. Keep as close as possible to the cliffs at the eastern side of the mountain and among these warty conglomerate boulders, pick up a path running southeast along the top of the precipice.

Follow the path to a fence at the tip of the spur, then turn southeast and descend steeply along the right-hand side of the fence. The path and fence lead all the way down to the road, where you turn left and walk 300m to the car park (1¼ hours from the River Mahon).

KNOCKMEALDOWN MOUNTAINS

Close western neighbours of the Comeraghs, the Knockmealdown Mountains have a similar geological history, but differ markedly in their form and landscape. A 25km-long, east-west aligned range, they lie between the River Tar to the north and the beautiful Blackwater River to the south. They're a proper mountain range with at least 15 distinct summits, the highest peak being Knockmealdown itself at 794m. There are several signs of glacial origins; apart from the Gap, which sharply divides the range and carries the main access road, there's Bay Lough, a corrie lake dammed by moraine, and the corrie on the northeastern side of Knockmealdown.

The Irish name for the main peak, *Cnoc Maol Donn* means 'bare, brown mountain', and accurately describes the appearance of the uplands. However, the jarringly straight-edged conifer plantations on the

SOUTHEAST

northern and southern slopes belie this to some extent, as does the spread of another exotic species, rhododendron. You'll go a long way to see a more striking example of the invasiveness of this plant than in the glen cradling Bay Lough (see the boxed text Scourge of the Rhododendron, p217).

Two walks are described in this section: a long traverse of the eastern half of the range, with a shorter alternative concentrating on Knockmealdown itself, and a shorter walk on the lower, gentler western part of the range.

ACCESS TOWN
See Clogheen (p90).

EASTERN KNOCKMEALDOWNS

Duration 6½–7 hours
Distance 21km
Ascent 1130m
Difficulty moderate–demanding
Start/Finish The Vee car park
Nearest Town Clogheen (p90)
Transport private

Summary Cross all the high points of the eastern half of the range, following amazingly bog-free, clear paths.

The long, sharply undulating eastern half of the Knockmealdown range just begs for an extended traverse, taking in as many of the summits as possible. The invitation is made all the more attractive by the existence of high paths, comparatively dry ground and ease of access from the road. This particular circuit takes in no less than five peaks and is one of the classic walks in the area, with a high point of 794m at the top of Knockmealdown. Although conifer plantations do little to enhance the landscape of the northern slopes of the range, the network of forestry tracks does serve walkers well, making for a relatively easy return from the mountain slopes.

Despite the high starting point, the amount of ascent accumulates into a healthy total over the course of the day. Add the distance covered, and the sting in the tail of a 190m climb in the final 3km, and it's easy to see why this route makes even the fittest of walkers feel their legs. If the prospect of the challenge is rather too daunting, consider the shorter alternative, which takes in Knockmealdown alone. This option involves one short section of heather-hopping, but otherwise follows good paths and tracks throughout.

PLANNING
Maps
The walk is covered by OSI 1:50,000 map No 74.

GETTING TO/FROM THE WALK
From Clogheen, head south along the R668 towards Lismore. The walk starts and finishes at a roadside parking area just uphill from the Vee, about 6km south of Clogheen.

THE WALK
From the car park, cross the road and follow the well-trodden path leading up to **Grubb's Monument**. This memorial commemorates one Samuel Grubb, a local property owner who was buried overlooking his domain. Continue up the hillside on a clear path to the broad, cairn-strewn summit of **Sugarloaf Hill** (663m, one hour from the start). From here the route to Knockmealdown is perfectly straightforward: simply follow the wide, undulating path beside or on top of an old stone wall, all the way to the trig pillar that stands alone on **Knockmealdown** summit (one hour from Sugarloaf Hill). Care is needed here in poor weather because steep cliffs lie just north of the summit. In good visibility however, the views are tremendous. Among much else, Dungarvan Harbour and the wide ribbon of the Blackwater River to the south are prominent features of the vista.

If you prefer to complete the short circuit, this is the place to turn around (see the Alternative Route, p84). To continue on the longer route, descend steeply east and southeast to a broad saddle. The stone wall peters out at this col, but reasserts itself on the way up to the double summit of **Knocknagauv** (655m, one hour from Knockmealdown). The path passes just north of a cairn on the first summit and just south of another cairn on the second. From here, descend northeastward along the wall for a few hundred metres to a slight knoll. Then, rather than crossing the wide col and going up to **Knocknafallia** (668m) – unless

LIAM LYNCH – REVOLUTIONARY

The wording on the impressive Liam Lynch Monument in the forest north of Crohan West is, perhaps understandably, entirely in Irish. Here's a brief explanation for those not versed in the language.

Liam Lynch was born in 1893 at Barnaguraha, near the small town of Anglesborough at the western end of the Galtee Mountains. His early passion for Irish history and the Irish language almost inevitably led him to determined opposition to British rule. As a member of the Irish Republican Army (IRA), he fought in the War of Independence and became the IRA's Chief of Staff. A fierce opponent of the Anglo-Irish Treaty, he advocated carrying on the fight – against the new Irish government. Early on 10 April 1923 he was shot dead, apparently by former comrades, in the Knockmealdown Mountains. Among his dying words were 'I am glad I am going from it all, poor Ireland' His successor declared a cease-fire soon afterwards. The memorial was unveiled in 1935 at a ceremony attended by about 15,000 people.

you really want to add this peak to the day's tally – keep beside the low wall and contour across the northern slopes of the mountain.

You meet a forest road in the gap between Knocknafallia and Knockmeal. The path now splits three ways. Take the leftmost trail and keep your eyes peeled for another turn about 50m along on a bend. Turn up the slope here, following a narrow path partially obscured by heather to

Knockmeal's (560m) summit plateau. Pass about 60m west of the small summit cairn and descend in a more northerly direction to a shallow gap. Continue over a bump then descend again along a narrow path. It's fairly rough going on the ascent to the final summit of **Crohan West** (521m, 1¾ hours from Knocknagauv), which is topped by a large cairn. The view from here is as good as from any of the higher summits, taking

SOUTHEAST

KNOCKMEALDOWN MOUNTAINS

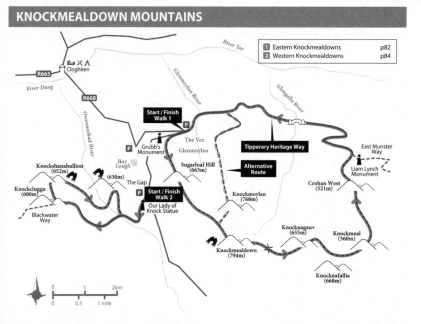

| | Eastern Knockmealdowns | p82 |
| 2 | Western Knockmealdowns | p84 |

in the Galtee Mountains and the vast patchwork of the vale of the River Suir.

Drop down towards the forest, following a line of old posts to where it meets a new section of fencing running in a northeasterly direction. Bear left here for 20m until you can turn north again along a wide clearing in the plantation. Descend beside the trees to reach the way-marked route of the East Munster Way. If you want to make a short detour to visit the impressive **Liam Lynch Monument** (see the boxed text Liam Lynch – Revolutionary, p83) follow signposts to the right for five minutes (30 minutes from Crohan West).

Retrace your steps away from the monument and turn left along the **East Munster Way**. About 3.5km further on, shortly before a **bridge** over the Glengalla River, the **Tipperary Heritage Way** joins the East Munster Way and the two continue in tandem from there to the end of the walk. The route continues partly through conifer plantations interspersed by more open stretches. Close to the deeply entrenched **Glenmoylan River**, look out for a left turn and head up the eastern side of the river to a left bend in the forest track. Continue ahead through bracken to a stile, then cross a footbridge. From here the path winds steeply uphill and brings you back to the Vee (2¼ hours from the monument).

ALTERNATIVE ROUTE: VIA KNOCKSHANE
4¼–4¾ hours, 11km, 830m ascent

Follow the route described to the top of Knockmealdown. From the summit trig pillar, turn around and retrace your steps northwest down the final ascent. Cross a slight dip and as you start to gain a little height, veer northeast to a prominent cairn on **Knockmoylan**, a rounded hill marked as point 768m on the map (2½ hours from the start). From here, head north down the broad spur mapped as Knockshane, to another cairn fringed with stones. Continue to descend, and as the gradient steepens, keep to the western side of the spur through deep heather to meet a track beside the forest fence. Turn right and follow the track into the forest and down to a T-junction; turn left here. This track soon meets the **Tipperary Heritage Way** at a bend (1½ hours from point 768m). Turn left and follow the way-marked route back up to the Vee.

WESTERN KNOCKMEALDOWNS

Duration 4–4½ hours
Distance 10.5km
Ascent 470m
Difficulty moderate
Start/Finish The Gap car park
Nearest Town Clogheen (p90)
Transport private
Summary A relatively gentle ramble over two modest, unassuming summits with lovely views far and wide.

The gentler, more rounded hills of the western Knockmealdowns are much less frequented than their higher, steeper associates to the east. Yet their summits are almost as scenic, and a far more amenable circuit takes you across the highest peaks. Access and route-finding are simplified thanks to the existence of the Blackwater Way, which crosses the mountains' southern slopes and offers waymarking posts to guide the walker across the lower part of the walk. From here the route branches cross-country, climbing an open mountain shoulder to reach the 652m-high summit of Knockshanahullion. Fences provide guidance for around half of the mountain section, but care is still required because it wouldn't be good to be caught on the high ground in mist.

Besides the views, the other attraction of the route is its archaeological significance. Excavations in the area have revealed many links with the Bronze Age: the remains of a Bronze Age settlement were discovered at Croughatoor, about 2km north of Clogheen, and an axe head – which can now be seen in the Tipperary County Museum in Clonmel – was found at Carrigmore, 3km west of the village. The mountains themselves hold their fair share of cairns and burial places, the most notable of which is the cairn that marks the top of Knockshanahullion and is visited on this route.

PLANNING
Maps
Use OSI 1:50,000 map No 74.

GETTING TO/FROM THE WALK
From Clogheen, drive south along the R668 towards Lismore. Continue past the Vee to the top of the Gap, and park in a car park on

the western side of the road (GR S031100). In the car park you'll find information boards for the Tipperary Heritage Way and the Blackwater Way.

THE WALK

From the car park, pass through the metal turnstile and follow a path towards the white statue of **Our Lady of Knock**. Veer left and pass a nearby domed shelter, then continue across the hillside to a steep rocky track. Climb beside this to reach a much more amenable track on the left, which leads towards a small forestry plantation. Waymarking posts for the **Blackwater Way** indicate the correct route. Follow the grassy track past the plantation and just as the ground starts to drop away, turn right along another track that leads into a valley to the west. Follow this through a wide zigzag to reach the valley head, marked by a gate and a junction of fences. Take note of this point; this is where you will rejoin the route after completing the mountain circuit.

Avoid the temptation to cross a now-obsolete stile or to continue straight ahead. Instead you must leave the track here and veer right slightly, tracing the line of a fence as indicated by a waymarker. Follow a small, peaty footpath through the heather and grass, keeping the fence on your left. The path rejoins a track near another gate. Turn right here and follow this track along the edge of the forest. At the tip of the plantation, follow the track around a sharp left bend and continue to a prominent metal stile at the northwestern corner of the trees. Cross the stile and you are now out onto open moorland. A line of fluorescent posts marks the route up the side of **Knock-clugga** (600m), and a steep path eases your progress underfoot.

As the path starts to level at the top of the rise, leave the Blackwater Way and turn right across a patch of bare ground. Head north along a narrow footpath through the heather, climbing gently across a broad spur. The path peters out before the top, but it's not long till you reach the prominent trig pillar that marks **Knockshanahullion** summit (two hours from the start). The excellent panorama takes in the Galtees to the northwest, while to the east the remainder of the Knockmealdown range is backed by the Comeragh Mountains. The huge pile of stones nearby is actually a burial cairn dating from the Bronze Age.

Descend southeastwards across open ground, dropping steeply at first over springy heather. Aim for the corner of a fence below. Here you join a rough path that heads generally eastward beside the fence, crossing intermittently wet ground underfoot. Having gained some height, the direction changes to southeast, though you keep climbing with the fence to your right. More or less on a crest, turn north with the fence and continue up to the flat summit known simply as **point 630m** (an hour from Knockshanahullion). From here the most arresting part of the view is Sugarloaf Hill and Knockmealdown across the Gap to the east.

Descend eastwards slightly to reach a fence corner, then turn right and follow the fence south. This brings you back to the gate at the head of the valley that you passed on your outward journey. Rejoin the track and turn left, retracing your initial steps back to the start (an hour from point 630m).

GALTEE MOUNTAINS

The Galtees are the highest inland mountain range in Ireland. They stand slightly aloof from the other mountain groups in the south, rising comparatively gradually from the sprawling 'Tipperary Plain' to the south, and much more steeply from beautiful Glen of Aherlow to the north. The range extends west from Cahir for 23km, with the highest peak, Galtymore, 919m, towering over at least 12 other distinct summits. Valleys bite deep into the main ridge, so that the Galtees (pronounced with a short 'a' as in 'fact') are characterised by long spurs reaching out from a relatively narrow main ridge.

The range is composed largely of old red sandstone, though most of the uplands are covered with blanket bog and the lower slopes are cloaked by conifer plantations. It's thought the peaks once measured in excess of 5000–6000 metres in elevation, but many millennia of erosion has significantly reduced their height. During the last ice age, however, Galtymore was still tall enough to reach above the glaciers. The series of rocky tors that lie scattered along the ridge are former nunataks, which today offer a frost-shattered glimpse of the massif's geological skeleton. One of the most notable formations is a heap of conglomerate boulders known as O'Loughnan's Castle, which can be seen on the Lough Muskry walk. The north face of the massif is punctuated by two deep corries containing hidden loughs. These are also relics of the ice age, where the water has been impounded by massed moraine.

There are several good walks in the range and two of the best are described in this section: a fine horseshoe route over Galtymore, and a less strenuous excursion to Lough Muskry. See More Walks (p89) for summaries of and alternative routes up Galtymore and a walk to Lough Curra.

PLANNING
Books
Four leaflets published by the Glen of Aherlow Fáilte Society describe low-level, way-marked walks to Lough Curra, Lake Muskry, Slievenamuck and Galbally. Each leaflet has descriptive notes and shows the route on a topographical map at 1:10,000 or 120,000. The leaflets are available from the Society's office in Glen of Aherlow.

ACCESS TOWN
See Glen of Aherlow (p92).

GALTYMORE WALK

Duration 5¾–6¼ hours
Distance 12km
Ascent 1020m
Difficulty moderate–demanding
Start/Finish Clydagh Valley car park
Nearest Town Glen of Aherlow (p92)
Transport private

Summary A classic horseshoe route over the highest peak in the Galtees, with magnificent panoramic views and awesome corries far below.

At 919m, Galtymore is one of Ireland's 12 Munros – peaks that reach over 900m high (see the boxed text The Irish Munros, p26). It stands proud of the rest of the range by almost 100m and is a prominent landmark far and wide. The route described is the most scenic and satisfying among several approach options; surprisingly perhaps, it's over virtually trackless ground, boggy in places but not excessively so.

Along the spine of the main ridge you're treated to thrilling views over Lough Dineen and Lough Curra, tarns that lie far below at the base of sheer-sided corries. At 574m, Lough Curra is the highest lake in the Galtees, and also the most secluded and scenically dramatic of all the lakes along the northern flank of the range. It lies in a hollow that predates glaciation, though the lake itself only formed after the last ice age when the valley was blocked off by moraine. The frozen theme continued right up to the era of refrigeration, with a track known locally as the 'old ice road' allowing winter ice to be drawn from the lough to service the large estates of the area.

Lough Curra is the subject of a local walk developed by the Glen of Aherlow Fáilte Society, which crosses the same ground as the final section of the route described here. The waymarks provide a useful guide from the descent of Knocknanuss to the end. See More Walks (p89) for more information about the Lough Curra walk, and also for an outline of a shorter, more direct ascent of Galtymore.

PLANNING
Maps
OSI 1:50,000 map No 74 covers the walk.

GETTING TO/FROM THE WALK
To reach the start, drive along the minor road on the south side of Glen of Aherlow – known as Glen of Aherlow Scenic Drive – to a junction about 100m east of Clydagh Bridge (at GR R874280). Drive south along the narrow road into the Clydagh River valley for about 300m to an informal car park at a junction with a forest track on the right.

THE WALK
Walk south along the bitumen road from the car park. Not far beyond the forest edge, climb a flight of concrete steps on the left then cross a stile. Go up a foot track beside a fence and cross a stile onto open moorland. Steer a southeasterly course up the generally steep spur of Cush, picking your

GALTEE MOUNTAINS

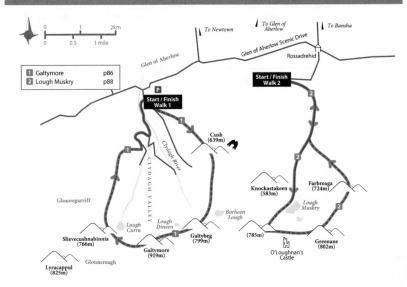

1	Galtymore	p86
2	Lough Muskry	p88

own course as there's no consistent path across the turf and sheep-grazed grass. Continue to the unadorned summit of **Cush** (639m), 1¼ hours from the start). The views are lovely: patchwork plains and hills merge with the northern horizon, while closer to hand, rugged cliffs tower above steep cirques.

Descend steeply southwards following a low, turfed wall to a soggy col. Then there's nothing for it but to tackle the ascent to Galtybeg, with little relief from the relentlessly steep terrain except good views of teardrop-shaped Borheen Lough. The small summit of **Galtybeg** (799m), like that on Cush, lacks a crowning cairn (1½ hours from Cush). Next, descend sharply southwestwards to the col above Lough Dineen. The driest route through the maze of peat hags is on the south side, below the crest; the scenic route along the rim is very soft in places and extremely hard to negotiate. Happily most of the ascent to **Galtymore** is relatively firm and dry. The mountain's highest point is marked by a cairn beside a broken trig pillar, with a large, white memorial cross located about 30m to the west (45 minutes from Galtybeg). To the

southeast the Comeragh and Knockmealdown Mountains are prominent, and to the northwest the Shannon estuary is visible on a clear day.

Descend southwestward from the summit to meet a curving stone wall. Follow this northwest along the ridge, passing through some patches of peat and enjoying a breathtaking view of Lough Curra far below. This wall dates back to about 1880 and once marked the boundary between the estates of two local families. Leave the wall at a corner just east of **Slievecushnabinnia** (766m) and head north across the heather and grass-cloaked summit dome.

Now start to descend in a north-northeast direction. After a while, aim for a tall cairn on the broad spur of Knocknanuss. Continue down from the cairn and when the slope on the right eases, change your course to northeast, heading towards a prominent waymarking post. Here you join the route of the local Lough Curra walk. Cross a grassy knoll and follow a line of waymarkers down to the edge of the forest. Cross a stile and follow a path between the wall and some conifers to a forest track. Turn left and continue along the track for a rather

SOUTHEAST

circuitous kilometre and a half, where you come to a junction beside the remains of an old chimney known as Saunders Lodge. Turn left here and follow this track through the trees and back to the start (2¼ hours from Galtymore).

LOUGH MUSKRY WALK

Duration 4–4½ hours
Distance 13km
Ascent 730m
Difficulty moderate–demanding
Start/Finish track junction at GR R920283
Nearest Town Glen of Aherlow (p92)
Transport private

Summary A fine circular walk above a spectacular glacial lake on the northern face of the Galtees.

Lough Muskry is the largest of the glacial lakes in the Galtees, sitting beneath imposing cliffs and steep green slopes at an altitude of 520m. Given its wild and unspoilt setting, you'd scarcely guess that the lough now contributes to the local water supply. This walk takes you up past the lake to **Greenane** (802m), the highest peak east of Galtymore. The lofty views from the summit provide a fantastic juxtaposition to the confines of the lake below. Up on the ridge you also pass O'Loughnan's Castle, not a ruined building but a natural formation consisting of flat, angular boulders set amid a clutter of pebbly rocks.

The first part of the route follows the 'Lake Muskry' walk, one of the local walks developed by the Glen of Aherlow Fáilte Society. The advantage of this is that the initial section, through the forestry plantation and as far as the lake, is fully way-marked. Beyond the lough the route crosses some mildly challenging open mountain terrain; there are some peat hags to negotiate but nothing too horrendous. If you prefer a shorter walk and don't mind missing the mountain section, it's well worth following the way-marked route as far as Lough Muskry and back. Allow two to 2½ hours for this 8km alternative.

PLANNING
Maps
Use OSI 1:50,000 map No 74.

GETTING TO/FROM THE WALK
Reach the hamlet of Rossadrehid at a crossroads on the south side of the glen. Drive south from here along a narrow bitumen road signed to 'Lake Muskry', then round a sharp right-hand bend and head west for 400m. Park at the start of a gravel forestry road on the left, where tracks enclose a small island of trees (GR R920283).

THE WALK
Within a few metres of the track's double entrance you will come to a junction. The waterworks building can be seen along the track to the south, but you should head east past an information panel, following the blue waymarkers for the local 'Lake Muskry' walk. After roughly 10 minutes, veer left at a fork and head into a long valley. Just over a kilometre later you come to a stile beside a gate at the plantation boundary. This is where you will rejoin the track on your return journey.

Though it isn't shown on the OSI map, the forest road actually continues ahead. Follow it as it rises steeply across the eastern slopes of **Knockastackeen** (583m), crosses a stream and reaches a point above tranquil and secluded **Lough Muskry** (one hour from the start). There are now two options for reaching the crest of the ridge above the lake. For a safer and more gradual ascent, return along the track as far as the stream, then follow the watercourse southwest up the slope. The steeper alternative is to start from the end of the track and climb directly up the steep grassy slope, making sure to keep well west of the cliffs that tumble into the lake.

Whichever route you choose, aim to emerge onto the ridge around the unnamed top marked as '785'. Turn east at this point and descend to the broad, peaty col between 785 and Greenane. Here you'll find not merely a 'cairn' as the map has it, but the cluster of boulders known as **O'Loughnan's Castle**. Continue eastwards and climb to the trig pillar on the summit of **Greenane** (1½ hours from Lough Muskry). The peak provides a great perspective over the rest of the Galtee range to the west, as well as more distant views of the Comeraghs and Knockmealdowns to the southeast.

The next objective is **Farbreaga** (724m), 1.5km northeast down a fairly well defined

THE MOST BEAUTIFUL BIRD IN THE WORLD

The ancient name for Lough Muskry was *Lough Beal Sead*, meaning 'Lake of the Jewel Mouth'. Local legend recounts how the lake was once home to Coerabar Boeth, the daughter of the fairy mansions of Connacht. A powerful and talented lady, Boeth was attended at the lake by some 150 maidens. Every other year, both she and her maidens were metamorphosed into birds. The most elegant creature was always Coerabar herself, who became the most beautiful bird in the world. As a sign of her rank and beauty, she was allowed to wear a necklace of red gold with a sparkling jewel at the centre. It's this jewel that became the namesake of the lough.

spur. You pass a cairn roughly half way down, while Farbreaga itself is marked by a spread-eagled mass of stones on a slight mound. Here, with a bit of imagination, you can make out the shape of a small one-time dwelling, possibly a booley (see the boxed text Booleying – Summer in the Mountains, p171). Keep to the crest of the spur for no more than 200m beyond Farbreaga, then turn decisively northwest and descend into the valley below. The upper part of the descent is littered with fantastically eroded peat hags, and negotiating a way through them is reminiscent of a ballbearing in a pinball machine. Your eventual aim is the forest boundary that you crossed earlier in the day. This means you'll have to ford the anonymous stream flowing through the glen – an interesting but not impossible proposition even after heavy rain.

Cross over the stile beside the gate, then retrace your initial steps down the forest road to the start (1½ hours from Greenane).

MORE WALKS

BLACKSTAIRS & BARROW
Brandon Hill
This broad hill (515m) comes and goes in the outlook from the Barrow Way (p72) and gives marvellous panoramic views west to the Galtees, Knockmealdowns and Comeraghs, and south to Waterford Harbour. From Graiguenamanagh follow the South Leinster Way for about 4km; the Brandon Way – way-marked with granite stones inscribed 'B.W.' and an arrow – loops around the eastern half of the mountain on minor roads, forests tracks and a moorland path. The waymarkers assume a clockwise course but the reverse direction gives better views. Allow 4¼ to five hours for this 12km walk involving 600m ascent. Use the OSI 1:50,000 map No 68.

COMERAGH MOUNTAINS
Seefin Circuit
Seefin (726m) is the highest point on a long ridge rising from the lovely Colligan River valley in the southwest corner of the Comeragh Mountains. Although the mountain lacks the spectacular corries found elsewhere in the Comeraghs, the eastern face is very steep. Start at a car park on the southern slopes of Coumaraglin Mountain (GR: 276018). Head north up a rough track then climb northwest along a long spur, past a communications mast to Coumaraglin Mountain (617m). Follow a fence north into a broad saddle then climb to Seefin's summit, which is blighted by an ugly building but allows panoramic views of the south coast. Follow a vehicle track northwest then southwest for almost 2km to a gate. Continue straight ahead to a minor road and turn left (at GR S255049). At a T-junction and make another left turn, cross the Araglin River and turn left again. Pass a track on the left and almost immediately bear left at a fork, then continue up to the car park. Use OSI 1:50,000 map No 75 and allow 4½ to 5 hours for the circuit, which involves 14.5km and 620m ascent.

GALTEE MOUNTAINS
Lough Curra
This dramatic lake on northern flanks of the Galtees is a good option if poor weather prevents excursions to the summits themselves. Follow a blue way-marked route from the Clydagh Valley car park (see Galtymore walk, p86) to the stile at the forest boundary. Follow a line of waymarkers southwest up the lower slopes of Knocknanuss to a grassy knoll. Here you pick up a track, known as the 'old ice road' and shown on the OSI map, and contour

southward across the hillside. Follow the track to the shore of the lough, and return by reversing your outward route. Allow three to 3½ hours for this 12km walk, which involves 470m ascent. Carry OSI 1:50,000 map No 74.

Galtymore Direct

If time is short you can tackle Galtymore head on, leaving the longer Galtymore Walk (p86) for another day. Start from the Clydagh Valley car park and follow blue waymarkers and signs to a stile over a forest fence. From there go up beside a burn then southwest to a skyline spur. Ascend steeply to the ridge, reaching it near the summit. Return by the same route. Allow 3½ to four hours for this 10km walk involving 770m ascent; carry the OSI 1:50,000 map No 74.

WAYMARKED WAYS

As well as the Barrow Way (see p72), there are four official Waymarked Ways in the southeast: the 100km South Leinster Way from Kildavin to Carrick-on-Suir, the 70km East Munster Way from Carrick-on-Suir to Clogheen, the 168km Blackwater Way from Clogheen to Shrone, and the 56km Tipperary Heritage Trail from the Vee to Cashel. For full route descriptions see www .walkireland.ie.

TOWNS & FACILITIES

BALLYMACARBRY

☎ 052 / pop 200

This village is the ideal base for the western Comeraghs, provided you're content deep in the countryside, far from town. The nearest tourist office and banks are in Clonmel (see p91). Facilities in the village itself are limited to one shop-service station, a couple of bars and a post office.

Sleeping & Eating

The closest camping and caravaning ground is **Powers the Pot** – see Clonmel (p91) for details.

There are also several B&Bs around the village. The family-run **Cnoc Na Ri** (☎ 613 6239; Nire Valley; s/d €45/80) can provide maps, packed lunches and a drying area for soggy gear. To reach it, head towards the Nire Valley, turn left over the bridge, and it's the second house on the right.

Clonanav Farm Guesthouse (☎ 613 6141; www.clonanav.com; s/d €70/100; open Easter-Sep) has en-suite rooms and does a great breakfast. It's signed off the R672 at the northern edge of Ballymacarbry.

The most luxurious accommodation in the area is 19th-century **Hanora's Cottage & Restaurant** (☎ 613 6134; www.hanoras cottage.com; Nire Valley; s/d €95/170; adults only). Facilities include hot tubs, a conservatory spa, free packed lunches and an excellent gourmet **restaurant** (dinner €40-50, open Mon-Sat). Take the Nire Valley road east out of Ballymacarbry and the cottage is about 5km further on.

Bar snacks are also available at **Melody's Nire View** (☎ 613 6169), a great pub in the heart of Ballymacarbry where the genial staff have free leaflets on local walks.

Getting There & Away

Bus Éireann (☎ 051-879 000) has limited services between Ballymacarbry and Clonmel (€5.40, 40 minutes, once on Tue and twice on Fri).

Ballymacarbry is on the R671 Clonmel–Dungarvan road, 16km south of Clonmel.

CLOGHEEN

☎ 052 / pop 1000

This village is close to the Knockmealdowns and is the northern access point for the famous road through the Vee. It has just enough facilities to make it a convenient base for walks in the range. The nearest tourist offices and ATMs are in Cahir or Clonmel.

Sleeping & Eating

On the northern edge of the village, family-oriented **Parson's Green Caravan & Camping Park** (☎ 746 5290; www.clogheen .com; camping per person/site €4/8) doubles as an open farm, offering pony rides and a walking trail past pigs, deer, emus and alpacas. Facilities include a coffee shop, takeaway restaurant and indoor playground for children.

Ballyboy House (☎ 746 5297; s/d €40/70) is a superbly restored, 400-year-old country house located 2km northeast of Clogheen along the R665. Evening meals are provided by arrangement.

Within the village itself, the friendly **Hermitage B&B & Restaurant** (☎ 746 5876; www.thehermitagehouse.com; s/d €40/80) has a fantastic location next to the river. Non-residents are also welcome at the popular in-house **restaurant** (mains from €15; open dinner Wed-Sun).

In the village you'll find several shops including a supermarket, as well as a selection of pubs and take-away restaurants.

Getting There & Away

Bus Éireann (☎ 051-879 000) service No 7 links Clogheen to Clonmel (€8.70, 35 minutes), Cork (€14.30, 1¼ hours) and Kilkenny (€16.50, one hour 35 minutes), with three buses daily Monday to Saturday and two on Sunday.

Clogheen is located around the intersection of the R668 and R665, 13km south of Cahir and 24km southwest of Clonmel.

CLONMEL & AROUND

☎ 052 / pop 16,000

Clonmel (*Cluain Meala*; 'Meadows of Honey') is Tipperary's largest and most commercial town, with an attractive riverside setting and innumerable small shops. It's a convenient base for walks in Comeragh Mountains, but if you have your own transport it can also be used for day trips to the Knockmealdowns and Galtees.

The town's **tourist office** (☎ 612 2960; www.clonmel.ie; St Mary's Church, Mary St; open Mon-Fri) is set in quiet church grounds, and sells maps and local walking guides. For OSI maps and guidebooks you could also drop in to **Eason's** (19-20 Gladstone St) or **The Book Centre** (O'Connell St).

Clonmel has two supermarkets for self-caterers: in Gladstone St and in Market Place, off Emmett St.

Sleeping

The most convenient camping and caravaning ground for the Comeraghs is **Powers the Pot** (☎ 23085; www.powersthepot.net; Harney's Cross; campsites €15; open May-Sep), set high on the northern slopes of the range. Meals (€10-15) are served in the adjacent thatched bar. It's 9km southeast of Clonmel, signposted from the R678 road to Rathgormack.

Also close to the mountains is **Rathgormack Hiking Centre & Hostel** (☎ 051-646 969; Rathgormack; dm €15). Part of the local community centre, facilities are simple but clean and guided walks are available on request. It's located beside the church in Rathgormack, 16km southeast of Clonmel along the R678. Phone ahead for access.

Other amenities in the village include a supermarket and two pubs.

In Clonmel itself you'll find several B&Bs along Marlfield Rd, due west of the centre. **Hillcourt** (☎ 612 1029; www.hillcourt .com; Marlfield Rd; s/d €32.50/60) is one option in a comfortable family home with views to the Comeragh foothills.

In the centre of town, **Fennessy's Hotel** (☎ 612 3680; fennessyshotel.com; Gladstone St; r €45-80) is an attractive four-storey hotel opposite Saints Peter & Paul Church. Extras include room safes and whirlpool tubs in some rooms.

Refined **Hotel Minella** (☎ 612 2388; www.hotelminella.ie; Coleville Rd; r €90-250) dates from 1863 and sits amidst extensive grounds, 2km east of the centre. Luxuries include private hot tubs on terraces overlooking the River Suir.

Eating

Sean Tierney (☎ 612 4467; 13 O'Connell St; meals €7-20) is a narrow old bar that churns out vast portions of pub classics like roasts and lasagne for both lunch and dinner.

Alternatively, **Befani's** (☎ 617 7893; 6 Sarsfield St; mains €15-30; open breakfast, lunch & dinner daily) brings the Mediterranean to Clonmel, with a long tapas menu available throughout the day.

Getting There & Away

Bus Éireann (☎ 051-879 000) services head to Dublin (€14.50, 3½ hours, six daily), Cork (€16, two hours, three daily), Kilkenny (€8.10, one hour, 12 daily) and a number of other places. Tickets can be bought at the train station on Prior Park Rd, where the buses also stop.

The **train station** (☎ 21982) is on Prior Park Rd, 1km north of the town centre. **Iarnród Éireann** (www.irishrail.ie) have regular services to Limerick Junction and Waterford (three daily Mon-Sat), with connections to Dublin Heuston (from €10, three hours, four daily Mon-Sat) among others.

SOUTHEAST

GLEN OF AHERLOW
☎ 062

Lying at the northern foot of the Galtee Mountains, this beautiful glen is home to a community of scattered villages and isolated farms. It makes a peaceful and convenient base from which to explore the area.

The Glen of Aherlow Fáilte Society **tourist office** (☎ 56331; www.aherlow.com; Coach Rd, Aherlow; open daily Jun-Oct) is at Newtown, at the junction of the R663 and R664. Friendly staff can provide information on local walks and accommodation.

There are small shops selling basic supplies in Newtown, Lisvarrinane and Rossadrehid, but the nearest ATMs are in Tipperary or Cahir.

Sleeping & Eating

Located just west of Newtown, friendly **Glen of Aherlow Caravan & Camping Park** (☎ 56555; www.tipperarycamping .com; camping per person/site €4/13) has an incomparable view of Galtymore. Excellent facilities include a games room and campers' kitchen.

Also set against a great backdrop of the Galtees, **Ballinacourty House Camping Park & B&B** (☎ 56559; www.camping.ie, www.ballinacourtyhse.com; camping site & two adults €20, s/d €52/70; open mid-Apr–Sep) is up a side road around 2km west of Newtown. The B&B accommodation is in a renovated, 18th-century stone building, and facilities include a restaurant, wine bar and tennis court.

At the eastern end of the glen, period elegance and high ceilings characterise the Georgian **Bansha House** (☎ 54194; www .tipp.ie/banshahs.htm; Bansha; s/d €60/90). The house is signed 250m along a lane at the western edge of Bansha village, and is one of several accommodation options in the area.

The Glen Hotel (☎ 56151; www.the glenhotel.ie; s/d €70/115) is an older-style hotel just west of Newtown, and serves meals in both its restaurant and bar (mains from €12).

Getting There & Away

There are no bus services in the glen. The main road through the valley is the R663, which branches west from the N24 at Bansha. From Tipperary, take the R664 to reach the R663 at Newtown.

GRAIGUENAMANAGH
☎ 059 / pop 1400

Graiguenamanagh (pronounced 'greg-na-mana') is a pretty little town on the River Barrow that grew up when Duiske Abbey was founded in 1204. The nearest tourist office is in Kilkenny (see below).

Sleeping & Eating

On the banks of the river, popular **Waterside** (☎ 7924246; www.watersideguest house.com; s/d €59/98) occupies an impressive 19th-century corn warehouse. It sells local OSI maps and guidebooks, and the **restaurant** (mains €19-27; open dinner Mon-Sat) is well regarded.

Around 6km southeast Graiguenamanagh towards St Mullins, **Brandon View** (☎ 972 4625; www.brandonviewbandb .com; Ballyling Lower; s/d €48/72) is a hospitable and contemporary B&B.

For supplies, you'll find two supermarkets in Main St Lower, along with a wide selection of pubs and take-away restaurants.

For something more substantial, try **Boats Bistro** (☎ 972 5057; High St; mains from €10; open lunch & dinner daily). It's located at the eastern end of the bridge and offers an interestingly cosmopolitan menu.

Kilbride Coaches (☎ 051-423 633) run regular buses to Graiguenamanagh from Kilkenny (one hour, twice daily Mon-Sat). Graiguenamanagh is on the R703, 23km southeast of Kilkenny.

KILKENNY
☎ 056 / pop 8700

A busy town with an intriguing medieval centre, Kilkenny is an absorbing destination in its own right as well as a gateway to the mountain areas beyond.

The **tourist office** (☎ 775 1500; Rose Inn St; www.kilkenny.ie; open daily Jul & Aug, Mon-Sat Sep-Jun) is located in the 1582 Shee Alms House and also sells local maps and guidebooks.

Supplies & Equipment

For outdoor gear and camping supplies, head to **Padmore & Barnes** (☎ 772 1037; Wolfetone St).

Kilkenny Book Centre (☎ 776 2117; 10 High St) stocks hundreds of titles as well as a wide range of maps. There's also a good café upstairs.

Self-caterers can pick up groceries from **Dunnes Stores** (☎ 776 1756; St Keiran's St; open 24hrs).

Sleeping & Eating

Situated in a small park off the R700 1.5km south of Kilkenny, **Tree Grove Caravan & Camping Park** (☎ 777 0302; www.tree grovecamping.com; New Ross Rd; camping site & two adults €20) is a 20-minute walk from the centre of Kilkenny along a pleasant river path.

Kilkenny Tourist Hostel (☎ 776 3541; www.hostels-ireland.com; 35 Parliament St; dm/tw from €17/40) is a relaxed and friendly IHH hostel on Kilkenny's main street, within a few steps of numerous pubs and restaurants.

The wonderfully welcoming B&B **Celtic House** (☎ 776 2249; john376@gofree.indigo .ie; 18 Michael St; r €80-90) has clean, bright rooms, some with views of the castle.

The Pembroke Hotel (☎ 778 3500; Patrick St; www.pembrokekilkenny .com; r from €69) is a new, epicentral hotel with some 74 rooms. Guests have free use of swimming and leisure facilities just around the corner.

At **Café Sol** (☎ 776 4987; William St; dinner mains €16-28; open lunch & dinner daily), the varied flavours of the seasonally-changing menu all work together in symphonic harmony. Three-course set menus (€23) are great value.

There's a postmodern sense of experimentation at **Fléva** (☎ 777 0021; 84 High St; dinner mains €18.50-27; open lunch & dinner Tue-Sun), where locally sourced produce is complemented by flavoursome accompaniments.

Getting There & Away

Bus Éireann (☎ 051-879 000) operates from a shelter about 200m east of John St, adjacent to the train station (which also sells bus tickets). Buses also collect and deposit passengers at the very central Café Net on St Patrick's St. The extensive timetable includes services to Dublin (€10.80, 2¼ hours, five daily), Cork (€16.10, three hours, two daily) and Clonmel (€8.10, one hour, 12 daily).

The **train station** (☎ 772 2024) has been shoved 200m back from John St to make way for a vast new mall. **Iarnród Éireann** (www.irishrail.ie) have regular services to Dublin (from €10, 1¾ hours, five daily) and Waterford (from €10, 50 minutes, six daily).

ST MULLINS

☎ 051 / pop 140

A peaceful hamlet about 6km along the River Barrow from Graiguenamanagh, St Mullins is a wonderfully atmospheric place that originated as a monastic settlement around 1300 years ago. There are few facilities except the village pub, and the nearest tourist office is in Kilkenny (see p92).

Mulvarra House (☎ 424 936; www.mul varra.com; s/d €50/80) is a modern and comfortable B&B, in a superb location overlooking the river. Evening meals (€30) are available on request and guests can soothe aching muscles in the on-site body treatment centre.

By road, St Mullins is 11km from Graiguenamanagh. Take the R703 and R729 to the hamlet of Glynn, then turn right to St Mullins.

Southwest

HIGHLIGHTS

- Climbing Carrauntoohil, the highest mountain in Ireland, on the classic **Coomloughra Horseshoe** (p108)
- Exploring the tip of the **Sheep's Head** (p130), the most isolated peninsula in the southwest
- Discovering the wonderfully serrated coastline around Slea Head on the **Dingle Way** (p100)
- Challenging yourself with scrambles along the knife-edged ridges of the **MacGillycuddy's Reeks** (p110)

Highest peak in the region: Carrauntoohil, MacGillycuddy's Reeks, 1039m

Southwest Ireland is a region of superlatives. It boasts the country's highest peaks, receives its greatest volume of overseas visitors, and offers months of walking to challenge enthusiasts of all persuasions. Encompassing counties Cork and Kerry, the region is split into a series of peninsulas, each very different in character. The Sheep's Head in County Cork is the most remote and untouched by tourism, and is a place where solitude is still possible. The Beara Peninsula, on the border between Cork and Kerry, has a wild, craggy landscape juxtaposed with colourful and picturesque villages. The Iveragh Peninsula has the highest and most challenging mountain range in Ireland. Finally, the Dingle Peninsula draws walkers hoping for a clear day to climb majestic Brandon Mountain or to experience an iconic coastal landscape that has starred in several Hollywood films.

Each peninsula has its own Waymarked Way, offering excellent long-distance paths, as well as a wide selection of shorter, easier walks. Besides the stunning scenery, the main attraction of the region is the opportunity to experience Irish culture both past and present. From its numerous standing stones, *clochains* (beehive-shaped, dry-stone huts) and other historic relics, to the friendly pubs that so often provide the focal point for celebrations after a good day's activity, the southwest can be hard to beat.

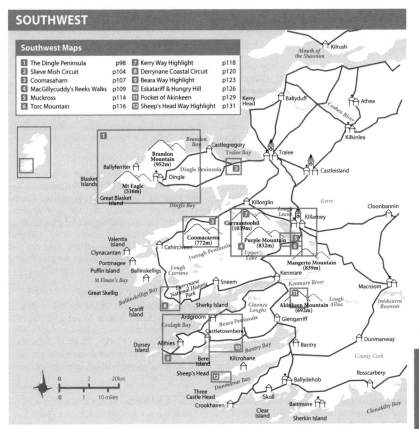

SOUTHWEST

Southwest Maps

1 The Dingle Peninsula	p98	7 Kerry Way Highlight p118
2 Slieve Mish Circuit	p104	8 Derrynane Coastal Circuit p120
3 Coomasaharn	p107	9 Beara Way Highlight p123
4 MacGillycuddy's Reeks Walks	p109	10 Eskatariff & Hungry Hill p126
5 Muckross	p114	11 Pocket of Akinkeen p129
6 Torc Mountain	p116	12 Sheep's Head Way Highlight p131

HISTORY

The landscape of the southwest is littered with evidence of its early history. Numerous promontory forts, stone circles, stone rows, mounds and cairns can be dated as far back as 5000 years.

By the 8th century the Vikings had arrived on the peninsulas, raided them and settled in Smerwick Harbour near Dingle. Four hundred years later it was the Normans turn to settle in the area, intermarry with locals and adopt the language. Soon after this, the area's recorded history becomes a series of battles against the English. In 1601 the Irish and Spanish fought the English at Kinsale, and O'Sullivan Beare's stronghold at Castletownbere, County Cork, was besieged.

The English forces were victorious, and a harsh regime of penal laws was put in place by 1695. Many Catholics were forced into the hills to worship; the many 'mass paths' in the region testify to this period of Ireland's history. It wasn't until the 19th century that a Kerryman, Daniel O'Connell, changed the course of Irish history when he successfully campaigned for Catholics to be emancipated. His ancestral home in Derrynane is featured on one of the routes in this chapter (see p120). O'Connell died in 1847 in the middle of the Great Famine. Other legacies of this traumatic period appear in the form of famine roads, mass graves and deserted villages.

During the early 20th century the countryside was further depopulated as young men and women emigrated abroad. More recently this displacement has been offset by a gradual influx of European settlers, and by a newfound affluence that owes much to the steady stream of tourists.

ENVIRONMENT

Southwest Ireland consists largely of old red sandstone, laid down 400 million years ago when the country lay beneath a shallow ocean. As marine life developed, the surface of this rock was overlaid with deposits of limestone and then coal. Tectonic movements 300 million years ago then threw these layers into tangled folds. Much of this folding is still evident on the glaciated flanks of the higher mountains. Weathering and the scouring effect of glaciers during successive ice ages eroded the limestone from the tops of the mountains but preserved it in the valleys. Glaciers also created corries (small, high, cup-shaped valleys) on the sides of the hills, and left the area strewn with high passes such as the Connor Pass on the Dingle Peninsula.

After the ice retreated Ireland entered a period during which the mild climate encouraged forests to grow. When humans first settled in County Kerry the region was covered in Scots pine, oak, yew, elm, juniper, birch and hazel. Today there are very few deciduous woods left, the most notable examples being the woods around Killarney and Glengarriff. Unfortunately rhododendrons, an introduced species, are endangering the remaining woodlands (see the boxed text Scourge of the Rhododendron, p217). Another foreign species that is now widespread across the region is the fuchsia. The striking red flowers of this plant border countless lanes throughout the southwest, but fuchsia is actually an import from New Zealand that only arrived in the area about 75 years ago.

The area is also well known for its abundance of Lusitanian plants, a group of species specific to the mild, moist, western coasts of Portugal, Spain, Britain and Ireland. Some Irish Lusitanian plants are not found in Britain and theories abound as to their origins. One is that the plants spread along land links with southern Europe after the link with mainland Britain had disappeared.

Pick up any stone on your travels and you may also encounter another unusual creature, the Kerry slug. A spotted slug that grows to 10cm, this creature is becoming harder to find because its natural habitat is slowly being destroyed by forestry activities.

PLANNING
Maps & Books

The best map for overall planning is the OSI 1:250,000 map *South*.

Kerry Walks by Kevin Corcoran describes 20 alternative routes in the region that keep away from the most popular summits.

PLACE NAMES

Several parts of the region – particularly on the Beara and Dingle Peninsulas – are designated Gaeltacht areas, where Gaelic is the first language written and spoken. In these places road signs and place names are often written in Gaelic only, without the usual English translation. To help you navigate through these areas, we give Gaelic names in relevant places in the text.

Information Sources

The official tourist office for the region is **Fáilte Ireland South West** (☎ 021-425 5100; www.discoverireland.ie/southwest; Grand Parade, Cork). Their website is a good source of general information, and includes accommodation listings and walk descriptions.

GATEWAYS

See Killarney (p110) and Tralee (p141).

THE DINGLE PENINSULA

Characterised by long sandy beaches, scattered villages and high coastal mountains, the Dingle Peninsula is one of the most popular tourist destinations in Ireland. Thankfully the north and west extremities of the peninsula have managed to escape the worst of the tour-bus invasion. While the influx of visitors has turned Dingle town into a surprisingly cosmopolitan place, the buzz that pervades the capital town doesn't extend far. The relative isolation of the rest of the peninsula means that the Gaelic language and associated traditions have managed to survive here intact. Today the area remains a Gaeltacht stronghold, and you will no doubt hear Gaelic spoken in shops and pubs.

The combination of challenging mountain terrain, spectacular coastline and relatively well-developed tourist infrastructure makes the Dingle Peninsula a perfect base for a week's walking holiday. Its greatest attractions are probably two of those described here: Brandon Mountain, the country's highest summit outside the Iveragh Peninsula, and the Dingle Way, one of its most scenic long-distance routes. However there are also plenty of options further off the beaten track, and we include a fantastic outing in the oft-overlooked Slieve Mish range to whet your appetite for further exploration.

PLANNING

Dingle tourist office (☎ 066-915 1188; www.dingle-peninsula.ie; the Pier, Dingle) is the main source of information for the area, and its website includes local accommodation listings.

ACCESS TOWN

See Dingle (p136).

BRANDON MOUNTAIN

Duration 5½–6½ hours
Distance 11km
Ascent 840m
Difficulty moderate–demanding
Start/Finish Faha car park
Nearest Town Cloghane (p135)
Transport private

Summary A steep climb through a lake-studded corrie leads to magnificent coastal views. One of Ireland's classic mountain walks, with a longer ridge-top alternative.

At 952m, Brandon is Ireland's eighth-highest peak, and the highest outside of the MacGillycuddy's Reeks on the Iveragh Peninsula. It's a mountain with two distinct sides: the western slopes present a uniformly rounded, grassy aspect, while the eastern flank has been gouged by ancient glaciers into a series of dramatic corries. These corries form huge, rocky steps, each of which is occupied by a lough. It's this line of paternoster lakes, leading steeply to the ridge above, that makes the mountain

so distinctive. The combination of dramatic terrain and magnificent summit views is unforgettable, and the sheer charisma of the peak makes it an inevitable favourite with walkers.

The main route described here makes an out-and-back trip to the summit from Faha, to the east. Though the terrain is steep in places, an informal path means route-finding is relatively straightforward in good visibility. However, the mountain's coastal location means it is notorious for bad weather; conditions can change very quickly and the proximity of steep cliffs means solid navigation skills are essential in poor visibility.

If you have the time and energy to spare, it's well worth considering the extended circuit described here as an alternative route. This outing explores the entire Brandon massif, climbing Brandon Mountain and then continuing across a cliff-lined ridge to the southern summits of Brandon Peak (840m) and Gearhane (803m). With 1150m of ascent there is no denying the trip is a strenuous one, but the scenery is wonderful throughout. Given a little luck with the weather, you should feel well rewarded for your effort.

PLANNING
Maps

Use the OSI 1:50,000 map No 70. Alternatively the OSI 1:25,000 weatherproof map *Brandon Mountain* offers more detail, though most names are marked in Irish only.

GETTING TO/FROM THE WALK

The main route starts and finishes from Faha car park. To get there, head northeast from Cloghane along the R585, then turn left 2km later along a minor road signed for 'Brandon Ridge Walk'. Continue along the single-track lane for 3km and park at the car park at the end of the road.

If you don't have your own transport, the best option is to follow the Dingle Way from Cloghane, beginning opposite O'Donnell's pub. The waymarking posts lead up a track and past a ruined church, then divert through fields to the right and out onto another lane. Leave the Dingle Way here and turn left along the road, climbing to Faha car park at road's end.

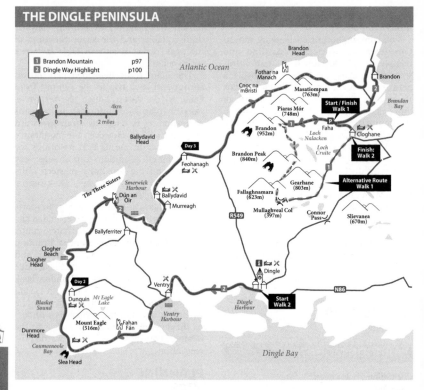

THE DINGLE PENINSULA

1 Brandon Mountain   p97
2 Dingle Way Highlight   p100

The alternative circuit over Brandon Peak starts and finishes in Cloghane village. However if you're lucky enough to have two vehicles at your disposal, the road sections can be avoided by leaving one vehicle at Faha car park, and the other at the end of the road at the top of the Cloghane River Valley. This will shave around 8.5km and 150m of ascent off the day's walk.

THE WALK

From Faha car park, an arrow painted on the rock directs walkers left, through a gate and out onto the open mountainside. Here another sign indicates the ascent route up a stony path marked by a series of white poles. The trail passes a well-tended grotto before beginning to climb steadily along the shoulder and around the ridge ahead. Here the landscape that makes Brandon so special is revealed. Hollowed out above **Loch Cruite** lies a deep rock corrie, with a network of small loughs filling the

depressions on the basin floor. The dark walls of the corrie are sheer and imposing, and it is difficult to see how the route might escape. It is a dramatic scene and the atmosphere of the place is powerful.

The path contours down to the corrie floor and picks through the rocky maze, crossing streams and passing alongside several of the smaller loughs. It gradually makes its way to the back left corner of the basin, where the ground steepens considerably. You'll need to use your hands for support in places as the path zigzags up the headwall, and some sections can be slippery in the wet. The climb is absorbing, and it is a shock to suddenly find yourself exiting the corrie and atop a ridge, with the coastline of the Dingle Peninsula in all its glory below.

A signpost at this point marks the descent for your return route to Faha. For the moment however you should turn left and head south along the ridge-line, climbing

A LEGENDARY SAINT FOR A MEMORABLE MOUNTAIN

The name Brandon Mountain comes from the Irish *Cnoc Bréanainn*, or 'Brendan's Hill', and recalls St Brendan 'The Navigator'. Born near Tralee, County Kerry, in AD 484, our knowledge of the saint's life stems from a lively mixture of recorded fact and legend. There is little doubt he was ordained as a priest in AD 512, and for the next 13 years he preached along the west coast of Ireland, building monastic cells at various locations including at the foot of Mt Brandon.

Accounts suggest it was in AD 530 that he climbed to the summit of his namesake mountain and received inspiration for a voyage to discover the Promised Land. Taking with him a number of dedicated pilgrims, he embarked across the Atlantic on a trip that is said to have lasted for seven years. His journey is described in various texts including the ninth-century *Voyage of St Brendan the Navigator*, though details slip into the mythological when they begin to describe encounters with sea monsters and people with swine heads. Nonetheless, the word spread and crowds of pilgrims soon began to flock to religious centres across the Dingle Peninsula.

Members of the St Brendan Society believe that Brendan was in fact the first westerner to discover America. In 1976, Irish explorer Tim Severin set out to demonstrate that it was feasible for Brendan to have crossed the Atlantic in a leather-clad boat such as the one described in the annals. He constructed a replica curragh and over two summers sailed from Ireland to Newfoundland via the Hebrides, Faroe Islands and Iceland. During the voyage he encountered icebergs, whales and porpoises, which he suggested might provide factual counterparts to the fantastic sights from the legends.

Whether real or imaginary, Brendan's voyages created one of the most remarkable and enduring of European legends. Today he is one of the Twelve Apostles of Ireland, and the patron saint of sailors and travellers. His achievements are commemorated worldwide, including at the United States Naval Academy in Annapolis, Maryland, where a large stained glass window bears his likeness. St Brendan's feast day falls on 16 May, and is celebrated in the Eastern Orthodox Church, the Roman Catholic Church and the Anglican Communion.

another 100 vertical metres before reaching the **summit of Brandon** itself (three to 3½ hours from the start). The peak is marked by a large metal cross and a stone oratory dedicated to St Brendan (see the boxed text A Legendary Saint for a Memorable Mountain, above).

Once you've fully appreciated the fine, 360° panorama that sweeps from the MacGillycuddy's Reeks to the Blasket Islands, return to the start by reversing your outward journey.

ALTERNATIVE ROUTE: BRANDON PEAK CIRCUIT

8–9 hours, 20km, 1150m ascent

Follow the route described above as far as **Brandon** summit. From here, head southeast around the top of the corrie and pick up the ridge that leads towards Brandon Peak. A fence and then a stone wall follows the ridge a safe distance from the sheer edge, and are good navigation guides in poor visibility. Be aware that in bad weather, visibility can be an issue and can make normally innocuous passage a more taxing challenge. The ridge undulates before climbing to the summit of **Brandon Peak** (840m); cross the stone wall to make the final climb to the summit cairn. The top provides fine views towards the Iveragh Peninsula across the waters of Dingle Bay to the southeast. This is one big horizon and it's worth taking the time to drink it in before pushing off again.

From Brandon Peak the route veers southwest, and the ridge narrows to a blunt knife-edge finale just before reaching **Gearhane** (803m). Pass through a gate at the summit of Gearhane and follow the southwest shoulder of the mountain over **Fallaghnamara** (623m) and down to the **Mullaghveal col** below. The waymarked Pilgrim's Route passes through this col on a bog track, and offers the easiest line of descent. Turn left along the track and follow it down to the Cloghane Valley road. If you have left a vehicle here this will mark the end of the route; otherwise it is a 6km walk along the quiet road back to the relative civilisation of Cloghane.

DINGLE WAY HIGHLIGHT

Duration 3 days
Distance 66km
Difficulty moderate
Start Dingle
Finish Cloghane
Nearest Towns Dingle (p136), Dunquin (p136), Feohanagh (p137), Cloghane (p135)
Transport bus

Summary Long sandy beaches, ancient ruins and a mountain crossing are highlights of one of the best stretches of Waymarked Way in Ireland.

The Dingle Way is an eight-day, 179km-long route that circumnavigates the Dingle Peninsula, starting and finishing at Tralee. Without a doubt one of the most scenic way-marked walks in the country, the three days described here represent the best section of the route. If you are walking the entire Way, these stages will provide the fourth, fifth and sixth days respectively.

The route described here follows country roads, sandy beaches and open mountainside as it explores the very tip of the Dingle Peninsula. The first day begins rather uninspiringly with 6km of largely road walking to Ventry, but by the end of the day the scenery is nothing short of spectacular. Recent route changes mean that roughly half of the second day is also along quiet lanes, though beautiful coastal scenery provides constant distraction. The third day crosses the wildest terrain and entails a climb to 610m on the northern slopes of Mt Brandon; for many walkers this is the metaphysical as well as the physical high point of the route. This section is frequently cloud-covered and the open slopes can prove challenging for anybody unused to mountain walking.

While the terrain is generally relatively flat or undulating, the daily sections are long enough to leave even the most experienced walker grateful to reach their accommodation at the end of the day. Those who have time on their hands will be forgiven for shortening the stages and spending longer exploring the scattered villages and intricate coastline of the area. For the energetic, possible side trips include Great Blasket Island (p158) and Brandon Mountain (p97).

PLANNING

The main challenge in planning your walk is organising accommodation. It's highly advisable to make reservations at any time of the year, and essential to do so during the busy summer months of June, July and August. Unfortunately there aren't enough camping grounds to make it possible to complete the route under canvas, so the cheapest option is to stay in a mixture of hostels and B&Bs.

The villages at the end of each day all have small shops or accommodation outlets that can supply food, so there is no need to carry more than one day's food or water with you. The route is fully way-marked, but it is still advisable to carry a map and compass. The third day – from Feohanagh to Cloghane – crosses mountainous terrain, so make sure to bring all the appropriate clothing.

Maps & Books

The route described here is covered by the OSI 1:50,000 map No 70, although you will need No 71 as well if you intend to complete the entire eight-day route.

The Dingle Way by Sandra Bardwell was fully revised in 2009 and has the most up-to-date route descriptions of all the guides available. It contains 1:115,000 strip maps, great photos and a comprehensive description of the route, including side trips and lots of background information.

Information Sources

The website www.dingleway.net is an invaluable resource when it comes to planning your trip. It provides full accommodation listings as well as trail notes, maps and a host of background information.

Guided Walks

Several local companies arrange self-guided trips along the Dingle Way. This means you walk on your own, at your own pace, but benefit from back-up support such as pre-paid accommodation, luggage transfers, route notes and maps. As well as the options listed below, all companies also offer 10-night itineraries. Prices are per person sharing a double room; expect to pay a supplement for singles.

Go Ireland (☎ 066-796 2094; www.govisit ireland.com; Dalys Ln, Killorglin, Kerry) A seven-night trip costs €640.

Southwest Walks Ireland (☎ 066-712 8733; www.southwestwalksireland.com; 28 The Anchorage, Tralee, Kerry) offers four/ seven nights for €338/555.

Tailor-Made Tours (☎ 066-976 6007; www.tailor-madetours.com; Ferry Rd, Keel, Castlemaine, Kerry) has four/seven night tours for €325/546.

GETTING TO/FROM THE WALK

The official start of this route is Dingle town. However if you prefer to avoid the 6km of largely road walking at the start, you could take the **Bus Éireann** (☎ 066-716 4700) service from Dingle to Ventry and start the route there (€2.60, 10 minutes, one service on Mon and Thur only).

Bus Éireann also runs scheduled services from Dingle to Dunquin and Feohanagh, the villages at the end of Days 1 and 2 respectively. Unfortunately there is no public transport between Dingle and Cloghane, at the end of the route. Without private transport, options for returning to Dingle include taking the Friday bus via Tralee, looking for a lift over the Connor Pass, or adding a fourth day's walking to your itinerary.

To return by foot, the easiest route is to follow the way-marked Pilgrim's Route (marked on the OS map). Follow the minor road that leads southwest from Cloghane, continuing up a track where the road ends to cross Mullaghveal col at 397m. Descend along the track to the Dingle–Ballycurrane road, turn left, and continue along the road to Dingle town. This final walk is 15km long and involves around 400m of ascent.

THE WALK
Day 1: Dingle to Dunquin
7 hours, 22km, 370m ascent

The first day's walk begins modestly but improves all the way to Slea Head, by which time the scenery is nothing short of spectacular. From Dingle, head west from the tourist office and harbour, and pick up waymarking posts at the roundabout at the western end of town. Follow the markers west, crossing the Milltown Bridge and continuing along the Slea Head road for 300m before turning right onto a minor road. The fields are littered with prehistoric standing stones, some decorated with patterns.

Roughly 3km along the road, the route turns right and makes a loop around to the north; this section is not marked on newer OS maps. Follow the marker posts as they direct you left after 300m, onto a muddy boreen that climbs across a southern spur of a hill. Rejoin a road and turn left, descending for 1.5km then turning right to rejoin the main road in the village of Ventry. There are several **shops** and **pubs** here, but the route continues straight across the main road onto the **beach**, where you turn right and continue along the sand for almost 3km. Along the way you will cross two streams; the second may need a 'boots off' approach depending on the tide and water levels. Almost at the end of the beach, watch carefully for a right turn onto a short track that leads inland past a red brick bungalow and onto a road. Waymarks then direct you swiftly left, right, and right again, and onto a narrow paved road.

The road terminates at a farm, but the Dingle Way continues to the right along a single-file path. This is a charming section that weaves between high hedges, though it can be muddy. Before long the path broadens into a track and rejoins the main road. Turn left onto the road and continue for 1km – care is needed here because the road is narrow and can be busy with traffic. Now turn right along a narrow lane that climbs uphill to a stile. Cross this and turn left, following waymarks and an informal path running along a stone boundary wall.

Sheep are likely to be in attendance as the route contours around the rock-studded slopes of **Mt Eagle** (516m). Keep an eye open on the seaward side of the route for several clusters of *clochains* (they lie on private land and can be visited from the road for €2-3, but good views are available from the path). These are known as the **Fahan** (*Fahan Fán*) group and there are around 500 ruins in all; it is thought that they are the remains of a late pagan/early Christian village. The various dwellings range from simple shelters to quite complex multi-roomed houses.

After crossing a stream and passing a particularly splendid *clochain*, the path begins to round **Slea Head** and great views of **Dunmore Head** and the Blaskets open up before you. It is a wonderful panorama, and one to treasure before you descend back to the main road. Turn right along the road and you'll soon pass a **café** and **Slea Head Farm B&B** (☎ 066-915 6120;

www.sleaheadfarm.com; s/d €45/70). Follow the busy road carefully for a little over 2km past Dunmore Head – the western-most point on the Irish mainland – to a marker post that directs you left past the departure point for the Blasket Island ferry. Cross a small stream to reach the Blasket Centre and Dunquin. See p136 for details of accommodation and facilities in the village.

Day 2: Dunquin to Feohanagh
7 hours, 20km, 120m ascent

The second day of the route is spent exploring the coastline around the tip of the Dingle Peninsula. Continue north from the Blasket Centre, cross the main road and climb a hill past Dunquin Hostel (see p137). The route then turns left onto a wide gravel track, with fine views ahead to Clogher Beach. The route returns to the main road, turns right and follows it for almost 1km before turning left down a minor road and onto a small path running around the back of **Clogher Beach**. You might want to take some time to explore the western end of the beach, where the cliffs are full of fossils of ancient sea plants and tiny, shelled creatures.

Five kilometres of road now separates you from the next stretch of sand at **Smerwick Harbour**. Walk through the car park and follow the marker posts back to the main road, turn left, and follow the road for almost 1km (a change from the coastal section marked on the OS map). Turn left onto a minor road, then right at a junction 1km later and pass a group of holiday bungalows and a hotel with a **coffee shop**. At the end of the road turn right and then quickly left again, following a lane up the eastern side of a golf course. The road crosses a windswept plain, through reed-filled marshes that are dotted with irises, mallows and blackberries. Ahead, the land rises to the sudden cliffs of the **Three Sisters**. The route makes two more right turns before reaching scenic Smerwick Strand. A short detour to the left just before the beach leads to the grassy mounds of **Dún an Óir promontory fort**. It was here that Elizabeth I's troops laid siege to Spanish and Irish rebels during the 1580 Irish uprising; the fort's 600 defenders surrendered after three days, and were immediately executed in a bloody massacre.

Continue along the beach to the far end. The route leaves the beach briefly at an unofficial camping ground, and follows a couple of lanes around a set of holiday

---

OGHAM SCRIPT

Ogham writing is thought to be pre-Christian in origin, and most of the 316 examples found in Ireland are concentrated in Cork and Kerry, particularly on the Dingle Peninsula. Ogham was the written language of the Celts and lasted until the 10th century AD, when it was supplanted by other scripts introduced by missionaries. Other examples of the text have been found in Wales and on the Isle of Man.

The writing system is extremely primitive and took archaeologists a long time to decipher. It consists of a series of strokes made across the corner of a piece of stone (you can see how it might have been difficult to make a shopping list to take to the market!). The strokes correspond to 19 of the characters of the Roman alphabet, plus the sound 'ng'. What is most interesting about Ogham writing is that it contains two consonants that are not present in Gaelic – 'h' and 'z' – suggesting that it did not originate in Ireland.

Most examples of the writing are found on standing stones representing boundaries or graves. Words that have been translated usually turn out to be a name and the patronymic. Some stones are also engraved with crosses, but these are generally thought to be later additions. Some of the Ogham stones on the Dingle Peninsula also bear another set of markings, thought to be later additions to the alphabet. At Ballintaggart, just outside Dingle, is a series of Ogham stones at an ancient burial site. Some of these bear only Ogham script, while others are carved with crosses, suggesting that the burial ground was used during the transitional phase between paganism and Christianity. In some areas, later groups have endowed these stones with their own spiritual significance, and they now form part of Christian holy sites. One such stone is at Coachford in County Cork, where a nearby holy well and boulder have become included in the site.

cottages. You are then directed back down onto the sand, where you head right to cross a stream via a narrow metal bridge. Now follow the beach northeast to **Murreagh**, where you join a road and turn left. Continue for 1km to **Ballydavid**, passing **Seashore House B&B** (☎ 066-915 5101; www.imeallnamara.com; Ballydavid; s/d €45/70) and a shop before turning left again at a T-junction. This brings you to Ballydavid pier and a couple of seafront **pubs**, both of which serve food.

The route returns to the coast for the next couple of kilometres, following a grassy footpath around a headland accompanied by extensive views. Now join the R549 road and turn left, soon passing **The Old Pier B&B and Restaurant** (see p137) on your way to Dooneen Pier and Feohanagh.

Day 3: Feohanagh to Cloghane
8 hours, 24km, 700m ascent

This long day includes a strenuous climb over the slopes of Brandon Mountain, which provides a fitting finale for the route. Keep an eye open for the small, black Kerry cow; one of the few herds still in existence is transported to the slopes of Brandon Mountain for summer pasture. Tired walkers will be forgiven for short-cutting some of the final, circuitous road sections, which will shave 4.5km off the day's total distance.

Continue past Dooneen Pier and follow the waymarkers through several road junctions. Instead of turning left off the R549 where indicated on the OS map, the route now continues east along the road for a further 500m, and turns left in front of a school. Turn right 400m later onto a narrow lane that soon becomes a track. A short stretch along a river bank brings you to another lane, where you turn left across a bridge. Here you pass two more B&B options: An Riasc and Coill an Rois (see p137). Before too long the lane turns to a track, then a path. A couple of stiles ease your passage across a section of open grassland, and wooden boardwalks spans the worst of a wet patch. You now rejoin a track, which brings you to a road. Turn left along the road, passing An Bóthar Pub and B&B (see p137) some 500m later.

Roughly 80m past the pub, turn right and climb along a lane to a junction. Turn left here, continuing straight ahead and winding between farm buildings to a large car park at the end of the road. This is the take-off point for the ascent of **Brandon Mountain** (952m), and you may want to pause to draw your breath for the climb.

A farm track continues ahead to the left, while a fence stretches away from the top right corner of the parking area. Avoid the temptation to follow the track to its end, and instead veer right after 50m or so and cross open ground towards the fence. Now follow the fence up the slope to a momentary break in the climb beside the knoll of **Cnoc na mBristi**. Here the fence turns away to the left (west). On a clear day it's worth leaving the way-marked route for a few minutes at this point, and following the fence to a junction with a wall. Here you can peer west at a system of ancient walls below known as **Fothar na Manach** (Fields of the Monks), where a community of monks once lived and farmed.

Back on the Dingle Way, the remaining ascent to the col between Brandon and **Masatiompan** (763m) is obvious in good weather; in poor visibility it can be lost beneath a blanket of cloud. Extra markers have been placed to guide walkers in the mist, but you still need to take care in bad weather. Once at the col (610m), walkers lucky with the weather will be rewarded by wonderful views. Cross a fence via a stile and pass an Ogham stone (see the boxed text Ogham Script, p102). Now pick your way down the steep, and occasionally boggy, slope to the northeast. Yellow paint splashes on the rocks mark the way, and great views open up across **Brandon Bay**, the Magharees and the Slieve Mish Mountains.

The descent soon becomes gentler, crossing open moorland and bringing you to the end of a track. Turn right and follow this for around 2.5km to a paved road. After 1km on the road you come to a junction and the route is indicated to the left. If you want to save yourself 3km of largely road walking and descend directly towards Cloghane, ignore the waymarking posts and turn right here.

The official route turns left again after 200m and loops through the scattered houses of Farran to Brandon village, passing a pub on the way. Now pass briefly around the back of Brandon Strand before rejoining the road and heading inland.

Around 2.5km later, turn right onto a more minor road towards Faha (again, continue straight ahead here for a more direct route to Cloghane). Cross a stile on the left after 2km and head across a field towards a forestry plantation, turning left again after 500m to head back towards the coast. You rejoin the road in the centre of Cloghane – see p135 for details of accommodation and facilities in the village.

SLIEVE MISH CIRCUIT

Duration 5–6 hours
Distance 11km
Ascent 900m
Difficulty moderate–demanding
Start/Finish GR Q743107
Nearest Town Tralee (p141)
Transport bus

Summary Follow a lofty ridge over the highest peaks in the Slieve Mish range, then descend to the serenity of a deep, lake-studded glen.

The Slieve Mish Mountains provide a wonderful vantage point over both the Dingle and Iveragh Peninsulas; catch a clear day for this route and you'll be treated to some of the finest coastal and mountain views in southwest Ireland. The route begins by tracing a high ridge over the summits of Gearhane (792m) and Caherconree (835m) to Baurtregaum, the highest point of the range at 851m. It then descends via the beautiful and secluded Derrymore Glen to the finish.

Derrymore Glen, the valley at the heart of the horseshoe, holds a series of three paternoster lakes. The pools are a hidden gem and many walkers make the trip up the valley to visit them as a route in its own right. Yet despite their beauty the lakes are at least partially artificial, having once been dammed to provide power for a water mill on the lower reaches of the Derrymore River.

Besides short sections of path at the start of the route and along Derrymore Glen, the circuit crosses open ground that shows few signs of passing feet. The feeling of isolation enhances the character of the walk but is deceptive – these mountains are accessible from a main road just a few kilo-metres southwest of Tralee. Well-defined topography makes navigation relatively straightforward in good visibility, though steep drops into the corrie mean caution is required in bad weather. It might also be worth packing a towel if you visit the area during the summer months. You wouldn't be the first walker tempted to cool off in the lough after the exertion of the ridge!

PLANNING
Maps
OSI 1:50,000 map No 71 covers the route.

GETTING TO/FROM THE WALK
The circuit starts and finishes at the end of a lane near Derrymore Bridge (GR Q743107). From Tralee, take the N86 southwest towards Dingle. Turn left onto a minor road after 10km, around 500m west of Derrymore Bridge. The bottom of the lane is marked with an 80km/h sign and has a yellow bungalow on the left. Continue steeply for 400m to a T-junction and turn right.

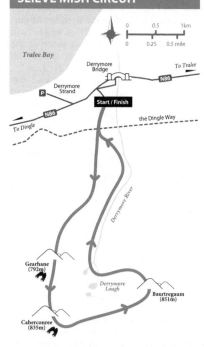

SLIEVE MISH CIRCUIT

The road ends beside a small cottage, and there is parking space in front of the building for around six vehicles. If further space is required use the large car park for Derrymore Strand, 1.5km northwest.

Scheduled **Bus Éireann** (☎ 066-716 4700) services ply the N86 on their way from Tralee to Dingle (four daily Mon-Sat and three on Sun). Though this is not an official stop, drivers should be able to drop you near Derrymore Bridge if you ask in advance.

THE WALK

From the end of the lane, follow a grass track past the cottage and round to the right. The track comes to an end after 100m; turn left here and cross a stile beside a gate. You are now out onto open ground beneath the Slieve Mish Mountains. Follow a rocky path south towards the base of the mountains. Within 400m, a prominent black waymarking post indicates a junction with the **Dingle Way**. The entrance to Derrymore Glen can be seen to the southeast, and you'll descend through this gap at the end of the circuit. For now however, set your sights directly ahead on the steep, heather-covered slope of Gearhane.

The initial part of the ascent is very steep. Expanding views north over Tralee Bay provide distraction but it's still something of a relief to arrive at the top of the spur, where the remainder of the circuit is visible ahead. Turn right and follow the ridge southwest, climbing more steadily over short grass. Several rock outcrops mark the summit of Gearhane (two hours from the start), while great views extend west over the undulating spine of the Dingle Peninsula.

Now climb gently around the southwestern corner of the horseshoe to the cairn at the top of **Caherconree** (835m; 20 minutes from **Gearhane**). The views are even better from here, particularly south over Dingle Bay to the MacGillycuddy's Reeks. The descent east from Caherconree is slightly trickier, and care is needed in poor visibility. The mountain narrows to a grassy ridge around one metre wide. The restricted space means a path has formed here, one of the only places on the route where you might see other footprints.

Follow the ridge down to a wide col strewn with boulders of old red sandstone.

The salmon-coloured sand between the stones gives the impression of walking across an upland beach. Climb steadily to the broad summit of **Baurtregaum** (851m; 45 minutes from Caherconree), whose trig point is set amid a circle of stones. You are now at the heart of the Slieve Mish Mountains and the various spurs of the range radiate around you.

Turn northwest at the summit and descend along the shoulder marked as 723m. As you lose height, arc gradually west then southwest, aiming for the northern shore of Derrymore Lough. The circuitous approach avoids steep ground to the southwest of the lough. **Derrymore Lough** (40 minutes from Baurtregaum) makes a good place for a rest. After the lofty terrain of the ridge, it's a novel feeling to be enclosed deep within the steep-sided basin.

When you're ready, follow the tumbling Derrymore River north along the base of the glen. After a relatively steep descent, cross to the river's western bank and join an intermittent path. The easiest ground can generally be found a short distance away from the watercourse rather than along its banks. The valley narrows to the exit portal and the path consolidates once more as you skirt around the lower slopes of Gearhane. Follow the path out of the valley, then veer northwest to the black waymarking post. Now simply retrace your initial steps over the stile to the start.

THE IVERAGH PENINSULA

If there is one place in Ireland that can be considered a mecca for walkers, the Iveragh Peninsula is it. The mountains of the MacGillycuddy's Reeks dominate the region, covering an area of almost 100 sq km and boasting no less than nine of the country's 10 highest peaks (see the boxed text The Irish Munros, p26). Granted such superlative terrain, it is little wonder that over 25,000 mountain enthusiasts are attracted to the region annually.

However, the high ground of the Reeks is not a place for the uninitiated. Weather is unpredictable, ridges are steep and exposure can be great, and the mountains claim lives on a yearly basis. Thankfully Iveragh has much more to offer walkers than these demanding peaks. Lower summits offer comparable views and as great a sense of achievement, without the degree of danger. The long-distance Kerry Way also provides almost 200km of walking through Iveragh's remote valleys and along its varied coastline.

Iveragh also has plenty to offer walkers who prefer an even more leisurely approach. Killarney National Park is not a place to seek solitude, but its gardens and lakeside nature trails are undeniably popular. The number of visitors to the region also means that tourist infrastructure is more developed here than in other parts of Ireland, and operators have many years of experience when it comes to catering to walkers' needs. If you are somebody who likes to walk without the hassle of preparing your own sandwiches or carrying your own luggage, this is the place for you!

PLANNING
Books
Jim Ryan's *Carrauntoohil and MacGillycuddy's Reeks: A Walking Guide to Ireland's Highest Mountains* details 20 popular walking routes in the Reeks, illustrated by clear photographs and full-colour OSI maps.

ACCESS TOWNS
See Glencar (p138) and Killorglin (p140).

COOMASAHARN

Duration 5–5½ hours
Distance 10km
Ascent 800m
Difficulty moderate–demanding
Start/Finish Junction at GR V636852
Nearest Town Killorglin (p140)
Transport private

Summary An impressively lonely circuit around a deep glacial corrie, featuring an exposed stretch of ridgeline and expansive views in all directions.

One of the revelations of walking on the Iveragh Peninsula is looking beyond the MacGillycuddy's Reeks to explore the wild coums and oft-overlooked ridges to the south. Coomacarrea (772m) and Teermoyle Mountain (760m) mark the high points of

an assertive mountain mass just west of the Reeks. The attraction here is the series of coums that have been gouged by glaciers from the mountains' northeastern slopes, and the dark lakes that lie within them. This walk circles the largest of these lakes, offering a brooding view into the dark recess before descending an airy ridge onto Coomreagh.

It is a wild and lonely walk; tumbling ravens are the most obvious sign of life as you skirt the high cliffs. It's easy to believe the story that the last wolf in Ireland was hunted to the very back of the main coum and killed for a five-pound reward. In penal times local people also made a pilgrimage of sorts along the shores of Coomasaharn Lake, to reach the mass rock at the lowering head of the corrie.

The route is best tackled in a clockwise direction to account for the steep, broken slopes of Knocknaman, which are safer to climb than descend. However, it's best to save the trip for a fine, dry day. Much of the route follows exposed cliff-tops, and finding the ridge onto Coomreagh can be particularly tricky in mist; a mistake here in poor visibility would have serious consequences. It's also worth noting that the route crosses numerous wire fences across the high ground, all of which should be negotiated with care at the lowest point.

Those who prefer a longer outing can extend the route north and encircle all three main corries in the area. From Teermoyle Mountain, pass over Mullaghnarakill and descend along the northern side of Coomnacronia before following the lake's outlet stream to a bog track. Follow this east to a lane and turn right, following the tracks and lanes marked on the OS map to return to the start. Allow seven hours for this 16km alternative, which involves 920m ascent.

PLANNING
Maps
The OSNI 1:50,000 maps No 78 and No 83 both cover the walk. No 83 is necessary if you want to extend the circuit around the corries to the north.

GETTING TO/FROM THE WALK
From Killorglin, take the N70 to the village of Glenbeigh and turn left beside Towers Hotel. Follow this narrow road southwest for 7km to a sharp right-hand bend, where

COOMASAHARN

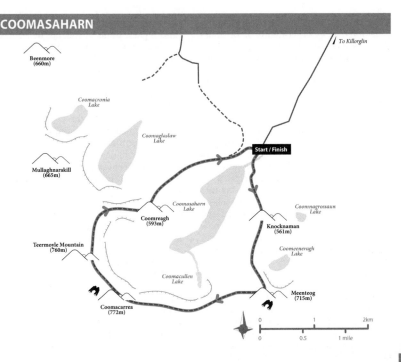

a track continues straight ahead (GR V636852). Park either in front of the ruined stone building just before the bend on the right, or carefully along the verges of the track.

There is no public transport to the area.

THE WALK

Set off along the track that leads around the north-eastern corner of the lake. Where this peters out, pass through a small gate and turn south, immediately beginning the climb up steep slopes of **Knocknaman** (561m). Weave through the rlocky outcrops and slippery gullies to arrive on a broad shoulder. Turn southwest here and follow the shoulder as it rises gradually to the summit of **Meenteog** (715m), 1.5km away. The terrain on this shoulder might be kindly described as squelchy, and provides the only unpleasant walking on the route. Meenteog provides a good outlook over Coomeeneragh Lake, as well as fine views in all directions.

From Meenteog, retrace your steps for a couple of hundred metres, then strike out west to reach the cliffs above beautiful

Coomacullen Lake, which lies tightly enclosed within rock walls below. Now follow the cliff-line west to the col between Meenteog and Coomacarrea. Navigation is aided here by a ditch and the remains of an old boundary wall, which lead you up onto the next climb. A steep haul brings you to the barren summit of **Coomacarrea**, marked by an iron cross. There's a fine view northeast down the length of Coomasaharn, while Valentia Island lies southwest of Dingle Bay.

A line of old stakes now descends northwest towards the col that separates Coomacarrea from Teermoyle Mountain. Just before the col you may notice a few small standing stones. A final, brief climb then brings you to the unmarked summit of **Teermoyle Mountain**. From here the best views lie north across Dingle Bay to the mountains of the Dingle Peninsula, with the long spit of Inch Strand particularly prominent in the foreground.

Precise navigation is now required to reach the sharp ridge leading down to

Coomreagh (593m), and extreme caution is required in poor visibility. If in doubt the slopes to the south and west of Teermoyle provide an escape route, though they leave you in need of a lift back to the start. Begin by descending north to point 702m. Now turn east, where a steep grassy slope gives access to the ridge, with a great deal of precipitous terrain on either side. The ground soon thins to a very narrow arête, though progress remains fairly straightforward despite the psychological effect of the exposure. To the left the slope drops to Coomaglaslaw, while to the right a series of gullies and buttresses fall away into Coomasaharn. A twist and short climb marks the return to broader ground and the flat top of Coomreagh. You can now draw your breath, take your eyes off your feet, and enjoy more great views of the Reeks.

After a little over 1km the shoulder narrows; keep the boulders and outcrops on your left-hand side and descend west towards the head of the lake. As you lose height, new aspects of the coum's cliffs open up across the water. As the ground flattens out pick up a rough track, which leads onto tarmac. Follow the lane as it winds down past houses and fuchsia-draped walls, and leads you back to the T-junction where the route began.

COOMLOUGHRA HORSESHOE

Duration 6–7 hours
Distance 11km
Ascent 1130m
Difficulty demanding
Start/Finish Lough Eighter Hydro Rd
Nearest Towns Glencar (p138), Killorglin (p140)
Transport private

Summary This spectacular and challenging mountain circuit crosses the three highest peaks in Ireland, featuring tremendous views and an exciting, narrow rock ridge.

This is arguably the finest circular walk in the country and probably the best way to climb Ireland's highest mountain, Carrauntoohil (1039m). A highly recommended and immensely rewarding day out, the route takes you across a narrow ridge as it passes over Carrauntoohil and the second and third highest peaks in Ireland: Beenkeragh (1010m) and Caher (1001m). Along with the MacGillycuddy's Reeks Ridge (p110), this route provides the highest-level walking in the country, with around 5km at an altitude of over 800m.

In fine weather the trip is strenuous but straightforward, with the exception of the rocky, knife-edge ridge linking Beenkeragh and Carrauntoohil, where you might need to use your hands for support (see Warning, p110). The outing becomes a serious proposition in poor visibility however. As well as reducing the dangers of a navigational error, it is well worth waiting for a fine day to fully appreciate the views from the roof of Ireland. See the MacGillycuddy's Reeks Walks map (p109).

PLANNING
Maps

Use either the OSI 1:50,000 map No 78, or Harvey's waterproof 1:30,000 Superwalker map *MacGillycuddy's Reeks*. The OSI 1:25,000 weatherproof map *MacGillycuddy's Reeks* also offers more detail, but most names are marked in Irish only.

GETTING TO/FROM THE WALK

The circuit starts and finishes at the bottom of the Lough Eighter Hydro Rd, 11km south of Killorglin and 23km west of Killarney. The road is shown on walking maps as a dotted track; follow signs for Glencar and keep your OS map handy to navigate the many junctions. The bottom of the track is marked by several wooden and metal gates, and an information panel erected by Kerry Mountain Rescue. Parking in the area is rather limited – the best options are either in a small lay-by on the eastern side of the road 100m north of the entrance, or in a larger lay-by with a map board around 800m south.

There is no public transport to the area.

THE WALK

Pass through the gate at the bottom of Lough Eighter Hydro Rd and begin to climb along the concrete track. Follow the road for 2km, all the way to the dam at the western end of the lough. You are now at the mouth of the impressive Coomloughra corrie, and Lough Eighter provides

MACGILLYCUDDY'S REEKS WALKS

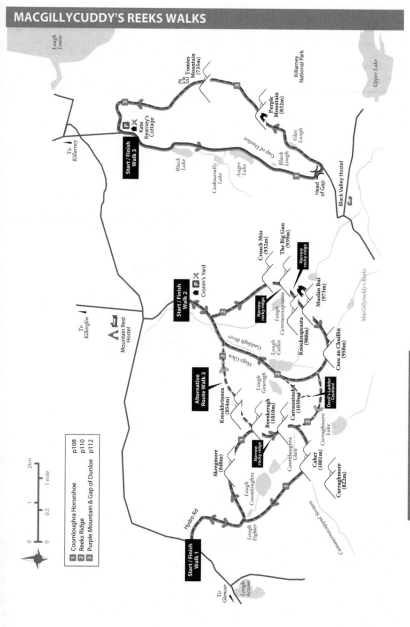

SOUTHWEST

a good spot to stop for a drink and admire the ring of mountains you are about to tackle.

Cross the outlet stream of the lough and immediately begin to climb steep slopes to the north, ascending to the shattered

WARNING

This walk features a section along a narrow and exposed ridge and will not suit walkers who don't have a head for heights. The ridge should be avoided in high winds, and becomes a serious undertaking in poor visibility or winter conditions. If there is a chance of encountering significant snow or ice, then an ice axe and other mountaineering equipment should be carried, and the route should only be attempted by those with winter mountaineering experience.

crest of **Skregmore** (848m). Faint tracks lead through the heather and springy turf, though these give way to boulders and shattered rock slabs near the top. The slopes converge to a spiky crest at the summit, and there are expansive views across Dingle Bay to the west. To the north, a patchwork of flat green fields leads across Kerry's rich dairy country.

The ridge now leads southeast for 1km, crossing a couple of unnamed summits to the foot of a broad, boulder-strewn ridge. A path twists and turns through the outcrops and leads to the small cairn marking Ireland's second-highest summit, **Beenkeragh** (1010m; three hours from the start). To the east, the ground suddenly falls away into Lough Gouragh, and a dizzying space leads the eye across to the cliffs on Carrauntoohil's northern face. Some walkers might find the sight of the ridge spanning this gap a little intimidating. Although it does require care in places, generally it is not as difficult as it looks.

Follow a path that descends steeply onto the ridge and, after picking your way along the crest for a stretch, follow it onto the right-hand (west) side of the arête. At about half distance, the path crosses to the steeper left-hand side for 100m (care should be taken here), before returning to the right again. Most of the difficulties are now over and it is a short, steep climb from the end of the ridge to the broad summit of **Carrauntoohil** (1039m; 45 minutes to one hour from Beenkeragh), the highest point in Ireland. New views open up from the summit, especially to the east along the saw-toothed ridge of the MacGillycuddy's Reeks. The

summit cross was erected in 1977 and originally featured a windmill that powered light bulbs on the cross.

Descend southwest to a col; a short, steep ascent where the ridge becomes narrow again leads to the summit of **Caher** (1001m). A small cairn marks the top, where another, slightly lower, summit (975m) comes into view just to the west. Pass over this and start the long descent northwest to Lough Eighter. After a bouldery section, a small path leads down the shoulder of Caher on springy turf. From Lough Eighter you might take a final look back into Coomloughra before heading back down the Hydro Rd to the start.

REEKS RIDGE

Duration 6–7 hours
Distance 13km
Ascent 1050m
Difficulty demanding
Start/Finish Cronin's Yard
Nearest Towns Gap of Dunloe (p138), Killarney (p139), Killorglin (p140)
Transport private
Summary The longest and most sustained ridge walk in Ireland, this route requires confidence over steep ground; the rewards are tremendous views.

Suitable for experienced walkers only, a trip along the Reeks Ridge is akin to a right of passage for ambitious Irish mountain enthusiasts. Here we present two route options for crossing what is arguably the finest section of ridge-line in the country. The main route described scales six summits over 900m (3000ft), including Knocknapeasta (988m) and Maolán Buí (973m), the fourth- and fifth-highest summits in Ireland respectively. But to really make this a route to remember, very fit walkers may want to add on the alternative finish, and extend the route west across Ireland's two highest peaks – Carrauntoohil (1039m) and Beenkeragh (1010m). This alternative makes for a particularly long, strenuous route that will challenge even the most accomplished walker, but it does give the immense satisfaction of completing eight of Ireland's 12 Munros in a single outing (see the boxed text The Irish Munros, p26).

The initial section of ridge between Cruach Mór and Knocknapeasta is a rocky knife-edge, and requires both a good head for heights and solid route-finding skills. You'll need to use your hands for support over this section, and basic scrambling manoeuvres are also required (see Warning, p111). Thereafter the ridge broadens. If you're a bit worried, it's worth walking at least as far as the summit of Cruach Mór. From here you'll get a good appreciation of the difficulties involved, and views that are more than worth the effort even if you decide to go back down the way you came. Refer to the *MacGillycuddy's Reeks* map mentioned in Planning, below.

PLANNING
Maps
The OSI 1:50,000 map No 78 covers the route, as does Harvey's waterproof 1:30,000 Superwalker map *MacGillycuddy's Reeks*. The OSI 1:25,000 weatherproof map *MacGillycuddy's Reeks* also offers good detail, though most names are marked in Irish only.

GETTING TO/FROM THE WALK
The walk starts and finishes at **Cronin's Yard** (☎ 064-663 4963; www.croninsyard .com; Mealis), the farm at the end of the road in Hags Glen (GR V836873). Facilities here include a tearoom, showers and toilets, a public telephone, and packed lunches are available on request. There is a daily fee of €2 for using the car park.

The farm is located 18km west of Killarney. Turn south off the N72 Killarney –Killorglin road at Beaufort, and follow signs initially for the Gap of Dunloe and then for Carrauntoohil. At a crossroads beside Kissane's Foodstore you should slow down; take the next left turn onto a narrow road that ends at Cronin's Yard after 3km.

There is no public transport to the area.

THE WALK
From Cronin's Yard, pass through a gate at the top right side of the car park. Follow a grass track along the side of a field and onto a stony track that climbs gently above the Gaddagh River. Leave the track where it crosses a tributary of the Gaddagh and head southeast across open ground, climbing towards the conspicuous summit of **Cruach Mór** (932m). Aim to the east of the summit to find easier ground. The top is marked

> ## WARNING
> This walk features sustained sections along a narrow and exposed ridge. It is not suited to walkers who suffer from vertigo, and should be avoided in windy conditions. The entire route becomes a serious undertaking in wet weather or poor visibility. In winter, if there is a chance of encountering significant snow or ice, then an ice axe and perhaps other mountaineering equipment should be carried, and the route should only be attempted by those with winter mountaineering experience.
>
> It is also best to avoid the Devil's Ladder, a loose and eroded gully that has traditionally provided the main route between Hags Glen and the Reeks. Numerous accidents – sometimes fatal – have occurred here over the years, often caused by people carelessly dislodging rocks onto walkers below. Use one of the two descent routes indicated in the walk description instead.

by a stone grotto, and has impressive views south across the Iveragh Peninsula (1½ to two hours from the start).

Your attention is likely to be drawn by the sight of the rock ridge running south towards **The Big Gun** (939m). Huge blocks of rock (known as gendarmes) adorn the crest of the ridge, making the job of keeping to the top very difficult at first. Follow informal paths below and to the west of the ridge, being careful not to lose too much height. Scramble back up to the ridge at a notch, and then climb – with care – directly along the exciting rock arête to reach The Big Gun. The ridge now swings southwest towards Knocknapeasta. Stick to the crest as you descend to a col, but where the ridge becomes difficult again you can drop to the left (south) of the arête before rejoining it just beneath the summit of **Knocknapeasta** (988m; around one hour from Cruach Mór).

The views from the highest point on the walk take in Ireland's three highest summits to the west and the serrated ridge you have just traversed to the east. To the north, wild cliffs fall away into the dark waters of Lough Cummeenapeasta, and beyond that the patchwork fields of north Kerry. To the south the mountain falls away to Black

Valley, and ridge after ridge of mountains extend towards the Atlantic.

Walk south from Knocknapeasta along a broad, stony ridge, then bear southwest as you drop to a col and climb a short distance to the summit of **Maolán Buí** (973m). Cross an unnamed top at 926m to reach **Cnoc an Chuillin** (958m; 1¼ hours from Knocknapeasta), the last major peak on the ridge. Now descend to a col and climb onto another unnamed summit. It is best to descend directly into Hags Glen from here, keeping to the west of steep ground. Many walkers still use the **Devil's Ladder** further to the west but this is best avoided (see Warning, p111). Once in **Hags Glen**, simply follow the stone track for 4km to the finish (two hours from Cnoc an Chuillin).

ALTERNATIVE ROUTE: REEKS RIDGE & CARRAUNTOOHIL
8–10 hours, 15km, 1450m ascent

From the col at the top of the Devil's Ladder, climb steadily northwest to the summit of **Carrauntoohil** (1039m). Then reverse the narrow ridge walk between Carrauntoohil and Beenkeragh described for the Coomloughra Horseshoe Walk (p108). Continue past Beenkeragh before making a long, steep descent northeast, over **Knockbrinnea** (854m), to the Gaddagh River at the base of Hags Glen. This descent is initially over boulders, but eases to heather and grass on the lower slopes. Join the track beside the river, turn left and complete the final distance to Cronin's Yard.

PURPLE MOUNTAIN & GAP OF DUNLOE

Duration 6–7 hours
Distance 14.5km
Ascent 890m
Difficulty moderate–demanding
Start/Finish Kate Kearney's Cottage
Nearest Towns Gap of Dunloe (p138), Killarney (p139)
Transport private

Summary Enjoy stunning views of Ireland's highest mountains from this airy, conical summit. Features a busy approach through the ever-popular Gap of Dunloe.

The sheer-sided valley of the Gap of Dunloe is one of Ireland's biggest natural tourist attractions, comparable to the Cliffs of Moher in terms of visitor numbers. Fortunately the mountain pass, gouged by glacial action aeons ago, manages to retain its imposing character despite the tourist chaos that sometimes takes place below.

Purple Mountain (832m) rises steeply to the east of the gap, and derives its name from the distinct, purple-tinged sweeps of sandstone talus near its top. Slightly further north is Tomies Mountain (735m), whose eastern slopes harbour the largest area of ancient Oakwood in the country (see the boxed text Killarney National Park – A Natural Success Story, p115). This route follows a ridge over the two summits, offering superlative views across the Reeks to the west. An informal path has formed along many stretches of the route, easing progress and aiding navigation.

If you must walk between June and August, consider making an early start to avoid the crowds. Alternatively, join the fun and take a jaunting car (a pony and trap) up the road from Kate Kearney's to the Head of Gap. Doing this will save around 6km of road walking; see Getting to/from the Walk (below) for details.

PLANNING
Maps
The OSI 1:50,000 map No 78 covers the route, although the extra detail given by Harvey's waterproof 1:30,000 Superwalker map *MacGillycuddy's Reeks* or the OSI 1:25,000 weatherproof map *MacGillycuddy's Reeks* might be preferable. (Note that most names are marked in Irish only on this last sheet.)

GETTING TO/FROM THE WALK
The start of the walk is 12km southwest of Killarney. Follow the N72 Killarney–Killorglin Rd to Beaufort, then follow signs south to the Gap of Dunloe. There is a large parking area at Kate Kearney's Cottage, at the bottom of the gap.

It is also possible to start the walk at the Head of Gap. The surface of the minor road through the gap is seriously broken in places, but it does carry traffic and there is space to park at the top. Unfortunately it is all but impossible to take a car through during the day in summer, when the road is blocked by a crawling procession of walkers, cyclists and jaunting cars (ponies and traps).

A jaunting car from Kate Kearney's to the Head of the Gap costs around €50. Services are led by demand and transport a maximum of four people.

THE WALK

From Kate Kearney's Cottage, follow the road heading south into the Gap and climb steadily through hairpin bends to the northern shores of **Black Lake**. On calm days, a wonderful reflection of the valley appears in the reedy waters of the lake. The road is then essentially flat for the next 1.5km, passing a tearoom before climbing again above **Auger Lake**, where imposing cliffs begin to close in on either side. Pass over a narrow bridge and climb steeply to **Black Lough**, where the gradient eases and the valley opens out again. A final ascent then brings you to the **Head of Gap** (1½ to two hours from the start).

Leave the road here and climb eastwards towards the steep, cliff-girt slopes that seem to bar progress. You should soon pick up traces of a path running along some old fencing. This will lead you steadily up and northeast beneath the crags to **Glas Lough**, which appears quite suddenly, hidden in a small hollow in the mountain.

Follow a path around the lough and then climb steeply onto the southern shoulder of Purple Mountain. There is a brief respite before the gradient increases once more, taking you across stunted heather and patches of talus to a small subsidiary summit at 793m. A few minutes later you reach the official summit of **Purple Mountain** (832m; 1½ to two hours from the Head of Gap), where you can rest and take in the lofty views in all directions. The Reeks demand most attention to the west, but the Killarney Lakes to the east and the patchwork of farmland to the north also catch the eye.

Descend along a pleasantly narrow ridge to the northeast and cross a small col before climbing to an unnamed summit at 757m. The route now doglegs to the north (be careful in mist), dropping into another saddle before making the final climb to the summit of **Tomies Mountain** (735m). Beside the summit cairn is a conspicuous sprawl of stones marking a **Neolithic burial site**.

The initial descent from Tomies Mountain is quite steep, leading to a flat shoulder. Contour around a slight rise and then descend steeply again, making a beeline for the small ridge above Kate Kearney's. As the angle of descent eases, bracken begins to appear and a small path winds through this to reach a track. Turn left onto the track, but only for a few metres. Now cross the gate on your left and follow a rough track down through a series of gates giving access to a sealed road. Follow the road for a short distance and then turn left to return to Kate Kearney's.

MUCKROSS

Duration 4–5 hours
Distance 14km
Ascent 150m
Difficulty easy
Start/Finish Muckross House car park
Nearest Town Killarney (p139)
Transport bus

Summary This popular lakeside walk in Killarney National Park features interesting geology, ancient ruins and tracts of precious native woodland.

Forming the core of Killarney National Park, Muckross is a popular day trip for visitors to Killarney. Today the estate serves two main purposes. Firstly there's the maintenance of the Muckross Demesne, which includes formal gardens and an imposing mansion dating from 1843. Secondly there's the preservation of precious patches of native woodland (see the boxed text Killarney National Park – A Natural Success Story, on p115).

The most significant tract of woodland on this route can be found along Muckross Peninsula, the spur of land that separates Muckross Lake from larger Lough Leane. Much of this peninsula is covered by ancient oak wood, whose thick foliage once provided cover for troops fighting Oliver Cromwell. Yet the real treasure is Reenadinna Wood, the most extensive of Europe's three large yew woods. Yews date back to the great primeval forests that covered the earth before deciduous trees made an appearance, and the strangely shaped boughs, thick moss and deep shade still evoke an atmosphere of reminiscent of another age.

This route makes a circuit around Muckross Lake, following a series of structured pathways. It actually forms one of Ireland's National Loop Walks, though at the time of writing there were no signs on the ground to indicate this. The estate can be especially busy in the summer, when you'll find yourself sharing the lanes, tracks and footpaths with lots of other walkers. It's a chance to swap stories and re-connect with humanity but it perhaps isn't the solitary walk you might be looking for. However, on the more remote sections it's still possible to spot wildlife such as deer, herons and red squirrels. Keep an eye out too for the small, black Kerry cow; one of the few herds in existence grazes at Muckross.

Other options during your visit to Muckross include a tour of **Muckross House** (☎ 064-663 1440; www.muckross-house .ie; adult/child €7/3, combined ticket with farms €12/6; open daily) or a trip around the fascinating replica 1930s **Muckross Traditional Farms** (☎ 064-663 1440; adult/child €7/4; open daily May-Sep, Sat, Sun & public holidays mid-Mar–Apr & Oct).

PLANNING
Maps
The OSI 1:50,000 map No 78 covers the route, though the national park lanes are incorrectly marked. A much more accurate representation of the route is shown on Harvey's waterproof 1:30,000 Superwalker map *MacGillycuddy's Reeks*.

GETTING TO/FROM THE WALK
The walk starts and finishes at the main car park for Muckross House. To get there, follow the N71 Kenmare road south from Killarney for 4.5km, then turn left through the main entrance for Muckross Estate.

If you're walking or cycling from Killarney, the best option is to follow the signposted Kerry Way as far as Muckross Abbey and then complete this circuit from there. See Day 1 of the Kerry Way Highlight (p118) for details of the route.

All **Bus Éireann's** (☎ 064-663 0011) Killarney–Kenmare services pass along the N71, and will drop you off outside the main entrance if you ask the driver (at least three daily Jun-Sep and once daily Mon-Sat the rest of the year).

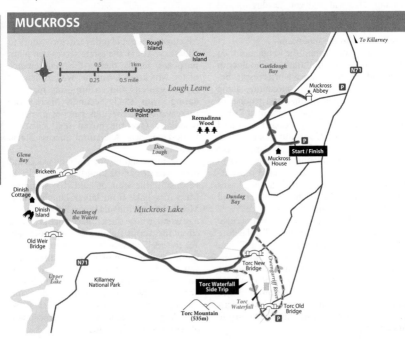

KILLARNEY NATIONAL PARK – A NATURAL SUCCESS STORY

Killarney National Park has long been a haven for species of flora and fauna that have found it hard to survive the pressures of modern life, and have been wiped out from elsewhere in the country. Most notable perhaps is the park's herd of Red Deer, the only animals in the country that are entirely descended from wild, native stock.

A more recent contender for the title of Most Charismatic Natural Inhabitant is the White-Tailed Sea-Eagle, which was re-introduced to County Kerry in 2007 following 100 years extinction from the country. A total of 15 young eagles from Norway were released in Killarney National Park in 2007, with a further 20 birds released in 2008. The eagles have since been tracked as far away as Northern Ireland, and by 2009 one of the Killarney birds had taken up residence at Glengarry, in Scotland. However, most of the surviving eagles still live in the tree-lined valleys of the MacGillycuddy's Reeks, flying to Kerry's coastal regions each day to feed.

The park's 10,236 hectares also offers a protective enclave for many plant species, and was designated a Unesco Biosphere Reserve in 1982. Today it harbours the largest area of ancient Oakwood remaining in the country, which can be found on the lower slopes of Tomies and Shehy Mountains, adjacent to Lough Leane. Other native tree species include holly, birch and beech, some of which are up 800 years old. The woodlands support an enormous range of bird life, as well as rare and elusive mammals such as the red squirrel and pine marten.

In another part of the park, Reenadinna Wood is the largest Yew forest in Europe. The trees, which consist largely of Irish yew, manage to find sustenance from a tiny layer of soil covering the limestone, with their roots burrowing into the rock for stability.

THE WALK

Begin by walking to the front door of **Muckross House**. Now head directly away from of the house along a tree-lined avenue, following signs towards Killarney and Muckross Abbey. Before long you reach a junction where Dinish-Cottage and the Meeting of the Waters are signed to the left. Though you will eventually make your way to Dinish-Cottage, it's well worth detouring first to Muckross Abbey.

Follow the signs to the abbey, heading along a footpath that weaves along the wooded shore of Lough Leane. Offshore lie several limestone pinnacles that have been sculpted into bizarre natural formations by the water. You arrive at the ruins of **Muckross Abbey** 1.5km and 30 minutes from the start. Founded in 1448 and burned by Cromwell's troops in 1652, the roofless building and graveyard offer an evocative place for exploration.

Retrace your steps along Lough Leane to the first junction marked for Dinish-Cottage and the Meeting of the Waters. Turn right here, then keep right at two subsequent junctions and join the lane that runs along the Muckross Peninsula. The next turn off the road isn't signed so you'll need to watch out for it. Around

500m from the last road junction, a vehicle track veers right beside a high wire fence. The start of the track is marked by a low plaque indicating the Arthur Young Nature Trail, which you now begin to follow in a reverse direction.

Follow the track as it climbs gradually into **Reenadinna Wood**, surrounded by the unusual shapes of yew trees. The vehicle track ends at a field; veer left around the boundary fence, then turn right through a gate into a meadow. The track consolidates again at the top left corner of the field, where you enter a section of fine oak woodland. Rejoin the road after 1km and turn right, again following signs to Dinish-Cottage and the Meeting of the Waters.

Continue to the end of the Muckross Peninsula and cross an old stone bridge to the island of **Brickeen**. Now follow the lane around the western end of Muckross Lake to **Dinish-Cottage**. A sign in front of the building directs you right, through pretty gardens of magnolias, azaleas and camellias, to an outlook over the **Meeting of the Waters**. There is a good view from here up the straights to the double-arched **Old Weir Bridge**, which guards the entrance to Upper Lake.

lonelyplanet.com

Follow the path back to the road and turn right, arriving at the N71 some 1.5km later. Now cross the road and join a gravel footpath that climbs a short distance up the vegetated slopes of **Torc Mountain** (535m) before contouring east for 1km. Near the end of this section you come to a junction and must make a choice. If you want to continue directly back to the start, turn left here, re-cross the N71 and follow signs back to Muckross House.

SIDE TRIP: TORC WATERFALL
1.5km return
If you still have energy to spare it's well worth turning right and making the 1.5km-detour to the impressive **Torc Waterfall**. From the junction, climb steadily through the trees and cross a bridge over the Owengarriff River just above the main falls. Turn left along a track, then left again to descend a series of steps to a viewpoint below the 12m-high cascade. Follow the river to the road bridge, and pass beneath this to re-enter Muckross Estate. The path weaves through more woodland before joining a lane for the final stretch to Muckross House.

TORC MOUNTAIN

Duration 3½ hours
Distance 8km
Ascent 490m
Difficulty easy–moderate
Start/Finish Torc Waterfall car park
Nearest Town Killarney (p139)
Transport bus
Summary A perfect introduction to Irish hill-walking, this relatively easy climb up a mountain path leads to superlative views over the Killarney Lakes.

The compact summit of Torc Mountain (535m) provides what are arguably the best views available over the Killarney Lakes and the backdrop of mountains to their south and west. Yet the route to the top of this modest hill involves very little of the difficult ground that is normally associated with Irish mountain walks. The Kerry Way provides a solid walking surface for the first half of the route and then a clear, constructed path ascends the remaining distance to the top. This ensures plenty of

gain for very little pain, and means this is a great option for those who want to experience the pleasure of standing atop a peak, but who are normally put off by the effort demanded to get there.

Despite its conveniences, the route does cross wild, open terrain and normal mountain precautions apply – you'll still need to carry all of the bad-weather equipment associated with mountain excursions, and those unfamiliar with compass navigation should avoid walking in poor visibility. Walkers who don't mind missing **Torc Waterfall** (an impressive cascade that is worth visiting at least once) can make an alternative start at the top of the falls; see Getting to/from the Walk (see below). Starting and finishing here will save you 1.5km and 110m of ascent. The walk can also be completed as a side trip from the Kerry Way (see p117).

PLANNING
Maps
The OSI 1:50,000 map No 78 covers the route. For extra detail, use Harvey's 1:30,000 Superwalker map *MacGillycuddy's Reeks*.

GETTING TO/FROM THE WALK
The car park for Torc Waterfall is 5.5km south of Killarney along the N71. The **Bus Éireann** (☎ 064-663 0011) Killarney–Kenmare service (up to three daily Jun-Sep and once daily Mon-Sat the rest of the year) will also drop you here if you ask the driver.

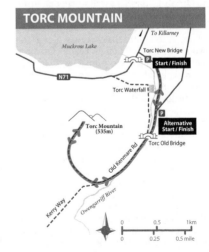

To start at the top of the falls, take the minor road signed for 'Old Kenmare Road' that leads south from the N71, 1km north of the waterfall car park. Follow this for 1.5km to a car park at the end of the road.

THE WALK

From the car park, follow a wide path through natural broad-leaved woodland to a viewpoint beneath the 12m-high **Torc Waterfall**. A flight of steps then leads to the left, climbing steeply through the trees to the top of the falls. Follow signs for the Kerry Way towards Kenmare and turn left at an **old stone bridge**, and then right at a paved road (passing the car park that is the alternative start/finish – see Getting to/from the Walk, p116). The road soon dwindles to a track, crosses the river, and exits the woodland.

Around 300m after the last trees, just as you reach the top of a rise, turn right onto an obvious pathway constructed of stone slabs. A blue sign for Torc Mountain confirms you're on the right trail. Follow the path up the hill, zigzaging up the grassy southwestern slopes on a mixture of stone steps and wooden boardwalk. The trail leads all the way to the mountain's small summit (two to 2½ hours from the start). Hopefully the weather will be clear and you can appreciate the fabulous panorama west across the Killarney Lakes to the MacGilly-cuddy's Reeks, with the sprawl of Killarney plainly visible north of Muckross.

Return by reversing your outward journey.

KERRY WAY HIGHLIGHT

Duration 2 days
Distance 41km
Difficulty moderate
Start Killarney
Finish Glencar
Nearest Towns Killarney (p139), Black Valley (p134), Glencar (p138)
Transport private, bus, boat

Summary A highly rewarding distillation of Ireland's most popular Waymarked Way, this route features waterfalls, forests, lakes and a section in the shadow of Ireland's highest mountain range.

The Kerry Way is a nine-day, 215km-long Waymarked Way that starts and finishes in Killarney and circumnavigates the Iveragh Peninsula. The two days described here are probably the wildest, most beautiful consecutive stages on the route, and together they offer some of the finest mountain scenery to be found on any low-level walk in Ireland. For walkers taking on the entire long-distance path, this section will probably form the first two days of the trip.

The majority of the walking is along tracks and informal paths, with most of the road sections encountered at the beginning and end of each day. The first section of the walk out of Killarney is particularly urban and a better start might be made at Torc Waterfall, leaving Muckross for another day's walk (see Muckross, p113). Starting at the waterfall will cut 5.5km from the first day's total distance. You can also finish at Lough Acoose rather than Glencar, thus dispensing with the last 4km of road walking. The route is well furnished throughout with waymarking posts, stiles and wooden boardwalks across boggy sections, easing your progress and making navigation a relatively straightforward task.

Unfortunately there is no public transport from Glencar, at the end of the second day, back to the start. If you can't arrange your own transport, consider walking only the first day of the route and returning to Killarney on the afternoon water taxi (see Getting to/from the Walk, p118).

PLANNING

Accommodation is limited along this part of the Kerry Way, so it's essential to book ahead. All accommodation outlets along the route can supply food, so there is no need to carry more than one day's food or water with you. Both days cross wild terrain beneath high mountains, so make sure to carry clothing suitable for all weather conditions. Despite the fact the path is fully way-marked, it's still advisable to carry a map and compass.

Maps & Books

The route described here is covered by the OSI 1:50,000 map No 78 and Harvey's 1:30,000 Superwalker map *MacGillycuddy's Reeks*. If you intend to complete the entire nine-day route you will also need OSI 1:50,000 maps No 83 and No 84.

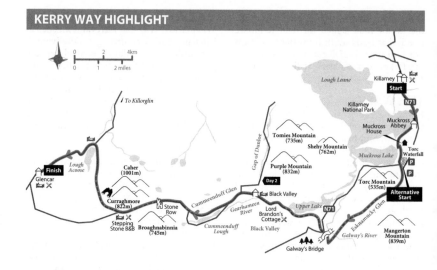

KERRY WAY HIGHLIGHT

Probably the best guide to the entire route is Sandra Bardwell's *The Kerry Way*, a full-colour production that includes a comprehensive route description and 1:118,000 strip maps, as well as plenty of background information and practical travel advice.

Information Sources
The website www.kerryway.net is a useful resource for planning your trip, offering accommodation listings, trail notes and a host of background information.

Guided Walks
Several local companies organise 'self-guided walking tours' along the Kerry Way, where you walk on your own, but benefit from back-up support such as pre-paid accommodation, luggage transfers, route notes and maps. Itineraries generally last for seven or 11 nights, though some 'mini-breaks' are also available. Prices are per person sharing; expect to pay a supplement for singles rooms.

Go Ireland (☎ 066-796 2094; www.govisit ireland.com; Dalys Ln, Killorglin, Co Kerry) seven/11 night trips cost €640/930.
Southwest Walks Ireland (☎ 066-712 8733; www.southwestwalksireland.com; 28 The Anchorage, Tralee, Co Kerry) offers four/seven/10 nights for €345/565/698.
Tailor-Made Tours (☎ 066-976 6007; www.tailor-madetours.com; Ferry Rd, Keel,

Castlemaine, Co Kerry) provides seven/11 night tours for €546/ €755.

GETTING TO/FROM THE WALK
The official start of the route is in Killarney – see p139 for details of transport services to/from the town.

To start the walk at Torc Waterfall head to the fall's car park, which is 5.5km south of Killarney along the N71. The **Bus Éireann** (☎ 064-663 0011) Killarney–Kenmare service will drop you off here if you ask the driver (up to three daily Jun-Sep and once daily Mon-Sat the rest of the year).

If you're ending the walk at Black Valley, the only public transport back to Killarney is provided by **O'Connor's Tours** (☎ 064-663 0200; www.gapofdunloetours.com; High St, Killarney), which runs a daily water taxi over the Killarney Lakes (€15 one way, Mar-Oct only). Boats depart at 10am and 11am from Ross Castle, 2km southwest of Killarney town centre. They return from the pier near Lord Brandon's Cottage on the Upper Lake at 2.15pm. The 1½-hour, 21km trip can be popular with tour groups in summer, but is nonetheless a great experience.

THE WALK
Day 1: Killarney to Black Valley
6 hours, 21km, 375m ascent
From the centre of Killarney, follow the N71 south, walking along a pavement on

the western side of the road. You'll pick up signs for the Kerry Way at the bridge over the River Flesk. Continue south along the N71 for a further 3km to **Muckross House**. Pass through the gates and follow the waymarkers through the estate grounds. At the turn-off to Rossnahowgarry, turn left and follow the waymarkers back across the main road to the car park for **Torc Waterfall** (an alternative starting point).

The way passes through natural broadleaved woodland to a viewpoint beneath the 12m-high waterfall. It then climbs steeply through the trees to the top of the falls, ascending flights of steps through a tunnel of vegetation before veering left at a stone bridge (the route marked on the OSI map is out of date here). The path joins a track and the route is signed to the right, following the first of many sections along the old road to Kenmare. Cross Torc Old Bridge and the woodland soon ends. The track crosses out onto open mountain terrain, and passes between the peaks of **Mangerton Mountain** (839m) to the left and **Torc Mountain** (535m) to the right. Torc Mountain is a possible side trip from the path – see the Torc Mountain walk (p116).

You soon leave the Owengarriff River behind and cross the Crinnah River in a low, wet valley, where the remains of the old road have long since sunken out of sight into the bog. Fortunately, a long section of wire-covered duckboard offers easy passage for walkers. The way rejoins the old road once it reaches firmer ground, and passes through the rocky ravine of **Esknamucky Glen**. It then descends to Galway's River and meets a paved track and a junction of alternate routes. The Kerry Way to Kenmare turns left here; you should turn right for Black Valley (four to 4½ hours from the start).

Pass Derricunnihy church and cross the N71 by **Galway's Bridge** and you will soon re-enter natural oak forest. The path cuts a wide trail through abundant woodland before crossing grasslands around the southwestern shores of **Upper Lake**. A large metal stile then gives access to the tearooms at **Lord Brandon's Cottage** (snacks €3-6; open daily Apr-Oct). This is a good place for lunch and the departure point for boats back to Killarney; it is likely to be a busy spot at midday in summer.

From the cottage your route follows a minor road alongside the picturesque Gearhameen River and exits Killarney National Park. Three and a half kilometres of road then runs from the east end of Black Valley to the west. How far you need travel depends on your chosen accommodation – see p134 for details of facilities within the valley.

Day 2: Black Valley to Glencar
7 hours, 20km, 500m ascent

Continue along the minor road towards the western end of Black Valley; ahead and to the right are the massive southern flanks of the MacGillycuddy's Reeks. The road runs out at a farm and you follow tracks into a small forest before setting off across open slopes with great views across Cummeenduff Lough and **Broaghnabinnia** (745m). Follow waymarks up and right along a lovely boreen lined with stone walls and gnarled holly. Pass a new bungalow and continue ahead onto a green road, passing the stark remains of an old farm framed by the slopes of **Caher** (1001m), Ireland's third-highest summit. The road ends at a couple of bungalows. Follow waymarks around these and up over open ground to the boulder-strewn pass between Broaghnabinnia and Curraghmore. Off to the left is a Neolithic stone arrangement (visible against the skyline on the ascent), which indicates that this pass has been important to people long before the days of waymarks.

From the pass descend steeply to reach a farmyard, looking carefully for waymarks and arrows painted on rocks. Walk along the paved road for a little over 1km to a set of prominent signs. Here you pass the welcoming **Stepping Stone B&B** (☎ 066-976 0215; www.steppingstonebandb.com; Maghanlawaun, Bridia Valley, Glencar; s/d €47.50/70), where snacks and meals are served in the attached **Cooky Monsters Café** (mains €11). The Kerry Way continues over steep grass slopes to the Lack Rd, an old droving route that is now being reassimilated into the mountain. The steep climb zigzags up to the pass (at almost 400m) between the brooding **Curraghmore** (822m) to the east and a smaller, unnamed peak (451m) to the west. From here there are fabulous views across the interior of

Iveragh before you begin the steep descent towards Lough Acoose.

At the bottom of this descent the Way meets the Gearhanagour Stream and traces its bank to a track. Follow this to a farm and onto a minor road (note the change of route from that shown on the OSI map), which you follow for almost 3km to the north end of Lough Acoose. At a junction with the main road, turn left (there are two B&Bs just to the right here – see Glencar, p138) and continue for 4km to Glencar.

DERRYNANE COASTAL CIRCUIT

Duration 3 hours
Distance 8km
Ascent 180m
Difficulty easy
Start/Finish Derrynane Dunes Nature Trail car park
Nearest Town Caherdaniel (p134)
Transport bus, private
Summary This varied, low-level circuit explores sandy beaches, an old mass path and Derrynane National Historic Park.

This relatively short circuit passes through a wide range of different habitats and points of interest in the southwestern corner of the Iveragh Peninsula. A long sandy beach, a rocky mass path, country lanes and the Kerry Way all provide passage along various sections of the route. Highlights include wonderful views over the islands and islets that litter the coastal waters in these parts, with the sharp outlines of the Skellig Islands prominent among them.

The route starts and finishes within the grounds of Derrynane National Historic Park, and it's possible to visit Derrynane House and gardens at the end of the walk (see the boxed text Derrynane National Historic Park, p121). Another site that is well worth a little extra exploration is the ruined abbey that sits on the northeastern shore of Abbey Island, at the western end of the beach. Dating from the 10th century and linked to St Finian, the wild coastal location of the ruined building and graveyard make it an atmospheric spot. It's easy to imagine locals in times gone by filing along the mass path that has provided access to the abbey for centuries.

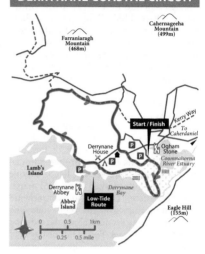

DERRYNANE COASTAL CIRCUIT

PLANNING
Maps & Booklets
The OSI 1:50,000 map No 84 covers the walk.

The visitor centre at Derrynane House sells two pamphlets that give more background to the area: *Derrynane Dunes* lists points of natural interest along the nature trail, while *Derrynane National Historic Park* offers a comprehensive history of the O'Connell family, the house and its surrounds.

GETTING TO/FROM THE WALK
The walk starts and finishes at the car park for 'Derrynane Dunes Nature Trail', around 200m east of the main car park for Derrynane House. From Caherdaniel, take the minor road west from the centre of the village, following signs for Derrynane House. Veer left at a junction after 1.5km, then turn immediately left again into the car park.

If you don't have your own transport, it's also possible to start and finish the walk in the village of Caherdaniel. Follow the directions above to the start point. At the end of the circuit, either return along the same road or head back to Caherdaniel along the Kerry Way. Allow an extra hour and add 3km to the distance if you opt for this approach.

DERRYNANE NATIONAL HISTORIC PARK

Derrynane National Historic Park was opened in 1975 to preserve the ancestral home of the 'Great Liberator', Daniel O'Connell. Daniel was one of a long line of O'Connells who fought against English oppression. The family had governed Ballycarbery Castle, near Cahirciveen, from the Middle Ages until the 17th century when, like most Irish landowners, they became involved in wars against Oliver Cromwell's forces. Like many of their peers, they destroyed their castle rather than give it up to the English, and the family fled to Waterford.

Connections with Kerry were maintained and the family were soon quietly reacquiring land in the area, despite anti-Catholic laws prohibiting them from doing so. **Derrynane House** (☎ 066-947 5113; adult/child €3/1; open daily May-Sep, Tue-Sun Apr & Oct, weekends only Nov-Mar) was built in 1702, then just a large farmhouse. Around a century later, Hunting Captain O'Connell adopted his nephew Daniel, and brought him to live at the house. Daniel was educated in London and Dublin, and went on to become a lawyer. He extended the house and transformed it into the mansion that stands today.

Daniel O'Connell is significant in Irish history because he mobilised the Irish people into their first mass movement. He demanded the state's anti-Catholic laws be removed, including the ban on Catholics becoming members of parliament. In this way, he is responsible for beginning the process by which Ireland gained its independence, though he was not a nationalist and sat in the British parliament. O'Connell's efforts eventually earned him a prison sentence, and one of the exhibits on display in the house is the ornate 'triumphal chariot' that was brought by his supporters to the prison gates to collect him on his release. O'Connell died in 1847 and his death bed can also be seen in Derrynane House. The village of Caherdaniel is now named in his honour.

THE WALK

From the car park follow the footpath that leads south, signed to 'Derrynane Dunes Nature Trail'. Turn left at the following junction and continue to the edge of expansive sand flats that adorn the **Coomnahorna River estuary**. Wading birds can often be seen picking over the spoils offered by the shallow water, and the slopes of **Eagle Hill** (155m) rise across the river.

Turn right and trace the river bank to the back of the dunes, and then continue through the dunes along a smaller footpath. Join the **beach**, turn right (northwest), and begin to walk along the wide, firm expanse of sand. The beach stretches for more than a kilometre; follow it to the end, passing several rock outcrops with painted current warnings along the way.

The route at the end of the beach depends on the tide. If the tide is out, simply continue along the sand, sweeping south at the end to reach **Abbey Island**. Here you'll find the evocative ruins of **Derrynane Abbey**, whose surrounding graves include one belonging to Mary O'Connell, wife of Daniel O'Connell. When you're ready, cross back to the end of the main beach and head left, following an access path and then a short section of tarmac to reach the pier and car park at the end of the road.

If the tide is in you will be forced off the beach soon after a yellow lifeguard hut, and should cross over the back of the beach to another parking area (where drinking water and toilets are available). Follow the minor road out of this parking area, turn left at a junction (signed to 'Abbey Island') and pass in front of **Keating's Bar** (☎ 066-947 5115), where snacks and limited **camping** facilities are available. Continue to the end of the road and you will arrive at Abbey Island pier and car park, where you rejoin the low-tide route.

Roughly 50m up the road from the pier, a waymarking post and steps in a stone wall indicate the start of the mass path. Follow this around the back of a building and you will soon find yourself weaving between seams of rock and climbing several flights of stone steps through a wonderfully wild coastal landscape. Descend to a stony cove and ignore two right turns off the path, continuing to trace the coastline till the path crosses a stile and joins a track. Follow this around the back of another small beach to a pier, where a minor road leads uphill to the right.

Follow the lane uphill and keep right at a junction. Around 1.5km from the pier you arrive at a sharp left-hand switchback, and a prominent signpost at the corner indicates the route of the Kerry Way. Turn right (east) here along a small lane and follow the marker posts for the next 1.5km. Watch for a left turn off the track soon after a metal gate and stile, where a footpath begins to climb across open ground. Cross a low spur of **Farraniaragh Mountain** (468m), the extra elevation affording fine coastal views. Descend through woodland on the other side of the spur to a minor road. The Kerry Way crosses the lane and continues to Caherdaniel; turn right along the road to return to the start of this circuit.

Descend for 1km and continue straight ahead at a junction, following signs for 'Derrynane Harbour'. Within 100m the white gateposts of **Derrynane House** appear on the left. Pass round the building to the flagpoles at the beach side of the house, then follow a grassy path away from the building to a wooden gate. This gives access to the back of the dunes. Now turn left and follow a grassy path back to the start of the route.

THE BEARA PENINSULA

The Beara Peninsula is characterised by rugged terrain and sudden sea views. The fringes of the peninsula provide its only flat ground and all of the settlements in the area are located along the coast. The interior rises abruptly to a mountainous mass of wild, rocky uplands, with sandstone erupting like broken bones through the skin of bog. Another characteristic of the peninsula is its profusion of ancient monuments. Standing stones, dolmens, ring forts, stone circles and Ogham stones are all liberally scattered around the area, testimony to its long history of human habitation. Today Beara is quieter than its northern neighbour, having thus far escaped the massive seasonal influx of tourists that can sometimes make Iveragh feel oppressive. Though they offer plenty of facilities for visitors, Beara's small villages retain much of their

traditional atmosphere and in many cases are still working communities.

Walking on Beara is generally split into two categories. On one hand, there are high mountain excursions with wonderful views; the Eskatarriff horseshoe and Hungry Hill are two such routes described here. On the other hand, there are low-level walks that explore the peninsula's narrow lanes, colourful villages and numerous prehistoric sites. The eight-day Beara Way is the long-distance showpiece of these routes, and a two-day highlight of this route is described in this section. However, for those who really want to explore further in this area the possibilities are numerous. Besides the routes mentioned here, there are great walks around two small islands (see Dursey Island, p161, and Bere Island, p161) and many other options in the surrounding hills.

PLANNING
The website www.bearatourism.com offers valuable information on the peninsula, including accommodation listings.

ACCESS TOWN
See Castletownbere (p135).

BEARA WAY HIGHLIGHT

Duration 2–3 days
Distance 39.5km
Difficulty easy–moderate
Start Castletownbere
Finish Ardgroom
Nearest Towns Castletownbere (p135), Allihies (p134), Eyeries (p137), Ardgroom (p133)
Transport bus
Summary This superbly varied way-marked route explores the colourful villages, rocky coastline and archaeological sites of the Beara Peninsula.

As mentioned above, The Beara Way is an eight-day, 220km-long Waymarked Way that starts and finishes in Glengarriff, at the eastern end of the Beara Peninsula. The route circumnavigates the peninsula and includes side trips to both Bere Island and Dursey Island, as well as several other 'spurs' which, if walked, can add several days to the route.

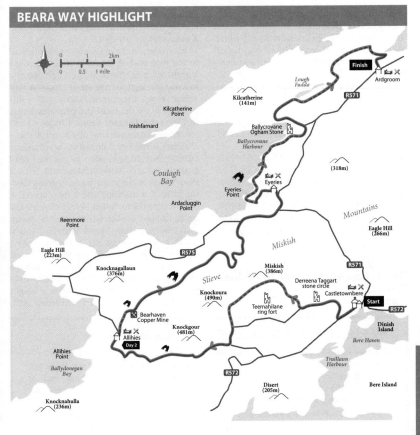

BEARA WAY HIGHLIGHT

The walk described here is a short highlight of the longer route. It can either be walked in three reasonably short days (finishing the second day at Eyeries), which would warrant a grade of easy to moderate, or in a combination of one short day followed by a fairly long day. Accommodation is plentiful, so how long you take depends purely on how quickly (or slowly) you want to travel. All the villages passed have shops or restaurants, so there is no need to carry more than one day's food or water with you.

Wonderful coastal and mountain views, quiet and colourful villages and a liberal sprinkling of ancient archaeological sites combine to make the route a memorable one. Terrain covered is a mixture of minor roads, farm tracks and open moorland, and the waymarking posts and stiles that

furnish the route make navigation relatively straightforward. Note that the markers are occasionally placed on telegraph poles.

PLANNING
Maps & Books
The route described here is covered by the OSI 1:50,000 map No 84. You will also need map No 85 if you are walking the entire route.

Beara Tourism produce *The Beara Way*, a 50-page official guide to the way-marked route, with text and photos by Dermot Somers. It's available from local tourist offices, and can also be downloaded from the website www.bearatourism.com/bearaway.html.

Guided Walks
Several local organisations arrange self-guided trips along the Beara Way,

SOUTHWEST

providing back-up support, luggage transport and accommodation booking. Longer itineraries complete the entire route, while others concentrate on selected highlights such as the sections describes here and Bere and Dursey Islands. Prices are per person sharing; expect to pay a supplement for singles rooms. Companies include:

Go Ireland (☎ 066-796 2094; www.govisit ireland.com; Dalys Ln, Killorglin, Co Kerry) eight-day trips cost €550.
Southwest Walks Ireland (☎ 066-712 8733; www.southwestwalksireland.com; 28 The Anchorage, Tralee, Co Kerry) offers a choice of eight and 11-day tours for €564/695.
Tailor-Made Tours (☎ 066-976 6007; www.tailor-madetours.com; Ferry Rd, Keel, Castlemaine, Co Kerry) provides eight or 10-day trips for €546/650.

THE WALK
Day 1: Castletownbere to Allihies
5½ hours, 13.5km, 500m ascent

Highlights of this day include several archaeological sites, and fine views during climbs over the shoulders of Miskish and Knockgour mountains.

From the centre of Castletownbere, head to the west end of the main street and take a right turn in front of the Olde Bakery, following a sign for the stone circle. About 1.5km along the minor road a gate leads into a field on the right and provides access to **Derreena Taggart Stone Circle**, a well-preserved, compact ring of 12 rock slabs.

After a further kilometre, waymarkers indicate a right turn onto an old turf road heading towards Miskish Mountain. After a short distance the route passes a great, rusting hulk of a machine and a map board. A short loop walk turns left here (following the route marked on the OS map as the Beara Way), but the Beara Way continues straight ahead before veering left onto a less obvious track. The marker posts now lead west over the southern shoulder of **Miskish Mountain** (386m), climbing steadily over open moorland. Here you reach a height of almost 300m, and are rewarded with

THE PUXLEYS & THE ALLIHIES COPPER MINES

The history of the Puxley family is so much like the plot of a romantic novel that Daphne Du Maurier turned it into one in her novel *Hungry Hill*. The Puxleys were originally from Wales, but in the 18th century the first Puxley settled near Castletownbere, buying land that had been confiscated from the O'Sullivan clan after the Battle of Kinsale. The area at this time was well known for its smuggling: wool and timber were exchanged for French wines and spirits.

The Puxleys at first took an active part in the smuggling, but in 1740 Henry Puxley was made Commissioner of the Peace and given a frigate and troops, so changed his allegiances. This caused a good deal of resentment among the local people, many of whom were the descendants of the O'Sullivan Beares and felt that they had a claim on the land. Tension grew as local O'Sullivans planned to enlist French privateers in an uprising against the English. In 1757 Henry, who went everywhere armed with a pistol, was shot and killed on his way to church.

Undeterred, the Puxleys continued to live and prosper in the area and in the early 19th century discovered a vast seam of copper ore on land that they owned at Allihies. The mine opened in 1811 and the family was soon reaping the rewards, demonstrating their new-found wealth by beginning to build the fabulously extravagant grand mansion that can still be seen in the grounds of Dunboy Castle. However they never finished building the house, and it lay unoccupied for most of the time while the Puxleys lived in Cornwall.

While mining brought wealth to the Puxley family, it brought low wages and dangerous, unhealthy working conditions for the workforce, which at one time numbered 1300. Experienced Cornish miners were brought into the area, and the dramatic ruins of engine-houses replicate those of Cornwall's coastal tin mines. As late as the 1930s, more than 30,000 tonnes of pure copper were exported annually, but supplies soon began to fall and the last mine closed in 1962.

Even as the mining activity began to wind down, things were hotting up on the political front. By 1920 the IRA was using the grounds of Puxley Manor to train recruits. In 1921, they burned down the house rather than have it used as a British army base.

far-reaching views over Castletownbere and Bere Island.

The descent is steep until you join a path, which leads across a stile and into a forestry plantation. The path through the trees follows a stream and can be rather wet underfoot. When you emerge onto a road, turn right and follow the tarmac for 500m to a T-junction, where the lane turns sharply left and the Beara Way is signed onto a forestry track to the right (three to 3½ hours from the start). The steepest ascent of the day can now be seen stretching up though the pine plantation ahead of you. Climb steadily straight up the track until finally, 2km after leaving the road, the terrain levels out and becomes a pleasant green road crossing a spur of **Knockgour Mountain** (481m). The dense forest is replaced by wonderful views across the entire western tip of the peninsula, and the coastline around Allihies lies spread out ahead.

The track meets a minor road alongside a prehistoric stone row. Follow the road down the hill, where a signed left turn and then two right turns will bring you into the centre of Allihies. See p134 for details of accommodation and facilities in the village.

Day 2: Allihies to Ardgroom
7 hours, 26km, 340m ascent

This fairly long and arduous day can be split into two with an overnight stop in the attractive little village of Eyries.

At the northern end of Allihies, waymarkers direct you onto a beautiful old boreen that takes you towards the smelter of the now-disused **Bearhaven Copper Mine** (see the boxed text The Puxleys & The Allihies Copper Mines, p124). Just beneath this building, ringed with fences and signs warning of old mineshafts, the way joins a small road, which it follows steeply uphill through rugged outcrops of sandstone to a broad col at almost 300m (45 minutes to one hour from Allihies). The excellent views southwest, across the furthest extremities of the Beara Peninsula, include the humped profile of Dursey Island.

These views are soon surpassed as the road becomes a gravel track, and you begin a long, gradual descent. A great panorama opens out across the Kenmare River to the Iveragh Peninsula, with the MacGillycuddy's Reeks, the highest mountains in

Ireland, serrating the skyline. After a descent of little more than 3km, the track becomes a sealed road again and you soon reach a waymark directing you up a narrow, fuchsia-lined boreen. You can cut almost 2km from the day's total by continuing straight ahead here. Otherwise, head off on a higher but unremarkable routing on the lower slopes of Miskish Mountain.

The remaining distance into **Eyries** (4km) is along sometimes-busy roads. See p137 for details of accommodation and facilities in the village. As you approach the village centre, the Beara Way turns left at a poorly marked junction just before O'Sullivan's Foodstore. A series of lanes and tracks then lead southwest to the coast. The next 3km are a delight, winding north along a **scenic coastline** of rocky headlands, coastal meadows and boulder-clad storm beaches. Numerous aluminium stiles ease your progress, though you'll need to beware of ankle-turning rocks when walking across the storm beaches. The routing differs from the OS map close to the end of this coastal section; soon after an old boat shed and slipway, the waymarks take you inland across a rough meadow, where you join a road. Turn left along the road, and in around 300m you will see a tall pillar in a field to the left – this is **Ballycrovane Ogham Stone**, at 5.3m-high the tallest Ogham stone in Europe (see the boxed text Ogham Script, p102).

Roads then lead around the bay of Ballycrovane Harbour, and northwest towards Lough Fadda. Here the route differs again from the OS map. Shortly before the lough, keep an eye open for a partially concealed marker post on the right-hand side of the road. Follow a path that angles around the southern shore of the lough, crossing rough and occasionally boggy grassland. At the end of the lough the path continues east across the moorland for a further kilometre. Here you join a lane and turn left, climbing northwest along the winding tarmac for 1km. A footpath short-cuts a hairpin bend near the top of the section, where you rejoin the route marked on the OS map. Now turn right off the road and set off once more across rough ground. Clever routing makes the most of rock terraces, and an informal path has formed underfoot. Cross a small gully and then descend to meet the final road at Cappul bridge. Ardgroom is slightly more than

1km south (right) along this road; see p133 for information about village facilities.

HUNGRY HILL

Duration 4–5 hours
Distance 9km
Ascent 710m
Difficulty moderate–demanding
Start/Finish Coomgira
Nearest Town Adrigole (p133)
Transport bus

Summary This complex climb up the highest peak on the peninsula includes a scramble across great blocks of sandstone to a pair of hidden mountain loughs.

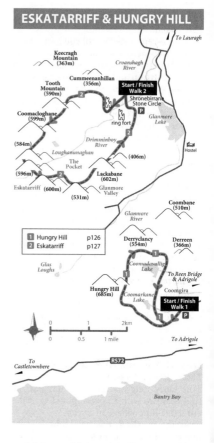

ESKATARRIFF & HUNGRY HILL

Hungry Hill (685m) is the highest point on the Beara Peninsula, and has a fascinating topography that makes it both compelling and difficult to climb. The sandstone that created the mountain has been gouged by glacial action on its eastern side into a complex system of cliffs and corries. These contain two hidden lakes, one of which feeds a waterfall that is arguably the highest in Ireland, plunging more than 200m over slabs and cliffs into the Coomgira Valley.

The route described here is the pick of several possible approaches, and is really only worth doing in good visibility because of the difficulty of route-finding and the constant proximity of steep and dangerous ground. The reward for reaching the summit is a significant sense of achievement, and amazing views over counties Cork and Kerry.

PLANNING
Maps

Use the OSI 1:50,000 map No 84, but bear in mind that the contours neither illustrate the complexity of some of the slopes, nor indicate the profusion of small cliffs.

GETTING TO/FROM THE WALK

To reach the start, turn west from the R572 at Reen Bridge, 1.5km southwest of Adrigole. If approaching from the north, cross the bridge before turning onto the narrow road lined with high fuchsia hedgerows. Follow this for 2km to a clearing on the left where several cars can be parked (GR V780493).

The R572 is used by buses travelling between Castletownbere, Bantry and Cork,

and drivers will deposit/collect you at Reen Bridge if requested in advance (for details of these bus services, see Getting There & Away for Castletownbere, p135).

It is not unusual for guests at the Hungry Hill Lodge in Adrigole to make the return trip up the mountain from there; add 1½ hours and 7km of easy road walking to the route.

THE WALK

Cross the stile at the back of the parking area and climb the slopes to the south, heading towards an obvious broken shoulder. A 20- to 30-minute climb should bring you onto the shoulder, which has a fence running along the top. Follow the fence west to a small stile; cross this to continue across rough ground to the base of Hungry Hill's southeast ridge.

The route ahead looks more difficult than it actually is. By following a line of least resistance to the right (north) or through the middle, a series of grassy ramps and easy scrambles lead to a vertical cliff. The easiest route heads around to the left (southwest) of this, but you can also find a slightly more adventurous route to the right. Either option will take you onto easier ground, where the way is now indicated by small stone cairns, and brings you in 10 to 15 minutes to a large cairn marking Hungry Hill's south summit (667m).

The trig pillar marking the actual summit of **Hungry Hill** is just a few hundred metres north across boggy ground. At this point the marvellous views you've been enjoying south across Bantry Bay will be joined by those to the west across the rest of the Beara Peninsula, and those to the north across Eskatarriff to the mountains of Iveragh.

The descent north from the summit begins gently, but soon steepens as eruptions of sandstone run at 45° to your angle of travel. Use the turf between these outcrops as ramps and zigzag down to the eastern side of the col between Hungry Hill and **Derryclancy** (554). You should now be able to see the lake in Coomadavallig. Don't descend to the lake shore but contour around the water, then walk down to the outlet, which is easily crossed.

Climb across a spur to Coomarkane, where another lake lies beneath tremendous rock walls. Descend to the outlet, cross it, and drop diagonally southeast across wet ground back to the parking area (20-30 minutes from the outlet stream of Coomarkane Lake).

ESKATARRIFF

Duration 5½–6 hours
Distance 12km
Ascent 750m
Difficulty moderate–demanding
Start/Finish Shronebirrane Stone Circle
Nearest Town Lauragh (p141)
Transport private
Summary Probably the most scenic mountain circuit on the Beara Peninsula, this route provides great views and an enjoyable descent.

Though it barely rises to 600m in height, Eskatarriff and its surrounding summits provide one of the most scenic mountain circuits in the southwest outside of the Iveragh and Dingle Peninsulas. Here ancient glaciers have hollowed out a mighty corrie known as 'The Pocket', which forms the centrepiece of this walk. The peaks loom over it, creating an air of challenge and foreboding, especially on an overcast day. Over the second half of the walk in particular, the ridges offer rewarding walking with great views.

However, there is also some rugged terrain to negotiate, which means you'll probably travel more slowly than you'd normally expect. You also need to pay careful attention to route-finding, even in clear weather, as there are only a few safe routes of ascent and descent. Think twice before starting the circuit if there is a chance of the cloud descending over the tops.

PLANNING
Maps
The OSI 1:50,000 map No 84 covers the route.

GETTING TO/FROM THE WALK
The start of the walk is along minor roads just south of Lauragh. From Lauragh, follow the R571 west for around 1km and look out for a left turn signed for the Rabach Way. Follow this road for a little less than 1km and turn right onto a narrow road with patches of grass in the middle. Follow this for around 2km until the road draws alongside the Drimminboy River. A track leads to the left, crossing the river on an old concrete bridge that is gated in the middle. The descent route off the mountain comes out here. Park the car at one of several small grass verges further along the road, taking care not to block gates or entries.

THE WALK
From your parking spot, walk southwest along the minor road to within sight of the final house in the valley. Set somewhat incongruously in the garden of this house are the largely untouched stones of **Shronebirrane Stone Circle**, probably dating to the Bronze Age. You may want to wander down for a closer look, but the route onto the mountain heads

up the faint spur to the right, towards a huge boulder set into the grassy slope. Cross the fence with care and climb past the boulder, continuing up steep slopes towards a band of rock outcrops. Move left and pick your way over some awkward terrain to the right of the cascading Shronebirrane stream to reach easier ground above. The views into the valley below are already superb.

Follow the stream as it veers to the west, heading towards a steep grass gully just north of the intimidating rock terraces of **Tooth Mountain** (590m). Sheep tracks make for easy progress up the gully and lead you to a broad col just below 500m (one hour from the start). From the col, cross the fence and follow it south, climbing over some rough ground to reach a broad shoulder southwest of Tooth Mountain, where there are fine views over Lackabane and across the Kenmare River to Scariff Island. Descend gently southwest into a col and then climb again to the trig point at the summit of **Coomacloghane** (599m).

Now you must descend, keeping left around jagged rock outcrops before climbing gently across grassy slopes east of a flat summit (584m) to reach a small cairn on the west top of Eskatarriff (596m; 1½-two hours from the col beneath Tooth Mountain). Progress to the main summit of **Eskatarriff** (600m) is hindered by rock terraces and peat hags set perpendicular to the direction you need to walk. The terrain remains difficult as you descend southeast from the summit towards a curious pyramidal summit at 531m, though views across the wild expanse of the Glanmore Valley to Hungry Hill are impressive. Either climb over or contour around the small summit and then veer northeast, climbing over easier ground to **Lackabane** (602m), the highest point of the route. From here, tremendous views open out across Kenmare Harbour towards the distant peaks of the Iveragh Peninsula.

Do not attempt to descend directly from Lackabane, but head northeast along an airy ridge across a small, unnamed summit at 406m. From here you can descend north across grassy slopes, aiming for a gate and track. At first this may not be very obvious but you may be able to make out the green outline of an old ring fort. The gate is a few hundred metres northeast of here, and should become apparent as you pick your way over some awkward ground near the valley floor. Be careful not to stray too far north on your descent, where the ground steepens into cliffs. Turn left along the track and follow it for 500m to the bridge and gate beside the minor road. Turn left at the road to return to your starting point.

WEST CORK

Although Cork is a large county, many of its best walking routes are clustered in the west; the landscape here tends to be wilder, less populated and more rugged. Outside of the Beara Peninsula (see the previous section), which is regarded as being in West Cork, it has few mountain ranges that can rival those of neighbouring Kerry. However, the region does contain several peaks that are worthy of note, including the Akinkeen Mountain and Knockboy, the county's highest summit at 706m, which are explored on one route in this section.

But for many the real character of West Cork is captured in quieter, less imposing places. With its warren of tiny country lanes enclosing lush pockets of natural habitat, many of the routes in the area are of a contemplative nature. One of the best of these can be found at the tip of the Sheep's Head, the most isolated peninsula in the southwest and a haven for the discerning walker.

PLANNING
Books
Kevin Corcoran's *West Cork Walks*, with detailed descriptions of several easy routes, makes it one of the best guides to the area. Also look for a series of local guides written by Damien Enright, who provides meticulously detailed and informative descriptions for walks in several parts of Cork.

Information Souces
The regional **tourist office** (☎ 027-50229; Wolfe Tone Sq) in Bantry can provide useful information on accommodation and transport links in West Cork.

POCKET OF AKINKEEN

Duration 4–4½ hours
Distance 6km
Ascent 500m
Difficulty moderate–demanding
Start/Finish Track at GR W023657
Nearest Town Glengarriff (p138)
Transport private

Summary This compact route leads around a dramatic mountain corrie, with an optional side-trip to the highest peak in County Cork.

Akinkeen Mountain is a distinctive peak of high drama that lies on the border of counties Cork and Kerry. Viewed from its namesake lough to the northeast, the peak looms darkly and precipitously overhead. Over 350m of sheer black cliff soar skyward, throwing down the gauntlet to all who dare to scale it. Yet despite its natural attractions and its status as the second highest summit in the Caha Mountains, the mountain remains largely overlooked by walkers. The cliffs are known to some hardy scramblers however, and there is a recognised scrambling route up one of the right-hand gullies on the otherwise unassailable face.

The route described here is a compact circuit, involving a direct ascent and descent of Akinkeen. The mountain's northern and eastern ridges curve around the lip of the corrie, providing a natural approach line. A fence provides navigational guidance across much of the high ground, but extreme caution is required near the cliff edge, particularly in poor visibility. Beware too of the cartographic confusion surrounding the labelling of the peak on the OS map – see below for more details.

To extend the route and take in the highest point in County Cork, consider adding the out-and-back detour to the summit of Knockboy (see Side Trip, p130).

PLANNING
Maps
The OSNI 1:50,000 map No 85 covers this walk, though the naming of Akinkeen Mountain and it surrounding peaks might be generously described as a right mess. Akinkeen Mountain is the 692m peak that lies just southwest of Lough Akinkeen. The

closest name on the map is 'Knockboy', though this 706m peak is marked again in its correct place some 2.5km to the south. The name 'Knocknamanagh', which hovers just north of Lough Akinkeen on the map, correctly refers to the 637m peak around 2.5km further northwest. It's all rather bewildering, but it's advisable to get to grips with the disorder before heading out.

GETTING TO/FROM THE WALK
The circuit starts and finishes at the bottom of a track along the Kilgarvan-Bantry road (GR W023657). Follow the N71 Bantry–Glengarriff Rd to Ballylicky, and turn northwest around 3km north of Ballylicky. Follow this minor road up beside Coomhola River and cross over the pass at the head of the valley. Around 2.5km down the other side of the pass you come to a sharp right-hand bend. A gated track leads off to the left from the apex of the bend, with space for a couple of vehicles to park without blocking access. If you need further space, continue 1km north along the road and park in a lay-by.

There is no public transport to the area.

THE WALK
From the bottom of the track, join the road and head east along the tarmac for 100m.

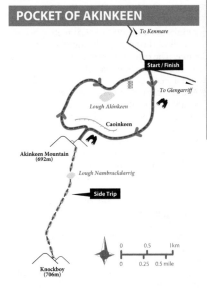

POCKET OF AKINKEEN

To Kenmare

Start / Finish

To Glengarriff

Lough Akinkeen

Caoinkeen

Akinkeen Mountain
(692m)

Lough Nambrackdarrig

Side Trip

0   0.5   1km

0   0.25   0.5 mile

Knockboy
(706m)

Turn right here along a smaller, rougher track and pass through a metal gate. You are now directly beneath the eastern arm of the horseshoe. Begin to climb south, making a diagonal ascent along a faint ramp. Rough tussock grass makes for awkward progress underfoot but magnificent views across **Lough Akinkeen** provide interest as you climb.

The top of the shoulder is marked by a fence. Join this and turn right, following the fence posts west along the ridge. You are now walking along the county border, with Kerry to the north and Cork to the south. Before too long you arrive at the base of a steep, craggy step. If you don't mind a piece of easy scrambling this can be climbed on the right-hand side of the fence. Alternatively, cross the boundary to find easier slopes to the left.

The scenery changes as you reach the top of the crag. You are now on the **ridge** proper, and the ground underfoot becomes studded with boulders and bare rock seams. Continue to follow the ridge-line as it curves northwest, taking care to stay back from the lip of the corrie and the precipitous drop to the north. As you near the top, fine views open out northwest towards the MacGillycuddy's Reeks – the unmistakable outline of the country's highest mountains. If you ease close to the cliff you'll also be able to enjoy an exhilarating birds-eye view over Lough Akinkeen, some 400 vertical metres below.

Follow the fence to the highest part of the ridge. The official **summit** of the mountain is set around 200m back from the cliff, and you'll need to head southwest to reach it. A small cairn marks the spot, and provides a fantastic vantage point for many of the mountains of Cork and Kerry.

Unless you want to make the detour to the summit of **Knockboy** (see Side Trip), retrace your steps northeast from the cairn to the top of the cliff. Turn left here and follow the fence down steeper ground on the mountain's northern shoulder. Cross the fence when the terrain allows and descend to a slight dip in the ridge. Head along the shoulder just north of the lough, passing several angular outcrops of rock as you descend to another fence. Turn right here and follow the fence down steep, grassy slopes to a gate and sheep pen at the base of the corrie.

Turn left and pass through the gate to join the end of a gravel track. The track leads east around the edge of Lough Akinkeen, though a conifer plantation along the shore prevents access to the water itself. Pass through another gate before joining a second track. Turn left here and continue to descend, pausing only to negotiate a stream where the path has been washed away by the water. A series of beautiful **waterfalls** near the bottom of the track heralds your return to the start. Pass through a final metal gate to reach the road itself.

SIDE TRIP: KNOCKBOY
2 hours, 5km, 270m ascent

From the summit of **Akinkeen Mountain** (692m), the rounded summit of **Knockboy** (706m) can be seen clearly to the south. If you want to make the detour to visit this mountain, descend gently south towards Lough Nambrackdarrig. A gradual ascent over rough ground then leads to the trig point at the top. Simply retrace your steps to return to the summit of Akinkeen.

SHEEP'S HEAD WAY HIGHLIGHT

Duration 5½–6 hours
Distance 16km
Ascent 380m
Difficulty easy–moderate
Start/Finish The Black Gate parking area
Nearest Town Kilcrohane (p139)
Transport private
Summary A high-quality coastal circuit, this walk explores wild scenery at the tip of the southwest's most remote peninsula. A shorter loop walk is also an option.

The Sheep's Head is the least known of all the peninsulas in southwest Ireland, yet it boasts wonderful views of the western seaboard and possesses a quiet, rural beauty in its interior. The entire headland is circumnavigated by the four-day, 88km-long Sheep's Head Way. The closing line of Seamus Heaney's poem *The Peninsula* has been adopted as an epithet for this long-distance path: 'water and ground in their extremity'. The motto is particularly relevant to the very tip of this isolated outpost of land, which provides the terrain for the one-day highlight described here.

Most of our walk uses the Sheep's Head Way, following obvious footpaths and taking advantage of the stiles, footbridges and marker posts that furnish the long-distance route. Ground covered is generally undulating, with the modest summit of Ballyroon Mountain providing the high-point at 239m. The route passes a series of steep cliffs at one point, offering a thrilling impression of height and space, but demanding that you take care near the edge. The circuit finishes with 3km of narrow lanes that are not part of the Sheep's Head Way. Views are wonderful throughout, with Mizen Head dominating to the south and the mountains of the Beara Peninsula rising across Bantry Bay to the north.

Those who prefer a shorter walk can complete a 4km alternative circuit from the car park at the end of the peninsula. This route is fully way-marked (like the longer circuit it forms one of the country's National Loops Walks) and takes in what is arguably the most impressive section of the longer route. Allow two hours for this option.

PLANNING
Maps & Books
The OSI 1:50,000 map No 88 covers this route.

The locally produced *Guide to the Sheep's Head Way* is available from shops and tourist offices around the peninsula. It includes a booklet describing the entire trail, and overview map showing the main route as well as various options for shorter, looped walks.

GETTING TO/FROM THE WALK
To reach the start of the walk, follow the main road 4km west from Kilcrohane to a junction where a road branches to the right (the junction is marked by a signpost reading 'The Black Gate'). One hundred metres further west is a roadside parking area, with space for eight to 10 vehicles.

THE WALK
From the parking area walk west along the main road for around 400m. A prominent waymarking stone directs you right, over a stone stile and across the left-hand side of a small field. Cross a second stile and walk between several farm buildings to a gate on the left. Negotiate this and you are out onto open terrain.

The path is well marked as it contours across the hillside. Marshy patches of ground need to be negotiated from time to time; pick the easiest-looking route around the edge of these. The route crosses a couple

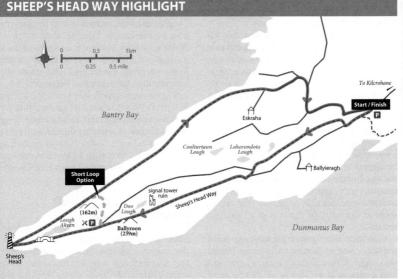

SHEEP'S HEAD WAY HIGHLIGHT

more stiles and passes close to two small loughs before descending onto a road. Turn left along this for just 20m before veering up a lane to the right. Pass between three houses and the road will dwindle to a grassy boreen and then a footpath as you begin to ascend Ballyroon Mountain.

The climb up the boulder-studded hillside is steady but rarely steep. The path joins the summit ridge near a jumble of rocks that is actually a ruined 17th-century **signal tower**; the tower was standing until 1990 when it was blown down in a gale. Continue along the ridge to the trig point that marks the top of the hill at 239m (2½ hours from the start); views encompass the Beara and Iveragh Peninsulas to the north, and Mizen Head to the south.

A short descent leads past a building (built as a lookout during WWII) to the parking area at the end of the Sheep's Head road. If you are lucky the **café** in the car park will be open and you can treat yourself to lunch. This car park is also the start/finish point for the shorter loop options outlined under Planning (p129).

The path is now well-trodden all the way to the **lighthouse**. At the end of Lough Akeen a wooden bridge offers passage over a marshy ditch, and a final short climb leads to a helicopter landing pad encircled with white stones. The lighthouse is down a flight of concrete steps to the right (one hour from Ballyroon Mountain).

Return to the helicopter pad and veer left to join the return path along the north side of the peninsula. Several marshy hollows lie alongside the first section of this route; skirt around them to their immediate left or climb a little way up the ridge further to the left to avoid them. The path then passes along the top of sheer cliffs. The scenery is impressive, but care is needed near the steep drops.

Climb gently up a wide hollow; the short loop option back to the car park will soon be signed off to the right. Continue ahead for the longer route, where the landscape becomes more pastoral and less rugged. Intricate coastal scenery begins to take centre stage as the path descends past a beautiful sea inlet.

Continue over grassy undulations until the scattering of houses of Eskraha comes into sight. Cross a stile beside a gate and join a narrow lane. This is where you leave

the Sheep's Head Way; instead follow signs for the 'Poet's Way' until it turns across a stile on the right. Continue along the road here, keeping right at the following two road junctions and climbing towards the ridge of the peninsula. Turn left at two subsequent junctions to reach the main road along the south coast. Turn right here and within 100m you will return to the start point.

MORE WALKS

DINGLE PENINSULA
Mt Eagle
Several walks are possible around Mt Eagle (516m), on the tip of the Dingle Peninsula. Starting from Kildurrihy village, a moderate to demanding 14km, six-hour route climbs the mountain, skirting Mt Eagle Lake before reaching the summit. From there, it crosses a subsidiary summit, Beenacouma, to the southwest, and descends to meet the Dingle Way, which it follows back to Kildurrihy. There isn't any public transport to Kildurrihy, but it is possible to get off the Dingle–Dunquin bus about 2km west of Ventry (see Dunquin, p136). Use the OSI 1:50,000 map No 70.

Stradbally & Beenoskee
The twin summits of Stradbally (798m) and Beenoskee (826m) dominate the centre of the Dingle Peninsula. From a start at the parking area beside Lough Anscaul, 4km north of Anascaul village, you can follow a good track up past waterfalls to a col at almost 400m. From there turn northeast and make the long climb to the summit of Beenoskee, from where there are superb views over the Dingle Peninsula. Walkers can opt to continue for another kilometre to the slightly lower tip of Stradbally before retracing the outward route to Lough Anscaul. Total distance including Stradbally is 13km, with 770m of ascent and a grading of moderate to demanding. Use the OSI 1:50,000 map No 70.

IVERAGH PENINSULA
Mangerton Mountain
Mangerton Mountain (839m), south of Killarney, has two sides to its character; the summit plateau and southern slopes are rounded and wet, while to the north steep cliffs and sharp arêtes enclose the

dramatically named Devil's Punchbowl. A moderate to demanding route to the top starts and finishes at a car park at the end of a minor road at GR V983848; take the N71 south from Killarney and turn left where a sign indicates the way to Mangerton (just south of Muckross Hotel) and then turn right 1.5km later. Follow a path alongside the Finoulagh River to the lough that fills the Devil's Punchbowl, and climb the ridge to the east. The small summit cairn is 400m south of the edge of the plateau. The ridge to the west of the lough can be followed on the descent. The route is 10km long, involves 690m of ascent, and takes around four hours. Use the OSI 1:50,000 map No 78.

BEARA PENINSULA
Glanrastel
A mountain circuit on the north of the Beara Peninsula, this route starts and finishes at the end of a minor road 2km east of Lauragh (p141). Follow a track along the southern bank of Glanrastel River and then pick a way up beside the stream to the eastern end of the valley. Veer south past Caha Lakes and trace the cliff-line west over Cushnaficulla (594m) and Knockowen (658m) before descending to the start. The moderate to demanding route is 10km long, involves 700m of ascent, and should take four to five hours. Use the OSI 1:50,000 map No 84.

WAYMARKED WAYS
Additional Waymarked Ways in southwest Ireland include the Ballyhoura Way in counties Tipperary and Limerick, the Slieve Felim Way in County Limerick, the Blackwater Way in counties Cork and Tipperary, and the North Kerry Way in County Kerry. See www.walkireland.ie for full descriptions of each of these routes.

TOWNS & FACILITIES

ADRIGOLE
☎ 027 / pop 450
At the southern end of the Healy Pass, Adrigole is a disparate collection of scattered buildings rather than a village with a definite centre. However, it does offer enough amenities to make it a viable base

for walkers on the Beara Way or those climbing Hungry Hill.

Sleeping & Eating
Hungry Hill Lodge (☎ 60228; www.hungryhilllodge.com; Adrigole; campsites €15, dm/s/d €15/25/44; open Mar-Dec) is one of the best reasons to base yourself here. Excellent facilities include a pub, an evening take away menu, bike hire and fully-equipped kitchens for hostel guests and campers. It's located just west of the Healy Pass Rd junction.

B&Bs in the area include **Ocean View** (☎ 60069; s/d €29/58), set in a modern farmhouse. It's signed off the R572 Glengarriff–Castletownbere Rd just east of the junction with the Healy Pass Rd, and evening meals can be provided by prior arrangement.

Peg's Shop, near the junction of the R572 and the Healy Pass Rd, sells groceries and local walking maps, though the supermarket 2km east along the R572 has a larger range of goods.

Getting There & Away
All the bus services between Castletownbere and Cork stop in Adrigole; for details see Getting There & Away (p135) for Castletownbere.

ARDGROOM
☎ 027 / pop 860
Another small village, Ardgroom has a shop, a petrol station and several pubs.

Sleeping & Eating
B&Bs include the friendly **Bruach na hAbhann** (☎ 74983; Glenbeg Rd; s/d/tr €45/70/90). From the Village Inn, cross the bridge and turn left; the B&B is 200m along on the left.

Sea Villa (☎ 74369; www.seavilla1.com; s/d from €49/70) occupies a scenic coastal site around 5km north of Ardgroom. Walkers arriving on the Beara Way from Eyeries should turn left instead of right at Cappul Bridge, and follow the lane for 4km to the house; phone ahead for a lift if you're too tired to walk. A three-course dinner is also available from Monday to Friday for €26 per person.

In the centre of the village, **Harrington's** offers a small but well-stocked shop as well

SOUTHWEST

as an internet café serving snacks and lunches.

The Village Inn (☎ 74067; mains from €12), on the main street, serves food in its bar and restaurant and is the best place for evening meals.

Getting There & Away
Ardgroom is served by public transport in July and August only. During these months the **Bus Éireann** (☎ 064-663 0011) Castletownbere–Kenmare service 282 passes through the village, stopping outside the post office. See Castletownbere (p135) for full details of this service.

ALLIHIES
☎ 027 / pop 650
A small village set above a sandy beach, Allihies (*Na hAilichí*) has a remarkably wide range of accommodation options. The small tourist information kiosk, located beside the church, opens in summer only.

Sleeping & Eating
Allihies Village Hostel (☎ 73107; www .allihieshostel.net; Allihies; dm/d from €18/50) is a model hostel at the northern end of the village. There are smart dorms, a courtyard and barbecue area.

B&Bs in the centre of Allihies include **Veronica's** (☎ 73072; s/d €35/70), where breakfasts and daytime snacks are served in the attached café.

Also very central is **Sea View Guesthouse** (☎ 73004; www.seaviewallihies.com; s/d €45/75), which offers 10 clean rooms and a great breakfast.

There is a reasonable-sized supermarket in the main street.

O'Neill's Bar & Restaurant (☎ 73008; mains €7-15), adjacent to the Village Hostel, specialises in steaks and locally-caught seafood and is the best place for an evening meal.

There is no public transport to Allihies.

BLACK VALLEY
☎ 064 / pop 60
This valley feels remote after the bustle of nearby Killarney, and the tiny shop at the back of the hostel is the only place to get fresh supplies. There are no banking facilities and accommodation options are limited, so you should book your room in advance.

Sleeping & Eating
The An Óige **Black Valley Youth Hostel** (☎ 663 4712; www.anoige.ie; dm €17; open Mar-Oct) is in the centre of the valley, just east of the Gap of Dunloe. Simple facilities include a drying room and a small shop stocking basics such as milk, pasta and tinned food. Packed lunches can be provided by arrangement.

Shamrock Farm House B&B (☎ 663 4714; http://shamrock.kerry-ireland.com; s/d €40/60) is alongside the Kerry Way at the western end of the valley. Evening meals, packed lunches and luggage transfers can also be arranged.

Alternatively, **Hillcrest Farmhouse** (☎ 663 4702; www.hillcrestfarmhouse .com; s/d €52/76; open mid-Feb–Oct) is located in an attractive farmhouse, 100m off the Kerry Way at the eastern end of the valley. Evening meals, luggage transport and a drying room are all available if required.

There is no public transport along the Black Valley.

CAHERDANIEL
☎ 066 / pop 350
Nestling between Derrynane Bay and the slopes of Eagles Hill, Caherdaniel is a tiny hamlet with a Blue Flag beach and plenty of facilities. There's a small grocery shop selling OSI maps, a petrol station, several cafés and pubs, and a range of accommodation.

Sleeping
There are several camping grounds around the village, including **Wave Crest** (☎ 947 5188; www.wavecrestcamping.com; campsites €16; open mid-Mar–mid-Oct), which enjoys a superb coastal setting 1.6km southeast of Caherdaniel along the main road. Excellent facilities include an on-site deli and a shop stocking OSI maps.

On the main road in the village centre, **Travellers' Rest Hostel** (☎ 947 5175; dm/d from €17/40) has the quaint feel of a country cottage and offers an optional breakfast. Call at the garage opposite if there's nobody about.

Local B&Bs include **Olde Forge** (☎ 947 5140; theoldeforge.com; s/d €40/74), 1.2km southeast of town on the N70. There are six attractive rooms and fantastic views of Kenmare Bay.

At the heart of the village, **Kerry Way B&B** (☎ 947 5277; www.activity-ireland .com/bab; s/d €45/60) occupies a pleasant old house with good sized en-suite rooms.

Eating

Caherdaniel also has a good choice of eating places, most of which are clustered around the crossroads in the centre of the village.

Blind Piper (☎ 947 5126; bar food €10-18; open lunch & dinner daily) is a local institution that serves quality pub grub including deep-fried monkfish.

A cheaper alternative is **Courthouse Café** (☎ 947 5834; dinner €10; open lunch & dinner Jun-Sep), with fish, chips and burgers a mainstay of the menu.

Getting There & Away

During July and August, **Bus Éireann** (☎ 064-663 0011) service 280 runs once-daily around the Ring of Kerry, linking Caherdaniel to Killarney (€17, two hours 55 minutes), Killorglin (€16, two hours 25 minutes) and Tralee (€17, 2¼ hours). There is no public transport at other times of the year.

CASTLETOWNBERE

☎ 027 / pop 850

A bustling little town and home to one of Ireland's largest fishing fleets, Castletownbere (*Baile Chais Bhéara*) is by far the largest settlement on the Beara Peninsula.

The helpful **tourist office** (☎ 70054; www.bearatourism.com; Main St; open Tue-Sat) is just outside the Church of Ireland. The town also has a good range of visitor facilities and several shops selling local walking maps and guides, including **The Shell** bookshop on the main street.

Sleeping & Eating

Situated off Main St, **Harbour Lodge Hostel** (☎ 71043; www.harbourlodge.net; Old Convent; dm/d €18/36) occupies a large former convent building. It's a strange old place with a refectory-like dining room and worn but spacious rooms.

Rodeen B&B (☎ 70158; www.rodeen countryhouse.com; s/d €45/70; open Mar-Oct) is a delightful haven tucked away above the eastern approach to town, and features fantastic sea views.

More central is **Cametringane Hotel** (☎ 70379; www.camehotel.com; the

Harbour; s/d €70/140), behind the harbour at the eastern end of town.

There's a large supermarket and a good selection of pubs around the town centre. Eateries include **Copper Kettle** (☎ 71792; the Square; mains €10-12; open daily for lunch), a convivial little café near the water.

One of the best restaurants in town is **Olde Bakery** (☎ 70869; oldebakerybeara @eircom.net; Castletown House; mains €13-21; open for dinner), which serves good-value international grub within rustic, wood-panelled surrounds.

Getting There & Away

Castletownbere bus services arrive and depart from the square. **Bus Éireann** (☎ 021-450 8188) runs via Bantry to Cork (€19, 3¼ hours), with three services daily Monday to Saturday and two on Sundays. In July and August only service 282 runs via Eyeries, Ardgroom and Lauragh to Kenmare (€11.40, one hour 20 minutes; twice daily Mon-Sat), with frequent onward connections from Kenmare to Killarney.

Harringtons (☎ 74003) also runs a private service between Cork and Castletownbere, once daily except Thursday and Sunday; **O'Donoghue's** (☎ 70007) operate on Thursday and Sunday instead. All Cork services pass via Bantry, Glengarriff and Adrigole.

CLOGHANE

☎ 066 / pop 280

A picturesque village, Cloghane (*An Clochán*) makes a good base for walkers climbing Brandon and is a pleasant stop over on the Dingle Way. The village's small **tourist office** (☎ 713 8137; open May-Sep) is opposite the church. It sells OSI maps and walking guides, and the staff can provide local walking and accommodation advice.

Sleeping & Eating

By the seafront you'll find **Mount Brandon Hostel** (☎ 713 8299; www.mountbrandon hostel.com; dm/s/tw €20/30/50; open Mar-Jan), a small, simple hostel with a patio overlooking the bay and relaxation treatments such as Shiatsu massage.

The village has several B&Bs, including **Benagh** (☎ 713 8142; mcmorran@eircom .net; s/d €35/70). Set 500m northeast of the

SOUTHWEST

village, this place offers four breezy rooms and sweeping views of the bay.

Mount Brandon Lodge (☎ 713 8117; s/d €50/70; open Jun-Aug) also occupies a scenic location at the back of Brandon Bay. Luggage transfer and packed lunches are available by arrangement.

Alternatively, head to **O'Connors** (☎ 713 8113; www.cloghane.com; s/d from €50/70; meals €14-18), a welcoming village pub that provides both rooms and bar food.

There is a small grocery shop on the ground floor of the hostel.

O'Donnell's pub (☎ 713 8301; mains from €10.50), also beside the hostel, is another good option for bar food, and serves lunches and dinners.

Getting There & Away

On Fridays only, **Bus Éireann** (☎ 716 4700) runs two bus services between Cloghane and Tralee (€10.30, 1¼ hours). By car, Cloghane is 13km north of Dingle via the Connor Pass.

DINGLE
☎ 066 / pop 1800

Despite its cosmopolitan cluster of restaurants, pubs and accommodation, Dingle town (*An Daingean*) manages to retain its character thanks to its working harbour and thriving fishing industry. It's the largest settlement on the Dingle Peninsula and most visitors pass through even if they chose to stay somewhere a little quieter.

The **tourist office** (☎ 915 1188; www .dingle-peninsula.ie; the Pier; open daily) is on the waterfront, and offers walking maps, guidebooks and information on the entire peninsula. **Mountain Man Outdoor Shop** (☎ 915 2400; www.themountainmanshop. com; Strand St) stocks a basic range of camping and outdoor gear, as well as offering guided walks.

Sleeping

Dingle has a host of accommodation options at all levels, but you would be advised to book ahead during July and August.

Some 1.5km west of Dingle town centre, **Rainbow Hostel** (☎ 915 1044; www .rainbowhosteldingle.com; camping per person €9, dm/d €16/40) is a rural, house-like hostel that offers the closest camping to Dingle.

Tucked away near the centre of town, the dinky **Grapevine Hostel** (☎ 915 1434; www.grapevinedingle.com; Dykegate Ln; dm €16-18, d €42) has en-suite bathrooms and a fire-lit lounge.

The town also has numerous B&Bs. **Kirrary** (☎ 915 1606; Avondale; collinskirrary@eircom.net; s/d from €50/90) has friendly owners and a cheerful atmosphere.

Set above a travel agency at the quiet end of town, **Sráid Eoin House** (☎ 915 1409; www.sraideoinbnb.com; John St; s/d €60/80; open Mar-Oct) offers an impressively wide breakfast selection.

Another great choice is the handsome **Captain's House** (☎ 915 1531; captigh @eircom.net; the Mall; s/d €60/100; open mid-Mar–mid-Nov), with its streamside garden and beautiful interior furnishings.

Eating

There is a large supermarket near the quay, while restaurants, pubs and cafés are numerous. One of the best spots for dinner is **Global Village Restaurant** (☎ 915 2325; Main St; mains €18-25; open dinner Mar-Oct), which has the sophisticated feel of a continental bistro and offers a fusion of global recipes.

Alternatively, **Half Door** (☎ 915 1600; John St; mains €22-50, set menu €25; open lunch & dinner) is an outstanding seafood restaurant where fish and shellfish are superbly presented in cosy surrounds.

Getting There & Away

Bus Éireann (☎ 716 4700) buses stop outside the car park behind the supermarket. Scheduled services go to Tralee (€11, 1¼ hours) and Killarney (€13, 2¼ hours). There are four services Monday to Saturday and three services on Sunday to each destination.

DUNQUIN
☎ 066 / pop 180

A scattered collection of houses, Dunquin (*Dún Chaion*) lacks any real focal point. However, its unusual pier is the departure point for ferries to Great Blasket Island, and the village is also home to the informative **Blasket Centre** (*Ionad an Bhlascaoid Mhóir*; ☎ 915 6444; www.heritageireland.ie; adult/child €4/2; open daily mid-Mar–Oct), with exhibits covering all aspects of the island's history.

Sleeping & Eating
The cheapest place to stay is the An Óige **Dunquin Hostel** (☎915 6121; oigedun @eircom.net; dm €15-19; tw €42; open Feb-Nov), which is conveniently located near the Blasket Centre. There are stunning views, but the doors are closed between 10am and 5pm.

B&B options in the village include **De Mórdha** (☎915 6276; www.demordha .com; s/d €45/70; open Easter-Oct), a pleasant little place with great views and all mod cons.

An Portán B&B (☎915 6212; www .anportan.com; s/d €40/70; open Easter-Sep) has 14 rooms in its guesthouse and serves traditional Irish meals in a separate **restaurant** (mains €12-25).

Rooms are also available at **Kruger's** (☎915 6127; s/d €35/70; open Easter-Aug), the village pub and the most westerly bar in Europe. Evening meals are served in the **bar** (mains from €12) and packed lunches are also available.

Getting There & Away
Bus Éireann (☎716 4700) has a limited service between Dunquin and Dingle (€5.40, 30 minutes), with two services on Mondays and Thursdays only.

EYERIES
☎027 / pop 200
Eyeries would be a solid contender in the 'brightest village in the world' contest, and its rainbow array of colourful buildings make it a popular visitor attraction.

Sleeping & Eating
Accommodation in the village is limited to B&Bs. These include **Coulagh Bay House** (☎74013; www.coulaghbayhouse.com; s/d €40/70), on the main road (and on the Beara Way), opposite the turn-off into Eyeries.

Colourful **Formanes House** (☎74360; s/d €35/60) is on the outskirts of the village. Instead of turning left into the village, continue to walk along the main road for another couple of minutes. The B&B is on the right just after the sports ground. Dinner can be served by prior arrangement.

Eyeries has a small supermarket for self-caterers. The only restaurant in the village is **Auntie Mays** (☎74477; mains from €12.50, dinner from Thu-Sun).

Getting There & Away
Eyeries is served by public transport in July and August only, when the **Bus Éireann** (☎064-6630011) Castletownbere–Kenmare service 282 passes through the village. See Castletownbere (p135) for full details of this service.

FEOHANAGH
☎066 / pop 390
One of the most remote villages on the peninsula, Feohanagh (*Fheothanach*) is little more than a disparate scattering of houses. The accommodation options are convenient for walkers however, as they all lie directly along the route of the Dingle Way.

Sleeping & Eating
Walkers coming from Dunquin will arrive first at the large **Old Pier B&B** and **Restaurant** (☎915 5242; www.oldpier.com; s/d €50/80), which is located along the coast road at the southern end of the village. Specialties in the restaurant include a wide selection of freshly caught seafood.

B&Bs in the centre of the village include **Coill an Rois** (Forest of the Roses, ☎915 5475; www.dinglebb.com; s/d from €47/70). Breakfast options include American-style waffles – a good choice considering the owner is a former professional pastry chef.

Alternatively, **An Riasc** (☎915 5446; www.anriasc.ie; s/d from €65/90) is a modern, family-friendly place that offers three guest bedrooms within a stone-fronted farmhouse.

Closer to the foot of Brandon Mountain you'll find pretty and comfortable **An Bóthar Pub and B&B** (☎915 5342; www.ireland-discover.com/botharpub.htm; Cuas; s/d €38/70; mains from €10.50). Food is served in the bar and restaurant, and packed lunches are also available.

Getting There & Away
Bus Éireann (☎716 4700) has a limited service from Feohanagh to Dingle (€4.50, 10 minutes), with one bus on Tuesdays and Fridays only.

SOUTHWEST

GAP OF DUNLOE & AROUND
☎ 064

While there is no village as such at the Gap of Dunloe, there is some accommodation in the area.

Sleeping & Eating

Mountain Rest Hostel & Camping (☎ 664 4272; Carnahone, Beaufort; campsite & two people €14, dm/d €15/32) is located behind Kissane's Foodstore, 5km east of Kate Kearney's and at the bottom of the road to Cronin's Yard. The cosy little hostel offers 12 beds but the facilities for campers are rather aged.

There are a few B&Bs are scattered around the Gap's southern entrance. **Wayside B&B** (☎ 664 4284; www.waysidebnb .com; s €60/80) occupies a large family home with beautiful gardens, and is 1km south of Kate Kearney's Cottage.

A kilometre further east in the direction of Killarney is homely **Purple Heather** (☎ 664 4266; http://homepage.eircom.net /~purpleheather; s/d €48/70; open Mar-Oct), where breakfasts are served in the conservatory beneath fine mountain views.

At the base of the gap itself, **Kate Kearney's Cottage** (☎ 664 4146; mains from €10.50; open lunch & dinner) is a 19th-century pub that serves bar food as well as more formal evening meals in its restaurant.

There is no public transport to the Gap, so you'll need your own means of reaching the area.

GLENCAR
☎ 066

More of a geographic area than a village, many of Glencar's houses are a kilometre or more apart.

Sleeping & Eating

The one focal point is **The Climbers Inn** (☎ 976 0101; www.climbersinn.com; dm/ s/d €25/35/70), which offers guided walks, luggage transfer, a drying room, packed lunches and a pub serving bar meals.

The other most convenient accommodation options are situated about 3.5km northeast of The Climbers Inn, where the Kerry Way joins the main road on the northeastern shore of Lough Acoose. **Lake View Farmhouse** (☎ 976 0136; camping per person €10, s/d €35/60) has fantastic views of Carrauntoohil and allows campers to stay outside. Evening meals are also available.

Next door, friendly **Lough Acoose House** (☎ 976 0105; www.acoose-house-glencar .com; s/d €40/60) offers homely rooms and a large garden, and can also provide evening meals, packed lunches and luggage transfer.

There is no public transport to or from Glencar.

GLENGARRIFF
☎ 027 / pop 1100

Hidden deep in Bantry Bay, Glengarriff (*Gleann Garbh*) is an attractive village with a happy holiday feel. Walkers will also enjoy exploring the network of short trails in the mature oak forests of Glengarriff Woods Nature Reserve – the entrance is 1.5km north of the village along the N71 to Kenmare.

The Fáilte Ireland **tourist office** (☎ 63084; Main St; open daily Jun-Aug) provides information for the area. The post office on the main street has a *bureau de change* but the nearest ATMs are in Bantry or Castletownbere.

Sleeping

The well-organised **Dowlings Camping & Caravan Park** (☎ 63154; Castletownbere Rd; campsites €18; open Easter-Oct), 4km west of Glengarriff on the road to Castletownbere, occupies a woodland setting. Amenities include a games room and a licensed bar staging traditional music every night from June to August.

Right at the heart of Glengarriff, **Murphy's Village Hostel** (☎ 63555; Main St; dm/d €15/50; open Jun-Sep) is a cheerful, well-run hostel with spacious, bright rooms. The owners also run the **Village Café** downstairs.

Modern **River Lodge B&B** (☎ 63043; Castletownbere Rd; s/d €50/80; open Feb-Nov) lies on the edge of the village and is one of several B&Bs in the area.

Eccles Hotel (☎ 63003; www.eccleshotel .com; Glengarriff Harbour; r €100-140) has a long and distinguished history; the decor is slightly parochial but the rooms are large and sunny.

Eating

There are several small supermarkets in the village for self-caterers.

At pleasant **Hawthorne Bar** (☎ 63440; Main St; lunch €9-15, dinner €14-20), the emphasis is on local seafood.

Alternatively, **Martello Restaurant** (☎ 63860; Garinish Ct, Main St; lunch €11-18, dinner €20-28; open Tue-Sun Jun-Aug, Thu-Sun Sep-May) is a smart but casual bistro offering dishes such as flambéed Bantry Bay scallops. Booking is advised.

Getting There & Away
Bus Éireann (☎ 021-450 8188) services travel from Glengarriff, through Bantry, to Cork (€17, 2½ hours) three times daily Monday to Saturday and twice on Sunday. There are also less frequent services along the Beara Peninsula to Castletownbere – see p135 for details.

KILCROHANE & AROUND
☎ 027 / pop 300
A small, quiet village, Kilcrohane has just enough facilities to make it a viable base for the walk around the tip of the Sheep's Head. There is a café and a small, old-fashioned grocery shop that sells the guide to the Sheep's Head Way. There are no banking facilities and the area **tourist office** (☎ 50229; Wolfe Tone Sq; open Mon-Sat Apr-Oct) is in Bantry.

Sleeping & Eating
Carbery View Hostel (☎ 67035; camping per person €7, dm €14) is set in a small annex to a family house. The friendly owners request that guests telephone in advance wherever possible.

Occupying a large, restored home near Kilcrohane church is **Bridge View House & Restaurant** (☎ 67086; www.bridgeview house.com; s/d €44/68). Rooms include a family suite that sleeps five, and evening meals in the restaurant are available by arrangement to guests and non-guests alike.

In the centre of the village you'll find the friendly **Bay View Inn** (☎ 67981; www .thebayviewinn.net; s/d €40/70 mains from €12). Food is served by prior arrangement and there are frequent music sessions in the downstairs bar.

Getting There & Away
Bantry Rural Transport (☎ 52727; www .ruraltransport.ie; 5 Main St, Bantry) run buses between Kilrochane and Bantry, twice a day on Tuesdays and Thursdays only (€4, 55 minutes). From Bantry there are frequent onward connections to Cork and Killarney.

KILLARNEY
☎ 064 / pop 16,900
Killarney is a well-oiled tourism machine located in the midst of sublime scenery. The town has been practising the tourism game for over 250 years and competition keeps standards high.

As well as providing visitor services details, the **tourist office** (☎ 663 1633; www.discoverireland.ie/southwest; Beech Rd; open daily) sells OSI maps and gives out a good, free map of the national park.

Sport Corran Tuathail (☎ 662 2681; www.sct.ie; Killarney Outlet Centre) is the best outdoor shop in Killarney, stocking a good range of gear, maps and guidebooks. It's located in a shopping arcade beside the train station.

Sleeping
Killarney has a huge choice of accommodation – unless you are booking well in advance you could let staff at the tourist office reserve a place for you (€4).

Flesk Caravan & Camping Park (☎ 663 1704; www.campingkillarney.com; Muckross Rd; campsites €19; open Easter-Sep) is the closest camping ground, about 1.3km south of town on the N71. Facilities include bike hire, a supermarket, restaurant, bar and café.

Hostels include the central **Neptune's Killarney Town Hostel** (☎ 663 5255; www .neptuneshostel.com; Bishop's Ln, New St; dm €14-20, d €40-50), whose dorms can sleep over 150.

Modern **Railway Hostel** (☎ 663 5299; www.killarneyhostel.com; Fair Hill; dm €13-22, s/d €38/52), near the train station, is about as inviting as hostels get. A basic breakfast is included in the price.

Welcoming **Rathmore House** (☎ 663 2829; rathmorehousekly@iol.ie; Rock Rd; s/d €50/80; open Mar-Oct) is a long-established B&B set amid a group of family-run establishments at the northern entrance to town.

Another option is **Elyod House** (☎ 663 6544; www.elyodhouse.ie; Ross Rd; r €60-80), a friendly, quietly located modern house on the road to Ross Castle, and a few minutes' walk from town.

Fairview (☎ 663 4164; www.fairview killarney.com; Lewis Rd; s/d €80/130) is a highly recommended guesthouse within walking distance of the centre, with alluring touches such as antique furniture and Jacuzzi baths.

Eating
Killarney also has countless eateries serving all manner of food. One of the best spots is **Brícín** (☎ 663 4902; 26 High St; mains €18-20; open lunch & dinner Tue-Sat), a Celtic Deco restaurant that doubles as the town museum.

The award-winning **Gaby's Seafood Restaurant** (☎ 663 2519; 27 High St; mains €18-50; open dinner Mon-Sat) specialises in exquisite Gallic dishes such as lobster in a cognac and cream sauce.

Getting There & Away
Bus Éireann (☎ 663 0011) is based beside the train station. Buses head from here to all parts of the country, including Tralee (€8, 35 minutes, hourly), Cork (€16, two hours, 15 daily), Dublin (€23, six hours, six daily) and Galway (€22, seven hours, seven daily).

There are also regular bus services to **Kerry Airport** (☎ 066-9764644; www.kerry airport.com) at Farranfore, about 15km north of Killarney. Buses run every two hours, daily between June and September, but just once or twice daily outside this period (€5, 20 minutes).

Killarney's **train station** (☎ 663 1067) is on Park Rd, east of the centre. **Iarnrod Éireann** (www.irishrail.ie) has connections to most major Irish cities, including three direct trains a day to Cork (€20, 1½ hours), nine to Tralee (€9, 45 minutes), and hourly services to Dublin Heuston (€36, 3½ hours).

KILLORGLIN
☎ 066 / pop 3900
This pretty town spans the River Laune and is significantly less hectic than Killarney. It offers plenty of amenities, but is short on budget accommodation.

The helpful **tourist office** (☎ 976 1451; Library Pl; open Mon-Sat) also sells OSI maps and walking guides.

Sleeping
The closest camping and caravaning ground is **West's Holiday Park** (☎ 976 1240; enquiries@westcaravans.com; Killarney Rd; campsites €18; open Apr-Oct), a small site with views of Carrauntoohil. It's located off the N72, just under 2km east of the bridge. Facilities include a tennis court.

The friendly and homely **Laune Valley Farm Hostel** (☎ 976 1488; camping per person €7; dm/d €16/36) is 1.8km out of town and signed off the Tralee Rd. Attractions include fresh farm produce and views of the Reeks, and campers can use the hostel facilities for free.

In Killorglin itself is **Riverside House** (☎ 976 1184; www.riversidehousebnb.com; s/d €48/70; open Mar-Nov), a family-friendly guesthouse with beautiful gardens sweeping down to the river. It's located beside the town's Roman Catholic Church.

Another recommended B&B is **Coffey's River's Edge** (☎ 976 1750; www.coffeysri versedge.com; The Bridge; s/d €50/100), which occupies an unbeatable location beside the bridge over the River Laune.

Eating
For self-caterers, there's a good supermarket on the Square, Upper Bridge St.

For a taste of the Mediterranean head to **Sol Y Sombra** (☎ 976 2347; Lower Bridge St; dishes €5-13; open Wed-Mon Jun-Aug, Wed-Sun Sep-Jan & Mar-May), a tapas bar set in a beautifully renovated church.

An enduring favourite is **Nick's Seafood Restaurant** (☎ 976 1219; info@nicks .ie; Lower Bridge St; mains €20-38; open dinner daily Jun-Sep, Wed-Sun Oct-May), where French-Irish flair produces finely-prepared dishes such as shellfish mornay and Kerry beef.

Getting There & Away
Regular **Bus Éireann** (☎ 064-663 0011) services run to/from Tralee (€7.60, 40 minutes) and Killarney (€6.40, 30 minutes). Both destinations have at least five services daily Monday to Saturday and four on Sunday. During July and August, service 280 also runs once-daily around the Ring of Kerry, linking to Killorglin to Caherdaniel (€16, two hours 25 minutes).

LAURAGH
☎ 064 / pop 170

The houses and facilities at Lauragh (*Laith Reach*) are even more spread out than most villages on the Beara Peninsula. The only identifiable centre is the road junction where the road from the Healy Pass joins the R571. The nearest shops are in Ardgroom (p133), 10km west, and the nearest tourist office is in Castletownbere (p135).

Creeven Lodge Caravan & Camping Park (☎ 668 3131; www.creevenlodge.com; site & two adults €16; open Easter-Oct) is 1.5km south along the Healy Pass Rd. It has grassy sites, a children's play area and a commonroom with cooking facilities.

The remote An Óige **Glanmore Lake Hostel** (☎ 668 3181; www.anoige.ie; Glanmore Lake; dm adult/child €17/14; open end-May–end-Sep) has a timeless atmosphere and a beautiful location. It's 5.6km from Lauragh; take the road for Glanmore Lake and keep going.

Mountain View B&B (☎ 668 3143; s/d €45/70) is a friendly family home 800m along the Healy Pass Rd. Evening meals can be provided and the owner offers a lift back to the Beara Way in the morning.

An Sibin (☎ 668 3941), the only pub in the village, is located just south of the crossroads. It offers bar snacks and frequent music sessions.

Getting There & Away
Lauragh is served by public transport in July and August only, when the **Bus Éireann** (☎ 663 0011) Castletownbere–Kenmare service 282 passes through the village. See Castletownbere (p135) for full details of this service.

TRALEE
☎ 066 / pop 22,100

Despite having plenty of facilities, Tralee remains a down-to-earth working town rather than a tourist destination. The helpful **tourist office** (☎ 712 1288; Denny St) is beside the Ashe Memorial Hall.

Landers Outdoor World (☎ 712 6644; Unit 4, Mile Height Retail Park) is the best gear shop in the area, stocking a wide range of equipment, clothing, maps and guidebooks. It's located just off the N21 at the eastern side of town.

Sleeping
The small **Bayview Caravan & Camping Park** (☎ 712 6140; bayviewtralee@eircom .net; Killeen; campsites €14; open Apr-Oct) has good facilities and a pleasant tree-lined location. It's 1.5km north of the centre on the R556.

Finnegan's Holiday Hostel (☎ 712 7610; www.finneganshostel.com; 17 Denny St; dm/s/d €17/30/50) has an elegant Georgian facade, en-suite bathrooms and a sizeable kitchen and lounge.

One of a line of B&Bs, **Conn Oriel** (☎ 712 5359; www.connoriel.com; 6 Pembroke Sq, Pembroke St; s/d €40/70) has friendly owners and cheery decorative art on the walls.

Friendly **Imperial Hotel** (☎ 712 7755; www.imperialtralee.com; Denny St; s/d €65/120) has modern bedrooms and good facilities, including a wood-panelled bar with traditional music sessions at weekends.

More stylish again is the **Grand Hotel** (☎ 712 1499; www.grandhoteltralee.com; Denny St; r €85/150). Built in 1928, it maintains the feel of a traditional county-town hotel in its pleasantly aged rooms.

Eating
There's a supermarket in the Mall for self-caterers, and plenty of good eateries in and around the town.

La Scala (☎ 712 2477; the Square; mains €6-19; open lunch & dinner daily) is a popular Irish-Italian restaurant where locals banquet on pizza, pasta and meatballs.

At stylish **Restaurant David Norris** (☎ 718 5654; Ivy Tce; mains €18-24; open for dinner Tue-Sat), the exciting menu features dishes such as crisp-fried calamari, steaks and shanks. A €25, four-course special is available before 7pm Monday to Friday.

Getting There & Away
Bus Éireann (☎ 716 4700) operates from next to the train station, east of the town centre. Services include eight daily buses to Dublin (€23, six hours), and hourly services to Killarney (€8, 40 minutes) and Cork (€17, 2½ hours).

From the **train station** (☎ 712 3522), there are three direct daily services with **Iarnród Éireann** (www.irishrail.ie) to Cork (€32, 2¼ hours), nine to Killarney (€9.50, 45 minutes) and one to Dublin (€36, four hours).

Atlantic Islands

> Highest peak in the region: Knockmore, Clare Island, 462m

Ireland's wonderfully fragmented Atlantic coast provides countless opportunities for walkers. Perhaps the most engaging and adventurous of these can be found on the country's many islands. Contrast the ruins of Great Blasket Island, melancholy and redolent of hardship, loss and emigration, with the vibrancy of the Aran Islands, given new life by tourism, internet-assisted business and an influx of people eager to live on a far-flung fringe of Europe.

The islands have long and often turbulent histories, intertwined with fascinating and unusual cultures. The people are resilient and pragmatic, qualities derived from the need to survive in a wild and ultimately unforgiving environment. The natural world seems closer here too: cars are few, meadows grow uncut, and relinquished lands provide a haven for a huge diversity of insect and plant life. Birds, in particular, thrive on the islands, more whales than you would imagine cruise by in the deep, offshore waters, dolphins and porpoises hunt in the quiet bays, and seals find rocky headlands on which to rest. Of course walkers benefit too, able to travel in peace along soaring cliffs and grassy boreens (country lanes), with the restless ocean a constant companion.

ATLANTIC ISLANDS

ATLANTIC ISLANDS

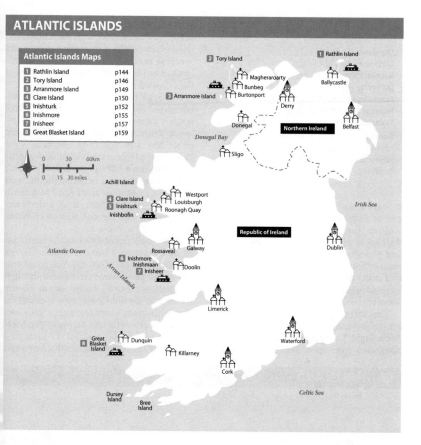

PLANNING

The official website www.irelandsislands
.com covers all the islands in this chapter,
as well as a host of others.

Place Names

On many of the islands, Gaelic (Irish) is the
first language written and spoken. Places,
road signs and place names are often
written in Gaelic only, without the usual
English translation. To facilitate navigation through these areas, Gaelic names
have been given as appropriate throughout
this chapter.

FERRY DELAYS & RESERVATIONS

Heavy swells and rough seas can halt ferry sailings at any time of the year. If you are planning
a visit to the islands, try to wait for settled conditions, or allow an extra day or two in case you
have to wait out the weather. Visitors staying overnight on the islands are not guaranteed return
passage the following day if the weather turns bad. Outside the summer months, services to
more remote islands like Tory can sometimes be disrupted for weeks on end.

Whatever the weather, it's always best to call ferry operators in advance to confirm sailing
times and make any necessary reservations.

ATLANTIC ISLANDS

RATHLIN ISLAND

Duration 3½–4½ hours
Distance 14km (8.7 miles)
Ascent 150m (492 ft)
Difficulty easy
Start/Finish Church Bay ferry pier
Nearest Town Rathlin Island (p163)
Transport boat
Summary Enjoy pleasant coastal panoramas on the way to West Lighthouse, where spectacular sea stacks team with thousands of nesting seabirds.

L-shaped Rathlin Island lies 7km northeast of Ballycastle and the coast of County Antrim. Just 6.5km long and 4km wide, Rathlin is famous for its coastal scenery and plentiful bird life. This walk makes the most of both features, focussing on the cliffs and stacks around West Lighthouse and the wetland area of surrounding Kebble Nature Reserve.

The cliffs support Northern Ireland's largest seabird colony, and the excellent **RSPB West Light Viewpoint** (☎ 048-2076 0062; admission free; open daily Apr–mid-Sep)

at the lighthouse provides stunning views of the rock faces, thick with guillemots, kittiwakes, razorbills and puffins during the breeding season from May to July. Binoculars can be hired to give you a better view of the crowded burrows and rock ledges.

Although the main route starts and finishes from the harbour, there are a couple of options for avoiding the road walk and starting at Kinramer Wood instead. You could either hire a bicycle from Soerneog View Hostel (see p163), or take the minibus shuttle with **McGinn's** (☎ 048-2076 3451), which operates on demand between the harbour and West Lighthouse from April to August.

On its own, the 5.5km circuit around Kebble Nature Reserve and Kinramer Wood should take 1½ to two hours.

Other walk possibilities on the island include an easy road trip out to Ushet Lough and Rue Point (8km return). You could also follow the short way-marked trail through the National Trust's Ballyconagan Nature Reserve to the old Coastguard Lookout on the north coast, where there are great views along the sea cliffs and across to the Scottish islands of Islay and Jura. Although a trip along the rugged north coast looks

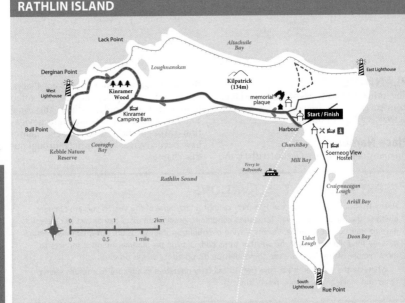

RATHLIN ISLAND

WHAT DO ROBERT THE BRUCE & RICHARD BRANSON HAVE IN COMMON...?

For a relatively small island, Rathlin has been the location of a remarkable number of notable events over the years.

The island's most illustrious visitor was Scottish hero Robert the Bruce, who retreated to the island after his defeat by Edward I in 1306. Watching a spider's resoluteness in repeatedly trying to spin a web gave him the courage to have another go at the English, whom he subsequently defeated at Bannockburn. The cave where he is said to have stayed is beneath the East Lighthouse, at the northeastern tip of the island.

Rathlin's strategic position in the turbulent waters between Scotland and Ireland has also left a legacy of massacres and conflict. In both 1575 and 1642 the island's population was decimated, first by the forces of the English Earl of Essex and then by the Scottish Campbell clan.

In 1898 Marconi made the world's first radio communication from Rathlin, contacting Ballycastle on the mainland from the East Lighthouse. The concrete base for the apparatus, inscribed with the Lloyds of London name, can still be seen at the beacon.

A century later in the 1990s, the Virgin tycoon Richard Branson also ended up on Rathlin after crash-landing in the sea a short distance to the north, the culmination of his transatlantic balloon flight.

See *Rathlin – Its Island Story* by Wallace Clark for a more detailed account of the island's colourful history.

tempting on the map, the route encroaches on private land and is not accessible to the public.

PLANNING
Maps
Use OSNI 1:50,000 map No 5.

GETTING TO/FROM THE WALK
Ferries to Rathlin leave from Ballycastle on the mainland, courtesy of **Rathlin Island Ferry** (☎ 048-2076 9299; www.rathlin ballycastleferry.com). There are eight or nine crossings daily from April to September (adult/child return £11/5), half of which are fast catamaran services (20 minutes), the rest via a slower car ferry (45 minutes). A reduced service also operates throughout the winter.

THE WALK
Walk left (west) from the harbour, past the shop, and turn right at the Church of Ireland church. Climb steeply along a narrow road and turn left at a junction, passing the island's Roman Catholic church. Continue to climb steeply to reach a **memorial plaque** commemorating the 500 islanders who emigrated during the Great Famine (10 minutes from the start). Already there are great views to the south across Church

Bay, Rue Point and out to the cliffs of Fair Head on the mainland.

Follow the road through quiet countryside to a left-hand bend, with the eastern boundary Kinramer Wood on the right. This is where the off-road circuit rejoins the road – leave your bike here if you have opted to cycle. Meanwhile the walk continues ahead along the road, past **Kinramer Camping Barn** (see p163), to arrive at the boundary of **Kebble Nature Reserve** 1km later (one hour from the famine memorial).

A gravel road leads on from the reserve entrance, past the warden's cottage and out towards West Lighthouse. Walk only 100m along this before turning left along a faint, grassy path. You soon reach a red metal gate. It's possible to make an optional detour of around 800m here by passing through the gate and following a

CALLING RATHLIN

If you're phoning Rathlin Island from within Northern Ireland, you only have to dial the eight-digit number supplied in this chapter. To call from the Republic of Ireland, use the special area code of ☎ 048, followed immediately by the eight-digit number.

ATLANTIC ISLANDS

somewhat overgrown path to the top of a flight of concrete steps with a metal handrail. This old access path leads down to a pier in the cove below – it was via this route that the construction materials for the West Lighthouse were brought to the headland. The path winds steeply and impressively beneath the cliff face, although vertigo sufferers will not appreciate the views. Follow it for as long as you want before retracing your steps back to the red gate.

Walk west across a field to a wooden gate, from where the cliff-line can be followed to the lighthouse. Hexagonal basalt columns and wildflowers line the coast, and care should be taken along the cliff edge. The seabirds circling below become more numerous as you progress, and free-standing sea stacks break up the swells beyond the foot of the cliffs. The way is undulating and stiles provide crossing points over a couple of fences as you near the lighthouse.

To access **West Lighthouse** and the RSPB viewing platform, follow the obvious concrete path down through a series of gates. It's hard not to be impressed by the natural spectacle spread out along the adjacent cliffs; the main seabird colony supports over 90,000 guillemots as well as thousands of fulmars, kittiwakes, razorbills and puffins. Once you've visited the lighthouse you can continue northeast along the cliff-tops, past Derginan Point and down past a small waterfall to the fringe of Kinramer Wood. Continue along the cliffs to a fence on the eastern boundary of **Kinramer Wood**, where there are good views across

Loughnanskan and Lack Point. Follow the fence south to reach the lighthouse road almost a kilometre east of the reserve boundary. Turn left along the road and retrace your steps to the harbour (one hour from the junction with the lighthouse road).

TORY ISLAND

Duration 3½–4 hours
Distance 11km
Ascent 100m
Difficulty easy
Start/Finish West Town ferry pier
Nearest Town Tory Island (p163)
Transport boat
Summary A 10th-century round tower, puffin colonies and a wonderfully rugged coastline are among the highlights of this remote island walk.

Tory Island (*Oileán Thóriagh*) is a fascinating place to visit, with some great, easy walking along its storm-battered coastline. It lies 12km off the northwestern tip of County Donegal and, because ferry services can be affected by winds from every direction, it is often difficult to get to (and leave!). Its isolation and its size – Tory is only 5km long and rarely more than 1km wide – contribute to a palpable feeling of remoteness. Standing on the highest point of Dún Balair on a stormy day is quite an experience, especially as you look out across the cliffs of the north coast with spray blowing across the entire island.

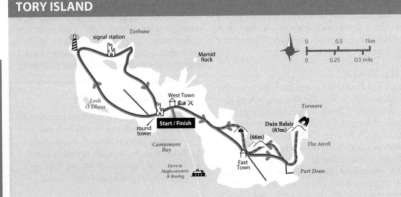

THE LONG BATTLE FOR ISLAND SURVIVAL

With nothing to shield it from savage Atlantic squalls, it's a tribute to the hardiness of Tory Islanders that the island has been inhabited for over 4500 years. Today the earliest visible signs of habitation are the round tower and Tau Cross, both legacies of the monastery founded here in the 7th century by St Columba. The 16m-high round tower is one of the most prominent buildings on the island, while the Tau Cross is one of only two T-shaped cruciforms in Ireland.

Throughout the centuries, physical isolation has shaped both the island's landscape and its culture. Much of Tory's desolate appearance stems from the fact that islanders have long since stripped every morsel of peat from the island to use as fuel. Separation from the mainland has also engendered a resourcefulness and resilience in the islanders that has led to peculiar but necessary customs. For example, it was common until a few decades ago for couples to continue to live in their respective family homes after marriage, such was the shortage of land. However isolation also had its blessings – the potato blight that devastated crops throughout Ireland during the Great Famine never reached Tory.

In 1974, after an eight-week storm that lashed the island mercilessly, the government made plans to evacuate Tory permanently. Thankfully this did not happen, due in part to the efforts of Father Diarmuid Ó Peícín, who spearheaded an international campaign to raise funds, create a proper ferry service, establish an electrical supply and more. Since then emigration and the demise of the fishing industry have brought their own share of problems, but the community still doggedly perseveres.

This route has two distinct loops that can be readily split into two short walks. The first loop (5km) explores the low-lying western half of the island and visits the lighthouse. The second loop (6km), takes in Dún Balair and the magnificent cliffs at Tory's eastern tip. The walk is feasible as a day trip depending on the ferry schedule, but an overnight visit adds to the experience. The island also has a National Looped Walk; the western part largely mimics the route described in this book, while the eastern section hardly leaves the road and would have you miss the best views over the cliffs.

Early summer is the best time to visit if you are interested in birds: over 100 species of seabird inhabit the island, and around 1400 puffins breed on the northern cliffs. Tory is also a stronghold of the endangered corncrake, whose distinctive cry (similar to the raspy call of a cricket) can often be heard in early summer.

For more practical and background information about Tory, see www.oileanthorai.com.

PLANNING
Maps
Carry OSI 1:50,000 map No 1. Note that many of the small tracks on the western side of the island are not shown on this map.

GETTING TO/FROM THE WALK
Ferry services to Tory Island are operated by **Donegal Coastal Cruises** (*Turasmara Teo*; ☎ 074-953 1340; adult/child return €26/15) from both Magheraroarty (35 minutes) and Bunbeg (1½ hours). Sailing times vary according to weather and tides. Bring waterproofs for the trip and check the forecast before travelling.

Magheraroarty (*Machaire Ui Rebhartaigh*) is reached by turning off the N56 at the western end of Gortahork near Falcarragh; the road is signposted 'Coastal Route/Bloody Foreland'.

From Bunbeg (part of the assembly of villages known as Gweedore, or *Gaoth Dobhair*), **Feda O'Donnell** (☎ 074-954 8114; www.fedaodonnell.com) runs a bus service twice daily (three on Fri-Sun) to Letterkenny (€7, 1½ hours), Donegal (€10, 1¾ hours), Sligo (€12, 3¼ hours) and Galway (€20, 5½ hours). **John McGinley** (☎ 074-913 5201; www.johnmcginley.com) buses also stop in Bunbeg on their way to Letterkenny (€7, 1½ hours) and Dublin (€16, 5¼ hours) between two and four times daily.

THE WALK
From the pier walk up past the Tau Cross onto the main road running through West Town. Turn left, walk past the **round**

tower, and at the edge of the town turn left at a fork, following a narrow road out past Loch Ó Dheas to the **lighthouse**. A high wall encloses the lighthouse but you can walk around this to reach the most westerly point on Tory. A small stone enclosure acts as a graveyard for eight bodies recovered from *HMS Wasp*, which sank close to Tory in 1884. The navy vessel was on its way to Tory to collect overdue rents; since then, no rents have been paid on the island.

Continue along a track to the ruins of a Lloyds signal station and turn left, following another track up to a small house, which the acclaimed landscape and portrait artist Derek Hill used on his visits to Tory. Follow a faint footpath along the eastern shore of the small peninsula to return to the main track. Turn left along this and follow it back down into West Town (1½ hours from the start).

Walk through the town and head east across a gentle rise to reach East Town. Turn left at a junction and follow the road out to Port Doon. Where the main road swings right, continue straight ahead, following the minor road to where it ends on a thin neck of grassy land, giving access to the wonderful cliff-ringed eastern promontory. Walk out across the open ground, climbing steadily past stone cairns to **Dún Balair** (one to 1¼ hours from West Town). At 83m, this is the modest highpoint of the island, named after the pre-Celtic mythical god Balor, the one-eyed chief of the Fomorians.

Although a promontory fort once graced this spot, little evidence is visible today. Instead, panoramic views predominate. To the south the mountainous north coast of County Donegal is spread out along the horizon, with the summits of Muckish, the Aghlas and Errigal prominent. To the east, a 500m-long, knife-edged fin of rock, some 50m high, thrusts out into the ocean. A couple of small stone cairns on the furthest point prove that some brave souls have ventured that far. The eye is also led west across the rest of the island by the sweep of dizzying granite cliffs that protect Tory's northern shores.

Descend back to the road and then trace the cliffs west along the north coast, passing some amazingly jagged sea stacks, to a large hole set back from the cliffs. This is actually a collapsed cave, and it is possible to scramble down into the grassy depression to get a better look at the natural tunnel that still connects it to a cliff-ringed inlet. Now descend back onto the road, turn right and continue back into West Town.

ARRANMORE ISLAND

Duration 5–5½ hours
Distance 14.5km
Ascent 320m
Difficulty moderate
Start/Finish Leabgarrow ferry pier
Nearest Town Arranmore Island (p161)
Transport boat

Summary An outstandingly scenic circuit on one of Donegal's more accessible islands, featuring precipitous cliffs, rocky islets and sea caves.

Measuring just 9km by 5km, Arranmore Island (*Árainn Mhór*) has been inhabited since the early Iron Age (800 BC). Its proximity to the mainland makes it relatively easy to maintain contact with the modern world, and there are more visitor facilities than on nearby Tory. Irish is still the main language spoken however, and the wild and rugged northwestern part of the island still exudes a palpable sense of isolation.

The walk described here is an anticlockwise circuit that takes in both the dramatic cliff faces and spectacular coastal scenery of the island's northwestern corner, and the highest point (227m) near Cluidaniller (226m), in the boggy centre. The walk starts and finishes on narrow roads, although you are unlikely to be bothered by much traffic. Elsewhere much of the ground covered is heavily grazed grassland, which makes for generally easy walking.

The route begins by following part of the Arranmore Way (*Slí Árainn Mhór*), a way-marked 14km route that also starts and finishes at the ferry pier. However, the signed route concentrates largely on the island's interior bog tracks and heads no further west than Lough Shore, which means it misses out on the spectacular coastline that provides the undisputed scenic highlight of the island. For more information on the Arranmore Way, as well as a host of practical and background information on the island, see www.arranmoreco-op.com.

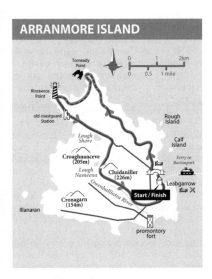

PLANNING

Maps

Use OSI 1:50,000 map No 1 for this walk. The Arranmore Way is not marked, nor is the lighthouse.

GETTING TO/FROM THE WALK

Ferry services to Arranmore operate from Burtonport on the mainland. **Arranmore Ferry** (☎ 074-952 0532; www.arainnmhor .com/ferry) makes regular crossings of the 1.5km stretch of water (passenger/car and driver €15/30 return; 20 minutes; seven or eight daily Jul & Aug, five Mon-Sat and three Sun Sep-Jun).

The same route is also covered by **Arranmore Fast Ferry** (☎ 087 317 1810) with a fast, passenger-only ferry (€15 return; two to three daily; five minutes) and a car ferry service (passenger/car and driver €15/30 return; 20 minutes).

Lough Swilly (☎ 074-912 2863) buses from Dungloe (€1.90, 15 minutes) stop in Burtonport once daily en route to Falcarragh, Dunfanaghy, Letterkenny and Derry.

THE WALK

From the ferry pier, follow the road around in front of Bonner's B&B and bear right over a bridge. Turn left onto the road that crosses the island to the lighthouse. Walk uphill for about 400m, passing Glen Hotel, and take the first road on the right. Turn

left after 1km and, 500m later, take a right, following waymarkers for the Arranmore Way. Turn left onto a vehicle track of yellow stone and follow it gently uphill for 1km, then leave the Arranmore Way opposite a marker post and turn right onto a smaller bog track.

The track turns into a peaty path, then dwindles away completely as you cross open slopes of heather and tussock grass, heading towards a line of fence posts that runs along the top of the ridge ahead. The fence marks the edge of the cliffs at **Torneady Point** (two hours from the start), where a sudden, dizzying view is revealed across the cliffs of the north coast. The cliffs reach 150m in height and sweep around in a kilometre-long horseshoe towards **Rinrawros Point**. The bay is littered with the debris of millions of years of erosion – huge, sheer-sided islands, stacks and pinnacles still defying the pounding swells.

Follow the cliffs first southwest and then west, descending across short grass to the **lighthouse** and keepers' residences at Rinrawros Point. Built at the end of the 19th century, this was the first lighthouse in County Donegal, and its beam is the most powerful of any lighthouse in Ireland.

Now walk southeast along the obvious road, passing an old coastguard station (used during World War I and later burnt by the IRA during the civil war). Climb steadily towards the island's interior; Lough Shore, which you pass on the right 30 to 45 minutes from the lighthouse, is famous for its stock of rainbow trout. Turn right onto a track shortly before a concrete filtering plant, following waymarks for the Arranmore Way for a short distance. Where the signed route turns right, continue ahead. Follow the track up onto the island's boggy centre, where a short detour (a few minutes return) to the southeast allows you to take in the top of **Cluidaniller** (226m). The views from here are superb, particularly of the Donegal mountains to the east.

The track then swings around to the southeast. At this point you can detour southwest to the island's unnamed high-point at 227m, 10 to 15 minutes return, where there are good views of Slievetooey to the southwest. The track now descends steadily to reach a paved road along the **Owenballintra River**. Follow the road down to its junction with the island's main road. Turn left to arrive at Leabgarrow and the ferry pier in 20 to 25 minutes.

CLARE ISLAND

Duration 5–5½ hours
Distance 15km
Ascent 600m
Difficulty moderate
Start/Finish Fawnglass Island ferry pier
Nearest Town Clare Island (p162)
Transport boat
Summary This is an impressive walk along high sea cliffs, the stiff climb to Knockmore rewarded by great views of the mainland coast.

Situated at the mouth of Clew Bay, Clare Island is the most mountainous of the Atlantic Islands. It boasts some tremendous walking packed into 10 sq km of rugged, cliff-fringed terrain. Any number of short, easy walks are possible along the roads and tracks of the south – indeed there are two way-marked National Loop Walks, 3km and 8km long respectively, that explore the southeastern corner. However to get the best from Clare Island you really need to visit the cliffs on its northwestern shore. The climb to the summit of Knockmore (462m) rewards walkers with panoramic views and is one of the most memorable outings on all Ireland's islands, though the

amount of ascent means it is also one of the toughest walks in this chapter.

Visitors to Clare Island stand on well-trodden soil; there is ample archaeological evidence to indicate that the island was inhabited by Neolithic communities from around 3000 BC. However the island's most infamous resident was Grace O'Malley (1530–1603), whose much-modified castle still overlooks the harbour. This 'pirate queen' controlled much of Connacht and was a thorn in the side of the English and their allies as she plundered their ships in Clew Bay.

Today the entire island has been designated a Special Area of Conservation. When the celebrated Irish naturalist Robert Lloyd Praeger (1865–1953) organised the world's first area-specific biological survey on the island between 1909 and 1911, he uncovered 585 species that were new to Ireland, 55 that were new to the British Isles and 11 that were new to science.

Walkers looking for an easier variation of the walk described can follow the route to the lighthouse, then proceed a couple of kilometres along the cliffs before heading back inland towards Fawnglass along any one of several tracks. Such circuits are around 11km long and avoid the steepest part of the climb – allow four to 4½ hours.

Also check www.clareisland.info for more information on the island. It's a basic, but nonetheless, very useful and informative site.

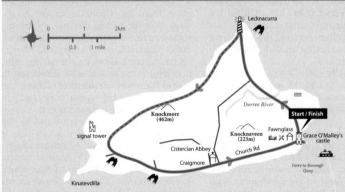

CLARE ISLAND

PLANNING
Maps
Use OSI 1:50,000 map No 30.

GETTING TO/FROM THE WALK
Ferries depart the mainland at Roonagh Quay, around 28km west of Westport via Louisburgh. **Clare Island Ferries** (☎ 098-28288, 087 241 4653; www.clareislandferry .com) and **O'Malley's Ferries** (☎ 098-25045, 086 600 0204; www.omalleyferries .com) both make the 20-minute trip (adult/child return €15/8). There are around 10 sailings daily in July and August, and around two daily the rest of the year.

There is no public transport to Roonagh Quay.

THE WALK
From the pier, turn right (north) and follow a small road around the back of the beach. Continue uphill past the community centre, following signs for the lighthouse. The road winds inland and climbs across a modest spur, before descending gently towards the coast. At a junction, turn right and climb steadily north to reach the **lighthouse**, perched impressively on the cliff edge, one to 1½ hours from the pier.

Now begin to follow the cliff edge southwest, staying on the landward side of a fence. Several steep climbs and descents follow, but the close-cropped turf is generally firm underfoot and the tremendous views of Knockmore and the cliffs are worth the effort. The route swings around to the west as you progress onto the eastern ridge of **Knockmore**, climbing unrelentingly to the summit trig point (1½ to two hours from the lighthouse). Views encompass numerous islands to the south including Inishturk and Inishbofin, the mountains of Connemara and County Mayo, Croagh Patrick and Achill Island. The cliffs beneath your feet also provide nesting sites for numerous birds – most prominently fulmars, but also choughs, an increasingly rare bird that looks like a small raven with a red beak.

Continue along the broad summit ridge for 500m, passing a large stone cairn. Descend steeply to the southwest, following a shoulder towards the prominent track and bungalows below. Out to the west you can see the ruins of a **Napoleonic signal tower**. Once on the road, turn left and begin the

walk back to Fawnglass. The 5.5km of paved road will take 1½ to two hours, depending on your pace, and is enlivened by good views of the County Mayo coastline and a chance to visit the **Cistercian Abbey** (c 1460). The abbey contains some unusual wall paintings of medieval origin, and a canopy tomb inscribed with the words 'Invincible on land and sea', believed to be the burial place of Grace O'Malley.

INISHTURK

Duration 3½–4½ hours
Distance 10km
Ascent 290m
Difficulty moderate
Start/Finish Ferry pier
Nearest Town Inishturk (p163)
Transport boat
Summary This charming island combines rugged coastal scenery and a modest mountain summit with a warm welcome.

Situated 12km off the shore of County Mayo, Inishturk vies with Tory Island for the title of most remote inhabited island in Ireland. Yet Inishturk never feels like a lonely outpost. Instead it finds the perfect balance between rugged scenery and welcoming hospitality, with friendly inhabitants, sandy coves and a picturesque harbour thrown in for good measure.

The island has two way-marked National Loop Walks, 5km and 8km long. The route described here starts and finishes by following the waymarks, but diverts off to visit the island's best natural assets – 191m-high Mountain Common and the soaring sea cliffs at the western side of the island, both of which are by-passed by the marked routes. The island's 60% of commonage means walkers can wander freely over much of the open land, while short-cropped grass and outcrops of rock offer a firm surface that is perfect for walking. The logistics of a visit are simple too. During the summer months frequent ferry services allow the circumnavigation of the island to fit into a single day, though there are enough visitor facilities for a comfortable overnight stay and it's tempting to linger longer to soak up that special island atmosphere.

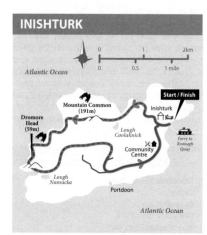

The only practical consideration for completing the walk is that much of the route passes along exposed cliff-tops, and care is required near the edge. Avoid walking in poor visibility and be extra vigilant in windy conditions.

See www.inishturkisland.com for more practical and background information about the island.

PLANNING
Maps
The OSNI 1:50,000 map No 37 covers the island itself, though Roonagh Quay lies on OSI 1:50,000 sheet 30. If you cross with Inishturk Ferries you'll also receive a free map of the island. This shows the terrain in much more detail than the OS map and has most of the walking route marked.

GETTING TO/FROM THE WALK
Ferries to Inishturk leave from Roonagh Quay, around 28km west of Westport via Lousiburgh. **Inishturk Ferries** (☎ 098-45541, 086 202 9670) and **Clare Island Ferries** (☎ 098-28288) both run between Roonagh Quay and Inishturk (adult/child return €25/12.50, 45 minutes). Both companies have at least two sailings daily during July and August, with more limited daily services during May, June and September. Contact the operators for winter schedules.

There is no public transport to Roonagh Quay.

THE WALK
From the ferry pier, walk around the harbour and head northwest along the island's only real road. After roughly 300m, turn right onto another lane that climbs towards the rock-studded hills, following the purple and green arrows of the loop walks. After 500m the lane ends at a metal gate; pass through this and you'll see a rough stone track continuing across the commonage ahead.

The route will return to the track shortly, but for now it's worth making a quick detour north to the coast. Turn right and follow a wall north to a sheer coastal inlet marked as Ooghdoul on the island map. The sound and smell of seabirds heralds your arrival at the 80m-high chasm, and during the summer you should be able to spot nesting fulmars and their chicks on the cliffs below.

Turn left and follow the coastline southwest, with fantastic views across the bay to

INISHTURK PAST & PRESENT
Inishturk, which translates from the Irish *Inis Toirc* as 'the island of the wild boar', attracted its first human inhabitants around 4000 BC. The majority of the island's Neolithic remains lie clustered around the little natural harbour of Portdoon on the south coast. Some 5000 years later this secluded inlet re-emerged as the centre of island activity, when (according to legend) a band of Danish pirates constructed the promontory fort marked on the OS map. This base was chosen because the rocks surrounding the creek shielded their boats from passing vessels, providing the perfect hiding place from which to launch their raids.

The present phase of inhabitation was under way by 1700. The famine years proved hard for the islanders however, and many families chose to emigrate during the 19th and 20th centuries. From a total of 567 inhabitants in 1821, the population had dwindled to just 91 by 1997. Small-scale farming and fishing for lobsters and crabs are the two main industries that allow today's population to survive.

Mountain Common. This summit is your next goal, but the easiest way to reach it is to swing back south to rejoin the track. Turn right onto this and climb gently to **Lough Coolaknick** – the island's only reliable source of fresh water. Just past the lough, leave the track again and turn right, beginning the ascent northwest to **Mountain Common** (191m). A steady climb brings you to the old Napoleonic signal tower and trig point at the summit (1½ hours from the start). The view is predictably impressive in all directions, with Achill Island, Clare Island and the mountains of Mayo arranged from north to south on the horizon.

Now head west over hummocky ground to the coast. Take care as you near the edge because the cliffs here are the highest on the island, dropping 140m directly to the sea. Several rock stacks decorate the base of the precipice, and the whole effect is quite exhilarating. Turn left at the cliffs and begin to trace the coastline south. You'll pass above several more chasms and viewpoints before the cliffs begin to lose height. Descend across two pretty streams then climb out to the final promontory of Dromore Head, where there's a great view south to the island of Inishbofin.

At Dromore Head, turn inland and follow an inlet east past Lough Namucka. Continue heading east until you meet a stone wall, then turn left and follow the wall north. After roughly 600m the wall swings east; turn right and continue to follow it, now back on the way-marked loop walk. After 1.5km you join a gravel road beside the island's Gaelic football pitch. Turn right and follow the lane to a junction with the coast road after 1km. Turn left here and follow the tarmac all the way around the island's southeast corner to return to the ferry pier approximately 2.5km later.

If you have time to spare, it's well worth making a couple of stops near the top of the hill before the final descent to the pier. On the right a metal gate signed for 'Tránaun' gives access to a sloping field, at the bottom of which you'll find a delightful sandy cove, perfect for cooling off on a hot day. Just 20m beyond the gate is the **Community Centre**, where refreshments are served in the bar.

THE ARAN ISLANDS

The three Aran Islands all offer easy walks through fascinating landscapes clad with limestone pavement and patterned with mosaics of gravity-defying stone walls. In this section we offer full descriptions of routes around Inishmore and Inisheer, while Inishmaan is featured on p161. On all three islands, some of the distance you will cover will be along quiet roads, but there are still considerable stretches of green lanes or boreens that wind between the fields. On Inisheer, in particular, you can also wander along the wild rocky shores, free from the confines of roads or tracks. Many of the tiny, walled fields and much of the limestone pavement is richly endowed with wildflowers during spring and early summer. On all three islands there are numerous archaeological features including early Christian chapels and huge, pre-Christian forts (see the boxed text Dúns of the Aran Islands, p156).

ENVIRONMENT
The geological make-up of the Aran Islands is almost identical to that of the Burren – see the boxed text Karst Wonders of the Burren, p197.

The sandy northern coasts of the Aran Islands are set apart from the Burren because of the presence of machair, a low-profile, slender strip of sand. This consists mainly of glacial debris originally blown ashore from a shallow, offshore platform after the last ice age, mixed with varying quantities of crushed shells. In many places this sandy landscape is covered with a hardy community of sedges, grasses and wildflowers. In the past it was used for grazing and growing crops. Machair, common on the west coast of Scotland's Western Isles, reaches its southern limit on the Aran Islands.

PLANNING
The website www.aranislands.ie provides accommodation listings and background information for each of the three islands.

Maps & Books
The OSI 1:25,000 map *Oileáin Árann* covers the islands and marks archaeological

ATLANTIC ISLANDS

and historic features; the islands are also featured on OSI 1:50,000 map No 51. Tim Robinson also produces a 1:28,160 *Oileáin Árann* map, which indicates a wealth of archaeological and historic features, and has a companion booklet explaining marked features in lots of detail.

The Burren and the Aran Islands by Tony Kirby details 15 walking routes, four of which are on the Aran Islands. The book was first published in 2009 so information is up to date.

ACCESS TOWNS

See Galway (p203) and Doolin (p202).

GETTING THERE & AROUND
Air

It is possible to fly to each of the Aran Islands. The mainland departure point is Connemara Regional Airport at Minna, near Inverin (I*ndreabhán*), about 35km west of Galway. **Aer Arann Islands** (☎ 091-593 034; www.aer arannislands.ie) offers return flights to any of the islands several times daily (adult/child €45/25, 10 minutes); groups of four or more should ask about group rates. A bus to the airport from outside Galway's Kinlay House Hostel (see p204) costs €3 each way.

Boat

Ferries to the Aran Islands leave from both Rossaveal, at the western end of Galway Bay, and from Doolin (see p202), in County Clare.

Companies operating from Rossaveal include **Island Ferries** (☎ 091-568 903, 572 273; www.aranislandferries.com; 4 Forster St, Galway; adult/child €25/13; year-round), which serves all three islands and also links Inishmaan and Inisheer. **Aran Direct** (☎ 091-566 535; www.arandirect.com; return adult/child €25/15) also serves Inishmore from April to late September. Both companies have at least one sailing daily, and several boats a day during July and August. The crossing can take up to one hour.

In Galway (see p203), ferry ticket agents can be found at the tourist office, and in offices on and around Eyre Square. Buses from Galway to Rossaveal connect with each sailing (€6 return); ask for details when you book.

From Doolin, **Doolin Ferries** (☎ 065-707 4455, 707 4466; www.doolinferries.com;

Doolin Pier) has frequent sailings to Inisheer (€15 return, 25 minutes, two to five daily) and Inishmore (€20 return, 75 minutes, twice daily), with a stop at Inisheer on the return leg. Services run from Easter to October.

Inter-island services run in high season only; from October to Easter connections require a trip back to Rossaveal.

INISHMORE

Duration	6–6½ hours
Distance	22km
Ascent	230m
Difficulty	moderate
Start/Finish	Kilronan ferry pier
Nearest Town	Inishmore (p162)
Transport	boat, plane

Summary This circuit follows green lanes and quiet roads past two prehistoric forts, dramatic cliffs, beaches and plenty of wildflowers.

At 14.5km long and up to 4km wide, Inishmore (*Inis Mór*) is the largest of the three Aran Islands, and by far the most developed and populous. As you contend with the tour operators hustling for business, you begin to appreciate why many locals are wondering whether perhaps mass tourism is not a mixed blessing. Nevertheless, it is possible to get away from it all on the quiet roads and lanes. Inishmore has most of the finest archaeological sites, the highest coastal cliffs and the greatest number of sandy beaches of the three islands, and is best explored by a combination of walking and cycling.

The way-marked Inis Mór Way wanders all over the island, making much use of roads, as well as boreens. It is marked fairly consistently with yellow arrows and 'walking person' symbols discreetly painted on stones. The walk described here is based on part of the way. Only about 10km of this route follows public roads; a further 8km follows green roads that are largely surfaced with coarse gravel. The rest of the distance is along grass and gravel paths, and across open limestone pavement. If the hard surfaces sometimes make for less than ideal walking conditions, there are compensations: fine, wide-ranging views, opportunities for exploring fascinating

INISHMORE

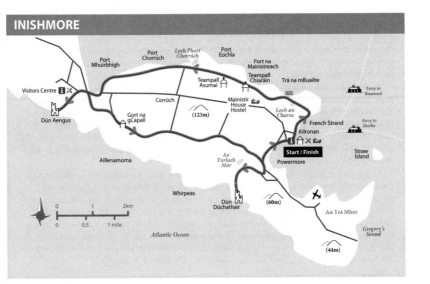

limestone pavement, and many archaeological and historic features.

Although the summer schedule of the Rossaveal ferries makes it possible for fast walkers to complete the described walk on a day trip, an overnight stay is recommended to make the most of your visit. You could then consider hiring a bike to explore more of the many green lanes, especially those leading to the cliffs in the northwest.

PLANNING
Maps & Books
Use either the OSI 1:25,000 map *Oileáin Árann*, or the OSI 1:50,000 map No 51. The leaflet *Inis Mór Way* also has a handy map and descriptive notes, and is available locally.

GETTING TO/FROM THE WALK
For details of ferry services to Inishmore, see Getting There & Around for The Aran Islands (p154).

The airstrip is 2km southeast of Kilronan; minibuses meet each flight and a ride to Kilronan costs €5 return.

THE WALK
From the pier, head northeast along a sealed road. After almost 1km, turn left along a green lane that skirts **Loch an Charra**. Take the second track on the right and follow

it down to the sands of Trá na mBuailte. At the western end of the beach, leave the shore along a green lane, follow this up to a road and turn right.

Opposite the next shingle-fringed bay, Port na Mainistreach (Port of the Monastery), a signed path leads to **Teampall Chiaráin** – the site of the first church on the island. Continue northwest along the road; after another 400m you come to the signed path to the tiny Teampall Asurnaí, perched on a ledge against a low cliff and dedicated to a female saint, Soarney.

Continue past Port Chorrúch for about 1km, passing the remains of a seaweed processing factory that once produced fertiliser and iodine, and leave the road along a green lane, way-marked with a 'walking person' symbol. The lane rises gently southwards; after about 250m go through a gap in the wall on your right and follow a very pleasant, grassy path along the top of an escarpment. This path develops into a wider lane and leads on to a road; turn left and continue around the sands of Port Mhuirbhigh.

Follow the road past waiting horses and carts to the small **Dún Aengus Visitor Centre** (☎ 099-61008; www.heritageire land.ie; adult/child €3/1; open daily), which houses informative displays and controls access to the gravel path leading to **Dún**

DÚNS OF THE ARAN ISLANDS

The seven dúns on the Aran Islands are among the most impressive archaeological sites in Ireland. These forts, dominating the skyline or perched unnervingly on cliff edges, are thought to date from about 200 BC.

The typically massive walls are in fact double walls filled with rubble. They can reach over 6m high, and taper from a base 6m thick to a top of 2m. Within the walls, a tight cluster of stone huts would have provided shelter for people and probably stock. The best examples of these, having been restored, are Dún Dúchathair on Inishmore and Dún Chonchúir on Inishmaan. The most convincing explanation of the origins of the forts is that they were built by powerful, well-to-do farming people to demonstrate their wealth and influence, to house cattle and to provide shelter from occasional raiders.

Excavations at Dún Aengus (or Aonghasa) on Inishmore have uncovered the remains of huts, the bones of a tiny child and some moulds used to cast artefacts in bronze, suggesting to archaeologists that the land was already occupied between 500 and 800 BC, several centuries before the fort was built. The fort is perched on the rim of a 200m-high cliff on the island's southern coast, and encloses an area of nearly six hectares. The fort proper is protected on the landward side by an intimidating jumble of sharp-edged stones, up to 1.8m high, that stand on end. It has four, roughly crescent-shaped walls, three of them with each end on the cliff edge; the outer wall is 400m long and was probably built with defence in mind.

Aengus (three hours from the pier; see the boxed text Dúns of the Aran Islands). Beside the visitor centre is **An Sunda Caoch coffee shop**. The best angle from which to appreciate the fort is the northwest, where slightly higher ground also offers fine views of the vertical cliffs on this side of the island.

Back on the road, return to the junction opposite Port Mhuirbhigh and head south along a way-marked green lane. This passes a clump of limestone bluffs and meets a sealed road – turn right. Follow the road through the small village of Gort na gCapall and climb steeply, with good views of the surrounding mosaic of walled fields opening up. The road becomes a track once you've gained the highest ground, where heather-studded grassland replaces the limestone pavement. After about 1km – ignore all cross tracks unless you decide to explore the coastline – the track starts its steep descent and the grass gives way to limestone and hazel scrub. Continue to the road by the shore and head right for 300m before turning right again along a narrow road signed to Dún Dúchathair.

Climb steeply to a T-junction and follow a sign to the dún; the narrow road soon yields to coarse gravel. The track passes above the bright green vegetation of An Turlach Mór, a turlough, and climbs onto limestone pavement. Leave the track where a low wall crosses it and head southeast, following a dún sign across the pavement. Breaks in the low stone walls and strips of grass between the clints make for fairly easy walking to the fort, perched on the edge of the cliff. Unburdened by official signs and in a more remote setting, **Dún Dúchathair** is more atmospheric than the larger, better known Dún Aengus.

Return to the main road, from where it's little more than 1km back to the start at Kilronan.

INISHEER

Duration 4½–5 hours
Distance 12km
Ascent 100m
Difficulty moderate
Start/Finish Ferry pier
Nearest Town Inisheer (p162)
Transport boat, plane
Summary A varied circuit of a fascinating storm-swept island, following quiet lanes and rock platforms beside the Atlantic Ocean.

Although Inisheer (*Inis Oírr*) lacks the great prehistoric forts of the other two Aran Islands, it encapsulates perfectly the

INISHEER

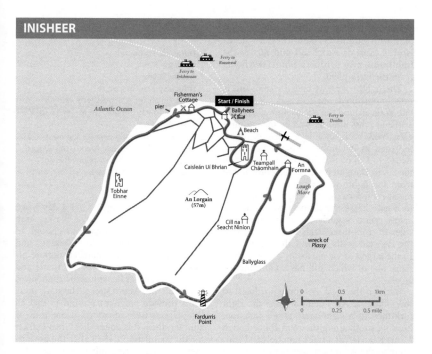

windswept limestone landscape, the web of stone-walled fields and the wealth of wildflowers in a beguiling, on-the-edge-of-the-world experience. There is also a host of other sites with historic and prehistoric significance, several of which can be visited during the walk. This is the smallest of the three Aran Islands, and can be explored during the summer on a day trip from Doolin.

The route described here virtually circumnavigates the island and takes you through the settled northern fringe, past the stone-walled fields in the centre and south, and around the wild and rocky south coast. For all but 2km along the southern shore, the walk follows quiet lanes. You'll come across yellow waymarks on some sections of the walk. These mark the route of the 10.5km Inis Oírr Way, which confines itself to the northern two-thirds of the island.

PLANNING
Maps
Use either the OSI 1:25,000 map *Oileáin Árann*, or the OSI 1:50,000 map No 51.

GETTING TO/FROM THE WALK
For details of ferry services to Inisheer, see Getting There & Around for The Aran Islands (p154).

THE WALK
From the ferry pier, walk west along the narrow road parallel to the shore and continue past **Fisherman's Cottage** restaurant. Ignore the waymarker pointing left at the next junction and go on to the small **fishing pier** at the northwest corner of the island. Continue along the road, now with a gravel surface, past another acute-angled junction on the left (where the waymarkers reappear). The shingle shore now lies on one side and a dense mosaic of fields, enclosed by remarkably intact stone walls, on the other.

About 1km from the acute junction, turn left with the painted sign, and about 100m along the paved lane is **Tobhar Eínne**, an old holy well situated within a walled enclosure.

Return to the coast road and continue southwest as it becomes a rough track. After about 600m, head roughly south across the limestone pavement and strips of grass to the shore. Follow the gently sloping rock platform around the southwestern headland (Ceann na Faochnaí) and east to the **lighthouse** near Fardurris Point (two hours from the ferry pier).

The lighthouse was built in 1857 and is now uninhabited, but access is not permitted. Walk around the enclosing wall and use a stile to cross another wall by the entrance gate. Now back on a level surface, follow the road as it climbs gradually northeast. Access to **Cill na Seacht Ninfon** (Church of the Seven Daughters) is from a point 1.5km from the lighthouse, almost opposite two metal-roofed sheds on the right; a pillar next to a gate bears the chapel's name and an arrow points vaguely in its direction. Use stiles to cross three fields to a rusty gate in the ivy-clad walls around the chapel site. In the largest stone enclosure are five grave slabs, one of which still has a faint, incised cross.

Back on the road, continue northeast to the village of **An Formna**. Take the right fork then turn right again at a T-junction, heading south along the road above Lough More. Keep left at a track junction and continue to the Atlantic shore, with the wreck of the *Plassy* just ahead (one hour from the lighthouse). This coastal freighter and one-time armed trawler was driven onto the rocks in March 1960. Miraculously, local lifeboat crews, helped by about 60 islanders, brought all 11 crew members safely ashore (Tigh Ned's pub, near the harbour, has a collection of photographs and documents detailing the rescue).

Follow the track north, which becomes a sealed road at the northern end of Lough More. Continue to follow the road along the island's north shore, past the airstrip where you can diverge, if you wish, to the sandy hummock that shelters the ancient **Teampall Chaomháin** (Church of St Keevaun). The small, 10th-century church is dedicated to the island's patron saint, and is remarkably intact considering it was buried under sand until its rediscovery in the 19th century.

A little further along the road, turn left to reach the 15th-century **Caisleán Uí Bhrian** (O'Brien's Castle), the most prominent structure on the island. From here follow the narrow road northwest, turn right at a T-junction and make your way through the maze of lanes back to the pier.

GREAT BLASKET ISLAND

Duration 3½ hours
Distance 8km
Ascent 300m
Difficulty easy–moderate
Start/Finish Great Blasket ferry landing
Nearest Towns Dunquin (p136) Dingle (p136)
Transport boat
Summary Exploring perhaps the most evocative of the Atlantic Islands, this rugged little walk features an abandoned village and excellent coastal views.

If you're lucky enough to get a day when the boats are running to Great Blasket, grab it. The island is mountainous enough to provide some exhilarating walking, and exudes a wonderfully natural, remote atmosphere; there are no paved roads and the only buildings lie within the abandoned village on the eastern shore. The stark stone ruins provide poignant reminders that all the Blaskets were inhabited at one time or another; the last islanders left Great Blasket for the mainland in 1953 after the government and remaining inhabitants agreed it was no longer feasible to live in such remote and challenging conditions.

Situated 5km out into the Atlantic, the Blasket Islands (*Na Blascaodaí*) are the most westerly islands in Europe, severed from the mountainous spine of the Dingle Peninsula by oceanic forces. At 6km by 1.2km, Great Blasket (*An Blascaod Mór*) is the largest and most visited of the six islands in the group. Yet it's impossible to forget you're on a tiny outpost, surrounded by, and at the mercy of, the elements. Despite the harsh environment some 208 species of plant have been identified on the island, and most visitors will be rewarded with sightings of seabirds, rabbits and seals.

Good weather is a prerequisite for the walk, both because boats don't run in adverse conditions and because the island has limited shelter (you'll be waiting in the open for the return boat). For those catching the ferry from Dunquin, it's also worth combining the trip with a visit to **The Blasket Centre** (*Ionad an Bhlascaoid Mhóir*; ☎ 066-915 6444; www.heritageireland.ie; adult/child €4/2; open daily mid-Mar–Oct), a wonderful interpretive centre located just a short distance from the pier in Dunquin.

HISTORY

Great Blasket Island has been inhabited since the Iron Age – Doon promontory fort (of which little is now visible) is thought to date to around 800 BC. When parish records began in 1821, the island had 128 inhabitants. Each family had a potato garden and kept sheep on the hills, and food was supplemented by wild rabbits, seabirds, seals, fish and shellfish. Thanks to this varied diet, the islanders suffered less than people on the mainland during the Great Famine.

A school was constructed in the early 20th century and a post office with a telephone was built in the 1930s. Unfortunately it was probably this progress into the modern world that ended the viability of island life. With a dwindling population, the school became redundant. Hospitals, priests and markets for produce were all a short but dangerous boat journey away. In 1953, the last remaining families were rehoused on the mainland.

GREAT BLASKET ISLAND

Given the number of visitors that now arrive on the island during the summer, it is easy to wonder whether tourism could have offered a lifeline for a viable island existence had the community just managed to hold on for another generation. It's a question that will never be answered, however, and today it's the inhabitants of Dunquin and Dingle who benefit from activities on Great Blasket.

STRUGGLES & JOYS OF ISLAND LIFE

Thomas O'Crohan (1856–1937) lived on Great Blasket Island all his life. Raised – as all islanders were – speaking only Irish, he spent the latter years of his life teaching his language to scholars seeking to document the Gaelic vernacular. His novel, *The Islandman*, is an entertaining, autobiographical work that describes his childhood and adult life on Great Blasket. Thanks to a sensitive translation into English by Robin Flower, the book also conveys a sense of the lyrical phraseology and creative expression that is at the heart of the Irish language.

The book paints a colourful picture of island life at the turn of the 20th century. Like many of the island children, O'Crohan kept a pet 'gully' when he was young; a seabird that he had risked his life to snatch from a cliff edge. He also had a dog, one of the best 'rabbiters' on the island, who would be sent into warrens to fetch the rabbits from inside. Returning to the village after a day's rabbiting with eight fat animals slung over his shoulder was ample reward for a hard day's work on the hills.

The back-breaking toil of turf cutting, constructing his own house with no help from others, and braving the dangerous waters around the island on fishing trips were all normal aspects of island life. Other anecdotes are more revealing – O'Crohan once had a chunk bitten from his leg by a huge seal that he was trying to bring home for the cooking pot. With the closest medical assistance on the mainland, such incidents could be fatal. According to O'Crohan, islanders managed to prevent infection by strapping a raw chunk of the offending seal to the wound!

The Islandman has a poignant note too; O'Crohan's wife died young and several of his children were killed before adulthood. The population of Great Blasket was sliding into irreversible decline, and O'Crohan was acutely aware that his life's experiences would soon be lost forever. The incident that finally pushed the islanders to desert their home was to come after his death. One of the young men on the island became ill, but was prevented from seeing a doctor by a week-long storm. The man died; had he lived on the mainland he probably would have been saved.

PLANNING
Maps & Books
OSI 1:50,000 map No 70 covers Great Blasket Island.

To get yourself into the mood, you might also like to read one of the books written by islanders about life on Great Blasket. Thomas O'Crohan's *The Islandman* is guaranteed to add to your experience (see the boxed text 'Struggles and Joys of Island Life'.

An Old Woman's Reflections by Peig Sayers is another well-known account by a former islander.

GETTING TO/FROM THE WALK
Ferry services to Great Blasket are frequently disrupted by bad weather and large swells, and can be rather chaotic at other times. Inhospitable terrain and awkward landing sites mean a dingy transfer is required on arrival at Great Blasket, and may also be necessary at Dunquin depending on the state of the tide. Retain your boarding pass whilst on the island; it's collected on the return trip and allows ferry operators to verify that everyone is accounted for. If you intend to stay overnight on the island, inform a crew member on your outward journey.

Most visitors approach the island from Dunquin. **Blasket Island Ferries** (☎ 066-915 6422, 087 672 6100; www.blasket island.com; adult/child return €20/10, 20 minutes, hourly Easter-Sep) and **Blasket Islands Ferry** (☎ 066-915 4864, 087 231 6131; www.blasketislands.ie; adult/child return €20/10, 15 minutes, hourly Easter-Oct) are the two main operators.

It is also possible to take a boat directly from Dingle. As well as their Dunquin service, **Blasket Island Ferries** (☎ 066-915 1344) also run a fast, 12-passenger ferry to the island from Dingle marina (adult/child return €35/25, 40 minutes, every two hours Easter-Sep).

It is possible to camp wild on the islands, but there are no facilities.

THE WALK
From the ferry landing, follow the main green track up through the **ruined stone cottages** towards the top right corner of the village. Here you join a grassy track; turn left (southeast) and begin to climb around the slopes of Tur Comhartha (231m). After an initial steep climb the track levels out and offers easy walking as you begin to head southwest, with fine views over the Iveragh Peninsula and the distant Skellig Islands.

At the western end of Tur Comhartha, the track veers back towards the northeast and a narrow footpath continues west. Follow this footpath through bracken and climb past rock-studded viewpoints to the rounded summit of **Slievedonagh** (281m, one to 1½ hours from the start).

The island now narrows to a blunt ridge with a steep, rocky drop to the north and more gentle, grassy slopes to the south. The arête is enjoyably narrow without really being dangerous. Continue along the footpath, dropping down to a col before making the final ascent to **Croaghmore**, the highest point on the island at 292m. From the summit trig point there are great views across the remainder of Great Blasket to the isles of Inishvickillane and Inishnabro. A small circle of stones, perhaps the remains of an ancient *clochain*, is clearly visible below.

It is possible to continue to the end of the island, although most people turn around and begin their return journey at Croaghmore. Retrace your steps over Slievedonagh to the track, then turn left to return via the island's north shore. Wonderful views of the mainland open up as you reach the village. The white sand cove and turquoise waters of An Traigh Bhan are ahead, although the track emerges near the **café** and this might claim your attention first. However you decide to end your visit, make sure to return to the ferry landing in good time for your boat.

MORE WALKS

Inishbofin
Some 9km from the coast of Connemara, Inishbofin (*Inis Bo Finne*) is a generally low-lying island that is 6km long by 3km wide. It has some fine sheltered beaches, a ruined monastery and a Cromwellian fort. Rare bird species that can be seen here include corncrakes, choughs and corn buntings. Numerous short, circular walks are possible, and a full circuit of the island adds up to almost 20km. Ferries leave from Cleggan, 16km northwest of Clifden (see p201), and are operated by **Island**

Discovery (☎ 095-45894, 45819; www .inishbofinislanddiscovery.com; adult/child return €20/10, 30-45 minutes, two to three times daily). The island has a hostel, camping and a couple of good hotels – the **tourism association** (☎ 095-45861; www.inishbofin .com) provides good online information and descriptions to local walks. Use the OSI 1:50,000 map No 37.

Inishmaan

Inishmaan (*Inis Meáin*) is the middle of the Aran Islands and is probably the most natural of the three – visitors are left much more to their own devices than on the other two islands. A way-marked route keeps to the central lanes, but tracks are few in the wild and rocky southern half of the island. A full day can easily be spent completing a coastal circuit, with plenty of off-track walking along the limestone pavements. One place not to miss is Dún Chonchúir, regarded as Ireland's finest hill fort, near the highest point of the island. See the introductory section to the Aran Islands (p153) for mapping options and details of air and ferry connections. The island has plenty of B&Bs – contact the helpful **Inishmaan Island Co-operative** (☎ 099-73010; open daily), northwest of the pier, for more information.

Bere Island

Just 1km off the coast of the Beara Peninsula, Bere Island is about as convenient as islands get. The island hosts a spur of the Beara Way, as well as two way-marked National Loop Walks. The pick of the routes is the 10km Ardnakinna Lighthouse Loop, which starts and finishes at the pier on the northwestern tip of the island. To get there, take the **Bere Island Ferry** (☎ 027-75009; www.bereislandferries.com; adult return €8, at least five daily Jul-Sep, at least three daily Oct-Jun) from Castletownbere (p135). The walk begins by heading out to the striking Ardnakinna Lighthouse, then climbs to 258m for tremendous views over Bantry Bay and the Beara and Sheep's Head Peninsulas. Terrain is a mixture of footpaths, track and lanes, and you should allow at least four hours for the circuit. There are a couple of pubs and small shops on the island, but tourist accommodation is limited. Use OSI 1:50,000 map No 84.

Dursey Island

Separated from the Beara Peninsula by a narrow channel, Dursey is similar in topography to Great Blasket Island. However, Dursey is still inhabited, and can be explored on an 11km-long, way-marked section of the Beara Way, which takes in the island's highest point at 252m. The signed route can also be extended by walking out to Dursey Head and back (add 4.5km). The coastal scenery is impressive and many species of bird frequent the cliffs and fields. The fun starts as you make your way to the island. Dursey is reached by Ireland's only cable car, which sways precariously 30m above Dursey Sound. Access is from Ballaghboy, 11km west of Allihies on the R575 and R572. There is no accommodation on the island, although it is possible to wild camp. Use the OSI 1:50,000 map No 84.

TOWNS & FACILITIES

ARRANMORE ISLAND

☎ 074 / pop 600

The main settlement on Arranmore Island is Leabgarrow, the village clustered around the ferry pier. It has no bank or ATM, but does offer plenty of other facilities for a comfortable overnight stay.

Sleeping & Eating

The 32-bed **Arranmore Hostel** (☎ 952 0015; www.arainnmhor.com; Leabgarrow; dm/d €17/39) is a short walk left of the pier, at the back of a sandy beach. The owners live off-site so call ahead.

Long-established **Glen Hotel** (☎ 952 0505; http://theglenhotel.weebly.com; s/d €35/70; open Apr-Oct) is set amid mature gardens. It's a short distance west of the pier, at the eastern end of the road that crosses the island. Meals are served in both the bar and restaurant.

There are also several B&Bs scattered about the island's southeastern corner, including **Bonner's** (☎ 952 0532; s/d €40/80), near the ferry pier.

There is a small, well-stocked shop at the back of the long, sandy beach. Near the ferry pier you'll also find **Ferryboat**

ATLANTIC ISLANDS

Restaurant (☎ 952 0532; mains from €8), which specialises in chips and burgers.

See Getting to/from the Walk on p149 for details of ferry services to Arranmore.

CLARE ISLAND
☎ 098 / pop 130

Most of Clare Island's amenities are clustered in the town of Fawnglass, around the harbour and beach. There are no banking facilities but there is a small shop and post office around 2km from the harbour, along the road to the island's western tip.

Sleeping & Eating
At the back of the beach is a small, grassy **camping ground** (☎ 26525; per tent €10); campers use the shower and toilet facilities at the nearby Community Centre.

There are also several B&Bs, all of which serve evening meals on request (from €15). **Sea Breeze B&B** (☎ 26746; s/d €40/70) occupies a family home, and overlooks the harbour and beach.

Right beside the pier, **Granuaile House** (☎ 26250; www.granuailehouse.net; s/d/tr €50/80/105) offers clean, comfortable rooms and a resident's lounge.

O'Grady's Guesthouse (☎ 22991; www.ogradysguesthouse.com; s/d €75/90), also at the back of the beach, has six luxurious, modern bedrooms and a guest sitting room. The on-site **restaurant** (mains from €15) is open for lunch and dinner daily and welcomes guests and non-residents alike.

Take-away food is also served from the Community Centre from June to September.

Clare Island is well served by frequent ferries – see Getting to/from the Walk on p151 for details.

INISHEER
☎ 099 / pop 300

All inhabited buildings on Inisheer (*Inis Oírr*) are clustered around the northern shore. In July and August a small **tourist kiosk** at the harbour provides visitor information and literature. The island has a small shop and post office, but no banking facilities.

Sleeping & Eating
There is free **camping** (with toilets & showers) at an official site by the main beach.

Beside the pier, **Brú Radharc Na Mara Hostel** (☎ 75024; maire.searraigh@oceanfree.net; dm €18; open Mar-Oct) is a spotless IHH hostel with ocean views and bikes for hire. The owners also run an adjacent **B&B** (d €50), with basic en-suite rooms.

Just a five-minute walk from the pier, **South Aran House B&B** (☎ 75073; www.southaran.com; s/d €45/70; open Apr-Oct) has simple yet stylish rooms, and is run by the same people as the adjacent Fisherman's Cottage café.

Óstán Inis Oírr (☎ 75020; r €55-90; open Apr-Sep) is a modern hotel just up from the strand. It has homey rooms and serves hearty meals in its pub and **restaurant** (mains €8-14, open lunch & dinner).

Most of the island's pubs offer bar meals. The cosy **Fisherman's Cottage** (☎ 75073; mains €12-20; open lunch & dinner Apr-Oct) also specialises in fresh seafood and organically grown vegetables.

For transport services to Inisheer, see Getting There & Around for The Aran Islands (p154).

INISHMORE
☎ 099 / pop 1300

Tourism turns the wheels of Inishmore's economy, and an armada of tour vans greets each ferry. The main settlement on the island is Kilronan, the village huddled around the ferry pier.

The **tourist office** (☎ 61263; open daily) is on the waterfront, just west of the pier. Other facilities in Kilronan include a good-sized supermarket with ATM.

Reservations are advised in high summer; the tourist office can book rooms for a €4 fee.

Sleeping & Eating
Two minutes from the ferry pier is **Kilronan Hostel** (☎ 61255; www.kilronanhostel.com; dm €21-27), perched above Tí Joe Mac's pub. Rooms are spotless and have en-suite bathrooms.

Alternatively, the quirky 60-bed **Mainistir House Hostel** (☎ 61169; www.mainistirhousearan.com; Mainistir; dm/d €17/50; buffet dinner €16) is on the main road north of Kilronan. A simple breakfast and free pick-up are included in the rates, and there's an option of an organic, largely vegetarian dinner.

Less than a five-minute stroll from the centre of town, **Ard Mhuiris B&B** (☎ 61333; ardmhuiris@eircom.net; s/d €70/80) is quiet, tidy and welcoming, with good sea views.

Just 100m from the ferry, **Pier House Guest House** (☎ 61417; www.pierhouse aran.com; r €90-120; open Mar-Oct) has 10 bright and comfortable rooms. The on-site **restaurant** (☎ 61811; mains €22-30; open lunch & dinner) is also open to non-residents and fresh seafood is a speciality.

Another option for daytime and evening dining is **O'Malley's @ Bayview** (☎ 61041; Kilronan; mains €7-23), where dishes include seafood chowder, burgers and fresh fish.

See Getting There & Around for The Aran Islands (p154) for transport information to Inishmore.

INISHTURK
☎ 098 / pop 100

The main settlement on friendly Inishturk lies within a short distance of the ferry pier. There's a small shop just northwest of the pier but it's best to bring most supplies with you. Also bring all the cash you need because the island has no bank or ATM.

Sleeping & Eating

The island has several B&Bs, all of which can provide evening meals if required. **Tránaun House** (☎ 45641; s/d/tr €35/66/90; mains €15) is a 10-minute walk south of the harbour, next to the Community Centre and overlooking Tránaun beach. Facilities include a guest lounge.

Friendly **Ocean View House** (☎ 45520; s/d €40/70; three-course dinner €25) is just a short stroll northwest of the pier.

The more remote but scenically positioned **Teach Abhainn** (☎ 45510; s/d €40/76; three-course dinner €25; open Apr-Oct) lies on a working farm at the centre of the island, along the route of the walk and around 2km southwest of the harbour.

The Community Centre, located along the road 600m south of the pier, serves bar drinks and is the island's main focus for socialising.

For information on ferry services to Inishturk, see Getting to/from the Walk on p152.

RATHLIN ISLAND
☎ 028 / pop 110

The main settlement on Rathlin Island is clustered around the harbour at Church Bay. The **Boathouse Visitor Centre** (☎ 2076 2024; open daily May-Aug), south of the harbour, provides information and walking advice for the island, and also sells books. There are no banking facilities but there is a tiny grocery shop a few paces west of the ferry berth (turn left as you come off the pier).

Make sure to book accommodation in advance.

Sleeping & Eating

There's free **camping** in a field on the eastern side of Church Bay, not far from the harbour.

Kinramer Camping Barn (☎ 2076 3948; alison.mcfaul@rspb.org.uk; Kinramer; dm £9) is a basic bunkhouse on an organic farm, 5km west from the harbour and along the route of the walk. Bring your own food and bedding.

A 10-minute walk south of the harbour, **Soerneog View Hostel** (☎ 2076 3954; www .n-irelandholidays.co.uk/rathlin; Ouig; s/d £12.50/20; open Apr-Sep) offers basic, hostel-style accommodation in a family home. Bikes can also be hired for £8 per day.

Coolnagrock B&B (☎ 2076 3983; Coolnagrock; s/d £30/50; closed Dec) is a well-appointed guesthouse on the eastern side of the island, with great sea views. It's a 15-minute walk from the ferry, and the owner will pick you up by arrangement.

The island's biggest (12 rooms) and most pleasant place to stay is the 18th-century **Manor House** (☎ 2076 3964; www.rathlin manorhouse.co.uk; s/d £40/70). It's on the north side of the harbour and run by the National Trust. The on-site **restaurant** serves lunches and evening meals and is open to non-residents from May to September (booking necessary).

Alternatively there's a café/chip shop at **McCuaig's Bar** (☎ 2076 3974), just east of the harbour.

Rathlin Island is well served by frequent ferries – see Getting to/from the Walk on p145 for details.

TORY ISLAND
☎ 074 / pop 190

The remote crag of Tory Island (*Oileán Thoraí*) has just two recognisable villages.

West Town (*An Baile Thiar*) surrounds the ferry pier and contains most of the island's facilities, while smaller East Town (*An Baile Thoir*) is little more than a scattering of bungalows a 20-minute walk east of the harbour.

Tourist information is available from the **Tory Island Co-op** (*Comharchumann Thoraí Teo*; ☎ 913 5502; www.oileanthorai .com), near the pier and next to the playground. At the time of research, a new tourist office was also due to open near the pier. There is a small shop on the island, but you should bring most supplies with you. Also bring plenty of cash because there is no bank or ATM.

Sleeping & Eating

Teach Bhillie/Tory Hostel (☎ 916 5145; www.toraigh.net; West Town; dm/s/d €20/35/50) is a cheery B&B that also offers shared, hostel-style accommodation, with a light continental breakfast included in the price. From the ferry pier, it's a 300m walk to the left.

Another option for B&B is **Graceanne Duffy's** (☎ 913 5136; East Town; d without/with ensuite €66/70; dinner €16; open May-Oct) in quieter East Town. There are three simple but comfortable bedrooms and meals are available by arrangement.

The largest accommodation is **Tory Hotel** (*Óstán Thoraí*; ☎ 913 5920; www .toryhotel.com; West Town; s/d €50/100, mains €8-11; open May-Oct). Located by the pier, this modern, 14-room hotel also offers good pub food.

Caife an Chreagáin (☎ 913 5856; three-course menu €20, mains €10-15; open Easter-Sep) is an all-day café/restaurant that serves great value snacks and meals.

For details of ferry services to the island, see Getting to/from the Walk for Tory Island (p147).

Central West

HIGHLIGHTS

- Exploring some of Ireland's finest cliff walking around remote and peaceful **Dún Caocháin** (p176)
- Spending several days discovering the marvellous variety of routes on **Achill Island** (p169)
- Negotiating the rugged slopes of Mayo's highest peak, **Mweelrea** (p185)
- Wandering across the unique limestone pavements of the **Burren** (p196)

Highest peak in the region: Mweelrea, Mayo, 814m

The Central West of Ireland stretches from the Burren in County Clare, north through Connemara and County Mayo, to the hills of County Sligo. It is a region encapsulated by themes of both unity and contrast. The Atlantic Ocean is a constant presence, and the landscape is wild and rugged. At the same time, variety is everywhere, and distinct areas are readily identified according to their unique character. From the amazing limestone formations of the Burren to the sharp, crag-bound peaks of the Twelve Bens; from the country's most holy mountain, Croagh Patrick, to the dramatic cliffs of north Mayo; there is little in terms of Irish topography that is not represented within this region.

In these stimulating settings, walkers are presented with different opportunities from one area to the next. One day you could be exploring the finest collection of wildflowers in the country and the next, challenging yourself over a long, strenuous mountain massif. Yet, wherever you go, it's virtually impossible to avoid fine views of the mountains, glens and coastline. It would take years to fully explore a region that offers so much – all most people can do is take their time, open their senses and enjoy!

CENTRAL WEST

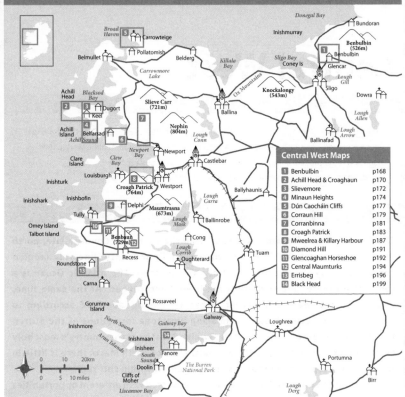

Central West Maps

1	Benbulbin	p168
2	Achill Head & Croaghaun	p170
3	Slievemore	p172
4	Minaun Heights	p174
5	Dún Caocháin Cliffs	p177
6	Corraun Hill	p179
7	Corranbinna	p181
8	Croagh Patrick	p183
9	Mweelrea & Killary Harbour	p187
10	Diamond Hill	p191
11	Glencoaghan Horseshoe	p192
12	Central Maumturks	p194
13	Errisbeg	p196
14	Black Head	p199

PLANNING
Maps & Books
The OSI 1:250,000 Holiday Map *West* neatly covers the region and is useful for general trip planning.

West of Ireland Walks by Kevin Corcoran describes 14 walks across counties Clare, Galway and Mayo, and has plenty of fascinating natural history and environmental information.

PLACE NAMES
Several parts of the region – particularly in the Burren, Connemara and County Mayo – are designated as Gaeltacht areas, where Gaelic is the first language written and spoken. In these places, road signs and place names are often written in Gaelic only, without the usual English translation. To facilitate navigation through these areas, Gaelic names are given in relevant places in the text.

Information Sources
Fáilte Ireland West (☎ 091-537 700; www .discoverireland.ie/west; Forster St, Galway) is the tourism body responsible for counties Galway and Mayo.

GATEWAYS
See Galway (p203) and Sligo (p207).

SLIGO

The walk described in this section is located just north of Sligo town, in an area often referred to as Yeats Country in deference to the region's most famous son – the poet

William Butler Yeats (1865–1939). The romantic quality of Yeats' poetry was fuelled by the landscapes he explored in his youth, and walkers can easily imbibe the same heady draughts of inspiration. Sprawling plateaus fall away in crumbling escarpments and sweeping slopes, while the Atlantic Ocean provides an ever-changing backdrop of light and mood.

The focal point of the route is Benbulbin, one of the country's most iconic peaks. The mountain lies at the western end of a long, flat-topped plateau covered by a heavy layer of blanket bog, and the best and most interesting walking is to be found around its edges. For botanists the Benbulbin Plateau is one of the most interesting upland areas of Ireland, though many of the more unusual species cling to rock faces and are difficult to see. The fringed sandwort is found nowhere else in the British Isles, while the clustered alpine saxifrage and chickweed-leaved willowherb are found nowhere else in Ireland.

The walk begins in Glencar, often called Ireland's 'Swiss Valley' in reference its near-Alpine grandeur. The glen is bordered by huge, limestone cliffs and is one of the best examples of a U-shaped, glacial valley in Ireland. Several waterfalls streak the rock walls before running into Glencar Lough, and while you're in the area it's well worth following the short, paved walkway to view beautiful Glencar Waterfall at the northeastern corner of the lough.

BENBULBIN

Duration 4–5 hours
Distance 12.5km
Ascent 600m
Difficulty moderate
Start/Finish Glenvale B&B
Nearest Towns Sligo (p207), Glencar (p138)
Transport private

Summary The classic route to Sligo's most famous summit, this superbly scenic walk takes you up a gully and out to the mountain's precipitous western tip.

Benbulbin (526m) is one of Ireland's most distinctive mountains. Its lofty promontory dominates the flat coastal plains of north Sligo like the prow of a ship thrusting west

GLENIFF OFF LIMITS

A quick glance at a map of the Benbulbin Plateau reveals the possibility of a wonderful circular walk round the Gleniff Valley. It is a fantastic circuit and would certainly be included in this book were it not suffering from a particularly embittered access problem. Unfortunately the area – especially around the lower slopes of Ben Whiskin – is currently off limits and if you do decide to walk there you are likely to come into conflict with the landowners.

into the Atlantic gales. For the walker it is a fascinating summit endowed with views and terrain as fine as any in Ireland's northwest.

The mountain is shaped like a wedge, its broad eastern end merging with the rolling and featureless Dartry Plateau. It's a different story to the west however, where slopes fall away in vertical escarpments over 100m high. These cliffs taper inexorably in to a single sharp point at the western-most tip. It is this point, which is the ultimate goal of any walk on Benbulbin, and where the thrilling aerial views of Donegal Bay are at their most impressive.

The mountain's distinctive morphology is a result of the different speeds of erosion between the resistant upper layer of Dartry Limestone and the much softer shales below. Just as the mountain's geology is something of a mix, so is its name. The peak goes by a variety of spellings, all anglicisations of the Irish name *Binn Ghulbain*, which has been translated variously as 'jaw-shaped mountain' or 'Gulban's mountain'. Gulban was a 5th-century Irish monarch who founded the kingdom of Tyrconnell, which extends north from here into County Donegal.

Note that it's best to avoid this route in poor visibility, as the proximity of many sheer drops makes navigational accuracy essential.

PLANNING
Maps & Books
Use OSI 1:50,000 map No 16.

A good walking guide to the area is *North Leitrim Glens* by David Herman. The guide describes a variety of day walks, and includes notes on local history and geology, accompanied by quotes from Yeats.

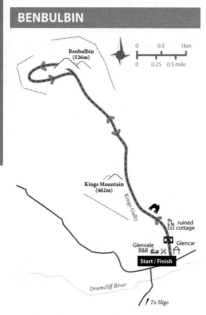

BENBULBIN

GETTING TO/FROM THE WALK

The only public transport option to Glencar also involves some walking. **Bus Éireann** (☎ 071-916 0066) Sligo–Manorhamilton services and Sligo–Enniskillen services both pass along the N16, close to Glencar. Check that the driver will stop near Glencar, and ask to be dropped off near the Glencar exit closest to Sligo. It is then a 2km walk to Glenvale B&B and the start of the route.

If you are approaching by car, take any of the minor roads off the N16 signed for Glencar. At the western end of Glencar Lough, watch for a signpost for Glenvale B&B. Head west along this road to reach the B&B. There is parking for several vehicles along the roadside here, but please don't park directly in front of the B&B.

THE WALK

The route starts just to the left of the B&B at an old gate. Go through this and walk along a muddy track, through a second gate and into a field. At the top of this field a third gate must be negotiated. The track now becomes very rough as you enter an area of rushes and rough pasture surrounding a **ruined cottage**, with fine views ahead to the cliffs and pinnacles of the Glencar

escarpment. To the left of the slope you should be able to make out a grassy path starting from the bottom of a large boulder field and running diagonally up the steep slopes into Kings Gully. This is your access route onto the plateau above.

Make for the upper left corner of the field, where a fence on the left can be crossed with ease. Cross the bottom of the boulder field and join the grassy track. This fantastic mountain path is very old and provides a quick and efficient means of gaining height on slopes that would otherwise be very taxing on the ankles. As you climb the views open out across Glencar to the east and Sligo town to the south.

At a small cairn the path turns north and delves into **Kings Gully** itself. Take care to stay on the path as the grassy sides of the gully are virtually sheer in places. The angle of ascent eases as you reach the top of the gully, where the path peters out among a jumble of peat hags. Cross a fence and follow the normally dry stream bed further north. There is plenty of evidence that this stream carries torrents of water when the bogs above reach saturation.

Cross the watercourse and climb northwest onto flat ground close to point 459m. If the weather is clear you should now be able to see the triangulation pillar on the summit of Benbulbin, approximately 2km northwest. The route to get there from point 459m is quite straightforward in good visibility. Continue almost due north across rougher ground, climbing gently to an unnamed top at just over 500m. Here the escarpments on the northern side of Benbulbin begin to reveal themselves. The views to the north open out too, all the way across Bundoran to Donegal's Blue Stack Mountains.

Change direction now and follow a broad ridge northwest all the way to the trig point on top of **Benbulbin**. The views from the summit are hampered by the flat surrounds, so it's well worth continuing out to the mountain's western tip. Simply head west from the summit, descending gently across a series of small dips and past a couple of peculiar bog pools. The sides of the mountain funnel remorselessly inwards until there is nowhere left to go; a small ramp of cropped grass drops off into space and all around is a dizzying sense of height and space. The views are sensational, but the need to take care is unquestionable. Be especially vigilant in windy conditions.

The simplest way to return to the start is to retrace your steps directly back to Kings Gully. However, if the visibility is good it's well worth varying your trip by walking along the rim of the northern cliffs before descending down the gully to the finish.

ACHILL ISLAND

At 147 sq km, Achill (*An Caol*) is Ireland's largest off-shore island. It is also one of its most accessible, thanks to a short bridge that connects it to the mainland. Despite this convenience, Achill retains plenty of its unique island atmosphere. Yet it's the breathtaking coastal scenery that makes the island a walker's paradise. Achill is blessed with soaring cliffs, rocky headlands and sheltered sandy beaches, all balanced inland by sharp mountains and broad expanses of blanket bog. There is enough to keep walkers busy for several days, and it's tempting to stay much longer to really explore the island at leisure.

Achill is at its most dramatic during winter, when high winds and lashing seas can make it seem downright inhospitable, despite a year-round population that remains as welcoming as ever. Few visitors choose to appreciate this temperamental side of the island, however, preferring its milder summers, when the beaches buzz with family activity and the area's holiday chalets, hotels and camping grounds reach full occupancy.

In this section we describe three walks on the island, all climbing to lofty outlooks that make the most of the incredible coastal views. If you don't have your own transport, it's quite possible to base yourself in Keel – the largest village and main centre of activity on the island – and complete all three routes with the help of a bike. Bikes can be hired from **O'Malley's Island Sports** (☎ 098-43125; jomalley@eircom.net; Keel; open Jun-Aug), next to the post office in Keel. Call ahead, as they disappear quickly during peak season.

PLANNING

Achill Tourism (☎ 098-47353; www .achilltourism.com; Cashel; open Mon-Fri Jun-Sep) is the best source of visitor information for the island. The website includes extensive accommodation listings and personal help is available in the office, which also sells local OSI maps and guidebooks. It's situated beside Lavelle's petrol station along the R319 between Achill Sound and Keel.

Maps & Books

Achill Tourism produces A *Bilingual Guide to Walking in Achill* detailing 14 low-level, easy circular walks on the island. Bob Kingston's *Achill Island Map & Guide*, at approximately 1:33,000, contains a wealth of background information and locates numerous points of interest on the map. The exhaustive reference containing plenty of intriguing history is *Achill Island* by Theresa McDonald. All publications are available from the tourist office.

ACCESS TOWN
See Keel (p205).

GETTING THERE & AROUND
Bus Éireann (☎ 096-71800) service 440 links Achill to Westport, running twice daily Monday to Saturday and once on Sunday. There are nine stops on the island including Achill Sound (€12.50, 1¼ hours), Dugort, and Keel (€16, two hours).

ACHILL HEAD & CROAGHAUN
Duration 5–5½ hours
Distance 13km
Ascent 920m
Difficulty moderate–demanding
Start/Finish Keem Strand
Nearest Town Keel (p205)
Transport private
Summary A truly spectacular walk above Ireland's highest sea cliffs, with sweeping mountain and sea views.

Lying at the western tip of Achill Island, the sea cliffs of Croaghaun are generally regarded as the highest in Europe (though the title is contended by Slieve League in County Donegal, see p228). Yet even leaving superlatives to one side, there is little doubt that together Achill Head and Croaghaun (688m) offer one of the most dramatic coastal walks in the country.

From inland Croaghaun has a rather unexciting, whale-back appearance, a profile that gives little indication of the drama waiting to the north. Here the erosive power of the Atlantic has chiselled away enough rock to create a two-kilometre stretch of cliffs over 550m high. Without chartering a boat, the only way to appreciate the multi-tiered battlements of schist and quartzite is to explore the area on foot.

In general the terrain is good, consisting largely of well-grazed grass and low heather. However, achieving the right weather for the route can be another matter. Much of the walk passes near precipitous drops, and extreme caution is required in wet, windy or cloudy conditions. Unfortunately the mountain forces the damp, oceanic winds to rise so abruptly that they often form a persistent cap of cloud over the summit of Croaghaun. The rest of Achill may be basking in glorious sunshine, but Croaghaun remains obscured from view. If possible it's well worth waiting for fine weather to complete the route safely and with the best views.

PLANNING
Maps
The OSI 1:50,000 map No 30 covers the walk entirely, and map No 22 shows all but a short section of the walk south of Keem Strand, where a map isn't really required. The path marked on both maps from Keem Strand along the cliff-top to Achill Head does not exist as a continuous path on the ground.

GETTING TO/FROM THE WALK
The walk starts at Keem Strand, 7km west of Keel along the R319. There are two large parking areas (and toilet facilities) at the end of the road above the beach.

The closest it is possible to get to the walk without your own transport is Dooagh, 2km west of Keel; add around 9km of (scenic) road walking to your day's itinerary if you use this village as your start/finish point.

THE WALK
From Keem Strand, climb steeply south-west up the grassy slope to the cliff edge above. From the top of the ridge, a short

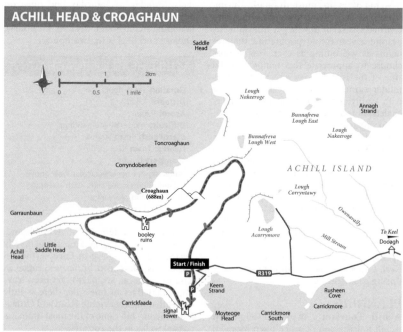

ACHILL HEAD & CROAGHAUN

BOOLEYING – SUMMER IN THE MOUNTAINS

Transhumance is the rather impersonal term for the age-old practice of taking animals to graze in mountain pastures during the summer. In Ireland it is known more colourfully as booleying, from the Irish word *buaile* (to milk).

This seasonal nomadism was an essential part of farming under the rundale system, which prevailed before fields were formally divided or enclosed by stone walls or fences. Each summer, families took their cattle up to the mountain foothills, where they could be let loose on the lush grass. Several members of the family would go with the animals and live beside them in simple, stone huts. The cows were milked and some huts may have included a semi-underground storage area where milk could be kept cool and stored until needed. Other family members visited from time to time with supplies of fresh food. In the autumn, people and cattle returned to the *clachan* – the cluster of houses and farm buildings that was home for the rest of the year – and the animals were put out on harvested fields.

The village of Dugort beneath Slievemore on Achill Island is a good example of an old, clustered, clachan-style settlement. Between Achill Head and the western ridge of Croaghaun you can also see the relatively well-preserved remains of the booley village of Bunowna.

Traditional rundale lands were reorganised in Ireland between the early 19th century and the 1930s; good land was divided into square fields and the poorer uplands into long strips. Clustered clachan settlements were also gradually replaced by separate houses or villages spread out along the side of roads – a pattern of habitation still evident today.

detour left (southeast) leads to the **signal tower** perched high above Moyteoge Head. From here it is simply a matter of turning round and walking northwest along the cliff-top, either contouring below the rim to avoid a series of undulations, or keeping to the high ground and taking them in your stride. The rises include a high point at 332m, where precious little separates the edge of the cliff from the sea far below. The wide views extend from the hills above the Dún Caocháin cliffs in the northeast to Croagh Patrick and beyond to the southeast.

After about 1½ hours you come to a point where the headland narrows to a relatively low but very exposed cliff. If you have the skill and confidence to negotiate this airy stretch, it is possible to continue a short distance towards the long, reptilian spine of **Achill Head**. Retrace your steps when the ridge becomes too demanding.

From the exposed cliff, veer east and drop down to the wide, flat col beneath Croaghaun. Here you cross a stream and pass the remains of a cluster of stone huts that once made up the **booley village** of Bunowna (see the boxed text Booleying – Summer in the Mountains). The best way to tackle the climb up the steep hillside to

Croaghaun is to begin by heading southeast, then sweep round to northeast as the angle of the slope allows. An effort of about 45 minutes brings you to the crest of the summit ridge, where you'll discover a well-trodden path and a vertiginous drop to the north. Follow the path northeast along the arête to **Croaghaun summit** (688m), marked by a modest cairn. To the northeast Saddle Head points its cliff-fringed arm towards the Belmullet Peninsula, while the crags of Achill Head make an impressive spectacle to the west.

Continue northeast along the ridge, then veer eastwards to reach another great outlook above the beautiful, pear-shaped **Bunnafreva Lough West**, its shore tidily lined with stones. From here, turn south and make a gradual, diagonal descent to the rim of the glacial corrie holding Lough Acorrymore, which now provides water for the whole island. Head southwest around the corrie and across Croaghaun's broad western spur, where Keem Strand comes into view below. The easiest line of descent down the heather-covered slope can be found along a strip of grass, near the eastern edge of a small stream. This will lead you directly back to Keem Strand where the route began.

SLIEVEMORE

Duration 4 hours
Distance 10.5km
Ascent 750m
Difficulty moderate
Start/Finish Dugort
Nearest Town Keel (p205)
Transport bus
Summary Strenuous but scenic walking over a steep ridge, followed by a descent into the deserted village of Slievemore.

Slievemore (*An Sliabh Mor* or 'Big Mountain') is the second-highest peak on Achill Island at 671m. It consists of a great keel of quartzite rising above Dugort on the north coast, and dominates the Achill landscape. A steep and engaging eastern ridge, a cliff-fringed north-eastern corrie, and fantastic summit views are all part of the mountain's charms. With the added interest of the deserted village of Slievemore, the traverse of the mountain provides a great half-day of walking. Although the ascent is steep and strenuous, the otherwise straightforward nature of the route lends it an easier grading than the longer route of Achill Head & Croaghaun (p169).

The circuit starts and finishes in the hamlet of Dugort – sometimes also spelled Doogort. This charming little settlement is gathered around a beautiful sandy cove at the eastern base of Slievemore. Visitor facilities are limited however, so the best option is to stay in the larger village of Keel (see p205).

PLANNING
Maps & Books
Use OSI 1:50,000 maps No 22 or No 30.

Bob Kingston's *The Deserted Village at Slievemore* is a small but interesting historical guide to the settlement, and is available in the tourist office.

GETTING TO/FROM THE WALK
For details of bus services to Dugort, see Getting There & Around for Achill Island, p201.

Dugort is about 4km north of the R319 Achill Sound–Keel road; there is a signed turn-off to the village about 3km north-west of Cashel. Park in the car park at the western end of the beach. If you have two vehicles, it is possible to avoid the 4km road section back to Dugort by leaving a car at the deserted village of Slievemore (GR F640072). There is ample parking at the base of the track near the cemetery.

THE WALK
From Dugort strand, take the minor road that leads northwest and passes in front of **The Strand Hotel** (☎ 098-43241; www .strandhotel.ie; s/d €45/80). Access to the mountain is from a road junction opposite a wide, grass verge (where you can also park), about 200m from the main road. A faint path starts immediately to the left of a prominent bungalow and leads up onto the mountain, winding between boulders to reach open ground above Dugort. The slope soon becomes steeper and a long, strenuous ascent begins, although some judicious zigzagging will ease the strain of the gradient. Climb for 30 to 40 minutes to reach an even steeper section (thankfully short-lived), which brings you out onto a fairly level shoulder beside the rocky pinnacle so conspicuous from the bottom of the mountain. Take in the superb view back down along the ridge to Dugort, over numerous coastal bays to the wild emptiness of north Mayo. There are also fine views to the south across Keel and the Minaun Cliffs.

From this point, about halfway to the summit, the climb becomes more interesting. On the right the ridge falls away in steep cliffs and to the left the slopes curve out of sight, revealing more airy views across Keel. A rough, mucky path becomes evident underfoot, winding up through the

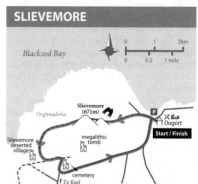

SLIEVEMORE

ACHILL'S DESERTED VILLAGE

The abandoned village of Slievemore, on the southwestern slopes of Slievemore mountain, provides a haunting reminder of the depopulation of rural Ireland during the 19th and early 20th centuries. Roughly 100 houses are strung out in linear fashion along an old boreen (country lane), all now ruined and overgrown. Take a peek inside the ruins and you'll see fascinating relics of former lifestyles: the metal rings on the walls were used to tether the animals that were brought in at night for security and warmth; stone slabs were covered with heather and rushes to make simple beds.

The exact reason for Slievemore's abandonment is not known, but it was most likely a combination of the Great Famine and the evictions of the Achill Mission. The Mission was an evangelical-Protestant endeavour that used the threat of rent increases as an aid to proselytising. It is almost certain that mass evictions took place at Slievemore, but probably not enough to depopulate the entire settlement. The rest of the inhabitants eventually moved to their summer booley village (see the boxed text Booleying – Summer in the Mountains, p171) at Dooagh, which was probably closer to their most reliable source of food – fish. Slievemore was then used as a booley village for a while, before being abandoned to the ghosts.

boulders that litter the crest of the ridge. In places many walkers will choose to descend slightly off the crest to the left to avoid some exposed rocky outcrops, though braver souls can scramble over these, enjoying the airy location. The ridge levels out only a short distance east of the summit. Descend slightly before climbing gently up to the trig point marking the top of **Slievemore** (two to 2½ hours from the start). On a clear day, fine views in all directions encompass many of the summits of Mayo and Galway, including Croagh Patrick, the Sheefry Hills and Mweelrea.

Descend gently from the summit along a broad ridge, heading in a westerly direction. Cross a flat, boggy area and then descend steeply onto a shoulder. At the end of this shoulder a steep outcrop of rock must either be skirted or descended directly with care, using grassy slopes that wind between the rocks. At this point walkers with the energy might want to view **Ooghnadirka**, an impressive gully running steeply down to the ocean from close to the ridge top. You'll need to descend a little to the north to fully appreciate this feature, which has been attributed to the weathering of a fault zone. Climb back onto the ridge to continue the route.

From the bottom of the outcrop, turn south and descend steeply towards the old linear settlement of **Slievemore village**, which lies strung out along the southeastern foot of the mountain. Old boundary walls, animal pens and many stone-built dwellings are visible, and as you reach the lower fields, lazy-beds are also obvious (see the boxed text Achill's Deserted Village, above, for more information).

Join the track that runs through the village and turn left. This leads past a parking area and cemetery to a minor road. Turn right and follow the road south, then turn left at a T-junction 400m later. Walk along this road all the way back to Dugort, some 4km away. The journey that can be enlivened after 1km by an optional detour up a signed path on the left to an interesting **Megalithic tomb** on the hillside above.

MINAUN HEIGHTS

Duration 5–5½ hours
Distance 13km
Ascent 540m
Difficulty moderate
Start/Finish Dooega beach
Nearest Town Keel (p205)
Transport private

Summary This impressive route takes you along a series of spectacular sea cliffs, offering a bird's-eye view of Achill Island.

Achill's most famous sea cliffs lie beneath Croaghaun, on the westernmost tip of the island. But these are not the only cliffs on Achill – far from it. Though not as high as Croaghaun, the Minaun cliffs are equally as impressive and far more accessible thanks to a road that leads all the way to the top.

The Minaun Heights (spelled *Menawn* on the OS map) rise to 486m and provide a wonderful viewpoint across the entire island. From the moment you reach the cliff-top you're met by a breathtaking view over the 4km-long sweep of Trawmore Strand, and it's difficult to imagine that the scenery could improve. Improve it does, however, all the way to Dooega Head, where profiles of Clare Island and the south Mayo hills are added to the panorama.

As you walk along the cliffs, you'll also notice a line of stone cairns extending from the summit of Minaun Heights to the col marked as 234m on the map. Some of these are old funeral stones, a legacy from the days when Kildavnet Church, on the south-eastern tip of Achill, was the only graveyard on the island. Funeral processions from villages in the northwest would pass over

Minaun on their way to the cemetery, and the cairns mark the spots where coffins were laid while the pallbearers took a rest.

The route described here is a circuit, but if you have two vehicles you can make it into a linear route with the rare benefit of 540m descent, but just 135m ascent. Leave the first vehicle at the summit car park (GR F670028), and follow the route southwest to your second vehicle at Dooega beach. Allow four hours for this 8km shortened route.

PLANNING
Maps
Use OSI 1:50,000 map No 30.

GETTING TO/FROM THE WALK
To reach the start of the route, follow the R319 over Achill Sound towards Keel. Around 4km from Achill Sound, turn left along the road to Dooega (*Dumha Eige*). Almost 4km later, turn left at a crossroads

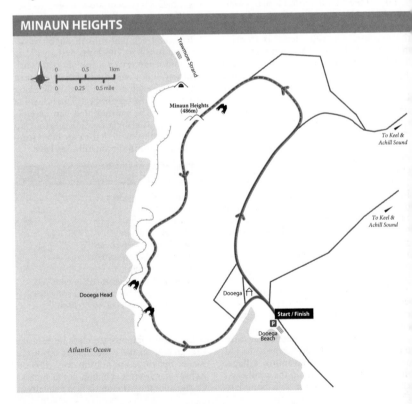

in the village. Park on the right, around 300m later, in the car park at the back of Dooega beach.

THE WALK

From Dooega beach car park, follow the road northwest towards the centre of the village. Continue straight over a crossroads after 300m, then keep right at two subsequent junctions. You are now on the minor road that leads along the southeastern foot of the Minaun Heights. Continue along this road for roughly 2.5km, where there's a break in the fence on the left of the road. Here you must begin to climb directly up the steep, heather-covered slope to the communication mast at Minaun's eastern summit. The angle of ascent is unrelenting, but the reward at the top will make the effort worthwhile.

At the top of the slope (two hours from the start) you'll find a car park, a fenced building and various communication masts. Turn left and follow a track, then a peaty path, towards the prominent cairn and statue that marks the top of **Minaun Heights** (486m). The view over Trawmore Strand and northern Achill is simply fantastic. The statue of the Virgin Mary was donated to the islanders by an American woman of Irish descent, and was placed on this high point as a blessing to all those living beneath it.

Continue southwest, descending across broad slopes for around 800m before swinging east around an inlet to a col. The quartzite cairns on these lower slopes may well stem from the days of funeral processions over the mountain. Veer southwest at the col and climb to the top of the next rise, where you are rewarded by the first real views along the **sheer rock face** of the cliffs themselves. The furthest cliffs, situated at the eastern end of Trawmore, harbour a series of **caves** that can be visited from the beach at low tide.

Now you have joined the cliff-line proper, it is essentially a case of tracing the edge of the cliffs around the western and southern reaches of Dooega Head. The terrain underfoot is a mixture of short heather and cropped grass, and a faint path is visible for most of the way. As you progress, the **coastal scenery** becomes yet more spectacular. First you round a series of small inlets where the rock drops 250m vertically to the ocean. Then, as you near the tip of the headland, the lighthouse and cliffs of Clare Island come into view some 12km across the sea.

The cliffs now begin to lose height and a relatively steep, heathery descent brings you almost down to sea level near the end of the headland (two to 2½ hours from the communication masts). Aim for an old stone wall that runs along the top of the shoreline, and follow this past several small fissures and rock arches that have been sculpted by wave action below. Continue around the southeastern corner of the promontory, passing between the wall and the shore. At times you may be forced onto the rocks themselves in an effort to avoid the occasional boggy patch. The OS map indicates two promontory forts in this area. Though there is no obvious sign of these above ground, archaeologists have identified them as part of a chain of Iron Age forts that were once scattered all around Achill's shoreline.

As you turn northeast towards Dooega, a rough track begins to consolidate underfoot. Follow the track to a junction with a tarmac lane, and continue straight ahead along the road. Keep right at another junction 300m later, then turn right at the next T-junction. Keep straight ahead at one more crossroads to return to Dooega beach car park.

MAYO

Mayo is a county of great geographical contrasts, offering walkers a generous variety of walks with the ocean as an ever-present backdrop. The cliffs of the north coast and on the western edge of Achill Island provide some of the county's finest coastal walking. The lonely Nephin Beg Range is a world apart from popular Croagh Patrick just across Clew Bay. Then there is Mweelrea, the highest peak in this chapter and a classic route for any serious walker.

HISTORY

The county was created in the 16th century and given the name *Maigh Eo*, meaning 'plain of the yew trees'. The area has been settled for over five millennia, as illustrated by the discovery of the Ceide Fields on

Mayo's north coast. Under the layers of bog archaeologists discovered the stone walls of an extensive farming community, now recognised as the oldest enclosed landscape in Europe and the largest Stone Age monument in the world. However walkers are more likely to encounter the forts (dúns or raths) that enclose isolated summits or coastal promontories and date from 800 BC to AD 1000.

St Patrick visited the area during the 5th century, inspiring the construction of monastic settlements and the designation of Croagh Patrick as a key site of religious pilgrimage (see the boxed text Ireland's Holy Mountain, p184). Later, during the 17th century, Mayo experienced the effects of Cromwell's plantation of settlers, but the tide began to turn when it became a centre for active opposition to the eviction of tenants; one of the founders of the Irish Land League, established in 1879, was Mayo man Michael Davitt.

Although Mayo was little affected by the civil war in the early 1920s, it nonetheless suffered from a continuing population drain as people abandoned the uncertain income of farming for a more secure life elsewhere. It was only during the 1990s that the population actually increased as the local economy diversified, with tourism playing a significant part.

ENVIRONMENT

The principal building block of Mayo's mountains is hard, white quartzite, a rock that transformed from the silts, sands and grits laid down in an ancient ocean about 500 million years ago. The county's foundations are exposed only on its highest peaks however; the north of the county is largely covered by blanket bog, while further south peat bog occupies most poorly drained areas. The combination of thin, poor soils, exposure to wind and high rainfall, and the ravages of grazing sheep, yields a limited range of vegetation besides heather or grass moorland. Natural woodlands are rare, though cultivated conifer plantations do now occupy many of the glens and hillsides. The scarcity of trees and shrubs means the ~f wildlife is also limited. Irish hares es are the species you're most likely though bird life is more diverse. On ast fulmars, gulls, guillemots and

cormorants are plentiful. Inland skylarks and meadow pipits are the tuneful moorland denizens, together with the occasional grouse and kestrel.

PLANNING

The internet is a good source of information about the area, try www.mayo-ireland.ie/motm.htm for links to walking information, accommodation and local history.

ACCESS TOWN

See Westport (p208).

DÚN CAOCHÁIN CLIFFS

Duration 5½–6½ hours
Distance 17km
Ascent 530m
Difficulty moderate
Start/Finish Carrowteige
Nearest Towns Belmullet (p201), Pollatomish (p207), Portacloy (p207)
Transport private
Summary This impressive route takes you past a profusion of dramatic cliffs, chasms and sea stacks along the remote north Mayo coast.

The remote and rugged coastline of northwest Mayo is one of Ireland's best-kept secrets. The cliffs reach just half the height of Slieve League in Donegal but are far more extensive, continuing almost without interruption for 30km. The walk described here is a one-day circuit that explores the cliffs' eastern reaches and provides a great introduction to the sort of walking available in the region. With more time and suitable transport arrangements, the entire 30km stretch of coast from Carrowteige to Belderg is worth exploring, either in a series of day walks or as a three-day backpacking trip, camping en route.

The Irish name for the area perpetuate Caocháin – a mythical, one-eyed giant though his dún (fort) on the coast has long since tumbled into the sea. The cliffs themselves consist of ancient Precambrian schist and quartzite that is about 600 million years old. Both the cliffs and their attendant offshore stacks are home to a large population of seabirds; fulmars and great black-backed gulls are the most common species you' see, though guillemots, kittiwakes and cormorants also live here.

There are two options for the route described: a longer version of 17km, or a 12km alternative that uses a short-cut to avoid the eastern part of the circuit. This eastern section follows a National Loop Walk and is fully way-marked, though the posts along the cliff sections are set 20m back from the edge with signs warning walkers not to approach any closer. It is a given that cliff walks present an inherent danger, but airy views over the precipice are a large part of what makes them so appealing. Most walkers will exercise commonsense and walk a sensible distance back, but still close enough to fully enjoy the location.

Northwest Mayo is one of the least visited areas of Ireland, and accommodation is rather sparse. Apart from one B&B within 2km of the route in Portacloy, the closest facilities can be found either 20km southwest in the village of Pollatomish, or 33km southwest in the larger town of Belmullet.

PLANNING
Maps & Books
The walk is covered by two OSI 1:50,000 maps, Nos 22 and 23.

An excellent, locally produced guide in English and Irish, *Dún Caocháin Walks*, by Uinsionn MacGraith and Treasa Ni

DÚN CAOCHÁIN CLIFFS

> ## WARNING
> Grass grows right to the very edge of these cliffs. Take care – it's all too easy to find yourself teetering on the brink as you line up a photo. Particular caution is required in wet or windy conditions.

Ghearraigh, contains plenty of background information and good walk descriptions; it is available from the tourist office in Belmullet (see p201).

GETTING TO/FROM THE WALK
The route starts and finishes outside the shop in the centre of Carrowteige (*Ceathrú Thaidhg*), at a road junction marked by a walk information board and waymarking post (GR F819419). Carrowteige is accessed via a minor road that leads north from the R314, 2km west of Glenamoy post office. Although the village is signed, you'll appreciate the help of your OSI maps to negotiate the network of secondary roads in the area.

There is no public transport to the area.

THE WALK
From the Carrowteige shop follow the red waymarks southwest, descending along a narrow road towards Broad Haven Bay. Cross a crossroads after 1km and continue to where the road ends at a **graveyard**. A sandy track continues towards Binroe Point, where you join another narrow road with fine beaches on either side. Climb inland along the road for 200m, then turn left along a rough track. Before long you meet the black ditch, an old wall made of stone and sods. Turn right and follow this to the top of the 100m-high cliff known as **Alt Breac**, where there's a dizzying perspective over coastline below.

Continue to follow the black ditch north, descending towards a series of rugged headlands. The next 40 or 50 minutes are a delight, with each twist and turn revealing a dramatic new coastal vista. Begin by dropping across a small valley, then climb onto a flat headland and curve east in line with the cliffs. Skirt around a deep inlet and continue past a couple of blunt promontories to reach a curious circular bog pool perched on the cliff edge. The next landmark is the **Children of Lir sculpture**, a metal and stone construction on the clifftop at the end of a narrow lane (2½ hours from the start).

Continue east with the red markers, climbing the steep slope above the sculpture. Before long the posts veer inland – this is where the alternative route joins the main walk (see Alternative Route: Via Bog Track Short-cut). Leave the waymarkers here and head northeast across open country, keeping close to the rim of the cliffs. A steady 2km climb brings you to the crowning height of **Benwee Head** (255m; *An Bhinn Bhui* or Yellow Peak). The wide-ranging view takes in Slieve League to the north and Achill Island to the south.

Cross a fence near the summit and continue to follow the cliffs northeast. Descend across the wide indentation of Doonvinalla to the next peninsula, where a ruinous line of boulders across a narrow ridge is all that remains of an Iron Age promontory fort (about 400 BC to AD 600). A little further on, near the end of a second finger of land at the western side of Portacloy Bay, are two relics from World War II: a small, derelict lookout building and the word 'EIRE' formed from flat stones on the ground. The letters are a common feature along the coast and reminded wartime pilots they were about to cross neutral Ireland.

Descend steadily south across the hillside, cross a stream and pass through a gate to reach **Portacloy pier** (two hours from the Children of Lir sculpture). At the top of the pier, join a narrow road and follow this south for about 300m, then take the first right turn. Keep left at a fork and continue southwest along the road, which turns into a track as you pass the last house. The track swings west about 800m from the fork and begins to climb uphill. Roughly 200m later, watch out for a gap in the bank on the left, marked by a waymarking post. Turn left here and descend across a moorland hollow, joining another bog track around 300m later. This track winds southwest across the hillside, then turns into a surfaced road beside a house. Turn left at the subsequent road junction and descend to the main road. Turn right for 350m to arrive back at the shop in Carrowteige.

ALTERNATIVE ROUTE: VIA BOG TRACK SHORT-CUT
4–4½ hours, 12km, 440m ascent

This short-cut follows the red waymarkers in an anti-clockwise direction, running opposite to the marked route. From Carrowteige shop, follow the main road west for roughly 1km to a junction. Turn right here and climb along a stone track across open bogland. Near the top of the slope, turn left at a marked junction and follow a newer track towards the coast. When the waymarking posts swing west across open ground, continue ahead to the cliff-line and join the main route described above.

CORRAUN HILL

Duration 5–5½ hours
Distance 11.5km
Ascent 640m
Difficulty moderate–demanding
Start/Finish Belfarsad bridge
Nearest Town Achill Sound (p201)
Transport private

Summary A great but rarely walked mountain circuit, featuring steep ridges, deep corries and fantastic coastal views.

The Corraun Peninsula tends to be a place that is registered simply as the last stretch of mainland before Achill Island. However, this does the area an injustice; the walk up Corraun Hill (*An Corran* or 'the Sickle') boasts characteristics that rival many of the better-known mountain routes in the country. Although the southern flanks of the mountain drop to the sea in a rather uniform fashion, the cliffs of the northern slopes offer the perfect juxtaposition. Here deep-sided corries are adorned with small loughs and separated by the bony fingers of sharp ridges. It is unusual to find these features on a mountain of such modest height. Corraun Hill has two main summits, with the highest reaching just 541m. Nonetheless, the views over Achill Island, Clew Bay and the west Mayo coast are outstanding, and provide the other major attraction of the route.

A blanket of thick heather covers the lower slopes of the mountain, while the summit plateau is strewn with a mixture of white quartzite and the pink-tinged rock that is characteristic of the area. A 1km-long section of bog towards the end of the route can be very wet, so gaiters are strongly recommended. The route also involves fording the outlet stream of a small lough, so avoid walking immediately after heavy rain.

In clear weather the well-defined topography of the mountain makes route-finding fairly straightforward for those with good map-reading skills, but care must be taken in poor visibility to avoid descending via the wrong ridge.

PLANNING
Maps
OSI 1:50,000 map No 30 covers the route.

GETTING TO/FROM THE WALK
For details of bus services to Achill Sound, see Getting There & Around for Achill Island, p169. It is possible to walk to Belfarsad bridge from Achill Sound, though your approach will depend on the state of the tide. At low tide it's an easy 2.5km walk across the beach to the east of the town, where you join the road heading south towards Corraun village. At high tide the coastal option is inaccessible and there's no option

but to begin by heading east along the R319, covering the entire 4.5km by road.

By car, approach the area on the N59 and turn west onto the R319 (signed for Achill Sound), 1km west of Mallaranny. Follow this road round the north of Corraun Peninsula. After around 9km, turn left towards Corraun village. Belfarsad bridge (GR L748985) is 3km along this road. Park either just south of the bridge or in front of the wooden church 80m further on.

THE WALK
From the bridge over the Belfarsad River, walk north along the road for around 20m and turn right onto a stone track marked with a waymarking post for a local loop walk. The track climbs gently as it leads southeast onto the open bog north of Corraun Hill; follow it for around 1.5km until you come to a prominent white stone in the centre of a fork. Veer right here. The track peters out within a few metres, but it sets you in the right direction for the ascent of Corraun.

Continue southeast across broken ground, descending briefly to cross a small depression before reaching the bottom of a prominent shoulder. The ascent up the

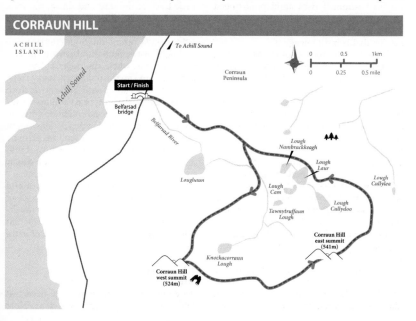

CORRAUN HILL

shoulder is steep, but eases off as it narrows into a more defined ridge with steep drops and great views on either side. The ridge is enjoyably narrow without being dangerous, and the heather gives way to rock as you gain height.

The ridge broadens out for a spell and then a final steep climb leads onto the summit plateau. Veer southwest and pick your way over the quartzite to reach the cairn and concrete trig point that mark the **west summit** (two to 2½ hours from the start). At 524m this point is 17m lower than the eastern summit, but the views are arguably better. The great ridges of Achill Island rise to the west, Clare Island lies beyond the mouth of Clew Bay to the south, and the intricate coastline of west Mayo stretches north. It is a wonderful viewpoint and certainly makes the climb worthwhile.

Continue east and then southeast from the summit, descending across a col before climbing more gently up broad slopes towards the east summit. A series of prominent cairns keeps you on the right track as you cross the rather featureless terrain. Be wary of steep cliffs to the north in poor visibility. The cairn marking the **east summit** (541m, 45 minutes to one hour from the west summit) rises amid pink-tinged sandstone rocks, and it is the view south across the islands of Clew Bay to Croagh Patrick that is most engaging.

From this summit another prominent cairn is visible on the far eastern edge of the plateau. Continue in this direction for 500m before veering north onto the ridge that provides the descent route (take care here to avoid descending the even steeper ridge immediately north of the east summit). Bear northwest as you lose height, heading towards the corner of a forestry plantation and a network of small loughs below.

The ground at the bottom of this ridge can be so wet that it glistens from above, and acrobatic skills are sometimes called on to avoid wet feet. Follow the fence of the forestry plantation as it skirts the eastern shore of **Lough Laur** and cross the outlet stream on stepping stones. Continue northwest from the stream, climbing a small mound ahead. The track that you followed at the start of the route should soon become visible; retrace your initial steps back to the road and turn left to return to Belfarsad bridge.

CORRANBINNA

Duration 5½–6 hours
Distance 14km
Ascent 1020m
Difficulty demanding
Start/Finish Carheenbrack
Nearest Town Westport (p208)
Transport bus, private

Summary A fine circuit over three summits on the western side of the Nephin Beg Range, with splendid views and a short, exciting scramble.

Few ranges in Ireland are as remote as the Nephin Begs, extending as they do into the vastness of the north Mayo boglands. The highest point of the range, the solitary massif of Nephin to the east, is actually the second-highest peak in Connaught at 806m. The circuit described here, around the Glendahurk Valley, is just one of many fantastic routes in the area – see Nephin Beg, p199, for another possibility.

As well as memorable topography, this route has the advantages of easy access and, by Nephin standards, a modest quota of peat bogs. Apart from short sections along a vehicle track at the start and finish, the walk crosses rough, trackless country as it make its way over Bengorm (582m), Corranbinna (714m) and Corranbinna South (681m). The highlight of the route lies between the two Corranbinnas, where the ridge narrows for a few hundred metres to a sharp, rocky arête. Here walkers can choose between a steep traverse below the crest or a thrilling scramble along the top. In good conditions the trip along the crest is not as bad as it looks, but in wet or windy conditions it requires extreme caution. Note that ice and snow turn it into a serious undertaking that requires winter experience and an ice axe as a minimum.

Mountain enthusiasts can also extend the route by adding a visit to the peak of Glennamong (628m), about 2.5km north-northeast of Corranbinna, a sidetrip that adds around two hours and 370m of extra ascent to the day.

PLANNING
Maps

To complete this circuit you will need two OSI 1:50,000 maps, Nos 30 and 31. Note that the route's main summits are not named on these maps. Corranbinna is the peak of 714m at the northeastern corner of the circuit, while Corranbinna South is the 681m-high peak at the northwestern corner.

GETTING TO/FROM THE WALK

Bus Éireann (☎ 096-71800) services on the Westport–Achill Island route pass along the N59, about 1.5km south of the start of the walk (twice daily Mon-Sat, once on Sun). It's not a scheduled stop, so arrange with the driver in advance to be dropped off or picked up here.

By car, follow the N59 north from Westport and then west from Newport. About 7.5km west of Newport, turn north onto a minor road marked by a modest sign on a wall for 'Carheenbrack' (most easily spotted approaching from the east). The turn is roughly 100m east of a white roadside statue of the Virgin Mary. Follow the minor road northwest for about 2km and cross the bridge over the Owengarve River (you'll need to open and close a gate in order to cross). Vehicles can be left in a gravel parking area at a junction of tracks just 50m north of the bridge (GR L911979). This is also the car park for a series of local lowland walks known as the Burrishole Loop Walks.

THE WALK

From the parking area, walk southwest along the track and re-cross the bridge over the Owengarve River. On the southern bank of the river, turn left and pass through a gate into open country. Head upstream fairly close to the river; a couple of narrow footbridges cross small tributaries and a ditch or two must be negotiated. After about 500m, as a low spur takes shape ahead, change course and climb eastwards up the long, grassy slope of Bengorm's broad southern spur. The western bank of a tributary stream, grazed by the ubiquitous sheep, provides the firmest passage for the long haul up the spur. A rocky stretch then leads to the small summit of **Bengorm** (582m) – 1½ hours from the start, crowned with a cairn. Variety is the essence of the panoramic view: Bellacorrick power station and a nearby wind farm in the north; Achill Island's peaks to

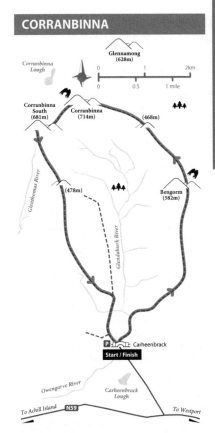

the west; and to the south Clew Bay, with its flotilla of islets overlooked by vigilant Croagh Patrick.

Descend steeply northwest to a small col and press on over two broad bumps on the spur, keeping left at the second one to keep well clear of the slabs to the right. For the final pull to Corranbinna, steer clear of the steepest boulder fields to the left. From the survey pillar at the top of **Corranbinna** (714m) – 1½ hours from Bengorm, the coast-and-mountain panorama is augmented by a fine perspective over the Nephin Begs.

A short descent now brings you to a notch in the ridge where the wind roars up from the coums below. This is the start of the rather intimidating-looking arête leading to Corranbinna South. Either bear left for a steeply-angled traverse across boulder-strewn slopes, or – if you have a good head for heights – scramble up along the crest. The exposure on the ridge top is sensational, but the only real problem is seeing ahead to the next move. You'll find it almost impossible to keep to the arête all the way along however as a couple of overhanging steps force you back down to the left.

The grassy upper section of the ridge soon gives way to the flat summit plateau of **Corranbinna South** (681m), where the ground falls steeply north to the elongated Corranbinna Lough. The corries holding both this lough and Corryloughaphuill Lough to the north are of ice age origin – see the boxed text Signs of a Glacial Past, (p30) for more information.

The long descent southeast begins over wet ground, though rocks and peat hags intrude as you pass over the ridge's intermediate bumps. The spur becomes more dissected and eroded as it broadens at its southern end. Keep to the crest until you can see the southern tip of the forestry plantation in Glendahurk Valley below. Head down to meet a forestry track at the point where it emerges from the plantation. Turn right and follow the track south, then turn left at a T-junction and head back to the car park at the start of the walk (2½ hours from Corranbinna).

CROAGH PATRICK

Duration 4–4½ hours
Distance 10km
Ascent 960m
Difficulty moderate–demanding
Start Belclare bridge
Finish GR L875808
Nearest Towns Murrisk (p206), Westport (p208)
Transport bus, private

Summary Scale Ireland's most important pilgrimage mountain to enjoy wonderful views over Clew Bay.

Croagh Patrick (764m) occupies a special place in Irish tradition as the country's most hallowed place of pilgrimage, and attracts tens of thousands of pilgrims to its summit every year. For those not primarily concerned with spiritual enlightenment, superb views over the island-studded inlet of Clew Bay more than reward the effort of the climb. The most frequently travelled route to the top is the tourist path (see Alternative Route, p185), a track as wide as a country road in some places that can be seen scarring the mountainside for kilometres around. However the mountain has much more to offer walkers than this well-trodden route. The traditional Pilgrim's Path follows the *Tóchar Phádraig* (Patrick's Causeway) from Ballintubber Abbey, some 40km away. Once at Croagh Patrick it makes an east-to-west traverse of the entire mountain ridge, offering a far superior route to the tourist path if you can organise transport logistics at each end.

The traverse crosses wild, open, but generally firm, mountain terrain. You are largely on your own to find the route up the eastern approach, though each minor summit along the ridge is topped with a cairn. After a short section on the tourist path, the western section is marked by large, widely spaced cairns and a rough path underfoot. Inevitably, an A-to-B traverse such as this depends on your ability to arrange transport at each end, though the Westport-Louisburgh bus may be of help (leave your car at the end then catch the bus back to the start).

If you opt for the tourist path from Murrisk, you'll start and finish at the **Croagh Patrick Visitor Centre** (☎ 098-64114; www.croagh-patrick.com; open mid-Mar–Oct), which sells local maps and guidebooks, and also offers a café and shower facilities. The path could never be described as subtle – it's rocky and often busy, and climbs the mountain in one steep slog – though its width does mean it's virtually impossible to get lost.

Bear in mind that the national day of pilgrimage is the last Sunday in July (known as Reek Sunday), when thousands of the faithful (some in bare feet) climb Croagh Patrick from Murrisk – see the boxed text Ireland's Holy Mountain, (p184).

ENVIRONMENT

Croagh Patrick has a distinctive volcanic profile, but its origins are anything but volcanic; it is composed largely of white quartzite, derived from sedimentary rocks

CROAGH PATRICK

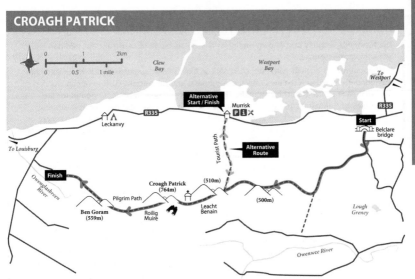

laid down hundreds of millions of years ago and later completely transformed by upheavals of the earth's crust. The quartzite has been fractured and shattered into the whitish mantle of scree that gives the mountain its beautiful, Fuji-like outline. While 'The Reek', as it is known locally, bears slight evidence of the impact of the ice age, Clew Bay below is a textbook study of the effects of a retreating glacier. As the ice melted, debris that had accumulated inside the glacier was deposited in a cluster of hills called drumlins. When the valley was later flooded by rising sea levels these drumlins became islands, their west-facing slopes carved into steep cliffs by the sea, while the protected eastern slopes remain relatively unchanged.

PLANNING

Maps

Croagh Patrick sits rather inconveniently on the corners of four OSI 1:50,000 maps. Nos 30 and 31 are the most important, covering the northern approaches and the main ridge. No 37 shows the descent to Roilig Muire and part of the climb towards Ben Goram. No 38, covering the approach to the mountain from the southeast, is not strictly necessary in good visibility.

GETTING TO/FROM THE WALK

The **Bus Éireann** (☎ 096-71800) Westport –Louisburgh service 450 plies the R335, and includes a scheduled stop at Murrisk, at the bottom of the tourist path (€3.50, 17 minutes, two to four times daily Mon to Sat). The same service can be used to reach the start and finish of the Pilgrim Path route – check the timetable and make advance arrangements with the driver as these are not scheduled stops.

By car, Murrisk is located on the R335, around 8km west of Westport. It's also possible to cycle between Murrisk and Westport; bicycles can be hired at Westport's Old Mill Holiday Hostel (see p208).

If you're travelling by car to Belclare bridge, at the start of the Pilgrim Path walk, follow signs to Louisburgh and Croagh Patrick from the N59 on the southwestern edge of Westport. There is very limited parking space just west of the bridge, and more about 75m east of the bridge. Alternatively, two cars only can be parked at the end of the public road along the route of the walk.

To reach the western end of the Pilgrim Path walk, turn south off the R335 1.5km west of Leckanvy and 4.5km west of Murrisk, along a road with a sign reading 'Rapid Signs'. Take the first left after

IRELAND'S HOLY MOUNTAIN

The history of Ireland's best known mountain is a classic blend of myth, ancient tradition and archaeological evidence.

The mountain's ancient name (*Cruchán Aigli* or Aigle's Peak) suggests that it was linked with the founder of the harvest-time Festival of Lughnasa, and the ancient custom of sun worship may well have centred on the mountain. The peak was certainly important enough for the early kings of Connaught to build a road to the summit from Ballintubber, about 40km east. Archaeological excavations have also uncovered evidence of a sizable prehistoric settlement on the summit dating from at least 300 BC, consisting of the remains of a substantial enclosure and numerous circular huts.

However it's the mountain's association with Patrick, Ireland's patron saint, that is most enduring. It's believed the saint fasted on the mountain for 40 days and 40 nights, emulating the biblical accounts of Moses and Christ. The mountain also became crucial in his campaign to convert the Irish people away from paganism, in which he performed Catholic rituals at sacred Celtic sites, thus 'Christianising' previously pagan practices. Legend also has it that Patrick evicted snakes from Ireland during his time on the mountain.

The chapel at the summit of Croagh Patrick is Ireland's highest church, and was built in 1905 on the remains of the first Christian chapel, dated between AD 430 and 890. Historic records of pilgrimage to the site date back to the 12th century. Today, the national day of pilgrimage is the last Sunday in July, when services are conducted on the summit, as they are on the last Friday in July (Garland Friday) and on 15 August (the Feast of the Assumption). For many years the national pilgrimage was made at night, although this practice was stopped during the 1970s.

An integral feature of the pilgrimage is the traditional performance of penance at designated stations along the way. There are three stations in all: Leacht Benain, commemorating Benignus, a disciple of Patrick; three separate substations on the summit; and Roilig Muire (the virgins' cemetery) on the western slope, possibly a pre-Christian burial site. Each year at each of these stations, thousands of pilgrims walk around large cairns whilst repeating key religious texts a prescribed number of times.

For further information about the mountain or to make a 'virtual pilgrimage', see www.croagh-patrick.com.

1km and park beside the road on the left, about 200m below a group of houses (GR L875808).

THE WALK

The walk starts quietly from Belclare bridge, heading south along a narrow, leafy lane. After about 500m, where the lane bends sharply left, you meet the way-marked Western Way; continue ahead and bear right at a fork about 400m further on. After 1km the road bends sharply right and a rough vehicle track, marked by a waymarking post, continues ahead. Go through the gate and climb steadily along the track for about 600m, where a stile on the right allows access to the mountainside. Waymarks leading onto the hillside beyond the stile are for the relatively new Croagh Patrick Heritage Trail, a 61km route from Balla to Murrisk. Do not follow these waymarks as they lead off the side of the mountain.

Instead climb the hill to the west. You will soon come to an old stone wall; gaps have developed in its otherwise sound structure, and it's not difficult to cross and continue up to the crest of the heathery ridge. Several mounds and hillocks then lie between you and the prominent slopes of Croagh Patrick ahead. Pass over these rises, crossing a peaty col with the remains of another stone wall, and then descend to join the eroded scar of the **tourist path** (1½ hours from the start). The col where you meet this motorway of Irish paths contains what could be described as an open-air autograph book: the names and initials of pilgrims and walkers are written in stones on the ground. A **toilet block**, complete with flushing water, can also be found slightly further along the track.

The wide path is covered with stones, and doesn't make for particularly easy progress; one can only wonder at the hardiness of pilgrims who make the ascent unshod. Wonder may turn to bemusement or admiration, depending on your beliefs, as you pass the pilgrims' first station (Leacht Benain) and read the plaque with the prescribed ritual.

About half an hour's steady plodding up the steep, stony highway brings you to the **summit of Croagh Patrick** (764m), which can be crowded at almost any time of the year. Here you'll find a chapel, a survey pillar, an offerings box, several shelters, a second station cairn (with even more challenging instructions for pilgrims) and more toilets. Thankfully the views over Clew Bay to the north are adequate compensation for any lack of tranquillity that might result from such a well-visited place.

Continue west from the summit along a narrower stone path and begin a zigzagging descent to the third and last station, **Roilig Muire**. From here a modest path continues west down to a narrow col. Climb northwest over **Ben Goram** (559m), a small plateau, and continue in the same direction, soon beginning to lose height. Two large cairns mark the start of the final, steep descent. Keep heading northwest at least until you meet a prominent, pillar-like cairn, to avoid precipitous crags on the western flank of the ridge. As the gradient eases, bear left and head down to the road (1¼ hours from the summit of Croagh Patrick). If you need to continue back to the R335, head right along the road for 600m, then turn right again to meet the main road 1km later.

ALTERNATIVE ROUTE: FROM MURRISK
3–3½ hours, 8km, 750m ascent

The tourist path begins from a large car park beside Croagh Patrick Visitor Centre in Murrisk. Head south along the obvious trail, beginning to climb almost immediately. Pick your way up the rocky ground to a col on the ridge of the massif. This is where the Pilgrim Path comes in from the east. Veer right (west) and follow the trail steeply to the summit. When you're ready to descend, simply retrace your outward journey back to the car park.

MWEELREA WALK

Duration 6½–7 hours
Distance 12km
Ascent 1150m
Difficulty demanding
Start/Finish Doo Lough
Nearest Town Leenane (p205), Delphi (p202)
Transport private
Summary The highest peak in the province of Connaught, this challenging mountain has great character, with spectacular corries and panoramic views.

Mweelrea (814m) can be climbed by several routes, all of which entail a good deal of steep ground. The mountain's allure lies not only in its size and terrain, but also in its wonderfully contrasting setting. The steep southern flanks soar dramatically above the shores of Killary Harbour. To the east, a deep pass separates the mountain from the sprawling Sheffry Hills and the Ben Gorm massif. Northwards, Mweelrea overlooks low-lying pastoral lands fringing the shores of Clew Bay. And at the mountain's western feet, superb sandy beaches face the Atlantic. Although Mweelrea's Irish name, *Cnoc Maol Réidh*, translates as 'grey, bald mountain', the upper reaches are generally grassy – at least where the sheep haven't stripped the protective cover from the stony ground.

The approach described here, via the cliff-lined, glacial corrie of Coum Dubh to the northeast, offers the mountain's most spectacular ascent option. A diagonal grassy terrace known as 'The Ramp' provides the only route for walkers through the improbable cliffs to Ben Bury (795m) on the northern rim of the central arc of the massif, still a good 2km from Mweelrea's summit. After walking out and back to the summit of Mweelrea you can enjoy another 2km of superb ridge walking around the rim of Coum Dubh to the top of Ben Lugmore (803m) and back.

As an alternative to the out-and-back route, you could also consider descending via the mountain's southeastern spur and finishing at Delphi Mountain Resort and Adventure Centre. For details of the accommodation and activity facilities available at the centre, see p202.

Whichever route you choose, it is worth waiting for a good, clear day to climb Mweelrea. With so much steep and dangerous ground, the consequences of a navigational error in poor visibility could be severe.

PLANNING
Maps
The OSI 1:50,000 map No 37 covers the walk. Note that Ben Lugmore, the summit of 803m situated southeast of Ben Bury, remains unnamed on this map.

GETTING TO/FROM THE WALK
The route starts and finishes from the northwestern tip of Doo Lough, situated alongside the R335 around 15km northwest of Leenane and 13km south of Louisburgh. There are a few parking spaces on the verge here. The alternative finish is 4.5km south of the start along the R335. Walkers are requested not to use the car park at Delphi Mountain Resort, but limited parking spaces are available along the road close to the centre.

There is no public transport to the area.

THE WALK
Follow a rough vehicle track away from the road, passing parallel to the northwestern shore of Doo Lough. Here you must cross a small stream, using either stepping stones beside a ford, or a footbridge about 100m upstream. Rejoin the track on the opposite bank, which soon dwindles and disappears. Continue generally south and, above a stock pen, cross the stream that drains Coum Dubh and follow it up into the corrie.

The ground underfoot is rough and occasionally marshy until, about 45 minutes from the start, you reach the foot of 'The Ramp' – the only break in the lower line of cliffs around the head of the corrie. Climb a grassy spur between two streams and bear right, following the natural line of the slope with cliffs close to your left. After a few hundred metres, move further to the right and continue up on a grassy spur. Eventually you reach a narrow path across a scree slope, which leads to a grassy col on the edge of the plateau where there is a substantial cairn (one hour from the bottom of the corrie).

Turn northwards at the col and climb to **Ben Bury** at the northern corner of the massif. The views from either of the small cairns on the flattish summit extend far across Clew Bay into north Mayo. The driest route southwest and south to the col below Mweelrea's summit is on the left, across flat, stony outcrops. From the col

DOO LOUGH FAMINE WALK

As you pass along the road beside Doo Lough you'll notice a monument erected 'To commemorate the hungry poor who walked here in 1849, and walk the Third World today'. The earlier remembrance recalls one of the great human tragedies of Irish history. During the mid-19th century, Ireland was in the dark grip of the famine years, which would ultimately result in the country's population being cut in half, with almost a million people dying and almost three million emigrating overseas.

The event that inspired the memorial was a death march that took place in this valley on 30–31 March 1849. After seeking admission to the poorhouse in Louisburgh, hundreds of starving locals were told they would have to apply to the Board of Guardians, which was meeting the following day at Delphi Lodge. The group duly set off on the 16km journey on foot, enduring freezing conditions and spending the night in the open. When they arrived at Delphi Lodge (on the northeastern shore of Finn Lough), they were told the board was at lunch and could not be disturbed. Eventually they did meet, but were refused assistance. That day it rained and snowed, and some people died of cold and hunger in the lodge grounds, while others perished on the long journey back to Louisburgh. It is thought a total of around 400 people died while the region's landlords stood by and did nothing.

To learn more about this and other poignant events of the period, visit the **Famine Museum & Granuaile Visitors Centre** in Louisburgh (☎ 098-66134; Church St, Louisburgh; adult/child €3.50/1.50; open Tue, Thu, Fri & Sat).

MWEELREA & KILLARY HARBOUR

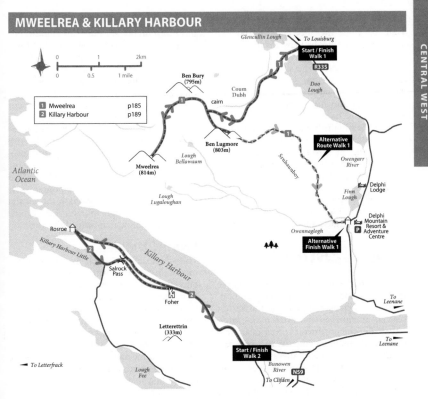

climb steeply, veering left for an aerial view of the wide and deep corrie embracing Lough Lugaloughan. The flat summit of **Mweelrea** (814m) – one hour from the cairn at the top of The Ramp – is adorned with a modest cairn perched on the very edge of the mountain's eastern face. The vista to the south and southeast sweeps impressively across the Twelve Bens and the Maumturks, while expansive Atlantic views include Clare and Achill Islands.

Return to the cairn at the top of The Ramp by working your way across the slope of Ben Bury, passing just below the most extensive drifts of scree. If you have the energy it's well worth continuing southeast from the cairn to experience some of the most entertaining and exhilarating walking on the mountain. Follow a faint path along the airy crest of the ridge, which although rocky at times, proves straightforward. To the east huge cliffs drop away into Coum

Dubh, while to the west the slopes become increasingly steep. Descend across a small col and then climb steeply to the pinnacle of **Ben Lugmore** (803m), the penultimate summit on the ridge.

From Ben Bury you can either continue to the Alternative Finish at Delphi, or return to Doo Lough by retracing your steps back along the ridge to the large cairn marking the top of The Ramp. Descend with care into Coum Dubh, then continue back out to Doo Lough.

ALTERNATIVE FINISH: DELPHI MOUNTAIN RESORT
1–1½ hours, 4km, 780m descent

From Ben Lugmore, descend southeast into a grassy gap and then climb a short distance to a broad, unnamed summit with a fine view back to Mweelrea. Now turn northeast and enjoy some excellent, easy walking along a broad ridge, passing over point 760 on the map. The rim of Coum Dubh lies to your left while the Sheefry Hills and Ben Creggan dominate the view ahead.

At the end of this ridge turn slightly south of east and descend the shoulder running down towards Delphi Mountain Resort. This deposits you on some boggy and rough ground in the Owennaglogh Valley; follow an old boundary wall towards Delphi. Just before the buildings you must ford the Owennaglogh River, a straightforward undertaking in normal water levels, but probably impossible in flood. If you are stuck there are two iron girders carrying a water pipe that with care will suffice as a makeshift bridge. All that remains is to cross a fence and follow a forestry track for a few hundred metres to Delphi and the R335.

CONNEMARA

The very name of Connemara is enough to capture the imagination. Mist-veiled mountains, lonely glens, rugged crags, the restless sea; all are images evocative of the area. Situated in the northwest corner of County Galway, Connemara consists of a compact group of mountains, valleys and moorlands, with Killary Harbour bordering the region to the north, and a seemingly endless maze of lakes and lower hills stretching away to the east and south. Dominated by the formidable peaks of the Twelve Bens and the Maumturks, but also including the Connemara National Park, the area has a great deal to offer walkers.

Connemara is reasonably well served by public transport and has a good range of inexpensive accommodation. Not surprisingly, it also experiences the worst of the notorious west coast weather, although on good days there are few finer places in which explore the Irish hills.

HISTORY

From prehistoric times and until at least the 12th century, people shunned the inhospitable and infertile interior of Connemara and clung to the narrow, coastal fringe and nearby islands. They left behind a large number of burial tombs and intriguing arrangements of stones, believed to be linked with rituals surrounding the solstice.

During the 19th century, Connemara was more favourably regarded by landowners; roads and piers were built and the town of Clifden was founded between 1810 and 1820. However, the population, which had grown phenomenally during the 19th century, was decimated by the Great Famine of the late 1840s (see the Killary Harbour route, p189, and the boxed text Doo Lough Famine Walk, p186). From 1891 the Congested Districts Board, and later the Irish Land Commission, guided a huge improvement in the fortunes of the area, putting the fishing industry on a firmer foundation and redistributing land holdings among former tenant farmers. Fishing and farming are still vital today, although tourism has become another economic mainstay of the area.

ENVIRONMENT

The principal building block of most of the mountains in Connemara is hard, white quartzite; rock that has been transformed from the sand and grit of an ancient ocean about 500 million years old. Beds of limestone also began transforming around this period, becoming bands of marble that form another a distinctive feature of Connemara today. Volcanic rocks are less common in the area, being mainly confined to the hard, black gabbro that makes up a few of the smaller hills in Connemara, including Errisbeg.

During the last ice age most of Connemara was buried under ice; the advance and retreat of the glaciers carved out and deepened valleys, and gouged sharp corries in the mountainsides (see Signs of a Glacial Past, p30). One of the most spectacular glacial features in the region, Killary Harbour, is explored on p189.

PLANNING
Maps & Books

Paddy Dillon's *Connemara* is a comprehensive guide to 30 varied walks in the region. Tim Robinson's *Connemara: Part 1, Introduction and Gazetteer* and the accompanying 1:63,360 *Connemara* map are beautifully written and designed, and are invaluable for historical, archaeological and geological background.

Information Sources

The region's main tourist office is located in Clifden (see p201). However, the best

online resources for the area are www.con
nemara.ie and www.goconnemara.com,
both of which detail an impressive list of
accommodation and a variety of other visitor information.

ACCESS TOWNS

See Clifden (p201), Leenane (p205) and
Letterfrack (p206).

KILLARY HARBOUR

Duration 3½–4 hours
Distance 10km
Ascent 180m
Difficulty easy
Start/Finish GR L814619
Nearest Towns Leenane (p205),
Letterfrack (p206)
Transport private

Summary A low-level circuit exploring the
southern shores of Killary Harbour, including a deserted hamlet, a famine road and
wonderful mountain scenery.

Killary Harbour is the 16km-long sea inlet
that marks the northern boundary of Connemara. More accurately described as Ireland's only true fjord, it was sculpted by the
glaciers of the last ice age, then submerged
when the climate warmed and the ice melted
about 10,000 years ago. The surrounding
backdrop is one of rugged mountain scenery, with steep, craggy peaks framing the
harbour on all sides. The slopes of Mweelrea, the highest mountain in Connaught,
rise steeply from the northern shores of the
inlet, while the summits to the east and
south are no less impressive.

Yet the natural splendour of the setting
is only one of the attractions of this route
along the harbour's southern shore. There
is also a poignant human history associated with the area. This part of the country
was particularly badly affected by the Great
Famine of 1845–49, and evidence of the
hardship of that era is impossible to avoid.
Ruined buildings of the now deserted settlement of Foher, which was depopulated
around the time of the famine, are visited
on this route. A famine relief road dating
back to 1846 – constructed by locals in
return for food rations – is followed over
another section.

The route also offers the opportunity to
explore the tiny fishing community of Rosroe at the mouth of Killary Harbour. This
hamlet can also be used as an alternative
start and finish point, though the hostel
that once made it possible to stay overnight
has now closed.

The terrain covered is a mixture of quiet
tarmac lanes, grassy boreens and rugged
paths. Salrock Pass marks the modest high-
point of the circuit at 130m, making this
an ideal option if clouds are lying low over
higher peaks in the area. Despite the route's
low altitude, boots are still required because
some sections of the trail are rough and
muddy.

PLANNING
Maps

The OSI 1:50,000 map No 37 and Harvey's
waterproof 1:30,000 Superwalker map *Connemara* both cover this route.

GETTING TO/FROM THE WALK

The route starts and finishes at the end
of a minor road (GR L814619) heading
northwest from the N59 on the southern
side of Killary Harbour. The turn-off from
the N59 is marked by signs for the Slí na
Chonamara, and is located 300m south of
the Bunowen River, around 7.5km west
of Leenane and 12km east of Letterfrack.
Parking at the end of the road is limited to
three cars – other small parking spots are
available further back along the road.

Large groups would do better to start
the circuit at Rosroe, where there is plenty
of parking space by the pier (GR L769650).
To reach Rosroe, turn west from the N59,
700m south of the Bunowen River and
400m south of the turn-off above. Continue for 7.5km, veering right, to the end
of the road.

There is no public transport to the
start of the route, although **Bus Éireann**
(☎ 091-562 000) Clifden–Leenane services
pass by on the N59 and could be used if the
timetable is convenient (see Getting There
& Away for Leenane, p205).

THE WALK

The start of the route is marked by two
gates and a sign indicating that private vehicles may not proceed any further. Pass
through the right-hand gate and continue

along the lane for a little over 1km. Lines of floats securing salmon pens bob in the harbour to the north and will be a constant presence for the first half of the route. The lane soon becomes a gravel track underfoot. Pass through a couple of gates and cross a bridge over a waterfall, where the track narrows again to a grassy boreen.

Around 3km from the start you come to a semi-ruined cottage, the first of several ruinous stone buildings that once made up the village of **Foher**. Follow the boreen along the front of the ruins, and pass over a stone stile in the wall to the west. The boreen now dwindles to a single-file path and climbs around a rock outcrop. The retaining walls of the famine road are obvious at the side of the path.

The rugged landscape is now dotted with boulders and bands of rock, though the buildings and boats of Rosroe soon come into view ahead (1½ to two hours from the start). Pass along the south side of a large stone wall enclosing a field, and exit the boreen beside a cottage. Join a minor road and turn right towards Rosroe harbour; the pier is a couple of hundred metres away, and well worth the short detour.

From the pier, retrace your steps along the road, continuing past the point where you descended from the boreen. Killary Harbour Little (or 'Little Killary') is the picturesque inlet to the south, its shape mimicking the larger-scale fjord further north. Follow the road for around 1km, climbing to a sharp right turn. Leave the lane here, continuing ahead (east) through a wooden gate. A short but steep ascent now leads to **Salrock Pass**, where Killary Harbour and Little Killary are both visible.

The descent down the eastern side of the pass is even steeper, though it's not long before you come to a junction of a fence and stone wall on your right. Cross the low wire fence at the corner and then turn immediately left through a gate in the wall. You are now at the top of the ruined settlement of Foher that you passed on your outward journey. Turn right and trace the wall as it descends gradually through the ruins, rejoining the boreen at the eastern end of the hamlet. Retrace your initial steps back to the road and your starting point.

DIAMOND HILL

Duration 2½–3 hours
Distance 7km
Ascent 420m
Difficulty easy–moderate
Start/Finish Connemara National Park Visitor Centre
Nearest Town Letterfrack (p206)
Transport bus
Summary Fantastic views and an enjoyably narrow summit make this charismatic little peak a lot of gain for very little pain.

Connemara National Park was established in 1980, and spans almost 3000 hectares of bog, mountain and heathland stretching from sea level to the 729m-high summit of Benbaun. Dominating the western section of the park, the quartzite-crowned peak of Diamond Hill (445m) offers fantastic views. Despite its modest size, this peak has all the character of neighbouring mountains that rise to almost twice its height.

The route described is one of Ireland's network of National Loop Walks and is fully signposted, following a mixture of gravel, stone and wooden paths throughout. It begins along the Sruffaunboy Nature Trail, which highlights the flora, fauna and geology of the area. It then combines the Lower Diamond Hill loop walk with the Upper Diamond Hill loop to reach the mountain's crowning fin of quartzite.

Just because there is a path, don't be fooled into thinking the mountain has been entirely tamed. True, route-finding is no longer an issue, but on the steep upper sections of the climb you'll still find yourself using your hands for assistance in places. Even though Diamond Hill is not high by local standards, it is no less prone to sudden onslaughts of mist, rain and strong wind, and in wet weather the quartzite becomes dangerously slippery underfoot.

The route starts at the national park **Visitor Centre** (☎ 095-41054; www.connemara -nationalpark.ie; Letterfrack; admission free; open daily Mar-early Oct), which offers exhibits on the park's history, geology and ecology. There's also a tearoom serving drinks and snacks, an indoor eating area and rudimentary kitchen facilities for walkers. The park grounds are open year-round.

DIAMOND HILL

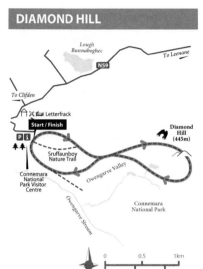

PLANNING
Maps & Books
Use either Harvey's Superwalker 1:30,000 map *Connemara* or OSI 1:50,000 map No 37, though neither map shows the path in its entirety.

A leaflet guide to the Sruffaunboy Nature Trail is also available from the visitor centre, and covers the early stage of this walk.

GETTING TO/FROM THE WALK
The entrance to the national park is signed off the N59, 500m southwest of the Letterfrack crossroads. For transport details to Letterfrack, see p206.

THE WALK
From the car park, walk around the northern side of the visitor centre and follow a wide gravel path northeast past a children's play area. Climb gently along the left side of a field, following the Sruffaunboy Nature Trail with Diamond Hill rising imposingly ahead. Pass through a sprung gate and climb round a sharp corner to a junction. Turn left here to continue along the Lower Diamond Hill Walk, which uses sections of boardwalk to span wet terrain. Within long you reach another junction, marked by a huge boulder. Turn left onto

the Upper Diamond Hill path, which soon begins to gain height as you approach the base of the summit pyramid.

At the next trail junction, turn left and climb a steep, winding staircase of flagstones. The path skirts under some very steep slopes and then climbs diagonally through a series of **quartzite outcrops** before swinging back to the left and exiting onto the upper section of the ridge. The gradient now eases and the path takes you gently to the **summit cairn** (1½ hours from the start). From here you can fully appreciate the intricate nature of the Connemara coastline, as well as the offshore islands of Inishturk, Inishbofin and Inishshark. Inland, the views across the Twelve Bens are sensational, while below to the northeast the gothic turrets of Kylemore Abbey are conspicuous on the shore of Kylemore Lough.

Continue to follow the path across the summit, onto an initially steep descent down the eastern side of Diamond Hill. A largely flat section then leads along a large terrace on the southern side of the mountain. As you work your way back to the western flank you return to a junction passed on the outward journey. Turn left here and descend to the boulder that marks the junction with the lower loop. Turn left again and descend steeply to an old bog road in the **Owengarve Valley**. Make a final right turn and follow the wide track back to the visitor centre.

GLENCOAGHAN HORSESHOE

Duration 7–7½ hours
Distance 12km
Ascent 1670m
Difficulty demanding
Start quarry near Glencoaghan River
Finish Ben Lettery Youth Hostel
Nearest Towns Clifden (p201), Glencoaghan (p204)
Transport bus

Summary A classic among Irish mountain walks, this exhilarating route demands fitness, surefootedness and confidence over steep and rocky ground.

A walk over some of the renowned Twelve Bens is akin to a rite of passage for walkers in Connemara, if not Ireland in general. This immensely rugged mountain range dominates the heart of Connemara and is arranged in a cluster of five interlocking horseshoes, with peaks ranging in height from Benbaun (729m) to Benlettery (577m). Intervening cols are extremely steep and bands of cliffs run around the central summits, lending the range an almost impregnable demeanour.

Despite appearances the Bens offer a variety of exhilarating walking routes, all of them strenuous in nature. The six southern summits fit neatly into the Glencoaghan Horseshoe, and form what is probably the most popular walk in the range. The route is immensely rewarding, but demands a high degree of fitness and hill-walking experience. It involves a large amount of ascent and the terrain can be rough; in several places steep slopes call for the use of hands, and rock steps demand minor scrambling manoeuvres. It is only possible to escape the ridge in one or two (rather inconvenient) places, and navigation in poor visibility is far from straightforward. In many places along the crest a rutted path has been worn by the passage of feet, but on many of the steeper slopes you are left to pick your own way through the boulders.

Other circuits in the Twelve Bens share many of the difficulties and rewards associated with this route. See the Benbaun Circuit (More Walks, p200) for details of another route around the range's northern summits.

PLANNING
Maps
Harvey's Superwalker 1:30,000 map *Connemara* is the ideal map for this route. Alternatively, you'll need two OSI 1:50,000 maps: Nos 37 and 44 (note that Bengower is misnamed Glengower on map 37).

GETTING TO/FROM THE WALK
To reach the start of the walk, turn north off the N59 onto a minor road, around 7km west of Recess, 15km east of Clifden and 1.7km east of the Ben Lettery Youth Hostel. The start is about 2.5km along this road. Park at a small quarry just west of the bridge over the Glencoaghan River, around 1.5km from the N59; alternatively, there are individual spaces about 1km further on. At the end of the walk, parking is available on the old road close to the hostel entrance.

Bus Éireann (☎ 091-562 000) and Citylink (☎ 091-564 163; www.citylink.ie) both ply the N59 on their Clifden–Galway services. Ask to be dropped off at the minor road near the start of the walk, or at Ben Lettery Youth Hostel. See Getting There & Away for Clifden (p202) for full transport details.

THE WALK
From the roadside around 1km northeast of the Glencoaghan River, head east and begin to climb towards the crest of the ridge. The ground becomes steeper as you gain height, and the bog gradually gives way to rock. At the top of the shoulder turn north and follow a worn path up the western side of the ridge to the summit of **Derryclare** (673m, 1½ hours from the start). The views south across the Connemara lake lands to the low ridge of Errisbeg (p195) are particularly fine.

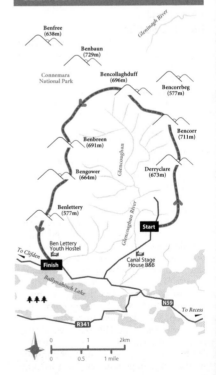

GLENCOAGHAN HORSESHOE

An easy descent, by Twelve Bens standards, takes you north to a peaty col. Then a steep, rocky ascent leads to a sprawling cairn on the compact summit of **Bencorr** (*Binn Chorr*, 711m, 45 minutes from Derryclare). The extra elevation here brings Mweelrea and the Benchoona massif into view to the north. Continue northwest along the ridge over a couple of dips and bumps to a cairn that marks the top of the next, very steep, descent. Veer westwards here and negotiate your way down some unstable scree, then stride over massive rock slabs to reach a narrow peaty col, *Mam na bhFonsaí* (30 minutes from Bencorr).

The next ascent begins over rock slabs, but moves to more broken rock as you near the small summit of **Bencollaghduff** (*Binn Dhubh*, 696m, 30 minutes from the col). This peak lies right in the midst of the Bens, at the apex of the horseshoe. Head west down another steep drop, though the gradient eases for the descent to a slender col. Here you make a major change in direction, turning southwest and beginning the trip along the western arm of the horseshoe – with some interesting route-finding problems beckoning you on.

The next climb starts easily enough, but as the ridge steepens, the rocks become less dissected. Keep to the left to surmount a bluff guarding the edge of the elongated summit arc of **Benbreen** (*Binn Bhraoin*, 691m). Keep to the crest and cross a series of hummocks to reach the mountain's southern tip, where a cairn marks the highest point (1¼ hours from the last col). Ribbons of scree now lead south to the next col, where the most exciting ascent of the day looms ahead. At the first apparent barrier a well-defined ramp provides a good route up; next, a narrow gully is climbed via its own, in-built 'steps'; and the last obstacle is overcome by bearing right along a path around the bluff. The reward for your effort is the summit of **Bengower** (*Binn Gobhar*, 664m, 30 minutes from Benbreen), and great views of the Connemara lake lands to the south.

Descend southwest to a broad, grassy col, then make the final climb of the day to **Benlettery** (*Binn Leitir*, 577m, 40 minutes from Bengower). Now follow an eroded path south from the summit, keeping west for the best route through the crags. On the

way down aim for the ruinous stone building just north of the hostel. Go through a gap in the fence above the ruin, which you pass on your left, and continue towards the hostel, crossing its enclosing fence via a stile.

CENTRAL MAUMTURKS

Duration 5–5½ hours
Distance 12km
Ascent 750m
Difficulty moderate–demanding
Start/Finish Maumeen car park
Nearest Town Clifden (p201)
Transport private

Summary A high-level walk across an intricate, rocky ridge in the heart of the magnificent Maumturk Mountains.

Any walk in the Maumturk Mountains is a serious undertaking. The terrain is more rugged than it looks from below, accurate route-finding is a challenge, and maps don't show the intricate jumble of knolls, spurs and tarns along the main summit ridge. For fans of such high rocky ground, however, this is an immensely rewarding route across a marvellously scenic range, and a classic outing within the Connemara region.

The walk described here crosses the central section of the Maumturk Mountains, and includes a visit to the range's highest peak, *Binn Idir an Dá Log* (Peak Between Two Hollows), at 702m. It begins by following an old pilgrimage route – now part of the Western Way – to a tiny chapel set evocatively within the confines of a mountain pass. The site is graced by an outdoor altar, a holy well and a collection of small, stone-carved Celtic crosses, one for each station of the cross. St Patrick himself is said to have blessed the land of Connemara from this point, and he couldn't have picked a more scenic spot to do it from – walkers may well be inspired to do the same thing! After a tough but highly rewarding upland section, the route finishes with 4km along a quiet minor road, although this can be avoided if two vehicles are available.

Unless you are confident of your navigation skills, it's best to tackle the Maumturks only in good weather – route-finding is particularly tricky in poor visibility.

PLANNING
Maps
Harvey's Superwalker 1:30,000 map *Connemara* is best for this walk. Alternatively, use the OSI 1:50,000 maps Nos 37 and 44.

GETTING TO/FROM THE WALK
If you are approaching the route by car, turn northeast from the N59 along a minor road signed to 'Mamean', 12km west of Maam Cross and 2km east of Recess. The car park is 3.2km further on (GR L892495). To avoid the road walk back to the start, there are small parking spaces near the bridge at GR L873521.

The closest you can get by public transport is Recess, about 4km southwest of the start of the walk. **Bus Éireann** (☎ 091-562 000) and **Citylink** (☎ 091-564 163; www.citylink .ie) buses all stop here as part of their Galway – Clifden routes – for more details see Getting There & Away for Clifden (p202).

THE WALK
From the Maumeen car park, go through the large gate and walk up the wide track that climbs steadily northeast towards the

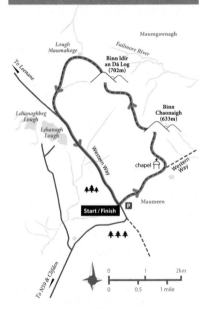

CENTRAL MAUMTURKS

mountains. After about 30 minutes you reach the tiny, stone **chapel** in the col of Maumeen, near the highest point on the track. The outdoor altar is topped with a slab of green-seamed Connemara marble, and the cairns marking the stations of the cross are scattered nearby.

From here, set a northeasterly course towards a grassy spur at the foot of low bluffs, soon crossing the path to the holy well on the left. Cross a fence and climb steeply northwest towards the crest of the spur. Here you meet the fence again – it provides an occasionally useful guide as you continue northwest, climbing to a bumpy plateau strewn with rock slabs and masses of shattered white quartzite. The summit, **Binn Chaonaigh** (633m), is set about 100m northwest of a tiny lough (one hour from the chapel).

From this summit, descend steeply west for about 700m before veering north close to the edge of cliffs. Continue down along a narrow ridge to a col. There are occasional traces of a stony path underfoot, although it isn't continuous enough to provide reliable guidance. Climb to a small cairn that marks the first of a cluster of tops, the highest (659m) marking a change in direction at an eastern extremity of the ridge.

Then comes another descent, followed by a steady climb first west then north over a jumble of bumps and hollows, now following a clear path underfoot. Continue to **Binn Idir an Dá Log** (702m), the main summit of the range, which is marked by a cairn on a chunky crag (1½ hours from Binn Chaonaigh).

Sporadic cairns indicate the route onwards, north across a plateau to the descent route along a narrow ridge tending northwest. A squat cairn on the northwest edge of a sloping shelf marks the start of a very steep section down through broken crags, although there are alternative routes down to the left that involve more grass and less rock. At the base of the descent lies the delightful **Lough Maumahoge** (45 minutes from the summit).

Cross the rocky spur west of the lough to reach a small col, where a steep descent leads down a grassy passage to the wide valley below. The gradient soon eases and an easy amble beside a picturesque stream brings down you to the road; the Maumeen car park is 4km along the lane to the left.

BRAVING THE MAUMTURKS CHALLENGE

Twenty-four kilometres of horizontal distance and 2336m of ascent probably aren't the criteria for most walkers' notion of a pleasant day's outing. Nevertheless, each Easter since 1975 a couple of hundred walkers have thought otherwise and taken part in the National University of Ireland Mountaineering Club's Maumturks Challenge.

The walk starts about 3km south of Maam bridge on the road to Maam Cross and finishes in Leenane. Check-in opens at 5am and most participants cover the distance in about 10 hours, although six hours is not unknown. The event is unsupported and all participants must be self-sufficient, though walkers are required to punch their Walk Cards at several checkpoints along the route. Cut-off times are also implemented, and those who fail to progress fast enough are requested to descend the range via the nearest designated exit route.

Apart from the physical challenge of completing the route, the event is further enlivened by the unpredictable climate. The Maumturks make their own weather within an area already infamous for its meteorological mayhem. In 1975 conditions were so bad that only a handful of the 70 starters completed the distance. In 2002 the event was cancelled altogether, while in 2008 snow covered much of the high ground, and visibility was severely affected by snow showers that fell throughout the day. The combined with the rugged terrain makes it little wonder a helicopter has had to be summoned on several occasions to lift injured walkers to safety.

For more information about the annual event, contact **NUIG Mountaineering Club** (www .maamturkswalk.com; Aran na MacLeinn, National University of Ireland, Galway City, County Galway).

ERRISBEG

Duration 2–3 hours
Distance 6km
Ascent 300m
Difficulty easy–moderate
Start/Finish Main St, Roundstone
Nearest Town Roundstone (p207)
Transport bus

Summary A short ascent of a rugged little hill, rewarded by far-reaching views across the loughs, bogs, coast and mountains of Connemara.

Southern Connemara is slightly off the beaten track, but exudes an atmosphere of peace and tranquility that can be hard to find in the region's more popular centres. If you do make it this far, don't miss the short but immensely scenic walk to the summit of Errisbeg. On a good day the views from the top – though only 300m high – embrace most of the major peaks, coastline and boglands of Connemara. The geology of Errisbeg is also unusual in that it has formed from an isolated outcrop of the volcanic rock gabbro, a rock type not common in Ireland.

The walk starts conveniently from the village of Roundstone, a popular weekend destination with a beautiful harbour view that has attracted the eye of many painters. Despite the route's modest distance, you'll still need to cross some rough, open ground. Although the summit plateau and its approaches are littered with cairns of all shapes and sizes, there aren't any clearly defined paths. The terrain underfoot consists of grass, heather and rock with some minor boggy patches, and decent boots are a necessity.

If you prefer a longer outing, consider extending the route into a coastal circuit by descending steeply south from the summit of Errisbeg to Dogs Bay and Gurteen Bay. Rough ground is covered on the descent and you'll need to avoid walking across private land close to the many cottages along the R341. Good coastal walking then leads from Gurteen Bay back to Roundstone. Allow an extra 1½ to two hours for this 9km circuit.

PLANNING
Maps
Use OSI 1:50,000 map No 44 for this walk.

THE WALK
From the main street in Roundstone, turn uphill at the corner of O'Dowd's pub onto

CENTRAL WEST

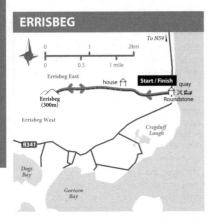

a narrow road. Climb steeply for a short distance to gain more level ground above the village. Continue straight along the road for the next 1km, passing over a crossroads before climbing steeply again to reach a house at the road end. To the left of the house is a wooden gate. Pass through this and follow the eroded path out onto the open hillside. Aim for easier slopes slightly north of the mountain's east summit. As you gain height the path becomes fainter and diverges into many separate, barely discernible trails, before disappearing altogether. Continue ahead, climbing towards the unnamed eastern summit at 252m, crossing wonderfully rugged terrain with tussock grass and heather filling the hollows between outcrops of rough gabbro.

Looking back to the east from this first top, views extend across the many inlets and islands of Galway Bay. To the north the vast mosaic of bog and loughs extends all the way to the slopes of the Twelve Bens. Head west across several intervening hummocks to reach the trig point that marks the official summit of **Errisbeg** (around 1½ hours from the start). On a clear day the panorama opens out to the west and it

WARNING

Note that the volcanic gabbro rock that makes up most of Errisbeg has magnetic properties that can affect compass needles, so great care is needed if navigating in mist.

can be difficult to discern exactly where the mainland ends and the ocean begins, such is the chaotic complexity of the coastline. To the south the low profiles of the Aran Islands are conspicuous Atlantic landmarks, and beyond these Black Head (p198) and the limestone pavements of the Burren show up either white or grey depending whether the sun is shining.

Turn around at the summit and return to Roundstone by retracing your outward journey.

THE BURREN

The Burren landscape is one of Ireland's most famous natural attractions, and justly so. This is a unique area, characterised by expanses of pale grey limestone pavement and terraced hillsides that stretch right down to the Atlantic (see the boxed text Karst Wonders of the Burren, p197). The name comes from the Irish word *boireann*, meaning 'place of rocks'. In reality, however, only 20% of the Burren is bare rock, while the remainder of the terrain is composed of vivid green fields and hills that boast the richest concentration of plant species in Ireland. The geological and botanical wonders of the area are offset by the ancient human interests; the Burren also has a remarkable number of archaeological features, especially prehistoric burial tombs, forts and early Christian chapels.

Curiously, given the wealth of natural and historic interest concentrated in the area, the Burren is not as accessible for walkers as most other parts of the country, and there are comparatively few good, sustained walks. Fortunately one or two routes are possible, and provide a highly recommended way to appreciate the unusual beauty of the area.

HISTORY

Communities have been living in the Burren for about 5000 years. For the earliest peoples of the Neolithic and Bronze ages, the building of tombs for their dead was of great importance, and the region is liberally sprinkled with ancient burial sites. Most impressive of these are the dolmens, upstanding slabs of stone that support a massive lid or capstone. From about 600 BC, Celtic people settled in the area and built round or oval enclosures known as raths, dúns, cashels or lios. The Burren has the best collection of these structures in Ireland, with as many as 450 different sites still identifiable.

ENVIRONMENT

The Burren is one of the finest 'botanical showplaces' in Europe, earning this distinction on two main counts: the wealth of species of flowering plants (especially rare ones) and the presence of species happily flourishing far from their normal habitats. Species of flower that usually grow high in the European Alps are abundant in the Burren, and many plants that are otherwise rare in Ireland also find a suitable habitat here; of the 27 species of orchid in Ireland, 23 are resident in the Burren.

Small herds of feral goats are quite common in the region, usually under the command of a fearsome billy with long horns and a wonderfully shaggy, dark coat. The goats, who feed enthusiastically on young trees, actually ensure the proliferation of wildflowers by keeping down the spread of hazel scrub. Other unusual, albeit domestic, native mammals that can be seen in the area are bog ponies – small, rotund horses about the same size as Shetland ponies, with wide, flowing manes. Traditionally used as working animals by farmers, these miniature wonders are now relatively rare. Several small herds are managed by enthusiasts in the Burren area, and you may be lucky enough to spot one of them.

PLANNING
Maps & Books

Tim Robinson's 1:31,680 map *The Burren* may be impractical for walking purposes, but it marks the area's geological and archaeological landmarks in exhaustive detail and is well worth a look.

The Burren and the Aran Islands by Tony Kirby details 15 walking routes, varying from 5km-long casual strolls to 15.5km-long routes over the region's limestone hills. It was published in 2009 so information is as up to date as possible.

KARST WONDERS OF THE BURREN

Few landscapes anywhere in Ireland, except perhaps the Giant's Causeway in Antrim, have the surreal, other-worldly appearance of the limestone pavements and terraces of the Burren.

The limestone itself is about 340 million years old and began as vast quantities of lime-rich material, such as shells and skeletons of marine creatures, that dissolved in the warm, shallow sea under which 'Ireland' was then submerged. Long after the sea had retreated, these beds were then stripped of a relatively thin layer of overlying material during the last ice age. Subsequent erosion, accelerated by the clearing of trees by early farmers, left what looks like a rock desert, with precious few spaces where soil could develop. The Burren limestone is up to 780m thick, and the bare pavements and terraces cover an area of 250 sq km.

The limestone beds are imprinted with lines of weakness – cracks or joints. When rainwater works its way down into these spaces the limestone, being a water-soluble rock, dissolves a little along the lines of the cracks. In their widened form these are called grikes; the slabs in between are the clints. Intricate networks of hollows, channels and pinnacles are the result of this water erosion. When rainwater has penetrated as far as it can go into the limestone, it then turns sideways, still dissolving the rock, and eventually forms networks of underground caves. The landform resulting from the process of disappearing water and underground cave formation is called karst, after an area in (former) Yugoslavia where it was first studied. The Burren is Ireland's best known karst area, and has the longest cave system in the country.

Typically for karst country, the Burren is virtually river-less. However, turloughs are a feature of the limestone country unique to Ireland. Derived from the Irish words *tur* loch, meaning 'dry lake', they are ephemeral lakes. They appear in shallow hollows only after heavy rain, when the water table (the level at which the ground is permanently saturated) rises and allows water to spill out and quickly fill the hollow, usually to a depth of about 2m. During a dry spell the water seeps away into the ground and the turlough recedes and may even disappear. Some turloughs materialise during autumn and fade away the following spring and summer.

Information Sources

The area's main **tourist office** is in Bal-lyvaughan (☎ 065-707 7464; www.bally vaughantourism.com; open daily Mar-Oct, weekends only Nov-Feb). It's located in The Village Stores on the village's main street. Staff can answer most tourist-related que-ries, and also sell maps and local books.

BLACK HEAD

Duration 5 hours
Distance 14.5km
Ascent 410m
Difficulty moderate
Start/Finish St Patrick's Church, Fanore
Nearest Towns Fanore (p203), Doolin (p202)
Transport bus, private

Summary A wonderful circuit exploring the unique, shattered limestone landscape and ancient stone enclosures of the Burren.

On the northwestern tip of the Burren, Black Head (Ceann Boirne) has some of the finest expanses of limestone pavement in the area. This route explores the terraces and pavements of the mountainous head-land, offering far-reaching coastal views and providing a showcase for many of the plant species that make the region a bota-nist's delight.

The circuit begins with a 3.5km section of paved road that traces the Caher River, the only surface river in the Burren. It then joins the route of the Burren Way for a short distance before heading across two rocky mountain summits. Ascents are not long or steep, but negotiating the shattered rock terrain demands constant attention. Stepping into one of the numerous fissures is a sure way to break an ankle! The final attraction of the route is a visit to the Iron Age stone fort of Cathair Dhúin Irghuis, before one of the region's evocative old green roads is followed back to Fanore. The route can be followed in either direction, though sea views are better in the direction described.

PLANNING
When to Walk

May, June and July are the optimum months for observing the region's profu-sion of wildflowers.

What to Bring

Make sure to bring plenty of water with you as there is none available en route.

Maps

The OSI 1:50,000 map No 51 covers the route.

GETTING TO/FROM THE WALK

Bus Éireann (☎ 091-562 000) operates a limited service through Fanore. Bus 432 passes through on its way from Galway (€14.30, 1½ hours) to Doolin (€4.50, 25 minutes), running once daily Monday to Friday during July and August, but on Tuesdays and Thursdays only the rest of the year.

By car, Fanore is located along the R477 'coast road', around 11km west of Bally-vaughan and 16km north of Doolin. For this walk, park in the car park for St Patrick's Church, which is signed 150m along the Khyber Pass road near the northern end of the village.

THE WALK

From the entrance to St Patrick's Church, turn right and begin walking east along the Khyber Pass. This narrow road climbs steadily for most of the 3.5km that you are on it, but traffic is light and the tum-bling waters of the Caher River to your left offer distraction. Around an hour from the church another road joins from the right, and waymarking posts signal that you are now on the route of the Burren Way. Con-tinue ahead for another few steps, then turn left to follow the Burren Way up a winding stone track.

Follow the track to the brow of a hill, passing a jumble of ruined farm buildings and the just-discernible fort of Cathair an Aird Rhois on the right. At the top of the rise, leave the track and cross a stone wall on the left, heading north across open mountain terrain. The green mound that marks the summit of **Gleninagh Mountain** (317m) is prominent to the north, and this is where you are heading. The route veers west and then east to reach the top, fol-lowing a natural line along the top of the rounded ridge. Numerous stone walls will need to be negotiated at the start of this sec-tion, and the grassy terrain is interspersed with sections of limestone pavement.

From the concrete trig pillar at the **summit** of Gleninagh (2½ to three hours from the start), sweeping views allow full appreciation of the Burren landscape; grey, rock-terraced hills stretch away on three sides, while the waters of Galway Bay offset the scene to the north. The large cairn of **Dobhach Brainin** (possibly of Neolithic origin) dominates the skyline to the northwest, and marks the second (unnamed) summit of the route at 314m.

A ridge links Gleninagh and this next peak. The ridge takes you down into a col and several short cliffs will need to be negotiated on the descent – easier points can generally be found by skirting a short distance along their edge. Once in the col, keep close to a wall running along its northeastern edge. The terrain now consists almost entirely of limestone pavement and this will continue for the remainder of the mountain crossing.

Veer to the east as you make the final climb to the summit (45 minutes from Gleninagh), which gives you a fine viewpoint for the coasts of Clare and Galway. The three Aran Islands are visible a few kilometres across the Atlantic to the east. Descend northwest from the summit carefully, negotiating several more cliff-like terraces along the way. The round walls of **Cathair Dhúin Irghuis** soon come into view ahead; cross a couple of stone walls and pass alongside the ruins on your descent towards Black Head.

Shortly after the fort the coast road comes into view, and you soon reach the grassy line of an old green road, enclosed on both sides by stone walls. Join the green road and turn left (southwest) to follow it the remaining 2.5km back to Fanore. Several stone walls now span the breadth of the old road and will need to be crossed; it's a bit of an obstacle course but nothing takes away from the delightful experience of following this ancient route through wildflower meadows and sections of dramatic limestone pavement. The end of the green road is obscured by a jumble of rocks; avoid this by passing along the edge of the field to the left. Cross a final wall to emerge on a gravel track just above Fanore. Follow the track downhill to a junction with the main road (the R477) and turn left. After 400m turn left again to rejoin the Khyber Pass, with St Patrick's Church just a short distance ahead.

MORE WALKS

MAYO
Nephin Beg
Nephin Beg (617m) lies in a remote area of bog and forestry plantations, north of Clew Bay. The walk starts from a track north Srahmore Lodge, at the point where the Bangor Trail and Western Way split (GR F968055). Follow the way-marked Bangor Trail for the first 6km, then climb the southwest ridge of Nephin Beg. Summit views encompass most of Mayo. The steep eastern slopes are then descended to reach the Western Way, and a 7km walk along tracks leads back to the start. Allow six to seven hours for this moderate to demanding, 18km-long route. Use OSI 1:50,000 map No 23. Access to this route is by private transport only.

BLACK HEAD

Galway Bay

Black Head

Cathair Dhúin Irghuis stone fort

Coolsiva Quay

R477

To Ballyvaughan

Dobhach Brainin cairn (314m)

Rocky View Farmhouse B&B

Fanore bridge

St Patrick's Church

Gleninagh Mountain (317m)

Start / Finish

Khyber Pass

Fanore

Caher River

To Doolin

(303m)

Cathair an Aird Rhois stone fort

Maumtrasna & the Devil's Mother

A challenging mountain circuit that is best kept for a fine day, this walk starts and finishes from the N59 at Glennacally Bridge, 6km east of Leenane (GR L935656). The demanding route traces a clockwise horseshoe around Glennacally River, beginning with a steep ascent to the wide summit plateau of Maumtrasna (673m). From here the route veers southwest, passing over Knocklaur to a 3km-long section of ridge that sweeps over the Devil's Mother (645m) before descending steeply back to the road. The route is 14km long and involves 1040m of ascent; allow at least seven to eight hours. OSI 1:50,000 maps Nos 37 and 38 cover the route. The **Bus Éireann** (☎ 091-562 000) Leenane–Westport service plies the N59 during July and August only, and will drop you at the start/finish of this route if you ask the driver; see Leenane (p205) for full service details.

CONNEMARA
Benbaun Circuit

This strenuous but scenic route traverses some of the major northern summits of Connemara's famous Twelve Bens, including the highest peak, Benbaun (729m). It traces a clockwise horseshoe around the Gleninagh River, also crossing Bencorr (711m) and Bencollaghduff (696m). The OSI 1:50,000 map No 37 and Harvey's Superwalker 1:30,000 map *Connemara* both cover the walk, which is also described in Paddy Dillon's book *Connemara*. The walk starts and finishes along the R344, at the bridge over Tooreenacoona River (GR L824555). Allow seven hours for the 13km circuit, which involves 1190m of ascent. Access to the bottom is by private transport only.

Tully Mountain

Tully Mountain (356m) rises in splendid isolation to the west of Connemara's highest peaks. A surprisingly complex hill littered with crags, tarns and rocky summits, it is an ideal option for days when higher summits are covered by cloud. Access to the route is by private transport only. From the N59 at Letterfrack, head north along the minor road to Tully Cross, and turn off after 3km towards the Ocean's Alive Visitor Centre. The circuit starts from the quay on the northern side of Ballynakill Harbour (GR L688598). From here, follow the road west for 300m then turn right onto a track. Pass around the left side of a quarry, then climb northwest and follow the mountain's shoulder up to the summit. Continue northwest along the ridge to Loughan, then descend south to a road. Turn left along the road to return to the start. This easy to moderate outing is 7km long, involves 375m of ascent, and takes around three hours. Use OSI 1:50,000 map No 37.

THE BURREN
Turlough Hill & Slievecarran

Set at the northeastern tip of the Burren, Turlough Hill (280m) and Slievecarran (326m) offer another chance to get close up and personal with the region's fascinating limestone pavement. Fine coastal views are another bonus. The moderate route starts and finishes at the bottom of a gravel track in the townland of Shanvally (GR M297086). Reach this point by turning south of the coast road between Kinvara and Ballyvaughan. Head up the track to its end, then climb east over limestone pavement to the col just south of Slieve Oughtmama. Turn south here and continue to the summit of Slievecarran. Then retrace your steps north, veering west past an Iron Age hill fort to visit the summit of Turlough Hill before descending back along the track to the road. OSI 1:50,000 map Nos 51 and 52 cover the 15km walk, which involves 500m ascent and takes 4½ to 5½ hours to complete.

WAYMARKED WAYS

There are plenty of Waymarked Ways in the central west, ranging from 26km to 118km long. In counties Sligo, Leitrim and Cavan there's the Cavan Way, the Leitrim Way, the Sligo Way and the Miners Way & Historical Trail. In County Mayo you'll find the Bangor Trail and the Foxford Way. In counties Galway and Roscommon there's the Western Way and the Suck Valley Way, and in County Clare there's a choice between the Burren Way, the Mid Clare Way and the East Clare Way. For full descriptions of all these routes, see www .walkireland.ie.

TOWNS & FACILITIES

ACHILL SOUND
☎ 098 / pop 255

The town of Achill Sound (*Ghob a'Choire*) spans the access bridge for Achill Island and has a wide range of visitor facilities, including an ATM and a large supermarket that sells local walking maps.

Sleeping & Eating
Occupying a former a train station, **Railway Hostel** (☎ 45187; camping per person €7.50, dm €15) now serves as a rather austere, no-frills hostel. It's located just before the bridge on the mainland side of the channel.

The town also offers also a wide choice of B&Bs. Try **Murrayville B&B** (☎ 45123; www.murrayvilleachill.com; Springvale; open Mar-Sep; s/d €25/60), a traditional family home within five minutes of the village centre.

Alternatively, friendly **Anvil House** (☎ 20908; www.anvilhouse.ie; Convent Road; s/d €35/60) is located in the heart of Achill Sound, near to the House of Prayer.

The newest hotel in town, **Óstán Oileán Acla** (Achill Island Hotel; ☎ 45138; www.achillislandhotel.com; s/d €45/90; mains from €12), is located beside the bridge on the mainland side. The bar food is extremely popular.

Lunch and evening meals are also served in almost all of the town's other bars and hotels.

For details of transport to Achill Sound, see Getting There & Around for Achill Island (p169).

BELMULLET
☎ 097 / pop 2100

The functional little town of Belmullet (*Béal an Mhuirthead*) lies at the entrance to the Irish-speaking Mullet Peninsula, and is the largest settlement in northwest Mayo.

Erris tourist office (☎ 097-81500; Barrack St; open Mon-Fri Easter-Sep) is small, friendly, and can help with most inquiries.

Sleeping & Eating
B&Bs in the area include the modern and cheerful **Chez Nous** (☎ 82167; chez_nous _belmullet@esatclear.ie; Church Rd; s/d €50/80; open Mar-Dec). It's a five-minute walk from the town's central roundabout along the road signed to the Garda station.

Nearby **Drom Caoin** (☎ 81195; www.belmullet-accommodation.com; Church Rd; s/d €40/90) is also five minutes' walk from the central roundabout. This peaceful home is set on a gentle slope and enjoys a serene outlook, with panoramic views of Blacksod Bay.

Right in the centre of town, **Western Strands Hotel** (☎ 81096; www.westernstrandshotel.com; Main St; s/d €48/70) also serves good food in its downstairs **bar** (mains from €10).

The town centre also has a reasonable-sized supermarket and several other eateries.

Getting There & Away
Bus Éireann (☎ 096-71800) services link Belmullet to Ballina (€12.50, 1¼ hours, once daily Mon-Sat with additional services in Jul & Aug), where there are onward connections to Sligo, Westport and Dublin. **McNulty's Coaches** (☎ 81086; www.mcnultycoaches.com; Chapel St) also run daily buses to and from Castlebar (€10, 1½ hours) from their office near Belmullet post office.

CLIFDEN
☎ 095 / pop 1900

A lively town, Clifden (*An Clochán*) holds the title of capital of Connemara. It offers a wide range of tourist facilities and is a good base for exploring the region.

The town's **tourist office** (☎ 21163; www.clifdenchamber.ie; Galway Rd; open daily Jul & Aug, Mon-Sat Easter-Jun & Sep) offers advice on local accommodation and activities.

Connemara Walking Centre (☎ 21379; Island House, Market St; open year-round) stocks a good selection of maps and guidebooks and arranges guided walks. There are also several bookshops and a large supermarket in the compact town centre.

Sleeping
Located in a peaceful spot off the bottom of Market St, **Brookside Hostel** (☎ 21812; www.brooksidehostel.com; Fairgreen; dm €16, d €40-50; open Mar-Oct) has the River Owenglin trickling past.

Clifden Town Hostel (☎ 21076; www
.clifdentownhostel.com; Market St; dm €17-
21, d €44) is a cheery IHH hostel right in
the centre of town. It has 34 beds in its
sunlit rooms.

Unbeatable for the price, elegant **Mall-
more House** (☎ 21460; www.mallmore
countryhouse.com; Ballyconneely Rd; d
€80; open Mar-Sep) is a colonnaded Georgian manor house is set in 14 hectares of
woodland about 2km from town.

Also highly recommended is **Sea Mist
House** (☎ 21441; Market St; www.seamist
house.com; r €80-120). With immaculate
rooms and a homey atmosphere, this place
is right in town but opens onto a private
fairytale garden.

Clifden's oldest hotel, **Foyle's** (☎ 21801;
www.foyleshotel.com; Main St; s €72,
d €114-170; open Jun-Aug) is a landmark
in the centre of town, with a well regarded
on-site **restaurant** (mains €15-20) specialising in seafood.

Eating

The wide selection of cafés, pubs and restaurants clustered around Clifden's town
centre means you won't be stuck for eating
options. For evening meals, try **Fogerty's**
(☎ 21427; Market St; mains €17.50-25;
open Thu-Tue). Set in a thatched stone cottage, the menu includes traditional Irish
and seafood dishes.

For a special treat, reserve ahead for **Ab-
beyglen Castle** (☎ 21201; www.abbeyglen
.ie; Sky Rd; set menu €49; open Feb-Dec),
where specialities include Connemara
lamb and crustaceans plucked from the
live tank.

Getting There & Away

Bus Éireann (☎ 091-562 000) services stop
on Market St near the library. There are
regular buses between Clifden and Galway
(€12.50, 1¾ hours, at least three daily Mon-
Sat & on Sun), and more limited services to
Letterfrack (€4.50, 35 minutes) and Leenane (€9.80, 55 minutes) on Tuesdays and
Saturdays only. During July and August
only there is also a service to/from Westport (€21, one hour 35 minutes, once daily
Mon-Sat), which also stops at Letterfrack
and Leenane.

Regular **Citylink** (☎ 091-564 163; www
.citylink.ie) buses also run from Clifden's

main square to Galway (€11, 1½ hours,
at least four daily) and Letterfrack (€5, 25
minutes, at least three daily).

DELPHI
☎ 095

Situated amid starkly beautiful mountain
scenery on the lower slopes of Mweelrea,
it's no accident that one of the country's top
spas chose to locate itself at Delphi.

Delphi Mountain Resort (☎ 42987,
42208; www.delphiescape.com; Leenane;
dm/s/d €40/134/198; dinner mains €15-28)
is a world-class spa-hotel that offers luxurious private rooms as well as (ultra-pricey)
eight-bed dorms. Spa treatments utilise
hand-harvested seaweed, and activities at
the adjacent adventure centre are open to
guests and visitors alike.

Delphi is situated 10km west of Leenane
along the R335.

DOOLIN
☎ 065 / pop 250

A scattered but popular village with a reputation for traditional Irish music, Doolin
has an extensive choice of accommodation.
It makes a good base for walks in the Burren and is also a departure point for ferries
to the Aran Islands. There is no post office
or bank, though several places will change
foreign currency.

Sleeping

Just 100m from the pier for the Aran Islands
ferry, **Nagles Doolin Caravan & Camping
Park** (☎ 707 4458; www.doolincamping
.com; site & two adults from €17; open
Apr-Sep) has great views of the Cliffs of
Moher.

In a picturesque spot by the river in the
upper village, **Aille River Hostel** (☎ 707
4260; ailleriver@esatclear.ie; Roadford;
campsites from €16, dm €18-25, d €50;
open mid-Mar–Dec) occupies a converted
17th-century farmhouse and provides free
laundry facilities.

Paddy's Doolin Hostel (☎ 707 4421;
www.doolinhostel.com; Fisher St; dm/d
from €17/50) is a modern, IHH-affiliated
hostel with a choice of four or eight-bed
dorms, or private en-suite rooms.

The impressive, purpose-built guesthouse
Doolin Activity Lodge (☎ 707 4888; www
.doolinlodge.com; Fisher St; s/d from

€45/70) has 14 newly furnished rooms as well as self-catering apartments.

On a bend in the Aille, **O'Connors Guesthouse** (☎ 707 4498; www.oconnors doolin.com; s/d from €50/70) is located in a rather plush farmhouse on a working farm.

Hotel Doolin (☎ 707 4111; www.hotel doolin.ie; Coast Rd; s/d €90/170) is a new, upmarket boutique hotel with 17 well-appointed rooms. There's a modern bar for those who want sport instead of music.

Eating

Self-caterers should head to the well-stocked **Doolin Deli**, along the road to the pier.

Whether you're looking for good food or traditional music, one of the best pubs in the village is **O'Connor's** (☎ 707 4168; Fisherstreet; mains €10-22), right on the waterfront.

Another excellent restaurant for evening dining is **Cullinan's** (☎ 707 4183; one-/ two-/three-courses €25/32/40; open dinner Thu-Tue), attached to the guesthouse of the same name.

Getting There & Away

Bus Éireann (☎ 091-562 000) runs one to three buses daily from Doolin to Limerick (€15, 2½ hours), with onward connections to Dublin. Buses also go to Galway (€14, 1½ hours, one or two daily) via Ballyvaughan. During the summer, various backpacker shuttles often serve Doolin from Galway and other points in Clare. These are amply marketed in hostels.

By car, Doolin is 7km west of Lisdoonvarna and 16km south of Fanore.

FANORE
☎ 065 / pop 150

The village of Fanore (*Fan Óir*) lies at the rocky heart of the Burren and is a convenient base for the Black Head route. It's a scattered settlement with limited amenities; the nearest **tourist office** is 11km east in Ballyvaughan (☎ 707 7464; www.bally vaughantourism.com; open daily Mar-Oct, weekends only Nov-Feb).

The small but well-stocked shop, **Siopa Fan Óir** (☎ 707 6131), just across from O'Donohue's pub, sells walking maps as well as groceries.

Sleeping & Eating

Rocky View Farmhouse (☎ 707 6103; www. rockyviewfarmhouse.com; s/d €45/80), is the most convenient accommodation for the Black Head walk. It occupies a charming old house, and is signed towards the coast from the northern end of the village.

Alternatively, **Seacoast Lodge** (☎ 707 6250; s/d €50/70) is a new family home with clean facilities. It's located beside O'Donohue's pub at the southern end of the village.

O'Donohue's (☎ 707 6119; mains €6-15; open Apr-Oct), 4km south of the Black Head walk, serves as a community centre and offers pub grub along with its genuine local character.

For transport information to Fanore, see Getting to/from the Walk for Black Head (p198).

GALWAY
☎ 091 / pop 72,000

Galway is a city that never sleeps, renowned around the world for its nightlife, music and cultural spirit. For walkers it serves as a natural gateway to the Burren and Connemara, as well as a departure point for trips to the Aran Islands.

For general tourist information, contact **Ireland West Tourism** (☎ 537 700; www .discoverireland.ie/west; Forster St; open daily Easter-Sep, Mon-Sat Oct-Easter), where efficient staff can help arrange accommodation and ferry trips.

Supplies & Equipment

The best places for outdoor equipment are **River Deep Mountain High** (☎ 563 938; Middle St) and **Great Outdoors** (☎ 562 869; Eglinton St). Both stock a wide range of gear, maps and guidebooks.

Maps and books can also be found at **Eason's** (☎ 562 284; Shop St), along with Galway's biggest rack of periodicals.

Sleeping

The closest camping to the city is peaceful **Ballyloughane Caravan & Camping Park** (☎ 755 338; galwcamp@iol.ie; Bally loughane Beach, Renmore; site & two adults €24; open Apr-Sep), 5km east of Galway on the N6 Dublin road. The beachside location gives it sweeping views across the bay.

There are plenty of hostels around the city. **Barnacle's Quay Street House** (☎ 568 644; www.barnacles.ie; 10 Quay St; dm €15-40, d €64-98) is a well-run establishment in the midst of Galway's night spots.

Kinlay House (☎ 565 244; www.kinlay house.ie; Merchant's Rd; dm €19-30, d €60-70) is probably the best all-round hostel in the city; it has free wi-fi and an ultra-central location just off Eyre Sq.

If you prefer a B&B, try **Griffin Lodge** (☎ 589 440; www.irishholidays.com/griffin .shtml; 3 Father Griffin Pl; s €45-60, d €55-80), which has eight immaculate rooms.

On the main drag, **Spanish Arch Hotel** (☎ 569 600; www.spanisharchhotel.ie; Quay St; r €95-150) is a boutique hotel housed in a 16th-century former convent, with an excellent on-site restaurant.

For something more upmarket, luxurious **Hotel Meyrick** (☎ 564 041; www .hotelmeyrick.ie; Eyre Sq; r €165-250) is a stately showpiece that dates from 1852.

Eating

The city centre offers delicatessens and supermarkets alike to tempt self-caterers.

The city's best selection of restaurants is on Quay St. **Ard Bia** (☎ 539 897; www.ar dbia.com; 2 Quay St; mains €16-30), offers a café menu during the day and full dinners in the evening.

Another option is **McDonagh's** (☎ 565 001; 22 Quay St; mains €15-25), the city's best chipper and an essential ingredient of any trip to Galway. There's a take-away counter on one side and a formal restaurant on the other.

Getting There & Away

Galway airport (☎ 755-569; www.galway airport.com; Carnmore) is situated 8km east of the city centre. Just one or two buses run between the airport and the city centre from Monday to Saturday (€3, 15 minutes). Alternatively a taxi costs about €20.

From the bus station just off Eyre Sq, there are frequent **Bus Éireann** (☎ 562 000) services to all major cities in the Republic and Northern Ireland, including Dublin (€14, 3¾ hours, hourly), Sligo (€16, 2½ hours, five daily) and Westport (€14.40, two hours, eight daily).

A variety of private bus companies also provide services to/from the city, leaving from the new coach station on Fairgreen Rd (around 100m from the train station, and 200m from Eyre Sq). **Bus Nestor** (☎ 797 484; busnestor@eircom.net) runs services to Dublin (€10, five to eight daily) via Dublin airport (€10). **City Link** (☎ 564 163; www.citylink.ie) also have hourly buses to Dublin (€12), as well as regular services to Clifden (€11, 1½ hours, at least four daily) and Letterfrack (€11, one hour 55 minutes, at least three daily).

From the **train station** (☎ 564 222), just off Eyre Sq, there are up to five trains daily to/from Dublin's Heuston Station (€35, three hours). Connections with other lines can be made at Athlone.

GLENCAR
☎ 071

A tiny collection of houses in a very beautiful setting, the valley of Glencar runs along the southern base of the Benbulbin plateau and makes a more convenient base for walkers than Sligo, 10km away.

Sleeping & Eating

It's hard to get closer to a walk than friendly **Glenvale B&B** (☎ 914 5937, 087 941 7995; s/d €35/70), situated right at the start of the Benbulbin route. The owners have made their land freely available to walkers for years, and it's nice to support such generosity by giving them your business.

The closest place for an evening meal is **Yeats Tavern** (☎ 916 3117; Drumcliff; mains €12-24). This vast and popular pub/restaurant is open all day, and located on the N15 at the northern edge of Drumcliff village, 4.5km west of Glenvale B&B.

For transport information to Glencar, see Getting to/from the Walk for Benbulbin (p167).

GLENCOAGHAN
☎ 095

If you're planning an assault on the classic Glencoaghan Horseshoe, there are a couple of convenient accommodation options close to the walk. However, you'll need to bring all supplies with you as there are no other facilities in the area.

Sleeping & Eating

Ben Lettery Youth Hostel (☎ 085 271 3588; www.anoige.ie; dm/d €16.50/38;

open Mar-Nov) is situated at the base of the mountain right at the end of the walk.

Canal Stage House B&B (☎ 51064; s/d from €45/70; open Jul-Aug) is along the minor road leading to the start of the walk.

Getting There & Away

Glencoaghan is 13km east of Clifden on the N59. The **Bus Éireann** (☎ 091-562 000) Galway–Clifden service passes in front of the youth hostel – ask to be dropped at the gate. **Citylink** (☎ 091-564 163; www.citylink.ie) plies the same route and will also let you off on request. See Getting There & Away for Clifden (p202).

KEEL
☎ 098 / pop 540

An open-plan village with a 3km-long Blue Flag beach and wide array of facilities, Keel (*An Caol*) is a perfect base for exploring Achill Island. Self-caterers can re-supply at the **Costcutter** (☎ 43125) supermarket, which also has an ATM.

Sleeping

On a trim patch of greenery overlooking Keel Strand, laidback **Keel Sandybanks Caravan & Camping Park** (☎ 43211; www.achillcamping.com; site & two adults from €16; open June–mid-Sep) is just a short stroll from the town.

Rich View House (☎ 43462, 086 231 5546; richviewhostel@hotmail.com; dm/s/d €15/18/36) is a relaxed hostel-cum-home-stay with simple facilities.

A short walk outside the village, **Fuchsia Lodge** (☎ 43350; fuchsialodge@eircom.ie; s/d €45/70) is popular and cosy and one of the few B&Bs on the island open all year round.

Overlooking the northern end of the beach, welcoming **Joyce's Marian Villa** (☎ 43134; www.joycesachill.com; s/d €60/90; open Easter–mid-Oct) is a highly recommended, memorable guesthouse.

Achill Head Hotel (☎ 43108; Pollagh; s/d €65/90) offers 19 modern rooms, 10-minutes' walk from central Keel along the road to Dooagh.

Eating

For lunch or afternoon tea it's hard to beat **Beehive Craft & Coffee Shop** (☎ 43018; snacks around €7; open Apr-Oct), with its wonderful homemade soups and sinful selection of cakes.

The award-winning **Calvey's Restaurant** (☎ 43158; mains €10-20; open lunch & dinner Easter–mid-Sep) serves a mix of fresh local seafood and meat from its attached butchery.

Getting There & Away

See Getting There & Around for Achill Island (p169) for details of bus services to Keel. By car, Keel is situated on the R319, 13km west of Achill Sound.

LEENANE
☎ 095 / pop 120

The small village of Leenane (also spelled Leenaun) is a compact settlement on the eastern shore of Killary Harbour. It manages to provide a large number of visitor facilities without sacrificing its traditional atmosphere.

Leenane Cultural Centre (☎ 42323; open Apr-Sep), just north of the bridge, provides basic tourist information, stocks local books and walking maps, and also has a café. The village has a small supermarket but no banking facilities.

Sleeping & Eating

Occupying a renovated 19th-century building, **Sleepzone Connemara** (☎ 42929; www.sleepzone.ie; campsites €12, dm €20-26, s/d €50/70; open Mar-Oct) is 6km from Leenane on the N59 Clifden road. Modern facilities include a bar, tennis court and bike hire.

In Leenane itself you'll find **Killary House** (☎ 42254; www.connemara.com/killaryhouse; r €50-80), a cosy B&B on a working farm that can provide evening meals by arrangement.

Friendly and comfortable **Portfinn Lodge** (☎ 42265; www.hotelinconnemara.com; s €30-50, d €60-100) offers great package rates if you're staying for two nights or more. The celebrated seafood **restaurant** (mains €16-26) is open to non-residents and also has an early-bird menu (€23.50, 6-7.30pm).

The largest hotel in the area, **Leenane Hotel** (☎ 42265; www.leenanehotel.com; s €55-69, d €110-138; open Apr–mid-Nov), is over 300 years old. It's located on the water's edge just south of the village centre and has an on-site bar and restaurant.

For meals, **The Village Grill** (☎ 42253; mains from €6) offers an array of burgers and fried stuffs.

The unexpectedly contemporary **Blackberry Café** (☎ 42240; mains €14-25; open lunch & dinner Easter-Sep) serves informal lunches and fabulous fresh seafood in the evenings.

Getting There & Away
Bus Éireann (☎ 091-562 000) service 419 stops at Leenane on Tuesdays and Saturdays only, on its journey to Galway (€12.50, one hour 20 minutes), Letterfrack (€6, 30 minutes) and Clifden (€10, 55 minutes). During July and August there is also an additional service that operates once daily Monday to Saturday, linking Leenane to Clifden, Letterfrack and Westport (€9, one hour 10 minutes).

LETTERFRACK
☎ 095 / pop 200
Founded by Quakers in the mid-19th century, the small village of Letterfrack (*Leitir Fraic*) has just enough facilities to make it a convenient base for walks in northern Connemara. There's a well-stocked grocery shop selling walking maps, but the closest banking facilities are in Clifden (p201).

Connemara National Park Visitor Centre (☎ 41054; www.heritageireland.ie; open Mar-early Oct), 500m west of the village and just inside the entrance to the park, is the closest source of tourist information. It also sells a range of hiking maps and guides.

Sleeping & Eating
The closest camping ground, **Renvyle Beach Caravan & Camping** (☎ 43462; www.renvylebeachcaravanpark.com; Renvyle; site & two adults €16; open Easter-Sep), is 7km north of Letterfrack through Tully Cross. It boasts fantastic views and has direct access to a sandy beach.

In Letterfrack itself, **Old Monastery Hostel** (☎ 41132; www.oldmonasteryhostel.com; campsites from €9, dm €13-15, d €40-50) occupies a spacious 19th-century stone building 400m east of the main crossroads. Breakfast and evening meals are available.

The newly-built **Letterfrack Lodge** (☎ 41222; www.letterfracklodge.com; campsites from €12, dm €10-20, d €50-60) is also very central, with en-suite rooms and three fully-equipped kitchens. Breakfast is available for €5 extra.

Mountainside B&B (☎ 087 971 0957; www.mountainsidebandb.com; s/d €30/€50) nestles at the base of Diamond Hill and offers a warm welcome in a typical Irish family home.

Amongst the pubs clustered around the crossroads, **Veldon's** (☎ 41046; mains from €10), adjacent to the shop, is best for food.

Alternatively, try **Pangur Ban** (☎ 41243; www.pangurban.com; Letterfrack; mains €15-24; open daily Jul-Aug, Tue-Sat Mar-Jun & Sep-Dec), set in a 300-year-old thatched cottage 100m west of the crossroads. The menu is filled with inventive Irish cuisine such as pot roast pheasant.

Getting There & Away
Bus Éireann (☎ 091-562 000) service 419 stops at Letterfrack on Tuesdays and Saturdays only, on its journey to Galway (€17.50, one hour 50 minutes), Leenane (€6, 30 minutes) and Clifden (€4.50, 35 minutes). During July and August only, there is also an additional service that operates once daily Monday to Saturday, linking Letterfrack to Clifden, Leenane and Westport (€13, one hour 10 minutes).

More regular **Citylink** (☎ 091-564 163; www.citylink.ie) buses also connect Letterfrack to Galway (€11, one hour 55 minutes, at least three daily) and Clifden (€5, 25 minutes, at least three daily).

By car, Letterfrack is 15km northeast of Clifden on the N59.

MURRISK
☎ 098 / pop 240
Murrisk is the village at the base of the tourist path up Croagh Patrick. Most walkers climbing the Reek make a day trip from Westport, but there are enough facilities to stay in the village too.

Croagh Patrick Visitor Centre (☎ 64114; www.croagh-patrick.com; open mid-Mar–Oct) is located at the start of the tourist path. It sells local maps and guidebooks, and also offers a café and shower facilities.

Sleeping & Eating
The closest camping ground is the small **Croagh Patrick Caravan & Camping Park** (☎ 087 659 7842; site & two adults €15), 3km west of Murrisk along the R335.

In Murrisk itself, B&Bs located along the N59 include **Elmgrove** (☎ 64819; s/d €45/70).

Béal-an-tSáile (☎ 098-64012; www.beal antsaile.com; s/d €40/66) also has sea views.

Also along the N59 is **The Tavern** (☎ 64060; www.tavernmurrisk.com; mains from €15; open lunch & dinner), an award-winning pub and restaurant that uses local Irish produce wherever possible.

For transport information to Murrisk, see Getting to/from the Walk for Croagh Patrick (p183).

POLLATOMISH
☎ 097 / pop 150

Irresistibly remote and pretty, Pollatomish (*Poll an Tómais*), also spelled Pullathomas, is a small village with a sandy beach some 16km east of Belmullet.

Sleeping & Eating
The main reason for basing yourself here is friendly **Kilcommon Lodge Hostel** (☎ 84621; www.kilcommonlodge.net; dm/d €16/40). It's great fun exploring the bric-a-brac in the surrounding gardens, and the beach is just a short stroll away. Breakfast (€6) and dinner (€16) are also available.

There is a small shop in the village, and of the two pubs McGrath's can provide bar food.

There is no public transport to the area.

PORTACLOY
☎ 097 / pop 70

A small hamlet scattered around a picturesque harbour, Portacloy (*Port a'Chlóidh*) offers the only accommodation within close proximity to the Dún Caocháin Cliffs. The nearest shop is in Carrowteige.

Sleeping & Eating
Friendly **Stag View B&B** (☎ 88853; s/d €35/70) occupies a peaceful family home, and is signed 1km to the right of the road as you enter Portacloy from Carrowteige. Evening meals are available on request.

There is no public transport to the village.

ROUNDSTONE
☎ 095 / pop 400

A small, picturesque fishing village, Round-stone (*Cloch na Rón*) has great views of the Twelve Bens and is a popular spot with visitors during the summer. There's a good choice of restaurants, cafés and shops, including **Roundstone Book Shop** (☎ 35832; The Quay), which sells OSI maps and local interest guides. The nearest tourist office is in Clifden (see p201).

Sleeping & Eating
The peaceful, well-equipped **Gurteen Beach Caravan & Camping Park** (☎ 35882; www .gurteenbay.com; Roundstone; campsites €15) is in a great spot 2.5km west of town, set at the back of the beach.

St Joseph's (☎ 35865; www.connemara .net/st josephs; Main St; d €64-72) is a central B&B that offers a warm welcome and has beautiful views over the harbour.

Also centrally located is **Roundstone House** (☎ 35864; www.roundstonehouse hotel.com; Main St; r €65-120; open Apr-Oct), a sprawling inn with 13 restful rooms. The pub also serves food, with plenty of local seafood.

O'Dowd's (☎ 35809; Main St; mains €15-22; open lunch & dinner) is an authentic, comfortable old pub that serves both bar food and more formal dishes in its adjoining restaurant.

Getting There & Away
There are regular **Bus Éireann** (☎ 091-562 000) services from Roundstone to Galway (€12.50, 1½ hours,) and Clifden (€6.40, 35 minutes). Buses operate twice daily during July and August, and once daily from Wednesday to Saturday the rest of the year.

By car, Roundstone is well signed from the N59 Galway–Clifden road.

SLIGO
☎ 071 / pop 19,400

Sligo is a vibrant town arranged around the River Garavogue. It's a good base for exploring Yeates Country and other parts of northern County Sligo, and also serves as a gateway to Donegal in the north.

North-West Regional Tourism (☎ 916 1201; www.discoverireland.ie/northwest; Temple St; open daily Jun-Aug, Mon-Sat Mar-May & Sep, Mon-Fri Oct-Feb) is south of the centre, and offers general information as well as accommodation bookings for the area.

The best place in town for outdoor supplies, walking maps and guidebooks is **Call of the Wild** (☎ 0914 6905; Rockwood Pde). For a wider selection of books, try **Keohane's Bookshop** (☎ 914 2597; Castle St).

Sleeping

The closest camping is **Greenlands Caravan & Camping Park** (☎ 917 7113; Rosses Point; site & two adults €19), in the village of Rosses Point, 8km northwest of the town. The park has a fantastic sea-front location and is within 500m of village amenities.

In Sligo itself, **White House Hostel** (☎ 914 5160; Markievicz Rd; dm from €14; open Mar-Oct) is a laidback place in a central location.

If you're looking for a B&B, head to Pearse Rd, just south of the centre, where you'll find plenty of choice. Amongst other options, **Pearse Lodge** (☎ 916 1090; pearselodge@eircom.net; Pearse Rd; s/d from €45/70) offers impeccably clean rooms and superb breakfasts.

Alternatively, **McGettigan's** (☎ 916 2857; www.bandbsligo.ie; Connolly St; s €45-58, d €75-85) is an unfussy guesthouse centrally located above the pub *An Crúiscin Lan.*

Comfortable **Sligo Southern Hotel** (☎ 916 2101; www.sligosouthernhotel .com; Strandhill Rd; s/d from €88/110) is an elegant hotel with courtly gardens, located beside the bus and train station. Superb facilities include a swimming pool.

Eating

There are several large supermarkets in the town centre.

Amongst a host of other eateries along the river you'll find **Fiddler's Creek** (☎ 914 1866; www.fiddlerscreek.ie; Rockwood Pde; mains €9-23), a pub with an excellent menu and a dining room overlooking the quay.

Consistently rated among Sligo's best dinner options, **Coach Lane** (☎ 916 2417; www.coachlane.com; 1-2 Lord Edward St; mains €20-28) offers top-notch Irish and international cuisine with some intriguing specials such as roast Tipperary ostrich.

Getting There & Away

From **Sligo Airport** (☎ 916 8280; www .sligoairport.com; Strandhill Rd), 8km west of town, there are direct **Aer Arann**

(www.aerarran.com) flights to Dublin twice daily (from €25, 40 minutes).

Bus Éireann (☎ 916 0066) services leave from the terminal below the train station, on Lord Edward St. Destinations include Dublin (€17.10, four hours, at least six daily), Galway (€16, 2½ hours, five daily), Donegal Town (€14, one hour five minutes; seven daily Mon-Sat and three on Sun) and Belfast (€23.50, four hours, twice daily).

Feda O'Donnell (☎ 074-954 8114; www.fedaodonnell.com) also operates a service between Crolly (County Donegal) and Galway via Donegal Town and Sligo Town twice daily (four times on Friday). Buses leave from Matt Lyon's shop on the corner of Wine and Quay Sts.

From the **train station** (☎ 916 9888), there are regular connections to Dublin Connolly (€32, 3½ hours, four or five daily).

WESTPORT
☎ 098 / pop 5200

Westport is a thriving little town with lots of character and plenty of amenities, and has long been popular with visitors. Its location between Achill Island and Croagh Patrick make it an inevitable staging post for walkers.

The **tourist office** (☎ 25711; www.dis coverireland.ie/west; James St; open daily Jul & Aug, Mon-Sat Apr-Jun & Sep, Mon-Fri rest of year) is a good source of general information and sells OSI maps.

Maps and guidebooks are also available at **Bookshop** (☎ 26816; Bridge St). For outdoor clothing and equipment, try **Hewetson Bros** (☎ 26018; Bridge St).

Sleeping

Visitors to Westport are spoilt for choice in terms of accommodation.

Parkland Caravan & Camping Park (☎ 27766; www.westporthouse.ie; Westport House, Quay Rd; site & two adults from €28; open May-early Sep) is close to the funfair-like attractions at Westport House, making it a hit for families with young children.

Set in an impressively repurposed mill, **Old Mill Holiday Hostel** (☎ 27045; www .oldmillhostel.com; Barrack Yard; James St; dm/d/tr from €18.50/48/66) couldn't be more convenient in terms of location.

Abbeywood Hostel (☎ 25496; www .abbeywoodhouse.com; Newport Rd;

dm €20-24, d €60; open daily May-Sep, weekends only Oct-Dec & Mar-Apr) is also set in a characterful old house that was originally part of a monastery, and located at the northern end of town.

Amongst the local B&Bs, **Killary House** (☎ 27457; killaryhouse@msn.com; 4 Distillery Ct; s/d €45/70) provides a memorable stay. It was formerly home to an 18th-century distillery, but now offers rooms that are warmly decorated and well appointed.

Westport Inn (☎ 29200; www.westportinn.ie; Mill St; s/d from €49/98) is one of the town's snazzier hotels, and just around the corner from the main drag. Some rooms have four-poster beds and jacuzzi tubs.

Eating

There are several large supermarkets around the town centre.

There are plenty of pubs and restaurants around the town centre. **Cabot's Source** (☎ 50546; The Linen Mill; dinner mains €18.50-27; open for lunch Mon-Fri, dinner Tue-Sun) utilises locally sourced, organic produce to create a fusion of Italian/Irish cuisine in a converted linen mill.

Delightful **Quay Cottage** (☎ 26412; www.quaycottage.com; the Harbour; mains €15-26), down at the harbour, takes full advantage of its location and serves seafood hauled straight from the harbour boats.

Getting There & Away

Bus Éireann (☎ 096-71800) travels to Dublin (€18.50, five hours, three daily), Galway (€14.40, two hours, eight daily), Sligo (€17, two hours, two daily) and Achill Sound (€12.50, 1¼ hours, twice daily). Buses arrive and depart from the Mill St stop. There are more limited services on Sunday.

The **train station** (☎ 25253) is 800m east of the town centre. There are three daily connections to Dublin (€35, 3½ hours).

Northwest

HIGHLIGHTS

- Wandering along the delightful forest and coastal paths of the **Ards Peninsula** (p216)
- Enjoying far-ranging views across Glenveagh National Park from the conical summit of **Errigal** (p222)
- Gazing out over the Marble Arch and the spectacular coastal architecture of **Horn Head** (p218)
- Walking along some of the finest sea cliffs in Europe at **Slieve League** (p228) and **Glencolmcille** (p230)

Highest peak in the region: Errigal, Derryveagh Mountains, 751m

For many, County Donegal in Ireland's northwest corner is second to none among the country's generous collection of walking areas. Donegal is a favourite thanks to its sheer wealth of places to explore, including the spectacularly indented coastline (with towering cliffs and secluded inlets), as well as remote and rugged mountains, glens and moors. Although Donegal's mountains are quite modest when set against Ireland's other peaks (there is only one rising above 700m), they lack nothing in scenic quality and variety: the clean lines of Errigal's white cone contrast sharply with the sprawling, flat-topped massif of nearby Muckish.

Donegal is also a place of high cultural interest, where rural areas still revolve around traditional lifestyles. It contains large Gaeltacht areas, where Irish is the first language, and Irish culture is ardently promoted and nurtured. Overall, the northwest has a rather seductive and intriguing other-worldly feel, somewhat isolated from the rest of Ireland. It's often said that you can never leave Donegal for good; even after one visit, it's easy to agree.

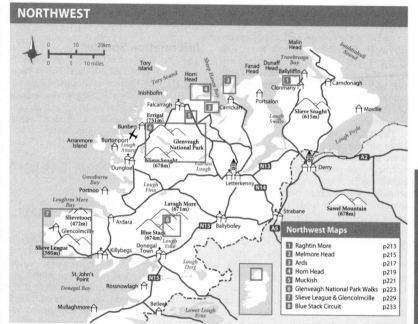

NORTHWEST

HISTORY

There are many reminders of Donegal's ancient past in the countryside, including prehistoric burial cairns, Iron Age forts and carved Celtic crosses. In historic times Donegal (meaning 'fort of the foreigners', most likely a reference to Viking invaders) was part of the old Irish kingdom of Ulster.

The county has been the setting for some crucial events in Ireland's history. These include the work of early Christian missionaries (led by Columba who was born in Glenties, County Donegal) and the flight of the Earls (the last of Ulster's Celtic chiefs) from Rathmullan on the Fanad coast in 1607. The latter event was the prelude to the colonisation of County Donegal as part of Ulster by English and Scots settlers.

At the start of the 19th century, Napoleon's empire-building activities alarmed British authorities and, in response, watchtowers were built along the Irish coast, in sight of each other. Many of these survive, to a greater or lesser extent, at prominent outposts in the region such as Horn Head. A few coastguard lookouts erected during WWI are also still standing.

Several places described in this chapter were caught up in the civil war of the early 1920s, notably the castle in Glenveagh National Park. Although Ireland remained neutral during WWII, the strife could not be ignored, as demonstrated by the prominent warnings to aircraft, in the form of the word EIRE written in stones, that can still be seen here and there along the coast.

ENVIRONMENT

County Donegal is perhaps the most geologically complex part of Ireland. Many of its most prominent peaks are composed of quartzite, schist and marble, which were deposited about 600 million years ago and folded and compressed 200 million years later. This was one phase of the major earth-building event known as the Caledonian orogeny. In another phase, the mountains were pushed up and granite formed below the surface. Aeons later this rock underlayer was exposed, and is now visible as the rounded Derryveagh and Glendowan Mountains. Later again, during the last ice age, ice-filled gaps and dykes in the surface rock wore away the surrounding stone to form U-shaped valleys, notably at Glen-veagh.

Today some alpine and arctic species survive in sheltered spots in the sparse soils of the mountain uplands. The glens and lower slopes support holly, rowan and juni-per, and orchids and butterworts are quite common. Remnants of native woodland are few, one of the most extensive being in Glenveagh National Park.

The most prominent feature of the Donegal landscape is peat bog, of which there are extensive tracts. While bogs are normally not places where walkers linger intentionally, they are relatively rich in wildlife, especially insectivorous plants and insects. The moorlands support a good range of birds, from the small and tune-ful skylark and meadow pipit, to the larger and much less harmonious red grouse, crow and raven. The corncrake, one of Ireland's threatened species, is making a comeback in north Donegal thanks to the Corncrake Project, a voluntary cooperative conservation scheme between farmers and BirdWatch Ireland. Under the scheme, grants are paid to farmers who are happy to delay mowing for hay or silage until 1 August. By then, young corncrakes are usu-ally sufficiently independent to survive the mowing. During spring and autumn you may see red deer in Glenveagh National Park, and golden eagles have also been reintroduced to the area.

PLANNING
Maps & Books
The best map for overall planning is the OSNI 1:250,000 Holiday Map *North*.

If you are looking for even more ideas for walks, try *New Irish Walks: West and North* by Tony Whilde and Patrick Simms, which includes 20 walks in Donegal. It has plenty of background information and is handy for its wide coverage, but is sometimes rather vague about parking places.

PLACE NAMES
A significant proportion of Donegal – especially around the coast – lies within a designated Gaeltacht area, where Irish is the first language written and spoken. In these places, road signs and place names are often written in Irish only, without the usual English translation. To facilitate navigation

through these areas, Irish names are also given in relevant places in the text.

Information Sources
The official tourist office for counties Don-egal and Sligo is **Fáilte Ireland North West** (☎ 071-916 1201; www.discoverireland.ie /northwest; Temple St, Sligo). The website is worth checking for transport and accom-modation information, and also has links to guided-walk operators in the area.

GATEWAYS
See Derry (p280), Donegal Town (p235) and Letterkenny (p238).

NORTH DONEGAL

North Donegal is a quietly beautiful region with an unspoiled and varied landscape. Sandy beaches, rugged coastal cliffs, wooded glens and rolling moorland are all crowned inland by the distinctive sum-mits of the Derryveagh Mountains. Many of the area's most compelling natural at-tractions are provided by the coastline, thanks to a series of rugged peninsulas that reach north into the Atlantic Ocean. Most of the routes in this section explore these fragmented headlands. The Inisho-wen Peninsula, which culminates in Malin Head, Ireland's northern-most extremity, can be viewed from the summit of Raghtin More. Horn Head and Melmore Head, at the tip of the Rosguill Peninsula, are both circumnavigated by fine coastal routes passing rugged cliffs and isolated beaches. The serene woodland of the Ards Peninsula offers a pleasant and less dramatic contrast, though the sandy coves and Atlantic swells remain ever-present.

Besides the scenery, another attraction of the area is its pleasantly laid-back atmos-phere; traditional lifestyles remain largely undisturbed during the winter, and there's a quiet holiday feeling during the summer, when visitors – mainly from the Republic and Northern Ireland – travel to their fa-vourite corner of the region. The fringe of small towns and villages along the coast offer a good range of reasonably priced accom-modation, cafés and other facilities. Though bus services are good along the main coast road, the more remote headlands can be hard to reach without your own means of transport.

ACCESS TOWN
See Dunfanaghy (p236).

RAGHTIN MORE

Duration 3½–4 hours
Distance 7km
Ascent 500m
Difficulty moderate
Start/Finish Glenevin Waterfall car park
Nearest Towns Clonmany & Ballyliffin (p234)
Transport private
Summary A visit to picturesque Glenevin Waterfall is followed by a steady climb to a wild quartzite summit with tremendous coastal views.

Raghtin More (502m) dominates the northwest corner of the Inishowen Peninsula, and is the highest summit of a range of mid-level quartzite mountains that includes the Urris Hills to the southwest. Despite its rounded and relatively uniform profile, the rock-strewn summit offers wonderful coastal views, encompassing Malin Head and the mountainous interior of north Donegal. The route described here – perhaps the easiest circuit over the mountain – begins by tracing woodland paths along a stream to the 10m-high Glenevin Waterfall. A track then leads up Butler's Glen, crossing alarmingly soft sphagnum moss sponges on its upper reaches. Once on the slopes of Raghtin More, heather and bilberry are widespread, and the ground is generally quite well drained.

Although Raghtin More is the highest peak in the area, Mamore Hill (423m) and the Urris Hills (with their high point at 417m) are a continuation of the range to the southwest. Without transport at both ends it is difficult to walk across all of the summits and avoid a lengthy return along roads. If you have two vehicles, however, one can be left at Clonmany and the other at Lenankeel, a tiny settlement to the north of the Urris Hills. A direct route can then be traced over the summits of Raghtin More, Mamore Hill and the peaks of the Urris Hills, with a descent along the western bank of the outlet stream of Crunlough. Terrain is generally rugged; crags and bluffs decorate the Urris

Hills, although informal paths have been worn along the summit ridge. Allow four hours for this 11km route.

PLANNING
Maps
OSI 1:50,000 map No 3 covers the walk. Note that the path to Glenevin Waterfall is not shown on this map.

GETTING TO/FROM THE WALK
Glenevin Waterfall car park is well signed; it's adjacent to Butler's Bridge on the minor road around the northeastern slopes of Raghtin More. From Clonmany, follow the road signed to Tullagh Bay, cross the river and bear right at an intersection. Butler's Bridge and the waterfall car park are about 1km further on, beside Glen House B&B.

THE WALK
The path to Glenevin Waterfall is well marked from the car park. A wide path leads upstream through pleasant birch and rowan woodland, crossing and recrossing the stream via wooden footbridges as the cliffs of a small gorge close in on either side. Benches and picnic tables are placed along the path, although you may feel that you don't deserve a rest just yet! The trail ends after 800m at **Glenevin Waterfall** itself.

Retrace your route downstream and take the first right at a junction of paths. This path climbs more steeply out of the gorge

RAGHTIN MORE

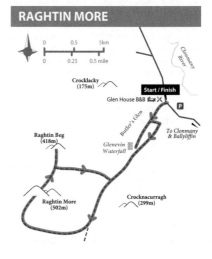

NORTHERN EXPOSURE AT MALIN HEAD

There is a special fascination about the extremities of land, and Malin Head is no exception. Although it is not visited directly in this chapter, it is a prominent feature in the views from many of the routes in North Donegal.

Despite its geographic significance, Malin Head is not a place of great scenic drama: it is a low, flat, grassy point fringed with modest cliffs. However, it has played a crucial role in the development of Irish communications and meteorological forecasting, and it's well worth taking a short stroll around the area, following various short paths that lead out from the roadside parking areas.

A watchtower was built at the head early in the 19th century to record the identity of passing ships. This information was then passed on to Lloyds, the shipping insurers in London. Lloyds was also at the forefront of the revolution in wireless communication, and in the following century they installed a new-fangled contraption in the tower. This device could 'catch' Morse code signals sent over relatively short distances at the rate of five words per minute. It wasn't until 1950 that the Irish government took over what was by then Malin Head radio station.

During WWII, Ireland's defence forces had a lookout post at the head, next to the old tower. The letters EIRE, formed from white stones set on the grass, were the simple but effective way of warning passing aircraft that they were entering the air space of a neutral nation.

Weather reports and storm warnings were first issued from Malin Head in 1870, a service that continues to this day. The buildings near the tip of the headland are now the base for both the meteorological station and the Irish Maritime Emergency Service.

and onto a track. Turn right and follow it as it climbs gradually southwest. Firm ground soon gives way to marshy terrain, and at times the track is more like a corridor of reeds and spongy mosses. The western edge of the track generally offers the firmest ground. Continue past a fenced area and climb until you are roughly level with the summit of Raghtin More, to the west. Leave the track here and head west, descending slightly to cross a stream before starting up the heather-clad slopes beyond.

Arc around to the northwest as you climb, aiming for the col between Raghtin More and Crockmain. Views over Mamore Gap and the Urris Hills become more extensive as you gain height. Heather begins to give way to jumbles of sharp quartzite as you near the wide summit plateau (2½ hours from the start). A high ring of rocks makes for a prominent summit cairn, although the views are better from the trig point 50m to the west. From here, the sweeping panorama embraces Malin Head to the northeast, the Urris Hills to the southwest and beyond that a maze of coastal inlets backed by the fascinating profiles of the Derryveagh Mountains.

Descend relatively steep ground northeast from the summit to the col between Raghtin More and Raghtin Beg. The summit of

Raghtin Beg (418m) is a short distance to the north and can be readily visited for more good views, especially across the sandy beach at Tullagh Bay. Return to the col and begin to descend through short heather, heading for the fenced area beside the track that you passed on the outward journey. Cross the stream in front of the enclosure, turn left at the track, and retrace your steps back to the car park at the start of the walk.

MELMORE HEAD

Duration 4–4½ hours
Distance 10km
Ascent 260m
Difficulty easy–moderate
Start/Finish GR C127425
Nearest Towns Downings (p236), Melmore Head (p239)
Transport private
Summary With the majestic Boyeeghter Strand as its centrepiece, the circuit of remote Melmore Head is one of Donegal's best-kept secrets.

Melmore Head lies at the very tip of the Rosguill Peninsula, and is a perfect place to ponder the intricate relationship between land and sea. The coastline here is fragmented into inlets, bays, islets and rock stacks, while just a few metres inland a series of rugged hills undulate to 160m high. These hills provide fine coastal views, while the grasslands below are rich in wildflowers, particularly in early summer. The shoreline is softened by a succession of tiny coves and long, sweeping beaches, among which lies the grandeur of Boyeeghter Strand. This is surely one of the wildest and most striking beaches in the country, its golden sand backed by dark cliffs and pounded by lines of Atlantic swell.

Few people venture this far north, and walkers completing the circumnavigation of the headland can revel in its 'end-of-the-earth' atmosphere. Progress is generally easy, with short grass underfoot, though the intricacy of the shoreline means you can expect to cover several times the distance that first appears on the map. Your exact route will also vary in many places according to the extent of the tide; low tide is generally best to allow easiest access between the coves and beaches.

PLANNING
Maps
The OSNI 1:50,000 map No 2 covers this walk.

GETTING TO/FROM THE WALK
Melmore Head lies on the northwest tip of the Rosguill Peninsula, which is accessed from the village of Carrickart on the R245. On the western edge of Carrickart, turn north onto the R248, signposted for Downings and the Atlantic Drive. About 2km out of Carrickart the main road turns left but minor road continues straight on, signposted for Melmore Head. Follow this winding road for the next 6km, keeping right at all major junctions. Eventually you drop down onto a flat stretch of machair; park on extensive grass verges anywhere before the turn signed to the youth hostel at GR C127425.

THE WALK
Begin by heading east across the machair to a wide gap in a fence, then cross some low dunes to reach the curving stretch of

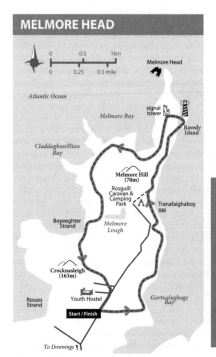

sand of **Gortnalughoge Bay**. Turn left and follow the shore to the northern end of the beach. Depending on the height of the tide, either hop over the rocks or follow the sand northwards around a series of coves and inlets.

After 1km, the coast turns northwest and reaches the larger beach of **Tranafaighaboy**. Avoid the deep gully just before the beach by keeping left of a fence and joining the minor road. Turn right and follow the lane for about 20m before turning right again onto a path back to the sand. At the northern edge of Tranafaighaboy lies **Rosguill Caravan & Camping Park** (see Melmore Head, p239, for details). The next stretch of shoreline is rather awkward, so it's best to avoid it by following the track north through the caravans. Return to the coast after roughly 200m and continue towards the small white **lighthouse** on Ravedy Island. If the tide is low you can descend a flight of steps and cross a causeway to reach the rocky islet itself.

From Ravedy, a faint path climbs west across grassy slopes to reach the remains of the old signal tower at the summit of **Melmore Head** (1¾ hours from the start). The coastal views are extensive: on a clear day you can look east to Malin Head, while to the west the 200m-high cliffs of Horn Head can be seen across Sheep Haven Bay.

Descend south towards the narrow neck of dune linking Melmore Head to the main peninsula and drop onto the cliff-backed beach in Melmore Bay. If the tide is low you can walk straight across the beach and scramble up the rocks at the western end. At high tide you may have to climb over Melmore Hill (70m), then descend northwest to rejoin the coastal route. The next stretch of coastline is flat and rocky with a conspicuous grassy headland commanding attention. Pass a storm beach and small enclosure before turning south again into wild **Claddaghanillian Bay**, where several shattered rock fingers thrust out into the Atlantic.

Continue to follow the shoreline until you reach a long, narrow inlet, where you should veer inland. Head south to the western end of **Melmore Lough**, a beautiful L-shaped lake set beneath steep slopes. From here, follow a high stone wall across the short rise to the west, where a gap in the wall lets you cross onto a promontory. It's more than likely that your breath will be taken away by the view over **Boyeeghter Strand** below (1½ hours from Melmore Head). This is a great place to take a little time out from the walk to enjoy the surrounds. To access the beach, cross back through the gap in the wall and head north for 100m to where you can descend through the dunes. If conditions permit, be sure to visit the cave at the back of the strand.

The way back to the start is through a steep grassy gully at the southern end of the beach. Climb this, and continue up the steep slope above it to reach a superlative viewpoint on the top of **Crocknasleigh**, some 163m above the beach. The climb is strenuous but the summit provides a fantastic 360° panorama of north Donegal and numerous photo opportunities. Descend southeast from Crocknasleigh, aiming for a strip of open, grassy ground to the right of a recently constructed house. This will bring you down to the road close to the turn for the youth hostel.

ARDS

Duration 2–2½ hours
Distance 7km
Ascent 160m
Difficulty easy
Start/Finish Ards Forest Park car park
Nearest Town Dunfanaghy (p236)
Transport private, bus
Summary A pleasant and straightforward route offering a scenic mix of coastal and forest walking.

Among the bold promontories of north Donegal, the Ards Peninsula is rather modest. Tucked away in a corner of Sheep Haven Bay, it constantly loses and regains its promontory status with the procession of the tides. On each low tide, the flats of the Campion Sands are exposed and flocks of eager, long-billed waders follow the receding waters in search of invertebrates. The humble rivers of the estuaries are left naked as thin, meandering ribbons of water. Just a few hours later the ocean returns to surround the peninsula, stretching down for 3km or more on either side. The craggy backbone of hills that leads southwest along the peninsula towards Muckish Mountain gives rise to the name Ards, derived from the Irish *ardai*, meaning 'heights'.

Much of the peninsula is taken up by **Ards Forest Park** (*Páirc Foraoise Na hArdaidh*; ☎ 074-912 1139). The forest is maintained by Coillte Teoranta (see p33) but is relatively varied by Irish standards; among the conifers you'll find stands of mature beech and small but important enclaves of semi-natural native woodland containing sessile oak, ash, birch, rowan, yew, hawthorn and elm. Areas undergoing felling are also being replanted with native broad-leaved species, reflecting the fact that Ards is in essence a recreational rather than a commercial forest. However the forest does have significant colonies of the invasive rhododendron, which will undoubtedly hinder the growth of new trees (see the boxed text Scourge of the Rhododendron, p217).

Although the forest park has a network of way-marked trails, this far more interesting route steps out of the park's boundaries and explores the nearby Capuchin Friary as well as the open coastline at the end of the peninsula. Using tracks and paths throughout, this route is perfect for an easy afternoon's stroll or for a day when the cloud is down on the hills.

PLANNING
Maps
The walk is covered by OSI 1:50,000 map No 2, although this map has insufficient detail to identify the smaller tracks and paths.

GETTING TO/FROM THE WALK
The entrance to Ards Forest Park is well signed along the N56, 3km north of Creeslough and 5.5km southeast of Dunfanaghy. From the entrance, follow the access road for 3km to a large parking area where you'll find toilets, a children's play area and picnic tables. There's a parking charge of €5 at peak times, and park gates close at sunset.

The Capuchin Friary is an alternative start/finish for the route. To get there, turn right from the N56 just over 1km north of Creeslough.

Buses running from Letterkenny to Dunfanaghy ply the N56, and pass by the entrance to Ards Forest Park; drivers will drop you at the entrance if you ask in

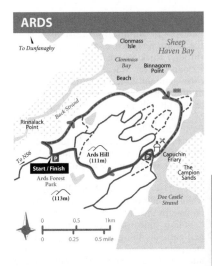

advance (see Dunfanaghy, p236, for details of these services).

THE WALK
From the car park it is a short stroll north to **Back Strand**. Here you can assess the state of the tide; if it is well out you can follow the sands right around to Clonmass

NORTHWEST

SCOURGE OF THE RHODODENDRON

In late spring and early summer the purple blooms of the rhododendron bring splashes of colour to the uniform greens, greys and browns of the Irish countryside. However, far from being an adornment, *Rhododendron ponticum* is threatening to engulf both native and introduced woodlands. Nowhere is this alarming prospect more striking than in Ards Forest Park and Glenveagh National Park in County Donegal, and in Killarney National Park in southwestern Ireland.

A native of the eastern Balkans, Turkey and Lebanon, the plant was introduced to Ireland early in the 19th century to beautify the grounds of many large estates. Surprisingly, in Ireland the rhododendrons found all the elements that made life comfortable for them on the fringes of the Mediterranean: a damp climate, no great extremes of temperature, acidic soils, freedom from disease and from the mouths of sheep and cattle (the leaves are poisonous). Add to this ideal environment the capacity to proliferate with alarming rapidity and you have an ecological disaster in the making.

Each bush can produce a million tiny, highly mobile seeds annually and, once established, the plants can spread rapidly – low level branches produce roots wherever they touch the soil. Rhododendrons develop a dense canopy of branches and thick leaves, shading out and choking less robust native species. The rhododendrons' fallen leaves also upset the normal chemistry of the soil, making it virtually impossible for native plants to regain a foothold until several years after the rhododendrons have been exterminated. However, getting rid of them is a long, slow process involving cutting down the tangled branches, then applying herbicides during successive growing seasons. In light of this, even one tree planted in innocence or ignorance in a private garden seems an avaricious monster.

Bay. If the tide is high then follow the obvious path running northeast parallel to the shore. Keep left at a junction, passing through thick woodland and several waterlogged areas where flag iris thrives in early summer. Once back in the open an optional wooden boardwalk on the left leads through marram grass to the edge of some high dunes overlooking Clonmass Bay. Return to the main path and follow it further east to reach the beautiful beach at **Clonmass Bay**, where the low-tide and high-tide routes are reunited (30 minutes from the start). There are fine views across Sheep Haven Bay to Rosguill Peninsula, while the hills of Fanad Head Peninsula can be seen in the distance to the east.

Follow blue waymarks along an informal path, climbing steeply uphill to a fine viewpoint across Clonmass Bay. A narrow but well-defined path leads straight ahead into thickets of birch. This delightful section, which can be muddy in places, winds through the trees and out to **Binnagorm Point**. Getting right out to the very tip of the point is complicated by a deep gully, which can be negotiated with a little scrambling. Shoals of fish often gather offshore here in the nutrient-rich waters at the mouths of the estuaries, and in spring and summer seabirds such as gannets and arctic terns come from the colonies on Horn Head to dive-bomb for a meal below.

The main path swings east near Binagorm Point and descends to a small beach. Cross the beach and climb the steep slopes on the other side using a gravel path and wooden steps.

At the top of the slope is a wide gravel path that soon splits in two at a junction. The path on the left is an optional loop around a small headland and will add five or 10 minutes to your walk. It rejoins the right-hand path a few hundred metres south of the junction. Once re-united, a single path continues south to a boundary wall and stands of mature broad-leaved trees. Pass through an old iron gate and beyond this a concrete path continues around a sandy bay. The path widens into a track, wooded on both sides, and after a few hundred metres brings you to the **Capuchin Friary** (1½ hours from the start). The friary was established in 1930 and visitor facilities include a large car park and a **café**.

Walk past the front of the house and follow the road uphill to the right of the car park. Take the second right from this road onto a forest track. Climb steadily to another junction where you should turn right and continue across the main spine of the peninsula. In spring this section is ablaze with the yellow blossom of gorse and the air is thick with the distinctive coconut fragrance. Keep straight ahead at junctions and then descend steeply through forest. At the bottom of this steep descent turn left and follow signs for the car park, which is only another 10 minutes' walk downhill.

HORN HEAD

Duration 5–6 hours
Distance 16km
Ascent 400m
Difficulty moderate
Start/Finish Hornhead Bridge
Nearest Town Dunfanaghy (p236)
Transport private
Summary An exhilarating walk along dramatic cliffs and beautiful coastline, past deep inlets, rock arches and quiet, unspoiled beaches.

Horn Head (*Corrán Binne* or 'Curve of a Horn') boasts the most impressive coastal scenery of north Donegal and for walkers, the trip around the headland is right up there among the country's classic coastal routes. Granted the cliffs aren't nearly as high as Slieve League (see p228), but they are exceptionally sheer in places and more than match the dimensions of Ireland's most celebrated sea walls at the Cliffs of Moher.

Apart from the obvious attraction of its tremendous rock architecture, Horn Head also has superb scenic variety. This route takes in a natural sea-arch, blowholes, beaches and megalithic tombs. The dunes are a delicate habitat and have been made a Special Area of Conservation along with New Lake, which is a wild-fowl sanctuary in its own right. In spring and early summer the cliffs also provide nesting sites for a plethora of seabirds including gulls, gannets, cormorants and puffins.

Though it was once possible to circumnavigate the entire peninsula on foot, the thick bracken that plagued the eastern part

HORN HEAD

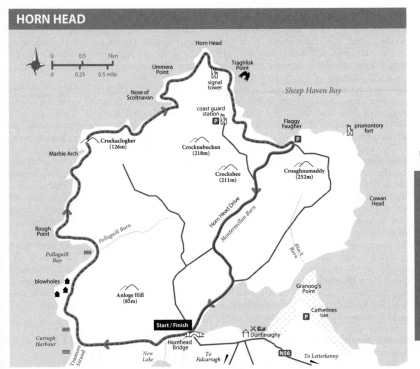

of the headland has rampaged out of control in recent years and has become too awkward to negotiate in comfort. This route avoids the area altogether and uses a scenic road to complete the loop. The walk is described in a clockwise direction, which avoids the danger of missing Marble Arch and means you save the most dramatic section of cliffs till last. On a warm day it's also worth considering that there is a safe swimming beach (Pollaguill Bay) near the start of the route. Swimming kit may be appreciated!

Most of the coastal section crosses short grass that is heavily grazed by sheep, making progress easy underfoot. The route is further defined for most of the way by an informal path, though it often passes vertiginously close to the cliffs. As always, caution is required when walking near the edge.

PLANNING
Maps
The walk is covered by OSI 1:50,000 map No 2. This does not show any of the paths,

the signal station ruins or some of the offshore rock features.

GETTING TO/FROM THE WALK
From the western end of Dunfanaghy, turn right along a minor road signed for 'Horn Head scenic drive'. You will arrive at Hornhead Bridge in around 1km. Park in a rough lay-by on the right-hand side of the road just north of the bridge.

If you have two cars the road section can be avoided by leaving a second vehicle at Flaggy Faugher parking area, at the northern end of the headland.

If you're reliant on public transport, it's also possible to start this circuit from Dunfanaghy village, thereby adding an extra 2km to the day's distance. See Dunfanaghy (p236) for details of bus services to/from the village.

THE WALK
Walk to the northern end of Hornhead Bridge and pass over a stone stile on the

western side of the road. Cross a long field and negotiate a large wooden stile at its western end. Continue ahead to a fork in the path and turn right, following the trail steeply uphill into the vast network of dunes. At the top of the climb you gain a fine view across New Lake and the neck of low-lying land joining Horn Head to the mainland. This land was under water and Horn Head was an island until as recently as the 18th century.

Descend through a metal turnstile and pass onto **Tramore Strand**, a beautiful beach over 2km long. Make your way to the northern end of the beach and scramble up some easy rocks to reach the grassy slopes above. As you reach the top of these slopes be sure to look back and savour the panorama of the Derryveagh Mountains towering over the sweeping sands of the bay.

On a stormy day the area's blowholes might be in operation. First up are two prominent **blowholes** separated by a narrow bridge of rock, known as The Two Pistols. A little further on and more impressive is McSweeney's Gun. In big Atlantic swells this was once audible over 30km away, though erosion has since widened the hole and reduced the impact of the noise. Continue around the coast onto steep grassy slopes and descend towards the sand and stone beach in **Pollaguill Bay**. Cross a fence, keeping close to the shore. A 'land preserved' notice warns against venturing inland, but this route simply crosses the beach and climbs the rocks at its northern end to gain the open grassy slopes above.

The next landmark is **Marble Arch**, which lies less than a kilometre away beneath an imposing headland. Cross a fence using a small stone stile and then walk out to the left to view one of the finest sea arches in the country. The route now continues up and across the headland, an ascent of almost 100m. The terrain becomes rougher underfoot as you pass an old circular stone shelter and climb over a steep rise. There is now a fine view to Horn Head in the distance; from this perspective the promontories do look unmistakably like a pair of thick horns.

Descend to the mouth of a deep channel then make a long steady climb to reach **Horn Head** itself (3½ to four hours from the start). Towards the top you join an eroded, peaty track that indicates you've reached the world of sightseers. However nothing can detract from the grandeur of the cliffs, and hundreds of seabirds can be seen wheeling and soaring on the air currents far below.

Follow the cliffs southeast past the prominent ruins of an old signal tower and around **Traghlisk Point**. There are fine views across to the bare vertical walls beneath Flaggy Faugher, where the cliffs are at their highest and most sheer. Rather than joining the road at this point it is well worth continuing the walk along the cliff-tops as far as Flaggy Faugher itself. This allows a view of the magnificent cliff-line beneath Horn Head, and also offers a glimpse down a gut-wrenching vertical drop of more than 200m to the turquoise water at its base.

If you haven't parked a car here, head southwest along the road for 4km to arrive back at Hornhead Bridge. Fortunately it's downhill all the way and the section is enlivened considerably by fine views across Dunfanaghy to Muckish Mountain.

DERRYVEAGH MOUNTAINS

The landscape of north Donegal is dominated by the rugged peaks of the Derryveagh Mountains. As well as providing an impressive backdrop as far as the eye can see, the range includes one of the most accessible and recognisable summits in the county, the distinctive cone of Errigal. In the heart of the mountains, Glenveagh National Park embraces a marvellous array of loughs, hills, glens, and expanses of wild and lonely moorland. With a host of surrounding peaks including Muckish and Slieve Snaght, this is a region where walkers are spoilt for choice; the routes described in detail are but a distillation of the best from a generous range of possibilities.

Yet this is also a remote and sparsely populated area, best suited to independent -minded visitors. Many of the routes are based around the tiny village of Dunlewy, which is conveniently located in the heart of the mountains but has a limited range of facilities. Public transport is non-existent, and you'll need your own vehicle to get around. It's worth bearing in mind too that midges can be a problem on calm days between May and September (see the boxed text Midges – A Walker's Bane, p323). Make sure to add a decent insect repellent to your pack to fully enjoy your walking experience during this time.

ACCESS TOWN
See Dunlewy (p236).

MUCKISH

Duration 2½–3 hours
Distance 6km
Ascent 420m
Difficulty moderate
Start/Finish GR C009309
Nearest Towns Dunfanaghy (p236), Dunlewy (p236)
Transport private
Summary A steep climb leads to the flat summit of a northern landmark, with marvellous panoramas of coastline and mountains.

A walk up Muckish (*An Mhucais* or 'The Pig's Back', 666m) looks to be a formidable proposition from any direction. In reality, however, ascents from either the north or south are steep, but relatively straightforward. The northern approach is more adventurous, passing through the remains of a sand quarry and following the old Miners' Path up through towering crags and pinnacles. Much of this path is eroded and you will need to use your hands for balance in a few places, although sporadic arrows indicate the line to follow. From Muckish Gap to the south there's the option of a more direct, less rocky route – see Alternative Route: From the South, p222. While most people arrive at the summit via an out-and-back route from one end or the other, a full traverse of the mountain is ideal if transport can be arranged.

In good weather it's worth allowing plenty of time to survey the marvelous views from the broad summit plateau. In poor visibility, however, the plateau can be a very confusing place; it is almost 1km long, virtually flat and has few distinguishing features to break the uniformity of the terrain. Locating the narrow descent paths is a serious proposition

in bad weather, and steep surrounding cliff faces mean that finding the right route is vital. In such conditions, consider turning back at the top of your ascent route rather than wandering too far onto the plateau.

Also see More Walks, p234 for a summary of a shorter route around Lough Agher, at the northern foot of Muckish.

PLANNING
Maps
The OSI 1:50,000 map No 2 covers the walk. On the northern approach, the Miners' Path is not marked above the quarry nor is the survey pillar shown (GR C005287). On the southern side, Muckish Gap is labelled only as 'Gleennaneor'.

GETTING TO/FROM THE WALK
For the northern approach, turn off the N56 7.5km south of Dunfanaghy or 2km north of Creeslough, almost opposite a large cemetery. Follow this minor road for roughly 6km and park on the left in a gravel parking area 100m before the road end.

MUCKISH

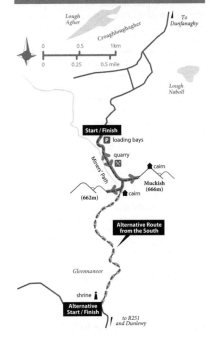

For the southern approach, turn north off the R251, 14km east of Dunlewy and 3km west of the entrance to Glenveagh National Park. Follow this minor road (signed to Falcarragh) for 3km to Muckish Gap, where there is a small shrine on the north side of the road. Park here or beside the bend just northwest of the shrine.

THE WALK

From the parking area, continue to the end of the road, where you'll find the large concrete loading bays of the former quarry. The hard, fine-grained grey and white quartzite of Muckish yields almost pure silica sand, which was once used to make high quality optical glass. The quarries on this side of the mountain were operational until 1955. Cross the stream on the right (west) and climb the spur between two small streams, largely following the rough steps of the well-graded Miners' Path. You will soon come to a maze of fallen rocks and disturbed ground; keep to the left and continue to climb up a rock-strewn gully, picking your way up the stony path to the left of a steep, heathery spur.

With the guidance of a series of painted arrows, stone cairns, rusty metal poles and wooden posts, follow the path as it weaves a way through the near-vertical cliffs. Cross a gully choked with fine sand and small rocks and climb beneath impressive bluffs to the site of the main **quarry**, now reduced to several pieces of old machinery and the remains of various concrete structures (45 minutes from the start). It is hard to imagine how these pieces of heavy, bulky machinery were brought up to this remote location.

From here, the path is on your left as you face the mountain; now much narrower, it squeezes past a crag and twists and turns up to the broad, rock-strewn **summit plateau** (another 20 minutes). The official summit, marked by a survey pillar, is about 400m to the east-northeast and is dwarfed by two enormous cairns, the largest about 7m high and 15m across. One **cairn** is on the northeast edge of the plateau, near the official summit, and the other to the southwest. The cairn close to the eastern rim is the best place for coastal views. To the northeast, the Urris Hills and Malin Head are prominent, while extensive sand dunes flank Horn Head nearer to hand. Inland,

the steep outlines of the Aghla Mountains and Errigal contrast with the more rounded Derryveagh Mountains further southeast.

Retrace your steps to the start.

ALTERNATIVE ROUTE: FROM THE SOUTH
2½–3 hours, 6km, 410m ascent

From the bend in the road, about 75m northeast of the shrine, a rather indistinct path leads north across soggy grassland towards the mountain. Aim for a steep gully (GR C001273) with a low, black crag on the northern side and climb through this to a col. Here you are faced with a very steep ascent over short heather, grass and bare rock. There is no real path, although as you approach the plateau rim (45 minutes from the gap) a trail does begin to form in the peat. On the rock-strewn **summit plateau**, small cairns mark the line of approach to an enormous cairn. The official summit, marked by a survey pillar, is 500m to the northeast. The **cairn** close to the eastern rim is the best place for coastal views (about 25 minutes from the plateau rim).

Return to Muckish Gap by retracing the outward route.

ERRIGAL

Duration 3½ hours
Distance 8km
Ascent 650m
Difficulty moderate
Start/Finish Errigal car park
Nearest Town Dunlewy (p236)
Transport private

Summary A classic of the northwest: climb the most distinctive and exciting mountain in Donegal for superb, panoramic views.

At 751m, the summit of Errigal is the highest point in County Donegal. The peak lies within Glenveagh National Park (see the boxed text, p225), and its volcanic profile means it has become an icon for Ireland's northwest. It is not surprising then that the trip to the top is the most popular mountain walk in the region. Once you've scaled the steep slopes it's easy to appreciate why it's such a favourite: although it takes only half a day to complete, this route has few rivals in terms of dramatic terrain or scenic splendour.

GLENVEAGH NATIONAL PARK WALKS

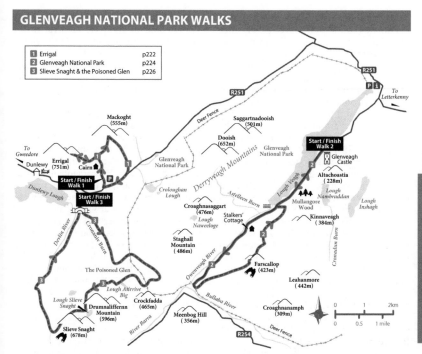

1 Errigal p222
2 Glenveagh National Park p224
3 Slieve Snaght & the Poisoned Glen p226

NORTHWEST

Unfortunately the effects of so many passing feet have caused quite serious erosion problems, although a program designed to combat the scarring of the hillside is now in place. The trip begins with a traverse of soggy grassland, but you soon come face to face with steep crags and scree-covered slopes. A well-worn path then climbs the quartzite rock of the southeast spur to the twin peaks on the summit ridge.

Conventionally, the return route retraces the outward climb. However this walk describes a variation that includes the trip over the neighbouring summit of Mackoght (555m). For the straightforward out-and-back route up Errigal, deduct around 150m of ascent, 2km and an hour of walking time from the statistics given for this route.

PLANNING
Maps
The walk is covered by OSI 1:50,000 map No 1.

GETTING TO/FROM THE WALK
Errigal car park is situated on the northern side of the R251, around 3km east of Dunlewy and 14km west of the entrance to Glenveagh National Park. There is adequate parking for around 20 vehicles.

THE WALK
Begin by taking the obvious path that leads north from the car park. Signs ask that you stick to the approach route marked by a series of poles; please do so to avoid exacerbating the mountain's erosion problems. Follow the path straight up the grassy slope ahead, keeping a small stream on your right. When the path peters out, continue to climb north–northwest across steep slopes and small hollows to reach the rocky col between Errigal and Mackoght. Here the path consolidates once again. Turn left (southwest) and begin the ascent of Errigal's magnificent eastern ridge, which sweeps in a graceful arc to the conspicuous twin summits.

As you gain height, the dissected cliffs of the Poisoned Glen and the dome of Slieve

Snaght dominate the views to the south. Landmarks are steadily revealed in other directions too: Arranmore Island just offshore to the west while the Aghlas and Muckish can be seen to the northeast.

Soon you reach the summit ridge, where the path is marked by a line of large cairns (1¼ hours from the start). The angular **cairn** close to the edge bears a plaque in memory of Joey Glover, a founding member of the North West Mountaineering Club who was killed by the IRA on 23 November 1976. A short amble along the ridge takes you to the twin summits of **Errigal**. The prospect now embraces a huge sweep of the Donegal coastline, stretching from Malin Head in the north as far south as Slieve League.

The quickest way to return to the start is simply to retrace your outward journey. However a more interesting variation is to return via Mackoght. Descend to the col on Errigal's eastern flank, then continue northeast. The spur on the right of a wide gully gives a good start for the relatively short climb to **Mackoght's** (555m) summit cairn. You are rewarded with a fine view of the Aghla Mountains and Inishfree Bay, framed by Errigal's spectacular cliffs.

Descend steeply southeast along a broad spur. Once on flatter ground, follow the line of an old fence for a few hundred metres to avoid the worst of the peat hags. Now head south to meet a wide path about 250m from the road. Turn right along the road for the final, 15-minute walk back to the car park.

GLENVEAGH NATIONAL PARK

Duration 5–6 hours
Distance 18km
Ascent 440m
Difficulty moderate–demanding
Start/Finish Glenveagh Castle
Nearest Town Dunlewy (p236)
Transport private

Summary In Ireland's largest national park, an easy walk beside beautiful Lough Veagh leads to a rugged, high-level return.

The U-shaped valley of Glenveagh was gouged out of the granite rock of the Derryveagh Mountains by the glaciers of the last ice age. Today the area's uplands consist of patches of exposed rock interspersed by large expanses of rough bog. The bare slopes stand in complete contrast to the luxuriant oak woodlands along the shores of Lough Veagh, one of the few stands of native trees surviving in County Donegal.

By simply following the southeastern shore of Lough Veagh, walkers gain a good overall impression of the landscape, flora and fauna of Glenveagh National Park. The road is paved as far as Glenveagh Castle, 3km from park entrance, and most people elect to ride the park shuttle bus across this section. At the castle the road turns into a gravel track. Visitors looking for an easy stroll can simply follow this track to and from the watershed of the Owenveagh River. However if your visit coincides with a spell of dry weather and you are used to walking over trackless country, the variation described here for the return from the watershed is well worthwhile. This takes you over the hill with the intriguing name Farscallop (on the OSI map) or Scollops (on the national park map), which rises to 423m above the upper reaches of the Owenveagh River. From the northeastern end of this hill, the views across Lough Veagh and to the northeast are outstanding, while the outlook across the bleak and empty moorland to the south conveys a profound sense of isolation. The only drawbacks are that a maze of peat hags pits parts of the hill and that tussocks of moor grass are widespread.

The route statistics assume you'll take advantage of the minibus service to Glenveagh Castle. If you chose to cover this distance by foot, add 6km and 1¼ hours to the length of the walk.

PLANNING

Deer culling takes place in the park between August and February each year. If you plan to walk over Farscallop during these months, contact the **park office** (☎ 074-913 7090) beforehand to find out when and where culling will be taking place.

Maps & Books

The walk is covered by OSI 1:50,000 map No 6.

A variety of publications giving more information about the park are available at the visitor centre. These include *The History* of Glenveagh, Glenveagh Gardens and the beautifully illustrated Glenveagh National Park – A Visitors' Guide.

GETTING TO/FROM THE WALK

The entrance to Glenveagh National Park is on the southern side of the R251, around 17km east of Dunlewy. The route to the park is well signed from the N56 to both the east and the west, and there is a large car park in front of the visitor centre.

The park **minibus service** (adult/child return €2/1) runs from the visitor centre to the castle roughly every 15 minutes during visitor centre opening hours. To make the journey on foot, simply follow the park road southwest from the visitor centre along the shore of Lough Veagh, arriving at Glenveagh Castle some 3km later.

GLENVEAGH NATIONAL PARK

Glenveagh National Park (Páirc Náisiúnta Ghleann Bheatha; www.glenveaghnationalpark.ie; admission free) consists of 140 sq km of the wildest, most rugged terrain in County Donegal. The parklands are split into four separate blocks: the largest is centred on the valley of Glenveagh and the surrounding Derryveagh Mountains. To the southeast is a tract of peat bogland around Lough Muck, in the northwest are the quartzite hills topped by Crocknafarragh, while the smallest block includes the conical summit of Errigal and the village of Dunlewy.

It is a neat historical irony that John George Adair, one of the more notorious characters in Donegal's history, was also indirectly responsible for the establishment of the park. By 1859 Adair had become landlord of a large area embracing Derryveagh and Glendowan. A series of disputes soon led him to forcibly evict his tenants amid scenes of appalling misery and heartlessness. Some resettled locally, others had to retreat to the Letterkenny poorhouse, while roughly 150 people emigrated to Australia and succeeded in making new lives in New South Wales.

Adair married a wealthy American widow and in the late 1860s built the delightfully showy Glenveagh Castle, which was modelled in miniature on Scotland's Balmoral Castle. After he died in 1885, Cornelia Adair devoted much of her time and money to improving the estate. Red deer were reintroduced to provide sport for the estate's guests and for lessees of the shooting rights. The first animals were a stag and five hinds from England and then, in 1910, 170 more deer were introduced from elsewhere in Ireland, England and Scotland. Today the herd numbers about 650 animals. The 45km-long, 1.8m-high fence that contains the deer was originally built in the 1890s and remains a quite remarkable construction, running in straight lines across the area's rugged hills, almost oblivious of steep crags and marshy boglands.

After several subsequent owners (including the IRA and the Irish Free State Army, who occupied the castle during the upheavals of the early 1920s), the estate was finally sold to the Office of Public Works in 1975. Glenveagh National Park was opened to visitors in 1984 and the castle two years later. Government work has concentrated on the preservation of the area's cultural and environmental heritage. Along with a daunting battle being waged against the rhododendron (see the boxed text Scourge of the Rhododendron, p217), a regeneration program is slowly allowing native woodland to expand. Fenced enclosures protect new seedlings of oak, holly, rowan, birch and hazel, which will eventually replenish the natural oak wood. Another ongoing project concerns Golden Eagles, which were successfully reintroduced to the park in 2000 after being hunted to extinction in the 19th century.

Glenveagh Visitor Centre (☎ 074-913 7090; open daily), at the entrance to the park, provides information, exhibits and audiovisual displays about the area and its natural history. It also has a **restaurant** (open Easter and Jun-Sep) that serves hot food and snacks.

Glenveagh Castle (adult/child €3/1.50; open daily Easter-Oct) is open to the public by guided tour only. You can wander around the castle's exotic gardens for free however. Lovingly nurtured for centuries, their cultured charm stands in marked contrast to the wild landscape that enfolds them. The castle **tearooms** (open Easter & Jun-Sep) also offer tasty cakes and snacks.

Camping is not allowed anywhere in Glenveagh National Park.

THE WALK

From the turning circle in front of Glenveagh Castle, walk around the left-hand side of the building and follow the track southwest along the shore of Lough Veagh, past an old sawmill on the left. After about 2km the track enters **Mullangore Wood**, the best of the natural oakwoods in Glenveagh. Sessile oak, birch and hazel are the main species. On the lough shore are some Scots pines, survivors of a former plantation. About 45 minutes' walk from the castle brings you level with the beach at the end of Lough Veagh. To the west, Astelleen Burn plunges 215m down the rocky hillside in three impressive cascades into the Owenveagh River.

Continue along the track, passing a small, white **stalkers' cottage** about 15 minutes from the beach. Beyond this the enormity of the rhododendron problem becomes obvious; the steep hillside ahead on the left is liberally blanketed with it and in early summer the plant's relentless spread is betrayed by patches of mauve on the northwest hillside as well. The walled enclosure nearby once protected a vegetable garden, cultivated by estate staff who lived here in the early 1920s; it also housed imported red deer before they were released.

The track becomes more like a path as it gains height, leaving the protection of the woodlands. A 45-minute walk from the cottage brings you to a gate in the deer fence. From here, you can either retrace your steps back to the castle or continue ahead towards the mountain of Farscallop. For the latter route, climb fairly steeply northeast from the gate. The northwestern edge of the slope provides the easiest passage. After about 1km the spur flattens out; continue in a northeasterly direction. The unmistakable peak of Errigal is dramatically framed above a dip in the Derryveagh Mountains to the northwest, while the moorland to the south has a compelling fascination in its bleakness and apparent emptiness. An hour's effort should bring you to the summit of **Farscallop** (423m). The views are best to the west and north, taking in wide stretches of the coast.

Continue along the ridge, which is now rather less bog-ridden. Cross a dip and climb to a lesser summit (378m). This modest top affords the walk's best views, spanning the full length of Lough Veagh with the Derryveagh Mountains rising steeply from the far shore. Continue down over damp and grassy ground to the woodland below and pick up an old bridle path, which descends generally west through trees to the lakeside track. Turn right and retrace your steps for the final 45-minute, 2.5km walk back to the castle.

SLIEVE SNAGHT & THE POISONED GLEN

Duration 6½–7 hours
Distance 14km
Ascent 800m
Difficulty demanding
Start/Finish Cronaniv Burn bridge
Nearest Town Dunlewy (p236)
Transport private

Summary A challenging ridge walk high above the spectacular Poisoned Glen, with some of the finest views from Donegal's peaks.

Slieve Snaght (*Sliabh Sneachta* or 'Mountain of the Snows', 678m) is the second highest peak in County Donegal and the crowning feature of the Derryveagh Mountains. A sprawling granite massif that is largely located within the boundaries of Glenveagh National Park, its summits are rounded domes interspersed by numerous loughs and pools. Though the mountain's rough terrain and awkward approaches make it a challenging proposition, experienced walkers will enjoy a superb ridge-top route that epitomises wild Irish hills at their best.

The route begins with a trip though The Poisoned Glen, on the northern flank of the mountain. This valley was filled by a northwest-flowing glacier during the last ice age, and has been described as the most perfect example of a glaciated feature in the area (see Signs of a Glacial Past, p30). The towering rock buttresses on either side of the glen were exposed and scraped smooth as the glacier melted, and the valley holds the remnant of a lake, held back by moraine left by the retreating ice.

Apart from a rough trail over the initial section, there are no clearly defined paths along the route. Although sheep and deer have cut a network of short paths in several places, these have a tendency to end abruptly on the edge of vertical cliffs. The route also entails negotiating the deer fence around the boundary of Glenveagh National Park in two places, though it is possible to squeeze between the wires without impairing their tension. Along the final section of the walk beside the Devlin River (*Abhainn Dhuibhlinne*), it's impossible to avoid patches of soggy swamp, made treacherous by extremely slippery mats of decaying moor grass. Fortunately a path of sorts gradually becomes clear as you pass above the river gorge, but the going remains rough and uneven underfoot.

PLANNING

Slieve Snaght lies on the northwest boundary of Glenveagh National Park. If you are planning to do the walk between August and February, the deer culling season in the park, it would be prudent to check with the **park office** (☎ 074-913 7090) about the location and time of the cull.

Maps

OSI 1:50,000 map No 1 covers the walk.

GETTING TO/FROM THE WALK

From the village of Dunlewy, follow the R251 east for 1km and turn right along a minor road, signposted to the Poisoned Glen. There are parking spaces about 1km along this road, either near the hairpin bend at GR B930189 or beside a large, roofless church nearby.

THE WALK

From the hairpin bend in the road, a rough path leads southeast, soon crossing a stream via an old stone, humpback bridge. Rocky in places and boggy in others, the path traces the northeastern bank of Cronaniv Burn and leads into the dramatic amphitheatre of the **Poisoned Glen**.

Cross a broad spur where the stream makes a right-angle bend and continue east. Ford the stream below a cascade and follow a tributary northeast, heading into a wide glen framed by broken cliffs. Negotiate the deer fence and continue through the glen to its head, ascending a rocky gully on the right (GR B956165). About two hours from the start you will emerge on the broad, dissected, rocky ridge.

> ## WHAT'S IN A NAME?
>
> Over the years, various accounts have been offered to explain how the dramatic, cliff-backed Poisoned Glen got its sinister name. Legend has it that when the ancient one-eyed giant king of Tory, Balor, was killed here by his exiled grandson, Lughaidh, the poison from the giant's eye split the rock and poisoned the glen. Other theories point to the one-time presence of Irish spurge; the milky juice from this plant was once used by salmon and trout poachers to poison water. The less interesting truth, however, probably lies in a cartographic gaffe. Locals were inspired to name the valley *An Gleann Neamhe* (the Heavenly Glen), but when an English cartographer mapped the area, he carelessly marked it *An Gleann Neimhe* – the Poisoned Glen.

Make your way generally southwest, keeping as close as safely possible to the rim of the steep crags on the right. The sections of bog become more sporadic and broad sheets of granite offer firmer terrain. After about 15 minutes, cross the deer fence again; the next major feature is the narrow **Lough Atirrive Big**, which you keep on your left. Climb the steep flank beyond and continue over the sprawling bump of **Drumnaliffernn Mountain** (596m). From here, impassable cliffs bar the route southwest; veer south instead and descend to **Lough Slieve Snaght** (about 1½ hours after arriving on the ridge).

A final, steep but straightforward climb brings you to the spacious summit plateau of **Slieve Snaght** (678m; 30 minutes from the lough). The large cairn marks a superlative vantage point; it is in the middle of the mountains but set back from the impressive trio of Errigal, the Aghlas and Muckish. The Donegal coastline, at least as far south as Slieve League, is included in the backdrop.

Start the descent on a south-southwesterly course, aiming to reach the valley just south of the col (GR B919146) via a steep, grassy gully between the crags. Then head generally north, but keep well to the east of a small stream, and drop down into the wide valley of the Devlin River. Follow the southern bank of this downstream past many small loughs; the going is rough and unavoidably wet in places. After about 1.5km the river straightens out and dives into a steep-sided gorge, which provides shelter for a luxuriant woodland of oak, birch, hazel, rowan and, unfortunately, rhododendron. Where the river turns north, continue northeast; cross Cronaniv Burn via the stone bridge and return to the start of the walk (about two hours from the summit).

SOUTH DONEGAL

In a country generously endowed with magnificent coastline, it is the southwestern reaches of County Donegal that stand supreme, offering some of the finest coastal walking in Europe. The cliffs of Slieve League in particular display a spectacular variety of rock formations. Standing on the narrow ridge of One Man's Pass, just beneath the summit of Slieve League, and facing the seemingly limitless Atlantic Ocean, there is a keen sense of being on the edge of the world. Yet this is an area that has been settled for 5000 years, and has a special place in Irish history as the heartland of Christianity as established by St Columba. Further inland, the rugged interior north of Donegal Town is dominated by the Blue Stack Mountains, part of the northwest that is least visited on foot.

SLIEVE LEAGUE

Duration 4½–5½ hours
Distance 15km
Ascent 570m
Difficulty moderate–demanding
Start Bunglass
Finish Malinbeg
Nearest Towns Kilcar and Carrick (p238), Malinbeg (p239)
Transport private, bus

Summary A truly exhilarating traverse of some of Europe's highest and most extensive sea cliffs.

The traverse of Slieve League is one of Ireland's outstanding coastal excursions. The cliffs reach almost 600m high, and are second to none in their diversity of form and colour. Local communities market Slieve League as the highest sea cliffs in Europe,

but the seaward slopes of Croaghaun on Achill Island (see p169) are nearly 100m higher. Slieve League devotees argue that it all depends on the definition of a cliff; the rock faces here are steeper and more continuous. Whatever the semantics there's no denying that the scenery is tremendously impressive, and it's deservedly popular with walkers and day-trippers alike.

The route includes a traverse of One Man's Pass, a narrow ridge between the two highest points on the Slieve League massif. The pass is actually less intimidating than it sounds, consisting of an arête about 1.5m wide, with steep but not vertiginous drops on either side. Fine days without much wind offer ideal walking conditions, both to make the most of the long views and to minimise the hazards of walking near such exposed terrain. Even on calm days, however, care is needed along the cliff edge.

The route described is the full traverse of the mountain, undoubtedly the most rewarding and fulfilling option available. Though it's presented from south to north, there's no reason why it can't be completed in the other direction too. The linear format presents logistical problems however, and many people make an out-and-back trip from one end or the other and turn around at the summit (a more popular option from Bunglass). Alternatively, why not complete the full traverse from Carrick, spend the night at Malinbeg, then walk the 7km of road to Glencolmcille the next day. From here you could complete the equally impressive Glencolmcille Circuit (see p230) before catching the bus back to Carrick.

PLANNING
Maps
The OSI 1:50,000 map No 10 covers the walk.

GETTING TO/FROM THE WALK
To reach Bunglass car park at the start of the walk, first head to the village of Carrick (*An Charraig*). From the centre of the village, turn south along a minor road signed to Bunglass. Pass through the village of Teelin after 2km, then turn right up a road signed to Bunglass. The car park is 5km beyond Teelin, along a very narrow road.

If you're travelling by public transport, the easiest option is to start the walk in

Carrick – see Alternative Start, p230. For transport options to Carrick, see Kilcar & Carrick (p238).

The traverse finishes at a car park at the end of the road in Malinbeg. Malinbeg is 7km southwest of the larger village of Glencolmcille. For details of public transport services to/from Glencolmcille, see p238.

THE WALK

Bunglass car park, perched 120m above the sea near the cliff edge, is a great start to the day, and provides the classic view of Slieve League's massive cliffs. Begin by heading northeast from the car park, following a well-used path that is paved at first before turning into an eroded line of peat. The path keeps close to the cliff edge as it climbs towards the summit of **Scregeighter** (308m). From there it turns northwest, still following the line of the cliffs. Ahead, views open up over a mosaic of

inlets and Rathlin O'Birne Island close to Malinbeg.

Continue up and over the aptly named **Eagles Nest** (323m), perched atop vertical cliffs. The path divides to traverse the heathery slopes of **Crockrawer** (435m) – the higher option is preferable – and the trails merge again higher up. Soon you are confronted with a steep, rocky ridge rising to a narrow crest. This narrows at one point to a fin of

SLIEVE LEAGUE & GLENCOLMCILLE

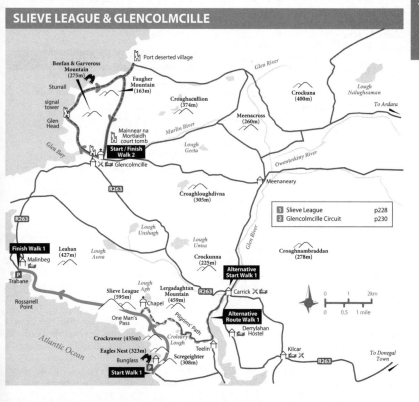

rock perhaps 1 metre wide (the real One Man's Pass?), with dangerous drops on either side. With care and balance this can be negotiated and enjoyed by the adventurous walker. The landward slope is cobwebbed with paths detouring away from the ridge, providing easier options that are preferable for the more cautious, or in wet or windy conditions. Either path brings you to a large cairn and onto open moorland (1½ hours from Bunglass). The Pilgrims' Path (see Alternative Start below) joins the main Slieve League route at this point, and walkers with plenty of energy might want to have a look at the ruined chapel along the pilgrims' route to the north.

It's not long now before the ridge suddenly narrows to **One Man's Pass**, a 250m-long arête with steep slopes on either side. The path along the top is wide and there is little danger – it is certainly not as difficult as the rocky crest encountered previously. Once across the pass, a final climb takes you up to the survey pillar and assorted cairns set on the broad summit of **Slieve League** (595m, 30 minutes from the cairn). In good visibility, the unmistakable profiles of Errigal to the north and flat-topped Benbulbin to the south can both be seen on the horizon.

To continue to Malinbeg, follow a rough path that descends steeply west, mostly over grass. Keep close to the cliff edge to locate the firmest terrain, crossing an unnamed stream just below a line of low crags. Then climb steeply over two spurs that extend seaward from the moorland dome of **Leahan** (427m) to the north. From here there are fine views back to Slieve League's cliffs, rock pillars and almost vertical drifts of scree. There is no clear path as you continue west around several small streams, but as you swing northwest you reach the end of a rough track. This track leads around the bay with the fine horseshoe beach of **Trabane** (White Beach) immediately ahead. Walk along the low cliff-top to finish at the car park above the beach (two hours from the summit of Slieve League).

ALTERNATIVE START: CARRICK
3–3½ hours, 7km, 560m ascent
For those without private transport, the easiest way to the summit of Slieve League is to start in Carrick and follow the Pilgrims' Path. The Pilgrims' Path is also a good option for vertigo sufferers and those who don't like the sound of One Man's Pass, although it misses out on the magnificent side view of Slieve League from Bunglass. The path is a straightforward route that ascends an obvious track for its duration.

To reach the start of the path, head south from the village of Carrick for 2km and then turn right along a minor road signed to Slieve League. Continue for 1.5km, following signposts to the informal car park near the end of the road.

Continue along the road, which turns into a stony track heading up to a shallow col above Lough Agh. Here there is a ruined stone **chapel** (marked on the OSI map as 'Ch') that is associated with a disciple of St Columba. It is set into the slope, just to the right of a cairn topped by a large, slender rock. Also nearby is a holy well, the water from which is believed to cure arthritis, once inducing hopeful sufferers to make what was no doubt a painful pilgrimage to the site.

GLENCOLMCILLE CIRCUIT

Duration 4–5 hours
Distance 13km
Ascent 500m
Difficulty moderate
Start/Finish St Columba's Church
Nearest Town Glencolmcille (p237)
Transport bus, private

Summary Dramatic coastline, ancient monuments and an atmospheric deserted village makes this an essential outing for any walker.

Situated amid some of the country's wildest coastline at the western tip of Donegal, the remote village of Glencolmcille is a place of unique character and other-worldly atmosphere. The area has long been a favourite with walkers, who come to follow its ancient pilgrimage route or explore its magnificent sea cliffs. The old village of Port, which was deserted in the 1940s, lies over the headland just north of Glencolmcille and makes a particularly evocative destination. The village's ruined cottages and stone enclosures lie amid starkly beautiful scenery, and are

WALKING FROM PAGANISM TO CHRISTIANITY

The tradition of walking goes back a very long time in Glencolmcille, and the village has been a major site of Christian pilgrimage (or Turas) for almost 1500 years. Human settlement dates back over 5000 years however, as the remarkable number of Neolithic monuments in the area attest.

The association with St Columba – the village namesake and the man who brought Christianity to the area in the 6th century – remains contested as there is no firm evidence of the saint actually visiting the village. There's no doubt however that a monastery was founded here in his name, and many of the existing Stone Age monuments were incorporated into Christian usage by inscribing them with a cross. An example of a previously pagan site being given new meaning within the Christian faith is Turas station No 9, passed near the end of the Glencolmcille Circuit. The site consists of a carved standing stone with a hole in the middle. This was once the location for pagan marriages, the union sealed when the couple joined fingers through the hole. Modern Christian practice involves walking around the stone three times and denouncing Satan. If the pilgrim achieves a state of grace, it should be possible to look through the hole and see paradise on the other side.

The tradition of a walking pilgrimage in Glencolmcille may also pre-date Christianity, but it certainly continued under the Catholic church. Even today thousands of modern pilgrims visit Glencolmcille on the 9th June each year to pray at the 15 ancient stations of the Turas, with traditionalists still completing the 5km route barefoot.

If you want to follow the route, get hold of the excellent guide *Gleann Cholm Cille*, which is available locally and marks the stations on a small-scale map of the village. Even with the guide in hand you should prepare for some detective work however because the signage is often misleading. Fortunately at least those monuments located alongside the modern walking routes are readily accessible, allowing visitors to appreciate the powerful symbolism of at least some of the ancient sites.

atmospheric reminders of the harshness of life in remote western Ireland.

The trip from Glencolmcille to Port was simplified in 2007 thanks to the development of two new National Loop Walks. Though the 10km-long Tower Loop and 13km-long Drum Loop don't lead directly to the ruins, they each provide marked paths for part of the way. As well as using these loops, the walk described follows part of the *Bealach na Gaeltachta* (Donegal Way), so roughly two thirds of the route is way-marked in some form. The remainder of the circuit crosses open coastline however, so a map and navigation skills are still required. Care is also required in the vicinity of the cliffs, especially in wet or windy conditions.

Maps

OSI 1:50,000 map No 10 covers the walk.

GETTING TO/FROM THE WALK

The route starts and finishes at St Columba's Church in the centre of Glencolmcille (GR G535849). Glencolmcille is located around 24km west of Killybegs along the R263. A small car park in front of the church provides space for around 10 vehicles.

For details of bus services to Glencolmcille, see p238.

THE WALK

Begin by heading west along the road from St Columba's Church, following the blue arrows of the Tower Loop. Within 80m you come to the first monument, one of the best cross-inscribed **early-Christian pillars** in Ireland. A set of stone steps allows access to the site.

Continue along the road for 50m and turn right at a junction. This lane leads along the sandy mouth of the Murlin River. Cross a bridge over a tributary stream then turn right again onto a smaller lane. Before long you pass Turas station No 3 on the left – a small mass rock beside a cairn. Continue towards a cottage, then veer right onto a grassy track in front of the house. Climb steeply to a junction with another lane and turn left. Roughly 80m later, turn through a gate on the right and head along a stone track. Columcille's Well, Turas Station No 7, is signed to the right here, though it's tucked into a hollow in the hillside and can be tricky to find.

Follow the track as it climbs the steep hillside in a series of switchbacks, with fantastic views southwest across Skelpoonagh Bay and Rossan Point. At the top of the slope the track forks. Turn left along the route signed to the signal tower and climb more gently across peaty ground. The **signal tower** is a huge, stone structure that was built in the wake of the French invasion of 1798 (see the boxed text A Tower of Strength, p44). The three towers in the vicinity of Glencolmcille were built between 1804 and 1806, but were only staffed for a few years before being abandoned completely in 1815.

Leave the way-marked route here and cross the final few metres to the cliff-top. Beneath your feet the Glen Head drops 200m to the Atlantic and there are fantastic coastal views to the north and south. Now begin to trace the coast northeast; an informal path in the grass marks the passage of previous feet. It's not long before the white cliffs of **Sturrall** jut into the sea. This dramatic fin of rock is surely one of the most impressive natural sights along the Irish seaboard.

Continue past the headland, taking care along the exposed cliff edge. Descend across a hollow then keep inland slightly as you cross rougher, heather-covered ground towards Port. The massive blocks of stone and countless seastacks that guard the entrance to Port bay beckon you on. Veer slightly inland to join a bog track marked by the waymarkers of the Bealach na Gaeltachta for the final descent to the **deserted village** (2½ to three hours from Glencolmcille).

It's easy to spend an hour or so wandering around Port, but when you're ready, relocate the bog track you used to arrive in the village. Follow the track as it climbs 260m to the radio mast at the summit of Beefan and Garveross Mountain. Here you meet the red arrows that indicate the Drum Loop. Keep straight ahead and descend along a tarmac lane towards the houses of Glencolmcille.

Near the base of the descent, some slabs of rock in a small field are actually **Mainnear na Mortlaidh**, a court tomb dating from 3000 BC. Shortly beyond this you pass Turas station No 9, a carved standing stone

with a hole in the middle (see the boxed text Walking from Paganism to Christianity, p231, for more on the symbolism of this site). A short climb and a final right turn then brings you back to St Columba's Church.

BLUE STACK CIRCUIT

Duration 6–7 hours
Distance 18km
Ascent 780m
Difficulty moderate–demanding
Start/Finish Edergole bridge
Nearest Town Donegal Town (p235)
Transport private
Summary A rugged walk that crosses rough and boggy ground but showcases the best of the beautiful Blue Stacks.

The Croaghgorm or Blue Stack Mountains, as they are more commonly known, rise above Lough Eske, a few miles north of Donegal Town and Donegal Bay. They are a wild, rough and very beautiful range of granite summits, which give good views of central and southern Donegal. This route takes in most of the main summits on a circuit that has Lough Belshade (*Loch Bel Sead* or 'Lake with the Jewel') at its centre.

The Blue Stacks drain poorly and the going can be exceptionally boggy after heavy rain. On the plus side, wet weather brings the best out of the 30m-high Eas Doonan waterfall and the many other small cascades along the Corabber River. Once up on the highest sections of the route, the rough terrain and lack of distinct summits and ridges makes navigation tricky in poor visibility.

PLANNING
Maps
Use OSI 1:50,000 map No 11.

GETTING TO/FROM THE WALK
To reach the start, take any one of three different turns that are signed for Lough Eske from the N15, between 4km and 7km northeast of Donegal Town. These will lead you onto the Lough Eske Drive, which runs anticlockwise around the lake. At the northern end of the drive, the road climbs steeply above the lake and there are two hairpins. The second of these has a small

BLUE STACK CIRCUIT

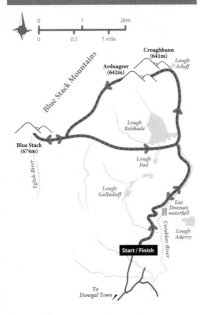

road running off its apex. Follow this road to its end at Edergole, where you'll find some outhouses, an old walker signpost and room to park several cars. Be careful not to block any of the nearby lanes or gates.

THE WALK

The walker post is an old marker from the Donegal section of the Ulster Way. Most of this route was never way-marked and it has now been abandoned. Go through the farm gate and follow a wide track along a small forestry plantation to a ford, then continue steeply to the splendid **Eas Doonan waterfall**. Pass a small boulder dam and head up along the banks of the Corabber River; a fairly distinct path leads across the boggy ground. After 1km you reach the point where the Corabber doglegs on its way down from Lough Belshade. Following along its bank on informal paths – if there's been rain you'll pass several powerful little waterfalls – to reach **Lough Belshade** (1½ hours from the start) and a sudden view of its encircling cliffs with the main Blue Stack summits behind.

Cross the Corabber at a boulder dam and head across the eastern shores of the lake,

aiming for a grassy notch in the spur that descends right to the lake in front of you. Pass through this and pick up a sheep track that leads into a wide gully. Climb north out of the gully when the stream peters out and continue across increasingly rocky, but drier, ground. A couple of outcrops are easily negotiated before reaching the summit of **Croaghbann** (641m) from where there are tremendous views across Lough Belshade and Lough Eske.

Turn west along a ridge and scramble down over slabs and rocky ground before climbing up to **Ardnageer** (642m), with its views across the rocky shelf above Lough Belshade. It's now a couple of kilometres over a number of rises to the main top of **Blue Stack** (674m), which is reached after a long, gradual ascent over grassy slopes. On the way to the summit you'll pass a conspicuous, brilliant-white outcrop of quartz, which from a distance looks like a patch of snow. The Irish for quartz, *grianchloch*, translates aptly as 'sunstone'.

The view from Blue Stack (three hours from Lough Belshade) is vast, in particular to the north where the pyramid of Errigal is prominent beyond the more prosaic outlines of the Derryveagh Mountains. To the south are Donegal Bay and the mountains of Yeats Country. About 600m to the northeast of the summit is the site where a WWII bomber crashed. A plaque marks the site but can be difficult to locate.

Retrace your steps from Blue Stack for 1km and descend eastwards back to Lough Belshade, moving down through a vague gully. The route is intricate, zigzagging down through outcrops and crossing delightfully rough granite slabs in a very wild situation.

When you reach the southeast corner of Lough Belshade, simply reverse the approach route back along the Corabber River to Edergole.

MORE WALKS

NORTH DONEGAL
Slieve Snaght

A northeast-to-southwest ridge of mountains stretches down the middle of the Inishowen Peninsula, with the summit of Slieve Snaght (the highest point on the headland at 615m and not to be confused with Slieve Snaght on the boundary of Glenveagh National Park) dominating the range. A moderate 10km walk exploring the area starts from a minor road between Buncrana and Carndonagh, at GR C438364. The route ascends Damph and Slieve Main (475m) to reach Slieve Snaght, crossing fields and rough, often boggy ground. The views from the summit are impressive. Allow four hours and use OSI 1:50,000 map No 3. The nearest bus route is the **Lough Swilly Bus Company** (☎ 074-912 2863) service from Derry, which runs along the R240 between Carndonagh and Quigley's Point, 5km to the northeast.

DERRYVEAGH MOUNTAINS
Dooish
For a rugged and challenging hill walk in Glenveagh National Park, try a circuit taking in Dooish Mountain (652m). Start from Glenveagh Castle as for the Glenveagh National Park route, p224, and follow the track described to the southwestern end of Lough Veagh. Ford the Owenveagh River and climb the steep slopes beside the Astelleen Waterfall. Now head north across rough ground in a very wild situation to the summit of Dooish. The descent runs northeast for 5km to reach the northeast end of Lough Veagh and the car park and visitor centre. The total distance of 13km includes 600m of ascent. Expect to take at least six hours for this route, which merits a grade of moderate-to-demanding for its rugged terrain alone. Use OSI 1:50,000 map No 6.

Lough Agher
This is an easy walk of 7km with only 50m ascent, in the shadow of the towering cliffs of Muckish. The route partly follows the track of a former narrow gauge railway between Letterkenny and Burtonport. To reach the start, follow directions for the northern approach to Muckish (p221), but park 1km before the end of the road in the bypassed hairpin of an older road. Follow the hill tracks generally southwest and west, then the old railway formation and the road on the northwest side of Lough Agher. Return via another section of the railway. Allow 1½ to two hours, and use OSI 1:50,000 map No 2.

SOUTH DONEGAL
Lavagh More
From a starting point in the Sruell Valley (GR G913881, OSI 1:50,000 map No 11), a wonderfully scenic and rugged circuit taking in the summits of Lavagh More (671m) and Lavagh Beg (650m) can be completed via Sruell Gap and the Grey Mare's Tail Waterfall. You'll need the OSI map to navigate the 12km of minor roads leading north from Donegal Town to the start. An old track leads up into Sruell Gap; from the end of this bear northwest and then northeast across Binnasruell, passing several loughs before reaching the summit of Lavagh Beg. Head southeast to Lavagh More and then descend steeply along the Sruell River back to the start. Expect to take 4½ to five hours for the 11km route, which has a total of 720m ascent and a grading of moderate to demanding.

WAYMARKED WAYS
County Donegal has two long-distance Waymarked Ways. *Slí Dhún na nGall* (The Donegal Way) is made up of four circular trails in the western part of the county, each of which is between 50km and 70km in length. Alternatively the Bluestack Way is a 47km route that starts in Donegal Town and ends in Ardara. See www.walkireland .ie for full descriptions of both routes.

TOWNS & FACILITIES

CLONMANY & BALLYLIFFIN
☎ 074 / pop 700
Clonmany is a small and relatively compact village in northwestern Inishowen. The village of Ballyliffin, around 2km northeast of Clonmany, has a wider range of accommodation thanks to its popularity as a summer golf resort. Both villages have small supermarkets, but the nearest bank is 8km east in Carndonagh, where you'll also find the helpful **Inishowen tourism office** (☎ 937 4933; www.visitinishowen.com; Chapel St, Carndonagh; open Mon-Sat Jun-Aug, Mon-Fri Sep-May).

Sleeping & Eating
The closest camping is at **Tullagh Bay Camping & Caravan Park** (☎ 937 8997;

campsites from €14; open Easter-Sep), around 3.5km northwest of Clonmany. This flat park is well located just behind sandy Tullagh Strand, though space is largely occupied by permanent caravans.

In Ballyliffin, try **Rossaor House** (☎ 937 6498; rossaor@gofree.indigo.ie; s €45-50, d €70-80), a B&B just outside town that offers pristine rooms, wonderful views and leafy little garden.

If you're doing the Raghtin More walk, it's hard to get more convenient than friendly **Glen House B&B** (☎ 937 6745; www.glenhouse.ie; Straid; s €70-80, d €90-110). Occupying a beautiful 1766 manor house, this place also has a tearoom serving daytime snacks, and an on-site **restaurant** (menus from €17; open Tue-Sun Jun-Sep, Thu-Sun from Sep-May). For location details, see Getting to/from the Walk, p213.

Ballyliffin also offers a range of hotels, the pick of which is **Ballyliffin Lodge** (☎ 937 8200; www.ballyliffinlodge.com; s/d €120/250, bar food €11.50-22.50, restaurant mains €16-26). Rooms are lavish, and leisure facilities include a state-of-the-art spa and golf course. Meals are served in both the hotel's restaurant and bar.

In Clonmany **The Village Diner** (mains from €6) offers simple meals for lunch and dinner, and all the hotels in Ballyliffin serve food.

Getting There & Away

Regular **North West Busways** (☎ 938 2619; www.foylecoaches.com) services link both Clonmany and Ballyliffin to Letterkenny (€7.30, one hour five minutes, four daily Mon-Fri & twice on Sat).

John McGinley (☎ 913 5201; www.john mcginley.com) run buses from Ballyliffin only, passing through Derry (€5, 45 minutes) on the way to Dublin (€20, five hours, twice daily Mon-Sat & once on Sun).

DONEGAL TOWN
☎ 074 / pop 2400

Normally marked on maps and road signs simply as Donegal, this is the gateway to walks in the southwest of the county. Accommodation is plentiful but on summer weekends it can be booked out, so it's wise to phone ahead.

The **tourist office** (☎ 972 1148; donegal@failteireland.ie; Quay St; open daily Jul-Aug, Mon-Sat Sep-Jun) is in the new 'Discover Ireland' building and sells a range of local guidebooks and OSI maps. **Four Masters Bookshop** (☎ 972 1526; the Diamond) also stocks local maps and guides.

There are no outdoor equipment suppliers in town, but there are several small grocery shops around the centre.

Sleeping & Eating

Situated 1.2km northwest of town off the Killybegs Rd (N56), **Donegal Town Independent Hostel** (☎ 972 2805; www.don egaltownhostel.com; Killybegs Rd, Doonan; dm €18, d €42-46) is within walking distance of town. Pick up can also be arranged.

Bluestack Centre (☎ 973 5564; www .donegalbluestacks.com; Drimarone; dm/f €17/50) is a remote hostel-cum-community centre with squeaky-clean rooms and a basketball court. It's 7km north of the centre, signposted from the roundabout northwest of town. It's often left unstaffed, so call ahead.

Friendly **Bridges B&B** (☎ 972 1082; thebridgesguesthouse@gmail.com; Waterloo Pl; s €40, d €60-70) overlooks the castle and the river, and offers five simple but spotless rooms.

In a great stone building at the heart of town, **Abbey Hotel** (☎ 972 1014; www .abbeyhoteldonegal.com; the Diamond; s/d from €80/130) offers access to a gym and has a stylish restaurant and bar.

For daytime meals and snacks, the snug **Blueberry Tearoom** (☎ 972 2933; Castle St; mains €7-10; open Mon-Sat) is a local favourite.

Serving lunches and evening meals, quaint **Market House** (☎ 972 1014; the Diamond; mains €17-28) tackles surf and turf mainstays with a fresh, contemporary ethos.

Getting There & Away

Frequent **Bus Éireann** (☎ 913 1008) services connect Donegal with Sligo (€12.50, 1¼ hours, six daily), Galway (€19, 3½ hours, two to three daily), Derry (€14.30, 1½ hours), Belfast (€19.50, 3½ hours) and Dublin (€18, four hours, six daily). The bus stop is on the western side of the diamond.

Feda O'Donnell (☎ 954 8114; www.feda odonnell.com) runs to Galway (€20, 3½ hours, twice daily, three on Fri & Sun) via Sligo. Call to confirm departure point.

NORTHWEST

DOWNINGS

☎ 074 / pop 1000

Downings is the main settlement on the Rosguill Peninsula, and a quietly popular holiday destination thanks to its long sandy beach, links golf course, and fantastic coastal scenery. Village facilities include a good-sized supermarket.

Sleeping & Eating

Located right beside the Blue Flag beach, **Casey's Caravan Park** (☎ 915 5301; rosap enna@eircom.net; campsites €10-20; open Apr-Sep) is both convenient and extremely popular, so it's best to book ahead during peak season.

Also near the beach, the family-run **Beach Hotel** (*Óstán na Trá*; ☎ 915 5303; www.beachhotel.ie; s/d €60/100; open Apr-Oct) offers plenty of personal touches. Most of the 30 rooms have sea views.

Downings Bay Hotel (☎ 915 5586; www .downingsbayhotel.com; s/d from €70/120; bar food €12.50-23.50, dinner menu €60-70 for two) offers contemporary luxury just a few steps from the strand. Rooms are immaculate, comfortable and spacious, and food is served in both the Haven Restaurant and JC's Bar.

There is no public transport to the area.

DUNFANAGHY

☎ 074 / pop 300

Dunfanaghy (*Dún Fionnachaidh*, 'Fort of the Fair-haired Warrior') is a compact village set amid beautiful scenery, and receives plenty of visitors during the summer. **McAuliffe's**, in the main street, stocks walking guidebooks. There's an ATM in the small supermarket on the waterfront, but the nearest tourist office is in Falcarragh (see p237).

Sleeping & Eating

Lovingly rebuilt, **The Mill House** (☎ 913 6409; www.corcreggan.com; Corcreggan Mill; camping per person €8-9, dm €18, s/d/ tr €35/50/70) is operated separately from the nearby Carriage Hostel. It has spotless rooms and optional breakfasts (from €5). It's 4km southwest of Dunfanaghy on the Falcarragh road (N56) and buses stop outside.

At the adjacent **Carriage Hostel** (☎ 910 0814; www.the-carriage-hostel-corcreggan .com; Corcreggan Mill; dm €14-17; s €25-35, d €35-42) there's a choice of sleeping

in a 19th-century railway carriage (open all year), or in a rustic stone Kiln House (open May-Sep).

With six flowery, spotless rooms, **Rosman House** (☎ 913 6273; www.rosman house.ie; Figart; s/d €45/60) is a homey B&B just down the road from the workhouse.

At the heart of the village, **Arnold's Hotel** (☎ 913 6208; www.arnoldshotel .com; Main St; s €55-85, d €130; mains €16-30; open Apr-Oct) has been in operation since 1922. It overlooks the waterfront in Sheep Haven Bay and serves fine Irish food in its elegant bar.

The best place for daytime snacks is **Muck 'n' Muffins** (☎ 913 6780; Main Sq; snacks €3-9.50; open daily), a three-storey café and craft shop in the centre of Dunfanaghy. During the summer it also opens some evenings as a wine bar serving tapas and cheeseboards.

Just south of the town on the Falcarragh road, **The Mill Restaurant & Guesthouse** (☎ 913 6985; www.themillrestaurant.com; Figart; three-course dinner €43.50; open Tue-Sun mid-Mar–Dec) serves perfectly composed meals, as well as offering high-class **B&B** (s/d €70/100).

Getting There & Away

Feda O'Donnell (☎ 954 8114; www.feda odonnell.com) buses from Crolly (€7, 40 minutes) to Galway (€20, five hours) stop in Dunfanaghy twice daily Monday to Saturday, three times Friday and Sunday.

John McGinley (☎ 913 5201; www.john mcginley.com) buses from Crolly stop in Dunfanaghy on their way to Letterkenny (€7, one hour) and Dublin (€20, 4¾ hours) between two and four times daily. **Lough Swilly Bus Co** (☎ 912 2863) services from Dungloe also stop in Dunfanaghy on their way to Letterkenny (€7, 55 minutes) and Derry (€7, 1½ hours).

DUNLEWY

☎ 074 / pop 700

The tiny settlement of Dunlewy (*Dún Lúiche*; also spelt Dunlewey) lies at the foot of Errigal, in the heart of the best hill-walking country of north Donegal. The village makes a convenient base for many of the routes in the Derryveagh Mountains, but facilities are limited to a small shop and petrol station.

Sleeping & Eating

On the northeastern edge of the village, the An Óige **Errigal Hostel** (☎ 953 1180; www .errigalhostel.com; dm/d €21/52) was completely rebuilt in 2007. State-of-the-art facilities now include a drying room, internet area and sitting room with log fire.

If you prefer a B&B, **Glen Heights** (☎ 956 0844; www.glenheightsbb.com; s/d €25/70) is a clean, new home where conservatory breakfasts are accompanied by panoramic views of the lakes and mountains. It's located 1.5km from the village centre, east along the R251 and then south along the minor road signed to the Poisoned Glen.

Also along the road to the Poisoned Glen, **Radharc an Ghleanna** (☎ 953 1835; http://radharcanghleanna.littleireland.ie; Moneymore; s/d €50/70) is a country bungalow with four clean, comfortable rooms.

The **Lakeside Centre** (*Ionad Cois Locha*; ☎ 953 1699; www.dunleweycentre.com; open Easter-Oct; snacks from €6), on the shore of Dunlewy Lough, offers various visitor attractions and serves food in its café.

For evening meals you'll have to head to one of the neighbouring villages – the closest options are a 10-minute drive west in Gweedore (*Gaoth Dobhair*). Here you'll find **Seaview Hotel** (*Óstán Radharc na Mara*; ☎ 953 1159; www.visitgweedore.com /seaview.htm; Bunbeg; s/d from €80/140), which occupies an unbeatable beachfront location along the main road. Chose between a decent selection of dishes in the **bar** (mains €12-26), or a four-course dinner in the elegant **bistro** (€45).

Getting There & Away

Dunlewy is situated on the R251, around 14km west of the entrance to Glenveagh National Park. There are no bus services to Dunlewy, although all three bus companies on the Dunfanaghy–Dungloe/Crolly route pass along the N56, 3km west of the village. Drivers will drop you at the Dunlewy turn if you ask in advance (see Getting There & Away for Dunfanaghy, p236, for details).

FALCARRAGH
☎ 074 / pop 850
Irish-speaking Falcarragh (*An Fál Carrach*) is a compact village with a workaday atmosphere, dominated to the south by the grey bulk of Muckish Mountain. You'll find more tourist amenities up the road in Dunfanaghy.

Falcarragh Visitor Centre (*An tSean Bheairic*; ☎ 918 0888; open Mon-Sat) is housed in the 19th-century former police barracks, and offers tourist information and a café.

Sleeping & Eating

The independent hostel **Loistin Na Seamroige** (Shamrock Lodge; ☎ 913 5057; Main St; dm/d €15/40; open mid-Jan–mid-Dec) is upstairs from Falcarragh's best pub. Dorms are basic but decent, and on a good night the pub seems like the town's living room.

B&Bs in the area include **Ferndale** (☎ 916 5506; s/d €36/46), around 200m west of the village centre.

Alternatively **Cuan-na-Mara** (☎ 913 5327; Ballyness; s/d from €32/64) offers B&B in a dormer bungalow with wonderful sea views over Ballyness Bay. It's 2km from the village centre along the road to the beach (signed Trá),

Lios an Easa (☎ 918 0581; www.donegal -bb.com; s/d €35/60) is situated at the western edge of the village, just before the bridge over the Tullaghobegley river. The beautifully furnished rooms are bright and spacious, and facilities include an attractive guest lounge.

There is a good supermarket at the bottom of the road signed to Muckish Gap, at the east end of the village. The village has two cafés serving daytime snacks, and a good fish and chip shop for take-away food. However the **Gweedore Bar** (☎ 913 5293; Main St; mains from €11.50) is the only place offering evening meals.

Getting There & Away

The **Feda O'Donnell** (☎ 954 8114; www .fedaodonnell.com) bus service from Crolly stops on Main St (twice daily Mon-Sat, three Fri & Sun) on its way to Letterkenny (€7, one hour) and Galway (€20, 5¼ hours).

John McGinley (☎ 913 5201) buses from Anagry also stop in Falcarragh on their way to Dublin (€20, five hours, three daily with additional services Fri & Sun).

GLENCOLMCILLE
☎ 074 / pop 300
The Gaeltacht village of Glencolmcille (*Gleann Cholm Cille*, 'Glen of Columba's

NORTHWEST

Church'; also spelt Glencolumbcille) is a remote and starkly beautiful coastal haven cut off from the rest of the world.

Teach Alasa (☎ 0973 0116; Cashel; open daily Apr–mid-Nov) dispenses limited tourist information. The village has a reasonable-sized shop but no banking facilities apart from the *bureau de change* at the post office.

Sleeping & Eating

The ageing IHO **Dooey Hostel** (☎ 973 0130; www.dooeyhostel.com; campsites/dm/d €7.50/15/30) is built into the hillside. The owner is a character and facilities are rustic. Drivers should take the road beside Glenhead Tavern for 1.5km; walkers can take a short cut beside the Folk Village.

Ionad Siúl (Glencolmcille Walking Centre; ☎ 973 0302; www.ionadsiul.ie; s/d €35/50) is a recently opened facility near the beach. It offers route information, guided walks, immaculate accommodation and cooking facilities. The owners live off-site, so call ahead.

You won't find a better spot to eat than **An Cistin** (The Kitchen; ☎ 973 0213; mains €10-22; open Easter-Oct). This café-restaurant is attached to Oideas Gael, an Irish language centre located 1km west of the village centre.

Getting There & Away

Bus Éireann (☎ 912 1309) has a regular service between Glencolmcille and Donegal Town (€12, 1¼ hours, at least twice daily Mon-Sat & once on Sun), passing via Kilcar and Carrick. There are extra daily services in July and August.

McGeehan Coaches (☎ 954 6150; www.mcgeehancoaches.com) also run from Glencolmcille to Letterkenny (€12.50, two hours, daily except Sun).

KILCAR & CARRICK
☎ 074 / pop 300

Kilcar (*Cill Chártha*) and its more attractive neighbour Carrick (*An Charraig*) are moderate-sized villages that make good bases for exploring Slieve League.

Kilcar Tourism is based at the village community centre, **Aisleann Cill Cartha** (☎ 973 8376; Main St, Kilcar; open Mon-Sat). Tourist information is also available from the **Tí Linn Centre** (☎ 973 9077; www.sliabhleague.com; Teelin, Carrick; open daily Easter-Sep, Fri-Tue Feb-Easter & Oct-Nov), in Teelin (*Tí Linn*), near Carrick. There are no banking facilities in either village.

Sleeping & Eating

Simple but homey **Dún Ulún House** (☎ 973 8137; dunulunhouse@eircom.net; Coast Rd, Kilcar; campsites €10, dm/d from €15/45) offers everything from a small camping ground ensconced in a tiered hillside, to hostel-style shared rooms, to traditional doubles. Breakfast is optional for €8 extra. The house is 1km west of the Kilcar village centre.

The well-run IHH **Derrylahan Hostel** (☎ 973 8079; derrylahan@eircom.net; Derrylahan, Kilcar; camping per person €8, dm/d €16/40) is another budget option. It's on a farm, 3km west of the Kilcar on the coast road. Pick-ups can be arranged.

In the heart of Carrick, **Ostan Sliabh Liagh** (☎ 973 9973; www.ostansliabhliag.com; s/d €35/70; bar food €6-12), offers B&B accommodation above the town's largest pub. Rooms are basic but clean, and decent bar food is served in the pub below.

Kilcar also has **Blue Haven** (☎ 973 8090; www.bluehaven.ie; Killybegs Rd; s/d €55/100; mains €14-26; open for dinner daily May-Oct, weekends only Nov-Apr), where all 15 guestrooms have access to a communal balcony. The stylish restaurant downstairs offers home cooking.

Both villages have good-sized grocery shops and a selection of pubs serving food.

Getting There & Away

All the buses to the area stop in both Kilcar and Carrick, which are about 10 minutes apart. **Bus Éireann** (☎ 912 1309) service 490 passes through the villages twice daily Monday to Saturday, and once on Sunday, on its way from Donegal Town (€10.50, 50 minutes) to Glencolmcille (€7.60, 25 minutes). There are also extra daily services during July and August.

LETTERKENNY
☎ 074 / pop 17,600

Letterkenny (*Leitir Ceanainn*) is Donegal's largest town, but is a working community rather less geared to tourism than other Irish gateways, and many visitors simply pass through on their way to Donegal's more alluring corners.

Northwest Tourist Office (☎ 912 1160; www.discoverireland.ie/northwest; Neil Blaney Rd; open daily Jun & Aug, Mon-Fri Sep-May) is 1km southeast of town centre at the end of Port Rd. There's an accommodation booking service and maps and guidebooks are also available.

The best place for outdoor equipment is **Wet & Wild** (☎ 912 5118; Ballyraine Retail Park), located in the town's eastern suburbs off Ramelton Rd.

Sleeping & Eating

Modern **Port Hostel** (☎ 912 5315; www .porthostel.ie; Port Rd; dm from €16, d €36-40) has a college dormitory atmosphere, and is a lively spot on holiday weekends. It's behind the An Grianán Theatre.

Letterkenny Court Hotel (☎ 912 2977; www.letterkennycourthotel.com; Main St; s €59-99, d €78-158) is a polished operation on the main drag. Service, style and location are its selling points.

For a luxurious experience, try **Castle Grove** (☎ 915 1118; www.castlegrove.com; Ramelton Rd; s/d €70/110; dinner menu €55), a grandiose Georgian manor 5km out towards Ramelton. The gardens are impossibly neat and award-winning Irish/French cuisine in the restaurant clinches the deal.

For self caterers, there are several supermarkets near the bus station and at the eastern end of the town centre.

There's no shortage of eateries around the town centre. **Simple Simon's** (☎ 912 2382; St Oliver Plunkett Rd; snacks €3-7; open Mon-Sat), is a natural-products shop with an on-site bakery and café.

Often touted as Letterkenny's best restaurant, **Yellow Pepper** (☎ 912 4133; www.yel lowpepperrestaurant.com; 36 Lower Main St; dinner mains €12-23), serves lunch also and stakes its reputation on excellent fish dishes.

Getting There & Away

Letterkenny is a major bus hub for northwestern Ireland. The bus station is by the roundabout at the junction of Ramelton Rd and the Derry road. It will look after luggage for €2.

Bus Éireann (☎ 912 1309) service 32 runs to Dublin (€19.50, four hours, nine daily). Service 64 arrives four times daily from

Derry (€9, 35 minutes) before continuing to Donegal Town (€9, 50 minutes), Sligo (€12, two hours) and Galway (€21, 4¾ hours).

John McGinley (☎ 913 5201; www.john mcginley.com) buses run to Dublin (€20, 3¾ hours) between two and four times daily.

Lough Swilly Bus Co (☎ 912 2863) stops in Letterkenny on its regular service from Derry (€7, one hour) to north Donegal.

Feda O'Donnell (☎ 954 8114; www.feda odonnell.com) runs a bus to Galway (€20, four hours, twice daily) via Donegal Town and Sligo. Buses stop on the road outside the bus station.

MALINBEG
☎ 074 / pop 100

Malinbeg is a small hamlet situated beneath the northern slopes of Slieve League. It boasts the beautiful cliff-ringed beach of Trabane and a grocery shop.

The best reason for staying here is the thoroughly modern and comfortable **Malinbeg Hostel** (☎ 973 0006; www.malin beghostel.com; dm/s/d €15/25/40; open mid-Jan–Nov). Great facilities include spotless rooms with private bathrooms. Call ahead for a pick-up.

There is no public transport to Malinbeg.

MELMORE HEAD & AROUND
☎ 074

Though there is no village at beautiful Melmore Head, a couple of accommodation options mean you can chose to stay here, right at the start of the walk. The nearest shops and ATM are in Downings, so bring all your own supplies.

At the end of the road along the headland you'll find the quiet **Rosguill Caravan & Camping Park** (☎ 915 5766; site and two adults €16; open May-Sep). Tranafaighaboy beach is just a few steps away and facilities include a tennis court and pitch and putt course.

Alternatively the An Óige **Trá Na Rosann Hostel** (☎ 915 5374; www.anoige.ie; dm €16; open end-May-Aug) has knockout views and a terrific atmosphere. It occupies a chalet-like former hunting lodge, and is the most northerly hostel in Ireland.

During summer months there is generally a **Fast Food Van** parked at the bottom of the road to the hostel.

There is no public transport to the area.

NORTHWEST

Northern Ireland

Highest peak in the region: Slieve Donard, Mourne Mountains, 850m

NORTHERN IRELAND

Northern Ireland has suffered a rather uninviting international reputation over the past 50 years, and the political turmoil has done a great job in masking the region's charms. But local walkers know the natural assets on their doorstep rival any in Britain or Ireland, and continued to enjoy their mountains and coastline throughout the years of unrest. Since the 1998 Good Friday Agreement, the region's inhabitants have been joined by an increasing number of visiting walkers keen to explore what is still an under-appreciated resource. If Northern Ireland's best walking venues were near Dublin, they'd be overwhelmed with people. But here it's still possible to stroll through fantastic scenery and feel like you're breaking new ground.

The real pleasure of Northern Ireland lies in the variety of its landscapes. One day you could be gazing over the clustered peaks of the Mourne Mountains, the next marvelling at the eroding forces of the ocean from a dramatic cliff-top path. Some routes begin in the urban heart of Belfast city, while others explore remote valleys where you'd be forgiven for thinking you were still in the 1970s.

The routes described in this chapter represent the elite of Northern Ireland's walking opportunities. Beginning in the region's capital, there are the cliffs of Cave Hill and the gentle North Down Coastal Path along the shore of Belfast Lough. In the south, you'll find a range of rugged outings in the Mournes, balanced by trips around the wooded grounds of historic manor-house estates. In the west are the relatively gentle Sperrin Mountains, along with the lakeland summit of Cuilcagh. The highlight of the northeast is the world-famous Causeway Coast, matched in beauty by walks through the beautiful Glens of Antrim. With so much on offer, it's easy to appreciate how you could spend a month exploring this region alone.

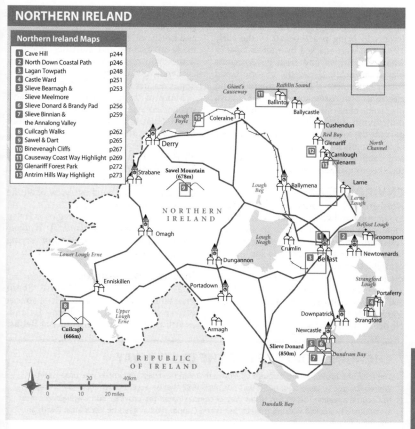

NORTHERN IRELAND

Northern Ireland Maps

HISTORY

The northeast of Northern Ireland was home to some of Ireland's earliest human inhabitants. Evidence suggests that Middle Stone Age people arrived on the Antrim Coast, from Scotland, 9000 years ago. The north was quickly settled and the countryside is littered with stone-built monuments from the Neolithic period. St Patrick later used the same area as a base from which to spread Christianity throughout the country.

By the 16th century, the north was the last stronghold of the Irish chiefs in their resistance against the increasing control of the British crown. The defeat of Hugh O'Neill, Earl of Tyrone, and his departure from Ireland in 1607 left the region leaderless. Soon after, Elizabeth I and then James

I set out the 'Plantation' of Ulster, removing Catholic landowners and replacing them with Scottish and English Protestants. This wholesale removal of people from their land, coupled with religious antagonism, initiated a conflict that still has two significant sections of the North's population at odds. It is also the source of the population pattern that led to partition. In 1921, while the rest of Ireland was gaining independence from Britain, the Anglo-Irish Treaty provided for the six predominantly Protestant counties of Ulster to remain within the United Kingdom, creating the province of Northern Ireland.

By the late 1960s, civil rights protests by Catholics in Derry and the unfortunate intervention of the police and British army ignited the Troubles, pitting Loyalists

NORTHERN IRELAND

against Republicans for more than 25 years of violence, killings and civil unrest. Attempts to bring peace began in the early 1990s and were marked by endless talks in which the British and Irish governments played key roles. Under the historic Good Friday Agreement of 1998, Northern Ireland elected its own Assembly and gained control over some of its own affairs. Early in the new millennium sectarian undercurrents still pervade the society, though the vast majority of inhabitants have grown tired of violence, and political parties, across the board work together to maintain the peace.

ENVIRONMENT

Northern Ireland packs a great variety of topography and geology into its small area, measuring only 150km east to west and 130km north to south. Lough Neagh, the largest lake in Ireland (383 sq km), is the centrepiece of the province, surrounded by the flat, low-lying valleys of the River Bann and its tributaries. Rolling drumlins of glacial origin and moorland between 300m and 500m high typify much of the rest of the North. In the southeast, the granite Mourne

Mountains stand out with their sharply angled peaks. Volcanic rock typifies the north and northeast; in the west, the Sperrins are made up of schists and quartzite. Limestone is the main rock type of the southwestern lakelands, giving way to sandstone on the upper reaches of Cuilcagh Mountain.

Many of the province's woodland and wetland ecosystems are managed by the National Trust, and large numbers have been designated as reserves.

PLANNING
Maps & Books

The OSI 1:250,000 map *North*, in the Holiday series, gives a good overview of all the areas covered in this chapter.

The best guidebook to the region is Helen Fairbairn's *Northern Ireland: A Walking Guide*, which describes 34 routes of varying difficulty from all around the province.

Information Sources

The Northern Ireland Tourist Board maintains an extensive network of tourist offices throughout Northern Ireland, as well as the region's main office at **Belfast**

CHANGING FORTUNES OF THE ULSTER WAY

The idea of a route passing through all Northern Ireland's varied landscapes was proposed by Wilfred Capper 50 years ago, but it was not until 1983 that an access order enabled his dream to become a reality. The 900km Ulster Way circumnavigated the province and was Ireland's most ambitious way-marked walking project, but when Capper died in 1998 he left a legacy with an uncertain future.

Despite its scope, legal status and strong popular image, the actual route never matched the original vision – long stretches of tedious road walking, unrelieved by even basic facilities, linked the more attractive off-road sections. Few walkers were prepared to spend five weeks walking the full distance, and large parts of the route were a commercial failure.

In a 1994 review it was generally agreed that the North needed several short, high-quality routes, rather than one often unattractive monster. By 2008, 11 new, two-day Waymarked Ways had been launched along the best sections of the original route (see the Cuilcagh Way Highlight, p263; Causeway Coast Way Highlight, p268; Antrim Hills Way Highlight, p273; and Waymarked Ways, p27).

At the same time as these routes were being developed, a consultation project was launched to decide what to do with the surviving sections of the original Ulster Way. In 2009, work began to re-market the Ulster Way as a whole. The route is now presented as several 'quality' sections – consisting largely of the recently launched routes – with intervening 'link' sections. The assumption is that few people will actually want to walk the link sections, but that public transport can be used to skip these and make a circuit around the quality sections. Walking the entire route still takes five weeks, but concentrating on just the quality sections takes two to three weeks.

For more information and descriptions of the various parts of the route, see the Ulster Way section on www.walkni.com.

CALLING NORTHERN IRELAND

If you're phoning a Northern Irish number from within the province, you only have to dial the eight-digit number supplied in this chapter.

To call Northern Ireland from elsewhere in the United Kingdom, use the area code ☎ 028, followed by the eight-digit number.

To phone Northern Ireland from overseas, the normal UK country code applies (+44), followed by the area code. However, there is also a cheaper option if you're calling the North from the Republic of Ireland; use the special area code of ☎ 048, followed immediately by the eight-digit number.

Welcome Centre (☎ 9024 6609; 47 Donegall Pl, Belfast). Their website www .discovernorthernireland.com is a great source of information for the entire province.

For route descriptions and general information on walking in the region, see www .walkni.com.

Daily weather forecasts for Northern Ireland are available from the Meteorological Office's **Weathercall** service (☎ 090 6850 0427; £0.60 per minute).

GATEWAYS

See Belfast (p278) and Derry (p280).

BELFAST & DOWN

Few would describe Belfast city as beautiful, but there are some surprisingly scenic walks lurking nearby. In the case of the Lagan Towpath, a historic route along the Lagan Navigation, the route starts at the urban heart of the city itself. Other routes, such as Cave Hill and the North Down Coastal Path, extend out from the edges of the suburbs, yet are still within easy reach of the city's extensive network of public transport.

Further away from the Northern Irish capital, County Down also has many quality walks to offer. The most renowned of these fall within the Kingdom of Mourne, and

are dealt with in the following section (see Mourne Mountains, p252). However, there are also several lowland routes between Belfast and the Mournes – we describe a circuit on the shores of Strangford Lough to whet your appetite for further exploration.

PLANNING
Maps

For navigating around the city, use the Collins *Belfast Streetfinder Atlas* or the OSNI 1:12,000 *Belfast Street Map*, both of which are available from local bookshops.

CAVE HILL

Duration 2–2½ hours
Distance 7km (4.5 miles)
Ascent 270m (886ft)
Difficulty easy–moderate
Start/Finish Belfast Castle car park
Nearest Town Belfast (p278)
Transport bus
Summary An easily accessible and highly rewarding circuit, climbing to the top of a cliff for fantastic views over Belfast city.

Just as Table Mountain looms over Cape Town, so Cave Hill rises above Belfast city. The trip to the top is one of those mandatory excursions; nobody can say they really know the city unless they've appreciated it from here. In terms of long-distance views that place the capital within its wider environment, no other vantage point even begins to compete.

The hill lies at the heart of Cave Hill Country Park, a 750-acre site at the northwestern corner of the city that also includes Belfast Castle and Belfast Zoo. The 368m-high summit is cut on its eastern side by a series of sheer escarpments, the long line of cliffs culminating at the prow of McArt's Fort. Among the city's inhabitants this promontory is popularly known as Nelson's Nose, a reference to the hill's face-like profile when viewed from the south. Though little remains visible today, the prow once held an Iron Age ringfort. In more recent times the lookout was visited by members of the United Irishmen, including Wolfe Tone, who looked down across the city in 1795 and pledged to fight for Irish independence.

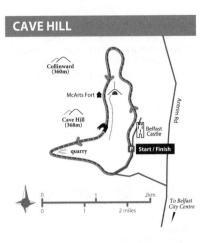

CAVE HILL

Three way-marked walking trails explore
Cave Hill from Belfast Castle, varying between 1.5km and 7km in length. This walk
is based on the longest route, the green Cave
Hill Trail. It follows a mixture of surfaced
and unsurfaced paths, and includes short
sections that are steep or rough underfoot.
Signposting is good until you arrive near
the top of the hill, but thereafter you'll need
to remain alert to locate the right path. The
route also passes along the top of exposed
cliffs, where care is needed in wet or windy
conditions.

Why not round off your walk with a
visit to **Belfast Castle** (☎ 9077 6925; www
.belfastcastle.co.uk; Antrim Rd; admission
free; open daily). This ornate building was
built in 1870 and was presented to the City
of Belfast in 1934. Upstairs the Cave Hill
Visitor Centre sheds light on the folklore,
history and ecology of the park, while downstairs you'll find the Cellar Restaurant.

PLANNING
Maps
OSNI 1:50,000 map No 15 covers the
walk.

GETTING TO/FROM THE WALK
The route starts and finishes at a car park
beneath Belfast Castle. From the city centre, head northwest to Antrim Rd then
follow signs for Belfast Castle. Pass through
the entrance gates and follow the driveway
uphill to a fenced parking area on the left
shortly before the castle.

Metro (☎ 9066 6630; www.translink.co
.uk) city buses also serve Belfast Castle –
take buses 1A to 1H from Donegall Sq
West.

THE WALK
Begin from the information board beside
the **car park**, where a low plaque signals the
green Cave Hill Trail uphill along a gravel
path. Turn right at a trail junction after
100m and head north along the slope into
deciduous woodland. Follow the waymarkers through several more junctions in the
trees. Occasional flights of steps punctuate
the ascent as the path weaves its way uphill.
A steep section of trail then climbs out of
the trees to a lookout, exposing the first real
views over Belfast Lough.

Follow the gravel path to a signed junction beneath the cliffs, around 40 minutes
from the start. The Cave Hill Trail branches
left here onto a smaller, earthen footpath
known as the Sheep's Path. The gaping
mouth of the lowest **cave** can be seen in
the cliff face ahead. The cliff holds no
less than five caves, all of which have
been chiselled from the basalt rock by
humans.

Follow the narrow trail as it swings to
the right beneath the cave and climbs
around the top of a hollow known as
the Devil's Punchbowl. A steady ascent
then leads past another viewpoint to a
stile. On the opposite side of this, turn
left and climb the northern shoulder of
Cave Hill. The prominent mast to the
northwest marks the 360m-high summit
of **Colinward**.

Another stile must be crossed before
the prow of **McArt's Fort** comes into view
ahead. Follow the cliffs south to the base
of the promontory, where a turnstile (30
minutes from the bottom of the cliffs) allow access to the top
flight of steps allow access to the top
minutes from the bottom of the cliffs).
Your reward for reaching this point is a
fantastic panorama over Northern Ireland's
eastern seaboard, with views stretching
from the Antrim Hills in the north to the
Mourne Mountains in the south. Belfast
lies immediately beneath you with the
ship yard prominent at the centre of the
city.

Retrace you steps off the prow and turn
left onto a gravel path. Follow the path south
along the cliffs, then cross a stile and swing

away from the edge. The best views now lie southwest over the rounded hummocks of the Belfast Hills. Descend through gorse and hawthorn to another stile. You now need to take care because the next turn is not marked. Continue to another stile that lies to the left of the main path. Cross the stile and join a gravel and grass path. Follow this into a meadow, bearing right and passing through gaps in two hedges. Turn immediately left after the second hedge and follow the path as it descends along the edge of an old **quarry**, a pretty spot that has been reclaimed by nature (20 minutes from McArts Fort).

Pass through a turnstile and cross a small stream. A steep, rough section of path now leads back into the woodland. Join a wider gravel path and turn right, continuing your descent through the trees. Turn left at the next fork to arrive at the entrance driveway for Belfast Castle. Turn left and follow the road uphill for 500m to return to your starting point.

NORTH DOWN COASTAL PATH

Duration 4½–5 hours
Distance 21km (13 miles)
Ascent 50m (164ft)
Difficulty easy
Start Holywood
Finish Groomsport
Nearest Towns Belfast (p278), Bangor (p277)
Transport train, bus
Summary A varied coastal path passing several harbours, sandy beaches, secluded woodlands and sites of historic interest.

The North Down Coastal Path begins just outside Belfast and heads east along the southern shore of Belfast Lough. Despite its urban beginnings, the route spends a surprising amount of time in relatively natural surrounds. The coastline is home to seals, wildflowers and many species of shore bird, with oyster catchers, cormorants, lapwings, eider duck and curlew all relatively common. The path forms part of the Ulster Way and is well surfaced for most of the way. Excellent public transport links mean it's also easily accessible, and can either be completed in its entirety or broken into shorter sections.

These days North Down is home to many of Belfast's more affluent citizens, and you'll pass several golf and yacht clubs along the route. In times past, the shoreline had a more strategic significance however, and the Normans built a series of coastal castles here during the 12th century. That theme endured over the following centuries and it wasn't surprising when Grey Point was chosen as the site for the lough's war defences some 800 years later. Built in 1907, Grey Point Fort saw service during both world wars and was closed in 1957. During its years of operation it had two six-inch (15cm) artillery guns trained across the water and, together with a similar emplacement at Kilroot on the lough's northern shore, provided a formidable barrier for unwelcome vessels approaching Belfast. The haven was put to good use during WWII when British and US warships gathered in Bangor Bay en route to Normandy and the D-day invasions.

There are several opportunities for snacks and drinks along the route; in Holywood, Crawfordsburn Country Park, Bangor and Groomsport. In rough sea conditions some sections of the route are awash at high tide, so if a big swell is running check the tide times before heading out. Though the section described here finishes at Groomsport, the official route continues east for another 3km, passing around the shingle bays of Orlock Point and finishing at a layby on the A2 at GR: 565828. At the time of writing this section was obscured by the construction of a housing development, but check locally if you want to extend the route around the headland.

PLANNING
Maps & Booklets
The OSNI 1:50,000 map No 9 covers the walk. A free leaflet entitled *The Coastal Path* is also available from local tourist offices and provides further background information on the route.

GETTING TO/FROM THE WALK
There are frequent **NIR** (☎ 9066 6630) trains from both Belfast Great Victoria St and Belfast Central to Holywood at the start of the walk (£2.40, 10 minutes). The service

NORTHERN IRELAND

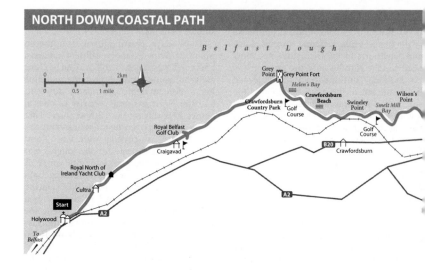

NORTH DOWN COASTAL PATH

also continues to/from Bangor (£4.60, 20 minutes), with intermittent stops at Cultra and Helen's Bay meaning you can shorten the route as required. Services run at least every 30 minutes Monday to Saturday and hourly on Sundays.

From Groomsport at the end of the route, you'll need to catch **Ulsterbus** (☎ 9066 6630) service No 3 back to Bangor bus and train station (£1.60, 10 minutes, 22 daily Mon-Fri, hourly on Sat & four on Sun). If you continue to Orlock Point you'll also find an Ulsterbus request stop in the final lay-by, which is served by buses on the same line.

THE WALK

From the entrance to Holywood train station, turn left and take the first left under the railway to the promenade. Turn right here and begin to follow the concrete path northeast, soon passing an Ulster Way signpost. Right from the start there's plenty of water-borne activity, with local yachts vying with large ferries heading to and from Scotland. Twenty minutes or so brings you to the **Royal North of Ireland Yacht Club** at Cultra, then 2km later you pass the sweeping fairways of Royal Belfast Golf Club at **Craigavad**. Between here and Grey Point you're likely to see oyster catchers and curlews on the rock shelves along the shore.

An hour or so of walking brings you to the dense deciduous woodland on the western boundary of **Crawfordsburn Country Park** (☎ 9185 3621; admission free; open daily). Continue for another 20 minutes to a side-path leading to **Grey Point Fort** (☎ 9185 3621; admission free; open Wed-Sun Easter-Sep, Sun only Oct-Easter), which is well worth a visit. Pass around Grey Point and along the beach at Helen's Bay to reach the wide, sandy expanse of **Crawfordsburn Beach**. Here signs point you a few hundred metres inland to Crawfordsburn Country Park's café and visitor centre, where you'll find excellent displays about the local wildlife. The park was established in 1971 and stretches along the coast for 3.5km, embracing flower-filled fields and the timbered glen around Crawfordsburn. Its name perpetuates the Crawfords, a local post-Plantation family who planted native and exotic trees in the glen.

Back on the coast, in clear conditions you should be able to make out the coastline of Scotland on the northeast horizon. Another 5km of varied walking takes you along Swineley Bay, around Swineley Point, Smelt Mill Bay and Wilson Point. The feeling of seclusion along this section is seldom disturbed, so it comes as something of a shock to enter **Bangor** with its noisy fun park and crowded marina (1¼ hours from Grey Point). Follow the seaside promenade

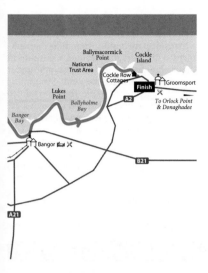

around Lukes Point to quieter Ballyholme Bay. From the eastern end of the bay, pick up a path beside the sea wall and continue along the edge of a field through the National Trust property at **Ballymacormick Point**. For the next 2km you're back in relatively wild surroundings where seabirds congregate on the rocky shore.

Just beyond the point lies the sleepy fishing village of Groomsport, with its picturesque harbour (one hour from Bangor). Continue to the main road, passing **Cockle Row Cottages** (☎ 9145 8882; admission free; open daily Jun-Aug), two restored 17th-century thatched cottages. Groomsport has few facilities but there is a small supermarket, pub and coffee shop in Main St, where you can slake your thirst whilst waiting for the bus.

LAGAN TOWPATH

Duration 4¼–4¾ hours
Distance 17.7km (11 miles)
Ascent 30m (98ft)
Difficulty easy
Start Belfast (p278)
Finish Lisburn (p284)
Transport train

Summary A riverside path leads out of Belfast into peaceful countryside beside a historic waterway.

The Lagan Towpath follows a corridor of greenery from the southwestern fringe of Belfast, through a patchwork of parks, woodland and meadows, to the city of Lisburn. At the heart of the route lies the Lagan Valley Regional Park, created in 1967 to protect 16 sq km on either side of the old Lagan Navigation. The trip relives the journey of the 19th-century horse-drawn barges that once steered a way along this navigation – see the boxed text Industrial Breakthrough of the Lagan Navigation, p249. Although many sections of the canal are now blocked, enough of the old locks and bridges remain intact that the journey is reminiscent of another age.

The route is well signed throughout and the entire distance is on surfaced paths, making it suitable for walkers of all persuasions. Despite its linear format, frequent transport links mean it's a simple matter to travel from the end back to the start. Albert Bridge serves as a convenient starting point but it's possible to join the towpath at several places along the route, especially if you can organise car transport. The rural scenery begins about an hour from Albert Bridge at the end of the Stranmillis Embankment, where you'll find a car park for the Lagan Valley Regional Park on Lockview Rd. There are no easy-to-reach refreshment stops along the way, so bring your own supplies.

PLANNING
Maps & Booklets
Two OSNI 1:50,000 maps, No 15 and No 20, cover the walk.

A *Towpath Leaflet* is also available free from local tourist offices, providing background information and a map of the route.

GETTING TO/FROM THE WALK
The walk starts at Belfast's Albert Bridge, which is close to **NIR's** (☎ 9066 6630) Central Station. Trains from all across the city and province arrive and depart from here. The station is also linked by numerous **Metro** (☎ 9066 6630) bus services to all parts of the city.

At the end of the walk, the easiest way to get back to Belfast from Lisburn is to take the train. NIR services run to Belfast Great Victoria St, Botanic and Central Station (£3, 30 minutes, at least half-hourly Mon-Sat &

hourly on Sun). To reach Lisburn station
from Union Bridge, cross the bridge and
the dual carriageway, then head uphill along
Bridge St to the centre of town. Take Castle
St and then Railway St to the station.

THE WALK
From Albert Bridge follow a paved path,
signposted to Stranmillis, that leads south
along the western side of the river. Pass
several apartment blocks and cross a lifting
bridge beside a small boat harbour. Across
the river are restored warehouses and a
gantry at the famous **Harland & Wolff
shipyard**, where the ill-fated *Titanic* was
built. Then comes Central Station on your
right and the green expanses of Ormeau Park
across the water. Near Ormeau Rd bridge

look out for Republican murals on house
walls nearby. Cross Ormeau Rd and follow
a roadside path beside Stranmillis Embankment with parkland beyond. Continue in
this fashion past King's Bridge, and under
Governor's Bridge. Beyond Stranmillis
Wharf apartments, leave the riverside to
divert around boat sheds and through a car
park to **Lagan Valley Regional Park** (about
an hour from Albert Bridge).

The path soon rejoins the river near a
weir and the scene is set for the rest of
the walk – tranquil river, wooded banks
and occasional pastoral views. After about
15 minutes you draw alongside an island
between a filled-in section of canal and
the river, where the native woodland is
being restored. Further on, with Belvoir

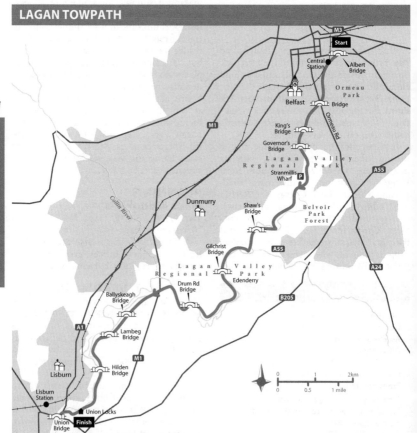

INDUSTRIAL BREAKTHROUGH OF THE LAGAN NAVIGATION

The Lagan Navigation played a pivotal role in Northern Ireland's industrial development. During the mid-18th century, output began to boom across a host of industries in the region's inland counties, yet muddy cart tracks provided the only means of transporting goods to the Port of Belfast. The solution to the transport crisis was the resource Ireland has in plenty – waterways. Between 1756 and 1796, the Lagan Navigation was built to link Lough Neagh and its tributary rivers to Belfast. Navvies flocked to the construction site from all corners of Ireland, bringing their own shovel or pick, to be paid the equivalent of £0.03 per day for the backbreaking work of digging through boggy ground and clearing dense thickets of trees. First a channel was dug from Lough Neagh to Lisburn, where the five Union Locks overcame the height difference down to the River Lagan. From there barges would navigate the river wherever possible, but where the gradient was too steep they would divert onto short sections of canal and use locks to descend in safety.

In its heyday the project was a resounding success. Teenage boat boys, often barefoot and ill-clad, led the barge-pulling ponies along the towpath. The horses dragged 21m-long timber barges loaded with large quantities of raw materials and goods destined for foreign ports. The trade allowed canal-side towns and industries to thrive for 150 years, with brewing, grain milling and linen production chief among them. Fortunes plummeted during the early 20th century however, as rail and road systems exerted their superiority. The navigation was finally closed in several stages between 1947 to 1958.

Park Forest reaching down to the opposite bank, cross the river via Red Bridge, then follow another bridge over the canal at what is the third lock with the boarded-up lock keeper's house nearby. Continue with the canal on the right; go under a modern road bridge and up a ramp to cross **Shaw's Bridge** to a car park. The first Shaw's Bridge was built as an oak bridge by Captain John Shaw from Cromwell's army in 1655 during the Cromwellian occupation of Ireland (though it is believed that there has been a bridge of some description in this spot since 1617); it was replaced in 1709 by the surviving, but now disused, five-arch structure. Follow a path back down to the tree-lined river and continue to the timber **Gilchrist Bridge** – named after John Gilchrist – the founder of the Lagan Valley Regional Park, an hour from Stranmillis.

The river soon heads off independently and you continue beside a relatively long section of canal, past two locks. As tall Drum House, a 19th-century home, comes into view, rejoin the river and soon pass under Drum Rd bridge, which has three arches and six flood arches and predates 1832. Next, cross a footbridge and go on, back beside the river. You're now passing through more open countryside, though the muted roar of traffic intrudes slightly. The canal

takes up again as the river meanders away northwards, and before long you pass beneath the motorway via a subway. Continue along the canal to the elegant double-arched **Ballyskeagh Bridge**, built of red sandstone and dating from around 1760.

Reuniting with the river, you soon pass a Coca-Cola bottling plant – located here because of its need for a reliable water supply. Past the ninth lock and cross Tullynacross Rd beside **Lambeg Bridge** – a small but still interesting iron suspension bridge. Still tree-lined, the river spills over a weir and another section of canal takes off with the houses of Hilden not too far away. Cross a road near Hilden Bridge and pass under a pedestrian bridge a little further on. Suburbia is now beginning to intrude – indicating that the lazy, bucolic rambling part of the walk is drawing to a conclusion, and it's not long before you pass through a portal of two metal arcs and join Canal St. Walk past the five tiers of **Union Locks**, with the impressive Lisburn Civic Centre occupying the site of a former spinning mill on an island beside you. Continue along the bank of the canal for another couple of hundred metres to the end of the towpath at Union Bridge (2¼ hours from Gilchrist Bridge).

NORTHERN IRELAND

CASTLE WARD

Duration 2–3 hours
Distance 8km (5 miles)
Ascent 40m (131ft)
Difficulty easy
Start/Finish Castle Ward car park
Nearest Towns Strangford (p286), Portaferry (p285)
Transport bus, private
Summary A varied lowland circuit around an historic National Trust estate on the shores of Strangford Lough.

Strangford Lough is the largest sea lough in Britain or Ireland, covering some 150 sq km. The inlet is replenished twice daily by tidal waters rich in plankton and nutrients, and supports a wealth of wildlife unrivalled in Europe. This is home to Ireland's largest breeding colony of common seals, 75,000 wildfowl including 75% of the world's population of Brent Geese, and around 2000 marine species. Relatively little of the intricate shoreline is accessible to walkers, but the best waterside trails can be found at the southwestern corner of the lough, in the National Trust estate of Castle Ward.

The house at the centre of this estate was built in the 1760s for Lord and Lady Bangor, an odd couple whose widely differing tastes in architecture resulted in an eccentric double-fronted residence. For walkers however, the 850 acres of grounds surrounding the house are likely to be of more interest. This route combines the best features of the estate's own walking trails with a section of the Lecale Way. It follows a mixture of surfaced and unsurfaced paths through woodland and along the lough shore, and is well way-marked throughout.

Among various sites passed along the route, two tower houses on the shore stand

HARNESSING STRANGFORD'S POWER

Despite its significant size, Strangford Lough is almost landlocked, connected to the sea by just a 700m-wide strait known as The Narrows. In fact the Vikings named this stretch of water Strangfjörthr, meaning 'powerful fjord', because when the tide turns, as it does four times a day, 400,000 tonnes of water per minute churn through the gap at speeds of up to eight knots (15km/h). You get some idea of the tide's remarkable strength when you see the ferry being whipped sideways by the current.

Until recently the current was little more than a nuisance for mariners, but in 2003 a British company called Marine Current Turbines proposed the site as an ideal place for the world's first commercial tidal power station. After a lengthy period of consultation and development, the £10 million project got underway in early 2008. A large underwater turbine known as a SeaGen was moored to the lough floor some 400m from the shore. Working much like an underwater windmill, the turbine has two rotor blades that are driven by tidal currents. Revolving 10 to 15 times a minute, the blades move slowly enough that they are unlikely to threaten marine wildlife such as the common seals that breed in the lough. The turbine operates for about 20 hours each day, because no energy is generated at slack tide when the current drops below two knots.

The turbine began operating at full capacity in December 2008, generating 1.2 megawatts of power. This power is purchased by a local electricity company and used to supply around 1000 homes in Northern Ireland and the Republic. At the time of writing, this was the greatest amount of power ever produced by a tidal project anywhere in the world. For many people it was seen as proof that marine power can play a role in reducing our dependency on fossil fuels, particularly for countries with coastlines as fragmented as Britain and Ireland. The current cost of installing the turbines is relatively high at £3 million for every megawatt they generate (compared to £2.3 million per megawatt for offshore wind), though the costs are likely to drop if the technology is more widely adopted.

Drawing on its experience of Strangford Lough, Marine Current Turbines hope their next project will be a 10.5 megawatt project that uses seven SeaGen turbines. Situated off the coast of Anglesey in north Wales, this tidal farm should be commissioned in 2011 or 2012.

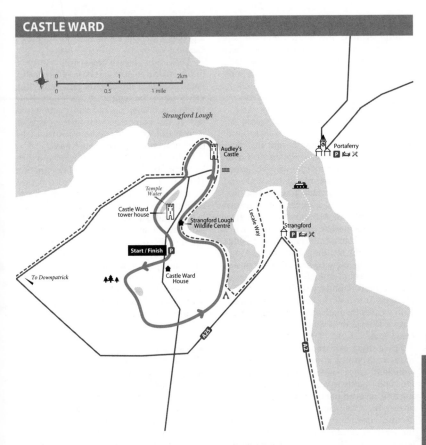

CASTLE WARD

Strangford Lough

Audley's
Castle

Portaferry

Temple
Water

Castle Ward
tower house

Strangford Lough
Wildlife Centre

Lecale Way

Strangford

Start / Finish P

To Downpatrick

Castle Ward
House

A25

A2

out. Castle Ward and Audley's Castle are simple stone forts, consisting of tall, square keeps. The region is dotted with similar buildings, which date back to the 15th and 16th centuries when Portaferry, the town at the mouth of the lough, was a major port. Most of the construction was spurred on by King Henry VI's offer of £10 to anyone who would erect a tower to protect the coastline.

The grounds at **Castle Ward** (☎ 4488 1204; adult/child £5/2.50) are open daily. House tours cost £2.80/1.90 extra. The house, wildlife centre and tearooms are open daily during Easter Week, July and August, and on weekends and public holidays from April to June and in September. Other facilities include an open farm and an adventure playground for children.

PLANNING
Maps
The OSNI 1:50,000 map No 21 covers the walk, but doesn't show much detail. The free trail map you receive at the entry kiosk is much more useful for walking purposes.

GETTING TO/FROM THE WALK
The circuit starts and finishes at the main car park for the Castle Ward estate. The entrance is signed off the A25 Downpatrick –Strangford Rd, around 12km northeast of Downpatrick and 2km southwest of Strangford.

It's also possible to walk to the estate from Strangford village. Rather than walk along the main road, join the Lecale Way at a footpath that starts from the end of Castle St. This leads over the hill behind the village, past fine views over the lough, before continuing around the shoreline to Castle Ward. You join the route described near the camping ground. Adding this start/finish to the route extends the day's walk by 4.5km.

THE WALK

From the southern end of the car park, follow signs for the adventure playground. The walking trail begins beside the playground at a wooden gate signed for Castle Ward Forest. Begin by following the green trail markers. Pass through the gate and head along a grass track towards the forest. Climb gently to a T-junction and turn left into the trees. Around 50m later, turn right along a narrow footpath to reach a small **lough**. Join a track at the water's edge and turn right, heading around the lough and along the edge of several open meadows. Pass a stand of majestic beech trees at the southern boundary of the estate before plunging into a dark pine wood. A smaller path weaves through the trees and emerges onto a tarmac driveway near the main entrance gate.

Leave the green trail here and cross the road, continuing straight ahead along a woodland track signed with red markers. Descend slightly to reach the estate's **camping and caravan park** (see p286 for details), cross a road, and continue ahead to a wide avenue. For the next 3km the route follows the waymarkers for the Lecale Way. Turn left and follow the avenue north along the lough shore to a T-junction roughly 1km later. Turn right here to reach **Strangford Lough Wildlife Centre** (☎ 4488 1411), around 1¼ hours from the start. It's well worth popping inside to learn more about the area's rich diversity of bird and marine life.

The lane then leads to a courtyard containing a farm and the **old tower house** of **Castle Ward**, the original estate building built in the 1570s. Turn right here and pass beneath a stone archway to reach the lough shore. Continue along the shore on a gravel track, now following markers for the blue trail and signs for the Lecale Way. Pass in front of Strangford Sailing Club, where there are great views east across the lough to Portaferry and The Narrows (see the boxed text Harnessing Strangford's Power,

p250). Join a footpath and continue across a pebble beach to arrive beneath **Audley's Castle**.

Turn right along a grassy trail and trace the shoreline around the base of the castle. Pass through a metal gate, past more fine views along the length of the lough. Now head back into woodland and swing left to join a gravel lane just west of the castle. A turnstile allows a quick detour to visit the fifteenth century tower house itself.

Follow the lane to a minor road and turn left. This brings you to another junction 150m later. Leave the road here and turn right through a stone gateway onto a track. Continue past the pretty lough of Temple Water and swing left onto a tree-lined pathway. Where the trees end, continue straight ahead along the yellow route, following signs for the house. Climb a grass bank and pass under a stone bridge, then turn right along a track. After 80m veer left and use a tunnel to reach the back of the main estate house. Either turn left to visit the mansion itself, or turn right to return to the car park.

MOURNE MOUNTAINS

The Mourne Mountains dominate the southeastern corner of Northern Ireland and are the highest, steepest and most rugged range in the province. The compact cluster of granite peaks includes seven summits above 700m high, and their accessibility has made them one of the most visited walking areas in Ireland. Routes here tend to be enjoyably adventurous in nature, and the ground is fantastically bog-free, with firm, short grass across many of the higher peaks. Though the possibilities for walkers are numerous, the four walks described in this section take in the most outstanding features of the range. Also see p275 for a summary of a fine alternative route over Slieve Muck in the southwestern corner of the region.

The Mournes were formed around 50 million years ago and are probably the youngest mountain group in Ireland. The steep slopes and acidic soils don't support a great variety of flora and fauna, but they are well endowed with evidence of glaciation. Distinctive features on several summits are huge craggy tors, or rock towers. These were formed during the last ice age when the very tops of the mountains poked through the ice sheet and avoided scouring by glaciers. Frost shattered the weaker rock away, leaving pinnacles of harder rock that are visible today.

Apart from decorating the summits, Mourne granite has travelled far and wide across the globe. In the past, stone quarrying was a major industry in the region, and blocks were transported down from the hills on carts to harbours at Newcastle, Annalong and Kilkeel. Kerbstones of Mourne granite can be found in Belfast, Liverpool, London, Manchester and Birmingham. There are still several working quarries today, and Mourne granite was used in the 9/11 British Memorial Garden in New York.

PLANNING
Books
Paddy Dillon's *The Mournes Walks* details a mixture of 32 low-level and mountain routes, and was fully updated in 2004.

ACCESS TOWN
See Newcastle (p285).

GETTING AROUND
During the summer months there are two bus services catering specifically for those who want to explore the Mournes. In July and August only, the **Ulsterbus** (☎ 9066 6630) Mourne Rambler service 405 runs a circular route from Newcastle, calling at a dozen stops around the Mournes, including Trassey Bridge (eight minutes), Meelmore (17 minutes), Silent Valley (40 minutes), Carrick Little (45 minutes) and Bloody Bridge (55 minutes). There are six buses daily and a £4 all-day ticket allows you to get on and off as many times as you like.

Also operating in July and August only, service 34A runs from Newcastle to the Silent Valley car park (30 minutes, four daily Mon-Fri, three Sat, two Sun), calling at Donard Park (five minutes) and Bloody Bridge (10 minutes).

You'll need your own transport to reach most mountain trailheads at all other times of the year.

SLIEVE BEARNAGH & SLIEVE MEELMORE

Duration 5–5½ hours
Distance 12.5km (8 miles)
Ascent 900m (2953ft)
Difficulty moderate–demanding
Start/Finish Trassey Track car park
Nearest Town Newcastle (p285)
Transport bus, private
Summary A neat circuit in the northwestern corner of the Mournes that includes one of the most distinctive summits in the range.

This compact circuit visits three peaks that all offer superlative vantage points. The highlight of the route is Slieve Bearnagh (739m), whose combination of fine granite tors and magnificent views make it one of the best-loved peaks in the Mournes. Though not as craggy, Slieve Meelmore (704m) and Slieve Meelbeg (708m) offer equally fine panoramas, with summit views encompassing almost all of the Mournes' clustered peaks as well as their intervening loughs and reservoirs.

The route largely follows tracks and well-trodden mountain paths, and includes a return section along the way-marked Mourne Way. This, combined with the

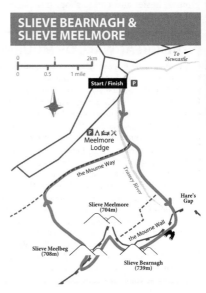

SLIEVE BEARNAGH & SLIEVE MEELMORE

presence of the Mourne Wall over the high ground, means that route-finding is a relatively simple matter. If you prefer a shorter outing the route can easily be split into two parts, either climbing Slieve Bearnagh on its own and descending northeast from the col between Bearnagh and Meelmore, or using this path as your outward route and climbing just Slieve Meelmore and Meelbeg.

PLANNING
Maps
Use either the OSNI 1:50,000 map No 29 or, for more detail, the waterproof OSNI 1:25,000 Activity Map *The Mournes*.

GETTING TO/FROM THE WALK
The circuit starts and finishes at the Trassey Track car park, around 9km west of Newcastle (GR: 312314). From Newcastle town centre, head west towards Bryansford. Turn left in Bryansford and join the B180 to Hilltown. Around 4km later, turn left onto a minor road. The car park is situated on the left, 1.5km along this road.

If you prefer to pay for secure parking, continue 400m beyond the public car park to **Meelmore Lodge** (☎ 4372 6657; www.meelmorelodge.co.uk; 52 Trassey Rd, Bryansford; camping per person £5, dm/tw £17/50). As well as a family camping ground, hostel and coffee shop, this place offers all-day parking for £4. To access

mountains from here, follow the marked track south to the Mourne Way, then turn left to reach the top of the Trassey Track.

The **Ulsterbus** (☎ 9066 6630) *Mourne Rambler* service from Newcastle visits the area during July and August only – see Getting There & Away on p285. Get off at the Trassey Bridge stop.

THE WALK
From the entrance to the car park, turn left and follow the road for 100m. Here a gravel track leads off on the left, marked by an information board for the Trassey Track and a signpost for the Mourne Way. Pass over the stile and begin to follow the track south. Two further gates are passed before you reach the open terrain of the Mournes. At the final gate, a stone wall can be seen extending west around the base of Slieve Meelmore. This marks the line of the Mourne Way, and your return route.

For now, continue south along the Trassey Track. Wind through a couple of gentle switchbacks before straightening up for the ascent to **Hare's Gap**, at the southeastern head of the valley. Keep left at a track junction beneath the northern slopes of Slieve Bearnagh and continue uphill over rougher, bouldery ground to the **Mourne Wall** (1¼ hours from the start). Cross this on a large wooden stile. You are now at the very head of the Silent Valley, and if you

THE GREAT WALL OF MOURNE

The Mourne Wall is one of the area's most distinctive features, and has been compared to a mini Great Wall of China. As well as providing a handy navigation guide for walkers, it is a magnificent feat of dry-stone wall construction. Entirely cement-free, it runs for some 35km across 15 major summits, and is generally about 2m high and 1m wide. Experienced walkers may be interested in replicating one of the region's greatest physical challenges – the trip around the entire wall in a single day. The route is a long-standing trial of stamina that involves around 3000m of ascent, and is definitely not for the faint hearted.

The wall itself was built between 1904 and 1922 to mark the watershed of the Silent and Annalong Valleys. Once it was finished, work began on the Silent Valley dam. The Mourne granite proved an awkward foundation for construction however, and the dam was eventually completed after 10 years of difficulties. The experience deterred the authorities from building another dam planned for the adjacent Annalong Valley; instead they transferred a considerable flow from the Annalong catchment through a tunnel beneath Slieve Binnian. In the 1950s increased demand prompted the building of the higher Ben Crom dam. Today the Silent and Annalong Valleys provide 130 million litres of water per day, much of it piped underground to Belfast. To learn more head to the **Silent Valley Reservoir** (☎ 0845-744 0088; car/motorcycle £4.50/2, plus per pedestrian adult/child £1.60/0.60; open daily), where you'll find an interesting exhibition on the building of the wall and dam.

walk a few paces to the left you will be able to enjoy tremendous views along the deep basin of Ben Crom.

Turn southwest at Hare's Gap and climb up a short flight of steps beside the wall. A section of flatter ground offers brief respite before the slope steepens again, until you arrive at **Bearnagh's North Tor**. Follow a path around the southern side of North Tor and rejoin the Mourne Wall in the col between Bearnagh's twin tops. The name Slieve Bearnagh translates as 'gapped mountain' and probably refers to this feature. A short climb brings you up to the huge Summit Tor, with more fantastic views (40 minutes from Hare's Gap).

Continue to follow the south side of the wall as it zigzags on top of Bearnagh, then plunges steeply west to the col between Bearnagh and Slieve Meelmore. Two walls now make their way up the slopes of Slieve Meelmore: the most direct route is alongside the new wall on the right. This leads to the conspicuous stone shelter, built in 1921, that adorns the summit of **Slieve Meelmore** (45 minutes from Slieve Bearnagh). A wooden stile allows you to cross the wall and appreciate the view in all directions, which include Cave Hill to the north and Lambay Island, northeast of Dublin, to the south.

From the summit head south, keep the wall on your right as you descend to another col. If you have the energy it's well worth adding the short, 100m climb to **Slieve Meelbeg**. This summit is marked only by a slight bend in the wall and a small cairn, but the new vantage point allows Spelga dam and reservoir to come into view to the west.

Return along the wall to the col between Slieve Meelmore and Slieve Meelbeg and cross a wooden stile. Now begin to descend down the centre of the valley to the northwest. Follow the left bank of a stream, with the grassy terrain merging into a stone track towards the bottom of the slope. Follow the track to a junction with the Mourne Way. Turn right onto this footpath, cross the stream and pick up the line of a boundary wall. Follow the path along the wall for almost 2km, crossing several small streams before arriving back at the Trassey Track. Turn left onto the track and retrace your initial steps back to the car park (two hours from Slieve Meelmore).

SLIEVE DONARD

Duration 4½–5 hours
Distance 9km (5.6 miles)
Ascent 850m (2789ft)
Difficulty moderate–demanding
Start Bloody Bridge car park
Finish Donard Park car park
Nearest Town Newcastle (p285)
Transport bus
Summary An extremely scenic yet relatively straightforward route over Northern Ireland's highest mountain.

Slieve Donard (850m) is a real magnet for outdoor enthusiasts. Its status as the highest summit in Northern Ireland and its dominating presence over the town of Newcastle makes it irresistible even to those who rarely venture so high. On a clear day the summit views encompass most of Northern Ireland.

Though not truly circular, this route offers the chance to see two different sides of the mountain. Many choose to ascend the mountain via an out-and-back trip from Donard Park, but the variety offered here is preferable. Good public transport links mean there is no problem completing the walk from a base in Newcastle. Both approach paths are well used and the Mourne Wall serves as a handrail across higher ground.

The two cairns on Donard summit have existed in one form or another since early Christian times, when the mountain went by the name Slieve Slanga, after Slainge, son of Partholan, who was buried under one of the piles of rock. The peak later became associated with St Domangard, a 5th-century follower of St Patrick, and his name (anglicised to Donard) has stuck. Bloody Bridge derives its name from gruesome events in 1641 when nine local Protestants and their minister were massacred there. In more light-hearted vein, the mountain's eastern sweep to the sea apparently inspired Percy French to write the famous song *The Mountains of Mourne*.

PLANNING
Maps
Carry either the OSNI 1:50,000 map No 29 or the waterproof OSNI 1:25,000 Activity Map *The Mournes*.

NORTHERN IRELAND

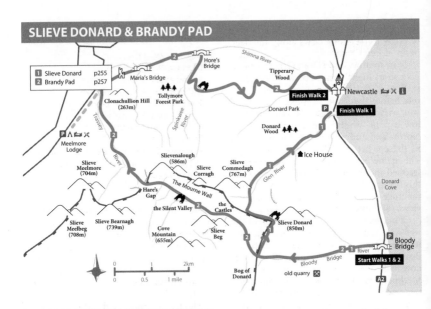

SLIEVE DONARD & BRANDY PAD

1 Slieve Donard   p255
2 Brandy Pad   p257

GETTING TO/FROM THE WALK

The walk begins at the Bloody Bridge car park, 3km south of Newcastle along the A2 coast road. **Ulsterbus** (☎ 9066 6630) service 37 stops here on its way from Newcastle to Annalong and Kilkeel (hourly Mon-Sat, seven on Sun). During July and August only, Bloody Bridge is also visited by the Mourne Rambler service 405, and service 34A. See Getting Around on p253.

Donard Park car park is situated at the southern end of Newcastle's main street, the Central Promenade.

THE WALK

From the southern end of Bloody Bridge car park, cross the road and pass through a wooden pedestrian gate. Follow a gravel path to the river, where you'll see the original bridge set just behind the new road bridge. The clear path climbs along the river bank; in spring and early summer the vivid yellow, aromatic gorse is quite spectacular here. After about 1km, immediately above some cascades, you can either cross to a wide vehicle track set just above the river to the south, or stay on the northern bank, following a well-defined walker's path. About 1km further on you pass an **old quarry** on the left, the source of large quantities of granite, some of which finished up in the foundations

of the Stormont parliament building near Belfast. Here you join a wide, rough path leading up from the quarry, which takes you up to the **Mourne Wall** at the Bog of Donard (1½ hours from Bloody Bridge).

Turn right in front of the wall and follow it northeast, climbing directly up the steep slope to the summit of **Slieve Donard**, marked by a stone Belfast Water Works shelter and a sprawling cairn (40 minutes from the Bog of Donard). With luck you'll be able to pick out the features of the unrivalled vista. To the north, the drumlin-dotted landscape merges with Strangford Lough and the Belfast Hills, with Scotland's Mull of Kintyre beyond. To the west the vast expanse of Lough Neagh is backed by the rounded Sperrin Mountains. The Isle of Man lies to the east and Howth Hill near Dublin can be seen in the south.

Turn westwards at the summit and descend steeply beside the wall to the col between Slieve Donard and Slieve Commedagh (767m, about 25 minutes from the top). Turn right here and leave the wall behind, following the Glen River Track northeast down the deep valley. The path is partially paved with stone slabs and the gradient eases as you progress. The views ahead of long beaches and jumbled dunes are superb. Shortly before arriving at the forest edge you'll notice a curious beehive structure across the river on the right, which is a restored **ice house** built in the mid-19th century to service the local estate. A short distance further on, a large sign explains the history of the estate and these ingeniously built structures.

Pass through a gate and enter **Donard Wood**. The path continues to descend alongside the Glen River for 1km, the stream's cascades and the mixture of mature Scots pine, oak, larch and beech trees providing a fitting finale to the walk. You cross the river on solid old bridges twice on the way down to the lawns of Donard Park. Once at this open area, keep right to reach the car park (1½ hours from the col).

BRANDY PAD

Duration 6½–7½ hours
Distance 22.5km (14 miles)
Ascent 745m (2444ft)
Difficulty moderate
Start Bloody Bridge car park
Finish Newcastle tourist office
Nearest Town Newcastle (p285)
Transport bus

Summary Follow an old smuggling trail across the Mournes, then switch to the woodland paths of the Mourne Way. The route can also be split into two easier days.

This is a route of two halves. The first part follows a traditional smuggling path from the coast, across the mountains, to join the Trassey Track at the Mournes' northwestern corner. The second part returns to Newcastle via the tumbling rivers and woodland of Tollymore Forest Park, following the waymarked Mourne Way for the duration. It's a great trip for those who lack confidence in their compass-reading skills, because established paths are followed throughout and no major peaks are scaled. Yet the route still allows you to experience a range of fantastic scenery and takes you through the very heart of the Mourne Mountains.

When Tollymore Forest Park was established in 1955 it became the first such park in Ireland or Britain. Today the 630-hectare park encompasses lakes and gardens, deciduous woodland, dense conifer plantations and the tumbling rapids of the Shimna and Spinkwee rivers. For walkers the highlight

is the network of waterside paths, some of which are followed by this route. The section along the banks of the **Shimna River** is particularly beautiful, the fast-flowing water spanned by a series of stone bridges and stepping stones dating back over 200 years. It's also worth keeping an eye open for wildlife, as it's not uncommon to spot deer among the trees and kingfishers or cormorants along the streams.

The route can either be walked in a single day, or split into two sections with an overnight stop at Meelmore Lodge, near the bottom of the Trassey Track. This would give a first day of four hours, 11.5km and 580m ascent, and a second day of three hours, 11km and 165m ascent. The route can also be finished at the bottom of the Trassey Track; see Getting to/from the Walk for Slieve Bearnagh & Slieve Meelmore for transport details (p254).

PLANNING
Maps
Carry either the OSNI 1:50,000 map No 29 or the OSNI 1:25,000 Activity Map *The Mournes*.

GETTING TO/FROM THE WALK

For transport details to Bloody Bridge at the start of the walk, see Getting to/from the Walk for Slieve Donard (p256).

The route finishes at the tourist information office at the southern end of Newcastle's Central Promenade. The closest large car park is in Donard Park, a couple of hundred metres further south along the road.

THE WALK
The first part of this walk follows the Slieve Donard route (see p255), climbing from Bloody Bridge to the Mourne Wall at the Bog of Donard (1½ hours from Bloody Bridge). The Mourne Wall marks the spot where the two walks diverge. From here, cross the stile over the wall and head west along a wide path, soon veering north across the lower slopes of Slieve Donard. The path descends slightly into the upper reaches of the Annalong Valley and sets out on a very scenic traverse below the **Castles**, a collection of purple-grey weathered granite blocks.

After crossing some eroded streams, the path leaves the Annalong Valley and crosses the wide col between Slieve Commedagh and Slieve Beg. Now descend, into the **Silent Valley**, where there's a fantastic view south over the Ben Crom Reservoir. Continue ahead to **Hare's Gap**, where you can celebrate a reunion with the Mourne Wall (1¼ hours from the Bog of Donard). The fine view north and northwest takes in fertile plains that merge seamlessly with the sea.

Cross the wall via a large stile and begin to descend northwest. There is a path of sorts through the rocks and heather, which soon brings you to the end of the stony Trassey Track. Follow this down the valley, with the **Trassey River** to your left. Just beyond a couple of gentle switchbacks you arrive at a gate, where the way-marked Mourne Trail comes in from the left. Continue along the track, passing two further gates – each with adjacent stiles – to reach the Trassey Rd (one hour from Hare's Gap).

To continue directly to Newcastle, turn right at the entrance to the Trassey Track, now following the signs for the Mourne Trail. After 80m (and just before the Trassey Track car park), turn right and follow a narrow lane through beech woodland into **Tollymore Forest Park**. A small signpost here indicates the way to the King's Grave, a megalithic tomb dating from 1000–1500 BC.

Cross **Maria's Bridge** and turn left at a track junction, crossing the Shimna River via the Boundary Bridge. A beautiful section of a little over 1km now follows the northern bank of the river, past the stone Parnell's Bridge and a lengthy series of rapids. Shortly after the confluence of the Shimna with the Spinkwee, turn right across a set of stepping stones. Keep right across Altavaddy Bridge then follow the western bank of the Spinkwee upstream, past a 10m-high cascade. As you might imagine, the cascade is a popular resting spot for walkers. Turn left at a track junction and descend across **Hore's Bridge**. Keep right at the next three track junctions, climbing steadily through the thick conifers at the park's southeastern corner.

When the trees end you're met by fine views east over Dundrum Bay and south over Slieve Commedagh. Turn right and descend to a road junction, continuing ahead onto Tullybrannigan Rd. Turn left 400m later onto Tipperary Lane and descend to Bryansford Rd. Turn left across the bridge over the Shimna, then turn right and follow a path along the river's northern bank. After 400m cross a footbridge and pass though Islands Park. Cross Shimna Rd and enter Castle Park, passing the boating lake on your left. Exit the park onto Newcastle's Central Promenade, and turn right to reach the tourist office (three hours from Trassey Rd).

SMUGGLING IN THE MOURNES

The paths through the Mournes may carry legions of walkers and climbers today, but they were originally created by the boots of smugglers and the hooves of their heavily laden packhorses. Until the coast road was built in the early 19th century, the region was cut off from the outside world, and the only access was on foot or by sea. The wild coastline made a perfect entry point for smuggled goods, which were transported under the cover of darkness on small, schooner-rigged craft called wherries. After a signal from the smugglers waiting on shore, the contraband was landed on an isolated beach. The illicit trade was particularly strong during the 18th century, when the Isle of Man was outside the control of British Customs and could be used as a convenient staging post.

Cargoes of tobacco, wine, leather, silk and spices all arrived in this manner, though French spirits were particularly popular. The goods were then whisked off into the wilderness to avoid the excise men at Newcastle. A favourite escape route, especially for those with a convoy of ponies, was along the route that was to become known as the Brandy Pad. The goods were then distributed inland; the village of Hilltown was a common destination and in 1835 almost half the houses there were pubs.

The tracks are now used for entirely innocent pursuits, though smuggling still goes on between the North and the Republic. Nowadays the cargoes of cigarettes or diesel fuel are carried largely by road transport.

NORTHERN IRELAND'S FIRST NATIONAL PARK?

Northern Ireland is unusual in the western world due to its lack of a national park. The Republic of Ireland has six such protected areas, while Britain has 13. In September 2002 the Northern Irish Assembly Minister for the Environment Dermot Nesbitt created history when he announced that the Mourne area was to be considered for designation as the province's first national park.

From 2003 to 2007 a working party collated information about the possible impact of such a park, and consulted with landowners and inhabitants to gather local reaction to the proposal. It proved a divisive proposal, and many strong opinions were aired both for and against the idea. Many people live within the proposed boundaries, and farmers were particularly concerned about the impact any legislation might have on their livelihoods and traditional working practices. The main issue for others was whether park regulations might prevent them from building houses and developing businesses that would otherwise be permitted.

The challenge facing the people of Northern Ireland is to create a 'Celtic Model' of park management that would suit the particular conditions here, and could support agriculture and sustainable development at the same time as promoting environmental conservation and public recreation. At the time of writing, work on the consultation process is on-going. However, there's little doubt that an area as beautiful and unspoiled as the Mournes deserves protection, and that walkers would be one of the main beneficiaries in the event of a positive outcome.

SLIEVE BINNIAN & THE ANNALONG VALLEY

Duration 5–5½ hours
Distance 13.5km (8.5 miles)
Ascent 950m (3117ft)
Difficulty moderate–demanding
Start/Finish Carrick Little car park
Nearest Towns Newcastle (p285), Annalong (p276)
Transport bus, private
Summary A fine circuit over the peaks guarding the southwestern Annalong Valley, with spectacular, far-ranging views.

This is a route that explores two distinct mountains at the southwestern corner of the Annalong Valley. The principle peak is Slieve Binnian, the third-highest point in Northern Ireland at 747m, and one of the province's most fascinating summits. The mountain owes its character to its incredible topography – the summit ridge stretches for almost 1.5kms and is littered with towering granite tors. The bulbous pinnacles display a fascinating morphology, and are great examples of landforms created by periglacial activity. Only the summit of Slieve Bearnagh can compete, though Binnian's tors are more complex, more extensive and eminently more suited to whimsical exploration. Given kind weather conditions it's

easy to spend an hour or more scrambling around the boulders.

The other major peak on the route is Slievelamagan (704m). This mountain enjoys the distinction of lying right at the heart of the Mournes, and its central location lends it some of the best views in the range.

Route-finding is aided by the existence of firm tracks along the lower sections,

SLIEVE BINNIAN & THE ANNALONG VALLEY

while informal paths cover much of the high ground. If you're feeling really energetic it's also possible to extend the route into a circuit of the entire Annalong Valley, adding ascents of Slieve Donard and Rocky Mountain. Allow at least eight hours for this tough, 21km alternative.

PLANNING
Maps
The OSNI 1:50,000 map No 29 and the waterproof OSNI 1:25,000 Activity Map *The Mournes* both cover this walk.

GETTING TO/FROM THE WALK
Turn off the A2 from the northern end of Annalong village, taking the road that leads west beside the Halfway House pub. Follow this for around 2.5km to a T-junction. Turn left here and descend across Dunnywater Bridge; Carrick Little car park is on the right around 1km further on.

The **Ulsterbus** (☎ 9066 6630) *Mourne Rambler* service from Newcastle visits the area during July and August only – for details see Getting Around on p253. Get off at the Carrick Little stop.

THE WALK
From the car park, walk up the Carrick Little Track for about 1km to a gate where the track meets the Mourne Wall. Cross a stile and turn left, following the wall northwest up the slope. Before too long you pass an information panel marking 23 features of the view, many of which you'll pass on the route. The terrain becomes steeper as you approach the foot of the summit tors, where you should swing right to gain **Slieve Binnian's** broad summit ridge between two large clumps of boulders. If you're feeling adventurous, the highest outcrop will succumb to a moderately easy scramble on the far side (about 1½ hours from the start).

Follow the ridgeline north then northwest, weaving your way through **The Back Castles**, a string of fascinating tors, some the size of large buildings and others not much bigger than a garden shed. The path keeps west of the first cluster and east of the second. Another short climb brings you to the mountain's **North Tor** (678m), where a huge granite monolith also makes for fascinating exploration.

From here you begin a steep descent to the deep, boggy col between Binnian and Slievelamagan. At the col, veer northeast and follow a faint footpath up the boulder-strewn slopes ahead. The ascent is steady, with little respite in the gradient until you reach the simple cairn that marks the summit of **Slievelamagan**, 1½ hours from Slieve Binnian. This is probably the most central peak in the Mournes, and the 360°-view sweeps around the entire range. Especially memorable is the outlook to the northwest, where Slieve Bearnagh looms over the dark waters of Ben Crom.

Continue to follow the path north from the summit, dropping down the northern shoulder of the mountain. Once you've reached the col between Slievelamagan and Cove Mountain, turn right and descend steeply over rough slopes, soon picking up a path leading south. This descends steeply past the western buttresses of Upper Cove and joins up with the top of the Carrick Little Track. Turn right and follow this track south along the base of the Annalong Valley, which narrowly escaped being flooded during Victorian times (see the boxed text The Great Wall of Mourne, p254).

Follow the track beneath the eastern slopes of Slievelamagan to a junction at the southern end of the valley. Turn left here and continue past the conifers of **Annalong Wood**. Here you re-encounter the stile you crossed on your outward journey. Cross the wall and retrace your initial steps back to Carrick Little car park (1¾ hours from Slievelamagan).

THE WEST

The area west of Lough Neagh is generally more rural and less urbanised than the eastern side of the province. The most significant topographical feature is the Sperrin Mountains, a sprawling range of rolling, bog-covered hills that form the largest upland area in Northern Ireland. The range includes 10 summits above 500m, the rounded hills separated by beautiful, rural valleys. From the Glenelly Valley in the heart of the region it's possible to reach several summits; one walk described here strides across the highest peak, Sawel Mountain at 678m.

Further southwest in County Fermanagh lies a very different landscape known as the lakelands – in fact, one-third of the county is covered by water. The maze of loughs is dominated to the south by Cuilcagh (665m), a mountain that also owes its distinctive shape to water erosion of the surrounding limestone landscape. The peak and surrounding area boast a unique natural history, and are the focus of the other two walks in this section.

ACCESS TOWN
See Enniskillen (p281).

CUILCAGH MOUNTAIN

Duration 5–5½ hours
Distance 13km (8 miles)
Ascent 480m (1575ft)
Difficulty moderate
Start/Finish Cuilcagh Mountain Park car park
Nearest Towns Belcoo (p278), Enniskillen (p281), Florencecourt (p282)
Transport private
Summary A straightforward approach to the top of Fermanagh's most intriguing peak, with an alternate finish at Florence Court.

Cuilcagh (665m) is the highest peak in the lakeland region of counties Fermanagh, Cavan and Leitrim. The summit of the massif straddles the border between Northern Ireland and the Republic and on a clear day it's possible to see both the Irish Sea off County Louth and the Atlantic Ocean near Sligo. A long, flat-topped peak rising from a sea of bog, Cuilcagh's northern slopes are protected as part of a European Geopark. The area's unique ecology can be attributed to its geological foundations; much of the lower ground around the peak is made of soft limestone and shale, while the summit itself consists of hard gritstone that is much more resistant to the erosive power of the elements. The result is an abrupt plateau flanked by a band of steep cliffs.

Geological features associated with both rock types can be seen on this route, from the vertical pinnacles surrounding the summit to the limestone sink holes evident near the start and end of the walk. The name Cuilcagh apparently derives from the Gaelic

Cailceach, meaning 'chalky'; something of a misnomer because chalk is one substance that does not exist on the mountain.

This route follows the Legnabrocky Trail to the summit, a straightforward out-and-back route that uses a gravel track to reach the mountain. The entire route is marked with frequent, yellow-topped posts, and forms part of the 33km-long Cuilcagh Way. The lowland section of this Waymarked Way is featured in the next walk, Cuilcagh Way Highlight (see p263). If you like the idea of walking the entire Cuilcagh Way over two days, it is perfectly feasible to link these two sections together. From the summit of Cuilcagh, continue to follow the waymarkers northeast and cross some rather wet blanket bog to Florence Court Forest Park (see Alternative Route: Via the Hiker's Trail, p262). Stay overnight near Florence Court (p263) and complete the Cuilcagh Way Highlight the next day. (If you need help with transport logistics to complete this route, consider using a taxi – there are numerous companies in Enniskillen, or call **Belcoo Cabs** (☎ 6638 6105) in Belcoo.)

PLANNING
Maps
The OSNI 1:50,000 map No 26 covers the walk.

GETTING TO/FROM THE WALK
The route starts and finishes at the car park for Cuilcagh Mountain Park (GR H121335). To reach the area, follow signs for Marble Arch Caves from the A4/N16 Enniskillen–Blacklion road. The car park is located 300m west of the entrance to Marble Arch, and contains information boards for the Geopark and the Cuilcagh Way.

There is no public transport to the area.

THE WALK
Climb the stile beside a wooden gate in the southwestern corner of the car park. To the right is Monastir Sink, a collapsed cave that is linked via an underground river to Marble Arch in the north. Follow the gravel track south through limestone meadows, crossing several stiles and a stone bridge in the early stages. The landscape then changes to the **blanket bog** that dominates much of the route. To get a closer look at

the bog, follow a short boardwalk loop that detours off the track to the left.

The track climbs gradually towards Cuilcagh, coming to an end after roughly 4km (one hour from the start). A well-marked footpath now continues ahead, dipping across a stream and continuing to climb towards the flat-topped escarpment. The band of cliffs surrounding the summit plateau is now clearly visible. Follow the footpath across a mixture of moss and tussock grass, which can be wet underfoot. The route passes just east of **Lough Atona** before beginning a steep ascent along a muddy trail to reach the top.

Once you have reached the flat ground of the summit plateau you have a choice of routes. The most impressive cliffs can be found to the west, above Lough Atona. It is well worth making the 1km detour along the plateau to visit these. To continue directly to the summit, turn left and head east instead.

Pick a route across the heather and stone plateau, passing a small pool and crossing a fence on your way to the eastern edge of the mountain. Here you'll find the **summit** (1½ hours from the end of the track), marked by a trig point and a large cairn that is in fact a Neolithic burial chamber. The 360° views encompass much of Fermanagh, Cavan and Leitrim, and on a very clear day you may be able to see both the Irish Sea to the east and the Atlantic Ocean to the west.

The return is simply back the way you came, though the outlook north over the pastoral landscape to Lough Erne offers an interesting change of perspective.

ALTERNATIVE ROUTE: VIA THE HIKER'S TRAIL

6–7 hours, 18km (11 miles), 540m ascent

Follow the route described to the summit of Cuilcagh. Instead of retracing your steps,

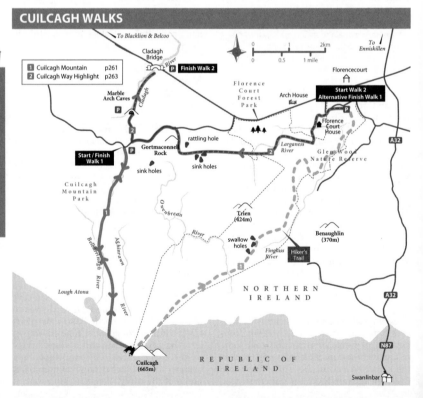

CUILCAGH WALKS

1 Cuilcagh Mountain   p261
2 Cuilcagh Way Highlight   p263

THE UK'S FIRST EUROPEAN GEOPARK

Between the Cuilcagh massif and the limestone grasslands to the north lies one of the most extensive areas of blanket bog in Ireland. Responding to the damage wrought in other areas by draining bogs for mechanised, large-scale peat extraction, Fermanagh District Council set up Cuilcagh Mountain Park in 1998. The aims were to protect undisturbed bogland, restore damaged areas and raise awareness of the crucial environmental importance of bogs.

The geological foundations of the area are also unique, consisting of a mixture of soft limestone and hard gritstone. In 2001 the park and nearby Marble Arch Caves, whose subterranean caverns are typical of limestone rock, became a Unesco European Geopark, the first park of its kind in the UK. At the time of writing there was a growing network of 32 such parks across 14 European countries, though Marble Arch remains one of just two designated reserves in Ireland, the other being the Copper Coast Geopark in County Waterford.

The park's geology and ecology are explained in the cave's visitor centre. To learn more about Geoparks in general, check out www.europeangeoparks.org.

zigzag down the escarpment to the north, using the waymarkers to guide you down the steep slope. At the bottom of the cliff, turn northeast follow the posts between the hills of Trien and Benaughlin. You have almost 5km of undulating **bog** to cross, and the ground is so wet underfoot that at times you might feel as if you're walking on water.

The landscape begins to change as you approach Benaughlin and return to limestone bedrock. Farm buildings can be seen to the right as you cross from moorland to firm, grassy meadows. Follow the posts to the edge of Florence Court Forest and cross a wooden stile marked for the Hiker's Trail (two hours from the summit).

Enter the trees and soon join a track that leads through Cove Wood to a forest road. Follow this down through several sweeping bends to a T-junction. Turn right here and pass through **Glen Wood Nature Reserve**, partly following the wooded banks of the beautiful Finglass River. The waymarkers now direct you along the edge of an open field, with the 18th-century Florence Court House sitting commandingly atop a rise to the left. Cross a river via a wooden bridge and keep left at the next three junctions. You now pass Ladies Well and reach the estate's main entrance driveway. Cross over the road and follow a final 100m section of path to the finish at the Florence Court Forest Service car park (1½ hours from the Hiker's Trail stile).

CUILCAGH WAY HIGHLIGHT

Duration 3–3½ hours
Distance 12km (7.5 miles)
Ascent 250m (820ft)
Difficulty easy–moderate
Start Florence Court Forest Service car park
Finish Cladagh Gorge car park
Nearest Towns Belcoo (p278), Enniskillen (p281), Florencecourt (p282)
Transport private

Summary An immensely varied lowland route passing a stately home, limestone pavement, Marble Arch Caves and a beautiful wooded glen.

This walk explores the forests and woodlands of the Florence Court estate, then takes you across a wild limestone landscape to Marble Arch Caves, the most famous show cave in Northern Ireland. The entire route is part of the 33km-long Cuilcagh Way, and navigation is simplified by frequent, yellow-topped marker posts. The route can also be combined with the previous outing over Cuilcagh Mountain (p261) to make a two-day circuit around of the entire Cuilcagh Way.

Though the walking time is relatively short, you'll probably want to allow extra time to visit the various attractions along the way. First up is **Florence Court Estate** (☎ 6634 8249; house tour adult/child £5/2; open daily Easter Week, Jul & Aug, Wed-Mon Jun, Sat, Sun & public hols Apr, May & Sep), an 18th-century stately home

NORTHERN IRELAND

surrounded by formal gardens, with an adjacent 1200-hectare forest park run by the Northern Ireland Forest Service. The manor house was the traditional seat of the Earl of Enniskillen, and was acquired in 1954 by the National Trust. The building is famed for its rococo plasterwork and antique Irish furniture, and can be visited on a house tour. Whether you decide to visit the house or not, walkers will certainly pass through the **grounds** (car/pedestrian £3.50/free; open daily) which include manicured lawns and a walled garden.

A highly enjoyable section then leads across open countryside and past patches of limestone pavement to Marble Arch Caves, which has been described as 'one of Europe's finest show caves'. Here you'll find another **Visitor Centre** (☎ 6634 8855; www.marblearchcaves.net; open daily Easter-Sept), offering regular – and highly recommended – 1¼-hour tours of the cave system (adult/child £8/5). The day's finale is a trip down Cladagh Gorge, past beautiful cascades and fine deciduous woodland.

Visitor facilities at both Marble Arch and Florence Court include shops that stock local OS maps, and cafeterias that serve snacks and lunches.

PLANNING
Maps
Carry the OSNI 1:50,000 map No 26.

GETTING TO/FROM THE WALK
The route starts at the Forest Service car park inside Florence Court estate. From Belcoo, cross the bridge south to Blacklion, turn left, and drive 11.8km southeast to a junction on the right, following signs to Florence Court. The entrance to the estate is 500m further along. Once inside the entry gate, follow the driveway for 300m and veer left into the forest service car park, marked by a toilet block and an information panel for the Cuilcagh Way. The closest public transport is the **Ulsterbus** service 192 from Enniskillen to Swanlinbar (twice daily Mon-Sat), which can drop you at Creamery Cross, about 2km from the house.

To reach Cladagh Gorge at the end of the route, take the same road from Belcoo and stop at the signed Cladagh Gorge car park some 6km later. The car park is situated just east of Cladagh Bridge, and also marked by a Cuilcagh Way information panel.

If you need help with transport logistics, the closest taxi company is **Belcoo Cabs** (☎ 6638 6105), who charge around £1 per mile.

THE WALK
Pick up the Cuilcagh Way markers outside the toilet block at western side of the car park. From here, follow a gravel pathway west towards Florence Court House. Soon there is an opportunity to turn right across a wooden footbridge and explore the estate's walled garden. Then continue ahead, crossing over a road junction to reach the National Trust courtyard buildings. Turn left here for house tours, and to visit the shop and tearooms.

The route continues past the courtyard, then turns left along the rear of **Florence Court House**. Follow a gravel track past a restored water-powered sawmill, then turn right and left across a footbridge over the Larganess River. Turn right and climb gradually to a junction of forest tracks, where you should turn right again. This leads into the conifer plantation. Follow forest tracks to a farm lane that passes alongside a wonderful karst outcrop. At the end of the lane, follow the posts across open farmland, using stiles to cross several fences. Along the way you pass more limestone pavement, and have the opportunity to explore many features typical of limestone karst topography (see the boxed text Karst Wonders of the Burren, p197). The route veers north at the bottom of Gortmaconnell Rock, and the waymarkers bring you to the Marlbank Loop Rd (1¾ hours from the start).

Turn left and follow the road west for 1.5km to the entrance to Marble Arch Caves. Turn right here and follow the driveway to the visitor centre. The route passes to the left of the building and turns left at its rear. Pass through two gates to enter Marble Arch National Nature Reserve, an ash woodland that harbours rare mammals such as red squirrels and pine marten. Keep right at a junction and descend a series of wooden steps, passing several impressive sink holes. You now come to a viewing platform for Marble Arch itself – a collapsed cave consisting of a limestone archway, with the Cladagh River rushing out over boulders below. Continue down the steps to a gravel path that follows the river downstream past several chutes and rapids. The deciduous woodland is carpeted with bluebells and other wildflowers in spring, and is a beautiful way to finish the walk. Continue past two gates to the car park at the bottom of the glen (1¼ hours from the Marlbank Loop Rd).

SAWEL & DART

Duration 5–5½ hours
Distance 14km (8.7 miles)
Ascent 650m (2789ft)
Difficulty moderate–demanding
Start/Finish B47 road at GR H639944
Nearest Towns Gortin (p284), Draperstown (p281)
Transport bus
Summary An ascent of the highest peaks in the Sperrin Mountains, featuring wonderfully wide views and a remote atmosphere.

The Irish name for the Sperrin Mountains – *Cnoc Speirín*, meaning 'pointed hills' – is something of a misnomer. This is a gently rounded, unassuming range, with few rocky outcrops poking through the deep blanket bog. The mountains' discreet charm derives more from their setting – the summits overlook a mosaic of green fields, hedgerows and woodlands in the rolling valleys below.

The main ridge of the Sperrins stretches for some 30km along the border of counties Derry and Tyrone. This circular walk takes you straight to the top, heading over the highest peak in the range, Sawel Mountain (678m), and the adjacent summit of Dart (619m). Though it covers some rough ground, the route is straightforward and presents few navigation problems, especially as there are convenient fences to follow over the upper slopes – very helpful in poor visibility. However, you should beware of old fencing wire lurking in the heather, just waiting to trip you into the nearest bog. The ground can also be rather soggy after a few days' rain, so it's best to wait for a dry interlude if at all possible.

For a greater understanding of the area, it's well worth stopping at **Sperrin Heritage**

SPERRINS OUT OF BOUNDS

Some landowners in the Sperrins are happy for responsible walkers to cross their land; others aren't so keen. If you encounter a landowner who asks you to turn back (and they are within their rights to make such a request), then do so. It's unlikely that you will have any problems on the walk described, but note that there is no access west of the summit of Dart Mountain.

Centre (☎ 8164 8142; 274 Glenelly Rd, Cranagh; adult/child £2.70/1.65; open daily Easter-Oct), situated just west of the walk. The exhibits explain the region's ecology and history. The discovery of gold was the most exciting event in recent times, and for an extra £0.85/0.45 you can try your luck at panning for gold in a nearby stream. The centre also sells OSNI maps and organises a program of walks in the surrounding hills.

For details of an alternative route in the Eastern Sperrins, see p276.

PLANNING
Maps
Use the OSNI 1:50,000 map No 13 or, for more detail, the waterproof OSNI 1:25,000 Activity Map *Sperrins*.

SAWEL & DART

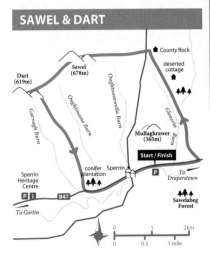

GETTING TO/FROM THE WALK

The walk starts and finishes from the B47, around 16km west of Draperstown and 500m east of the crossroads in Sperrin village. Park here in a lay-by on the southern side of the road (GR H639944).

Ulsterbus (☎ 9066 6630) service 403, known as the Sperrin Rambler, runs along the B47 twice daily Monday to Saturday on its way between Omagh, Gortin, Drapers-town and Magherafelt. The closest official stop to this walk is the Sperrin Heritage Centre, some 1.5km west of the route, but if you ask nicely the driver should be able to drop you a few kilometres further east along the line of the walk itself.

THE WALK

From the lay-by, walk east along the B47 for almost 1.5km. Within a kilometre the road descends through a steep dip to cross the **Glenerin Burn**. Beyond this you pass a small conifer plantation on the left, then an adjacent farm. About 200m further on, there's a rickety gate set at an angle to the road. This is your access into the mountains.

Negotiate the makeshift gate and follow the track as it curves into lonely Glenerin. About 1.5km from the start, the well-graded track crosses an unnamed tributary of Glenerin Burn, which could be difficult after heavy rain. A few metres further on, join a firm vehicle track and climb north-westwards above Binleana Burn, passing a deserted cottage in a small conifer plantation. On the horizon you may spot the profile of **County Rock**, a conspicuous boulder that stands, as does much of the Sperrin range, on the border between counties Tyrone and Derry.

Follow the track up to a tarmac road near the rock (1½ hours from the start). Cross the road and, with a fence on your right, ascend a cluster of rock outcrops. Then continue up the occasionally soggy, unremittingly steep slope ahead. Fortunately the ground becomes firmer underfoot as you gain height. At the point where another fence comes up on the left, cross the fence on your right and continue uphill. Where this fence bends away southwards, continue west for about 150m to reach the summit of **Sawel Mountain**, marked by a trig pillar, a cairn, and sweeping views stretching as far as Donegal (an hour from the road).

Cross a stile over a nearby fence and descend southwest to the col between Sawel and Dart. The peat hags and mosses here are less malevolent than they look. You'll soon meet a fence that runs generally southwest towards **Dart Mountain**. Dart, dotted with rocks, is a hill of greater character though less elevation than Sawel. Follow the fence up to the summit, 45 minutes from Sawel. The views of the immediate area are better than from its taller neighbour as you're closer to beautiful Glenelly. Also prominent in the scene are the towers on Mullaghcarn to the southeast and the huge corrie and slopes of Mullaghclogha to the west.

The descent is simply a matter of following a fence, first back down Dart's eastern spur, then south from a rocky knoll down the broad, tussock-covered spur of Oughtmame. At a fence across your line of travel, go through a gate on the left beside a small pine plantation (this plantation is not shown on the OSNI map). Around 250m further south a green lane materialises. This makes for an easy final stage down through three more gates to the B47 (an hour from Dart).

Turn left and head along the B47 for 2km to return to the start.

THE NORTH

The northern part of Northern Ireland is blessed with some of the finest scenery in the province. The area's most celebrated feature is the coast of County Antrim, where the pounding Atlantic Ocean has sculpted an eclectic array of sea stacks and pinnacles, cliffs and caves, all interspersed by long, sandy beaches. From a walker's perspective, the highlight of the shoreline is the Causeway Coast Way, which takes in the best of the scenery along with world-famous sites such as the Giant's Causeway and the thrilling rope bridge at Carrick-a-Rede.

Antrim also boasts a range of coastal hills, cut in the north by no less than nine distinct glens. The best of these environments are also explored by excellent waymarked trails. The rock that underpins the entire region is basalt, which was deposited during a period of intense volcanic activity some 60 million years ago. The lava stretched west into Country Derry, where more dramatic landforms remain as testament to the geological upheaval. The best example of this is the towering escarpment of Binevenagh, where a short but exhilarating route rivals any in Antrim.

BINEVENAGH CLIFFS

Duration 2–3 hours
Distance 6.5km (4 miles)
Ascent 200m (656ft)
Difficulty easy–moderate
Start/Finish Binevenagh Lake car park
Nearest Town Limavady (p284)
Transport private
Summary Get among the cliffs and pinnacles of Binevenagh to explore one of the most unusual landscapes in the north.

The cliffs of Binevenagh tower over the Magilligan lowlands of northern County Derry. With a vertical drop of more than 100m, the basalt escarpment dominates the landscape for miles around. In some places the cliffs rise unopposed, while elsewhere they are cut into sharp defiles or shattered into a maze of free-standing stacks and pinnacles. It all makes for a highly unusual landscape, and a wonderful location for a walk.

The cliffs are not only intriguing from an aesthetic point of view; they are also unique in Ireland thanks to their unusual geology and ecology. The precipice harbours both arctic-alpine and coastal flora, and has been classified an Area of Special Scientific Interest. The rock itself was created by massive lava flows and invites inevitable comparisons with the more famous basalt formations of the Giant's Causeway, some 30km to the east. And if local myth is to be believed, the connection doesn't stop there. One of the pinnacles at the base of the cliff is known as the Finn MacCool Finger Stone, a reference to the same giant who gave his name to the causeway in County Antrim.

The walk starts beside a lake at the top of the cliffs, which is kept stocked with trout and is a popular spot among the local fishing community. It then makes a circuit around the main escarpment, exploring the rock walls from above and below. Though it's relatively short, the quality of the route

is such that it's recommended even for those who generally prefer longer outings. Navigation is generally straightforward; waymarking posts of the old Ulster Way provide initial guidance and informal paths cover much of the rest of the route. However, there's no getting away from the fact that half the walk takes place beside a sheer drop. Make sure to exercise due care and attention when close to the edge, especially in wet or windy conditions.

PLANNING
Maps
Use the OSNI 1:50,000 map No 4.

GETTING TO/FROM THE WALK
Binevenagh Lake car park is situated right at the top of the cliffs. From Limavady, take the A2 northeast to Artikelly, then head along the B201 to Coleraine. Two kilometres east of Artikelly, turn left. After 5km, turn left again, following signs for Binevenagh Forest. The forest entrance is located on the left 1km further on. Follow the track uphill to the car park at the end of the road.

There is no public transport to or from Binevenagh.

THE WALK
From the car park, head northwest towards the cliffs on a footpath marked with an Ulster Way post. Keep right at a fork and follow the trail to the cliff edge, where you are greeted by wonderful views. The flat farmland that stretches beneath you to the spur of Magilligan Point is in fact the largest coastal plain in Ireland, while the hills of

Inishowen rise across Lough Foyle to the west.

Follow the path northeast along the clifftop, aiming for a narrow strip of trees that hugs the cliff edge. At the apex of the trees you'll find another waymarking post. The trail splits three ways here. The best option is to keep far left and continue along the very edge of the escarpment, descending carefully between the forest and cliff edge. After almost 100m, the path veers right into the trees and begins to zigzag down through the forest. You may miss the left turn however, because the most obvious trail heads right from the junction, descending a muddy slope between the trees and an area of felled forestry. If you find yourself on this path don't worry, just head back left into the forest after 100m, where you will rejoin the original trail.

The path through the forest is steep and can be muddy after rain. You reach the bottom of the slope and join a gravel vehicle track around 30 minutes from the start. Turn left here and follow the track to its end, then cross a stile beside a metal gate. You are now out into the open, directly beneath the Binevenagh cliffs. Follow a faint path along the right-hand side of the field. When the trees fall away to your right, begin to traverse across the field to the left, climbing very gradually towards the base of the sheer escarpment. Along the way you'll need to cross several more fences, each bridged by a wooden stile. The path eventually becomes lost in the grass, though the stiles indicate the general line of the route.

Towards the centre of the cliff a steep gully cuts down the precipice. Beneath this, cross another stile at the top of an old stone wall. The ground now begins to undulate across a series of hummocks; keep climbing, gradually drawing closer to the base of the cliffs. Two distinct waves of rock now lie to your left, the nearer stacks having broken off the main escarpment. Several curious rock towers and pinnacles also lie scattered beneath the precipice, sculpted by the forces of erosion.

Continue ahead, passing between several sharp hummocks. Around 40 minutes beyond the track you will see a distinctive tooth of rock lying just beneath the main precipice, with a grassy ramp to its left. The path consolidates again near the base of this ramp. Join the trail and follow it up the cliff.

As you reach the top of the escarpment, veer left and climb north across the grass-covered slope. Pass through a metal gate and continue along the edge of the precipice until you are forced to the right by the lip of a steep gully. The path then leads inland to the shore of Binevenagh Lake. Turn left, cross the concrete outlet dam, and follow the track back to the car park.

CAUSEWAY COAST WAY HIGHLIGHT

Duration 5–5½ hours
Distance 18.5km (11.5 miles)
Ascent 150m (492ft)
Difficulty moderate
Start Carrick-a-Rede car park
Finish Giant's Causeway Visitor Centre
Nearest Towns Ballintoy (p277), Giant's Causeway (p282), Bushmills (p280)
Transport bus, train
Summary A superb coastal journey past sandy beaches, sea arches and cliff-tops to reach the spectacular Giant's Causeway.

The official Causeway Coast Way stretches for 53km from Portstewart to Ballycastle, but the most scenic section – the walk between Carrick-a-Rede and the Giant's Causeway – can be done in a day and offers one of the finest coastal walks in all of Ireland. The route is way-marked throughout and follows generally firm paths, interspersed with sections of beach walking and rock hopping.

The Giant's Causeway and Carrick-a-Rede, with its thrilling rope bridge, are two of the country's premier natural tourist attractions. Both sites are now owned and maintained by the National Trust, who have also purchased intervening coastal lands and negotiated access agreements with local landowners to ensure a continuous path between the two points. The rest of the Causeway Coast Way (not described here) involves a 9.5km road walk east to Ballycastle, and attractive though less dramatic coast west from the causeway to Portstewart.

Despite the linear format, good transport services during the summer mean there's no problem returning from one end of the route to the other. The walk can also be split into shorter segments, with major access points at White Park Bay and Dunseverick Castle. Beside the heritage sites, rock formations and cliffs, the flora and fauna are another pleasant aspect of the route. Many species of seabird frequent the cliffs, including razorbills, guillemots and puffins. Among the summer wildflowers along the path, the lovely blue harebell, yellow tormentil and pink thrift make frequent appearances.

Note that parts of the walk follow a narrow path along the top of unfenced cliffs, and can be dangerous in wet and windy weather. Also, high tides can temporarily block the way at either end of White Park Bay; check tide times at any tourist office and avoid walking this section at high water.

PLANNING
Maps & Books
The path is marked on OSNI 1:50,000 map No 5 and the waterproof OSNI 1:25,000 Activity Map *Glens of Antrim*.

The illustrated leaflet-guide *Causeway Coast Way* provides further background for walkers; it's available to purchase from the Causeway Visitor Centre and local tourist offices. For a more in-depth treatment of the walk and its surrounds, consider Philip Watson's *A Companion to the Causeway Coast Way*.

Information Sources
The website www.northantrim.com provides local accommodation listings as well as a host of background information for many of the locations visited on this route.

GETTING TO/FROM THE WALK
There are several transport services for tourists visiting the popular Causeway Coast, making it easy to complete the walk in either direction.

Ulsterbus (☎ 9066 6630) operate the buses in the area. Service 172 links Ballycastle, the Giant's Causeway, Ballintoy, Bushmills, and Coleraine (six daily Mon-Fri, one on Sat, three on Sun) and is the main, year-round service along the Causeway Coast. The Antrim Coaster service 252 from Coleraine also includes stops at Bushmills, the Giant's Causeway and Ballintoy. There are two buses daily from Monday to Saturday, with one service continuing to/from Belfast's Europa Bus Centre.

There are also extra summer services that shuttle between the area's main tourist attractions. From July to mid-September, the Causeway Rambler service 402 links Bushmills and Carrick-a-Rede (£4, 25 minutes, seven daily) with stops at the Giant's Causeway, Dunseverick Castle, White Park Bay and Ballintoy. The ticket allows unlimited travel in both directions for one day.

An interesting alternative for getting away from the end of the walk is the

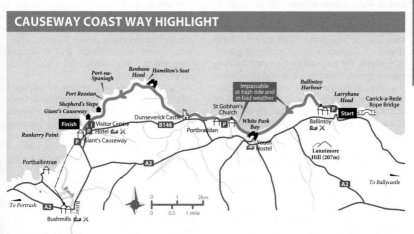

CAUSEWAY COAST WAY HIGHLIGHT

A MYTHICAL BRIDGE TO SCOTLAND

The Giant's Causeway is Ireland's first World Heritage site. Legend has it that the 40,000 hexagonal columns were built by the Irish giant Finn MacCool during his attempt to construct a bridge to Scotland. Prosaic geologists, however, have spoiled a good story with their scientific explanation.

The rocks are a product of the volcanic activity that blanketed this region with lava around 60 million years ago. As successive lava flows slowly cooled, the rock fractured along lines of tension and force, much as the surface of drying mud often cracks in a roughly hexagonal pattern.

The process wasn't uniform throughout and the Causeway's columns sometimes have four, five, seven or even eight sides. In fact, from the cliff path you can make out three distinct layers in the cross-section of basalt exposed along the cliffs. The lowest layer has the best columns, the middle layer is column-free and the top layer has quite irregular formations. Another product of the cooling process was ball-and-socket jointing within the columns. The sockets survive as bowl-like depressions on the top of the columns, which local people used to evaporate sea water to make salt in the 19th century.

Giant's Causeway & Bushmills Railway
(☎ 2073 2844; www.freewebs.com/giants causewayrailway; adult return £6.75). The locomotives (two steam and one diesel) run from Bushmills to the Giant's Causeway, departing hourly between 11am and 5.30pm. Services operate daily in July and August, and weekends only from Easter to June, September and October.

If you bring your own vehicle, note that it costs £6 to park at the Giant's Causeway. Parking is free at Carrick-a-Rede, though there is a charge to visit the rope bridge itself.

THE WALK

Before setting out on the main walk, it's worth taking time to visit the famous **Carrick-a-Rede Rope Bridge** (☎ 2076 9839; adult/child £4/2; open Mar-Oct). The 20m-long, 1m-wide footbridge spans the chasm between the mainland cliffs and the little island of Carrick-a-Rede, swaying gently 30m above the rock-strewn water. Crossing the bridge is either exhilarating or terrifying, depending on your head for heights. Once on the island there are good views of Rathlin Island and Fair Head to the east. It's a 2km, 45-minute round trip from the car park along a good path. There's a National Trust information centre beside the car park, as well as a café serving light meals and drinks.

To begin the route proper, follow the road west past the main car park. Where the road descends towards the overspill car park in the quarry below, head left onto a grassy cliff-top path. Follow this for a

kilometre above Boheeshane Bay to reach a minor road beside a church. Turn right here and follow the road down to picturesque Ballintoy harbour. Though it's rather early in the day, **Roark's Kitchen** (☎ 2076 3632; mains £3-6; open daily Jun-Aug, Sat & Sun only May & Sep) is a cute little tearoom on the quayside that makes a very tempting place for a quick pit stop.

Continue along the shoreline past a series of conical stacks and sea arches, then cross a couple of fields and round a low headland to reach **White Park Bay** (45 minutes from Carrick-a-Rede). This fine, sandy beach is more than 2km long; progress is easiest at low tide, when you can walk on firm sand. Partway along, **White Park Bay Hostel** (☎ 2073 1745; www.hini .org.uk; 157 White Park Rd, Ballintoy; dm/ tw £17/40; open Apr-Oct) lies among the dunes. This modern hostel boasts exceptional views of the beach and is located just a few minutes' walk from a Causeway Rambler bus stop.

The beach ends in a jumble of boulders at the base of high limestone cliffs. Scramble across the rocks, which may be slippery when wet, to reach the secluded harbour of Portbraddan. If you've timed it wrong and the way is blocked by high tide, detour back to the hostel and follow the B14 road to Portbraddan. Beside the second house in the hamlet sits **St Gobhan's**, the smallest church in Ireland.

Beyond Portbraddan white limestone gives way to black basalt, and the path threads through a natural tunnel in the rocks before weaving around several rocky coves. At Dunseverick Harbour, follow a minor road for roughly 200m before turning right at a waymark and descending a flight of steps. The path then wanders along the grassy foreshore, rounds a headland and crosses a footbridge above a waterfall before reaching a car park opposite the skeletal remains of windswept and dramatic 16th-century **Dunseverick Castle** (1½ hours from White Park Bay).

From here the path climbs steadily, passing an old salmon fishery in a rusty-roofed cottage on the shore far below. You are now approaching **Benbane Head** and the most dramatic coastal scenery of the route. The cliffs soar to their highest point beneath the viewpoint known as **Hamilton's Seat**, some 45 minutes beyond Dunseverick Castle. It's certainly worth pausing to soak up the panorama from the 100m-high cliff-top, with views stretching as far west as Malin Head in Donegal.

The path continues along the rugged cliff-line for a further 4km before reaching Giant's Causeway. Around half-way along you pass Port-na-Spaniagh – Bay of the Spaniards – the final resting place the *Girona*, the last known wreck of the Spanish Armada, which sank in 1588. A kilometre or so further on, a signpost indicates the Shepherd's Steps heading down to the right. If you prefer to continue directly to the end of the route, keep straight ahead along the cliff-top.

If you want to visit the unique rock formations around the **Giants Causeway**, descend the flight of steps. Once at the lower-level path, a 500m detour to the right leads past the formation known as the Organ (a stack of vertical basalt columns) and the Giant's Eyes (a pair of rust-red sockets where huge boulders have fallen out of the rock face) to a viewpoint near Port Reostan. Turn left at the lower path to reach the causeway itself (one hour from Benbane Head). After exploring the area, follow the paved road uphill for 1km to reach the **Causeway Visitor Centre** (☎ 2073 1855; www.giantscauseway centre.com; open daily). The adjacent gift shop and tearoom, which serves a selection of drinks and light meals, are good spots to relax if you're waiting for transport away.

GLENARIFF FOREST PARK

Duration 2½–3 hours
Distance 10.5km (6.5 miles)
Ascent 260m (853ft)
Difficulty easy
Start/Finish Glenariff Forest Park car park
Nearest Town Glenariff (p283)
Transport bus
Summary Follow firm trails through this magnificently scenic forest park, past thundering waterfalls, towering trees and extensive views down the glen.

Often referred to as 'the Queen of the Glens' and once glorified as 'Switzerland in miniature', Glenariff is a classic U-shaped glacial valley. With its towering rock escarpments, it certainly has the most dramatic features of any of the nine Glens of Antrim. A focal point of the valley is the 12-sq-km Glenariff Forest Park, a dense woodland bisected by the Glenariff and Inver rivers. These rivers cut steeply down through the basalt in a series of narrow gorges and spectacular waterfalls, with some 22 falls within one kilometre alone.

The park is readily accessible to walkers thanks to its network of walking trails, which vary in length between one and nine kilometres. The route described combines the red Scenic Trail and the blue Waterfall Trail, and takes you past all the best spots. Maintained paths and walkways are followed throughout and frequent waymarking posts make navigation a simple task.

From an ecological point of view, the most interesting environment in the park can be found within a 1km stretch of gorge along the Glenariff River. Here the narrow rock walls and surrounding trees ensure a constantly damp, humid microclimate. Such conditions support an abundance of mosses, liverworts and ferns, all protected in a National Nature Reserve. Another section of the route crosses the line of an old narrow-gauge railway, which was built in 1873 and was the first such railway in Ireland. The line once linked the mines at Cloghcor, where iron ore was extracted, to the coast at Red Bay. Though the mining activity itself was short-lived, in many ways the railway heralded the modern era by giving birth to tourism in the glen.

Glenariff Forest Park (☎ 2175 8232; car/motorcycle/pedestrian £4/2/1.50; open daily) is near the main car park, and **Glenariff Tea House** (☎ 2175 8769; mains £7-13) is the perfect place for a rewarding snack after your day's exertion.

PLANNING
Maps
The OSNI 1:50,000 map No 9 and the OSNI 1:25,000 Activity Map *Glens of Antrim* put the walk in its wider geographical setting. However the park's own brochure shows the waymarked trails much more clearly; it's available at the park entrance or from the tea house.

GETTING TO/FROM THE WALK
Ulsterbus (☎ 9066 6630) service 150 links Glenariff Forest Park to Waterfoot (£2.30, 11 minutes), Cushendun (£4, 30 minutes) and Ballymena (£4, 40 minutes). There are four services daily from Monday to Friday, and two on Saturday.

In Waterfoot you can connect to the Antrim Coaster service 252, which stops in Coleraine, Bushmills (£7, one hour 20 minutes), the Giant's Causeway, Ballintoy, Glenarm and Larne (£5.80, one hour). There are two buses daily from Monday to Saturday, with one service continuing

to/from Belfast's Europa Bus Centre (£4.50, two hours).

By car, Glenariff Forest Park is 7.5km south of Waterfoot via the A43 road.

THE WALK
From the northeastern corner of the main car park, follow the white way-marked path and pass below the tea house. At a three-way junction go straight on, now following the red waymarkers of the Scenic Trail. Descend steadily northeast along the banks of the tumbling Inver River; the wild garlic around here is particularly aromatic in springtime. You soon arrive at a bridge spanning the river. Avoid the temptation to cross here – you will return this way at the end of the route. Continue downstream to another bridge over Glenariff River and join a path on the opposite bank (30 minutes from the start). If you fancy a break, the **Laragh Lodge** restaurant (see Glenariff, p283) is located just a few metres to the right. To continue on the route, turn left, now following the blue waymarkers of the Waterfall Trail.

Follow the turbulent water upstream past numerous small falls. The rock walls soon draw closer and the path is forced onto a wooden walkway attached to the side of the cliff. At the head of the gorge lies perhaps the most famous waterfall in the Glens of Antrim, the powerful, double drop of **Ess-na-Larach**, meaning The Mare's Fall. The path continues upstream through more open woodland, passing several more cascades. Follow the blue waymarkers through a junction and cross another bridge to arrive at Hermit's Fall. Cross the river again at a third bridge and pick up the red waymarkers again on the opposite bank.

A short detour along the path to the left will bring you back to the visitors centre. To continue on follow the red Scenic Trail away from the river. Cross the park's two access roads and climb through the pines to a large clearing with views down the length of Glenariff. In summer the clearing is covered by swathes of Purple Loosestrife.

The path now undulates towards the route's highpoint, crossing the upper Inver River and two tributaries around 1¼ hours from the first Glenariff bridge. Soon the track begins to descend, past more fine

GLENARIFF FOREST PARK

views along the glen. Wind down through several switchbacks and cross the line of the old narrow-gauge railway to reach the bottom of the slope. Here you cross the bridge over the Inver that you passed on your outward journey. Turn left on the opposite bank and retrace your initial steps to the car park.

ANTRIM HILLS WAY HIGHLIGHT

Duration 5–6 hours
Distance 21km (13 miles)
Ascent 480m (1575ft)
Difficulty moderate
Start Ballyboley Forest car park
Finish Glenarm (p283)
Transport bus

Summary This scenic Waymarked Way explores the sheer escarpments and coastal summits of the Glens of Antrim.

The Antrim Hills Way is a two-day, 34.5km trail that stretches from the coastal village of Glenarm to the volcanic plug of Slemish Mountain, crossing hilltops and open farmland along the way. The walk described here is the best section of the longer route: a one-day stretch that explores a high coastal plateau and encompasses perhaps the most enjoyable upland walking in County Antrim. Firm terrain, dramatic scenery and fantastic views are just some of the treats on offer.

The trail can be walked in either direction, and our route opts for a north-bound trajectory. It begins with an ascent of 474m Agnew's Hill, then heads north across a series of summits between 300m and 400m high. These hills rise gently to the west but fall away steeply to the east, forming a conspicuous geological landform that is a legacy of the last ice age. The most striking formation is Sallagh Braes, a semi-circular basalt escarpment that has been designated an Area of Special Scientific Interest. This natural amphitheatre was created when glaciers cut into unstable slopes and caused a massive land slip, leaving the vertical cliffs 2km long and 100m high that are visible today.

Frequent stiles and waymarking posts make route-finding simple in good conditions. In many places the path is faint or non-existent however, and the amount of open terrain means navigation skills are still required in bad weather.

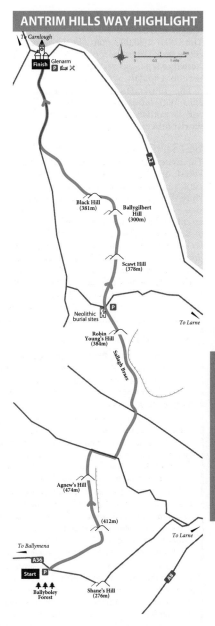

ANTRIM HILLS WAY HIGHLIGHT

To Carnlough

Finish   Glenarm

Black Hill (381m)

Ballygilbert Hill (300m)

Scawt Hill (378m)

Neolithic burial sites

To Larne

Robin Young's Hill (384m)

Sallagh Braes

Agnew's Hill (474m)

(412m)

To Larne

To Ballymena

A36

Start

Ballyboley Forest

Shane's Hill (276m)

NORTHERN IRELAND

PLANNING
Maps & Booklets
The OSNI 1:50,000 map No 9 covers the entire walk. The waterproof OSNI 1:25,000 Activity Map *Glens of Antrim* also shows all but the very start of the route.

The illustrated leaflet-guide *Antrim Hills Way* offers more background detail and is available to purchase from local tourist offices.

GETTING TO/FROM THE WALK
The route starts at a car park in Ballyboley Forest, on Shane's Hill. The car park contains an information panel for the Antrim Hills Way, and is situated on the southern side of the A36 Larne-Ballymena road, around 10km west of Larne and 21km east of Ballymena. The official end of the route is Glenarm village, at the Coast Rd car park just north of the bridge. Glenarm is generally accessed via the A2 Larne-Carnlough road.

Despite the walk's linear format, it's still possible to complete the route relying on the local bus network. Park your car in Glenarm, then use the **Ulsterbus** (☎ 9066 6630) service 162 to reach Larne (£3.30, 25 minutes, eight daily Mon-Fri, five on Sat). Change in Larne to service 130 to Ballymena, and ask to be dropped at the Ballyboley Forest car park (£2.60, 20 minutes, at least four daily Mon-Sat).

THE WALK
From Ballyboley Forest car park, cross the road and join a grassy footpath beside a signpost for the Ulster Way. Follow the path along a fire-break in the forest, then cross a stile to reach open, mountainous terrain. The cairn that marks the southern summit of Agnew's Hill is now visible to the northeast. Head directly towards the cairn until you meet a track that once formed part of an old droving road. Turn right onto the track and begin the gradual ascent towards the southern summit. You'll need to cross a large stile before reaching the top, where you're rewarded with your first real views. The outlines of the Belfast Hills, the Mourne Mountains, the Sperrins and

SLEMISH MOUNTAIN

All the routes in this section are underpinned by the same rock: basalt. This was deposited during Tertiary times, when the entire region was subject to intense volcanic activity lasting for two million years. Besides the hexagonal pillars visible at places like the Binevenagh and the Giant's Causeway, one of the best places to appreciate the region's geological past is from the top of Slemish Mountain (437m).

Lying just west of the Antrim Hills Way Highlight, Slemish is in fact the core of an ancient volcano. It's the best example among numerous extinct volcanoes that lie dotted around the Antrim plateau. Sixty million years ago, Slemish was simply magma filling the crater of a much larger volcano. The magma cooled relatively slowly and became dolerite, a hard rock typical of volcanic plugs. Subsequent erosion stripped the surrounding volcano away, exposing the plug and leaving the distinctively shaped peak that is visible today.

The mountain also has strong association with St Patrick. Patrick was first transported to Ireland around AD 400 and sold as a slave to a chieftain in County Antrim. For six years he was forced to work as a herdsman, tending sheep and pigs around Slemish. During this time, he underwent a profound spiritual development, often praying on the mountain top as he tried to reconcile himself to his life of captivity. He would later return to the country of his epiphany, and his success at converting the Irish people is well documented.

As you tour around the region, it's well worth detouring past Slemish and making the short climb to the top. Begin at Slemish car park (GR D217057), which is signed from Broughshane, 5km northeast of Ballymena. Follow an informal footpath towards the base of the mountain, then climb directly up the steep slope, following the route of least resistance. The reward for reaching the narrow summit ridge is incredible views in all directions. Head along the ridge to its southern edge, then descend steeply southwest. Having reached flatter ground at the base of the mountain, join a path and head north for 800m to return to the car park. The 2km circuit involves 200m of ascent and takes about 1½ hours to complete; use OSNI 1:50,000 map No 9.

Scotland decorate the horizon all around. It's a wonderful panorama, and one that stays with you for the duration of the walk.

Turn left at the southern cairn and descend slightly, then begin a steady climb along the broad ridge to the cairn at the far northern edge of the plateau. This is the highest point of **Agnew's Hill** (474m), and indeed the route, reached one hour from the start. From the summit, the remainder of the walk can be seen stretching away to the north. Descend along the marker posts and cross a stile, then turn right beside a fence. Descend to a road and turn right along the tarmac, where there are good views back across the sheer eastern cliffs of Agnew's Hill.

After almost 1km, turn left off the road and cross another stile. Follow the path through a field and cross a stream above an artificial lough. Here you join a grass track between high stone walls. Follow the track north, negotiating several wooden gates and another stream to reach a minor road. Turn left and follow the road for roughly 120m, then cross into a field on the right. A series of stiles now leads across the fields to heathery ground above the amphitheater of **Sallagh Braes** (1¼ hours from Agnew's Hill). Follow a fence around the lip of the escarpment, with steep gullies allowing the occasional glimpse into the void below. The airy sensation and the view over the curving cliffs make this a very memorable piece of walking.

The path eventually veers away from the edge of Sallagh Braes to climb northwest over the shoulder of **Robin Young's Hill** (384m). You then descend along a short section of stony track and more cropped grass to reach a **car park** at Linford. The two prominent mounds near the car park are thought to be **Neolithic burial sites** dating from around 4000 BC.

Cross the road beside the car park and climb along the right side of a field to the summit of Ballycoos (one hour past Sallagh Braes). A gradual descent and ascent then brings you to **Scawt Hill** (378m). Continue in the same vein across a series of grassy undulations, keeping to the high ground near the eastern edge of the plateau. The coastal views remain impressive throughout, with the rocky outcrops of the Maidens or Hulin Rocks visible out to sea.

The trail eventually swings west across rougher ground to reach the trig point at the summit of **Black Hill** (381m), around 45 minutes from Ballycoos. The concrete pillar also marks the start of a diagonal descent northwest off the plateau. Follow the marker posts down through the fields and across several rocky hummocks. Eventually you meet a stone wall at the right side of a field and descend through gorse bushes to a road. Turn right here and follow the tarmac for almost 2km, then turn left onto a smaller road. This brings you to the top of Altmore St in Glenarm village; continue to the end of the street to arrive at the seafront itself.

MORE WALKS

BELFAST & DOWN
Divis & Black Mountain
In 2004 the National Trust purchased 600 hectares of the Belfast Hills, including Divis and Black Mountain at the heart of the range. The rounded summits are covered in rough moorland, but provide excellent views over Belfast city and further afield. Start at a parking area at GR J265742. A map board near the entrance explains the four trail options, which range from 1¾ hours to six hours long. Paths are fully way-marked and fitted with route infrastructure where necessary. Approach the area via Belfast's Upper Springfield Rd, then take a signed right turn onto Divis Rd – the National Trust car park is 800m further on the left. Alternatively, take the **Metro** (☎ 9066 6630) city bus No 106 from Belfast city centre and alight along Upper Springfield Rd beside the brown National Trust sign. Walk up Divis Rd to the site entrance. Use the OSNI 1:50,000 map No 15.

MOURNE MOUNTAINS
Slieve Muck
This rewarding moderate to demanding route in the southern Mournes allows a different perspective over the most scenic summits in the range. Start at a car park at the bottom of the track known as Banns Rd (GR J284214), along the B25 roughly 13km southeast of Hilltown and 7.5km north of Kilkeel. This is also the 'Slievenagore' stop on the summer-only Mourne Rambler bus

NORTHERN IRELAND

service (for details, see Getting Around on p253). Head northeast along the track, climbing gradually to Lough Shannagh, the largest natural lake in the Mournes. Pass around the northeastern corner of the lough, then climb to meet the Mourne Wall in the col between Carn Mountain and Slieve Loughshannagh. Turn left and follow the wall over Carn Mountain (588m) to the trig point at the top of Slieve Muck (674m). Now descend southwest along the main ridge for 1.5km to a point where the ground descends steeply in all directions. Pick your way carefully southeast down the slope, heading for a point where the Yellow River meets a stone wall. Cross the river on stepping stones and rejoin the Banns Rd, turning right and retracing your initial steps to the car park. Allow 4½–5½ hours for the 13km-route, which involves 560m ascent. Carry either the OSNI 1:50,000 map No 29 or the OSNI 1:25,000 Activity Map *The Mournes*.

THE WEST
Castle Archdale

Castle Archdale lies on the eastern edge of Lower Lough Erne in County Fermanagh, and offers some of the best opportunities for walking along the lough shore. Two public parks, **Castle Archdale Country Park** (☎ 6862 1588; www.ni-environment.gov .uk/archdale; Lisnarick; admission free), and Castle Archdale Forest Park, lie side by side, each offering a variety of marked walking trails. The best option for walkers wanting to fully explore the area is an easy 10km figure-of-eight loop that takes in both parks. Begin from the Courtyard car park (GR H176588) in the country park, which is signed off the B82 Enniskillen-Kesh road around 11km north of Enniskillen. The adjacent **visitor centre** (open daily Easter-Sep, Sun only Oct-Easter) can provide trail maps and also houses exhibits about the estate's role during WWII. Other attractions include a short boat trip to view the ruins of a 12th-century monastic site on nearby White Island. Use OSNI 1:50,000 map No 17, or the OSNI 1:25,000 Activity Map *Lough Erne*.

The Eastern Sperrins

This compact circuit in the eastern Sperrin Mountains offers fine views and crosses the third-highest summit in the range.

The route starts and finishes beside Glenedra Bridge (GR C706003), around 9km northwest of Draperstown on the B40 Draperstown-Feeny road. From the northern side of the bridge, follow a forest track southwest into Banagher Forest. Turn right at the first track junction and left at the second. Around 300m later, turn right along a wide firebreak to reach open mountainside. Climb to the summit of Mullaghaneany (627m), then continue southeast and northeast over the top of Oughtmore (569m) and Spelhoagh (568m). Descend northeast towards Craighagh Hill, then follow a gully northwest to a forest track. Turn right and follow the track back to the start. Use OSNI 1:50,000 map Nos 13, 7 and 8 and allow three to four hours for the moderate to demanding, 9km (5.5 mile) trip, which involves 450m ascent.

WAYMARKED WAYS

As well as the Ulster Way (see the boxed text Changing Fortunes of the Ulster Way, p242), Northern Ireland has 11 short Waymarked Ways, each two days long. The best of these routes are described in this chapter – see the Cuilcagh Way Highlight, p263; Causeway Coast Way Highlight, p268 and Antrim Hills Way Highlight, p273. However fans of long-distance walking may also want to check out the Lecale Way and the Mourne Way in County Down; the Newry Canal Way and Ring of Gullion Way in Armagh; the Sliabh Beagh Way in County Fermanagh; the Central Sperrins Way and North Sperrins Way in the Sperrin Mountains; and the Moyle Way in County Antrim. For full descriptions of all these routes, see www.walkni.com.

TOWNS & FACILITIES

The telephone area code for all of Northern Ireland is ☎ 028 from Britain and the rest of the world, and ☎ 048 from the Republic of Ireland.

ANNALONG
pop 1900

The fishing village of Annalong is scattered around the A2 road coast road around

12km south of Newcastle. A range of visitor facilities make it a quieter and more convenient base for walks in the eastern Mourne Mountains.

There are two supermarkets, one of which has an ATM. However the nearest **tourist offices** are in **Newcastle** (see p284) and **Kilkeel** (☎ 4176 2525; kdakilkeel @hotmail.com; Rooney Rd; open Mon-Fri, also Sat Easter-Oct), a larger town 5km southwest.

Sleeping & Eating

The family-oriented **Cornmill Quay Hostel** (☎ 4376 8269; www.cornmillquay .com; Marine Park; dm/d £17/46) is set in a pretty little cottage courtyard above the harbour.

If you prefer a B&B, try friendly **Sycamores** (☎ 4376 8279; 52 Majors Hill Rd; s/d £37.50/55). It's within walking distance of the harbour, yet you can lie in the beautifully furnished rooms and contemplate views of the mountains.

Glassdrumman Lodge (☎ 4376 8451; www.glassdrummanlodge.com; Mill Rd; s/d £70/90) guesthouse also offers panoramic Mourne views, and the restaurant is recommended in several culinary guides (dinner £45 per person). It's located 1.5km west of the A2, and signed from the northern end of the village.

There are several restaurants and eateries in the village, including **Harbour Inn** (☎ 4376 8678; 6 Harbour Dr; mains £7-16). This attractive pub is beside the harbour, and has an upstairs restaurant with great views of the Mournes.

Getting There & Away

Ulsterbus (☎ 9066 6630) service 37 passes through Annalong on its way from Newcastle (£2.60, 20 minutes, hourly Mon-Sat, seven on Sun), via Bloody Bridge, to Kilkeel (£2.60, 20 minutes). There are onward connections from Newcastle to Belfast.

BALLINTOY

pop 200

Ballintoy is a pretty village tumbling down the hillside to a picture-postcard harbour. The village is just a short walk from Carrick-a-Rede Rope Bridge, the starting point for the Causeway Coast Way Highlight walk.

Sleeping & Eating

Sheep Island View Hostel (☎ 2076 9391; www.sheepislandview.com; 42a Main St; camping per person £6, dm/d from £14/30) is an excellent independent hostel offering dorm beds or space for tents. There's a free pick-up service from the Giant's Causeway, Bushmills or Ballycastle.

Right in the centre of the village, **Fullerton Arms Guest House & Restaurant** (☎ 2076 9613; www.fullertonarms.co.uk; 22 Main St; s/d £50/70) has rooms to suit parties of various sizes. Meals are served in both the bar and **restaurant** (mains £7-11), with a menu strong on lamb and steak.

Occupying a listed Georgian building in the heart of the village, **Ballintoy House B&B** (☎ 2076 2317; 9 Main St; s/d £30/50) is comfortable and very friendly. There's a discount if you opt for a continental breakfast.

Portcampley B&B (☎ 2076 8200; www .portcampley.com; 8 Harbour Rd; s/d £25/50) is a renovated traditional Irish cottage with eight bedrooms, some with enough beds to sleep families or small groups. It's along the road to Ballintoy Harbour, and the easiest way to reach Carrick-a-Rede is via the coastal path.

In the centre of the village there's a small supermarket and several pubs offering evening meals.

Getting There & Away

For details of bus services to Ballintoy, see Getting to/from the Walk for the Causeway Coast Way Highlight walk (p269). All the buses that stop at Carrick-a-Rede also stop in Ballintoy village.

BANGOR

pop 76,800

Bangor is a Victorian seaside resort that has undergone a recent renaissance as an out-of-town base for city commuters. Good transport links make it easily accessible from Belfast, and staying here is particularly convenient for walkers finishing the North Down Coastal Path.

The **Tourist Information Centre** (☎ 9127 0069; www.northdown.gov.uk; 34 Quay St; open daily Jul & Aug, Mon-Sat Sep-Jun) also sells a good range of maps and guides.

Sleeping & Eating

Set in a lovely Victorian townhouse just 300m north of the train station, **Ennislare House** (☎ 9127 0858; www.ennislarehouse .com; 7-9 Princetown Rd; s/d £35/60) offers large rooms, stylish decor, and a friendly welcome.

Cairn Bay Lodge (☎ 9146 7636; www .cairnbaylodge.com; 278 Seacliff Rd; s/d from £45/80) is a lovely seaside villa overlooking Ballyholme Bay, 1km east of the town centre. It oozes Edwardian elegance and provides gourmet breakfasts.

Combining traditional Victorian fittings with elegant modern decor, **Hebron House** (☎ 9146 3126; www.hebron-house.com; 68 Princetown Rd; s/d £55/80) provides memorable breakfasts around a communal dining table.

Offering views of the harbour, **Jeffers by the Marina** (☎ 9185 9555; 7 Gray's Hill; mains £13-17; open lunch & dinner Tue-Sun) is a chic little café-restaurant serving coffee and cakes during the day and an interesting dinner menu in the evening.

Upstairs from a busy bar, **Coyle's Bistro** (☎ 9127 0362; 44 High St; mains £13-18; open for dinner Tue-Sun) offers an intimate atmosphere and an acclaimed menu, with dishes such as pan-fried rabbit.

Getting There & Away

The bus and train stations are together on Abbey St, at the uphill end of Main St.

Ulsterbus (☎ 9066 6630) service B2 or 502 runs from Belfast's Laganside Bus Centre to Bangor (£3, 50 minutes, every 30 minutes Mon-Sat, eight on Sun).

There's also a regular train service from Belfast's Great Victoria St and Central stations to Bangor (£5, 30 minutes, half-hourly Mon-Sat, hourly on Sun).

BELCOO
pop 500

A scenic village set on the western shore of Lough MacNean Lower, many walkers prefer Belcoo's peaceful atmosphere to the hustle and bustle of nearby Enniskillen. The village runs up to the river; cross the bridge and you're in Blacklion in the Republic of Ireland. Blacklion has further sleeping and eating options, though you'll need to pay in euros.

There are two supermarkets in the village, but the nearest tourist information centre is in Enniskillen.

Sleeping & Eating

There are several B&Bs around Belcoo. **Rockview House** (☎ 6638 6534; Aughavass; s/d £25/48) is in an elevated bungalow roughly 1.5km from the centre of the village along Garrison Rd.

On the lake shore in the village itself, **Bella Vista** (☎ 6638 6469; Cottage Dr; s/d £35/50) is a welcoming, two-storey family home with friendly hosts and comfortable rooms.

The **Customs House Country Inn** (☎ 6638 6285; www.customshouseinn .com; Main St; s/d from £60/80) offers high-class accommodation in a restored building at the heart of the village. Downstairs is a welcoming pub and a cosy, candlelit **restaurant** (mains £9-15).

There's also luxury accommodation and gourmet dining a few hundred metres south across the border in Blacklion. **MacNean House & Restaurant** (☎ 00 353-71 985 3022; www.macneanrestaurant.com; Main St; s/d €80/140; five-course dinner menu €50-70; restaurant open Thu-Sun) is one of the country's finest restaurants, run by award-winning TV chef Neven Maguire. The food is truly outstanding, though you'll need to book well in advance to avoid disappointment.

Getting There & Away

Ulsterbus (☎ 9066 6630) service 64 links Belcoo to Enniskillen (£2, 25 minutes, seven daily Mon-Fri, three on Sat, one on Sun). **Bus Éireann** (☎ 071-916 0066; www .buseireann.ie) service 66 from Sligo to Belfast also stops in Belcoo (four daily Mon-Fri, three on Sat).

By road, Belcoo is 18km west of Enniskillen via the A4.

BELFAST
pop 277,000

It's something of an understatement to describe Belfast's history as colourful. The outbreak of the Troubles in 1969 made it notorious around the world, but since the 1998 Good Friday Agreement, massive swathes of the city have been redeveloped and tourism has taken off. Today the North's capital is remarkably cosmopolitan, and the logical place to start a visit to Northern Ireland.

Information Sources

The **Belfast Welcome Centre** (☎ 9024 6609; www.gotobelfast.com; 47 Donegall Pl; open daily) provides information about the whole of Northern Ireland, and can book accommodation for anywhere in Ireland or Britain.

Supplies & Equipment

Belfast has a fantastic range of outdoor shops, all selling walking gear, camping equipment, maps and guidebooks. The three best outlets are **Tiso** (☎ 9023 1230; 12-14 Cornmarket), **Surf Mountain** (☎ 9024 8877; 12 Brunswick St) and **Jackson Sports** (☎ 9023 8572; 70 High St).

For maps and books, you could also try **TSO Bookshop** (☎ 9023 8451; 16 Arthur St) or **Waterstones** (☎ 9024 0159; 44-46 Fountain St).

Sleeping

Belfast International Youth Hostel (☎ 9032 4733; www.hini.org.uk; 22-32 Donegall Rd; dm £11-15, s/d from £21/29) is a modern HI hostel conveniently located just off Shaftesbury Sq, though it can be a bit noisy at night when the pubs and clubs empty.

Another long-established hostel, **Arnie's Backpackers** (☎ 9024 2867; www.arnies backpackers.co.uk; 63 Fitzwilliam St; dm £9-12), occupies a cosy terraced house in the university area, with plenty of lively bars and restaurants nearby.

If you're looking for a B&B, **Camera Guesthouse** (☎ 9066 0026; www.camera guesthouse.com; 44 Wellington Park; s/d £48/62) is friendly and welcoming, occupying a Victorian building on one of South Belfast's peaceful, tree-lined terraces.

Park Inn (☎ 9067 7710; www.belfast .parkinn.co.uk; 4 Clarence St West; r from £60) is a brand new hotel only five minutes from City Hall and close to loads of good pubs and restaurants. It's excellent value, and family rooms can be arranged.

Just south of City Hall, **Ten Square** (☎ 9024 1001; www.tensquare.co.uk; 10 Donegall Sq South; r from £170) is an opulent, Shanghai-inspired boutique hotel.

Eating

Self-caterers will find several supermarkets dotted around the city centre.

Mourne Seafood Bar (☎ 9024 8544; 34-36 Bank St; mains £10-17; open for lunch daily, dinner Tue-Sat) occupies a pub-like space behind a fishmonger's shop, so the seafood is as fresh as it gets. It's hugely popular, so book ahead.

Northern Ireland's only Michelin-starred restaurant is **Deane's Restaurant** (☎ 9033 1134; 34-40 Howard St; mains £15-23; open lunch & dinner Tue-Sat), where chef Michael Deane takes the best of Irish and British produce and gives it the gourmet treatment.

Getting There & Away

Belfast's main **Europa Bus Centre** is behind the Europa Hotel and next door to Great Victoria St train station. It's the terminus for buses to Dublin (£13, three hours, hourly), Derry (£10, 1¾ hours, half-hourly Mon-Sat, 11 on Sun), and destinations in the west and south of Northern Ireland. The smaller **Laganside Bus Centre** (Oxford St), near the river, is mainly for buses to County Antrim, eastern County Down and the Cookstown area. Contact **Ulsterbus** (☎ 9066 6630; www.translink .co.uk) for regional timetables and fares.

There are also frequent bus connections between the Europa Bus Centre and Belfast's two airports. The Airport Express 300 (£7, 30 minutes, every 15 minutes between 7am and 8pm, hourly through the night) runs to **Belfast International Airport** (☎ 9448 4848; www.belfastairport.com), 30km northwest of the city. Airport Express 600 (£1.50, 15 minutes, every 20 minutes between 6am and 10pm) serves **George Best Belfast City Airport** (☎ 9093 9093; www.belfastcityairport.com), 6km northeast of the centre. For international flight information, see p305.

For trains, Belfast's **Central Station** (East Bridge St), east of the city centre, is the departure point for services to Dublin (£28, two hours, eight daily Mon-Sat, five on Sun) and all destinations in Northern Ireland. Trains for many destinations including Derry (£10, 2¼ hours, seven or eight daily Mon-Sat, four on Sun) can also be taken from **Great Victoria St Station** (Great Northern Mall), next to the Europa

Bus Centre. For service information, contact **Translink** (☎ 9066 6630; www.translink.co.uk).

Getting Around
Belfast's city bus network is operated by **Metro** (☎ 9066 6630; www.translink.co.uk). Most services depart from various stops around Donegall Sq, at City Hall. The **Metro kiosk** (open Mon-Fri), at the northwest corner of the square, sells tickets and provides free route maps. You can also buy tickets from the driver (change given). Fares range from £1 to £1.60 depending on distance, or you can opt for a Metro Day Ticket giving one-day's unlimited bus travel for £3.50.

There are local trains every 20 or 30 minutes connecting Great Victoria St and Central Station via City Hospital and Botanic Station, with a flat fare of £1 for journeys between any of these stops.

BUSHMILLS
pop 1350
The small town of Bushmills has long been a place of pilgrimage for connoisseurs of Irish whiskey; not surprising given that it's home to the world's oldest legal distillery. Good accommodation options also make it an attractive stop for walkers exploring the nearby Causeway Coast.

Sleeping & Eating
Modern **Ballyness Caravan Park** (☎ 2073 2393; www.ballynesscaravanpark.com; 40 Castlecatt Rd; campsites £17; open mid-Mar–Oct) has won numerous awards for its conservation standards. It's located about 1km south of Bushmills on the B66.

Just off the diamond in the centre of town, **Mill Rest Youth Hostel** (☎ 2073 1222; www.hini.org.uk; 49 Main St; dm £16-17, d £39; open daily Mar-Oct, Fri & Sat only Nov-Feb) is a modern and child-friendly hostel with a kitchen, restaurant, laundry and bike shed.

One of Northern Ireland's most atmospheric hotels, **Bushmills Inn** (☎ 2073 2339; www.bushmillsinn.com; 9 Dunluce Rd; s/d from £168/178) offers luxurious accommodation in its Mill House complex. The excellent **restaurant** (dinner mains £15-20) is set in the old 17th-century stables.

There's a supermarket and selection of eateries around the village centre. For daytime snacks, try the **Copper Kettle** (☎ 2073 2560; 61 Main St; mains £3-6), a rustic tea-room with great cakes and scones.

Getting There & Away
For details of bus services to Bushmills, see Getting to/from the Walk for the Causeway Coast Way Highlight (p269).

DERRY
pop 83,700
Derry – or Londonderry – is Northern Ireland's second largest city, and boasts the only set of city walls in Ireland to survive almost intact. With frequent flights to Britain and good road transport connections to the Republic, it also serves as an alternative gateway to the North.

Information Sources
For tourist information, head to **Derry Tourist Information Centre** (☎ 7137 7577; www.derryvisitor.com; 44 Foyle St; open daily Jul-Sep, Mon-Sat Mar-Jun & Oct, Mon-Fri Nov-Feb). It sells maps and books, and can book accommodation throughout Ireland.

The most useful map for getting around is the OSNI 1:10,000 *Street Map of Londonderry*, available from local bookshops.

Supplies & Equipment
The best place for outdoor equipment is **House of Value** (☎ 7137 3666; 5 Market St), located just inside Ferryquay Gate in the old city.

For maps and books, try **Easons** (☎ 7137 7133; Foyleside Shopping Centre, Foyle St).

Self-caterers can stock up at several large supermarkets situated just north of the city walls.

Sleeping & Eating
Set in a Georgian townhouse, friendly **Derry City Independent Hostel** (☎ 7128 0542; www.derry-hostel.co.uk; 44 Great James St; dm/d from £12/36) is just a short walk northwest of the bus station. They also have an annexe nearby with stylish double rooms aimed at couples.

Alternatively, **Derry Palace Hostel** (☎ 7130 9051; www.paddyspalace.com; 1 Woodleigh Tce, Asylum Rd; dm from £12) is central, comfortable and as friendly as they come.

Within a five-minute walk of the walled city, friendly **Saddler's House B&B** (☎ 7126 9691; www.thesaddlershouse .com; 36 Great James St; s/d £50/60) is set in a lovely, Victorian townhouse.

Da Vinci's Hotel (☎ 7127 9111; www.da vincishotel.com; 15 Culmore Rd; r from £75) is a sleek, stylish boutique hotel on the west bank of the Foyle, 1.5km north of the city centre.

Fitzroy's (☎ 7126 6211; 2-4 Bridge St; mains £10-15; open daily) does café-style lunches till 5.30pm, then tasty bistro dinners. The set two-/three-course dinner for £12/15 (available from 8pm Monday to Thursday) is good value.

Occupying a shiny glass-fronted venue on the riverfront, **Mange 2** (☎ 7136 1222; 110-115 Strand Rd; mains £13-19; open lunch & dinner Tue-Sun) serves top quality Irish produce with occasional Asian or French twists.

Getting There & Away
The bus station (☎ 7126 2261) is on Foyle St, just northeast of the walled city. **Ulsterbus** (☎ 9066 6630) services cover most of Northern Ireland and the Republic, including Belfast (£10, 1¾ hours, every 30 minutes Mon-Sat, 11 on Sun) and Dublin (£16, four hours, every two hours daily).

Lough Swilly Bus Company (☎ 7126 2017) has an office upstairs at the bus station, and runs buses to Letterkenny (£5, 30 to 45 minutes, nine daily Mon-Fri, five on Sat) and other destinations in County Donegal. **Bus Éireann** (☎ 00 353-74 912 1309) service 64 runs from Derry to Galway (£18, 5¼ hours, three daily, two on Sun) via Letterkenny, Donegal and Sligo.

The **Airporter** (☎ 7126 9996; www.air porter.co.uk; Quayside Shopping Centre, Strand Rd) bus runs direct from Derry to Belfast International (£18, 1½ hours) and George Best Belfast City (£18, two hours) airports. Buses depart hourly Monday to Friday, and every two hours at weekends.

Derry's train station (referred to as Londonderry in Northern Ireland timetables) is on the eastern side of the River Foyle; a free Rail Link bus connects it with the bus station on Foyle St. Trains to Belfast (£10, 2¼ hours, seven or eight daily Mon-Sat, four on Sun) are slower than the bus, but the section of line between Derry and Coleraine

is very scenic. Contact **Translink** (☎ 9066 6630) for more details.

DRAPERSTOWN
This market town lies at the eastern end of the Glenelly Valley and is the closest place of any size to the main Sperrin Mountains. The nearest tourist office is **Magherafelt Tourist Information Centre** (☎ 7963 1510; thebridewell@magherafelt.gov.uk; The Bridewell; 6 Church St; Magherafelt; open Mon-Sat).

Sleeping & Eating
Campers and caravaners should head to **Shepherd's Rest Campsite** (☎ 7962 8517; www.shepherdsrestpub.com; 220 Sixtowns Rd, camping per person £5) 4km southwest of Draperstown along the B47 towards Beaghmore stone circles. It's conveniently located beside The Shepherd's Rest, a family run country pub, and amenities include a garden cottage with cooking facilities.

There's B&B accommodation at the **Derrynoid Centre** (☎ 7962 9100; www .derrynoid.co.uk; Derrynoid; s/d £52/78), a large convention centre that also welcomes individuals. It's situated within a 250-acre forest, 2km northwest of the town centre along the B40. Facilities include an on-site restaurant, gym and spa.

In the heart of Draperstown, **Apparo Hotel & Restaurant** (☎ 7962 8100; www .apparohotel.com; 18 St. Patrick's St; s/d £55/85) is a new boutique hotel with a stylish interior and guest garden. The restaurant is rightly popular with residents and visitors alike.

Getting There & Away
Ulsterbus (☎ 9066 6630) services 403 and 112 both connect Draperstown to Magherafelt (£2.60, 30 minutes, seven daily Mon-Fri, four on Sat). From here there are onward connections, via Castledawson, to Belfast and Derry. Service 403 also heads to Omagh (£8, 1½ hours, twice daily Mon-Sat), where there are connections to most other destinations in the region.

ENNISKILLEN
pop 13,600
An attractively sited, prosperous town perched amid the web of waterways linking Upper and Lower Lough Erne, Enniskillen

is almost unavoidable en route to Cuilcagh mountain, Florence Court and the Marble Arch Caves.

The **Tourist Information Centre** (☎ 6632 3110; www.fermanagh.gov.uk; Wellington Rd; open daily Easter-Oct, Mon-Fri Nov-Easter) offers information about the county, as well as local OS maps. **Easons** (☎ 6632 4341; 10 High St) also stocks maps and local guidebooks.

Sleeping & Eating

The modern, purpose-built **Bridges Youth Hostel** (☎ 6634 0110; www.hini.org.uk; Belmore St; dm/s/tw £17/22/39) has a great location overlooking a river in the centre of town. Facilities include a restaurant, laundry and bike shed.

Rossole Guesthouse (☎ 6632 3462; 85 Sligo Rd; s/d from £30/50) is a modern, Georgian-style house overlooking a small lake. It's located 1km southwest of the town centre on the A4 Sligo road – along the route to Cuilcagh and Florence Court.

For a spot of country-house comfort, try **Mountview Guesthouse** (☎ 6632 3147; www.mountviewguests.com; 61 Irvinestown Rd; s/d from £45/65), a large, ivy-clad Victorian villa set in wooded grounds. It's just an 800m walk north of the town centre.

Westville Hotel (☎ 6632 0333; www.westvillehotel.co.uk; 14-20 Tempo Rd; s/d from £80/95) only opened in 2008, but its stylish interior, good food and welcoming staff quickly made it a firm favourite.

For evening meals, **Scoffs Wine Bar & Restaurant** (☎ 6634 2622; 17 Belmore St; mains £9-19) is a busy place with a modern vibe and an adventurous international menu.

Franco's (☎ 6632 4424; Queen Elizabeth Rd; mains £12-22, open lunch & dinner daily) is set in a former blacksmith's forge, and serves a range of Asian and seafood dishes as well as filling pizza and pasta.

Getting There & Away

The **Ulsterbus** (☎ 9066 6630) service 261 runs from Enniskillen to Belfast (£10, 2¼ hours, hourly Mon-Sat, two Sun). **Bus Éireann's** (☎ 071-916 0066) service 66 runs to Sligo (£8, 1½ hours, five daily Mon-Sat, two on Sun) via Belcoo, while service 30 heads to Dublin (£13, 2½ hours, seven daily Mon-Sat, four Sun).

FLORENCECOURT

A small, scattered village, Florencecourt has one guesthouse that can be used as a staging post for walkers completing the two-day Cuilcagh Way. The closest shops are in Belcoo (10km west), and the closest tourist office is in Enniskillen (13km north).

There is no public transport to the village.

Sleeping & Eating

The only B&B within walking distance is **Arch House** (☎ 6634 8452; www.archhouse.com; 59 Marble Arch Rd; s/d £40/60), a well-appointed guesthouse on a working farm, with an on-site **restaurant** (mains from £7.50). It's signed off the main road 500m west of Florencecourt village. If you're walking here from Florence Court estate, follow the Cuilcagh Way past the National Trust courtyard buildings and turn right along the exit driveway (the exit road from the Forest Service car park leads east along a more circuitous route).

GIANT'S CAUSEWAY

There are several accommodation options within a stone's-throw of the Giant's Causeway. These make useful bases for walkers finishing the coastal route late in the day, but advance booking is essential. The closest place with full amenities is Bushmills.

Sleeping & Eating

The closest B&B to the site is **Kal-Mar B&B** (☎ 2073 1101; 64a Causeway Rd, Bushmills; d £50), a small but friendly place in a traditional family home.

Just 200m along the road, **Ardtrabane House B&B** (☎ 2073 1007; www.ardtrabanehouse.co.uk; 66 Causeway Rd, Bushmills; s/d £45/65) is bright and modern. There are two rooms that can sleep four, and a footpath provides direct access to the causeway, less than a five-minute walk away.

The National Trust's **Causeway Hotel** (☎ 2073 1226; www.giants-causeway-hotel.com; 40 Causeway Rd, Bushmills; s/d £60/90) is unbeatable in terms of location – it's on the coast right beside the visitor centre and offers fine sunset views over the Atlantic.

For lunches and evening meals, try **The Nook** (☎ 2073 2993; 48 Causeway Rd, Bushmills; mains £7-16), at the turn-off to the visitor centre. The building dates from the 1850s and was originally used as a school house.

For details of transport to the Giants Causeway, see Getting to/from the Walk for the Causeway Coast Way Highlight (p269).

GLENARIFF

The valley of Glenariff stretches inland from Waterfoot, a village renowned for its 2km-long sandy beach. The nearest **tourist office** (☎ 2177 1180; 24 Mill St, Cushendall; open Mon-Sat Jul-Sep, Tue-Sat Oct-Jun) and the nearest ATM are in Cushendall, 3km north along the coast road.

Sleeping & Eating

There are several accommodation options within walking distance of Glenariff Forest Park.

The spacious, grassy terrain of **Glenariff Forest Caravan Park** (☎ 2955 6000; 98 Glenariff Rd; camping per person £11) is located along the A43, just 200m east of the park's main entrance. The tariff includes entry to the park.

There's hostel accommodation at **Ballyeamon Camping Barn** (☎ 2175 8451; www.ballyeamonbarn.com; 127 Ballyeamon Rd; dm £10). The attractive, cottage-like buildings are located along the B14, 1km north of its junction with the A43. A 1.5km walk southeast along the way-marked Moyle Way brings you to the main entrance of the forest park.

Dieskirt Farm (☎ 2177 1308; www.dieskirtfarm.co.uk; 104 Glen Rd; s/d £35/50) provides B&B on a secluded working farm. There are great mountain views and it's a walk of just over 1km to the park's eastern entrance beside Laragh Lodge.

Too far to walk but still just 6km from the park, the friendly **Sanda B&B** (☎ 2177 1785; www.sandabnb.com; 29 Kilmore Rd; s/d £35/50) is located just outside Waterfoot off the A43. Extras include a drying room and a pick-up service from the end of a walk.

The village of Waterfoot, at the seaward end of the glen, has a small supermarket.

Adjacent to the park's eastern entrance, on a side road off the A43, **Laragh Lodge** (☎ 2175 8221; 120 Glen Rd; mains £9-11; open lunch & dinner daily) offers a hearty menu in a cottage-style bar that dates back to the 1890s.

Getting There & Away

For details of bus services to Glenariff, see Getting to/from the Walk for Glenariff Forest Park (p272).

GLENARM

pop 600

Glenarm is the oldest village in the Glens of Antrim, and its neat Georgian houses contrast interestingly with its coastal location. The **tourist office** (☎ 2884 1705; 2 The Bridge; www.glenarmtourism.org.uk; open daily) is beside the bridge on the main road.

Sleeping & Eating

Accommodation in the village is limited to two B&Bs; for a wider choice, head 4km north along the coast road to the larger village of Carnlough.

A modern, homely place, **Castleview B&B** (☎ 2884 1587; 15B Altmore St; s/d £30/50) has two bedrooms, one a family room with four beds.

Riverside House B&B and Café (☎ 2884 1474; faith.pa@btopenworld.com; 13 Toberwine St; s/d £35/50) occupies a restored Georgian house in the heart of the old village. The cosy café downstairs also offers a relaxing place for lunch or afternoon tea.

In Carnlough, the best place to stay is the historic **Londonderry Arms Hotel** (☎ 2888 5255; www.glensofantrim.com; 20 Harbour Rd; s/d from £65/110). This former coaching inn dates from 1848 and has a wonderfully crusty, old-fashioned atmosphere. The **restaurant** (mains £15-20) specialises in local lamb and seafood.

Glenarm has two small supermarkets and several cafés for daytime snacks. The closest place for an evening meal is Carnlough, where you'll find a wide selection of eateries.

Getting There & Away

The **Ulsterbus** (☎ 9066 6630) Antrim Coaster service 252 links Glenarm to Coleraine, Bushmills (£9, 1¾ hours), the Giant's Causeway, Ballintoy, Waterfoot, Carnlough and Larne. There are two buses daily from Monday to Saturday, with one service continuing to/from Belfast's Europa Bus Centre (£7, one hour 35 minutes).

Service 162 also runs from Glenarm to Carnlough and Larne (£3.30, 25 minutes, at least six daily Mon-Sat).

GORTIN

The village of Gortin lies at the southwestern corner of the Sperrin Mountains. It's around 20km from the Sawel and Dart walk, but has the closest hostel accommodation. The nearest tourist office is **Omagh Tourist Information Centre** (☎ 8224 7831; tourism@omagh.gov.uk; Strule Arts Centre, Bridge St, Omagh; open Mon-Sat Apr-Sep, Mon-Fri Oct-Mar), 15km south.

Sleeping & Eating

The main reason for staying in Gortin is **Gortin Accommodation Suite** (☎ 8164 8346; www.gortin.net; 62 Main St; dm/f £10/50), a modern outdoor activity centre in the middle of the village. As well as dorms, the centre has en-suite family rooms with one double and two single beds.

In Main St you'll find several small supermarkets, along with various options for evening meals. Try **Foothills Bar & Restaurant** (☎ 8164 8157; 16 Main St; mains from £10) for local produce in a contemporary setting.

Getting There & Away

The **Ulsterbus** (☎ 9066 6630) service 403, known as the Sperrin Rambler, runs between Gortin and Omagh (£3, 25 minutes, twice daily Mon-Sat). Connections can be made in Omagh for Belfast, Derry and most other destinations in the region.

LIMAVADY

pop 12,000

Limavady is a quiet and prosperous town whose best feature is the lovely Roe Valley Country Park, where beautiful riverside walks stretch for 5km on either side of the River Roe. It is also the closest place of significant size to the cliffs of Binevenagh.

The **tourist office** (☎ 7776 0307; tourism @limavady.gov.uk; 7 Connell St; open Mon-Sat May-Sep, Mon-Fri Oct-Apr) is northeast of the town centre in the Limavady Borough Council Offices.

Sleeping & Eating

A long-established hotel and pub dating from 1875, the central **Alexander Arms Hotel** (☎ 7776 3443; 34 Main St; s/d £30/50) is now a friendly, family-run place that also serves pub grub and restaurant meals.

The closest accommodation to Binevenagh is **Ballyhenry House** (☎ 7772 2657; www.ballyhenry.co.uk; 172 Seacoast Rd; s/d £35/60). It lies at the heart of a 350-acre working farm and extras include a laundry, drying room and guided tours of the farm. The house dates from 1898 and is located off the B69 around 5km north of Limavady.

The most luxurious place to stay is **Radisson SAS Roe Park Resort** (☎ 7772 2222; www.radissonroepark.com; Roe Park; s/d from £75/100), a modern hotel complex including an 18-hole golf course and treatment spa. The hotel is located off the A2 Derry road, 1.5km from the town centre.

There are plenty of supermarkets and eateries around Limavady town centre.

The top spot for evening meals is **Lime Tree** (☎ 7776 4300; 60 Catherine St; mains £15-20; open for dinner Tue-Sat). Dishes promote local produce and an early-bird menu (two/three courses £13.50/16.50) is also available before 7pm Tuesday to Friday.

Getting There & Away

Ulsterbus (☎ 9066 6630) service 143 runs between Derry and Limavady (£4.50, one hour 50 minutes, hourly Mon-Fri, eight on Sat, four on Sun). There's no direct bus to Belfast, but service 146 goes to Dungiven (£3, 40 minutes, five daily Mon-Fri), where you can get a onward connection to Belfast.

LISBURN

pop 110,000

The southwestern fringes of Belfast extend as far as the rapidly growing Lisburn (*Lios na gCearrbhach*) – Northern Ireland's third-largest city, 12km southwest of the city centre. Lisburn is known for its shopping, heritage and horse racing. **Lisburn Tourist Information Centre** (9266 0038; Lisburn Sq; 9.30am-5pm Mon-Sat) is on the town's main square.

Getting There & Away

Buses 523, 530 and 532 from Belfast's Upper Queen St go to Lisburn (£2.60, 40 minutes, half-hourly Mon-Fri, hourly Sat & Sun), or catch the train (£3.50, 30 minutes, at least half-hourly Mon-Sat, hourly Sun) from either Belfast Central or Great Victoria St Stations.

NEWCASTLE

pop 7500

This coastal town combines Victorian architecture with modern facilities such as a new promenade, elegant sculptures and trendy coffee shops. Its natural setting between a 5km-long beach and Slieve Donard, Northern Ireland's highest mountain, is hard to beat, and it's a logical gateway to the Mourne Mountains.

Information Sources

The town's **Tourist Information Centre** (☎ 4372 2222; newcastle.tic@downdc .gov.uk; 10-14 Central Promenade; open daily) sells walking maps and provides all the normal tourist guidance. For expert advice on the mountains and trails themselves, head to the **Mourne Heritage Trust** (☎ 4372 4059; www.mournelive.com; 87 Central Promenade; open Mon-Fri). As well as selling maps and books, there are regular guided walks during the summer.

For outdoor equipment and camping supplies, head to **Hill Trekker** (☎ 4372 3842; 115 Central Promenade; open Tue-Sun), situated along the coast road at the southern end of town.

Sleeping

For campers there are grassy pitches and good facilities at spacious **Tollymore Forest Caravan Park** (☎ 4372 2428; 176 Tullybranigan Rd; campsites £9-13). The park is 3km northwest of Newcastle – you can walk there (along Bryansford Ave and Bryansford Rd) in 45 minutes from the town centre. The tariff includes entry to the surrounding forest park.

Just a few minutes' walk from the bus station, **Newcastle Youth Hostel** (☎ 4372 2133; www.hini.org.uk; 30 Downs Rd; dm £14; open daily Mar-Oct, Fri & Sat only Nov & Dec) is housed in an attractive 19th-century villa with sea views.

If you prefer a B&B, try **Briers Country House** (☎ 4372 4347; www.thebriers.co.uk; 39 Middle Tollymore Rd; s/d from £40/60). Offering peaceful farmhouse accommodation and great views of the Mournes, Briers is 1.5km northwest of the town centre (signposted off the road between Newcastle and Bryansford). Evening meals are available by prior arrangement.

Alternatively, at **Beach House** (☎ 4372 2345; beachhouse22@tiscali.co.uk; 22 Downs Rd; s/d £50/90), you can enjoy sea views with your breakfast. The elegant Victorian B&B has three rooms and a communal balcony overlooking the beach.

If only the best will do, **Slieve Donard Resort & Spa** (☎ 4372 3681; www.hastings hotels.com; Downs Rd; s/d from £80/100) is a magnificent, Victorian red-brick pile overlooking the beach. Established in 1897, it has been recently refurbished and equipped with a luxurious spa.

Eating

There's a wide range of restaurants and take aways around the town centre, as well as several supermarkets. **Maud's** (☎ 4372 6184; 106 Main St; mains £3-7) is a bright, modern café with stunning views that serves tasty food from breakfast to dinner daily.

Mourne Café (☎ 4372 6401; 107 Central Promenade; mains £6-8; open lunch & dinner daily) is a new, informal café that dishes up a kids menu (mains £5) as well as seafood chowder or beer-battered haddock and chips for the adults.

Getting There & Away

Newcastle bus station is situated off the northern end of Main St on Railway St. **Ulsterbus** (☎ 9066 6630) service 20 runs between Newcastle and Belfast's Europa Bus Centre (£7, 1¼ hours, hourly Mon-Sat, seven on Sun).

Newcastle can also be reached from Newry, which is on the Belfast–Dublin train line. From Newry bus station, take bus No 240 to Newcastle (£5, 50 minutes, six daily Mon-Sat, two on Sun) via Hilltown.

PORTAFERRY

pop 3300

Portaferry is a neat huddle of streets at the northern mouth of Strangford Lough. Frequent ferry services across the Narrows make it as convenient as Strangford village for walkers wanting to explore Castle Ward, with the added excitement of a boat trip to reach the start of the route.

The town's **tourist information centre** (☎ 4272 9882; tourism.portaferry@ards -council.gov.uk; Castle St; open daily Easter-Sep) is in a restored stable near the tower house.

Sleeping & Eating

Occupying a Victorian villa in a superb seafront location opposite the ferry slipway, **Barholm** (☎ 4272 9598; www.barholm portaferry.co.uk; 11 The Strand; dm/s/d £14/18/40) offers both hostel-style and B&B accommodation. Be sure to book ahead.

Fiddler's Green (☎ 4272 8393; www.fid dlersgreenportaferry.com; 10-12 Church St; s/d £46/65) is a popular pub and restaurant that also provides B&B in four homely rooms. The bar downstairs has traditional music sessions every weekend.

A charming seafront hotel with elegant, Georgian rooms, **Portaferry Hotel** (☎ 4272 8231; www.portaferryhotel.com; 10 The Strand; s/d £65/110) also has a family-friendly **restaurant** (mains £15-19) with a French-influenced menu.

Getting There & Away

Ulsterbus (☎ 9066 6630) services 9, 509, 10 and 510 travel between Portaferry and Belfast (£6, 1¼ hours, 12 daily Mon-Sat, four on Sun).

The **ferry** (☎ 4488 1637) plies the 700m-wide strait between Portaferry and Strangford (10 minutes, every half-hour). The one-way/same-day return fares are £5.30/8.50 for a car and driver, and £1.10/1.80 for car passengers and pedestrians.

STRANGFORD

pop 600

This picturesque fishing village is dominated by a 16th-century tower house and lies at the southern mouth of Strangford Lough. Accommodation is limited, but there's a wider choice in Portaferry, a short ferry journey north across the Narrows.

Sleeping & Eating

Campers should head to **Castle Ward Caravan Park** (☎ 4488 1204; 19 Castle Ward Rd; site & two adults £7.50/17.50 members/non-members; open mid-Mar–Sep). The entrance to this simple, wooded ground is signed from the A25 just 1km southwest of Strangford village, and the tariff includes entry to the National Trust estate.

Just around the corner from the ferry slipway, **Cuan** (☎ 4488 1222; www.the cuan.com; the Square; s/d £53/85, mains £9-15) has nine neat, comfortable rooms and an atmospheric restaurant serving lunches and dinners of local seafood, lamb and beef.

Alternatively, **Lobster Pot** (☎ 4488 1288; 9-11 the Square; bar meals £6-11, restaurant mains £10-17) is a charmingly old-fashioned pub overlooking the harbour, with a smart, modern bistro that serves excellent seafood.

Getting There & Away

Ulsterbus (☎ 9066 6630) service 16 runs between Strangford and Downpatrick (£3, 30 minutes, at least six Mon-Sat). From Downpatrick there are frequent onward connections to places such as Belfast and Newcastle.

For details of the ferry service across the Narrows, see Getting There & Away for Portaferry.

Walkers Directory

ACCOMMODATION

Ireland's towns and cities generally offer a great array of accommodation, ranging from plush hotels to cheap but friendly hostels. In more remote areas the choice is often restricted to B&Bs, with the odd camping ground or hostel thrown in for good measure.

For each walk we suggest a list of places to stay: information that is gathered under the Towns & Facilities heading at the end of each regional chapter. The list is not exclusive – they're usually the places we feel are best or most useful to hikers. We've also endeavoured to highlight properties that are committed to eco-responsibility. In many areas you'll find other options by contacting the regional tourist office.

In the listings, we begin by detailing the budget options (under €30/£20 per person),

then offer a selection of midrange places (€30-60 or £20-40 per person). Sometimes we also recommend places over €60/£40, either because there isn't a great choice in lower price bands, or because the quality of the establishment necessitates its inclusion. Rates are per 'room' per night, unless otherwise stated. Where a range of prices is given, it refers to rates for different rooms during high season.

Room prices in Dublin are disproportionately high and can be double what you would pay elsewhere in the country.

No matter where you are in the country, it's always best to book ahead in peak season (Apr-Sep). Fáilte Ireland and the Northern Ireland Tourist Board (NITB) will book serviced accommodation for a fee of €4/£2. Make telephone bookings through their booking system **Gulliver Ireland** (in Ireland ☎ 1850 61 61 61, in UK ☎ 0800 096 8644, in the USA ☎ 1 888 827 3028, from everywhere else insert freephone prefix before ☎ 6686 6866).

Fáilte Ireland and the NITB also publish annual accommodation guides detailing the camping grounds, B&Bs, guesthouses and hotels within their jurisdiction, and it's well worth getting hold of relevant guides to help you plan your trip. See Tourist Information for contact details, p303.

Camping & Caravan Parks

Though camping grounds are understandably absent from Ireland's city centres, you'll generally find a good sprinkling in more rural areas, especially near the coast and in popular holiday regions. Many cater mainly for caravans, but most also provide grassy spaces for pitching tents. Some hostels also offer camping space for tents along with use of house facilities, which makes them better value than the main camping grounds. At commercial parks the cost is typically somewhere between €12 and €22 (£8 and £15) for a site and two people, with electricity for caravans charged at about €4/£3 extra. Most parks only open from Easter to the end of September or October.

For more information on Ireland's camping grounds, contact the **Irish Caravan & Camping Council** (www.camping -ireland.ie; PO Box 4443, Dublin 2). Their website lists a wide range of graded sites in both the Republic of Ireland and Northern Ireland, and also has links to places that hire camper vans.

WILD CAMPING

Though the lack of multiday wilderness routes means wild camping is not as common in Ireland as in many countries, that doesn't mean it's entirely impossible. Providing you are not on private land and are well away from the public gaze, few will ever know if you spend a night outdoors. Discretion is paramount so mountain tops and remote stretches of coastline are probably the best – as well as the most rewarding – places to sleep under the stars. In more accessible areas such as popular beaches you will often see notices forbidding camping or overnight parking. Camping is also forbidden within Ireland's national parks.

See p34 for guidelines for responsible wilderness camping.

PRACTICALITIES

- Catch up on new walking routes, news and events with Ireland's top outdoor magazine, *Walking World Ireland* (www .walkingworldireland.com; €4.85/£3.95).

- The Republic of Ireland uses the metric system for weights, measures, speed limits and signposting – everything, in fact, except the good old pint in the pub.

- Northern Ireland uses a mixture of metric and imperial systems – road signs are in miles, but OS mapping is in kilometres.

- Plug appliances into the three flat pin sockets for (220V, 50Hz AC) power supply.

- Tune into RTE Radio One (88-90 FM or 567/729 MW) for culture and politics; Today FM (100-103 FM) for pop, rock and alternative music; or Newstalk 106-108 (106-108 FM) for commercial daytime current affairs and chitchat.

Guesthouses & B&Bs

Bed and breakfasts (B&Bs) and guesthouses are a major industry in many Irish towns and villages. B&Bs are generally run from small, family houses with fewer than five bedrooms. Standards vary enormously, but most have some bedrooms with bathroom at a cost of roughly €35 to €40 (£23-28) per person per night. In luxurious B&Bs, expect to pay €55 (£38) or more per person. Facilities in budget B&Bs may be very limited: TVs, telephones, kettles and the like are restricted to midrange and top-end establishments. Note that outside big cities, most B&Bs only accept cash.

Guesthouses are much like upmarket B&Bs. The difference lies in their size, with guesthouses generally having between six and 30 bedrooms. Prices vary enormously according to the standard but the minimum you can expect to pay is €35 (£23) per person (€40 in Dublin), and up to about €100 (£70) in popular areas. The majority of guesthouses are unlicensed but many have restaurants and good facilities, and can accept credit-card payment.

Single supplements are generally charged for sole occupancy of double rooms. No matter where you stay, a hearty cooked breakfast is almost always included in the price, along with lighter, continental-style alternatives.

Hostels

An Óige (☎ 01-830 4555; www.irelandyha .org; 61 Mountjoy St, Dublin 7; Mon-Fri) and **Hostelling International Northern Ireland** (HINI; ☎ 028-9032 4733; www .hini.org.uk; 22-32 Donegall Rd, Belfast BT12 5JN; daily) are the two associations that belong to Hostelling International (HI) – what used to be known as the Youth Hostel Association. An Óige has 23 hostels scattered around the Republic and HINI has six in the North. Some old-fashioned hostels still exist in remote areas – one or two even lack electricity – but many HI establishments have been modernised, and the most up-to-date now resemble guest houses, complete with ensuite bedrooms. To stay at a HI hostel you need to be a member or pay a supplement. Some hostels close between about 10am and 5pm while others are open all day, and a night-time curfew may also apply.

ACCOMMODATION PRICES & THE RECESSION

At the time of writing, the global financial downturn had hit Irish tourism very hard with the industry in the throes of its biggest crisis in recent history – the result being that price structuring is not nearly as predictable as it was previously. To date, B&B rates have remained more or less steady, but many hoteliers – particularly at the upper end of the scale – are in a desperate struggle to stay alive. Consequently, they're doing the previously unthinkable in an effort to sell rooms, dramatically slashing rates and offering a plethora of incentive deals to get you into their hotels: free add-ons like dinners and treatments are increasingly standard, as are three-nights-for-the-price-of-two offers.

Rack rates at the top hotels are no longer to be trusted and the standard prices quoted on the brochure or the website have become increasingly pie-in-the-sky – it's quite the norm these days to pay half the quoted rate in some of the country's top properties, particularly out of season. The key, however, is to ask: when making a booking, don't settle for the first rate quoted and be sure to ask for a better deal. More often than not, you'll get one.

Ireland also has a large number of independent hostels, some of which are excellent, while others are higher on character than facilities. **Independent Holiday Hostels of Ireland** (IHH; ☎ 01-836 4700; www.hostels-ireland.com; 57 Lower Gardiner St, Dublin 1) and **Independent Hostel Owners of Ireland** (IHO; ☎ 074-973 0130; www.holidayhound.com/ihi; Dooey Hostel, Glencolumbcille, Co Donegal) are both umbrella associations that do their best to offer a reliable standard of accommodation.

The prices quoted in this book for hostel accommodation are for those aged over 18. A dorm bed in high season generally costs from €13 to €25 (£8–16). Many hostels also offer family rooms or smaller private rooms for a small supplement.

Hotels

The range of hotels in Ireland covers everything from country pubs and stately mansions to the anonymous, city-based establishments belonging to international chains. Prices fluctuate accordingly, and may be either on a room-only basis or may include breakfast. You may even find that some hotels offer better rates than guesthouses. In city hotels cheaper rates may apply at weekends, when their main corporate clients disappear. Many hotels across the country offer packages for more than one night's stay including dinner, especially in low season, and it's always worth asking about special deals at the time of booking.

BUSINESS HOURS

The standard business hours are generally the same for both the Republic and Northern Ireland and are shown below, with any variations noted:

Banks 10am to 4pm (to 5pm Thu) Monday to Friday

Offices 9am to 5pm Monday to Friday

Post Offices Northern Ireland 9am to 5.30pm Monday to Friday, 9am to 12.30pm Saturday; Republic 9am to 6pm Monday to Friday, 9am to 1pm Saturday. Smaller post offices may close at lunch and one day a week.

Pubs Northern Ireland 11.30am to 11pm Monday to Saturday, 12.30pm to 10pm Sunday. Pubs with late licences open until 1am Monday to Saturday, and midnight Sunday; Republic 10.30am to 11.30pm Monday to Thursday, 10.30am to 12.30am Friday and Saturday, noon to 11pm Sunday (30 min 'drinking up' time allowed). Pubs with bar extensions open to 2.30am Thursday to Saturday; closed Christmas Day and Good Friday.

Restaurants Noon to 10.30pm; many close one day of the week.

Shops 9am to 5.30pm or 6pm Monday to Saturday (until 8pm on Thu and sometimes Fri), noon to 6pm Sunday in bigger towns only. Shops in rural towns may close at lunch and one day a week.

Tourist Offices 9am to 5pm Monday to Friday, 9am to 1pm Saturday. Many extend their hours in summer, and open fewer hours/days or close October to April.

CHILDREN

Walking with your children is very different from walking as you knew it before they came along. Fortunately if you can adjust happily to living with children, you'll probably also enjoy walking with them.

It's often said that kids slow you down, and that's never truer than when you set out on a walk. There's an age when children go at exactly your pace because you're carrying them all the way (a good backpack built for the purpose is worth its weight in chocolate), but their increasing weight, and a growing determination to get down and do everything for themselves, mean that phase soon passes. Once your first child is too big or too independent for the backpack, you simply have to scale down your expectations of distance and speed.

This is when the fun really starts. No longer another item to be carried – at least, not all the time – a walking child must be factored into your planning at the most basic level. Rather than get partway into a walk and ask yourself in desperation, 'Why are we doing this?', make this the first question you ask. While walking driven by statistics – kilometres covered and peaks bagged – isn't likely to work with kids, other important goals can surface: fun and a sense of something accomplished together; joy in the wonders of the natural world.

Easy and small is a good way to start – you can always try something harder next time. Too hard and what should be fun can become an ordeal for all – especially the child.

Don't overlook time for play. A game of hide and seek during lunch might well be the highlight of your child's day on the track. A few simple toys or a favourite book brought along can make a huge difference. Play can also transform the walking itself; a simple stroll in the bush becomes a bear hunt in an enchanted forest.

For the sake of sanity, or at least increased satisfaction, you may also need to plan for some walking 'without' children. This is harder to arrange away from home and the regular network of family, friends, babysitters, etc. Child-minding services are often accessible to travellers, although some parents will feel uncomfortable leaving kids with unfamiliar carers.

There's another alternative; if you're desperate to stretch the legs and enjoy some terrain that's simply beyond you as a family, split up for a few hours. Find a short but suitably challenging walk – maybe a peak close to a town or road, or a side trip – and take turns. Consider whether you could take your walking holiday with another young family. This enlarges the pool of both hikers and carers, and gives the kids company their own age.

Among the walks described in this book, the following are most suitable for children:

Dublin Area Phoenix Park (p38), Bray Head (p45), Howth Peninsula (p43), Great Sugar Loaf (p47)
Southeast Part of the Barrow Way Highlight (p72)
Southwest Muckross (p113), Torc Mountain (p116), Derrynane Coastal Circuit (p120)
Atlantic Islands Tory Island (p146), Inisheer (p156), part of the Great Blasket Island (p158), part of the Dursey Island (p161)
Central West Killary Harbour (p189), Diamond Hill (p190)
Northwest Ards (p216), part of the Glencolmcille Circuit (p230)
Northern Ireland Cave Hill (p243), part of the North Down Coastal Path (p245), River Lagan (p247), Castle Ward (p250), part of the Causeway Coast Way Highlight (p268), Glenariff Forest Park (p271)

Practicalities

On the whole you'll find that people in Ireland go out of their way to cater for you and your children. Most hotels and some B&Bs provide cots at no extra charge, and almost all restaurants have high chairs. Note that officially children are only allowed in pubs until 7pm. Car seats (around €50/£33 per week) are mandatory for children in hire cars between the ages of nine months and four years. Bring your own seat for infants under about nine months as only larger forward-facing child seats are generally available. Remember not to place baby seats in the front if the car has an airbag.

Nappy-changing facilities can generally be found in public conveniences in either the women's or disabled toilets.

Ireland has one of the lowest rates of breastfeeding in the world; nevertheless you should be able to feed your baby in all but a few public places without jaws dropping.

Two great websites are www.eumom .ie for pregnant women and parents with young children, and www.babygoes2.com, which is an excellent travel site about family-friendly accommodation worldwide.

For further general information, also see the latest edition of Lonely Planet's *Travel with Children*.

CLIMATE

Thanks to the moderating effect of the Atlantic Gulf Stream, Ireland's climate is relatively mild for its latitude, with a mean annual temperature of around 10°C. The temperature drops below freezing only intermittently during winter, and snow is scarce at low altitudes – perhaps one or two brief flurries a year. Even higher up, the mountains rarely carry snow for very long. Ranges away from the west coast tend to be

snowcapped for longest, with the Wicklow Mountains and the Mournes holding on to their white cloaks for up to two weeks in midwinter.

The coldest months are January and February, when daily temperatures range from 4° to 8°C, with 7°C the average. Wind chill is perhaps the biggest danger to hikers at this time. The combination of low temperatures and strong winds can catch people out, especially on mountain routes. As a rule the air temperature drops 2° to 3°C for every 300m of height gained. Add even a moderate wind chill factor and it soon becomes obvious that several layers of insulation might be needed to keep warm.

In summer, temperatures during the day are a comfortable 15° to 20°C. During the warmest months, July and August, the average is 16°C. A hot summer's day in Ireland is 22° to 24°C, although it can sometimes reach 30°C. There are about 18 hours of daylight

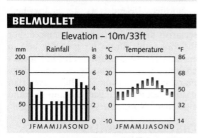

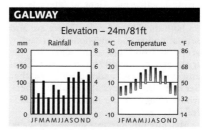

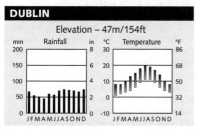

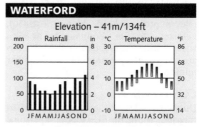

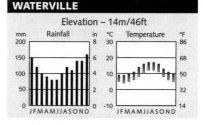

daily during July and August and it's only truly dark after about 11pm.

Rainfall varies markedly from west to east. The soggiest places in the southwest endure as many as 270 days of rainfall a year, whereas the dry southeast enjoys a more continental climate and has barely half that amount.

One thing you can be sure of about Irish weather is how little you can be sure of. It may be shirtsleeves and sunglasses in February, but winter woollies in May. Changes can happen quickly too, so it pays to always be prepared for 'four seasons in one day'.

For more information about when to visit Ireland, see p22.

Weather Information

Hikers in Ireland should never underestimate the changeability of the weather, and make sure to check the forecast before heading out. General forecasts are available following the main news bulletins on both the TV and radio. There are also several online and telephone information services. Good places to start are the Irish meteorological service, **Met Éireann** (www.met.ie) and the **BBC Weather Service** (http://news.bbc.co.uk/weather), whose charts for the British Isles include Ireland.

Met Éireann forecasts are also available via telephone through their **Weatherdial** service – call ☎ 1550-123 followed by the relevant provincial code: Munster (☎ 850), Leinster (☎ 851), Connaught (☎ 852), Ulster (☎ 853) and Dublin (☎ 854). Calls are charged at a premium rate of €0.95 per minute.

CUSTOMS

Duty-free sales are not available when travelling within the EU. Goods for personal consumption bought in and exported within the EU incur no additional taxes, if duty has been paid somewhere in the EU. Over certain limits you may have to show that they are for personal use. The amounts that officially constitute personal use are 3200 cigarettes (or 400 cigarillos, 200 cigars or 3kg of tobacco) and either 10L of spirits, 20L of fortified wine, 60L of sparkling wine, 90L of still wine or 110L of beer. There's no customs inspection apart from those concerned with drugs and national security.

Travellers coming from outside the EU are allowed to import duty free 200 cigarettes, 1L of spirits or 2L of wine, 60ml of perfume and 250ml of *eau de toilette*.

Dogs and cats from anywhere outside Ireland and the UK are subject to strict quarantine laws. The EU Pet Travel Scheme, whereby animals are fitted with a microchip, vaccinated against rabies and blood tested six months 'prior' to entry, is in force in the UK and the Republic of Ireland. No preparation or documentation is necessary for the movement of pets directly between the UK and the Republic. Contact the **Department of Agriculture, Food & Rural Development** (☎ 01-607 2000) in Dublin for further details.

DANGERS & ANNOYANCES

Ireland is safer than most countries in Europe, but normal precautions should be observed. Crime is at its worst in the big cities, where pickpockets, thieves, and drug-related incidents can be common.

Some parts of the country are notorious for car break-ins, and insurance policies often don't cover losses from cars. If you're leaving a vehicle for several hours while you complete a walk, be especially cautious and make sure to leave nothing of value inside.

Northern Ireland is as safe as anywhere else, but there are still areas where the sectarian divide is bitterly pronounced. For the foreseeable future, it's probably best to ensure your visit to Northern Ireland doesn't coincide with the climax of the Orange marching season on 12 July; sectarian passions are usually inflamed at this time and even many Northerners leave the province.

DISCOUNT CARDS
Heritage Discounts

In the Republic, the **Heritage Card** (☎ 01-647 6587; www.heritageireland.com; Visitor Services, 51 St Stephen's Green, Dublin 2; child/student/senior/adult/family €8/16/21/55) entitles you to free access to over 75 sites for one year.

In Northern Ireland, **National Trust Membership** (☎ 0870 458 4000; www .nationaltrust.org.uk; under 25/adult/family £21.50/47.50/82; Membership Dept, PO Box

39, Warrington WA5 7WD, UK) entitles you to free admission to its 18 properties in Northern Ireland, but only really makes financial sense if you're touring its English sites too. It's cheaper to join online.

Student & Youth Cards

The **International Student Identity Card** (ISIC; www.isiccard.com) attracts discounts on transport, commercial goods and services, and admission to theatres, cinemas, museums and sights.

The **International Youth Travel Card** (IYTC; www.isiccard.com) and **European Youth Card** (Euro<26 card; www.euro26 .org) offer similar discounts for nonstudents under 26. All these cards are issued by hostelling organisations, student unions and student travel agencies.

EMBASSIES & CONSULATES
Irish Embassies & Consulates
REPUBLIC OF IRELAND DIPLOMATIC OFFICES OVERSEAS

Australia (☎ 02-6273 3022; www.embassy ofireland.au.com; 20 Arkana St, Yarralumla, Canberra, ACT 2600)

Canada (☎ 613-233 6281; www.embassy ofireland.ca; 130 Albert St, Suite 1105, Ottawa, Ontario K1P 5G4)

France (☎ 01 44 17 67 00; www.embassy ofireland.fr; 4 rue Rude, 75116 Paris)

Germany (☎ 030-220 720; Friedrichstrasse 200, 10117 Berlin)

Italy (☎ 06 697 9121; www.embassyof ireland.it; Piazza di Campitelli 3, 00186 Rome)

Netherlands (☎ 070-363 09 93; www.em bassyofireland.nl; Dr Kuyperstraat 9, 2514 BA The Hague)

New Zealand (☎ 09-977 2256; consul @ireland.co.nz; Level 7, Citibank Bldg, 23 Customs St East, Auckland)

UK (*Embassy* ☎ 020-7235 2171; www .embassyofireland.co.uk; 17 Grosvenor Pl, London SW1X 7HR; *Consulate* ☎ 0131-226 7711; www.irishconsulatescotland .co.uk; 16 Randolph Cres, Edinburgh EH3 6TT; *Consulate* ☎ 029-2066 2000; Brunel House, 2 Fitzalan Rd, Cardiff CF24 0EB)

USA (☎ 202-462 3939; www.embassy ofireland.org; 2234 Massachusetts Ave, NW, Washington, DC 20008) There are also consulates in Boston, Chicago, New York and San Francisco.

UK (FOR NORTHERN IRELAND) DIPLOMATIC OFFICES OVERSEAS

Australia (☎ 02-6270 6666; www.ukin australia.fco.gov.uk; Commonwealth Ave, Yarralumla, Canberra, ACT 2600)

Canada (☎ 613-237 1530; www.ukin canada.fco.gov.uk; 80 Elgin St, Ottawa, Ontario K1P 5K7)

France (☎ 01 44 51 31 00; www.ukinfrance .fco.gov.uk; 35 rue du Faubourg St Honoré, 75383 Paris)

Germany (☎ 030-204 570; www.ukin germany.fco.gov.uk; Wilhelmstrasse 70, 10117 Berlin)

Italy (☎ 06 4220 0001; www.ukinitaly.fco .gov.uk; Via XX Settembre 80a, 00187 Rome)

Netherlands (☎ 070-427 04 27; www.ukin nl.fco.gov.uk; Lange Voorhout 10, 2514 ED The Hague)

New Zealand (☎ 04-9242888; www.ukinnew zealand.fco.gov.uk; 44 Hill St, Wellington)

USA (☎ 202-588 6500; www.ukinusa.fco .gov.uk; 3100 Massachusetts Ave NW, Washington, DC 20008)

Embassies & Consulates in Ireland

If you're even remotely responsible for any kind of trouble, your country's embassy won't be of any help to you – you're bound by Irish (and in the North, British) law. In genuine emergencies you might get some assistance: a free ticket is exceedingly unlikely but embassies might assist you with getting a new passport.

The following countries have embassies in Dublin:

Australia (☎ 01-664 5300; www.ireland .embassy.gov.au; 7th fl, Fitzwilton House, Wilton Tce, Dublin 2)

Canada (☎ 01-234 4000; 7-8 Wilton Tce, Dublin 2)

France (☎ 01-277 5000; www.ambafrance .ie; 36 Ailesbury Rd, Dublin 4)

Germany (☎ 01-269 3011; www.dublin .diplo.de; 31 Trimleston Ave, Booterstown, Blackrock, Co Dublin)

Italy (☎ 01-660 1744; www.ambdublin .esteri.it; 63-65 Northumberland Rd, Ballsbridge, Dublin 4)

Netherlands (☎ 01-269 3444; www.nether landsembassy.ie; 160 Merrion Rd, Ballsbridge, Dublin 4)

UK (☎ 01-205 3700; www.britishembassy .ie; 29 Merrion Rd, Ballsbridge, Dublin 4)
USA (☎ 01-668 8777; www.usembassy.ie; 42 Elgin Rd, Ballsbridge, Dublin 4)

The following countries have consular representation in Northern Ireland:

Germany (☎ 028-9024 4113; Chamber of Commerce House, 22 Great Victoria St, Belfast)
Netherlands (☎ 028-9077 9088; c/o All-Route Shipping Ltd, 14-16 West Bank Rd, Belfast)
USA (☎ 028-9038 6100; Danesfort House, 223 Stranmillis Rd, Belfast)

FESTIVALS & EVENTS

There are literally hundreds of festivals held in Ireland throughout the year, the largest of which is St Patrick's Day on 17th March. Local tourist offices can provide information about other events in their region. The Association of Irish Festival Events (AOIFE) also maintains a very useful website at www.aoifeonline.com; www.art .ie is worth perusing too.

Walking Festivals

Ireland hosts around 30 walking festivals each year, which last from two to four days each. Festivals take place all round the country and offer an opportunity to walk and socialise with like-minded enthusiasts. For a calendar of events, see the Walking Festival Calendar boxed text on p295.

FOOD

Our café and restaurant listings appear in order of price with the cheapest appearing first. In most towns you can expect to find at least one good bistro, café or restaurant where you can eat well for around €20/£15. Bar meals are less expensive (generally ranging from €10/£6 to €20/£15), and can be just as interesting, with an emphasis on fresh produce and hearty servings.

Vegetarians are almost universally catered for.

Local Food & Drink

Traditional Irish cuisine tends to follow the pattern of meat or fish, potatoes and vegetables, presented in a variety of

---

WALKING CLUBS & ASSOCIATIONS

The following umbrella organisations are good starting points for locating walking clubs, routes and events around the country:

Countryside Access & Activities Network (CAAN; ☎ 028-9030 3930; www.countryside recreation.com; The Stableyard, Barnett's Demesne, Belfast) A network organisation that manages outdoor activities in Northern Ireland. Their responsibilities include the administration of the Waymarked Ways in the province, and maintenance of the website www.hikeni.com, where you'll find descriptions of numerous walking routes around the region.

Mountaineering Ireland (☎ 01-625 1115; www.mountaineering.ie) Formerly known as the Mountaineering Council of Ireland, this is the representative body for hill hikers and climbers in Ireland. It takes a prominent role in access, safety and environmental matters, and also publishes the quarterly magazine *Irish Mountain Log*. Their website is full of useful information and links.

National Waymarked Ways Advisory Committee (NWWAC; ☎ 01-860 8823; www.hikeireland .ie; Irish Sports Council, Top fl, Block A Westend Office Park, Blanchardstown, Dublin 15) This group is responsible for the maintenance and development of Waymarked Ways in the Republic of Ireland. Their website includes descriptions of all the Waymarked Ways in the jurisdiction.

Ulster Federation of Rambling Clubs (www.ufrc-online.co.uk; 4 Woodvale Park, Dungannon) Acts as a governing body for Northern Irish rambling clubs and promotes the interests of hikers in the region. Amongst a host of walking-related information, their website includes contact details and activity programs for some 30 walking clubs across the North.

Walkers Association of Ireland (www.walkersassociation.ie) An online forum for hill hikers and ramblers all over Ireland. The website includes details of public walking events as well as links to walking clubs and associations from around the country.

WALKING FESTIVAL CALENDAR

The precise dates of Ireland's walking festivals vary from year to year, but most take place over weekends and stay around the same month. The list below indicates the main festivals.

FESTIVAL	COUNTY	CONTACT
MARCH		
Tain	Louth	Louth County Council (☎ 042-933 5457; www.louthcoco.ie)
Ardara	Donegal	Ardara Hiking Festival (☎ 074-954 1830; www.ardara.ie)
APRIL		
North Leitrim Glens	Leitrim	Holey Soles Hillwalking Club (☎ 086 841 8843; norlemglens@eircom.net)
MAY		
Achill	Mayo	Achill Tourism (☎ 098-47353; www.achilltourism.com)
Glen of Aherlow	Tipperary	Glen of Aherlow Fáilte Society (☎ 062-56331; www.aherlow.com)
Ballyhoura International	Limerick	Ballyhoura Fáilte (☎ 063-91300; www.ballyhouracountry.com)
Slieve Bloom	Offaly	Slieve Bloom Rural Development Co-operative (☎ 086 278 9147; www.slievebloom.ie)
West Cork	Cork	West Cork Tourism (☎ 086 898 709; www.westcork.ie)
Sliabh an Iarainn	Leitrim	Arigna Leader (☎ 071-964 1569; www.hikingwildireland.com)
JUNE		
Mourne International	Down	Newry & Mourne District Council (☎ 028-4175 2256; www.mournehiking.co.uk)
Glenullin	Tyrone	Sperrins Tourism (☎ 028-8674 7700; www.sperrinstourism.com)
JULY		
Castlebar International	Mayo	Castlebar International Walks Office (☎ 094-902 4102; www.castlebar4dayswalks.com)
AUGUST		
Sperrins	Tyrone	Sperrins Tourism (☎ 028-8674 7700; www.sperrinstourism.com)
SEPTEMBER		
Wee Binnians	Down	Wee Binnian Hikers (☎ 028-9066 9718; www.weebinnians.com)
OCTOBER		
Carlow	Carlow	Carlow Tourism (☎ 059-913 0411; www.carlowtourism.com)
Wicklow Mountains	Wicklow	Wicklow County Tourism (☎ 0404-20070; www.visitwicklow.ie)
Nire Valley	Waterford	Hanora's Cottage (☎ 052-613 6134; www.hanorascottage.com)

styles. One long-standing dish is Irish stew, a hearty broth of lamb or mutton (traditionally the neck joint), potatoes, onions, and carrots, simmered slowly with parsley and thyme. You'll find that potatoes are served with everything, even the traditional fried breakfast, where potato bread and hash browns (grated potato bound with egg and fried) are common components.

Irish cuisine has come a long way in the past years however, and fine dining experiences are now much more common. In the better restaurants, traditional dishes are often given a creative, contemporary makeover, then served with precise attention to presentation. The country boasts several chefs and restaurants that are renowned on a global stage, while local artisan producers offer a range of home-produced

WALKERS DIRECTORY

AN OUTDOOR FEAST

Somehow there's nothing quite as satisfying as a meal prepared and eaten alfresco. Though the lack of multiday routes in Ireland means eating in the wild is rarer than in some other countries, that doesn't mean it never happens.

One particularly memorable evening springs to mind, at the end of a summer's day on Inishturk Island. We had circumnavigated the island, enjoying the beautiful coastal scenery before returning to the harbour, where we happened to meet a fisherman just as he was landing his catch. A quick negotiation and a large lobster was ours. The local shop had a pot of cream, and the bar supplied a bottle of white wine. Then it was back to our tent near a secluded beach, with just enough time for a quick dip before settling down to the serious business of preparing our feast. The lobster was grilled over a fire, and served with pasta tossed in a butter, onion, cream and wine sauce. Who says camping wild means you have to rough it?

Helen Fairbairn

goods such as cheeses, breads, smoked fish, sausages, jams and relishes.

As far as traditional drinks are concerned, it's hard to avoid the cup of tea, which is almost always taken with milk. Coffee houses are now common in towns, but if you're offered a warm drink to welcome you to somebody's home it's invariably tea. In pubs and bars, the ubiquitous Guinness (a heavy black stout) is equally as dominant. Though there is generally a choice of other draught beers, mainly lagers, the company that owns Guinness has a virtual monopoly on drink supply in the country and it is surprisingly difficult to find much variety. Draft beer is served either in pints (570ml) or half-pints (285ml).

On the Walk

Most of the walks in this book are one-day routes that take you away from civilisation. On these walks there are no facilities so you'll have to come prepared with all the food and drink you need for the day. Irish hikers commonly carry a lunch

WATER

Mains tap water is safe to drink throughout Ireland. When you're on the walk, try to carry all the water you will need for the day. Most upland areas in Ireland are heavily grazed by sheep and other animals, and it's generally safest to regard all stream water as unfit to drink. If you think you might need to collect water in the wild, see water purification on p324.

of sandwiches, chocolate, and water or a flask of tea to drink. It's a good idea to pack slightly more than you think you might need in case of emergencies.

Some of the routes are multiday Waymarked Ways, but each stage invariably ends in a town or village where you'll find serviced accommodation, a pub or restaurant. As a result it is never necessary to carry more than your lunch on the walk. If you choose to camp along a multi-day route, check what facilities are available along the way. Some remote villages don't have shops where you can re-supply, so it may be necessary to carry a certain amount of food with you.

Buying Food

Supermarkets and convenience stores are everywhere in Ireland, although small, owner-run groceries, bakeries and butcher shops are still very much part of the shopping scene. In larger towns you can usually find at least one place specialising in Irish products. One of the most enjoyable ways to buy food is to visit a farmers market, where you'll find a lively atmosphere and plenty of fresh, authentic, local produce. Ask locally to find out about the markets in each area.

GUIDES

The following companies offer organised walking in Ireland:

Ireland

Croagh Patrick Walking Holidays (☎ 098-26090; www.walkingguideireland.com;

Belclare, Westport, Co Mayo) Concentrates on the Achill Island–Connemara–Burren area and the adjacent islands.

Footfalls (☎ 0404-45152; www .hikingireland.com; Trooperstown, Roundwood, Co Wicklow) Offers a host of tours around all the country's best walking spots, including Wicklow, Cork, Kerry, the Burren, Connemara, Donegal and Antrim.

Go Ireland (☎ 066-976 2094; www .goactivities.com; Old Orchard House, Killorglin, Co Kerry) Focusses on the west coast, from Donegal to Mayo, Galway and Kerry.

Irishways Walking Holidays (☎ 01-260 0340; www.irishways.com; Belfield Bike Shop, UCD, Dublin 4) Features walking holidays in Connemara, Kerry, Cork and Wicklow.

South West Walks Ireland (☎ 066-712 8733; www.southwestwalksireland.com; 6 Church St, Tralee, Co Kerry) Programs cover the west coast from north to south, as well as Wicklow and Antrim.

Tailor-Made Tours (☎ 066-976 6007; www.tailor-madetours.com; Ferry Rd, Keel, Castlemaine, Co Kerry) Regions covered include Wicklow, Cork, Kerry, the Burren, Connemara and Donegal.

UK

Joyce's Ireland Walking Tours (☎ 01179-628 235; www.joycesireland.co.uk; 52 Stoke Ln, Westbury on Trym, Bristol, BS9 3DN) Covers pretty much the whole county with a wide variety of tour options.

Ramblers Worldwide Holidays (☎ 01707-331 133; www.ramblersholidays.co.uk; Lemsford Mill, Lemsford Village, Welwyn Garden City, AL8 7TR) Runs week-long trips around the glens and coast of Antrim.

USA

Backroads (☎ 800-462 2848, 510-527 1555; www.backroads.com; 801 Cedar St, Berkeley, California 94710) Organises a week-long walking tour around counties Cork and Kerry.

Wilderness Travel (☎ 1800-368 2794, 510-558 2488; www.wildernesstravel.com; 1102 Ninth St, Berkeley, California 94710) Offers a nine-day walking tour exploring Galway, Mayo and Donegal.

HOLIDAYS

Public holidays can cause road chaos, as everyone tries to get somewhere else for the break. It's also wise to book accommodation in advance during holiday periods.

Public Holidays

Public holidays in both the Republic and Northern Ireland:

New Year's Day 1 January
St Patrick's Day 17 March
Easter (Good Fri to Easter Mon inclusive) March/April
May Holiday 1st Monday in May
Christmas Day 25 December
St Stephen's Day (Boxing Day) 26 December

Public holidays in Northern Ireland:

Spring Bank Holiday Last Monday in May
Orangeman's Day 12 July
August Holiday Last Monday in August

Public holidays in the Republic of Ireland:

June Holiday 1st Monday in June
August Holiday 1st Monday in August
October Holiday Last Monday in October

St Patrick's Day and St Stephen's Day holidays are taken on the following Monday should they fall on a weekend. In the Republic, nearly everywhere closes on Good Friday even though it isn't an official public holiday. In the North, most shops open on Good Friday but close the following Tuesday.

School Holidays

In the Republic, standardised primary and secondary school holidays generally fall around the following times:

Mid term break last week in October
Christmas/New Year 2½ weeks from the end of December to early-January
Mid term break one week in mid-February
Easter 2½ weeks around Easter
Summer July and August (June also for secondary schools)

For precise dates each year, visit the website for the Department of Education and Science (www.education.ie) and click on the link for School Holidays.

In the North, holidays for primary and secondary schools vary. Visit www.deni .gov.uk/schools/index.htm then click on school holidays for a comprehensive rundown.

INSURANCE

Insurance is important: it covers you for everything from medical expenses and luggage loss to cancellations or delays in your travel arrangements. Make sure to read the small print about 'dangerous activities' that are not covered – on some policies this includes walking in the mountains.

If you're an EU citizen, a European Health Insurance Card (EHIC; available from health centres, or from post offices in the UK) covers you for most medical care. Other countries, such as Australia, also have reciprocal agreements with Ireland and Britain, but many countries do not.

If you do need health insurance, remember that some policies offer lower and higher medical-expense options, but the higher one is chiefly for countries such as the USA that have extremely high medical costs. Everyone should be covered for the worst possible case, such as an accident requiring an ambulance, hospital treatment or an emergency flight home. You may prefer a policy that pays health-care providers directly rather than you

having to pay on the spot and claim later. See p320 for health insurance details.

All cars on public roads must be insured. If you are bringing your own vehicle check that your insurance will cover you in Ireland.

INTERNET ACCESS

If your computer isn't equipped to handle 220 volts AC or a three-point socket, you'll need a universal AC adapter and a plug adapter, which will enable you to plug in anywhere. All hotel rooms have phone lines and you can plug the phone lead into the back of your laptop; although most have direct-dial services, you'll most likely have to dial an outside line access number (usually 9) to get online. Provided you're dialling a local access number you'll be charged the price of a local call (which from a hotel is usually timed and 50% more than usual).

Major internet service providers (ISPs) such as **AOL** (www.aol.com), **CompuServe** (www.compuserve.com) and **AT&T Business Internet Services** (www.attbusiness. net) have dial-in nodes in Ireland. If you access your email account through a homebased ISP, your best option is to open an account with a local, global ISP provider: the most reliable ones are **Eircom** (☎ 1800 369 369; www.eircom.ie) or **O2** (☎ 1800 924 924; www.02.ie).

Although Ireland has one of the lowest rates of broadband penetration in Europe (26% in 2009), 60% of Irish households have broadband, including most B&Bs in and around the major towns of Ireland; you'll also find WiFi (wireless fidelity) in many midrange and top-end hotels. Most public libraries have free internet access, and many towns also have internet cafés, although they're closing as the rate of household broadband goes up. You can log on for €4–10 per hour in the Republic, or about £4 per hour in the North.

For a list of websites useful to hikers and travellers in Ireland, see Internet Resources on p24.

MAPS

A map is an essential piece of kit for the vast majority of walks in Ireland. The country's mountainous areas are generally devoid of formal trails and signposts, and a map is your only means of navigation. Details of

---

TRAVEL INSURANCE

Buy a policy that generously covers you for medical expenses, theft or loss of luggage and tickets, and for cancellation of and delays in your travel arrangements. It may be worth taking out cover for mountaineering activities and the cost of rescue. Check your policy doesn't exclude walking as a dangerous activity.

Buy travel insurance as early as possible to ensure you'll be compensated for any unforeseen accidents or delays. If items are lost or stolen get a police report immediately – otherwise your insurer might not pay up.

MAPS IN THIS BOOK

The maps in this book are based on the best available references, sometimes combined with GPS data collected in the field. They are intended to show the general routes of the walks we describe. They are primarily to help locate the route within the surrounding area. They are not detailed enough in themselves for route-finding or navigation. You will still need a properly surveyed map at an adequate scale – specific maps are recommended in the Planning section for each walk. Most chapters also have a regional map showing the gateway towns or cities, principal transport routes and other major features. Map symbols are interpreted in the legend on the inside front cover of this book.

On the maps in this book, natural features such as river confluences and mountain peaks are in their true position, but sometimes the location of villages and routes is not always so. This may be because a village is spread over a hillside, or the size of the map does not allow for detail of the path's twists and turns. However, by using several basic route-finding techniques (see p319), you will have few problems following our descriptions.

---

the specific map needed for each walk are provided as part of each route description.

Buying Maps

Large-scale OSI and OSNI maps are widely available in outdoor shops, bookshops, newsagents and tourist offices. In Dublin, the **National Map Centre** (☎ 01-476 0487; www.irishmaps.ie; 34 Aungier St; Mon-Fri) stocks the entire OSI and OSNI range, and you can order from their online catalogue through the website.

In the North, **OSNI** (☎ 028-9025 5768; www.osni.gov.uk/mapstore; Colby House, Stranmillis Rd, Belfast BT9 5BJ) also runs an online map shop.

Large-scale Maps

Ireland is covered by a collection of 89 maps at a scale of 1:50,000. These are published in the Republic as part of the Ordnance Survey of Ireland (OSI) *Discovery* series, and in the North as the Ordnance Survey of Northern Ireland (OSNI) *Discoverer* series. With a contour interval of 10m and detailed depiction of topographical features, these maps are the standard reference for hikers. They're priced at €8.60/£6.90.

The OSI also publishes a few 1:25,000 scale, weatherproof maps for areas of special interest to hikers, including the Brandon Mountain and MacGillycuddy's Reeks (€12.99). OSNI also has five water-resistant 'activity maps' at a scale of 1:25,000, covering areas such as the Mourne Mountains, the Sperrin Mountains and the Glens of Antrim (£8.30).

Harvey (☎ 01786-841 202; www.harvey maps.co.uk; 12-22 Main St, Doune, Perthshire FK16 6BJ, Scotland; maps £9.95) and **EastWest Mapping** (☎ 053 -937 7835; www.eastwestmapping.ie; Clonegal, Enniscorthy, Co Wexford; maps €11.45) are other companies that produce excellent, waterproof 1:30,000 maps aimed specifically at hikers. Regions covered include Connemara, MacGillycuddy's Reeks and the Dublin and Wicklow Mountains.

Details of other locally produced or specialised maps, such as those for national parks, are given with the relevant walks.

Small-scale Maps

The four 1:250,000 maps in the OSI *Holiday* series – North, South, East and West – cover the whole island and are good for trip planning and accessing walking areas. They cost €8.35/£6.50 each. Alternatively, the OSI *Complete Road Atlas of Ireland* covers the country at 1:210,000 and also

---

PLACE NAMES

Place names are now marked on OSI and OSNI maps in both English and Irish. Unfortunately the OSI's earlier policy of anglicisation extinguished many original Gaelic names, thus losing the insights into the appearance or significance of places, and usually obscuring the fact that the Irish name had a distinctive meaning.

includes large-scale city and town maps (€12.99/£9.75).

MONEY

The currency in the Republic of Ireland is the euro (€), which is divided into 100 cents. The reverse side of coins have a design particular to their country of issue (a Celtic harp in Ireland's case), but are legal tender in all countries that accept the euro (Austria, Belgium, Finland, France, Germany, Greece, Italy, Luxembourg, the Netherlands, Portugal and Spain). Remember that the UK is not a participant in the euro-zone, so if you're travelling to Northern Ireland you'll have to change into pounds.

The British pound sterling (£) is used in Northern Ireland. Northern Irish notes have a different design to UK notes, and though they are still legal tender, they may not be readily accepted by some shops in Britain. If you have any trouble British banks will swap them for you.

The best exchange rates are generally obtained at banks. *Bureaus de change* and other exchange facilities usually open for longer hours but the rate and/or commission will be worse. Many post offices operate a currency-exchange facility and open on Saturday morning. Exchange rates at the time of writing can be found on the inside front cover of this book.

To get a general idea of food and accommodation costs in Ireland, see p23.

ATMs & Credit Cards

Credit cards make the perfect travelling companions: they're ideal for major purchases and let you withdraw cash from selected banks and ATMs. ATMs are usually linked to international money systems such as Cirrus, Maestro or Plus. Bear in mind, though, that each transaction incurs a currency conversion fee and credit cards can incur immediate and exorbitant cash advance interest rate charges.

Charge cards such as Amex and Diners Club don't have credit limits, but may not be accepted in smaller establishments. Visa and MasterCard are more widely accepted, though many B&Bs and some smaller or remote petrol stations take cash only.

Remember to keep a note of the emergency telephone number to ring if your card is lost or stolen.

ON THE WALK

Many of the walks in this book visit remote areas where there are no banking facilities. Rural accommodation suppliers, shops and pubs often don't accept credit cards either. Make sure to carry enough cash to cover all your bills in these regions.

Cash & Travellers Cheques

Nothing beats cash for convenience – or risk. It's still a good idea, though, to arrive with some cash in the local currency (both euros and sterling, if travelling to the North) to tide you over.

Amex and Thomas Cook travellers cheques are widely recognised and they don't charge commission for cashing their own cheques. Eurocheques can also be cashed in Ireland. Travellers cheques are rarely accepted outside banks or used for everyday transactions (as they are in the USA).

International Transfers

The most practical way to receive money from overseas is by telegraphic transfer. There are two ways to do this. The first can take up to eight days through the banking system. Your bank sends money to an Irish bank nominated by you. You will need identification, most likely a passport, before the money is paid to you in the local currency, minus the transfer commission.

The quickest way to receive cash from home is to transfer it through Amex, Thomas Cook or Western Union.

It is not practical to receive money by bank draft. Irish banks are notorious sticklers about drafts and won't allow you to cash them unless you first open a bank account, a small bureaucratic nightmare. Even then, it can take three weeks to clear. If you're not planning a long stay, stick to telegraphic transfers.

Taxes & Refunds

Value-added tax (VAT) is a sales tax of 21.5% that applies to most luxury goods in Ireland, excluding books, children's footwear and second-hand clothing. Visitors from non-EU countries can claim back most of the VAT on purchases that are subsequently exported from the EU within three months of purchase.

Most shops in the Republic and Northern Ireland operate a taxback scheme – the most popular are Cashback and Ireland Tax Free – which operate roughly as follows: if you're a resident of a country outside the EU and buy something from a store displaying a Cashback or Ireland Tax Free sticker, you'll be given a relevant voucher with your purchase which can be refunded directly on to your credit card or in US, Canadian or Australian dollars, British pounds or euros at Dublin or Shannon airport. One advantage of Ireland Tax Free is that you can reclaim your tax at the nearest Travelex office, usually Thomas Cook.

If you reclaim more than €250 on any of your vouchers you'll need to get the voucher stamped at the customs booth in the arrivals hall at Dublin or Shannon airport before you can get your refund from the Cashback desk.

In Northern Ireland, shops participating in the Tax-Free Shopping refund scheme will give you a form or invoice on request to be presented to customs when you leave. After customs have certified the form, it will be returned to the shop for a refund.

Tipping

Tips of around 10% are expected in metered cabs and in restaurants where the service charge isn't included.

PERMITS & FEES

Permits are not required to walk anywhere in Ireland, nor are any fees payable. The most you'll have to pay is a parking charge if you decide to use some privately-owned car parks, or an entrance fee if the route enters a National Trust property, national park or some forest parks.

PHOTOGRAPHY & VIDEO

Natural light in Ireland can be very dull, so use faster film to capture the sombre atmosphere: 200ASA should do in most situations, though 400ASA might also be required. Print film and memory cards are both widely available.

In regard to taking photos in Northern Ireland, if you want to take photos of fortified police stations, army posts or other military or quasi-military paraphernalia, get permission first to be on the safe side. In the Protestant and Catholic strongholds of West Belfast it's best not to photograph people without permission: always ask first and be prepared to accept a refusal.

Ireland's major airports are all equipped with inspection systems that do not damage film or other photographic material carried in hand luggage.

TELEPHONE

Eircom is Ireland's largest telephone service provider, although deregulation of the telephone industry has seen the arrival of a number of other providers. In the North most public phones are owned by British Telecom (BT).

The cheapest calls are those placed from land-line phones to other land-line phones; international calls to mobiles can cost significantly more. Prices are also lower in the evening and at the weekend. Phone calls from hotel rooms cost at least double the

PUBLIC & PRIVATE PROPERTY

The vast majority of land in both the Republic and Northern Ireland is privately owned and the public has no automatic right to roam. Access across private land is either granted as traditional practice, such as in the main mountain areas, or by an agreement between the landowner and the local council. A few recognised rights of way do exist, but these aren't as numerous or well protected as in many other Western countries.

This lack of legal status means that an awful lot of walking in Ireland depends on the goodwill of landowners for its existence. There is a real danger that inconsiderate behaviour by hikers might lead to access being withdrawn and apparently established routes being lost. It is essential therefore to respect the landowner's wishes at all times. Unfortunately it can be hard to differentiate between public and private property, especially in the mountains, where there are few visible boundaries between commonage and privately-owned land. To avoid worsening the access situation, the best advice is to walk in a responsible manner at all times, and be polite to any farmers you might meet along the way. See p34 for more advice on responsible walking.

WALKERS DIRECTORY

standard rate. You can send and receive faxes from post offices or most hotels.

Rather than placing reverse-charge calls through the operator in Ireland, you can dial direct to your home-country operator and then reverse the charges or charge the call to a local phone credit card.

Local telephone calls from a public phone in the Republic cost €0.30 for around three minutes (around €0.60 to a mobile), regardless of when you call. The number for national directory enquiries is ☎ 11811, and for international it's ☎ 11818. In Northern Ireland a local call costs a minimum of £0.20. Call ☎ 118500 for national directory enquiries, and ☎ 118505 for international numbers.

Pre-paid phonecards by Eircom, BT or private operators are available in newsagencies and post offices, and work from all pay phones, dispensing with the need for coins.

Mobile Phones

Virtually everyone in Ireland has a mobile phone. Ireland uses the GSM 900/1800 cellular phone system, which is compatible with European and Australian, but not North American or Japanese, phones. SMS is a national obsession, especially with young people, who communic8 mostly by txt.

There are four Irish service providers: Vodafone, O2, Meteor and 3. There are three mobile codes – 085, 086 and 087 – but Mobile Number Portability (MNP) allows customers to hold on to their codes whilst switching between providers. All have links with most international GSM providers, which allow you to 'roam' onto a local service on arrival. This means you can use your mobile phone to text and make local calls, but will be charged at the highest possible rate. You can also purchase a pay-as-you-go package (for around €70) with a local provider with your own mobile

---

TAKING PHOTOS OUTDOORS

For hikers, photography can be a vexed issue – all that magnificent scenery but such weight and space restrictions on what photographic equipment you can carry. With a little care and planning it is possible to maximise your chance of taking great photos on the trail.

LIGHT & FILTERS

In fine weather, the best light is early and late in the day. In strong sunlight and in mountain and coastal areas where the light is intense, a polarising filter will improve colour saturation and reduce haze. On overcast days the soft light can be great for shooting wildflowers and running water and an 81A warming filter can be useful. If you use slide film, a graduated filter will help balance unevenly lit landscapes.

EQUIPMENT

If you need to travel light carry a zoom in the 28–70mm range, and if your sole purpose is landscapes consider carrying just a single wide-angle lens (24mm). A tripod is essential for really good images and there are some excellent lightweight models available. Otherwise a trekking pole, pack or even a pile of rocks can be used to improvise.

CAMERA CARE

Keep your gear dry – a few zip-lock freezer bags can be used to double wrap camera gear and silica-gel sachets (a drying agent) can be used to suck moisture out of equipment. Sturdy cameras will normally work fine in freezing conditions. Take care when bringing a camera from one temperature extreme to another; if moisture condenses on the camera parts make sure it dries thoroughly before going back into the cold, or mechanisms can freeze up. Standard camera batteries fail very quickly in the cold. Remove them from the camera when it's not in use and keep them under your clothing.

For a thorough grounding on photography on the road, read Lonely Planet's *Travel Photography*, by Richard I'Anson, a full-colour guide for happy-snappers and professional photographers alike. Also highly recommended is the outdoor photography classic *Mountain Light*, by Galen Rowell.

Gareth McCormack

phone. As you use up your airtime, you simply buy a top-up card (€10–€35) at a newsagency or petrol station. The other service providers have variations on this scheme. Similar schemes exist in Northern Ireland.

Phone Codes

When calling the Republic of Ireland from abroad, dial your country's international access code, followed by ☎ 353, followed by the domestic number minus the initial '0'. When calling Northern Ireland from abroad, dial your country's international access code, then ☎ 44 28, and then the local number. To call Northern Ireland from Britain, simply dial ☎ 028, then the local number. This changes to ☎ 048 when calling from the Republic. The area code for the whole of Northern Ireland is ☎ 028, so domestic callers need only dial the eight-digit local number.

To call UK numbers from the Republic dial ☎ 00 44, then the area code minus the initial '0', then the local number. Do the same for international calls, replacing 44 with the recipient country code. To call Britain from Northern Ireland, just dial the area code followed by the local number. To place an international call or to call the Republic from Northern Ireland, dial ☎ 00 followed by the recipient country code, then the area code (dropping any leading '0') and the local number.

TIME

In winter, Ireland is on Greenwich Mean Time (GMT), also known as Universal Time Coordinated (UTC), the same as Britain. From late March to late October, the clock shifts to 'summer time', which is GMT plus one hour.

TOILETS

Public toilets – often marked with the Irish *Fir* (Men) and *Mná* (Women) – are rarely seen outside the bigger towns, and even then they're usually only found in shopping centres. Most petrol stations have facilities for public use, though standards of cleanliness are not always high. Many pubs and restaurants display that annoying 'Toilets are for customer use only' sign, but if the place is crowded, who'll ever know you're not a customer?

TOURIST INFORMATION

The country's main tourist boards can provide invaluable information both before you travel and while you're in Ireland. In the Republic, contact **Fáilte Ireland** (from the Republic ☎ 1850 230 330, from the UK 0800 039 7000; www.discoverireland.ie). In Northern Ireland, the service is provided by **Northern Irish Tourist Board** (NITB; ☎ 028-9023 1221; www.discovernorthernireland.com; 59 North St, Belfast).

Both websites include an accommodation booking service, or telephone reservations can be made via the tourist boards' system **Gulliver** (in the Republic ☎ 1800 668 668, in the UK ☎ 0800 783 5740, in the USA & Canada ☎ 800 398 4376).

Fáilte Ireland also has an office in **Belfast** (☎ 028-9032 7888; 53 Castle St, Belfast) and NITB has an office in **Dublin** (within the Republic ☎ 01-679 1977, 1850 230 230; 16 Nassau St, Dublin).

In the Republic and the North there's a tourist office in almost every big town; most can offer a variety of services including accommodation reservations, *bureau de change* services, map and guidebook sales, and free publications. These smaller offices are detailed in the regional chapters.

Main Regional Tourist Offices in the Republic

Fáilte Ireland also has six regional offices, which can give more in-depth information on specific areas.

Cork Kerry (☎ 021-425 5100; www.discoverireland.ie/southwest; Cork Kerry Tourism, Áras Discover, Grand Pde, Cork)

Dublin (www.visitdublin.com; Dublin Tourism Centre, St Andrew's Church, 2 Suffolk St, Dublin)

East Coast & Midlands (☎ 044-48761; www.discoverireland.ie/eastcoast; East Coast & Midlands Tourism, Dublin Rd, Mullingar) For Kildare, Laois, Longford, Louth, Meath, North Offaly, Westmeath, Wicklow.

Ireland North-West & Lakelands (☎ 071-916 1201; www.discoverireland.ie/northwest; Temple St, Sligo) For Cavan, Donegal, Leitrim, Monaghan, Sligo.

Ireland West (☎ 091-537 700; www.discoverireland.ie/west; Ireland West Tourism,

Áras Fáilte, Forster St, Galway) For Galway, Roscommon, Mayo.

Shannon Region (☎ 061-361 555; www .discoverireland.ie/shannon; Shannon Development, Shannon, Clare) For Clare, Limerick, North Tipperary, South Offaly.

South East (☎ 051-875 823; www.dis coverireland.ie/southeast; South East Tourism, 41 The Quay, Waterford) For Carlow, Kilkenny, Tipperary, Waterford, Wexford.

Tourist Offices Abroad

Outside Ireland, Fáilte Ireland and the NITB unite under the banner Tourism Ireland, with offices in the following countries:

Australia (☎ 02-9299 6177; info@tourism ireland.com.au; 5th level, 36 Carrington St, Sydney, NSW 2000)
Canada (☎ 1800 223 6470; info.ca@tourism ireland.com; 2 Bloor St West, Suite 1501, Toronto, Ontario M4W 3E2)
France (☎ 01 53 43 12 35; info.fr@tourism ireland.com; Tourisme Irlandais, 33 rue de Miromesnil, 75008 Paris)
Germany (☎ 069-9231 8500; info.de @tourismireland.com; Gutleutstrasse 32, 60329 Frankfurt-am-Main)
Italy (☎ 02 5817 7311; Piazzale Cantore 4, 20123 Milan)
Netherlands (☎ 020-530 6050; info @ierland.nl; Iers Nationaal Bureau voor Toerisme, Spuistraat 104, 1012 VA Am-sterdam)
New Zealand (☎ 09-379 3708; info@tour ismireland.co.nz; Dingwall Bldg, 2nd fl, 87 Queen St, Auckland)
UK (☎ 0800 039 7000; info.gb@tourismire land.com; Nations House, 103 Wigmore St, London, W1U 1QS)

USA (☎ 212-1418 0800; info.us@tourism ireland.com; 17th fl, 345 Park Ave, New York, NY 10154)

VISAS

UK nationals don't need a passport to visit the Republic, but are advised to carry one (or some other form of photo identification) to prove that they *are* a UK national. It's also necessary to have a passport or photo ID when changing travellers cheques or hiring a car. European Economic Area (EEA) citizens (that is, citizens of EU states, plus Iceland, Liechtenstein and Norway) can enter Ireland with either a passport or a national ID card.

Visitors from outside the EEA will need a passport, which should remain valid for at least six months after their intended arrival.

For EEA nationals and citizens of most Western countries, including Australia, Canada, New Zealand and the USA, no visa is required to visit either the Republic or Northern Ireland, but citizens of India, China and many African countries do need a visa for the Republic. Full visa requirements for visiting the Republic are available online at www.dfa.ie; for Northern Ireland's visa requirements see www.ukvisas.gov.uk.

EEA nationals can stay for as long as they like, but other visitors can usually remain for up to three months in the Republic and up to six months in the North. To stay longer in the Republic, contact the local garda (police) station or the **Garda National Immigra-tion Bureau** (☎ 01-666 9100; www.garda .ie/angarda/gnib.html; 13-14 Burgh Quay, Dublin 2). To stay longer in Northern Ireland contact the **Home Office** (☎ 0870-606 7766; www.homeoffice.gov.uk; Immigration & Nationality Directorate, Lunar House, 40 Wellesley Rd, Croydon CR9 2BY, UK).

Transport

CONTENTS

GETTING THERE & AWAY

ENTERING THE COUNTRY

An increase in the number of foreign nationals seeking asylum during the last decade has meant a far more rigorous questioning for those from African and Asian countries or from certain parts of Eastern Europe. The border between the Republic and Northern Ireland still exists as a political reality, but there are few if any checkpoints left; for non-EU nationals it is assumed the screening process occurred upon entry to the UK. For information on visa requirements turn to p304.

Passport

EU citizens can travel freely to and from Ireland if bearing official photo ID. Those from outside the EU, however, must have a passport that remains valid for six months after entry.

AIR
Airports & Airlines

There are scheduled nonstop flights from Britain, continental Europe and North America to Dublin and Shannon, and good nonstop connections from Britain and continental Europe to Cork.

Cork (ORK; ☎ 021-431 3131; www.cork airport.com)
Dublin (DUB; ☎ 01-814 1111; www.dublin airport.com)
Shannon (SNN; ☎ 061-712 000; www.shann onairport.com)

Other airports in the Republic with scheduled services from Britain:

Donegal (CFN; ☎ 074-954 8284; www.don egalairport.ie; Carrickfinn)
Kerry (KIR; ☎ 066-976 4644; www.kerry airport.ie; Farranfore)
Knock (NOC; ☎ 094-67222; www.knock airport.com)
Waterford (WAT; ☎ 051-875 589; www.fly waterford.com)

In Northern Ireland there are flights to **Belfast International** (BFS; ☎ 028-9448 4848; www.belfastairport.com) from Britain, continental Europe and the USA.

Other airports in Northern Ireland that operate scheduled services from Britain:

Belfast City (BHD; ☎ 028-9093 9093; www.belfastcityairport.com)
Derry (LDY; ☎ 028-7181 0784; www.city ofderryairport.com)

> ## THINGS CHANGE...
> The information in this chapter is particularly vulnerable to change. Check directly with the airline or a travel agency to make sure you understand how a fare (and ticket you may buy) works and be aware of the security requirements for international travel. Shop carefully. The details given in this chapter should be regarded as pointers and are not a substitute for your own careful, up-to-date research.

The main Irish airlines:

Aer Árann (☎ 1890 462 726; www.aer arann.com) A small carrier that operates flights within Ireland and also to Britain.
Aer Lingus (☎ 01-886 8888; www .aerlingus.com) The Irish national airline, with direct flights to Britain, continental Europe and the USA.
Ryanair (☎ 01-609 7800; www.ryanair .com) Ireland's no-frills carrier with inexpensive services to Britain and continental Europe.

Nearly all international airlines use Dublin as their hub. Airlines flying into and out of Ireland:

Adria Airways (Czech number is ☎ +386 (0)13691010; www.adria.si)
Aer Árann (☎ 1890 462 726; www.aer arann.com)
Aer Lingus (☎ 01-886 8888; www.aerlingus .com)
Air Baltic (in Latvia ☎ +370 5 2356000; www.airbaltic.com)
Air Canada (☎ 1800 709 900; www.air canada.ca)
Air France (☎ 01-605 0383; www.airfrance .com)
Air Malta (☎ 1800 397 400; www.airmalta .com)
Air Southwest (in the UK ☎ +44 870 241 8202; www.airsouthwest.com)
Air Transat (in the UK ☎ +44 8705 561 522; www.airtransat.com)
American Airlines (☎ 01-602 0550; www .aa.com)

BMI (☎ 01-407 3036; www.flybmi.com)
British Airways (☎ 1800 626 747; www .britishairways.com)
City Jet (☎ 01-8700 300; www.cityjet.com)
Continental (☎ 1890 925 252; www.con tinental.com)
Delta Airlines (☎ 1800 768 080; www.delta .com)
EasyJet (☎ 048-9448 4929; www.easyjet .com; Belfast)
Etihad Airways (☎ 01-477 3479; www.eti hadairways.com)
Flybe (☎ 1890 925 532; www.flybe.com)
Flyglobespan (☎ 01-874 7666; www.fly globespan.ie)
German Wings (☎ 01-865 0125; www .germanwings.com)
Iberia (☎ 01-407 3017; www.iberia.com)
KLM (☎ 1850 747 400; www.klm.com)
Lufthansa (☎ 01-844 5544; www.lufthansa .com)
Luxair (☎ 00800-2456 4242; www.luxair .co.uk)
Malev Hungarian Airlines (☎ 01-844 4303; www.malev.com)
Ryanair (☎ 0818 30 30 30; www.ryanair .com)
S7 Airlines (☎ 01-663 3933; www.s7.ru)
Scandinavian Airlines (☎ 01-844 5440; www.flysas.com)
Swiss Airlines (☎ 1890 200 515; www.swiss .com)
Turkish Airlines (☎ 01-844 7920; www .turkishairlines.com)
US Airways (☎ 1890 925 065; www.usair ways.com)

Tickets

The emergence of the no-frills, low-fares model as the future of European air travel has made cheap tickets the norm rather than the exception. For point-to-point travel the best deals are almost always available on-line. Europe's largest carrier, Ryanair, will penalise passengers who don't avail of their online services (including check-in) – but more complicated travel arrangements are best handled by a travel agent, who knows the system, the options and the best deals. Be sure to check the terms and conditions of the cheap fares before purchasing.

Australia & New Zealand

There are no nonstop scheduled air services from Australia or New Zealand

---

BAGGAGE RESTRICTIONS

Airlines impose tight restrictions on carry-on baggage. No sharp implements of any kind are allowed onto the plane, so pack items such as pocket knives, camping cutlery and first-aid kits into your checked luggage.

If you're carrying a camping stove you should remember that airlines also ban liquid fuels and gas cartridges from all baggage, both check-through and carry-on. Empty all fuel bottles and buy what you need at your destination.

DEPARTURE TAX

A travel tax is built into the price of an air ticket for the Republic and Northern Ireland, and is also paid as part of the ticket if you leave the Republic by ferry. An exception is Ireland West Airport (Knock), which requires passengers boarding flights at that airport to pay a €10 'development fee'. This fee is not included in the price of your ticket and must be paid at the airport.

to Ireland; generally it's cheapest to fly to London or Amsterdam and continue from there. Most fares to European destinations can have a return flight to Dublin tagged on at little or no extra cost. Round-the-world (RTW) tickets are another good bet and are often better value than standard return fares.

The Saturday travel sections of the *Sydney Morning Herald* and Melbourne's *The Age* newspapers advertise cheap fares; in New Zealand, check the *New Zealand Herald* travel section.

Recommended agencies in Australia:

Flight Centre (☎ 133 133; www.flight centre.com.au)
Shamrock Travel (☎ 03-9602 3700; www .irishtravel.com.au)
STA Travel (☎ 1300 733 035; www.statravel .com.au)

Recommended New Zealand agencies:

Flight Centre (☎ 0800-243 544; www.flight centre.co.nz)
STA Travel (☎ 0508-782 872; www.statravel .co.nz)

Canada
Air Canada is the only carrier flying directly to Ireland, from Toronto to both Dublin and Shannon. Your best bet for cheaper fares may be to connect to transatlantic gateways in the USA or to fly to London and continue on to Ireland from there. Check the travel sections of the *Globe & Mail*, *Toronto Star*, *Montreal Gazette* or *Vancouver Sun* for the latest offers.

Recommended agencies in Canada:

Canadian Affair (☎ 1604-678 6868; www .canadian-affair.com) Cheap one-way fares to British cities.
Flight Centre (☎ 1888-967 5355; www .flightcentre.ca)
Travel CUTS (☎ 866-246 9762; www .travelcuts.com)

Continental Europe
Price wars have cut the price of flights to Ireland from continental Europe to their lowest rates ever. The two biggest players in the market are the one-time national airline **Aer Lingus** (www.aerlingus.com), now a no-frills airline in virtually every respect, offering competitive prices to over 40 destinations; and the king of all low-fares airlines, **Ryanair** (www.ryanair.com), which serves over 80 European destinations from Dublin and over 100 from its (now) main hub at London Stansted. Ryanair's success is predicated on using secondary airports in or around major cities, which can make for expensive and time-consuming transfers. Check when you book.

UK
There is a mind-boggling array of flights between Britain and Ireland. The best deals are usually available online, and it's not unusual for airport taxes to exceed the base price of the ticket on the lowest fares (generally for early morning or late-night flights midweek).

Most regional airports in Britain have flights to Dublin and Belfast and some also provide services to Shannon, Cork, Kerry, Knock and Waterford.

USA
In the USA, discount travel agencies (consolidators) sell cut-price tickets on scheduled carriers. Aer Lingus is the chief carrier between the USA and Ireland, with flights from New York, Boston, Baltimore, Chicago and Los Angeles to Shannon, Dublin and Belfast. Heavy competition on transatlantic routes into London might make it cheaper to fly there and then continue on to Ireland. The Sunday travel sections of the *New York Times*, San Francisco *Chronicle-Examiner*, *Los Angeles Times* or *Chicago Tribune* list cheap fares.

TRANSPORT

CLIMATE CHANGE & TRAVEL

Climate change is a serious threat to the ecosystems that humans rely upon, and air travel is the fastest growing contributor to the problem. Lonely Planet regards travel, overall, as a global benefit, but believes we all have a responsibility to limit our personal impact on global warming.

FLYING & CLIMATE CHANGE

Pretty much every form of motorised travel generates carbon dioxide (the main cause of human-induced climate change) but planes are far and away the worst offenders, not just because of the sheer distances they allow us to travel, but because they release greenhouse gases high into the atmosphere. The statistics are frightening: two people taking a return flight between Europe and the USA will contribute as much to climate change as an average household's gas and electricity consumption over a whole year.

CARBON OFFSET SCHEMES

Climatecare.org and other websites use 'carbon calculators' that allow travellers to offset the level of greenhouse gases they are responsible for with financial contributions to sustainable travel schemes that reduce global warming – including projects in India, Honduras, Kazakhstan and Uganda.

Lonely Planet, together with Rough Guides and other concerned partners in the travel industry, support the carbon offset scheme run by climatecare.org. Lonely Planet offsets all of its staff and author travel.

For more information check out our website: www.lonelyplanet.com.

Some of the more popular travel agencies in the USA:

Ireland Consolidated (☎ 212-661 1999; www.irelandair.com)
STA Travel (☎ 800-781 4040; www.statravel.com)

LAND
Bus
Eurolines (www.eurolines.com) has a three-times-daily coach and ferry service from London's Victoria Station to Dublin Busáras. For information on border crossings see p310.

SEA
There are many ferry and fast-boat services from Britain and France to Ireland. Prices quoted throughout this section are one-way fares for a single adult on foot and then up to two adults with a car, during peak season.

UK & Ireland
FERRY & FAST BOAT
There are numerous services between Britain and Ireland but it's definitely wise to plan ahead as fares can vary considerably, depending on the season, day, time and length of stay. Often, some return fares don't cost that much more than one-way fares and it's worth keeping an eye out for special offers. International Student Identity Card (ISIC) holders and Hostelling International (HI) members get a reduction on the normal fares.

These shipping lines operate between Britain and Ireland:

Irish Ferries (in the UK ☎ 0870-517 1717, in the Republic ☎ 1890 313 131; www.irishferries.com) For ferry and fast-boat services from Holyhead to Dublin, and ferry services from Pembroke to Rosslare.
Isle of Man Steam Packet Company/Sea Cat (in the UK ☎ 1800 805 055, in the Republic ☎ 01-836 4019; www.steam-packet.com) Ferry and fast-boat services from Liverpool to Dublin or Belfast via Douglas (on the Isle of Man).
Norfolkline (in the UK ☎ 0870-600 4321, in the Republic ☎ 01-819 2999; www.norfolkline.com) Ferry services from Liverpool to Belfast and Dublin.
P&O Irish Sea (in the UK ☎ 0870-242 4777, in the Republic ☎ 01-407 3434; www.poirishsea.com) Ferry and fast-boat services from Larne to Cairnryan and Troon, and ferry services from Liverpool to Dublin.

Stena Line (☎ 0870-570 7070; www.stena line.com) Ferry services from Holyhead to Dun Laoghaire, Fleetwood to Larne and Stranraer to Belfast, and fast-boat services from Holyhead to Dublin, Fishguard to Rosslare, and Stranraer to Belfast.

The main routes from the UK to the Republic include:

Fishguard & Pembroke to Rosslare These popular, short ferry crossings take 3½ hours (from Fishguard) or four hours (from Pembroke) and cost around £25/119; the cost drops significantly outside peak season. The fast boat crossing from Fishguard takes just under two hours and costs around £30/135.

Holyhead to Dublin & Dun Laoghaire The ferry crossing takes just over three hours and costs from £25/95. The fast-boat service from Holyhead to Dun Laoghaire takes a little over 1½ hours and costs £25/130.

Liverpool to Dublin The ferry service takes 8½ hours from Liverpool and costs £25/180. Cabins on overnight sailings cost more. The fast-boat service takes four hours and costs up to £40/240.

The main routes from mainland Britain to the North:

Cairnryan to Larne The fast boat takes one hour and costs £21/170. The ferry takes 1¾ hours and costs £15/120.

Fleetwood to Larne The six-hour crossing costs £122; no foot passengers are carried.

Liverpool to Belfast The 8½-hour crossing costs £40/155 (incl meals) during the day and £30/235 (incl cabin and meals) at night.

Stranraer to Belfast The fast boat takes 1¾ hours and costs £20/130. The ferry takes 3¼ hours and costs £16/85.

It's possible to combine bus and ferry tickets from major UK centres to all Irish towns on the bus network, but with the availability of cheap flights it's hardly worth the hassle. The journey between London and Dublin takes about 12 hours and costs about £43 one way. The London to Belfast trip takes 13 to 16 hours and costs £38 one-way. For details in London contact **Eurolines** (☎ 0870-514 3219; www.eurolines.com).

France
FERRY
Brittany Ferries (in the Republic ☎ 021-427 7801, in France ☎ 02 98 29 28 00; www.brittany-ferries.com) Weekly service from Roscoff to Cork from early April to late September. The crossing takes 14 hours and costs up to €85/490 without accommodation.

Irish Ferries (in Rosslare ☎ 053-33158, in Cherbourg ☎ 02 33 23 44 44, in Roscoff ☎ 02 98 61 17 17; www.irish ferries.com) One to three times a week from Roscoff to Rosslare from late April to late September; the crossing time is 17½ hours. Ferries from Cherbourg to Rosslare sail two to four times per week year round, except in late January and all of February; crossing time is 20½ hours. Both services cost up to €150/625 without accommodation.

GETTING AROUND

Travelling around Ireland can be short, simple and sweet – or maddeningly long and infuriatingly complicated. Distances are relatively short and there's a good network of roads, but public transportation can be infrequent, expensive or both and – especially with trains – not reach many of the more interesting places.

Your own transport is a major advantage and it's worth considering car hire for at least part of your trip. The growing network of motorways have cut journey times considerably, but the huge network of secondary and tertiary roads are much better if you want to 'experience' Ireland as you travel – although it is still true that smaller, rural roads can make for difficult driving conditions.

If you opt not to drive, a mixture of buses, the occasional taxi, plenty of time, walking and sometimes hiring a bicycle will get you just about anywhere.

AIR
Airlines in Ireland
Ireland's size makes domestic flying unnecessary unless you're in a hurry, and there are flights between Dublin and Belfast, Cork, Derry, Donegal, Galway, Kerry, Shannon and Sligo, as well as a

Belfast-Cork service. Most flights within Ireland take around 30 to 50 minutes.

The only domestic carriers are:

Aer Árann (☎ 1890-462 726, in Dublin ☎ 01-814 5240, in Galway ☎ 091-593 034, in Cork ☎ 021-814 1058; www.aerarann .com) Operates flights from Dublin to Belfast, Cork, Derry, Donegal, Galway, Kerry, Knock and Sligo; and a Belfast to Cork route. **Aer Lingus** (information & bookings ☎ 01-886 8844, flight information ☎ 01-705 6705, in Belfast ☎ 028-9442 2888; www .aerlingus.com) The main domestic airline.

BOAT
Ferry
There are many boat services to islands lying off the coast, including all of those included in the Atlantic Islands chapter. Services are relatively frequent during the summer but only the permanently inhabited islands have services in the winter months. Bad weather in the summer months can cause cancellations, particularly to islands served by small boats like Great Blasket Island. In the winter it is not unheard of for some islands to go for several weeks without the ferry being able to run.

BORDER CROSSINGS
Security has been progressively scaled down in Northern Ireland in recent years and all border crossings with the Republic are now open and generally unstaffed. Permanent checkpoints have been removed and ramps levelled. On most routes your only indication that you have crossed the border

---

FERRY, BUS & TRAIN DISCOUNT DEALS

FOR TRAVEL ACROSS EUROPE
Eurail (www.eurail.com) passes are for non-Europeans who have been in Europe for less than six months. They are valid on trains in the Republic, but not in Northern Ireland, and offer discounts on Irish Ferries crossings to France. Passes are cheaper when bought outside Europe. In the USA and Canada phone ☎ 1888-667 9734. In London contact **Rail Europe** (☎ 0870-584 8848; 179 Piccadilly).

    InterRail (www.interrail.com) passes give you a 50% reduction on train travel within Ireland and discounts on Irish Ferries and Stena Line services. Passes can be bought at most major train stations and student travel outlets.

FOR TRAVEL WITHIN IRELAND
Holders of the new **Student Travel Card** (www.studenttravelcard.ie) are entitled to 40% discount on Irish trains and 25% off Bus Éireann services. The card is available from **Usit offices** (www.usit.ie).

UNLIMITED-TRAVEL TICKETS FOR BUSES & TRAINS
The Open-Road Pass covers bus-only travel within the Republic, allowing for a variety of travel options from three days' travel out of six consecutive days (€54) to 15 days' travel out of 30 (€234).

    Irish Rover tickets combine services on Bus Éireann and Ulsterbus. They cost €83.50 (for three days' travel out of eight consecutive days), €190 (eight days out of 15) and €280 (15 days out of 30).

    Iarnród Éireann Explorer tickets cover train travel in the Republic. They cost €160 (for five days travel out of 15 consecutive days). The Irish Explorer rail and bus tickets (€245) allow eight days' travel out of 15 consecutive days on trains and buses within the Republic.

    Freedom of Northern Ireland passes allow unlimited travel on NIR, Ulsterbus and Citybus services for £15 for one day, £36 for three out of eight consecutive days, or £53 for seven consecutive days.

    Children aged under 16 pay half price for all these passes and for all normal tickets. Children aged under three travel for free on public transport. You can buy the above passes at most major train and bus stations in Ireland. Although they're good value, many of them make economic sense only if you're planning to travel around Ireland at the speed of light.

will be a change in road signs and the colour of number plates and postboxes.

BUS

Bus Éireann (☎ 01-836 6111; www.bus eireann.ie; Busáras, Store St, Dublin) is the Republic's bus line and offers an extensive network throughout the South. Private buses compete – often very favourably – with Bus Éireann in the Republic and also run where the national buses are irregular or absent.

The larger bus companies will usually carry bikes for free but you should always check in advance to avoid surprises. **Ulsterbus** (☎ 028-9066 6600; www.translink. co.uk; Milewater Rd, Belfast) operates the only bus service in Northern Ireland.

Bus Passes

Details of special deals and passes are given in the boxed text on p310.

Costs

Bus travel is much cheaper than train travel, and private buses often charge less than Bus Éireann. Generally, return fares cost little more than a one-way fare.

Some sample one-way (single) bus fares include the following:

Service	Cost	Hrs	Frequency (Mon-Sat)
BELFAST–DUBLIN	£13	3	7
DERRY–BELFAST	£10	1¾	10+
DERRY–GALWAY	£26.10	5¼	4
DUBLIN–CORK	€11.70	4½	6
DUBLIN–DONEGAL	€17.60	4	5
DUBLIN–ROSSLARE	€16.70	3	12
DUBLIN–TRALEE	€23	6	12
DUBLIN–WATERFORD	€12.20	2¾	7
KILLARNEY–CORK	€15.30	2	12
KILLARNEY–WATERFORD	€21.20	4½	12

Reservations

Bus Éireann bookings can be made online but you can't reserve a seat for a particular service.

CAR & MOTORCYCLE

Ireland has more cars than ever and the building of new roads and the upgrading of existing ones just cannot keep pace. Be prepared for delays, especially at holiday weekends. **AA Roadwatch** (☎ 1550 131 811; www.aaroadwatch.ie) provides traffic information in the Republic.

In the Republic, speed-limit and distance signs are in kilometres (although the occasional older white sign shows distances in miles); in the North, speed-limit and distance signs are in miles.

You'll need a good road map and sense of humour to deal with the severe lack of signposts in the Republic, and on minor roads be prepared for lots of potholes.

Petrol is considerably cheaper in the Republic than in the North. Most service stations accept payment by credit card, but some small, remote ones may take cash only.

All cars on public roads must be insured. If you are bringing your own vehicle in to the country, check that your insurance will cover you in Ireland.

Bring Your Own Vehicle

It's easy to take your own vehicle to Ireland and there are no specific procedures involved, but you should carry a vehicle registration document as proof of ownership.

Automobile Association members should ask for a Card of Introduction entitling you to services offered by sister organisations (including maps, information, breakdown assistance, legal advice etc), usually free of charge.

Automobile Association (AA; Northern Ireland ☎ 0870-950 0600, breakdown assistance ☎ 0800-667 788; Republic Dublin ☎ 01-617 9999, Cork ☎ 021-425 2444, breakdown assistance ☎ 1800-667 788; www.aaireland.ie)
Royal Automobile Club (RAC; Northern Ireland ☎ 0800-029 029, breakdown assistance ☎ 0800-828 282; Republic ☎ 1890 483 483; www.rac.ie)

Driving Licence

Unless you have an EU licence, which is treated like an Irish one, your driving licence is valid for 12 months from the date of entry to Ireland, but you should have held it for two years prior to that. If you don't hold an EU licence it's a good idea to obtain an International Driving

LOCAL TRANSPORT TO & FROM THE WALKS

There's no getting away from the fact that the majority of walks in Ireland are impossible to reach using public transport. Those that are served by public transport are often subject to services that are infrequent or shut down in the winter. For this reason most walkers on a tight schedule, or visiting between the months of October and April, will find it almost essential to have their own car.

However a quick glance at the Table of Walks on p16 will tell you that there are exceptions to this. Walks in and around Dublin and Belfast are well-served by year-round public transport, as are most of the walks in the Atlantic Islands chapter.

For the more remote walks in the west of Ireland there are generally compromise solutions for the determined traveller. For example, it is possible to rent bikes at many hostels and you may be able to reach some fairly remote trailheads using pedal power. Alternatively it may be possible to arrange a taxi, or your accommodation provider may be happy to arrange private transport. On top of this you can explore the option of joining a guided walk, where transport to and from the walk will be included.

Permit (IDP) from your home automobile association before you leave. Your home-country licence is usually enough to hire a car for three months.

You must carry your driving licence at all times.

Hire

Car hire in Ireland is expensive, so you're often better off making arrangements in your home country with some sort of package deal. In July and August it's wise to book well ahead. Most cars are manual; automatic cars are available but they're more expensive to hire.

The international hire companies and the major local operators have offices all over Ireland. **Nova Car Hire** (www.rentacar-ireland.com) acts as an agent for Alamo, Budget, European and National, and offers greatly discounted rates. In the Republic typical weekly high-season hire rates with Nova are around €150 for a small car, €185 for a medium-sized car, and €320 for a five-seater people carrier. In the North, similar cars are marginally more expensive.

When hiring a car be sure to check if the price includes collision-damage waiver (CDW), insurance (eg for car theft and windscreen damage), value-added tax (VAT) and unlimited mileage.

If you're travelling from the Republic into Northern Ireland it's important to be sure that your insurance covers journeys to the North. People aged under 21 aren't allowed to hire a car; for the majority of hire companies you have to be aged at least 23 and have had a valid driving licence for a minimum of one year. Some companies in the Republic won't rent to you if you're aged 74 or over; there's no upper age limit in the North.

You can't hire motorbikes and mopeds.

Parking

Ireland is tiny and the Irish love their cars; in cities parking can be expensive and difficult. Parking in towns and cities is either by meter, 'pay and display' tickets or disc parking (discs, which rotate to display the time you park your car, are available from newsagencies). Parking in smaller towns and villages is normally free and easy.

Parking for many of the walks in this book is in ad-hoc lay-bys. When parking on road verges, be careful to check for soft ground or anything hidden in vegetation that might damage your vehicle. Parking in front of gates, no matter how minor or apparently unused, is a definite no-no.

Purchase

It's more expensive to buy a car in Ireland than most other European countries. If you do buy a car (or intend to import one from another country) you must pay vehicle registration tax and motor tax, and take out insurance.

Road Conditions

Road surfaces in rural Ireland tend to be quite poor, particularly in mountainous areas. Ice and snow is rarely a problem, but when there is a spell of freezing weather do not expect anything except the major routes to be cleared.

Road Hazards

Visibility on rural Irish roads tends to be poor so you should temper your speed accordingly. Slow moving farm vehicles are a frequent hazard, and stock is often herded along public roads on its way from one field to another. If you do come across a flock on the move, sit still while the animals pass around you or until the farmer waves you on.

Many of the walks in this book also take you to areas where sheep are allowed to graze unconfined. On wet and cool days, sheep are irresistibly attracted to roads, when the paved surface provides the driest and warmest place for miles around. If you find yourself in such an area, proceed with caution, especially at night or when there are young lambs around.

Road Rules

A copy of Ireland's road rules is available from tourist offices. Here are some of the most basic rules which should serve as an essential starting point before you take to the roads:

- Drive on the left, overtake to the right.
- Safety belts must be worn by the driver and all passengers.
- Children aged under 12 aren't allowed to sit on the front seats.
- Motorcyclists and their passengers must wear helmets.
- When entering a roundabout, give way to the right.
- Speed limits are 120km/h on motorways, 100km/h on national roads, 80km/h on regional and local roads and 50km/h or as signposted in towns.
- The legal alcohol limit is 80mg of alcohol per 100ml of blood or 35mg on the breath (roughly two pints of beer an hour for a man, one for a woman). Note: three pints (1½ for a woman) will put you over the limit.

HITCHING

Hitching is becoming increasingly less popular in Ireland, even though it's still pretty easy compared to other European countries. Travellers who decide to hitch should understand that they are taking a small but potentially serious risk, and we don't recommend it. If you do plan to travel by thumb, remember it's illegal to hitch on motorways.

TRAIN

Iarnród Éireann (Irish Rail; ☎ 1850 366 222; www.irishrail.ie; 35 Lower Abbey St, Dublin) operates trains in the Republic on routes that fan out from Dublin. The system is limited though: there's no north-south route along the western coast, no network in Donegal, and no direct connections from Waterford to Cork or Killarney. **Northern Ireland Railways** (NIR; ☎ 028-9089 9411; www.translink.co.uk; Belfast Central Station) runs four routes from Belfast. One links with the system in the Republic via Newry to Dublin; the other three go east to Bangor, northeast to Larne and northwest to Derry via Coleraine.

Costs

Train travel is more expensive than bus travel and one-way fares are particularly poor value. Note a midweek return ticket is often about the same as a one-way fare. First-class tickets cost around €5 to €10 more than the standard fare for a single journey.

Some sample one-way fares:

Service	Cost	Hrs	Frequency (Mon-Sat)
DUBLIN–BELFAST	€38	2	HALF-HOURLY
DUBLIN–CORK	€66	3¼	8
DUBLIN–GALWAY	€34.50	3¼	5
DUBLIN–LIMERICK	€50	2½	13
DUBLIN–SLIGO	€32	3	3
DUBLIN–TRALEE	€68.50	4½	8
DUBLIN–WATERFORD	€27	2½	7

Reservations

Iarnród Éireann takes online reservations for all of its regular train services – see www.irishrail.ie.

TRANSPORT

TRAIN ROUTES

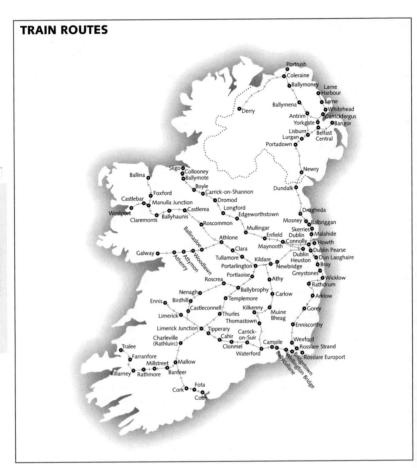

Train Passes

As is the case throughout Europe, you'll be able to source a wide range of rail passes for travel across Ireland. Details of special deals and passes are given in the boxed text on p310.

Clothing & Equipment

Irish weather forecasters have an admirable ability to say the same thing, and always with a smile on their faces. 'It might be sunny now, but don't worry, it won't be long before it's wet again.' While spells of fine, dry, and even warm weather are regular features of Irish climate, it is also true that rain, drizzle and showers recur with regularity at any time of the year. Consequently those braving the Irish outdoors – particularly walkers – need to be dressed and equipped for everything from prolonged sunshine to heavy rain, no matter what the skies look like when you set out.

CLOTHING
Gaiters
These are absolutely essential for rough, wet walking and, to a considerable extent, can replace overtrousers in all but the wettest, coldest conditions. They postpone the awful moment when water starts to seep into your boots and can help to minimise the discomfort of wading through shallow water.

Footwear
Boots are absolutely essential for most of the walks described in this book – those that involve hiking cross-country or only on rough tracks, or where you have to follow paths that are usually wet and muddy. Runners or specialised walking shoes are fine for canal walks, and those following firm, dry paths, such as the near-urban walks in and close to Dublin and Belfast.

You'll be very lucky if you don't finish at least one day with sodden boots; beware the eager B&B host who rushes to grab your boots and dry them in front of the fire. Stuff your boots with newspaper and make sure they're put in a warm room, well away from any direct heat source such as an open fire.

Layering
The secret to comfortable hiking is to wear several layers of light clothing, which you can easily take off or put on as you warm up or cool down. Most walkers use three main layers: a base layer next to the skin; an insulating layer; and an outer, shell layer for protection from wind, rain and snow.

For the upper body, the base layer is typically a shirt of synthetic material such as polypropylene, with its ability to wick moisture away from the body and reduce chilling. The insulating layer retains heat next to your body, and is often a windproof synthetic fleece or down jacket. The outer shell consists of a waterproof jacket that also protects against cold wind.

For the lower body, the layers generally consist of either shorts or loose-fitting trousers, polypropylene 'long-john' underwear and waterproof overtrousers.

Waterproof Shells
In addition to the advice given in the boxed text Buying Tips (p316), there are a few other points worth keeping in mind when you're deciding what you'll need to keep dry. A large cape, made of waterproof material, that drapes over you and your pack is recommended. It's less constricting than a jacket, doesn't leak through the seams (a common failing of jackets) and underneath a cape you're less likely to overheat than in a jacket. A cape would be most useful for lower-level walks rather than on exposed, windy ridges and summits. The same goes for an umbrella – not as daft as it sounds if there's little wind, the main advantage being that your all-round vision isn't restricted.

WINDPROOF JACKET
Given that Irish weather is windy as often as not, especially in western areas, protection against breezes and gales is worth serious consideration. Garments that serve this

BUYING TIPS

BACKPACK

For day walks, a day-pack (30L to 40L) will usually suffice, but for multiday walks you will need a backpack of between 45L and 90L capacity. A good backpack should be made of strong fabric such as canvas or Cordura, a lightweight internal or external frame and an adjustable, well-padded harness that evenly distributes weight. Even if the manufacturer claims your pack is waterproof, use heavy-duty liners.

FOOTWEAR

Runners or walking shoes are fine over easy terrain but, for more difficult trails and across rocks and scree, the ankle support offered by boots is invaluable. Nonslip soles (such as Vibram) provide the best grip. Buy boots in warm conditions or go for a walk before trying them on, so that your feet can expand slightly, as they would on a walk. Some walkers carry a pair of sandals or thongs (flip flops) to wear at night or at rest stops. Sandals are also useful when fording waterways.

GAITERS

If you will be hiking through snow, deep mud or scratchy vegetation, gaiters will protect your legs and help keep your socks dry. The best are made of strong fabric, with a robust zip protected by a flap, and secure easily around the foot.

OVERTROUSERS

Choose a model with slits for pocket access and long leg zips so that you can pull them on and off over your boots.

SLEEPING BAG & MAT

Down fillings are warmer than synthetic for the same weight and bulk but, unlike synthetic fillings, do not retain warmth when wet. Mummy bags are the best shape for weight and warmth. The given figure (-5°C, for instance) is the coldest temperature at which a person should feel comfortable in the bag (although the ratings are notoriously optimistic).

An inner sheet helps keep your sleeping bag clean, as well as adding an insulating layer. Silk 'inners' are lightest, but they also come in cotton or polypropylene.

Self-inflating sleeping mats work like a thin air cushion between you and the ground; they also insulate from the cold. Foam mats are a low-cost, but less comfortable, alternative.

SOCKS

Hiking socks should be free of ridged seams in the toes and heels.

STOVES

Fuel stoves fall roughly into three categories: multifuel, methylated spirits (ethyl alcohol) and butane gas. Multifuel stoves are small, efficient and ideal for places where a reliable fuel supply is difficult to find. However, they tend to be sooty and require frequent maintenance. Stoves running on methylated spirits are slower and less efficient, but are safe, clean and easy to use. Butane gas stoves are clean and reliable, but can be slow, and the gas canisters can be awkward to carry and a potential litter problem.

TENT

A three-season tent will fulfil the requirements of most walkers. The floor and the outer shell, or fly, should have taped or sealed seams and covered zips to stop leaks. Most walkers find tents of around 2kg to 3kg a comfortable carrying weight. Dome- and tunnel-shaped tents handle windy conditions better than flat-sided tents.

WATERPROOF JACKET

The ideal specifications are a breathable, waterproof fabric, a hood that is roomy enough to cover headwear but still allows peripheral vision, capacious map pocket, and a heavy-gauge zip protected by a storm flap.

purpose, that are waterproof except in steady downpours and weigh less than conventional rain jackets, are now fairly plentiful in outdoor shops; collectively they're known as soft shell tops.

EQUIPMENT
Sleeping Sheets
The vast majority of hostels – both the youth and the independent varieties – provide sheets, either for an additional fee or as part of the overnight tariff. In fact, in the more luxurious ones you might even find your bed made up for you. Even so, if you plan on doing a lot of hostelling, it would be worth taking your own sleeping sheet to save some money.

Stove Fuel
Canned gas and liquid fuels are stocked by the larger outdoor equipment shops (see Buying & Hiring Locally, below). Methylated spirits (labelled 'mineralised methylated spirits' in Ireland) may also be found in hardware shops and larger supermarkets.

BUYING & HIRING LOCALLY
Most large towns in Ireland have some sort of shop selling outdoor clothing and equipment, where you should find a range of quality international brands. The country's big cities and those towns located near popular hiking areas generally have the most comprehensive ranges and widest choice. For details of the main outdoor retailer in each town, see Towns & Facilities at the end of each regional chapter.

Hiring equipment is completely unknown, so you'll need to come fully equipped or prepared to visit the local outlets.

NAVIGATION EQUIPMENT
Maps & Compass
You should always carry a good map of the area you are hiking in (see Maps, p298), and know how to read it. Before setting off on your trek, ensure that you understand the contours and the map symbols, plus the main ridge and river systems in the area. Also familiarise yourself with the true north–south directions and the general direction in which you are heading. On the trail, try to identify major landforms such as mountain ranges and gorges, and locate them on your map.

This will give you a better understanding of the region's geography.

Buy a compass and learn how to use it. The attraction of magnetic north varies in different parts of the world, so compasses need to be balanced accordingly. Compass manufacturers have divided the world into five zones. Make sure your compass is balanced for your destination zone. There are also 'universal' compasses on the market that can be used anywhere in the world.

Global Positioning System (GPS)
Originally developed by the US Department of Defense, the Global Positioning System (GPS) is a network of more than 20 earth-orbiting satellites that continually beam encoded signals back to earth. Small, computer-driven devices (GPS receivers) can decode these signals to give users an extremely accurate reading of their location – to within 30m, anywhere on the planet, at any time of day, in almost any weather. The cheapest hand-held GPS receivers now cost less than €75 (although these may not have a built-in averaging system that minimises signal errors). Other important factors to consider when buying a GPS receiver are its weight and battery life.

Remember that a GPS receiver is of little use to walkers unless used with an accurate topographical map. The receiver simply gives your position, which you must then locate on the local map. At the time of writing there were no GPS compatible topographical maps for Ireland. The signals from a crucial satellite may be blocked (or bounce off rock or water) directly below high cliffs, near large bodies of water or in dense tree cover and give inaccurate readings. GPS receivers are more vulnerable to breakdowns (including dead batteries) than the humble magnetic compass – a low–tech device that has served navigators faithfully for centuries – so don't rely on them entirely.

Altimeter
Altimeters determine altitude by measuring air pressure. Because pressure is affected by temperature, altimeters are calibrated to take lower temperatures at higher altitudes into account. However, discrepancies can still occur, especially in unsettled weather, so it's wise to take a few precautions when using your altimeter.

CLOTHING & EQUIPMENT

HOW TO USE A COMPASS

This is a very basic introduction to using a compass and will only be of assistance if you are proficient in map reading. For simplicity, it doesn't take magnetic variation into account. Before using a compass we recommend you obtain further instruction.

1. Reading a Compass
Hold the compass flat in the palm of your hand. Rotate the **bezel** so the **red end** of the **needle** points to the **N** on the bezel. The bearing is read from the **dash** under the bezel.

2. Orienting the Map
To orient the map so that it aligns with the ground, place the compass flat on the map. Rotate the map until the **needle** is parallel with the map's north/south grid lines and the red end is pointing to north on the map. You can now identify features around you by aligning them with labelled features on the map.

3. Taking a Bearing from the Map
Draw a line on the map between your starting point and your destination. Place the edge of the compass on this line with the **direction of travel arrow** pointing towards your destination. Rotate the **bezel** until the **meridian lines** are parallel with the north/south grid lines on the map and the N points to north on the map. Read the bearing from the dash.

4. Following a Bearing
Rotate the **bezel** so that the intended bearing is in line with the **dash**. Place the compass flat in the palm of your hand and rotate the **base plate** until the **red end** points to N on the **bezel**. The **direction of travel arrow** will now point in the direction you need to walk.

5. Determining your Bearing
Rotate the **bezel** so the **red end** points to the **N**. Place the compass flat in the palm of your hand and rotate the **base plate** until the **direction of travel arrow** points in the direction in which you have been hiking. Read your bearing from the **dash**.

1	Base plate
2	Direction of travel arrow
3	Dash
4	Bezel
5	Meridian lines
6	Needle
7	Red end
8	N (north point)

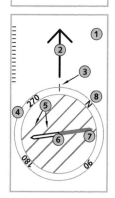

---

o Reset your altimeter regularly at known elevations such as spot heights and passes. Do not take spot heights from villages where there may be a large difference in elevation from one end of the settlement to another.

o Use your altimeter in conjunction with other navigation techniques to fix your position. For instance, taking a back bearing to a known peak or river confluence, determining the general direction of the track and obtaining your elevation will usually give you a pretty good fix on your position.

Altimeters are also barometers and are useful for indicating changing weather conditions. If the altimeter shows increasing elevation while you are not climbing, it means the air pressure is dropping and a low-pressure weather system may be approaching.

Route Finding
The maps in this book are intended to help you locate the route within the surrounding area. They are not detailed enough in themselves for route-finding or navigation. When you're on the walk, make sure to carry a properly surveyed map at an adequate scale – these are recommended in the Planning section for each walk.

Bear in mind however, that while accurate, these reference maps are not infallible. Inaccuracies in altitudes can be caused by air-temperature anomalies, and the location of villages and trails are not

CHECK LIST

This list is a general guide to the things you might take on a walk. Your list will vary depending on the kind of hiking you want to do, whether you're camping or planning on staying in hostels or B&Bs, and on the terrain, weather conditions and time of year.

CLOTHING

- boots and spare laces
- gaiters
- hat (warm), scarf and gloves
- jacket (waterproof)
- overtrousers (waterproof)
- runners (training shoes), sandals or thongs (flip flops)
- shorts and trousers or skirt
- socks and underwear
- sunhat
- sweater or fleece jacket
- thermal underwear
- T-shirt and long-sleeved shirt with collar

EQUIPMENT

- backpack with liner (waterproof)
- first-aid kit*
- food and snacks (high energy) and one day's emergency supplies
- insect repellent
- map, compass and guidebook
- map case or clip-seal plastic bags
- pocket knife
- sunglasses
- sunscreen and lip balm
- survival bag or blanket
- toilet paper and trowel
- torch (flashlight) or headlamp, spare batteries and globe (bulb)
- water container
- whistle

OVERNIGHT WALKS

- cooking, eating and drinking utensils
- dishwashing items
- matches and lighter
- sewing/repair kit
- sleeping bag and bag liner/inner sheet
- sleeping mat
- spare cord
- stove and fuel
- tent, pegs, poles and guy ropes
- toiletries
- towel
- water purification tablets, iodine or filter

OPTIONAL ITEMS

- altimeter
- backpack cover (waterproof, slip-on)
- binoculars
- camera, film and batteries
- candle
- emergency distress beacon
- GPS receiver
- groundsheet
- mobile phone**
- mosquito net
- notebook and pen
- swimming costume
- walking poles
- watch

* see the First-aid Check List (p321)
** see Mobile Phones (p327)

CLOTHING & EQUIPMENT

always perfect. This may be because a village is spread over a hillside, or the size of the map does not allow for detail of the trail's twists and turns. Trails themselves can also be re-routed, and these changes may not be updated immediately on printed references. The best advice is to combine the information on the reference map with the written descriptions in this book. In addition, use several basic route-finding techniques to keep yourself on the right track:

1. Be aware of whether the trail should be climbing or descending.
2. Check the north-point arrow on the map and determine the general direction of the trail.
3. Time your progress over a known distance and calculate the speed at which you travel in the given terrain. From then on, you can determine with reasonable accuracy how far you have travelled.
4. Watch the path – look for boot prints and other signs of previous passage.

Health & Safety

Keeping healthy on the trail depends on your predeparture preparations, your daily health care while travelling and how you handle any medical problems that develop. While the potential problems can seem quite daunting, in reality few travellers experience anything more than an upset stomach.

BEFORE YOU GO

While Ireland has excellent health care, prevention is the key to staying healthy while abroad. A little planning before departure, particularly for pre-existing illnesses, will save trouble later. Bring medications in their original, clearly labelled, containers. A signed and dated letter from your physician describing your medical conditions and medications, including generic names, is also a good idea. If carrying syringes or needles, be sure to have a physician's letter documenting their medical necessity.

Some of the walks in this book are physically demanding and most require a reasonable

level of fitness. Even if you're tackling the easy or easy–moderate walks, it pays to be relatively fit, rather than launch straight into them after months of fairly sedentary living. If you're aiming for the demanding walks, fitness is essential.

Unless you're a regular walker start your get-fit campaign at least a month before your visit. Take a vigorous walk of about an hour, two or three times per week and gradually extend the duration of your outings as the departure date nears. If you plan to carry a full backpack on any walk, carry a loaded pack on some of your training jaunts.

If you have any known medical problems or are concerned about your health in any way, it's a good idea to have a full check-up before you start hiking. It's far better to have any problems recognised and treated at home than to find out about them half-way up a mountain. It's also sensible to have had a recent dental check-up since toothache on the trail can be a miserable experience.

INSURANCE

If you're an EU citizen, a European Health Insurance Card (EHIC), available from health centres or, in the UK, post offices, covers you for most medical care. The EHIC won't cover you for non-emergencies, or emergency repatriation home. Citizens from other countries should find out if there is a reciprocal arrangement for free medical care between their country and Ireland. If you do need health insurance, make sure you get a policy that covers you for the worst possible case, such as an accident requiring an emergency flight home. Find out in advance if your insurance plan will make payments directly to providers, or reimburse you later for overseas health expenditures.

RECOMMENDED VACCINATIONS

No jabs are required to travel to Ireland. The World Health Organization, however, recommends that all travellers should be covered for diphtheria, tetanus, measles,

FIRST-AID CHECK LIST

Following is a list of items you should consider including in your first-aid kit – consult your pharmacist for brands available in your country.

ESSENTIALS

- adhesive tape
- bandages and safety pins
- elasticated support bandage – for knees, ankles etc
- gauze swabs
- non-adhesive dressings
- paper stitches
- scissors (small)
- sterile alcohol wipes
- sticking plasters (Band-Aids, blister plasters)
- thermometer (note that mercury thermometers are prohibited by airlines)
- tweezers

MEDICATIONS

- antidiarrhoea and antinausea drugs
- antifungal cream or powder – for fungal skin infections and thrush

- antihistamines – for allergies, eg, hay fever; to ease the itch from insect bites or stings; and to prevent motion sickness
- antiseptic (such as povidone-iodine) – for cuts and grazes
- cold and flu tablets, throat lozenges and nasal decongestant
- painkillers, eg, aspirin or paracetamol (acetaminophen in the USA) – for pain and fever

MISCELLANEOUS

- calamine lotion, sting relief spray or aloe vera – to ease irritation from sunburn and insect bites or stings
- eye drops – for washing out dust
- rehydration mixture – to prevent dehydration, eg, due to severe diarrhoea; particularly important when travelling with children

mumps, rubella, polio and hepatitis B, regardless of their destination.

INTERNET RESOURCES

There is a wealth of travel health advice to be found on the internet. For further information, **Lonely Planet** (www.lonelyplanet .com) is a good place to start.

IN TRANSIT

DEEP VEIN THROMBOSIS (DVT)

Blood clots may form in the legs during plane flights, chiefly because of prolonged immobility. The longer the flight, the greater the risk. The chief symptom of deep vein thrombosis is swelling or pain of the foot, ankle, or calf, often on just one side. When a blood clot travels to the lungs, it may cause chest pain and difficulty breathing. Travellers with any of these symptoms should immediately seek medical attention.

To prevent the development of DVT on long flights you should walk about the cabin, contract the leg muscles while sitting,

drink plenty of fluids and avoid alcohol and tobacco.

JET LAG & MOTION SICKNESS

To avoid jet lag (quite common when crossing more than five time zones) try drinking plenty of non-alcoholic fluids and eating light meals. Upon arrival, get exposure to natural sunlight and readjust your schedule (for meals, sleep etc) as soon as possible.

Antihistamines such as dimenhydrinate (Dramamine) or meclizine (Antivert, Bonine) are quite often the first choice for treating motion sickness. A herbal alternative is ginger.

IN IRELAND

AVAILABILITY & COST OF HEALTH CARE

Excellent health care is readily available and for minor self-limiting illnesses pharmacists can give valuable advice and sell over-the-counter medication. They can also advise when more specialised help is required and point you in the right direction.

COMMON AILMENTS

BLISTERS

To avoid blisters make sure your hiking boots or shoes are well worn in before you hit the trail. Your boots should fit comfortably with enough room to move your toes; boots that are too big or too small will cause blisters. Similarly for socks – be sure they fit properly and are specifically made for walkers – even then, check to make sure that there are no seams across the widest part of your foot. Wet and muddy socks can also cause blisters, so even on a day walk, pack a spare pair of socks. Keep your toenails clipped but not too short. If you do feel a blister coming on, treat it sooner rather then later. Apply a simple sticking plaster, or preferably one of the special blister plasters that act as a second skin.

FATIGUE

A simple statistic: more injuries happen towards the end of the day than earlier, when you're fresher. Although tiredness can simply be a nuisance on an easy walk, it can be life-threatening on narrow exposed ridges or in bad weather. You should never set out on a walk that is beyond your capabilities on the day. If you feel below par, have a day off or take a bus. To reduce the risk, don't push yourself too hard – take rests every hour or two and build in a good half hour's lunch break. Towards the end of the day, take down the pace and increase your concentration. You should also eat properly throughout the day; nuts, dried fruit and chocolate are all good energy-giving snack foods.

KNEE STRAIN

Many walkers feel the judder on long steep descents. Although you can't eliminate strain on the knee joints when dropping steeply, you can reduce it by taking shorter steps, which leave your legs slightly bent and ensure that your heel hits the ground before the rest of your foot. Some walkers find that tubular bandages help, while others use hi-tech, strap-on supports. Hiking poles are very effective in taking some of the weight off the knees.

INFECTIOUS DISEASES

Fungal Infections

Sweating liberally, probably washing less than usual and going longer without a change of clothes mean that long-distance walkers risk picking up a fungal infection, which, while an unpleasant irritant, presents no danger.

Fungal infections are encouraged by moisture, so wear loose, comfortable clothes, wash when you can and dry yourself thoroughly. Try to expose the infected area to air or sunlight as much as possible and apply an antifungal cream or powder like tolnaftate.

Lyme Disease

This is a tick-transmitted infection (see Ticks, p323). The illness usually begins with a spreading rash at the site of the tick bite and is accompanied by fever, headache, extreme fatigue, aching joints and muscles and mild neck stiffness. If untreated, these symptoms usually resolve over several weeks but over subsequent weeks or months disorders of the nervous system, heart and joints may develop. Treatment works best early in the illness. Medical help should be sought.

Tetanus

This disease is caused by a germ that lives in soil, and in the faeces of animals. It enters the body via breaks in the skin. The first symptom may be discomfort in swallowing, or stiffening of the jaw and neck; this is followed by painful convulsions of the jaw and whole body. The disease can be fatal. It can be prevented by vaccination, so make sure your shots are up to date.

TRAVELLERS DIARRHOEA

If you develop diarrhoea, be sure to drink plenty of fluids, preferably in the form of an oral rehydration solution such as dioralyte. If diarrhoea is bloody, persists for more than 72 hours or is accompanied by fever, shaking, chills or severe abdominal pain you will need to seek urgent medical attention. Walkers in Ireland who use untreated water from streams, rivers or lakes may be at risk of Amoebic Dysentery or Giardiasis.

Amoebic Dysentery

This is characterised by a gradual onset of low-grade diarrhoea, often with blood and mucus. Cramping abdominal pain and vomiting are less likely than in other types of diarrhoea, and fever may not be present. It will persist until treated and can recur and cause other health problems.

If you think you have amoebic dysentry, you should seek medical advice; treatment is the same as for giardiasis.

Giardiasis

Symptoms include stomach cramps, nausea, a bloated stomach, watery, foul-smelling diarrhoea and frequent gas. Giardiasis can appear several weeks after you have been exposed to the parasite. The symptoms may disappear for a few days and then return; this can go on for several weeks.

Seek medical advice if you think you have giardiasis, but where this is not possible, tinidazole or metronidazole are the recommended drugs. Treatment is a 2g single dose of tinidazole or 250mg of metronidazole three times daily for five to 10 days.

ENVIRONMENTAL HAZARDS
Bites & Stings
BEES & WASPS

These are usually painful rather than dangerous. However, in people who are allergic to them severe breathing difficulties may occur and urgent medical care is required. Calamine lotion or a commercial sting relief spray will ease discomfort and ice packs will reduce the pain and swelling.

TICKS

Always check all over your body if you have been hiking through a potentially tick-infested area as ticks can cause skin infections and other more serious diseases. Ticks are most active from spring to autumn, especially where there are plenty of sheep or deer. They usually lurk in overhanging vegetation, so avoid pushing through tall bushes if possible.

If a tick is found attached to the skin, press down around the tick's head with tweezers, grab the head and gently pull upwards. Avoid pulling the rear of the body as this may squeeze the tick's gut contents through its mouth into your skin, increasing the risk of infection and disease. Smearing chemicals on the tick will not make it let go and is not recommended.

Cold
HYPOTHERMIA

This occurs when the body loses heat faster than it can produce it and the core temperature of the body falls.

It is frighteningly easy to progress from very cold to dangerously cold due to a combination of wind, wet clothing, fatigue and hunger, even if the air temperature is above freezing. If the weather deteriorates, put on extra layers of warm clothing: a

MIDGES – WALKERS' BANE

The midge is a tiny black insect that gathers in dense, dark clouds and descends on humans. The female of the species uses her powerful mouth to break the skin, inject saliva and suck blood through her food tube. The saliva makes the bite itch, and the more you scratch it, the itchier it becomes. Discomfort generally lasts for a few hours, longer if you're allergic to the bite.

Midges usually appear in late May and infest certain parts of the Irish countryside until the first chilly weather in September. They congregate over damp ground, rushes and sphagnum moss, and are most virulent in the early morning, in hazy sunshine and during the evening. They don't like wind, dry ground, heavy rain or bright sunshine, and rarely venture indoors.

For protection, cover your arms and legs and wear a hat with a fine netting veil, available in most outdoor equipment shops. Liquid insect repellents should keep exposed skin midge-free for a few hours at a time. Some contain DEET, a slightly toxic chemical, others are made from plant oils including citronella and eucalyptus.

Permethrin, an insecticide derived from chrysanthemums, can be applied to clothing and equipment and lasts for a week or two, but only for several minutes on the skin. Read all labels carefully and follow the directions carefully.

WATER

Many diseases are carried in water in the form of bacteria, protozoa, viruses, worms and insect eggs etc. Tap water in Ireland is safe to drink but drinking untreated water from streams, rivers and lakes should be avoided.

WATER PURIFICATION

The simplest way of purifying water is to boil it thoroughly. Vigorous boiling for at least one minute should be satisfactory.

You can also use a chemical agent to purify water. Chlorine and iodine are usually used, available from outdoor equipment suppliers and pharmacies. Chlorine tablets will kill many pathogens, but not some parasites like giardia and amoebic cysts. Iodine is more effective in purifying water. Follow the directions carefully and remember that too much iodine can be harmful.

If you plan to camp wild for considerable periods of time you could consider purchasing a water filter. There are two main kinds of filter. Total filters take out all parasites, bacteria and viruses and make water safe to drink. They are relatively expensive. Simple filters (which can be a nylon mesh bag) take out dirt and larger foreign bodies from the water so that chemical solutions work much more effectively; if the water is dirty, chemical solutions may not work at all. It's very important when buying a filter to read the specifications, so that you know exactly what it removes from the water.

---

wind and/or waterproof jacket, plus wool or fleece hat and gloves are all essential. Have something energy-giving to eat and ensure that everyone in your group is fit, feeling well and alert.

Symptoms of hypothermia are exhaustion, numb skin (particularly toes and fingers), shivering, slurred speech, irrational or violent behaviour, lethargy, stumbling, dizzy spells, muscle cramps and violent bursts of energy. Irrationality may take the form of sufferers claiming they are warm and trying to take off their clothes.

To treat mild hypothermia, first get the person out of the wind and/or rain, remove their clothing if it's wet and replace it with dry, warm clothing. Give them hot liquids – not alcohol – and some high-energy, easily digestible food. Do not rub victims: instead, allow them to slowly warm themselves. This should be enough to treat the early stages of hypothermia. The early recognition and treatment of mild hypothermia is the only way to prevent severe hypothermia, which is a critical condition.

Heatstroke

Heat exhaustion (yes, even in Ireland it can still happen!) occurs following excessive fluid loss with insufficient replacement of fluids and salt. Symptoms include headache, dizziness and tiredness. Dehydration is already happening by the time you feel thirsty – aim to drink sufficient water to produce pale, diluted urine. To treat heat exhaustion drink water and/or fruit juice, and cool the body with cold water and fans.

Sun

Protection against the sun should always be taken seriously. Slap on the sunscreen and a barrier cream for your nose and lips, wear a broad brimmed hat and protect your eyes with good quality sunglasses with UV lenses, particularly when hiking near water or sand. If, despite these precautions, you get yourself burnt, calamine lotion, aloe vera or other commercial sunburn relief preparations will soothe the burn.

TRAUMATIC INJURIES

Detailed first-aid instruction is outside the scope of this book, but here are some tips and advice. Walkers should consider taking a first-aid course before hitting the trail to ensure they know what to do in the event of an injury.

Fractures

Indications of a fracture (broken bone) are pain (tenderness of the affected area), swelling and discolouration, loss of function or deformity of a limb. Unless you know what you are doing, you shouldn't try to straighten an obviously displaced broken bone. To protect from further injury, immobilise a nondisplaced fracture by splinting it, usually in the position found, which will probably be the most comfortable position.

Fractures of the thigh bone require urgent treatment as they involve massive blood loss and pain. Seek help and treat the patient for shock. Fractures associated with open wounds (compound fractures) also require more urgent treatment than simple fractures as there is a risk of infection. Dislocations, where the bone has come out of the joint, are very painful, and should be set as soon as possible.

Broken ribs are painful but usually heal by themselves and do not need splinting. If breathing difficulties occur, or the person coughs up blood, medical attention should be sought urgently, as it may indicate a punctured lung.

Internal Injuries

These are more difficult to detect, and cannot usually be treated in the field. Watch for shock, which is a specific medical condition associated with a failure to maintain circulating blood volume. Signs include a rapid pulse and cold, clammy extremities. A person in shock requires urgent medical attention.

Major Accidents

Falling or having something fall on you, resulting in head injuries or fractures, is always possible when hiking, especially if you are crossing steep slopes or unstable terrain. Following is some basic advice on what to do in the event of a major accident. If a person suffers a major fall:

- make sure you and other people with you are not in danger
- assess the injured person's condition
- stabilise any injuries, such as bleeding wounds or broken bones
- seek medical attention (see p327)

If the person is unconscious, immediately check whether they are breathing – clear their airway if it is blocked – and check whether they have a pulse – feel the side of the neck rather than the wrist. If they

are not breathing but have a pulse, you should start mouth-to-mouth resuscitation immediately. In these circumstances it is best to move the person as little as possible in case their neck or back is broken.

Check for wounds and broken bones – ask the person where they have pain if they are conscious, otherwise gently inspect them all over (including their back and the back of the head), moving them as little as possible. Control any bleeding by applying firm pressure to the wound. Bleeding from the nose or ear may indicate a fractured skull. Don't give the person anything by mouth, especially if they are unconscious.

You'll have to manage the person for shock. Raise their legs above heart level (unless their legs are fractured); dress any wounds and immobilise any fractures; loosen tight clothing; keep the person warm by covering them with a blanket or other dry clothing; insulate them from the ground if possible, but don't heat them.

Some general points to consider are:

- Simple fractures take several weeks to heal, so they don't need fixing straight away, but they should be immobilised to protect them from further injury. Compound fractures need urgent treatment.
- If you do have to splint a broken bone, remember to check regularly that the splint is not cutting off the circulation to the hand or foot.
- Most cases of brief unconsciousness are not associated with any serious internal injury to the brain, but as a general rule of thumb in these circumstances, any person who has been knocked unconscious should be watched for deterioration. If they do deteriorate, seek medical attention straight away.

Sprains

Ankle and knee sprains are common injuries among walkers, particularly when crossing rugged terrain. To help prevent ankle sprains, wear boots that have adequate ankle support. If you do suffer a sprain, immobilise the joint with a firm bandage, and, if feasible, immerse the foot in cold water. Distribute the contents of your pack among your companions. Once you reach shelter, relieve pain and swelling by keeping the joint elevated for the first 24 hours and, where possible, by putting ice on the swollen joint. Take simple painkillers to ease the discomfort. If the sprain is mild, you may be able to continue your walk after a couple of days. For more severe sprains, seek medical attention as an x-ray may be needed to find out whether a bone has been broken

SAFETY ON THE WALK

You can significantly reduce the chance of getting into difficulties by taking a few simple precautions. These are listed in the boxed text Walk Safety – Basic Rules below. GPS units used properly can greatly reduce your chances of becoming lost, however they should not be considered a substitute for traditional navigational skills, including the ability to read a map accurately and use a compass.

CROSSING RIVERS

Sudden downpours are common in the mountains and can speedily turn a gentle stream into a raging torrent. If you're in any doubt about the safety of a crossing, look for a safer passage upstream or wait. If the rain is short-lived, it should subside quickly.

If you decide it's essential to cross (late in the day, for example), look for a wide, relatively shallow stretch of the stream rather than a bend. Take off your trousers and socks, but keep your boots on to prevent injury. Put dry, warm clothes and a towel in a plastic bag near the top of your pack. Before stepping out from the bank, unclip your chest strap and belt buckle. This makes it easier to slip out of your backpack and swim to safety if you lose your balance and are swept downstream. Use a walking pole, grasped in both hands, on the upstream side as a third leg, or go arm in arm with a companion, clasping at the wrist, and cross side-on to the flow, taking short steps.

DOGS

During walks in settled and farming areas, you're likely to encounter barking dogs – tethered or running free. Regard any dog

as a potential attacker and be prepared to take evasive action: even just crossing the road can take you out of its territory and into safety. A walking pole may be useful, though use it as a last resort.

LIGHTNING

If a storm brews, avoid exposed areas. Lightning has a penchant for crests, lone trees, small depressions, gullies and caves, as well as wet ground. If you are caught out in the open, try to curl up as tightly as possible with your feet together and keep a layer of insulation between you and the ground. Place metal objects such as metal-frame backpacks and walking poles away from you.

RESCUE & EVACUATION

If someone in your group is injured or falls ill and can't move, leave somebody with them while another one or more goes for help. They should take clear written details of the location and condition of the victim, and of helicopter landing conditions. If there are only two of you, leave the injured person with as much warm clothing, food and water as it's sensible to spare, plus the

---

WALK SAFETY – BASIC RULES

- Allow plenty of time to accomplish a walk before dark, particularly when daylight hours are shorter.

- Study the route carefully before setting out, noting the possible escape routes and the point of no return (where it's quicker to continue than to turn back). Monitor your progress during the day against the time estimated for the walk, and keep an eye on the weather.

- It's wise not to walk alone. Always leave details of your intended route, number of people in your group, and expected return time with someone responsible before you set off; let that person know when you return.

- Before setting off, make sure you have a relevant map, compass, whistle, and that you know the weather forecast for the area for the next 24 hours.

whistle and torch. Mark the position with something conspicuous – an orange bivvy bag, or perhaps a large stone cross on the ground. Remember, the rescue effort might be slow, perhaps taking days to remove the injured person.

Emergency Communications

Dial ☎ 999 or ☎ 118 (the national emergency numbers) and ask for the mountain rescue or contact the nearest garda/police station. Be ready to give information on where the accident occurred, how many people were injured and the injuries sustained. If a helicopter needs to come in, what are the terrain and weather conditions like at the place of the accident? Also provide details on where you're calling from and stay put until someone arrives.

TELEPHONE

Mobile phone coverage in the areas most frequented by walkers is patchy, irrespective of which provider you use. It can vary from good to hopeless over an incredibly short distance, so using your mobile is really a matter of luck (see also Mobile Phones, p302).

DISTRESS SIGNALS

If you need to signal for help, use these internationally recognised emergency codes. Give six short signals, such as a whistle, a yell or the flash of a light, at 10-second intervals, followed by a minute of rest. Repeat the sequence until you get a response. If the responder knows the signals, this will be three signals at 20-second intervals, followed by a minute's pause and a repetition of the sequence.

Search & Rescue Organisations

The Irish **Mountain Rescue Association** (www.mountainrescue.ie) is a voluntary organisation. Member groups, which are locally based teams of highly trained, experienced and dedicated people, provide a rescue service to anyone in distress in the mountains. The local team will coordinate the rescue and organise a helicopter for evacuating the injured person if necessary.

Helicopter Rescue & Evacuation

If a helicopter arrives on the scene, there are a couple of conventions you should be familiar with. Standing face on to the chopper:

- Arms up in the shape of a letter 'V' means 'I/We need help'
- Arms in a straight diagonal line (like one line of a letter X) means 'All OK'

For the helicopter to land, there must be a cleared space of 25m x 25m, with a flat landing pad area of 6m x 6m. The helicopter will fly into the wind when landing. In cases of extreme emergency, where no landing area is available, a person or harness might be lowered. Take extreme care to avoid the rotors when approaching a landed helicopter.

Language

CONTENTS

In 2003 the government introduced the *Official Languages Act*, whereby all official documents, street signs and official titles must be either in Irish (Gaeilge) or in both Irish and English. While Irish is the official language, it's only spoken in isolated pockets of rural Ireland known as Gaeltachtaí, the main ones being Cork *(Chorcaí)*, Donegal *(Dhún na nGall)*, Galway *(Gaillimhe)*, Kerry *(Chiarraí)* and Mayo *(Mhaigh Eo)*.

Irish is a compulsory subject in schools for those aged six to 15, but Irish classes have traditionally been rather academic and unimaginative, leading many to consider it a waste of time. Ask people outside the Gaeltachtaí if they can speak Irish and nine out of 10 of them will probably reply, *ah, cupla focal* (a couple of words), and they generally mean it. Many adults do say, however, that they regret not having a greater grasp of it.

Recently, a new Irish curriculum has been introduced that will cut the hours devoted to the subject but make the lessons more fun, practical (with a focus on spoken language) and celebratory.

If you'd like a witty insight into the quirks of language in Ireland, get a copy of Lonely Planet's pocket-sized *Irish Language & Culture*.

PRONUNCIATION

Irish can be classified into three main dialects: Connaught Irish (Galway and northern Mayo), Munster Irish (Cork, Kerry and Waterford) and Ulster Irish (Donegal). The pronunciation guidelines given here are an anglicised version of modern standard Irish, which is essentially an amalgam of the three.

Vowels

Irish divides vowels into long (those with an accent) and short (those without) and, more importantly, broad (**a**, **á**, **o**, **ó**, **u** and **ú**) and slender (**e**, **é**, **i** and **í**), which can affect the pronunciation of preceding consonants.

a	as in 'cat'
á	as in 'saw'
e	as in 'bet'
é	as in 'hey'
i	as in 'sit'
í	as in 'marine'
o	as in 'son'
ó	as in 'low'
u	as in 'put'
ú	as in 'rule'

Consonants

Other than a few odd-looking clusters, like **mh** and **bhf**, consonants are generally pronounced as they are in English.

bh	as the 'v' in 'voice'
bhf	as the 'w' in 'well'
c	as the 'c' in 'cat'
ch	as the 'ch' in Scottish *loch*
d	as in 'do' when followed by a broad vowel; as the 'j' in 'jug' when followed by a slender vowel
dh	as the 'g' in 'gap' when followed by a broad vowel; as the 'y' in 'year' when followed by a slender vowel
mh	as the 'w' in 'well'
s	as in 'said' before a broad vowel; as the 'sh' in ship before a slender vowel and at the end of a word
t	as the 't' in 'toast' before a broad vowel; as the 'ch' in 'church' before a slender vowel
th	as the 'h' in 'house'; as the 't' in 'mat'; silent at the end of a word

MAKING CONVERSATION

Hello	*Dia duit*	dee·a gwit
(lit: God be with you)		
Hello (reply)	*Dia is Muire duit*	dee·as moyra gwit
(lit: God and Mary be with you)		
Good morning	*Maidin mhaith*	maw·jin wah
Good night	*Oíche mhaith*	eek·heh wah

Goodbye	*Slán leat*	slawn lyat
(said by person leaving)		
Goodbye	*Slán agat*	slawn agut
(said by person staying)		
Welcome	*Ceád míle fáilte*	kade meela fawlcha
(lit: 100,000 welcomes)		
How are you?	*Conas a tá tú?*	kunas aw taw too

SIGNS

Fir	*fear*	Men
Gardaí	*gardee*	Police
Leithreas	*lehrass*	Toilet
Mna	*m'naw*	Women
Oifig An Phoist	*iffig ohn fwisht*	Post Office

CUPLA FOCAL

Here are a few cheeky phrases *os Gaeilge* (in Irish) to help you impress the locals:

amadáin	fool
Dún do chlab!	Shut your mouth!
Póg ma thóin!	Kiss my arse!
Slainte! (slawn-cha)	Your health! (cheers)
Táim go maith!	
(thawm go mah)	I'm good!
Ní ólfaidh mé go brách arís!	
(knee ohl-hee mey gu brawkh u-reeshch)	
I'm never ever drinking again!	

BASIC WORDS & PHRASES

What is this/that?
Cad é seo/sin?   kod ay shoh/shin
I don't understand.
Ní thuigim.   nee higgim
I'd like to go to ...
Ba mhaith liom   baw wah lohm
dul go dtí ...   dull go dee ...
I'd like to buy ...
Ba mhaith liom ...   bah wah lohm ...
a cheannach   a kyanukh

Thank you (very) much.
Go raibh (míle)   goh rev (meela)
maith agat.   mah agut
..., (if you) please.
..., más é do thoil é.   ... maws ay do hall ay
(I'm) fine/good/OK.
(Tá mé) go maith.   (taw may) goh mah
What's your name?
Cad is ainm duit?   kod is anim dwit?
My name is (Sean Frayne).
(Sean Frayne) is   (shawn frain) is
ainm dom.   anim dohm
Excuse me.
Gabh mo leithscéal.   gamoh lesh scale
another/one more
ceann eile   kyawn ella

Yes/It is.	*Tá/Sea.*	taw/sheh
No/It isn't.	*Níl/Ní hea.*	neel/nee heh
nice	*go deas*	goh dyass

DAYS & MONTHS

Monday	*Dé Luaín*	day loon
Tuesday	*Dé Máirt*	day maart
Wednesday	*Dé Ceádaoin*	day kaydeen
Thursday	*Déardaoin*	daredeen
Friday	*Dé hAoine*	day heeneh
Saturday	*Dé Sathairn*	day sahern
Sunday	*Dé Domhnaigh*	day downick

NUMBERS

1	*haon*	hayin
2	*dó*	doe
3	*trí*	tree
4	*ceathaír*	kahirr
5	*cúig*	koo-ig
6	*sé*	shay
7	*seacht*	shocked
8	*hocht*	hukt
9	*naoi*	nay
10	*deich*	jeh
11	*haon déag*	hayin jague
12	*dó dhéag*	doe yague
20	*fiche*	feekhe

Irish
Language & Culture

Great craic!

Also available from Lonely Planet:
Irish Language & Culture

Glossary

Here you'll find some of the more commonly encountered Irish organisations and words, including those used in place names on maps; some are followed by an anglicised version in brackets. Also included are English terms that may not be familiar.

A

abhainn (ow, owen) – river, stream
achadh (agha, augh) – field
alt – height, high place
An Óige – Irish youth hostel association, literally 'The Youth'
arête – narrow ridge, particularly between glacial valleys

B

baile (bally) – village, settlement, town
bán (baun) – white
barr – top
beag (beg) – small
bealach (ballagh) – pass, *col*
beann (ben) – peak
bearna (barna) – *gap*
bia – food
binn – peak
bó – cow
bog – wet, spongy ground consisting of decomposing plant matter, see also *peat*, *peatland*
booleying – traditional practice of moving herds to upland pastures in summer
boreen – old country lane or narrow road
bóthar (boher) – road
breac (brack) – speckled
Bronze Age – the earliest metal-using period, about 2000 to 500 BC in Ireland, after the Stone Age and before the Iron Age
brook – stream
buaille (booley) – summer cattle pasture
buí – yellow
bullaun stone – stone with a depression, probably used as a mortar for grinding medicine or food and often found on monastic sites
bun – river mouth
burn – stream (Northern Ireland)

C

caher – prehistoric stone fort, city, *rath*, *dún*, *cashel*, *lios* **calladh** (callows) – lakeside or riverside grasslands prone to regular flooding
carn (cairn) – pile of stones
carraig (carrick) – rock
cashel – prehistoric stone fort, *rath*, *dún*, *caher*, *lios*
ceann (kin) – headland
Celts – people who arrived in Ireland about 300 BC
ceol – music
cill (kil) – church, chapel
cillin (killeen) – children's graveyard
clachan – beehive-shaped, *dry-stone* hut; *clochain*
clint – a natural cobblestone, the slabs between the cracks (*grikes*) found in a natural limestone pavement
cloch – stone
clochain – beehive-shaped, *dry-stone* hut; *clachan*
cluain – meadow
cnoc (knock, crock) – rocky hill
coill (kil) – woodland
coire – *corrie*
col – low point or pass between two peaks
cor – rounded hill
corrán (carraun) – serrated or crescent-shaped mountain
corrie – small, high, cup-shaped valley, often of glacial origin; cirque, *coire*, *coum*
coum – small, high, cup-shaped valley, often of glacial origin; cirque, *coire*, *corrie*
crag – steep cliff
crannog – an ancient lake dwelling on a natural or artificial island
cruach, **cruachan** – steep hill
cuan – bay
cúm (coum) – small, high, cup-shaped valley, often of glacial origin; cirque, *coire*, *corrie*
curragh – rowing boat consisting of a wooden frame with outer skin of tarred canvas
cutaway peatland – an area where *peat* harvesting has finished

D

Dáil Éireann – Irish Assembly
dearg – red
dheas – south

doire (derry) – oak wood
doline – a bowl-shaped depression down which water percolates in limestone country, *sink hole*
dolmen – chamber of prehistoric tomb comprising huge supporting stones and one or two large capstones
druim (drum) – ridge
drumlin – a rounded or teardrop-shaped hill formed from *moraine*
dry stone – a technique of building in stone without using mortar or cement
dubh (duff, doo) – black, dark
dún – prehistoric stone fort, *rath, cashel, caher, lios*

E

eaglais – church
eas – waterfall
Éire – Irish name for the Republic of Ireland
escarpment – steep slope or cliff

F

fen – flat *bog*
fionn (fin) – white, clear
fraoch (freagh) – heather
fulachta fiadh – Bronze Age cooking place

G

gabher (gower) – goat
Gaelige – Irish language
Gaeltacht – Irish-speaking area
gaoith (gwee) – wind
gap – mountain pass, *col*
garbh – rough
garda – Irish Republic police, plural gardaí
glas – green
gleann (glen) – valley
gorm – blue
gort – tilled field
green road – an old country route or unsealed road, usually with a grassed surface
grid reference – quoted in the text as GR followed by six figures, the accurate method of giving the location of a place, explained in the margin of Irish Ordnance Survey maps
grike – one of a network of semi-regular cracks between natural cobblestones (*clints*) found in limestone pavement

I

Iarnród Éireann – Irish Railways
inbhear (inver) – river mouth

inis (inish) – island
Iron Age – in Ireland the Iron Age lasted from around the end of the Bronze Age in about 500 BC to the arrival of Christianity in the 5th century

J

jaunting car – pony and trap

K

kil – church, chapel, woodland
killeen – children's graveyard
kin – headland
knock – rocky hill

L

lágh (law) – hill
leac – flat rock, flagstone
leataobh – lay-by, small roadside parking place
leithreas – toilets
leitir (letter) – rough hillside
liath (lea) – grey
lios – fort, defended settlement, *rath, dún, caher, cashel*
lough (loch) – lake, inlet
loughan – small lake, *tarn*
lug, lag, log – hollow

M

machair (maghera) – sandy plain or flat area near the sea
mám (maum) – pass
marriage stones – a pair of stones, often with a hole through which people made marriage vows
mass path – walking path created by Catholics going to hidden places of worship during times of religious persecution
meall, maol (mweel) – bare hill
móin, móna – turf
mór (more) – big
moraine – ridge or mound of debris deposited by retreating glacier
motte – a substantial, flat-topped earth mound on which a timber tower was built
mullach – summit

N

Neolithic – era characterised by the use of stone implements, from about 4000 to 2000 BC
North, the – the six counties constituting the political entity of Northern Ireland

nunatak – a mountain peak that poked above an ice sheet and escaped the scouring action of glaciers

O

Ogham stone – marker stone engraved with a primitive form of writing, known as Ogham
oifig an phoist – post office
oileán – island
ow, **owen** – river, stream

P

pairc – field
passage grave – Stone Age megalithic tomb in a large, domed cairn with a narrow passage leading to the burial chamber
peat – partly decomposed vegetable matter found in *bogs* and traditionally used as fuel
peat hags – area of *bog* where erosion or turf cutting has left small clumps of *peat* exposed
peatland – an area of land consisting of *peat bogs*
pitch – camp or tent site
pitched path – path laid with flat stones
plantation – the settlement of Protestants in Ireland in the 16th and 17th centuries
pobal – public
poll – hole, pond, small bay

R

radharc – view, scenery
raised bogs – areas of *peat* covered with heather and moss
rath – fort, defended settlement, *cashel*, *caher*, *dún*, *lios*
reek – ridge, crest
Republic, the – the 26 counties of the Republic of Ireland (*the South*)
riabhach – grey
ride – forest clearing, way or track for horse riding
ring fort – a term covering *rath*, *lios*, *dún* and *cashel* – all roughly circular structures of stones and earth that probably date from around 800 to 700 BC, some were still used into the Middle Ages
rinn – headland
roisin – small promontory
ros – promontory
round tower – tall, tapering circular tower possibly used for centuries as a lookout or refuge
route – a cross-country course where there isn't any path or track

rua, **ruadh** – red
rundale – system of land tenure based on the communal use of unenclosed grazing land

S

sceir (sker, skerry) – rock visible at sea, reef
scellig (skellig) – small rocky islands
sea stack – rock pinnacle close to the coast
sean – old
sidh (shee) – fairy, hill inhabited by fairies
sink hole – a bowl-shaped depression down which water percolates in limestone country, *doline*
slí – path
sliabh (slieve) – mountain
slidhe (slee) – road, track
slí geill – yield right of way (road sign)
souterrain – underground chamber, possibly of prehistoric origin but long in use, most likely for food storage
South, the – the *Republic* of Ireland
spate – flood
spinc (spink) – pinnacle
sráid – street
srón – nose-like mountain feature
sruth, **sruthán** – stream
stuaic (stook) – pinnacle
suí, **suidhe** (see) – seat

T

talus – scree
Taoiseach – Irish prime minister
tarn – small mountain lake or pool
teach – house
teampall – church
theas – south
thiar – west
thoir – east
thuaidh – north
tir (teer) – land, territory
tobar – well
togher – ancient wooden trackway across *peatland*
tombolo – narrow sand or shingle bar, which links an island to the mainland or to another island
tor – tower-like rock formed by frost shattering a *nunatak*
townland – a traditional rural area, which may be near a town of the same name
trá – sandy beach
trig point or **pillar** – summit survey marker

GLOSSARY

tulach – small hill
turas – journey, pilgrimage
turlach – seasonal lakes or ponds in limestone country, *turlough*
turlough – seasonal lakes or ponds in limestone country, *turlach*

W

Waymarked Way – a (marked) long-distance trail
waymarker – directional pointer on walking routes, usually a 'walking person' symbol on posts and direction signs

Behind the Scenes

THIS BOOK

This guidebook was commissioned in Lonely Planet's Melbourne office, and produced by the following:

Publisher Chris Rennie
Associate Publisher Ben Handicott
Commissioning Editors Bridget Blair, Janine Eberle
Cover Designer Brendan Dempsey
Cover Image Research Naomi Parker
Internal Image Research Jane Hart
Project Manager Jane Atkin
Thanks to Andy Lewis, Graham Imeson, Mik Ruff
Production [recapture]

THANKS FROM THE AUTHORS
HELEN FAIRBAIRN & GARETH McCORMACK

Our biggest thanks are due to Stuart Fairbairn, who twice came over for relentless, three-week stints to help us research the routes. Great walking and data collection Stu, and fantastic fun at the same time. Then Erin, who kept us all entertained and ensured the routine was interspersed with plenty of playground action. To Katie, Dermot and Diane for tireless babysitting services, though I fear your duties aren't going to get any easier. And to the Gawleys, especially Mervyn, for the frequent visits and coffee breaks that keep us sane when slaving at the computer.

OUR READERS

Many thanks to the travellers who used the last edition and wrote to us with helpful hints, useful advice and interesting anecdotes:

Kyle Barbour, Fernando Condal, C Dalton, Maureen Downes, Andrea Harchar, Dick Hazelwood, Marianne Mueller, Keith Tapp

ACKNOWLEDGMENTS

All photographs by Lonely Planet Images, and by: Eoin Clarke p2 (#1, #2), p12; Richard Cummins p4 (#5); Gareth McCormack p3 (#1, #2), p5 (#2, #3, #4), p6 (#1, #2), p7 (#4, #5), p8 (#1, #3), p9 (#2, #3), p10 (#1, #4), p11 (#2, #3).

BEHIND THE SCENES

THE LONELY PLANET STORY

Fresh from an epic journey across Europe, Asia and Australia in 1972, Tony and Maureen Wheeler sat at their kitchen table stapling together notes. The first Lonely Planet guidebook, *Across Asia on the Cheap*, was born.

Travellers snapped up the guides. Inspired by their success, the Wheelers began publishing books to Southeast Asia, India and beyond. Demand was prodigious, and the Wheelers expanded the business rapidly to keep up. Over the years, Lonely Planet extended its coverage to every country and into the virtual world via lonelyplanet.com and the Thorn Tree message board.

As Lonely Planet became a globally loved brand, Tony and Maureen received several offers for the company. But it wasn't until 2007 that they found a partner whom they trusted to remain true to the company's principles of travelling widely, treading lightly and giving sustainably. In October of that year, BBC Worldwide acquired a 75% share in the company, pledging to uphold Lonely Planet's commitment to independent travel, trustworthy advice and editorial independence.

Today, Lonely Planet has offices in Melbourne, London and Oakland, with over 500 staff members and 300 authors. Tony and Maureen are still actively involved with Lonely Planet. They're travelling more often than ever, and they're devoting their spare time to charitable projects. And the company is still driven by the philosophy of *Across Asia on the Cheap*: 'All you've got to do is decide to go and the hardest part is over. So go!'

Index

000 Map pages
000 Photograph pages

INDEX

INDEX

LONELY PLANET OFFICES

Australia
Head Office
Locked Bag 1, Footscray, Victoria 3011
☎ 03 8379 8000, fax 03 8379 8111
talk2us@lonelyplanet.com.au

USA
150 Linden St, Oakland, CA 94607
☎ 510 893 8556, toll free 800 275 8555
fax 510 893 8572
info@lonelyplanet.com

UK
2nd fl, 186 City Rd,
London EC1V 2NT
☎ 020 7106 2100, fax 020 7106 2101
go@lonelyplanet.co.uk

Although the authors and Lonely Planet have taken all reasonable care in preparing this book, we make no warranty about the accuracy or completeness of its content and, to the maximum extent permitted, disclaim all liability arising from its use.

PUBLISHED BY LONELY PLANET PUBLICATIONS PTY LTD

ABN 36 005 607 983

Cover photograph: Ireland coast landscape (Edmund Nägele, Photolibrary). Many of the images in this guide are available for licensing from Lonely Planet Images: www.lonelyplanetimages.com.

Printed by Fabulous Printers Pte Ltd
Printed in Singapore

Mixed Sources
Product group from well-managed forests and other controlled sources
www.fsc.org Cert no. SGS-COC-005002
© 1996 Forest Stewardship Council